THE
GALATIANS
DEBATE

York St John
Library and Information Services
Normal Loan

Please see self service receipt for return date.

Fines are payable for late return

THE
GALATIANS
DEBATE

Contemporary Issues in
Rhetorical and Historical
Interpretation

Mark D. Nanos, *Editor*

HENDRICKSON
PUBLISHERS

Printed in the United States of America

First Printing—November 2002

The image on the cover comes from a plaque depicting St. Paul disputing with Greeks and Jews, mid 12th century (champleve enamel on copper). The image appears courtesy of Victoria & Albert Museum, London, UK/Bridgeman Art Library and is used with permission.

Library of Congress Cataloging-in-Publication Data

The Galatians debate : contemporary issues in rhetorical and historical
    interpretation   /   Mark D. Nanos, editor.
        p. cm.
    Includes bibliographical references and indexes.
    ISBN 1–56563–468–3 (hardcover : alk. paper)
    1. Bible. N.T. Galatians—Socio-rhetorical criticism. I. Nanos, Mark D., 1954– .
    BS2685.52 .G35 2002
    227′.406—dc21
                                                    2002015497

TABLE OF CONTENTS

PART 1. RHETORICAL AND EPISTOLARY GENRE

Section A: Rhetorical Approaches

Section B: Epistolary Approaches

PART 2: AUTOBIOGRAPHICAL NARRATIVES

Section A: Rhetorical Approaches

Section B: Socio-Historical Approaches

PART 3: THE GALATIAN SITUATION(S)

ACKNOWLEDGEMENTS

A project such as this requires the cooperation of the contributors and, in many cases, the original publishers of their work; I am thankful to each for helping to make this volume a reality. Special thanks are extended to several contributors who were active agents in securing permissions, especially Paula Fredriksen, Walter Hansen, Jim Hester, and Joop Smit. To this list of facilitators should be added Duane Watson. Jim Hester also provided several unpublished manuscripts and other assistance, and Carl Classen helped me locate several elusive bibliographic entries. In addition, I am grateful for the help of many others. Halvor Moxnes facilitated interaction with Nils Dahl, who was hospitalized in Oslo. Dahl's original manuscript was made available to me by the gracious offer of Jerry Neyrey. Tom Olbricht kindly discussed certain elements of the introduction. Patrick Alexander facilitated the initial discussions that resulted in the contract with Hendrickson, and offered helpful guidance. Shirley Decker-Lucke of Hendrickson proved to be a friendly, helpful editor.

I want especially to express gratitude to Neil Elliott, who was originally the coeditor of this project. Although other obligations prohibited him from completing the process, I am grateful for the help and friendship Neil supplied. And I want to thank my parents, Arthur S. and Dorothy Nanos, who nurtured appreciation of the value of debate. I would like to dedicate my work on this project to the memory of Nils A. Dahl (1911–2001), whose own work exemplifies dedication to this task.

MARK D. NANOS

INTRODUCTION

Mark D. Nanos

In recent years, the sophisticated refinement and employment of rhetorical and sociohistorical tools have profoundly altered the interpretive landscape. The impact of these methodological developments is probably nowhere more clearly evident than in the contemporary discussions of Paul's letter to the Galatians. As a result, the student seeking to read the secondary literature on Galatians must often negotiate specialized language and complex lines of argument for which he or she may be largely unprepared. In addition to the theological jargon that traditionally characterizes discussion of Galatians, one now encounters a significant amount of rhetorical and sociohistorical terminology, and the reader's familiarity with this specialized language is increasingly assumed. Unless one has been trained in rhetorical theory, especially classical, is familiar with epistolography, has a grasp of historical, social scientific, and literary criticism, and enjoys some acquaintance with the increasing awareness of the interpreter's role in the interpretive process—and the kind of carefully measured phrasing this can produce—this language, which was designed to clarify and increase precision, may instead serve to obscure and perhaps alienate.

This volume is designed to help facilitate familiarity with the contemporary issues central to the interpretation of Galatians, the prevailing points of view as well as some recent challenges to them, and to help penetrate the specialist's technical terminology. Unfortunately, it is unable to address all of the current—much less the traditional—debates or include every pertinent participant and essay, especially the arguments offered only in monographs or commentaries, or as part of research made in the service of other topics and texts. The essays included, however, comprise a comprehensive introduction to significant research in the field, representing some of the best work available, and, for the most part, define the terms commonly employed, or at least provide a sense for how they are used. Those chosen for this volume concentrate around three important areas of particular interest. The first part of the volume examines contemporary rhetorical and epistolary analyses of the letter. The second part investigates recent interpretations of Paul's autobiographical narrative related in Galatians 1 and 2, especially Paul's view of his relationship with the Jerusalem authorities of this nascent movement and, even more specifically, his perspective on the incident with Peter at Antioch. The third part traces various ways of constructing the situation among the addressees in Galatia, whereby interpreters seek to discover the reasons Paul wrote just this response.[1]

Many issues arise in each of these areas of debate. For rhetorical analysis of Galatians, for example, consider but a few of the methodological matters that become immediately apparent in these essays. How should an interpreter approach the task in view of the fact that Paul wrote letters but the rhetorical handbooks addressed the delivery of orations? If analyzed according to rhetorical categories for oration, or, alternatively, within epistolary categories, or even by attending to elements that arise from both of these communication mediums, to what genre should Galatians be assigned, and with what results for its interpretation? Moreover, should analysis of Paul's first-century correspondence be confined to theories and examples that arise in ancient classical handbooks and extant texts, and if so, which ones, or should it include the insights available to us now from later rhetorical theories and examples? Naturally, the decisions made on these matters will impact the way the message of the letter is interpreted or its prior interpretation is confirmed.

In the area of sociohistorical methodology, consider the way that interpreters construct the context of the writer and the recipients of the letter. What were the contextual situations of Paul, his addressees, and those who were influencing them in a direction to which Paul objected? Why did he write this letter? Or more precisely, why did he perceive the need to write it, and what did he design it to accomplish? How might Paul's assessment have differed from the perceptions of the addressees in Galatia? or from the perceptions of those whose influence Paul sought to check? The construction of the situation(s) among the addressees and the perception of Paul upon which the interpreter settles directly influence the way that he or she perceives the nature of Paul's response or confirms a prior understanding thereof. Each interpreter variously draws, intentionally or not, upon a wealth of historical and cultural as well as rhetorical and philosophical—not to mention theological—ideas, traditions, and methods of enquiry and argumentation. Naturally, the different choices made in each of these areas combine to influence every interpreter to different conclusions.

It is interesting to note that both the more rhetorically and sociohistorically oriented approaches to the interpretation of this letter connect when attending to the issue of establishing a context for Paul's letter. Why? Because, in order to interpret Paul's language in Galatians, it is necessary to construct—or at least assume—the context for which it is imagined to have been used, so that the historical rhetorical meaning it may have held for the writer and his addressees can be proposed. We have the extant message Paul sent, but we do not know the situational context that prompted his decision to write it; we cannot know a priori what he meant to communicate, why he arranged it in this and not some other way, or what, for the recipients, it meant when received. In order to construct a context for understanding these his-

---

[1] Some interpreters refer to their hypotheses as reconstructions; discussing constructions, however, has the advantage of recognizing in the terminology that interpreters seek to conceptualize historical or rhetorical situations that are by nature perceptions for the original players as well as for the later interpreter, and thus not objectively measurable "constructions" (e.g., archaeological sites) that we then "*re*construct."

torical and rhetorical situations, that is, what might have been actually happening as well as what Paul thought was happening and hoped to effect by way of this letter, it is necessary to hypothesize from the language used therein, because apart from this letter we do not have any certain evidence from which to work. These are interdependent tasks. Circularity is thus built into the process of interpretation, since we do not know the context but must hypothesize it from the language of the letter, yet we do not know the meaning of the language of the letter—or the genre—without hypothesizing a context for its usage.

The construction of sociohistorical as well as rhetorical contexts to interpret Paul's language cannot be easily separated from the enterprise of interpretation itself, including theological. Each aspect involves analysis of Paul's rhetoric in a kind of back-and-forth process; moreover, none of this analysis takes place in a vacuum. The point can be illustrated with any of the essays included in this volume, but let us briefly consider the essay that initiated the contemporary interest in rhetorical analysis of Paul's letter, as it should help the reader qualify the results of each of the others.

Hans Dieter Betz makes is clear that he seeks to investigate the "possible criteria and methods" for "how to arrive at an *'outline'* of the letter."[2] Betz thereby announces that he does not seek to offer a hypothesis for, or an analysis of, the sociohistorical context of Paul or the addressees per se, or to offer an interpretation of Paul's language. He wants to determine the rhetorical genre exemplified by Paul's argument, and then outline the elements. Yet the choice of rhetorical genre requires the construction of a sociohistorical as well as rhetorical context provoking Paul's letter—in Betz's case, what is determined to be Paul's "defense" against "opponents." Naturally, this situational hypothesis requires an implicit, if not explicit, analysis of Paul's letter, from which the elements of its construction are gathered. That is, in order to determine the reason for the letter, it is necessary for Betz to have a working hypothesis for the author's perception of the situational exigence—why Paul felt compelled to respond. Only with a situation already postulated can Betz propose a reason for Paul choosing as most appropriate to the task ("inventing") just this kind of *defensive* reply ("forensic"/"judicial") instead of some other kind (e.g., "deliberative" or "epideictic"), or even an entirely different kind of discourse. And only after these stages of the interpretive process have been undertaken can Betz advance an argument for why and how Paul set out to arrange the elements (the outline) of his argument—that is, how Paul "organized" it. This process exemplifies the ineluctable circularity of the interpretive task already noted: from the rhetorical information supplied in the letter, in concert with any other information or conjecture that is also incorporated, the interpreter hypothesizes the historical as well as rhetorical situation giving rise to the letter and at the same time analyzes its rhetoric, including that from which he or she constructed that context, on the basis of his or her hypothesis of the context of its usage. Since the contemporary interpreter was not present, he or she can only hypothesize the historical situations as well as the rhetorical nature of Paul's epistolary response. Then these hypotheses must be tested, debated if you will.

---

[2] Betz, "Literary Composition," 3.

It should be noted that the importance of these contemporary discussions of the context and rhetoric of Galatians reaches well beyond the confines of the interpretation of this particular letter. Even discussions of those whose influence Paul opposes in other letters often turn on the identity and interests attributed to those supposed to be influencing his addressees in Galatia. The information contained in Paul's autobiographical narrative of Galatians 1 and 2 is the most important firsthand source that interpreters have available for comprehensive constructions of Paul and his activities, and it provides some of the earliest and most essential available evidence for research into the historical and theological origins of Christianity, reaching even beyond consideration of Paul's relationship with the Jerusalem apostles. For example, histories of early Christianity rely upon an interpretation of the "facts" about Paul, the Jerusalem apostles, and the developments in Jerusalem and Antioch that are related in these narrative units. And the interpretation of the situation in Galatia and of the nature of the message contained in Paul's response also plays a central role in such historical constructions. This last element, the interpretation of Paul's message in this letter, is of course essential to the theological enterprise. Indeed, for sociohistorical as well as rhetorical debates, Galatians holds pride of place.

No one should assume that he or she approaches the interpretation of this text without some presuppositions, whether gained from study of Galatians, Paul's other letters, the Acts of the Apostles, or other ancient texts believed to bear upon its interpretation, and without his or her own predisposition to the material and its meaning, even the perception of its relative importance. Some of these presuppositions may have become part of what he or she believes to be *known* about Galatians as well as its author, Paul, from sermons and classes, literature and newspapers, casual conversation or formal education, or prior reading and study of the letter. This exposure may have led to a negative or positive disposition to the language of the letter, to the person who wrote it, to those to whom he wrote, or to those whom he wrote to oppose. Some interpreters have internalized a particular understanding or seek to do so to direct their future thoughts; some may have other interests, including challenging a particular interpretation, for any number of reasons. The point is that the interpretation of this letter and the ends to which the conclusions drawn are applied represent aspects of a complex process; no one should assume that he or she is approaching the task without some bias. In this interpretive enterprise humility, the employment of interdisciplinary methodologies, and the role of debate to sharpen our awareness of the alternatives offer immeasurable benefits.

Certain debates that were once central for the interpreter of Galatians are now not the focus of most contemporary attention, and are thus not the topics of this volume. For example, the discussion of the precise location of the addressees (the so-called North or South Galatia hypotheses), while ongoing, is presently at an impasse. It is currently difficult to make much headway from the information internal to the letter itself. The arguments tend to focus upon comparisons with information available in the Acts of the Apostles, and are often undertaken as part of comprehensive portraits of Paul and his several journeys. At this juncture most interpreters concentrating upon Galatians summarize the evidence for both positions and, if taking up one side or the other, usually still seek to distance their conclusions from the necessity of being proven correct on this element.[3] Other debates not covered specifically here focus on particular passages, such as investigations of certain elements related in Paul's autobiographical accounts in Galatians 1 and 2. They seek to understand, for example, how or if the events noted there correspond to the events traced in the Acts of the Apostles, the timing of this letter vis-à-vis Paul's other letters, or the chronology and character of Paul's life and activities both before and after his "calling or conversion," or whether he argued on the basis of "faith *in*" or "the faith *of* Christ." Also not included are many essays on a wide variety of topics that include discussion of Galatians, or those that focus upon particular passages but do not aim to offer a comprehensive analysis of either the context or rhetoric of the letter per se. Many of the theologically oriented disputes fall into this category. They concern Galatians and may arise in and influence the arguments of the contributors to this volume, but represent broader topics than this project can hope to address.

A word about organization is in order. The volume is divided into three major parts, as discussed above. Two of these are subdivided further according to methodological emphasis. The essays within each part and subdivision appear in the order of their original publication date, with new contributions last; hopefully, this will offer the reader a sense of the way that the debates have developed to date. Below is a brief introduction to each of these parts and subdivisions, and a summary of each of the essays. Cross-references to essays within the volume have been updated to reflect the page numbers of the contributions as they appear now in *The Galatians Debate*. The footnote numbering in these chapters may not always exactly match that of the original articles. A Glossary of selected terms follows the last essay. Finally, there is a comprehensive volume bibliography, an index for citations of ancient sources, and an index of modern authors.

I am confident that the contributors join me in hoping that these essays will serve to stimulate deeper insight, further productive research, and facilitate lively debate for many years to come.

Part 1: Rhetorical and Epistolary Genre

Rhetorical Approaches

To whatever degree it may be argued that the analysis of Paul's letter has been characterized by attention to rhetoric in the past, it is clearly the case that Hans Dieter Betz's work initiated the modern debate. Betz hit a nerve when he proposed in his 1975 article—followed by the detailed articulation of the thesis in his 1979 Hermeneia commentary—that Galatians can be "analysed according to Graeco-Roman rhetoric and epistolography."[4] The reaction to his proposal was swift and significant, and its reach extends far beyond rhetorical analysis of Galatians. Within a few years

---

[3] In addition to the helpful discussions found in most contemporary commentaries (esp. R. Longenecker, *Galatians*, lxi–lxxii), see Bruce, "Galatian Problems 2"; Jewett, *Chronology*; Scott, *Paul*; Breytenbach, *Paulus*.

[4] Betz, "Literary Composition"; idem, *Galatians*.

many reviews, essays, monographs, and commentaries began to appear—pro and con, to be sure—with each interpreter concerned to discover the possibilities such rhetorical approaches might hold for Galatians, for Paul's other letters, and for other New Testament documents. The essays below will trace some of this development, and they will make clear that there are other important voices in this debate not represented directly in this volume. For example, the classicist George Kennedy was one of the first to interact with Betz's proposal and the challenge to apply classical rhetorical theory to the interpretation of the New Testament documents, including Galatians. His approach was in many ways methodologically similar to Betz, but he differed strongly over classification of the genre, with several notable results. The essay by Robert Hall, among others, brings Kennedy's voice directly to bear on this debate. Many influential voices should be noted besides those included in this volume; some gave papers in the same meetings and to the same societies, and these practitioners turned to others, especially those working in the fields of classical and modern rhetorical theory. The included essays trace the main lines of the argument in superb fashion and introduce many of the other central figures and ideas to which the reader seeking to join the debate should also attend.[5]

---

[5] Proponents of forensic classification include the essays herein by Betz, "Literary Composition," and by T. Martin, "Apostasy to Paganism"; and see, e.g., Betz, *Galatians;* Brinsmead, *Galatians;* Hester, "Rhetorical Structure"; idem, "Use and Influence." For criticism of this classification, see herein Hall, "Rhetorical Outline"; Smit, "Letter of Paul"; Classen, "St. Paul's Epistles"; and see Kennedy, *New Testament Interpretation,* 144–52; Aune, "Review of Betz, *Galatians*"; Meeks, "Review"; Lyons, *Autobiography,* 112–19; Fairweather, "Rhetoric: Parts 1 & 2"; Cooper, "*Narratio*"; and commentators, e.g., R. Longenecker, *Galatians,* cix–cxiii, Esler, *Galatians,* 60–61; Witherington, *Grace,* 27–31. See also the arguments of those listed below who challenge, to various degrees, the effort to classify this letter by rhetorical categories developed for orations.

Proponents of deliberative classification herein include Hall, "Rhetorical Outline"; Smit, "Letter of Paul"; and see, e.g., Kennedy, *New Testament Interpretation,* 144–52; Lyons, *Autobiography,* 119–20, 136, 173–75; Russell, "Rhetorical Analysis"; Fairweather, "Rhetoric: Part 3," 219, 240, though with caveat; Cosgrove, *Cross and the Spirit,* 25–30; Aune, *Literary Environment,* 206–8; commentators include, e.g., Matera, *Galatians,* 11; Esler, *Galatians,* 61, 137; Witherington, *Grace,* 25–41, passim. Note too Mitchell, *Reconciliation,* 22–23, although dealing directly with classification of 1 Corinthians.

Proponents of epideictic classification have generally argued from a more functional than formal basis and from epistolography; see herein Hester, "Epideictic Rhetoric and Persona," and see, e.g., Hester, "Placing the Blame"; Kraftchick, "Why Do the Rhetoricians Rage?" 67–71; J. White, "Apostolic Mission," 159–61; Sullivan and Anible, "Epideictic Dimension"; Nanos, *Irony,* 329–31.

Classification of Galatians within these rhetorical genres has been challenged to various degrees and for various reasons. For arguments about the inherent weakness of analyzing letters according to the classifications developed for oration, see Malherbe, *Ancient Epistolary Theorists,* 2–3, for both sides of argument (Demetrius, *De elocutione,* applies rhetorical terms to letters, and Cicero, *De or.* 2.11.49–50, may be taken this way, yet Malherbe notes that there does not seem to have been "an entire theoretical system"). See herein Classen, "St. Paul's Epistles," 98–99, 109–13; and, see e.g., Aune, *Literary Environment,* 158–59; Anderson, *Ancient Rhetorical Theory,* 93–109, 111–23, 141, 165–67, and esp. 34, 100, 103; Stowers, *Letter Writing,* 27, 51–52, 56; Porter, "Theoretical Justification"; idem, "Paul of Tarsus," esp. 539–47, 562–67; idem, "Ancient Rhetorical Analysis"; Weima, "Aristotle"; D. Watson, "Rhetorical Criticism"; Reed, "Epistle"; idem, "Using Ancient Categories." Among those working specifically on Galatians, note herein Berchman, "Galatians (1:1–5)"; Hester, "Epideictic Rhetoric and Persona"; Dahl, "Galatians"; and see, e.g., Hansen, *Galatians,* 22–24; idem, *Abraham in Galatians,* 55–71; Cosgrove, *Cross and the Spirit,* 23–31; Kern, *Rhetoric and Galatians,* 30–34, passim; Nanos, *Irony,* 323–31; and the commentaries of R. Longenecker, *Galatians,* ci–cxix; Dunn, *Theology,* 20; Williams, *Galatians,* 28–31; Martyn, *Galatians,* 20–23; Esler, *Galatians,* 18–19, 59–61.

In his seminal essay, "The Literary Composition and Function of Paul's Letter to the Galatians," Betz proposes to read Galatians as an example of forensic rhetoric expressed in the literary genre of an "apologetic letter." Betz deftly combines the strategies and techniques of Cicero and Quintilian, among others, to show us how he understands Paul to have employed these rhetorical devices in his letter, especially when he analyzes chapters 1–2, which he categorizes as the *exordium* (1:6–11), *narratio* (1:12–2:14), and *propositio* (2:15–21). Where the device is lacking or does not seem to exemplify the model rhetorical approach that Betz understands Paul to be otherwise engaged in constructing, these instances are still understood to represent rhetorical strategies. For example, where the *probatio* of 3:1–4:31 fails to exemplify the elements to be expected in an apologetic letter, Paul's language is understood to be calculated to, for example, "disguis[e] his argumentative strategy," as would be "expected" of "a skilled [Hellenistic] rhetorician": "Paradoxically, extremely perfected logic was thought to create suspicion and boredom, not credibility, while a carefully prepared mixture of some logic, some emotional appeal, some wisdom, some beauty, and some entertainment was thought to conform to human nature and to the ways in which human beings accept arguments as true" (18–19). When Paul places an allegorical proof at the end of the *probatio,* a move that fails to conform with Quintilian's advice, Betz finds the explanation in the adaptation of Pseudo-Demetrius's epistolary example, thus moving away from direct argumentation to a more inductive approach calculated to involve the readers/hearers in "find[ing] the 'truth' for themselves, thus convincing themselves, and at the same time clearing themselves from the blame of being ἀνόητοι Γαλάται" (24). Evaluation of the *paraenesis* (5:1–6:10) turns around advice not from rhetorical handbooks, where its consideration is incidental at best, but from the philosophical tradition, such as one finds articulated in Seneca's letters. Although a largely undeveloped observation, it is interesting that in his concluding comments Betz also considers Galatians to have some characteristics of a "magical letter," whereby Paul "overcomes the limitations of the 'apologetic letter'" (27–28). For Betz, a letter such as this one "presupposes the real or fictitious situation of the court of law, with the jury, the accuser and the defendant. In the case of Galatians, the addressees are identical with the jury, with Paul being the defendant and his opponents the accusers. This situation makes Paul's letter a self-apology" (26).

The next two essays in this volume employ similar analytical methods and assume that somewhat similar situations obtain for the addressees, yet represent direct challenges to Betz's classification of Galatians as forensic/judicial rhetoric. In "The Rhetorical Outline for Galatians: A Reconsideration," Robert Hall, drawing from the work of George Kennedy, also argues within classical categories, but to propose that Paul's argument exemplifies a "deliberative" rather than a defensive speech. Even though elements of the other genres may be at work, the functional characteristics of deliberative speech—exhortation and dissuasion to or from a particular future action on the grounds of expedience or harm—dominate Galatians. According to Hall, the participants in this debate are not primarily concerned about adjudicating Paul's *past* actions (forensic), or praising or denouncing a *past* action, or "merely" seeking "to change a *present* attitude" (epideictic). Rather, Paul is concerned with what decision the addressees will make "between two antithetical modes of life and behavior" and, as a result, with what direction their *future* actions will take—functions characteristic of a deliberative speech (31). Paul urges the addressees to "cleave to Paul and his gospel and to reject his opponents and their gospel" (31). He employs invective in the declamatory style of popular deliberative, although Quintillian deplored this kind of excess (31). In the style of deliberative, Paul's narratives seek not to remind of the facts of a case but to introduce "relevant matters external to the case"—in this instance, to prove that Paul's authority and gospel are from God and confirmed by the church but his opponents and their message are not (32). Paul calls for a choice, appealing to the addressees' advantage, a distinctive function of deliberative rhetoric, as is also the important role of exhortation throughout—"Galatians must be deliberative" (32). In the balance of his essay Hall explains how the outline of Galatians exemplifies just such a speech in ways that a forensic classification is ostensibly unable to match. The functions of salutation and *exordium* are combined in 1:1–5; the proposition of the letter is set out in vv. 6–9; the proof, which constitutes the bulk of the letter (including the *narratio* and exhortation of Betz's outline), explains the reasons the audience should accept the proposition. It consists of a narration (1:10–2:21) articulating Paul's ethos, followed by a variety of other arguments (3:1–6:10). The epilogue of 6:11–18 restates and summarizes the argument, as Quintilian would advise (cf. *Inst.* 6.1.1–2).

In "The Letter of Paul to the Galatians: A Deliberative Speech," Joop Smit joins Hall in arguing for a deliberative classification of Galatians in classical terms. From the start, he mounts criticism of Betz's analysis as judicial, yet he shares, even sharpens the concern to find exact formal as well as functional correspondence between Paul's construction of the letter's argument and what is advised in rhetorical handbooks that may have been available to Paul. Smit explains discrepancies between the claims Betz makes for Quintilian and for Paul's letter, and the elements Smit finds present in those references. He challenges the notion that the function of Paul's narratives is to seek a pronouncement of judgment by the addressees as a judicial body: "The story does not confront them with a precise legal question, but rather proposes two courses of action from which they should choose" (40).

Smit argues that Gal 2:15–21 does not exemplify the formal characteristics of a *propositio,* which sums up the points of agreement and disagreement between the parties besides enumerating and briefly explaining the argument to come, that is, making transparent the organization of the entire speech. Furthermore, he argues that 3:1–4:31 is poorly suited to the task of a *probatio,* to strengthen the position of the speaker's position. Instead of interrogation of witnesses to ascertain the legitimacy of a certain course of action, Smit finds the strengthening of assertions: Paul "makes the reproach that they would be acting foolishly and harming themselves if they change their behavior" (41). Smit finds fault not only with Betz's admitted problem of the lack of evidence for the type of exhortation expressed in 5:1–6:10, which Betz labels *paraenesis,* but also with Betz's classification of 6:11–18 as *peroratio,* since it does not sum up the main points of the *probatio* of 3:1–4:31 and it is missing the other two parts to be expected in a *peroratio,* namely, an effort to arouse anger and hostility *(indignatio)* and an appeal to pity *(conquestio).*

Smit instructively proposes consideration of four methodological matters that arise for the interpreter seeking to classify Paul's rhetoric in classical terms and that underscore his criticisms of Betz's approach (42–45). First, in terms of historical witnesses, he notes that Quintilian—whose writings are encyclopedic and thus easily mined for support of virtually any view relating to Paul—wrote around 90 C.E. in Rome and was influenced by the continuous adaptation of the Greeks by the Romans, so that reference to Cicero, writing around 85 B.C.E., provides a more reliable control for analysis of Paul's letter. Second, in addition to taking issue with Betz's genre classification of Galatians as judicial rhetoric on functional terms, he suggests the priority of the Hellenistic handbook *Rhetorica ad Alexandrum* (anonymous, ca. 300 B.C.E.), which precedes the priority position assumed by judicial rhetoric in the handbooks to which Betz appeals. Third, he seeks to challenge the traditional Lutheran theological assumptions he believes to be at work in Betz's analysis, as though at issue were justification by faith in the face of legalistic challenges. Although Smit argues that Paul "crossed the bounds of Judaism" and chose to "leave the hedge of torah" in order to accomplish his task (58), he nevertheless proposes to build his analysis around the recent trend to see at issue a dispute about the conditions that obtain for legitimating the incorporation of Christ-believing Gentiles in unity with Christ-believing Jews in the Christian community of faith. Fourth, he challenges the inclusion of 5:13–6:10 in the original letter's composition—though not necessarily denying that it was written by Paul—thereby seeking to explain the presence of exhortation unattested in the handbooks for preparing a deliberative speech, even as it is absent for the judicial genre. At the end of his essay, Smit returns to this topic and to overcoming the implicit admission of a problem arising for these classical rhetorical analyses.

In keeping with his suggested methodology, Smit finds throughout the letter functional equivalents of the deliberative genre of speech as defined by Cicero and the *Rhetorica ad Alexandrum.* He proposes that 1:6–12 constitutes the *exordium,* which aims "to make the listeners well-disposed, attentive and receptive" (46). Paul's argument here is political as expected, including terms (such as "deserting," "disturbing," and "subverting") to dissuade the addressees from following his opponents and to instead persuade them to remain true to him and the course on which they had begun with his teaching. Smit understands 1:13–2:21 to constitute the *narratio,* which should follow the *exordium* and, as such, be designed to set out the facts in a brief, clear, and plausible manner, bending what details are revealed to the speaker's rhetorical advantage. This is followed by the *confirmatio,* and Smit understands Paul to be occupied with proofs in 3:1–4:11. The absence here of a *divisio* or *partitio* between the *exordium* and *narratio* constitutes for Smit further evidence against classification as judicial, where the *narratio* would be expected to render an account of the earlier stated facts, defining the points of agreement between the parties and clarifying the precise point for which judgment is sought in the plea. Although the details are far too many to note, Smit sees Paul proceeding as he should in a *confirmatio,* clearly articulating a series of arguments based upon honor and advantage as well as baseness and disadvantage. Paul's *conclusio* is understood to consist of three parts that clarify the choice at hand: the *conquestio* of 4:12–20 seeks to arouse the audience's pity, the *enumeratio* of 4:21–5:6 briefly summarizes to refresh the memory of the listeners, and the *indignatio* of 5:7–12 intends to incite hatred of his opponents. Finally, since the *conclusio* ought to be the final word, Smit proposes that 6:11–18 constitutes an *amplificatio,* which arises because Paul's argument is sent as a letter and thus calls for a subscription in his own handwriting. In addition, he argues that its concerns are in keeping with the concerns of the deliberative genre. Galatians 5:13–6:10 is omitted from the outline, since the otherwise "clear structure and line of thought shown by the text without this passage" are understood to legitimate Smit's hypothesis. It instead "contains a rounded off fragment of Paul added to the letter at a somewhat later time" (58).

Rhetorical analysis of Galatians according to the classical handbooks also occupies Robert Berchman in "Galatians (1:1–5): Paul and Greco-Roman Rhetoric," but with a shift of focus. He notes the exegetical limitations of a methodology that has resulted in skilled critics reaching such different conclusions about the genre of Paul's argument. Berchman suggests this results from the fact that while theoreticians ascribed certain meaning to particular rhetorical forms, Paul "adjusted" these forms "to fit the persuasive context his letter(s) address. Thus the inventive and not the mimetic aspects of rhetoric are what interest him" (62). Formal parallels with Greco-Roman rhetoric may be found, but these forms do not exist in "pure form in Galatians."

To demonstrate the proposed gap between theory and Paul's practice of rhetoric, Berchman undertakes a form-critical analysis of a specific unit within the letter, the prologue or proem of 1:1–5. He approaches the formal structural dimensions of this text as if it were a speech act, investigating the aspects of logic, topic, and genre found there. A variety of elements are noted for each aspect in his detailed examination. For example, in terms of genre, Berchman detects argument from opposites, authority, relation, and the "more and less" in vv. 1–2 (characteristics of forensic); from authority, relation, parallel cases, and authority in vv. 3–4 (characteristics of deliberative); and from authority in the doxology of v. 5 (a characteristic of epideictic speech). For Berchman, within these five verses Paul argues judicially for the truth of his character, deliberatively for the self-interest and future benefits of the addressees, and epideictically to deepen their values. Working backward from these classifications, Berchman advances several suggestions for constructing the historical situation provoking such rhetoric. He finds Paul's creditability at issue behind the forensic arguments, yet the fact that Paul's deliberative rhetoric aims to influence the future course of action the addressees will take suggests a continued relationship and agreement on the importance of the gospel of Christ for themselves (the stasis). This agreement is also implied in the laudatory rhetoric of the doxology, for such epideictic speech appeals to shared values, apart from which such a hymn would not be used. Berchman's Paul is not only well studied in Greco-Roman rhetoric; he is comfortable enough with the formal aspects to employ them functionally beyond their prescribed handbook stereotypes.

In "Apostasy to Paganism: The Rhetorical Stasis of the Galatian Controversy," Troy Martin employs rhetorical theory—stasis theory in particular—to move from Paul's accusations and arguments to a reconstruction of Paul's understanding of the basic issues at dispute. The stasis represents the chief issue to be decided in a dispute, and secondary stases can also arise. If one is accused of some action and denies having done it, this denial constitutes the chief issue at dispute. If one accepts the fact of having done it but redefines it, or appeals to mitigating circumstances that alter the significance of the event, or perhaps challenges the jurisdiction of the case, then the defense chosen determines the stasis, the issues to be resolved, and thus the direction that the arguments to prove or refute one's claims will take. The interpreter of Paul's letter has only the remaining arguments of one party from which to construct the issues at dispute. Thus, to determine the stasis, he or she must both take account of Paul's accusations and seek to fill in the anticipated responses of the addressees.

Martin proposes two accusations. In 1:6–9, the charge is exchanging his gospel for another one that requires circumcision and observance of the Jewish law; in 4:8–11, the charge is apostatizing to paganism. In order to make sense of these two ostensibly irreconcilable alternatives, Martin argues that the addressees have accepted the terms of this other gospel as the legitimate definition of Christian gospel but they have declined to submit to its requirement of circumcision. Thus they understand themselves to have rejected the gospel of Christ, leaving open only the option of returning to paganism. He thereby determines that the principle stasis is the accusation, in 4:8–11, of a return to paganism and that this is a stasis of quality, which investigates the seriousness of an alleged action, rather than its denial, redefinition, or rejection on technical grounds. Since Martin understands 4:8–11 to constitute Paul's accusation of their past action of apostatizing in response to the unacceptable terms of the gospel, now believed to include circumcision, he determines the genre to be forensic. Paul is not defending himself, as Betz understands the case to be when assigning Galatians to this same genre, because Paul is engaged in accusing the addressees, like the prophets of old, "in the tradition of a divine lawsuit": "It is a pre-trial letter written to an offending party to summon that party back to the original agreement. . . . If this case should ever come to trial, the letter to the Galatians is one of the documents the plaintiff, Paul, would most certainly enter as evidence against the defendants, the Galatians" (93–94). Moreover, this stasis is, according to Martin, of the subcategory of shifting the blame to the proponents of this other gospel for leading the addressees into actions that are forbidden. In this way, Martin both classifies the rhetorical genre and clarifies the historical situation for which he understands it to have been invented. While the addressees will agree to the charge of returning to paganism, they will contend that they have done so innocently in response to learning the terms of the *true* gospel, inclusive of terms that Paul had not mentioned—namely, circumcision and the observance of Jewish law. Paul's argument at this point in the dispute, which is when Galatians is written, sets out the terms of the true gospel as he had delivered it, anticipates that their response will be to blame those influencing them otherwise, and makes it clear that they must not persist in their present course, which includes unjust behavior toward Paul and is without excuse before God. In the balance of the essay, Martin articulates the details of his approach.

The final essay in this section, by Carl Joachim Classen, "St. Paul's Epistles and Ancient Greek and Roman Rhetoric" offers a critique of methodological issues that arise—or at least should arise—for these approaches to rhetorical analysis in general and to the application to Galatians in particular. In addition, he traces examples of rhetorical analysis of Paul's letter that precede the contemporary debate touched off by Betz's essay and commentary on Galatians, especially the sixteenth-century work of Melanchthon, who invented a fourth genre to categorize Galatians, *instruction* rhetoric *(genus didacticum)* [cf. 101]. Although Classen recognizes that Paul would have "imbib[ed] applied rhetoric from others" through reading, "even if he never heard of any rules of rhetorical theory," he is comfortable with the notion that Paul probably had some direct knowledge of such theory [97–98 and n. 11]. Moreover, Paul's Tanak studies would have contributed to some level of rhetorical sophistication. Whatever the historical case, Classen's point is that the contemporary critic of Paul's correspondence should not limit himself or herself to the rhetorical resources available to a person of Paul's time, beyond an interest in, for example, demonstrating the extent of Paul's familiarity with such theories and practices. Otherwise, for the rhetorical analysis of texts, instead of adopting the author's limitations, "one should not hesitate to use the most developed and sophisticated form" (97). Furthermore, Classen observes another limitation to analysis of Galatians from ancient rhetoric alone: "The categories of ancient rhetoric fail us with respect to the structure of this epistle, because it is an epistle, and they were not made nor meant to fit such kinds of composition" (109). Such an observation introduces a fitting transition to the discussions arising in our next section.

Epistolary Approaches

While Betz was probing the application of ancient forensic rhetorical theory to this letter (which effort included noting formal features of the epistolary structure), Nils A. Dahl was focusing primarily on the promise of ancient epistolary theory. Whereas Betz combed the rhetorical manuals of Aristotle, Cicero, and Quintilian, to name a few, Dahl searched the epistolary handbooks of Pseudo-Libanius and Pseudo-Demetrius and the papyri exemplifying ancient correspondence. The product of Dahl's research was presented to the 1973 SBL seminar entitled "The Form and Function of the Pauline Letters." Until now this paper, "Paul's Letter to the Galatians," has been available only to a small number of Pauline scholars who met together to discuss the promise of epistolary and rhetorical approaches to Galatians, or those to whom they passed it on. Although it has not been entirely overlooked by recent interpreters, its influence can hardly be compared to that of the rhetorical approach.[6] The case for two different lines

---

[6] Those who refer to Dahl's paper in their analysis include, e.g., Hester; R. Longenecker; Hansen, a student of R. Longenecker; and myself, thanks to the gracious offer of a copy from Jerome Neyrey, who received it at a seminar at Yale that same year.

of research should not be overstated, however, because certainly both Dahl and Betz were participating in the same meetings and reviewing the same literature.[7]

In "Paul's Letter to the Galatians: Epistolary Genre, Content, and Structure," Dahl demonstrates the results of an epistolary approach to identifying the genre and structure of Galatians, although, for the sake of space, only two sections of the paper are included here, while three other sections and several charts and appendixes are omitted. Dahl combines the insights of epistolary specialists—who noted that the opening rebuke and expression of surprise were consistent with many examples, from ancient papyri letters, of a form that could be labeled "ironic rebuke"—with his recognition of the special place of irony in such expressions according to the ancient epistolary handbooks. This leads him to suggest that, although representing a change of style from Paul's other extant letters, the opening to Galatians is not a deviation from epistolary conventions. This is a very common letter style—in fact, more frequent in the extant papyri letters than thanksgiving openings—by which the writer expresses disappointment and disapproval through a statement of feigned surprise, that is, ironically. This ironically rebuking expression of surprise is often accompanied by rhetorical questions of the same nature. But rather than implying a bad relationship with the addressees, "even in reproaches θαυμάζω ["surprise"] is mainly used when the relationship between sender and recipient is basically good and has been good in the past"; moreover, "the ironic rebuke is an indirect 'expression of affection and concern' (φιλοφρόνησις) for the addressees" (119). The rebuke undermines the recipient's negligence, failure to comply with instructions, or some other inappropriate or foolish action, but it does so on the basis of an ongoing relationship, and thus the writer's continued expectations for a good-will response. Dahl discusses many examples that parallel the style, expressions, and message of Galatians.

Dahl's analysis of the structure and message of Galatians as a letter instead of a speech yields much to compare with the above analyses. He separates passages "that are more directly addressed to the epistolary situation (1:1–5, 6–10; 3:1–5; 4:8–11, 12, 13–20; 5:2–12; 6:11–16, 17, 18)," wherein the expressions of surprise and distress along with rebuking questions and all the explicit references to those influencing the addressees in Galatia are contained, from the four self-contained narrative units expressing more general information (1:12–2:21; 3:4–29 and 4:1–7; 4:21–31 and 5:1; and 5:13–6:10) [131]. For Dahl, 1:6–4:11 forms a structural unit in which Paul expresses his reaction to developments in the Galatian congregations, providing the background for the request or pleading section of 4:12–6:10. At 4:12, Paul, as the writers of other letters of ironic rebuke often do—and, mutatis mutandis, in ways that can be detected in the structure of many of his other letters—asks the recipients to do what they have thus far neglected. The letter body is framed by a salutation in

---

[7] Betz notes his debt to members of the seminar, mentioning Nils Dahl, Robert Funk, M. Luther Stirewalt, and John White specifically (Betz, "Literary Composition," 4 n. 9), and refers to Dahl's paper (9 n. 44). The exchange of ideas is obvious; note the many references in Betz's work to the epistolary handbooks and papyri, and in Dahl's paper to the classical rhetoricians.

1:1–5 and an autobiographical epilogue that summarizes the contrast between himself and the advocates of circumcision and draws attention to the importance of remaining on the course set by Paul (6:11–18).

There are many differences advanced for the formal, functional, and structural elements of the letter and the meaning of its various sections; yet the letter's purpose is for Dahl not that different from that of the rhetorical analysts noted above: "to make these churches dissociate themselves from the intruders and again follow the apostle and his gospel" (138). Nevertheless, the way the rhetorical data are understood to be organized may have significant results, for example, on how the interpreter identifies the players and situations in Galatia that Paul sought to influence and the ones whose influence he sought to obstruct.

In "A Paradigm of the Apocalypse: The Gospel in the Light of Epistolary Analysis,"[8] G. Walter Hansen develops a few specific insights on the topic of Paul's gospel that result from an epistolary approach similar to Dahl's. The theme and mood of the letter are stated in the opening expression of surprise (θαυμάζω) that the addressees have defected from the true gospel, and this rebuke extends from 1:6 to 4:11 (cf. 1:6, 9; 3:1–5; 4:9, 12). For Hansen, the request of 4:12 is the decisive turning point of the letter, and the request section is understood to run from 4:12 to 6:10. Paul turns from rebuking the addressees for their defection from the gospel to appealing to them to live instead according to it. His appeal in 4:12–20 becomes a focal point of this transition, not the subsidiary argument or digression of many rhetorical approaches. Instead of reading Paul's prior autobiographical comments (1:11–2:21) and arguments about Abraham (3:6–4:11) as a defense against accusations brought by Paul's supposed opponents, according to Hansen they represent parallel paradigms of the power of the gospel to prepare the way for the request Paul will make—namely, to make central to their lives the gospel of Christ. The authority of the gospel is at stake; it is the power of faith in that authority that the faithfulness of Paul and Abraham exemplify. Hansen proposes that the epistolary salutation (1:1–5) introduces the theme of the letter: "Paul's personal participation in the gospel—the death and resurrection of Jesus—was a participation in the apocalypse, the intervention of God within history which brought to an end the old world order and brought into being the new creation" (151). The subscription (6:11–18) restates the request to become like Paul, that is, to imitate his experience based upon the apocalyptic event of the cross of Christ.

Part 2: Autobiographical Narratives

Paul's autobiographical remarks in Galatians 1 and 2 have influenced not only the way that this letter has been interpreted but also represent the most extensive firsthand report of Paul's life before faith in Christ and both at and after his change of conviction about the meaning of Jesus (and the groups of Christ-believers). As a re-

---

[8] Hansen, *Abraham in Galatians,* 221 n. 22, for expression of his debt to Dahl's paper.

sult, constructions of Paul, of Paulinism, and of the early church all draw significantly from this material. The information is, however, embedded in a narrative fashioned to persuade the Galatian addressees in specific ways in view of Paul's perception of their situation. As a result, the interpreter who draws upon it must construct—or otherwise assume the shape of—the interpretive frame by which to analyze the relatively brief details of events that did not take place in Galatia, whether or not he or she is concerned specifically with interpreting the Galatian situation and Paul's rhetorical approach to it. In other words, the rhetorical analysis of the series of narrative units in Galatians 1 and 2 must consider the rhetorical issues that arise therein, but also their relationship to Paul's larger argument in the letter.

Part 2 of the volume presents several rhetorical and sociohistorical interpretations that exemplify the modern debate on the autobiographical narrative units of the first two chapters. The three rhetorical essays represent significantly different approaches, whereas the four sociohistorical essays often explicitly interact with each other. Indeed, most of them deal with the Antioch incident of Gal 2:11–21. As a result, this section provides the most comprehensive discussion to date of both the issues and the probable solutions for understanding the conflict between Paul and Peter around which this narrative turns.

Rhetorical Approaches

Paul Koptak's "Rhetorical Identification in Paul's Autobiographical Narrative: Galatians 1:13–2:14," employs the literary-rhetorical method of Kenneth Burke, specifically, his idea of identification. Unlike most of the approaches surveyed to this point, this method does not emphasize a contest of opinion in which the communicator seeks to persuade to his or her own side, certainly not in the sense of a defense; instead, it considers the way in which he or she goes about eliciting "consensus and cooperation by demonstrating what Burke calls a 'consubstantiality' between communicator and audience" (160). That is, it seeks to show how they "stand together" with a similar concern or interest. When the communicator identifies with the concerns of the audience, the audience in turn begins to identify with those of the communicator. Koptak thus seeks to understand how Paul rhetorically identifies with the audience and seeks to win their identification with himself. To the degree that they identify themselves standing with Paul, they will recognize also the distance that stands between themselves and those who do not share their (the addressees' and Paul's consubstantially united) understanding of the gospel of Christ.

A few examples will indicate the difference this method can make. The oppositional relationship Paul stresses in Galatians 1 is observed to be between human and divine authority in Paul's own life before and since his confession of Christ—a change of perspective that he shares with the other apostles in Jerusalem. Thus, even if pursuit of the divine course set for him kept them apart for many years, this does not imply, as it does for most interpreters, that "he was a rebel or did not agree with them" (163). Likewise, 2:1–10 is understood by Koptak to show that the Jerusalem apostles stand with Paul on the gospel God revealed to him, even in the face of opposition from those who did not identify with that gospel of Christ. The apostles also choose to please God rather than human authorities. Paul draws the Galatian addressees into this identification, approaching the choice as one of either identify-ing with the gospel of Paul, which the Jerusalem apostles and Paul preserved for them through "cooperative independence," or undermining it by choosing the other messengers and their gospel, which would parallel a choice to identify with the "false brothers" (v. 5). The Antioch incident of 2:11–14 is understood to illustrate the negative alternative, "how the consubstantial principles of unity and equality are betrayed when one chooses to base one's actions on the desire to please humans rather than God" (166). For Koptak, Paul "brings the Gentiles into fellowship with the Jewish church and he alone stands with them when all other Jewish Chris-tians withdraw" (168). By way of identification, Paul uses the autobiographical narra-tive "to create a rhetorical community that the Galatians were forced either to join or reject" (168).

In "Paul's Argumentation in Galatians 1–2," Johan Vos begins with an under-standing that Paul is engaged in a polemic against rival missionaries influencing the Galatian churches. Vos characterizes with "certainty" these "opponents" as Christ-believers who regard Paul's gospel as incomplete because it lacked inclusion of "the commandment of circumcision as a prerequisite for full membership among the people of God" (169). Then Vos sets out to demonstrate that the autobiographical narrative of Galatians 1 and 2 can be understood "as an answer to the sole demand of circumcision or obedience to the law of Moses and that it is unnecessary to recon-struct other charges" (170). With these decisions in hand about the nature of the his-torical situation and the specific limits of Paul's defensive rhetoric (in the sense of an apologetic for the truth of the gospel but not a defense of his apostleship per se), Vos explains why it is inadvisable to follow the consensus in understanding many of Paul's comments to indicate other charges at issue. For example, the prescript of 1:1–5 anticipates the core argument to follow but is offensive in focus: "The divine authorization of the apostle is the decisive argument against the other gospel" (171). Vos classifies 1:6–9 as the *propositio* and finds here the main thesis set out in rebuke and with a conditional curse: "The true gospel is not the gospel of the opponents, but only that of Paul" (173). He explains why the other classifications advanced by rhetorical critics fail to account adequately for the material. Galatians 1:10–12 constitutes a *confirmatio* argued by enthymemes, that is, by a series of syllogisms through which Paul draws attention to the fact that the tone and content of vv. 6–9 demonstrate that Paul is not a flatterer or servant of humans but a servant of God who speaks the truth. Such appeals to ethos as a way of legitimizing the content of a rhetor's speech can indicate he or she has rivals in mind, or they can represent stereotypical antithesis, but they need not indicate a prior accusation. According to Vos, Paul is not defending himself but proving the truth of his gospel. Vos describes 1:13–2:14(21) as the narrative *confirmatio*. Galatians 1:13–24 confirms Paul's legiti-macy by way of historical evidence (v. 12); 2:1–10 confirms that the Jerusalem au-thorities endorsed the truth of his gospel and his way of legitimizing it and demonstrates his faithful ethos in the face of challengers; and 2:11–14(21) confirms

Paul's faithful ethos even before Peter and at the same time demonstrates that even Paul's ethos is subservient to the truth of the gospel. Rather than one of the three genres of classical classification, Vos prefers Melanchthon's category of "didactic" to describe Paul's autobiographical narrative, wherein Paul "defended the truth of his gospel in the face of a contrary gospel and gave instructions as to its nature" (180).

James Hester's new contribution to the debate, "Epideictic Rhetoric and Persona in Galatians 1 and 2," serves several functions. It could have been included in part 1 to exemplify an argument for classifying Galatians as epideictic, a less represented position to date. And Hester pursues this rhetorical approach by attending to epistolary conventions in a way that contributes to the above epistolary discussions of Galatians. But the essay is included in part 2 because it concentrates upon analysis of the narrative discourse of Galatians 1 and 2, bringing to bear tools ranging from rhetorical and epistolary theories and practices, both ancient and modern, to the introduction of a new method to the discussion, symbolic convergence theory. Hester categorizes Galatians as a letter of blame, a letter style that expresses a benefactor's attempt to criticize and/or shame the recipients for a perceived wrong done by them to the benefactor and yet still attempts to maintain the relationship. This can be further refined as blame in the sense of reproach, wherein the accused party has benefited from the effort of the writer but now takes on an attitude or change of behavior that threatens the relationship, indicating a failure to remember the debt of gratitude owed. In addition, Hester notes elements of other letter styles, such as rebuke and censure for the addressees' choice of beliefs and behavior known to be wrong (1:8–9; 4:8–11, 21; 5:2, 13, 17), and he observes elements of vituperation (5:2–12), irony (1:6–7; 3:1–5 [sarcasm]), and *paraenesis* (5:16–6:10). These epistolary observations Hester links with elements that exemplify epideictic, not only Paul's expression of disapproval but, more important, the topics of encomium that arise in 1:13–2:14, since encomium "represents the aim and scope of epideictic literature" (188, quoting Burgess). Hester argues that "the narrative section is fashioned as an encomium because of the ability of the encomium to express character, and for its usefulness in fulfilling the argumentative purpose of character contrast" (190). In a detailed comparison of the topics of encomiums with Paul's autobiographical narrative, Hester uncovers many parallels. Most important, Hester argues that Paul begins to shift the blame from the Galatian recipients as observers to them as participants with the chreia in 2:14, followed by the elaboration of vv. 15–21, which changes to inclusive language. He concludes that Paul, "having established the issue (stasis [of quality of the gospel and relationship with Paul]), launches into an encomiastic narrative to illustrate the legitimacy of his gospel. Its character was so superior to anything the Galatians might have encountered subsequently that because of it he triumphed over his unnamed enemies in Jerusalem and shamed Peter in Antioch" (191). In sum, "Paul is the enactment of his own vision; he is proof of his own argument and an example of one who is led by his rhetorical vision" (195). He expects the addressees to both imitate his character and obey his persona.

Sociohistorical Approaches

Since 1983, James D. G. Dunn's essay, "The Incident at Antioch (Gal. 2.11–18)," has represented one of—if not the—most comprehensive examinations of the conflict narrated in Gal 2:11–21 (11–14 for some interpreters). Dunn questions the exegetical assumption of previous interpretations that simply the role of Jewish food laws was at issue. The historical evidence available suggests to Dunn that one problem with traditional readings is the failure to grasp that "earliest Christianity was not yet seen as something separate and distinct from Judaism"; even if holding "some distinct and peculiar beliefs about Jesus," it was a "religion of the Jews" (201, emphasis omitted). The questions that arose had to do with the requirements for the inclusion of Gentiles within these Jewish groups. The group in Antioch would have continued to understand itself in a dynamic relationship with the leaders in Jerusalem, "recognizing the church at Jerusalem as the fountainhead of their distinctive faith" (202). Paul shared this perspective also, Dunn argues, until after this incident. In addition, Dunn seeks to account for the political, religious, and economic constraints faced by Jewish groups in Antioch as well as in Judea during this period of life in the Roman Empire; these would have created inter- and intracommunal tensions for the Jewish groups believing in Jesus. Dunn concludes, "The open table-fellowship practised at Antioch was perceived by the Jerusalem church (and perhaps by other Jews) as a threat" to their "heritage"; "the mission of the men from James would then have been their reaction to that threat" (206). In this light, Dunn seeks to examine the way the table fellowship would have been perceived from the perspective of "the ones from James."

Dunn offers a detailed discussion of many sociohistorical features, including issues of purity, food, and the various active identity systems for approaching interaction with non-Jewish and even with diverse Jewish people, and the topics raised on these matters will occupy an important portion of the debates that arise in the following essays. As a result of Dunn's understanding of these historical—largely religious—issues, coupled with his interpretation of key terms in Paul's text, he proposes that three alternatives remain for interpreting the incident at Antioch. He decides against the first and second alternatives. For Dunn, it is unlikely that Peter and the other Jewish believers in Jesus "had completely abandoned the laws governing table-fellowship" or that Paul would have reacted so negatively if at issue were "merely that the Gentiles should observe the most basic laws of the Torah—the Noahic laws" (222–24). And it is unlikely that Paul would employ the terminology he did if at issue were the final stage of proselyte conversion; moreover, it is doubtful that "Peter would have abandoned in Antioch an agreement made in Jerusalem" (225). He settles on the third alternative, falling somewhere between the other two offered. Although some basic food laws were being observed by Jews and Gentiles alike at this table, "what the men from James would have called for was a much more scrupulous observance of the rulings on what the dietary laws involved, especially with regard to ritual purity and tithing" (225). The reasons Peter withdrew are suggested to be his acceptance of the logic of this demand; his native sensibilities to the pressure threatening Jewish groups, especially his fellow Christ-believers; his concern to preserve a good reputation among Jews; his acknowledgment of the authority of Jerusalem; and his deduction that these Gentiles would be willing to go along for the sake of their Jewish brothers and sisters. In turn, Paul is understood to have recognized "for the first time, probably," that "the principle of 'justification through faith' applied not simply to the acceptance of the gospel in conversion, but also to the whole of the believer's life" (230). Thus, Dunn concludes, Paul saw that to "live life 'in Christ' *and* 'in accordance with the law' was not possible; it involved a basic contradiction in terms and in the understanding of what made someone acceptable to God" (230, emphasis his).

"Judaism, the Circumcision of Gentiles, and Apocalyptic Hope: Another Look at Galatians 1 and 2" by Paula Fredriksen covers many substantial historical issues that need to be investigated by the exegete approaching this narrative. She seeks to understand Paul's arguments "within his own religious context, first-century Judaism" and, in particular, within the views that prevailed among certain Jewish people and groups toward Gentiles, that is, representatives of nations other than Israel (236). Fredriksen argues that Gentiles were generally seen as idolaters unless they chose to convert and become proselytes and observers of Jewish life. In between these two identities there is a third very broad category of "anomalous" Gentiles, Gentiles who adopt some Jewish ways of life, associate with Jewish communities in certain ways, become benefactors of Jewish communities, and so on, yet without electing to become proselytes. In some cases it is apparent that they continued to participate in public idolatry concomitant with their role in the larger non-Jewish community. These Gentiles are sometimes identified as "God-fearers." But there is also another category to consider, that is, the eschatological images of Gentiles: what is the place of Gentile people at the end of the ages? At the negative extreme were those who anticipated the destruction of the nations—in most cases, of the unrighteous Gentiles among them. At the positive extreme were those who anticipated that in the end "the nations participate in Israel's redemption" (244). The repudiation of idols to turn to the living God at the end represents a moral but not a halakic conversion; they will be included (saved) in the people of God as Gentiles who are no longer idolaters, yet they will still not be Jews/Israelites.

These conclusions in hand, Fredriksen discusses the political reasons that would account for Paul's prior persecution—disciplinary flogging—of Jewish believers in Jesus. Finding fault with the largely theological reasons usually proposed, she instead argues that Paul reacted to "apostles enthusiastically proclaiming the imminent subjection of the present order through the (returning) Messiah to the coming Kingdom of God," in synagogues that included Gentiles, some responding positively to this message, so that together these believers in Jesus "would constitute a committed, energetic, and vocal subgroup *within* the larger community" (253, emphasis hers). The larger Jewish community would have been concerned that proclamations to Gentiles of a crucified Messiah—a political troublemaker in Roman terms—would eventually become known in the larger non-Jewish community, posing a threat to working relationships they enjoyed with the local Roman government. Paul may have represented the synagogue court's jurisdiction over its Jewish members in order to avoid this risk. Fredriksen suggests that, in view of the failure of the expected events of the parousia, over the next decades some Christ-believing Jews began to seek the incorporation of Gentiles by proselyte conversion in order to further the Jewish mission in the meantime, since otherwise they faced a problem of creditability among Jewish groups. Faced with "too many Gentiles, too few Jews, and no End in sight," Paul came to see that, paradoxically, the restoration of Israel awaited the completion of his "work among the Gentiles, bringing their donation, and in a sense themselves, as an acceptable sacrifice to Jerusalem" (258). Central to Fredriksen's interpretation of Paul's proposition is the notion that he held to the conviction that Gentiles remain Gentiles.

Philip F. Esler challenges the usual way of viewing Peter's ostensible change of course between the Jerusalem meeting (2:1–10) and the Antioch incident (2:11–14[21]) in "Making and Breaking an Agreement Mediterranean Style: A New Reading of Galatians 2:1–14." Indeed, Esler magnifies the difference, suggesting Peter's withdrawal at Antioch represents an intentional breach of the agreement reached in Jerusalem. When it comes to setting out the Jewish context by which to evaluate the social values at issue, Esler understands both the prevailing norms and the situation described very differently than do the interpreters of the other essays in this section. Esler argues that Jews would not dine with Gentiles in the particular way that he believes would have been necessary to share eucharistic meals, which meals he understands to be the setting of the Antioch incident. The Jews would have been concerned to avoid the widespread Gentile habit of offering the gods a libation from the wine they drank and to avoid having to share a loaf of bread with someone who also ate idol food. This fear of idolatry led them to demand the circumcision (conversion) of the Christ-believing Gentiles if they were to return to the table (at Antioch) or avoid exclusion from it (in Galatia).

To make this case, Esler pursues several theses. Methodologically, he appeals to Mediterranean cultural studies to argue that Paul's narrative signifies an honor challenge. Esler explains the model he adopts, and when he applies it to the conflict that Paul relates, he concludes, in short, that the agreement that appeared to be reached in Jerusalem in response to Paul's initiation of an honor challenge was ultimately found to be nonbinding. Since it was not sealed with an oath, Paul was vulnerable to being shamed if he acted upon the ostensible agreement. Esler understands the agreement between the Jerusalem apostles and Paul to guarantee eucharistic table fellowship with Gentiles in the Diaspora without requiring proselyte conversion. It was opposed by a strict faction of Christ-believing Jews in Jerusalem, but they suffered defeat. They eventually brought sufficient pressure to bear, however, to persuade the Jerusalem apostles to renege on the agreement, thus avenging their earlier loss of honor. The ultimate termination of that table fellowship by Peter when he is in Paul's Diaspora zone signifies the leadership reneging on its earlier agreement. It is understood to be to Paul's shame because the agreement could not be proven, apart from an oath, to reflect their true intentions; hence, it was not their honor that was impugned but Paul's. Thus Paul cannot come right out and accuse Peter of breaking the agreement when calling for the circumcision of the Gentiles in Antioch after the arrival of the ones from James; instead, he merely accuses Peter of inconsistency.

In the final essay in this section, Mark D. Nanos offers a new contribution to the debate, "What Was at Stake in Peter's 'Eating with Gentiles' at Antioch?" Two particular questions are at the center of the investigation: 1) What did the "ones of/for circumcision" find objectionable about Peter's eating with Gentiles, and as part of that question, why did Peter fear them? 2) What did Paul find so objectionable about Peter's subsequent withdrawal and separation from those meals? To discover the answers, other issues are raised and discussed, such as the identities of the parties involved and the appropriateness of analyzing the sociotheological setting through a pre-Christian Jewish communal lens. From the start, the prevailing portraits of Paul—which naturally influence the kinds of hypotheses that have been considered in order to interpret his message—are challenged. Instead of assuming that Paul was against observation of a Jewish diet for Jewish believers in Jesus, or even just indifferent to the matter, it is assumed that he both held it to be important for these Jews and practiced it as significant for himself. Moreover, Nanos maintains that the Gentiles involved had already adopted the diet expected of Gentiles seeking to associate at mixed meals, so that the food laws were not themselves at dispute and neither was the fact that Jews and Gentiles were eating together, whether at a eucharistic meal or at some other kind. Nanos argues that "the ones ἐκ [for] circumcision" should be identified as non-Christ-believing Antiochene Jews, perhaps a special-interest group that advocates the prevailing view for how to incorporate Gentiles as equals within any Jewish group, regardless of what they believe about Jesus, and thus objects to the policies being advocated by the Christ-believing groups in Antioch. The "certain ones from James" are identified also as most likely representing non-Christ-believing interest groups, but with James' permission, or, alternately, as supportive of the mixed meals. Beyond the timing supplied by noting their arrival, the purpose of their coming and its relationship to the events that followed are not clear. It is specifically "the ones for circumcision" whom Peter is said to fear, not the "certain ones from James," and it is this group or groups that Nanos believes to be central to understanding the historical situation.

After discussing other views, especially those expressed in the above essays, Nanos argues that what was at stake was not the food or that it was being shared with Gentiles per se. Rather, it was the way it was being shared, that is, among equals, which is a pattern reserved for those who have become proselytes; but such a policy of equality is not extended to mere Gentile guests or those who have not embarked upon the course of becoming proselytes or declared any intention to do so. Thus, Nanos proposes, this mixed meal signified the novel and dangerous claims to status being made for the Gentiles within this Jewish group. It symbolized the claim that the end of the ages had dawned in the death and resurrection of Jesus, the time of eschatological *shalom*. Naturally, this claim—together with the social results its implementation would impose upon the larger Jewish minority communities and upon the larger Greco-Roman society into which the Jewish communities were intimately networked—was cause for concern and for action that can be understood to signify tensions both within the communities and between them. According to Nanos, it is just such social dynamics, and the theological claims they symbolize, that Paul's narration of the Antioch incident reveals, interpreted from Paul's perspective for the sake of achieving his rhetorical goals for the later Galatian addressees.

Part 3: The Galatian Situation(s)

The third section comprises essays that seek to construct the situation(s) of the addressees in Galatia. There is a distinction in Paul's letter between the narrative discourse units, in which Paul relates the stories of prior situations of his life (e.g., Jerusalem, Antioch), and the situational discourse units, in which Paul directly addresses the present situation of the recipients of the letter in Galatia. Although those narratives were designed and included to achieve his rhetorical aims for the addressees, they do not relate the events that are taking place in Galatia, and their relationship to the events of the addressees is a matter of interpretation. The organization of this volume is intended to help clarify this matter for the reader. For the most part, while the essays in part 2 concerned interpretation of the narratives in Galatians 1 and 2, the essays in this section focus upon the historical and rhetorical situations of the addressees. A range of rhetorical, literary, sociological, social scientific, historical, and theological approaches are employed in the process. The debates turn largely on how one constructs the identities, interests, and messages of those people whose influence over the addressees is opposed by Paul. What were their goals, their strategies, and the specific techniques employed to achieve them? Also important to these discussions are the ways that the addressees and their situations are conceptualized, the way Paul's former influence among them is understood, and the way that the purpose of the message he conveyed in this letter is perceived. Together, these kinds of elements constitute the discussion of the context of the addressees, and decisions—or assumptions—about these matters ineluctably shape the theological interpretation of Paul's language.

The section begins with A. E. Harvey's essay, "The Opposition to Paul," which offered a challenge to the prevailing lines of argument developed during the mid-nineteenth to mid-twentieth centuries. At the time of Harvey's article, these debates were framed by F. C. Baur's hypothesis that Paul's rhetoric reveals a mission to undo his work on the part of "opponents" originating from Jerusalem to execute the interests of James and Peter. Even the interpreters that challenged this hypothesis generally understood the issues to be framed by features of its construction and, in particular, the fact and nature of Paul's opposition, even if the reasons for it and the representatives of it were differently portrayed. Yet while Harvey retains the notion that Paul responds in Galatians to opposition—communicated in the title itself—he raises questions where many others had not. He cautions against mirror-reading prior opposition from Paul's arguments in the letter, noting in particular that some of Paul's arguments in 1 Corinthians reflect not prior opposition but failure to consider the implications in ways that Paul therein seeks to arouse.

It is clear to Harvey that there is pressure being exerted upon the addressees to get circumcised. To understand this pressure, Harvey argues for several preliminary situational elements: 1) the addressees are Christians, and most of them Gentiles who had been God-fearers in the synagogues of Galatia previously but without deciding to become proselytes; 2) when they "first became Christians they had made a clean break from the Jewish community" but then later "had already renewed their contact with the synagogue to the extent of observing the Jewish festivals and holy days, and were now contemplating the further step of accepting circumcision"; and 3) those bringing this pressure to bear must have been Jewish proselytes or those contemplating becoming such, on the basis of Harvey's understanding of the participle in 6:13: "those who get themselves circumcised" (324–26). The pressure is understood to be by the local synagogues upon former God-fearing Gentile members of the Christian churches. The goal is not to "wean the Christians from their new faith"; rather, it is "to make them conform to an outward pattern of Jewish observances" (328). "Reprisals" against these former "supporters from the synagogue" are considered "inevitable unless those who had defected could not merely be brought back to their former allegiance but made to commit themselves permanently by accepting circumcision and persuading their fellow-Christians to do the same" (328). This pressure was "sometimes supported by powerful propaganda, sometimes by the threat of persecution" (331–32). Thus "Paul's real opponents are those Christians in Galatia who are ready to yield to this pressure and are persuading others to do the same" (328). The addressees' concerns are fear and expediency, and thus they seek a compromise that they believe does not threaten their faith in Christ; after all, the pressure is "mediated by Jews or Gentiles within the church" (331–32). "Paul's task is not so much to meet their arguments as to show them up as having no arguments, indeed as having given the matter no serious thought at all" (330). Harvey signals that one significant result of this argument is that it moves the interest of the opposition from the traditional theological concern with Judaism to a more pragmatic one, which he believes befits the usual Jewish tolerance for a wide range of beliefs and interpretations: a greater concern that behavior conform with patterns of Jewish observance. Harvey's view represents a challenge to the theological, if not sociological, heart of the Baur hypothesis, including many of the elements shared by most, if not all, of arguments that have been mounted against it.

Robert Jewett's essay, "The Agitators and the Galatian Congregation," represents an argument that has been often cited, and its influence is evident in many monographs and commentaries. He opens with a brief but lucid discussion of the various prevailing views of the time, and he takes as his point of departure a challenge posed by Walther Schmithals that Jewett finds still unsatisfactorily answered at the time, even by Schmithals's conclusions. The question is also important for what it reveals about the framework of the discussion at the time: "Why would Jewish Christians suddenly lose their traditional disinterest in the Gentile mission and embark on a circumcision campaign in Galatia?" (336). Jewett constructs a situation in Galatia that includes people who "had come into Galatia with the aim of stirring up the congregation and perverting the gospel" (336). They require circumcision of the

Christ-believing Gentiles "on grounds that entrance into the elect spiritual community demanded prior admission into Abraham's covenant through circumcision" (336). Among other indications, Jewett identifies the "agitators" as "Christian believers," on the basis of his understanding of the implications of 1:7 and 6:12 (336–37); as Jews advocating the circumcision of these Gentiles, on the basis of his interpretation of the participle in 6:13 (337–39); as outsiders, on the basis of the implications of 1:6 and 4:17, among others (339); and as originating from, and oriented to, Jerusalem, for several reasons (339–40).

This relatively traditional construction in hand, Jewett sets out to explain an interesting paradox that arises from his understanding of Paul's remark in 6:12 that the advocates of circumcision in Galatia are motivated to succeed at this task in order to avoid "persecution for the cross of Christ." He understands the feared persecution to be anti-Pauline, yet the motivation to circumcise these Gentiles to be avoidance of that persecution. How can one make sense of this? To solve this apparent problem, Jewett offers a new construction of the situation in Galatia that is intimately linked with political constraints originating from Judea and Jerusalem. The leaders of the Christ-believers there were under pressure to comply with the norms of "the Zealots," whom Jewett understands to represent mortal danger to those "in the villages of Judea or Galilee who maintained close relationships with Gentiles or who did not zealously seek the purity of Israel" (340). During the late forties and early fifties, in order for the Christ-believers in Judea to "avert the suspicion that they were in communion with lawless Gentiles" and thereby "thwart Zealot reprisals," they sought to have the Christ-believing Gentiles circumcised (341). This program extended out to Antioch and Galatia in order to protect the Judean churches from reprisals. It was not primarily a theological interest that motivated this mission to Galatia, provoking Paul's letter, but an expedient political agenda, which, for Jewett, makes sense of several of Paul's statements that remain largely unexplained in the alternative views. Moreover, their strategy was "cleverly designed" to seem to the Galatians to "offer a completion" rather than opposition to Paul's work (342; cf. 343). They seemed to offer the promise of perfection in a way that would appeal to the Hellenistic sensibilities of the addressees, promising them entrance into Abraham's promise, identity as part of Israel, perfection in the Spirit. Their goal was, after all, to get the Galatians to comply so that they could return home with news that would get the pressure off the Judean churches; the level of commitment to Torah or the lifestyle of a proselyte thereafter were not really their immediate concern. Hence, Paul's ethical instructions are explained as addressing the failure of the Galatians to grasp the ethical imperatives of life in the Spirit or the suffering of an ultimate judgment. The puzzle of "pneumatic libertinism" at the same time as "nomism" is understood to be the result of their believing that circumcision promised perfection, but did not require a nomistic lifestyle, except for circumcision and some calendrical practices that would "ensure entrance into the mythical seed of Abraham" (347).

In the title, "A Law-Observant Mission to Gentiles," J. Louis Martyn signals the central thrust of his argument. Martyn's construction of the situation in Galatia depends largely upon the way he understands the identity of the ones whom Paul opposes, to which he immediately turns. He labels them "the Teachers" to avoid identifying them solely by way of their relationship with Paul; moreover, referring to them as "opponents" is "somewhat reductionist." For, even if Martyn finds them to be opposing Paul, he notes that Paul considers them opponents "not merely of himself" but "of *God*" (349, emphasis his). To begin with, the Teachers "have connections both with Diaspora Judaism and with Palestinian, Christian Judaism." They are "messianic Jews, at home among Gentiles," who are "in touch with—indeed understand themselves to represent—a powerful circle of Christian Jews in the Jerusalem church, a group utterly zealous for the observance of the Law" (351).

To further elaborate the Teachers' identity, Martyn employs data from a range of documents from Diaspora Jews, Judeans, and Christian Jews of various places that he understands to parallel his interpretation of "Paul's own references to the Teachers' work" (351). To fill out the portrait with incremental precision, Martyn offers ten arguments from the "direct references" of the letter itself and four from "allusions." The Teachers are (1) outsiders, (2) Jewish people who have arrived from outside Galatia, (3) Christian-Jewish evangelists with a gospel (4) that proclaims both Christ and Law; (5) and this Law—"the covenantal Law of Sinai"—is presented by them as good news for Gentiles in their "ecumenical mission." They (6) seek "to correct what they see as the Law-less evangelism of Paul," in order to "keep on good terms with some persons of considerable power" and "perhaps understanding it [their mission] to be the means by which God is filling out the infinite number of progeny he had promised to the patriarch." They (7) argue for and demonstrate that the Law is the source of the Spirit (8) and that the Galatians will be shut out from salvation if they do not accept the conditions of their message, (9) namely, by becoming proselytes, the males circumcised, and observing the Jewish calendar as well as dietary regulations. For them, (10) "Christ is secondary to the Law," "the Messiah of the Law." The Teachers argue (11) that they are descendants of Abraham, which the Gentiles can become, too, if they become circumcised and Law-observant; (12) that Jerusalem—"the Jerusalem church"—is their "mother"; (13) that the Gentiles will become part of the people Israel if they accept their message; and (14) that they will escape the "Impulsive Desire of the Flesh" that still plagues their daily life, whereas Paul, "an unfaithful student of the Jerusalem apostles," has left them without "potent ethical guidance." This portrait in hand, in the balance of the essay Martyn elaborates what these Teachers' "Sermon on Abraham" to the Galatians might have been like—an interesting exercise for which he draws from the various sources noted above and integrates his interpretation of these with his interpretation of Paul's language in Galatians.

The contribution of Nikolaus Walter, "Paul and the Opponents of the Christ Gospel in Galatia," represents Mark Nanos's translation of the author's original German essay. Accepting the prevailing theses that Paul responds in Galatians to a Jewish mission opposing his "Law-free Christian . . . gospel," Walter challenges the identification of the rivals in Galatia as Christians and of their message as about Christ.

Their message is "not another version of the Christ proclamation but the opposite of a gospel of Christ: a gospel without Christ Jesus" (362). They incorporate similar language in order to "trick" the Galatians into a decision that turns them away from Christ without realizing it. They reprove Paul and discredit his gospel as human and blasphemous; their own message of Torah is, however, from God, having been given to Moses. Walter understands Paul to respond to their charges in part by "depreciating his relations with the Jerusalem Christians" in 1:15b–22; thus, they must have "depicted his dependence as something that devalued the message" (363). If that is so, then it is unlikely that they are Judaic Christians, since they, too, would be dependent upon Peter and James. These opponents see Peter, James, and Paul joined in "betraying the essentials of Judaism," even if Paul seems to them to be "the most dangerous," since he is actively reaching out to the Gentiles (364). Paul thus seeks to uphold the "faithful Law keeping of the original apostles in Jerusalem"—even though he is ambivalent about this strategy—because "they see the Law-free mission to the Gentiles not as 'betrayal' of the Torah and Judaism but as fulfillment of the will of God newly revealed in Christ Jesus" (364).

Although this group opposes Paul's mission, this is not their primary purpose but a side effect with which they must be concerned because they, too, are engaged in a mission to the Gentiles, but one that promotes proselyte conversion instead. And they do so by proclaiming the theme of "Abraham as the Father of Believers," not unlike what Martyn proposes, except that Walter understands their message to proclaim this independent of a relationship to Jesus Christ. Thus, just as they adopted Paul's terminology of εὐαγγέλιον to make their case against his message of Christ, Paul responds in this letter with an argument about Abraham that is designed to undermine their message without Christ. The promise to Abraham precedes Torah and came directly to Abraham, not by a mediator. Abraham's justification is by faith, not Torah. And it was "linked with a 'seed' (σπέρμα) of Abraham (in the singular!)—and this seed has come in Christ Jesus, no one else (Gal 3:14–16)" (365). Walter argues that "if the opponents were Christians, then such an argument would not have scored the necessary point!" Finally, Walter understands Paul to deny legitimate status as children of Abraham "to any Judaism that is bound to the service of Torah" (365). This kind of polemic, which Walter does not find Paul using when writing of Abraham in Romans 4 or 9–11, for example, leads him to suggest that Paul is afraid of their winning his converts away from Christ, but it "is hardly appropriate to use against Christian competitors" (365). Moreover, other elements of the letter and its differences from, for example, the way Walter understands Paul to approach the opponents of 2 Corinthians, leads him to conclude, "Must we, then, not assume that the opponents actually stand outside the churches, outside of any relationship with Christ, and that they do not desire so much to specifically invade the churches as, rather, on the contrary, to undermine and eliminate the churches by means of 'compelling' the Galatians away from Christ toward Torah (cf. 6:12–13)?" (366).

John M. G. Barclay's essay, "Mirror-Reading a Polemical Letter: Galatians as a Test Case," offers a helpful methodological discussion as well as an argument for the implications on the study of Galatians. Whether the reader of Paul agrees with his arguments or not, in order to "*understand* their real import," Barclay proposes that he or she will need to construct the issues at dispute and "enter into the debate from *both* sides" (367, emphasis his). The obstacle is that we often are faced with constructing from the author's point of view the thoughts and identities of those whom the author opposes. The text we have that supposedly "answers the opponents" is then used as a "mirror" to "see reflected the people and the arguments under attack" (367). For Galatians, the problem is magnified in several ways: 1) Paul is not directly addressing the opponents even if he is addressing the audience about them and the effect they have had, so it is not merely the audience at the other end of his comments but a third party whom we seek to identify; 2) this is polemical rhetoric from someone who believes "his whole identity and mission are threatened," and thus "his statements about the character and motivation of his opponents should be taken with a very large pinch of salt" because Paul shows them "in the worse possible light, with the hope of weaning the Galatians away from them"; and 3) there is a problem of circularity: the way Paul used language in dialogue "remains obscure until we can hypothesize the other end of the dialogue, and yet . . . in order to reconstruct that dialogue," we must use the same verses (370).

Barclay examines several examples of mirror-reading in the interpretation of Galatians that he judges to be subject to methodological "pitfalls." These are 1) "*undue selectivity*" of the texts and criteria to discern the identity and message of the opponents; 2) "*over-interpretation*" of certain statements as rebuttals of counter-statements that may not constitute accusations; 3) "*mishandling polemics*" by taking at face value some of Paul's statements about those he opposes and by taking Paul's side "unduly" or, alternately, using this language to criticize him; and 4) "*latching onto particular words and phrases* as direct echoes of the opponents' vocabulary and then hanging a whole thesis on those flimsy pegs" (372–76, emphasis his). Barclay lays out several suggestions for improving the criteria, including the need to measure carefully the 1) type of utterance; 2) tone; 3) frequency of theme; 4) clarity of evidence; 5) unfamiliar elements as perhaps more telling; 6) consistency of the portrait; and 7) historical plausibility of the construction on offer (376–78). This last category gives rise to Barclay's concluding argument for measuring the plausibility of various aspects of the construction of the Galatian situation on offer and of his own suggestions. To review but one of the categories, Barclay concludes that it is "certain or virtually certain" that 1) "Paul's opponents were Christians"; 2) "they wanted the Galatians to be circumcised and to observe at least some of the rest of the law, including its calendrical requirements"; 3) "they brought into question the adequacy of Paul's gospel and his credentials as an apostle"; and 4) "their arguments were attractive and persuasive for many Galatian Christians" (380).

In "The Argumentative Situation of Galatians," B. C. Lategan begins with a helpful description of some of the elements of an argumentative situation. "No argument is necessary in a situation where matters are self-evident." But "when questions arise or doubt exists," then "argumentation is called for" (383). Argumentation is concerned with persuasion and involves a common language in order to facilitate communication; it also involves a communicator and audience. Lategan appeals to Perelman's distinguishing of three kinds of audiences: the universal audience, the single interlocutor, and the subject himself or herself. Moreover, however historically real the people whom the author addresses or argues about are, the audience is a construction in the mind of the one arguing, and it is from one's image of them and what one thinks will be important to them that one argues. The "quality of the argument and the strategy of the writer" are products of the author's perception of the audience, and by them he or she seeks to move the reader or hearer (384). For Lategan, argumentative situation and rhetorical situation are the same in concept but distinguishable in that the former emphasizes "the *issue* regarding which persuasion is attempted" whereas the latter attends to "the *strategies* used by the writer to effect persuasion" (384).

These definitions in hand, Lategan suggests that the audience for Galatians consists of the uncircumcised who are considering taking this step; those who are Jews by birth, "with whom he identifies himself by using the first person"; and maybe a universal audience inclusive of the contemporary reader, since Paul uses the first person in the autobiographical narrative of 2:17–20 in a way "which transcends the confines of a specific historical setting and which assumes a certain timeless quality" (385). After a brief discussion of the guidelines set out in Barclay's essay and a survey of some prevailing views, Lategan concludes that there is one direction of opposition facing Paul (against the two-front and some other views he surveys) and the tension concerns "two modes of existence—one of slavery under the law and one of freedom in Christ" (387). Lategan concludes that the central concern with Abraham in Paul's argument indicates that his position as "father of the believers" was emphasized by "the Galatians' opponents" and "a close link between Abraham and the law was taken for granted, which provided further authority for the demand that the law should be kept" (387). Paul accepts the premise of their argument but undermines the implications by arguing that Abraham as father must be taken as he was then, "uncircumcised, without the formalized law—in fact, a gentile—who trusted God and his promise and acted only out of faith" (388). The kinship relationship with Abraham, then, follows for the Gentile who has faith in Christ, Abraham's seed. The audience is moved to a new understanding of their socialization. Lategan also understands the cursing and rhetorical questions of 1:11–12 to indicate "a sensitivity to what appears to be an accusation by the opponents that Paul is playing for the gallery by preaching a soft or easy gospel" (389–90).

The ethical instructions of the last two chapters also illuminate the argumentative situation. These pivot around standing firm in the freedom made possible by Christ and in the command to walk in the Spirit, which flow from Paul's prior theological arguments. The ethical elements "are not cast in the form of commands or instructions, but represent a summary of the self-evident results flowing from a life controlled by the Spirit" (391). And these elements are typically Hellenistic as well as Jewish. Lategan understands the argumentative situation to concern Paul's response to such matters as the move from "independent ethical decisions" by his converts to "practical guidelines for the everyday life of the believer" on offer from

Paul's opponents. This response is grounded in Paul's theological convictions about "the new existence in faith" that Paul has argued (392). They must exercise freedom but also live in a spiritual way: "They will need neither him nor the crutches of a casuistic system" (393–94). So it seems to Lategan that there is an anti-Pauline opposition, that it seeks to convince the Galatians to observe Torah in addition to faith in Christ, and that this message was proving persuasive because of the disorientation of these Gentiles, who were "new to the Christian faith, but also unfamiliar with its Jewish roots," and thus needed "practical advice to guide their day to day life in an environment not very sympathetic to or supportive of their new convictions" (395).[9]

In "The Inter- and Intra-Jewish Political Context of Paul's Letter to the Galatians," Mark D. Nanos argues that in this letter Paul reacts to a situation in which his non-Jewish addressees, who had placed their faith in Paul's "message of good," were now having to negotiate the local communal constraints they faced in Galatia. Nanos asks, "How would Jewish communities in central Anatolia have responded to *Gentiles* claiming to be full and equal members of the communities of the righteous, on the basis of faith in Christ, apart from proselyte conversion?" (396). He suggests that a mixed response is implied by the way Paul frames his reaction in this letter. On the one hand, anyone claiming to have already gained full community status would have likely been denied, but on the other hand, anyone seeking to turn from idolatry to full membership among the people of God might be welcomed as potential proselytes. Nanos understands these Gentiles to be members of Jewish subgroups within the Jewish communities who are, after Paul's departure, beginning to interact more fully with other members of these larger local Jewish communities and, as a result, beginning to recognize some differences about their own (sub)group identity and expectations. Unwilling to return to the practices of family and civic idolatry and wishing to ensure their welcome as Gentile guests who did not seek to threaten the status quo—that is, the privilege the Jewish communities had negotiated with the pagan communities that allowed them to continue in their own way of life by, for example, abstaining from local civic expression of the imperial cult—these Gentiles may have considered proselyte identity, which had long-standing tradition on its side as well, very appealing. The central issue was not about their faith in Jesus per se; rather, the objection to these Gentile guests arose when they sought to legitimate identity claims or behavior that departed from prevailing communal norms by appealing to the meaning of Christ for themselves. These Gentile guests seeking full membership standing were told that they could avoid the marginality of disputed status, whatever they might believe about some Judean martyr of the Roman regime, and become "children of the quintessential proselyte and righteous one, Abraham himself" (397).

---

[9] Two excurses have not been reproduced here, the first one entitled "The Metaphorical Basis of the Family of God as Anti-structure" (270–73, original essay), and the second, "Social Consequences of the Believer's New Self-Understanding (Gl 3:28)" (273–76, original essay).

Nanos proposes that Paul's response to this development—from the θαυμάζω opening of 1:6, signaling a feigned "surprise," to the ironic turns of phrase, rebukes, sarcastic comments, and relentless questioning—represents an ancient letter of ironic rebuke. Drawing on Nils Dahl's essay, Nanos argues that such a letter, as described in the ancient handbooks and exemplified in many surviving papyri, effectively expresses the author's disappointment that his addressees have behaved inappropriately to their relationship, that they should have known better than to treat this "other" message of Torah observance—"that is really bad for them" because it "subverts the good news of Christ"—as "good news" (399). Challenging the identities and labels usually attributed to the people influencing the addressees—for example, "Judaizers," "opponents," and "agitators"—Nanos refers to them as "influencers." He separates references to them in the situational discourse of the letter from references to those who populate Paul's narratives about earlier situations in Jerusalem and Antioch, and he questions the prevailing view that they are in some way related to the Jerusalem Christ-believers, even that the situation involves an intramural struggle between supposed "Law-free" (Pauline) and other "Torah-observant" factions of "Christianity." Instead, the central issues, according to Nanos, revolve around points about which we should expect Paul and the Jerusalem apostles to agree. Representatives of Diaspora Jewish communities in which these coalitions function as subgroups, however, would be expected to disagree fervidly on these points. For Nanos, the various comments in Paul's narrative units work together with his situational comments and bring clarity to his message that the addressees must maintain faithfulness to the values of this coalition even in the face of seemingly overwhelming disapproval. The addressees must resist the temptation to comply with both prevailing Jewish communal and pagan societal norms for identity and behavior in "the present evil age." They may suffer in the present age for living according to this conviction but, according to Paul, they must do so in order to honor both the one in whom they believed and the one who brought them this message.

Dieter Mitternacht offers a new contribution to the debate, "Foolish Galatians?—a Recipient-Oriented Assessment of Paul's Letter." Drawing from his 1999 dissertation, Mitternacht argues that Galatians represents a "letter of petition," wherein Paul calls the addressees to imitate himself. He understands the situation in Galatia from Paul's perspective to involve "people in Galatia who are circumcised" but who do not "observe the whole law," "advising the Galatian Christ-believers to do the same, and the advice appeals to them" (409). Mitternacht suggests Paul's rhetoric indicates that Paul "expects weighty opposition from the addressees," for "whenever Paul appeals to the situation of the addressees, the rhetorical strategy shifts from argumentation to persuasion" (409). Paul creates "a rhetorical stage on which those whom he opposes are denigrated for their selfishness, those who are to be persuaded are ridiculed for their naiveté, and those of repute (especially Peter) are demonstrated to be inconsistent. The author himself emerges as the only reliable authority, divinely ordained and equipped" (409–10). Attending to the logic of Paul's rhetorical emphases and the historical social constraints on Jewish communities, Mitternacht argues that the conversion of Gentiles to faith in Christ led to their marginalization "from both their potential social and religious homesteads"; that is, it resulted in distance from their former social location yet also failed to gain them status equality on prevailing Jewish communal terms unless they became proselytes (411). Mitternacht surmises that the tensions might have resulted from the influence of other Christ-believers in Galatia who were already proselytes beforehand, who by "their affiliation with the uncircumcised Christ-believers . . . may have drawn negative attention to themselves, felt threatened, and therefore urged them to consider circumcision both for their own and for the uncircumcised Christ-believers' sake" (432). These kinds of social constraints resulted in questions about "the requirements of the life of faith working through love and in the imminent expectation of the new creation" (411). Galatians constitutes Paul's reply. While they are awaiting redemption from the present evil age, he instructed them, "any attempt to circumvent confrontation with social and political power structures amounted to a rejection of Christ Jesus, who himself had confronted and suffered the sword of Rome" (411). Although circumcision may seem to the addressees to be "the lesser of two 'trials,'" Paul called them to endure an even "bigger trial," for he held that "in this present evil age the Christ-like life is to be essentially marked by the cross" (412). To argue this reading, Mitternacht investigates the meaning of Paul's plea in 4:12 to "become as I, for I also as you!" and the correspondence of this understanding with his interpretation of the message of 3:1–5. One of the many methodological concerns Mitternacht raises in his rhetorical critique of Paul's stereotyping of the addressees' naiveté and the influencers' selfishness, for example, is the need for interpreters not to become collaborators with the author in his rhetorical strategy. "As long as one accepts as incontestable Paul's authority to correct, threaten, and judge, one will not come to terms with either the historical realities of the *first* communication situation or the rhetoric involved in any communication, and thus with the plausible effect of the letter on the addressees" (413, emphasis his). Mitternacht's recipient- rather than a sender-oriented reading of Galatians challenges many of the present approaches to Paul's rhetoric, the dynamics of the situation that it implies, and the meaning of Paul's response.

ABBREVIATIONS

General

ad loc.	*ad locum,* at the place discussed
B.C.E.	before the Common Era
C.E.	Common Era
ca.	circa
cf.	compare
ch(s).	chapter(s)
e.g.	for example
esp.	especially
f./ff.	following verse/verses
frg.	fragment
i.e.	that is
lit.	literally
n(n).	note(s)
no(s).	number(s)
NT	New Testament
OT	Old Testament
para.	paragraph
pars.	parallels
p(p).	page(s)
praef.	preface
sc.	*scilicet* (namely)
s.v.	*sub verbo,* under the word
v(v).	verse(s)
viz.	namely
vs.	versus

Biblical Editions

LXX	Septuagint
NA[27]	*Novum Testamentum Graece,* Nestle-Aland, 27th ed.
REB	Revised English Bible
RSV	Revised Standard Version

Bible with Apocrypha

1 Cor	1 Corinthians
1 Esd	1 Esdras
1 John	1 John
1 Macc	1 Maccabees
1 Pet	1 Peter
1 Sam	1 Samuel
1 Thess	1 Thessalonians
1 Tim	1 Timothy
2 Cor	2 Corinthians
2 Macc	2 Maccabees
2 Thess	2 Thessalonians
2 Tim	2 Timothy
3 Macc	3 Maccabees
4 Macc	4 Maccabees
Bar	Baruch
Bel	Bel and the Dragon
Col	Colossians
Dan	Daniel
Deut	Deuteronomy
Eph	Ephesians
Esth	Esther
Exod	Exodus
Ezek	Ezekiel
Gal	Galatians
Hab	Habakkuk
Heb	Hebrews
Isa	Isaiah
Jas	James
Jdt	Judith
Jer	Jeremiah
Josh	Joshua
Judg	Judges
Lev	Leviticus
Matt	Matthew
Mic	Micah
Num	Numbers
Phil	Philippians
Phlm	Philemon
Prov	Proverbs
Ps	Psalms
Rev	Revelation
Rom	Romans

Sir	Sirach
Tob	Tobit
Zech	Zechariah
Zeph	Zephaniah

Old Testament Pseudepigrapha

1 En.	*1 Enoch (Ethiopic Apocalypse)*
Jos. Asen.	*Joseph and Aseneth*
Jub.	*Jubilees*
Pss. Sol.	*Psalms of Solomon*
Sib. Or.	*Sibylline Oracles*
T. Mos.	*Testament of Moses*
T. Naph.	*Testament of Naphtali*

Mishnah, Talmud, and Related Literature

b.	Babylonian
m.	Mishnah
t.	Tosefta
y.	Jerusalem
ᶜAbod. Zar.	*ᶜAbodah Zarah*
ᵓAbot	*ᵓAbot*
ᶜArak.	*ᶜArakin*
B. Meṣᶜia	*Baba Meṣᶜia*
B. Qam.	*Baba Qamma*
Ber.	*Berakot*
Bik.	*Bikkurim*
ᶜEd.	*ᶜEduyyot*
Ḥag.	*Ḥagigah*
Ḥal.	*Ḥallah*
Ḥul.	*Ḥullin*
Ker.	*Kerithot*
Mak.	*Makkot*
Meg.	*Megillah*
Nid.	*Niddah*
ᵓOhal.	*ᵓOhalot*
Pesaḥ.	*Pesaḥim*
Qidd.	*Qiddušin*
Šabb.	*Šabbat*
Sanh.	*Sanhedrin*
Šeqal.	*Šeqalim*
Soṭah	*Soṭah*
Yebam.	*Yebamot*

Other Rabbinic Works

ʾAbot R. Nat.	ʾAbot de Rabbi Nathan
Deut. Rab.	Deuteronomy Rabbah
Gen. Rab.	Genesis Rabbah
Lev. Rab.	Leviticus Rabbah
Mek.	Mekilta
Midr. Exod. Rab.	Midrash Exodus Rabbah
Midr. Pss.	Midrash I Psalms
Pesiq. Rab.	Pesiqta Rabbati
S. Eli. Rab.	Seder Eliyahu Rabbah
Sipre	Sipre
Tanḥ.	Tanhuma

Dead Sea Scrolls

1QM	Milḥamah or War Scroll
1QpHab	Pesher Habakkuk
1QS	Serek Hayaḥad or Rule of the Community
1QSa	Rule of the Congregation (Appendix a to 1QS)
11QTᵃ	Temple Scroll
CD	Cairo Genizah copy of the Damascus Document

Apostolic Fathers

Herm. Sim.	Shepherd of Hermas, Similitude
Ign. Magn.	Ignatius, To the Magnesians
Ign. Phld.	Ignatius, To the Philadelphians

New Testament Apocrypha and Pseudepigrapha

Acts Pet. Paul	Acts of Peter and Paul
Acts Pil.	Acts of Pilate
Asc. Jas.	Ascents of James
Ps.-Clem.	
Ep. Pet. Jas.	Pseudo-Clementine Epistle of Peter to James
H.	Pseudo-Clementine Homilies
Recogn.	Pseudo-Clementine Recognitions

Ancient Christian Works

Clement of Alexandria	
Strom.	Stromata
Commodian	
Instr.	Instructiones

Cyril
   Ador.   *De adoratione in spiritu et veritate*
Eusebius
   Hist. eccl.   *Historia ecclesiastica*
   Praep. ev.   *Praeparatio evangelica*
Justin
   Dial.   *Dialogus cum Tryphone*
Origen
   Hom. Exod.   *Homiliae in Exodum*
   Hom. Lev.   *Homiliae in Leviticum*
   Princ.   *De principiis (Peri archōn)*
Tertullian
   Apol.   *Apology*
   Nat.   *Ad nationes*

Classical Works

Aristotle
   [Probl.]   *Problemata*
   Rhet.   *Rhetorica*
   [Rhet. Alex.]   *Rhetorica ad Alexandrum*
   Top.   *Topica*
Arrian
   Epict. diss.   *Epicteti dissertationes*
Cicero
   Amic.   *De amicitia*
   Att.   *Epistulae ad Atticum*
   Dom.   *De domo suo*
   Fam.   *Epistulae ad familiares*
   Fin.   *De finibus*
   Inv.   *De inventione rhetorica*
   Mur.   *Pro Murena*
   De or.   *De oratore*
   Part. or.   *Partitiones oratoriae*
   Princ.   *De principiis*
   Rab. Perd.   *Pro Rabirio Perduellionis Reo*
   [Rhet. Her.]   *Rhetorica ad Herennium*
   Sest.   *Pro Sestio*
   Sull.   *Pro Sulla*
Demetrius
   Eloc.   *De elocutione (Peri hermēneias)*
Demosthenes
   Cor.   *De corona*
   Ep.   *Epistulae*

Exord.   *Exordia (Prooemia)*
[4] Philip. *Philippica iv*
Dio Cassius
 Hist.   *Historia romana*
Dio Chrysostom
 Alex.   *Ad Alexandrinos (Or. 32)*
 Cel. Phryg. *Celaenis Phrygiae (Or. 35)*
 Dei cogn. *De dei cognitione (Or. 12)*
 1 Tars.   *Tarsica prior (Or. 33)*
Diodorus Siculus
 Bib. hist. *Bibliotheca historica*
Epictetus
 Diatr.   *Diatribai (Dissertationes)*
Hermogenes
 Inv.   *De inventione*
Herodotus
 Hist.   *Historiae*
Hippocrates
 Morb.   *De morbis* (Περὶ νούσων)
Homer
 Il.   *Ilias*
 Od.   *Odyssea*
Horace
 Sat.   *Satirae*
Isocrates
 Ep.   *Epistulae*
 Or.   *Orationes*
John Malalas
 Chron.   *Chronographia*
Josephus
 Ag. Ap.   *Against Apion*
 Ant.   *Jewish Antiquities*
 J.W.   *Jewish War*
 Life   *The Life*
Juvenal
 Sat.   *Satirae*
Libanius
 Or.   *Orationes*
Lucian
 Gall.   *Gallus*
 Sat.   *Saturnalia*
 Symp.   *Symposium*
Martial
 Epigr.   *Epigrammata*

Maximus of Tyre
    Or.   *Philosophical Orations*
Persius
    Sat.   *Satirae*
Petronius
    Sat.   *Satyricon*
Philo
    Abr.   *De Abrahamo*
    Contempl. *De vita contemplativa*
    Ebr.   *De ebrietate*
    Flacc.   *In Flaccum*
    Ios.   *De Iosepho*
    Legat.   *Legatio ad Gaium*
    Migr.   *De migratione Abrahami*
    Mos.   *De vita Mosis*
    Praem.   *De praemiis et poenis*
    Prob.   *Quod omnis probus liber sit*
    Somn.   *De somniis*
    Spec.   *De specialibus legibus*
    Virt.   *De virtutibus*
Plato
    Apol.   *Apologia*
    Ep.   *Epistulae*
    Gorg.   *Gorgias*
    Prot.   *Protagoras*
    Resp.   *Respublica*
    Symp.   *Symposium*
Pliny the Younger
    Ep.   *Epistulae*
Plutarch
    Adul. am.   *De adulatore et amico*
    Cic.   *Cicero*
    Adv. Col.   *Adversus Colotem*
    Inv. od.   *De invidia et odio*
    Mor.   *Moralia*
    Quaest. conv. *Questionum convivialium Libri IX*
Pseudo-Demetrius
    Typ. epist.   *Typoi epistolikoi*
Pseudo-Libanius
    Epist. char.   *Epistolimaioi charactēres*
    Typ. epist.   *Typoi epistolikoi*
Quintilian
    Decl.   *Declamationes*
    Inst.   *Institutio oratoria*

Seneca
  Ep.   *Epistulae morales*
Strabo
  Geogr.   *Geographica*
Suetonius
  Claud.   *Divus Claudius*
  Dom.   *Domitianus*
  Jul.   *Divus Julius*
Tacitus
  Ann.   *Annales*
  Hist.   *Historiae*
Theophrastus
  Char.   *Characteres*
Xenophon
  Cyr.   *Cyropaedia*
  Mem.   *Memorabilia*

Papyri, Epigraphica, etc.

BGU   *Aegyptische Urkunden aus den Königlichen Staatlichen Museen zu Berlin, Griechische Urkunden.* 15 vols. Berlin, 1895–1983

PSI   *Papiri greci e latini.* Florence, 1917

SB   *Sammelbuch griechischer Urkunden aus Aegypen.* Edited by F. Preisigke et al. Vols. 1– , 1915–

UPZ   *Urkunden der Ptolemäerzeit (ältere Funde).* Edited by U. Wilcken. Berlin and Leipzig, 1927

P.Bad.   *Veröffentlichungen aus den badischen Papyrus-Sammlungen.* 6 vols. Heidelberg, 1923–38

P.Cair.Zen.   *Zenon Papyri, Catalogue général des antiquités égyptiennes du Musée du Caire.* Edited by C. C. Edgar. 5 vols. Cairo, 1925–40

P.Corn.   *Greek Papyri in the Library of Cornell University.* Edited by W. L. Westermann and C. J. Kraemer Jr. New York, 1926

P.Gen.   *Les Papyrus De Genève.* First edition edited by J. Nicole. Geneva, 1896–1906

P.Grenf.   *An Alexandrian Erotic Fragment and other Greek Papyri chiefly Ptolemaic* (vol. 1; edited by B. P. Grenfell. Oxford, 1896). *New Classical Fragments and Other Greek and Latin Papyri* (vol. 2; edited by B. P. Grenfell and A. S. Hunt. Oxford, 1897)

P.Lips.   *Griechische Urkunden der Papyrussammlung zu Leipzig.* Edited by L. Mitteis. Leipzig, 1906

P.Mert.   *A Descriptive Catalogue of the Greek Papyri in the Collection of Wilfred Merton.* 3 vols. Variously edited by H. I. Bell, C. H. Roberts, B. R. Rees, J. W. B. Barns, and J. D. Thomas. London and Dublin, 1948–67

P.Mich.	Michigan Papyri
P.Oxy.	Oxyrhyncus Papyri
P.Paris	*Notices et textes des papyrus du Musée du Louvre et de la Bibliothèque Impériale.* Edited by J. A. Letronne, W. Brunet de Presle, and E. Egger. Paris, 1865

Secondary Sources

ANRW	*Aufstieg und Niedergang der römischen Welt: Geschichte und Kultur Roms im Spiegel der neueren Forschung.* Edited by H. Temporini and W. Haase. Berlin, 1972–
BAG	Bauer, W., W. F. Arndt, and F. W. Gingrich. *Greek-English Lexicon of the New Testament and Other Early Christian Literature.* Chicago, 1957
BAGD	Bauer, W., W. F. Arndt, F. W. Gingrich, and F. W. Danker. *Greek-English Lexicon of the New Testament and Other Early Christian Literature.* 2d ed. Chicago, 1979
BDAG	Danker, F. W. *A Greek-English Lexicon of the New Testament and Other Early Christian Literature.* 3d ed. Chicago, 2000
BDF	Blass, F., A. Debrunner, and R. W. Funk. *A Greek Grammar of the New Testament and Other Early Christian Literature.* Chicago, 1961
EncJud	*Encyclopaedia Judaica.* 16 vols. Jerusalem, 1972
GLAJJ	Stern, M. *Greek and Latin Authors on Jews and Judaism.* 2 vols. Jerusalem, 1980
HS	E. Hennecke, *New Testament Apocrypha.* 2 vols. Edited by W. Schneemelcher. Philadelphia: Westminster, 1963–65
KlPauly	*Der Kleine Pauly: Lexicon der Antike.* Edited by Konrad Ziegler and Walther Sontheimer. Stuttgart: Alfred Druckenmuller, 1964
LCL	Loeb Classical Library
LSJ	Liddell, H. G., R. Scott, and H. S. Jones, *A Greek-English Lexicon.* 9th ed. with revised supplement. Oxford, 1996
OCD	*Oxford Classical Dictionary.* Edited by M. Cary et al. Oxford, 1949
OTP	*Old Testament Pseudepigrapha.* Edited by J. H. Charlesworth. 2 vols. New York, 1983, 85
PGL	Patristic Greek Lexicon. Edited by G. W. H. Lampe. Oxford, 1968
PGM	*Papyri graecae magicae: Die griechischen Zauberpapyri.* Edited by K. Preisedanz. Berlin, 1928
RE	*Realencyclopädie für protestantische Theologie und Kirche*
Str-B	Strack, H. L., and P. Billerbeck. *Kommentar zum Neuen Testament aus Talmud und Midrasch.* 6 vols. Munich, 1922–1961

CONTRIBUTORS

John M. G. Barclay
Professor of New Testament and Christian Origins, Department of Theology and Religious Studies, University of Glasgow, Scotland

Robert M. Berchman
Associate Professor of Philosophy and Religious Studies, Dowling College, Oakdale, New York

Hans Dieter Betz
Shailer Mathews Professor (Emeritus) of New Testament, University of Chicago

C. Joachim Classen
Full Professor (Emeritus) of Classics, Georg-August-University Göttingen, Germany

Nils A. Dahl
Buckingham Professor of New Testament, Yale University, Emeritus

James D. G. Dunn
Lightfoot Professor of Divinity, University of Durham, UK

Philip F. Esler
Professor of Biblical Criticism, University of St Andrews, Scotland

Paula Fredriksen
Aurelio Professor of Scripture, Boston University

Robert G. Hall
Professor, Department of Religion, Hampden-Sydney College, Virginia

G. Walter Hansen
Associate Professor of New Testament and Director of the Global Research Institute, Fuller Theological Seminary, Pasadena

A. E. Harvey
Revd. Dr., formerly University Lecturer in Theology and Fellow, Wolfson College, Oxford, UK

James D. Hester
Professor of Religion (Emeritus), University of Redlands, California

Robert Jewett
Visiting Professor, University of Heidelberg, Germany

Paul E. Koptak
Paul and Bernice Brandel Professor of Communication and Biblical Interpretation, North Park Theological Seminary, Chicago

Bernard C Lategan
Professor and Director, Stellenbosch Institute for Advanced Study, South Africa

Troy Martin
Professor of Religious Studies, Saint Xavier University, Chicago

J. Louis Martyn
Edward Robinson Professor (Emeritus) of Biblical Theology, Union Theological Seminary, New York

Dieter Mitternacht
Ph.D., Research Scholar and Lecturer, Lund University, Sweden

Mark D. Nanos
Ph.D., Independent Scholar, Lee's Summit, Missouri

Joop Smit
Senior Lecturer in New Testament Exegesis, Catholic Theological University at Utrecht, The Netherlands

Johan S. Vos
Ph.D., Lecturer in New Testament, Vrije Universiteit, Amsterdam

Nikolaus Walter
Professor at Friedrich-Schiller-Universität Jena, Ruhestand, Germany

ORIGINAL LOCATION OF ARTICLES

Betz, H. D. "The Literary Composition and Function of Paul's Letter to the Galatians." *New Testament Studies* 21 (1975): 352–79.

Hall, R. G. "The Rhetorical Outline for Galatians: A Reconsideration." *Journal of Biblical Literature* 106, no. 2 (1987): 277–88.

Smit, J. "The Letter of Paul to the Galatians: A Deliberative Speech." *New Testament Studies* 35 (1989): 1–26.

Berchman, R. M. "Galatians (1:1–5): Paul and Greco-Roman Rhetoric." Pages 1–15 in *Judaic and Christian Interpretation of Texts: Context and Contexts*. Edited by J. Neusner and E. S. Frerichs. New Perspectives on Ancient Judaism 3. Lanham, Md.: University Press of America, 1987.

Martin, T. "Apostasy to Paganism: The Rhetorical Stasis of the Galatian Controversy." *Journal of Biblical Literature* 114, no. 3 (1995): 437–61.

Classen, C. J. "St. Paul's Epistles and Ancient Greek and Roman Rhetoric." Pages 1–28 in *Rhetorical Criticism of the New Testament*. Tübingen: Mohr Siebeck, 2000.

Hansen, G. W. "A Paradigm of the Apocalypse: The Gospel in the Light of Epistolary Analysis." Pages 194–221 in *Gospel in Paul: Studies on Corinthians, Galatians, and Romans for Richard N. Longenecker*. Edited by L. A. Jervis and P. Richardson. Sheffield: Sheffield Academic Press, 1994.

Koptak, P. E. "Rhetorical Identification in Paul's Autobiographical Narrative: Galatians 1.13–2.14," *Journal for the Study of the New Testament* 40 (1990): 97–115.

Vos, J. S. "Paul's Argumentation in Galatians 1–2." *Harvard Theological Review* 87, no. 1 (1994): 1–16. Copyright 1994 by the President and Fellows of Harvard College.

Dunn, J. D. G. "The Incident at Antioch (Gal. 2:11–18)." *Journal for the Study of the New Testament* 18 (1983): 3–57.

Fredriksen, P. "Judaism, the Circumcision of Gentiles, and Apocalyptic Hope: Another Look at Galatians 1 and 2." *Journal of Theological Studies* 42, no. 2 (1991): 532–64.

Esler, P. F. "Making and Breaking an Agreement Mediterranean Style: A New Reading of Galatians 2:1–14." *Biblical Interpretation* 3, no. 3 (1995): 285–314.

Harvey, A. E. "The Opposition to Paul." Pages 319–32 in vol. 4 of *Studia Evangelica*. Edited by F. L. Cross. Berlin: Akademie, 1968.

Jewett, R. "The Agitators and the Galatian Congregation." *New Testament Studies* 17 (1970–1971): 198–212.

Martyn, J. L. "A Law-Observant Mission to Gentiles: The Background of Galatians." Pages 7–24 in *Theological Issues in the Letters of Paul*. Nashville: Abingdon, 1997.

Walter, N. "Paulus und die Gegner des Christusevangeliums in Galatien." Pages 351–56 in *L'apôtre Paul: Personnalité, Style, et Conception du Ministère*. Edited by A. Vanhoye. Bibliotheca ephemeridum theologicarum lovaniensium 73. Leuven: Leuven University Press, 1986.

Barclay, J. M. G. "Mirror-Reading a Polemical Letter: Galatians as a Test Case." *Journal for the Study of the New Testament* 31 (1987): 73–93.

Lategan, B. C. "The Argumentative Situation of Galatians." *Neotestamentica* 26, no. 2 (1992): 257–70.

Nanos, M. D. "The Inter- and Intra-Jewish Context of Paul's Letter to the Galatians." Pages 146–59 in *Paul and Politics: Ekklesia, Israel, Imperium, Interpretation*. Edited by R. A. Horsley. Harrisburg: Trinity, 2000.

The above are used with the kind permission of the respective publishers.

PART

I

Rhetorical and Epistolary Genre

Section A
Rhetorical Approaches

1

THE LITERARY COMPOSITION AND FUNCTION OF PAUL'S LETTER TO THE GALATIANS[1]

Hans Dieter Betz

When discussing commentaries friends have repeatedly suggested to me that the commentary genre is at present not the most creative format within which to work. This may or may not be true, but the enterprise certainly provides for some strange experiences. It has been my experience that things go smoothly as long as one does not ask too many questions. The present paper, however, is the preliminary outcome of asking too many questions about how to arrive at an "outline" of the letter to the Galatians. Nearly all commentaries and *Introductions to the New Testament* contain such an outline, table of contents, or paraphrase of the argument. However, despite an extensive search, I have not been able to find any consideration given to possible criteria and methods for determining such an outline.

In the process of my studies I also found that the letter to the Galatians can be analyzed according to Greco-Roman rhetoric and epistolography. Apparently, this has never been realized before, with the possible exception of Joseph Barber Lightfoot. In his still valuable commentary he has an outline in which he uses the term "narrative" for the first two chapters, "argumentative" for chapters 3 and 4, and "hortatory" for 5:1–6:10. These are indeed the proper terms, if we analyze the letter according to Greco-Roman rhetoric, but Lightfoot never betrays whether or not he was aware of this fact.[2]

German scholarship at the end of the nineteenth and the beginning of the twentieth century was sharply divided on the question of how to classify Paul's letters, whether to classify them as literary or non-literary, and whether or not to assume influences of Hellenistic rhetoric. Although men like Ulrich von Wilamowitz-Moellendorrf[3] and Martin Dibelius[4] had included Paul among the great letter-writ-

---

[1] Sections of this paper were read at the 29th General Meeting of the Society for New Testament Studies at Sigtuna, Sweden, 13 August 1974.
[2] Lightfoot, *Galatians*, 65–67.
[3] Wilamowitz-Moellendorff, "Griechische Literatur," 159ff.
[4] Dibelius, *Geschichte*, 5ff.

ers of antiquity, it seems that the strong opposition against such a judgement expressed by scholars like Franz Overbeck,[5] Paul Wendland[6] and Eduard Norden,[7] has
prevailed. When one reads their arguments today, however, the heavy influence of ideology arouses suspicion. Scholars of the later twentieth century seem in basic agreement that Paul's letters are "confused," disagreeing only about whether the confusion
is caused by emotional disturbances, "Diktierpausen" or "rabbinic" methodology.[8]

1. The Form of the Letter as a Whole

It is my thesis that Paul's letter to the Galatians is an example of the "apologetic
letter" genre.[9] The evidence for this thesis must, of course, be derived from an analysis of the composition of the letter, but before we turn to this question at least a few
remarks on the literary genre of the "apologetic letter" are necessary.[10]

The emphasis upon the interrelationships between various literary genres is one
of the major contributions of Arnaldo Momigliano's 1968 lectures at Harvard University on "The Development of Greek Biography."[11] The genre of the "apologetic letter," which arose in the fourth century B.C.,[12] presupposes not only the existence of
the "letter" form but also the genres of "autobiography" and "apologetic speech,"
which are also older forms of literary expression. In Greek literature all of these genres are represented by famous examples, of which we need to mention only Plato's
pseudo-autobiography of Socrates, its imitation in Isocrates' *Antidosis (Or. 15)* (Περὶ
ἀντιδόσεως), an authentic apologetic autobiography, and Demosthenes' self-apology, *De corona*. These examples inspired later writers who imitated them, e.g., Cicero
in his *Brutus* or Libanius in his "Autobiography" (*Or. 1*).[13]

Momigliano also makes the Socratics responsible for creating the genre of the
"apologetic letter,"[14] the most famous example of which is Plato's *Ep. 7*. The authenticity of this letter and the other Platonic letters is presently very much a matter of
scholarly debate[15] but is of no substantive importance for the genre itself. "In any

---

[5] Overbeck, "Anfänge."

[6] Wendland, *Kultur*, 342ff. In regard to Galatians Wendland says (349): "*Eine Exegese, die sich zum Ziele setzt, den Inhalt dieses Briefes in eine planvolle Disposition zu fassen und von logischen Gesichtspunkten ihn als Einheit zu begreifen, geht in die Irre.*"

[7] Norden, *Die antike Kunstprosa*, 492ff.

[8] An example of this is Koepp, "Abraham-Midraschimkette," 181–87.

[9] At the outset I would like to acknowledge my great indebtedness to the members of the SBL Seminar on "The Form and Function of the Pauline Letters," in particular Nils A. Dahl, Robert W. Funk, M. Luther Stirewalt and John L. White. Although in the present paper I take a somewhat different approach, I would never have been able to do so without their continuous stimulation and gracious sharing of ideas.

[10] See also Betz, *Apostel Paulus,* chapter 2.

[11] Momigliano, *Development; Second Thoughts.*

[12] Momigliano, *Development*, 62.

[13] Ibid., 58–60, with further bibliography.

[14] Ibid., 60–62.

[15] Ibid., 60 n. 16, with the literature mentioned there. In addition see now the discussion about Edelstein, *Letter*; the reviews by G. Müller and Solmsen; papers by Gulley, *Authenticity,* and Aalders, *Political Thought*; and Goldstein, *Letters*, chapter 7: "The Forms of Ancient Apology and Polemic, Real and Fictitious."

case it is a remarkable attempt to combine reflections on eternal problems and personal experiences."[16] The subsequent history of the genre is difficult to trace, since most of the pertinent literature did not survive.[17] "We cannot, therefore, see the exact place of Plato's letter in the history of ancient autobiographical production. But one vaguely feels the Platonic precedent in Epicurus, Seneca, and perhaps St Paul."[18] Momigliano's last words—"and perhaps St Paul"—come rather unexpectedly and without any further explanation. Our analysis, however, will demonstrate that, whatever reason may have caused his remark, it is certainly correct, and that the cautious "perhaps" is no longer necessary.

2. The Epistolary Framework

The epistolary framework of the Galatian epistle can be easily recognized and separated from the "body"—in fact, it separates so easily that it appears almost as a kind of external bracket for the body of the letter. However, several interrelations between the epistolary framework and the body indicate that both elements are part of the same composition.[19]

(a) The Prescript (1:1–5)

Apart from some special features, the prescript follows the basic pattern of other Pauline prescripts. The basic sequence of *superscriptio, adscriptio,* and *salutatio* is "Oriental" in origin and character, but shows also "Hellenistic" and specifically Christian developments. Compared with other Pauline prescripts, this one has been expanded considerably, although not as much as that of Romans. It shows the following structure:

1:1–2a   Name of the principal sender, his title, a definition of the title, the stating of co-senders.

1:2b   The naming of the addressees.

1:3–4   The salutation, expanded by christological and soteriological "formulae."

1:5   A doxology, with the concluding "amen."

(b) The Postscript (6:11–18)

In 6:11–18 Paul adds a postscript in his own handwriting. This conforms to the epistolary convention of the time. An autographic postscript serves to authenticate the letter, to sum up its main points, or to add concerns which have come to the mind

---

[16] Momigliano, *Development,* 62.

[17] Momigliano does not mention the so-called Cynic Epistles, a body of epistolary literature that deserves to be carefully studied with regard to early Christian letters. See the editions by Hercher, *Epistolographi,* 208–17, 235–58; Reuters, *Briefe;* Mondolfo and Tarán, *Eraclito,* with bibliography. See also Strugnell and Attridge, "Epistles."

[18] Momigliano, *Development,* 62.

[19] It is precisely at the points of expansion where we find close relations between the prescript and various parts of the body of the letter: the title and its definition (Gal 1:1), and the christological-soteriological statements (1:4).

of the sender after the completion of the letter. As soon as we go beyond these general remarks, however, questions arise.

First, the handwritten postscript presupposes that the preceding letter has been written by a "professional" amanuensis. Was the amanuensis just a copyist, or did he have an influence in the composition of the letter itself? The very fact that Paul employed an amanuensis rules out a haphazard writing of the letter and presupposes the existence of Paul's first draft, or a sequence of draft, composition and copy. The highly skillful composition of Galatians leaves us the choice of attributing this high degree of epistolographic expertise to Paul, to the amanuensis, or to a combination of both. I am inclined to attribute the composition to Paul himself, because the letter does more than simply conform to convention. While making use of convention, it is nevertheless a highly original creation. Nowhere in it is there any indication of a separation of form and content. This is even true of the personal postscript, which is well composed in itself and fully integrated with the rest of the letter. Yet, given the employment of an amanuensis and the common practices in letter writing in Paul's time, the problem of "authorship" may be more complicated than we have previously imagined. If one adds to this the fact that there are co-senders named in the prescript and that the "secretary" could be one of them,[20] the letter itself assumes more and more the character of an official document and less the character of a "private" letter.

Secondly, the postscript must be examined not only as an epistolographic convention but also as a rhetorical feature.[21] As a rhetorical feature, the postscript of the letter to the Galatians serves as the *peroratio* or *conclusio*,[22] that is, the end and conclusion of the apologetic speech forming the body of the letter.[23] The general purpose of the *peroratio*[24] is twofold: it serves as a last chance to remind the judge or the audience of the case, and it tries to make a strong emotional impression upon them. The three conventional parts of the *peroratio* carry out this task: the *enumeratio* or *recapitulatio* (ἀνακεφαλαίωσις) sharpens and sums up the main points of the case,[25] the *indignatio* arouses anger and hostility against the opponent,[26] and

---

[20] Rom 16:22: ἀσπάζομαι ὑμᾶς ἐγὼ Τέρτιος ὁ γράψας τὴν ἐπιστολὴν ἐν κυρίῳ.

[21] For matters pertaining to Greco-Roman rhetoric we have used as major tools Ernesti, *Graecorum rhetoricae; Latinorum rhetoricae;* Volkmann, *Rhetorik;* Lausberg, *Handbuch,* and the reviews by Dockhorn and Schmid; Leeman, *Orationis ratio;* Kennedy, *Art of Persuasion;* idem, *Art of Rhetoric,* and the review by Clarke; on the "handbooks" see Fuhrmann, *Lehrbuch.*

[22] For a treatment of this subject see Aristotle, *Rhet.* 3.19; [*Rhet Alex.*] 20; *Rhet. Her.* 2.30.47–2.31.50; Cicero, *Inv.* 1.52.98–1.56.109; the longest discussion is found in Quintilian, *Inst.* 6.1.1ff.

[23] See below, section 3.

[24] See the treatment in Volkmann, *Rhetorik,* §27; Lausberg, *Handbuch,* §§431–442.

[25] See Quintilian, *Inst.* 6.1.1–2 (Winterbottom): "*Rerum repetitio et congregatio, quae Graece dicitur* ἀνακεφαλαίωσις, *a quibusdam Latinorum enumeratio, et memoriam iudicis reficit et totam simul causam ponit ante oculos, et, etiam si per singula minus moverat, turba valet. In hac quae repetemus quam brevissime dicenda sunt, et, quod Graeco verbo patet, decurrendum per capita.*" Cicero, *Inv.*1.53.98 (Hubbel, LCL): "*Enumeratio est per quam res disperse et diffuse dictae unum in locum coguntur et reminiscendi causa unum sub aspectum subiciuntur.*" See for more material Lausberg, *Handbuch,* §§334–435.

[26] See Cicero, *Inv.* 1.53.100: "*Indignatio est oratio per quam conficitur ut in aliquem hominem magnum odium aut in rem gravis offensio concitetur.*" See also Lausberg, *Handbuch,* §438.

the *conquestio* stimulates pity.[27] In an actual case, the *peroratio* can, of course, take many different forms, but it must conform to the case at issue, and it must be concise. It also must be clearly related to the individual parts of the speech, especially to the *exordium*.[28]

When we look at Paul's postscript (6:11–18) as a *peroratio*, some very interesting structures emerge, all confirming that we do, in fact, have this part of a speech before us.

6:11   The epistolary "formula" announcing and introducing the postscript.

6:12–17   A *peroratio*, which is almost identical with the *recapitulatio*.[29] Quintilian mentions that for certain "Greek" orators this was a preferred form.[30] Paul's *peroratio* is primarily a *recapitulatio* while others use the *recapitulatio* as only a part of the *peroratio*.

6:12–13   A sharp polemic against the opponents, denouncing them not only as "heretics" but also as "morally" inferior and despicable. This is clearly an expression of *indignatio*, with a good dose of *amplificatio*.[31] Its relation to the *causa* (1:6f.) is equally obvious.[32]

6:14   Restatement of Paul's own theological position, as he has advocated it throughout the letter.[33]

6:15   The κανών for the Galatians to follow in the future.[34] This κανών sums up the entire paraenetical direction advocated by Paul in the letter.[35]

6:16   A conditional blessing upon those who follow the κανών (6:14f.). This conditional blessing implies also a threat against those who do not intend to follow the Pauline κανών and who consequently fall under the curse (1:8–9). Quintilian recommends the inclusion of a threat in the *peroratio*, as he does for the *exordium*.[36]

---

[27] See Cicero, *Inv.* 1.55.106: "*Conquestio est oratio auditorum misericordiam captans.*" See also Lausberg, *Handbuch*, §439.

[28] See Lausberg, *Handbuch*, §432.

[29] That the final section of Gal conforms to the *enumeratio*, *indignatio* and *conquestio* and that Paul was influenced by Greek rhetoric has been proposed already by Starcke, "Rhetorik"; Stogiannou, "Ἀνακεφαλαίωσις"; differently Bahr, "Subscriptions."

[30] Quintilian, *Inst.* 6.1.7 (see the quotation below).

[31] Cf. *Rhet. Her.* 2.30.47: "*Amplificatio est res quae per locum communem instigationis auditorum causa sumitur.*" In 2.30.48 ten *loci communes* to be applied are listed; similarly Cicero, *Inv.* 1.53.101ff. See Lausberg, *Handbuch*, §438.

[32] Cf. Gal 2:4–5, 11–14; 3:1; 5:7, 10–12.

[33] Cf. esp. Gal 1:1, 11–12; 2:19–21; 4:12; 5:2, 10, 11; 6:17.

[34] Cf. Quintilian, *Inst.* 6.1.22.

[35] Cf. esp. 2:4–5, 11–14; 5:4–6, 25. It is interesting that according to Plutarch, *Adv. Col.* 1118b, and Cicero, *Fin.* 1.19.53, Epicurus' Canons were believed to have come down from heaven (διοπετεῖς). See J. Schneider, "Brief," *RAC* 2:572f.

[36] Quintilian, *Inst.* 6.1.13: "*Metus etiam, si est adhibendus, ut faciat idem, hunc habet locum fortiorem quam in prooemio.*" Cf. 4.1.20–21 and see below.

6:17   Paul concludes the *peroratio* with an apostolic "order" in regard to the future coupled with his self-description as a representative of the crucified Christ.[37] Paul's reason for making this remark at this point becomes understandable if we are anticipating the *conquestio*. Although reduced to a minimum, 6:17 does have the appearance of a *conquestio*. Among the examples mentioned by Quintilian as having been employed most effectively by Cicero is one that points out the defendant's "worth, his manly pursuits, the scars from wounds received in battle . . ." as a recommendation to the judge.[38] Gal 6:17 is such a *conquestio,* for it points to the στίγματα τοῦ Ἰησοῦ with which Paul has been inflicted as a result of his apostolic mission, a mission which is identical with the case presented.[39] However, it also is clear that Paul does not openly appeal for pity. Perhaps the lack of such an emotional appeal is due to the fact that, as Quintilian reports:

> The majority of Athenians and almost all philosophers who have left anything in writing on the art of oratory have held that the recapitulation is the sole form of peroration. I imagine that the reason why the Athenians did so was that appeals to the emotions were forbidden to Athenian orators, a proclamation to this effect being actually made by the court-usher. I am less surprised at the philosophers taking this view, for they regard susceptibility to emotion as a vice, and think it immoral that the judge should be distracted from the truth by an appeal to his emotions and that it is unbecoming for a good man to make use of vicious procedure to serve his ends. None the less they must admit that appeals to emotion are necessary if there are no other means for securing the victory of truth, justice and the public interest.[40]

Paul's restraint at this point with regard to the emotional appeal may reflect the same kind of caution which, according to Quintilian, was characteristic of philosophers.[41]

6:18   The letter concludes with a final benediction and an "amen." Both are part of the epistolary framework which we also find in other Pauline letters.[42]

---

[37] Cf. Gal 1:1, 12, 16; 2:19f.; 4:14; 5:24; 6:14.

[38] Quintilian, *Inst.* 6.1.21 (Butler). Its connection with the "catalogue of περιστάσεις" should be noted. See Betz, *Apostel Paulus,* 97ff.

[39] Cf. Gal 1:13, 23; 4:29; 5:11; 6:12.

[40] Quintilian, *Inst.* 6.1.7 (Butler).

[41] The refusal to ask for mercy was attributed to Socrates (cf. Xenophon, *Mem.* 4.4.4) and subsequently became part of the Socratic tradition. This tradition has influenced Paul, as I have shown in *Apostel Paulus,* 15ff.

[42] Cf. Rom 16:20; 1 Thess 5:28; 1 Cor 16:23; 2 Cor 13:13; Phil 4:23; Phlm 25.

3. The Body of the Letter (1:6–6:10)

(a) The Exordium (1:6–11)

The "body"[43] of Paul's letter begins on a note of ironic indignation, expressed by the words "I am astonished that . . . ,"[44] and then states what the apostle regards as the cause for writing the letter: "that you are so quickly deserting him who called you in [the] grace of Christ [and turning] to a different gospel—not that there is another [gospel]; but there are some who disturb you and want to pervert the gospel of Christ." This statement of the *causa* of the case, the reason why the letter was written, contains the "facts" that occasioned the letter, but these "facts" are stated with a partisan bias. This is indicated by the self-correction[45] in v. 7, where Paul denies that there is another gospel, and by the "political" language of vv. 6–7,[46] which describes the actions taken by the Galatians as "desertion" (μετατιθέναι) and those taken by the opposition as "creating disturbance" (ταράσσειν) and "turning things upside down" (μεταστρέψαι). This language is no doubt intended to discredit the opponents in the eyes of the addressees and to censure the Galatians for their own disloyalty.

Generally speaking this first part of the body of the Galatian letter conforms to the customary *exordium*, which is otherwise known as the *prooemium* or *principium*.[47] In the treatment of the *exordium* in Aristotle's *Rhetorica*,[48] the *Rhetorica ad Herennium*,[49] Cicero's *De inventione rhetorica*[50] and Quintilian,[51] there is considerable agreement in regard to the definition, composition and function of the *exordium*. This includes the understanding that various types of *exordia* must be distinguished and applied in accordance with the nature of the case. There is some disagreement and development among these authors in determining what the various types are and when they can best be applied.

Aristotle advises that if the audience is already attentive, the speaker may start his speech by directly introducing a summary of the "facts."[52] The *Rhetorica ad Herennium*[53]

---

[43] I am disagreeing here with White, "Introductory Formulae," who has the body of the letter begin with 1:11 (93, 94). The difference comes about because White takes "the private Greek letters of the papyri as a basis of comparison" (62). Our analysis shows that this basis is too small for a comparison with Paul. The clarification of the relationship between the "private" letters on papyrus, the "literary" letters and rhetoric is another problem of research.

[44] Θαυμάζω is a familiar rhetorical expression which became an epistolary cliché. It occurs often, e.g., in Demosthenes, Antiphon and Lysias. See Preuss, *Index demosthenicus*, s.v.; Holmes, *Index lysiacus*, s.v. Cf. also Plato, *Apol.* 17A, 24A; *Crito* 50C. For the epistles, see, e.g., Isocrates, *Ep.* 2.19; 9.8; also White, "Introductory Formulae," 96; for the term in connection with the exordium, see Lausberg, *Handbuch*, §270. A large collection is also found in Dahl, "Paul's Letter."

[45] On the *correctio* see Lausberg, *Handbuch*, §§784–786.

[46] For parallel language cf. Isocrates, *Ep.* 7.12f.

[47] On the *exordium*, see esp. Volkmann, *Rhetorik*, §12; Lausberg, *Handbuch*, §§263–288.

[48] Aristotle, *Rhet.* 1.1.9 (1354b); 3.14.1ff. (1419b19ff.); cf. [*Rhet. Alex.*] 29ff. (1436a32ff.).

[49] *Rhet. Her.* 1.4.6–1.7.11.

[50] Cicero, *Inv.* 1.15.20–1.17.25.

[51] Quintilian, *Inst.* 4.1.1–79.

[52] Aristotle, *Rhet.* 3.14.8 (1413b). Cf. [*Rhet. Alex.*] 29 (1437b35ff.).

[53] *Rhet. Her.* 1.4.7: "*Dociles auditores habere poterimus, si summam causae breviter exponemus et si adtentos eos faciemus.*"

names the summary of the *causa* as a means for making the hearers attentive and receptive. The handbook sets forth four methods for making the hearers well disposed: "by
discussing our own person, the person of our adversaries, that of our hearers, and the
facts themselves."[54] But in 1:6–7, Paul does more than simply present the bare facts. He
also discredits his adversaries by using the language of demagoguery[55] and expresses
his disappointment and disapproval of the Galatians for changing over to the side
of the opposition.[56] Speaking in the terms of the *Rhetorica ad Herennium*, Paul's
statement of the *causa* is a mixture of two types of *exordia*, the *principium* ("Direct
Opening") and the *insinuatio* ("Subtle Approach"). The former, the *principium*, is appropriate in addressing an audience where attention, receptivity and a favorable disposition can be obtained directly and without difficulty,[57] while the *insinuatio* should be
used in cases where, for example, the audience has been won over by the previous
speech of the opponent.[58] Paul's case stands in the middle: he can be certain of having
the attention and receptivity of the Galatians at once, but they have almost been won
over, though not quite.[59] This mixture of the *principium* and the *insinuatio* may be
peculiar, but it conforms precisely to the situation with which Paul sees himself
confronted.

Cicero's treatment in his *De inventione* is very similar to the *Rhetorica ad
Herennium*. Without going into the problems of the relationship between the two
works,[60] it may suffice to mention that Cicero has greater tolerance of variability and
mixture of cases and types. He places great emphasis upon discrediting the opposition. In comparison with Paul, it is noteworthy that he recommends the expression of
astonishment and perplexity as one of the means to regain the goodwill of an audience which has been won over by the opposition.[61]

The next section of the Galatian *exordium* (1:8–9) contains a double curse,
issued conditionally upon those who preach a gospel different from the Pauline gos-

---

[54] *Rhet. Her.* 1.4.8: "*Benivolos auditores facere quattuor modis possumus: ab nostra, ab adversariorum nostrorum, ab auditorum persona, et ab rebus ipsis.*" Cf. Aristotle, *Rhet.* 3.14.7 (1415a);
Cicero, *Inv.* 1.16.22.

[55] Cf. *Rhet. Her.* 1.5.8: "*Ab adversariorum persona benivolentia captabitur si eos in odium, in
invidiam, in contemptionem adducemus. In odium rapiemus si quid eorum spurce, superbe, perfidiose,
crudeliter, confidenter, malitiose, flagitiose factum proferemus. In invidiam trahemus si vim, si poten-
tiam, si factionem, divitias, incontinentiam, nobilitatem, clientelas, hospitium, sodalitatem, adfinitates
adversariorum proferemus, et his adiumentis magis quam veritati eos confidere aperiemus. In contemptionem adducemus si inertiam, ignaviam, desidiam, luxuriam adversariorum proferemus.*"

[56] Cf. Aristotle, *Rhet.* 3.14.2 (1414b), who names as the sources of epideictic *exordia* ἔπαινος ἢ
ψόγος (cf. 3.14.4 [1415a]).

[57] *Rhet. Her.* 1.4.6: "*Principium est cum statim auditoris animum nobis idoneum reddimus ad
audiendum. Id ita sumitur ut adtentos, ut dociles, uti benivolos auditores habere possimus.*"

[58] *Rhet. Her.* 1.6.9: "*Tria sunt tempora quibus principio uti non possumus, quae diligenter sunt
consideranda: aut cum turpem causam habemus, hoc est, cum ipsa res animum auditoris a nobis alienat;
aut cum animus auditoris persuasus esse videtur ab iis qui ante contra dixerunt.*"

[59] Note the present tense in Gal 1:6–7; 4:9, 21; also 4:11, 12–20; 5:1, 4, 7–12, 13; 6:12–16.

[60] See Adamietz, *Ciceros De inventione*.

[61] Cicero, *Inv.* 1.17.25: "*Sin oratio adversariorum fidem videbitur auditoribus fecisse—id quod ei
qui intelliget quibus rebus fides fiat facile erit cognitu—opportet aut . . . aut dubitatione uti quid
primum dicas aut cui potissimum loco respondeas, cum admiratione. Nam auditor cum eum quem
adversarii perturbatum putavit oratione videt animo firmissimo contra dicere paratum, plerumque se
potius temere assensisse quam illum sine causa confidere arbitratur.*"

pel. The way Paul states this curse indicates that he merely repeats (v. 9: ὡς προειρήκαμεν, καὶ ἄρτι πάλιν λέγω) a curse which had been issued at some earlier occasion (v. 8), so that what appears now as a double curse is really the reissuing of a previous curse. Also, this curse must be seen in connection with the conditional blessing in the postscript (6:16), a matter to which we will return later.[62]

How does this curse fit into the *exordium?* In his treatment of the *exordium* Quintilian discusses devices to be employed in cases where the judge is influenced by prejudice, most likely through the previous speech of an opponent.[63] One effective method, for which Cicero is cited as an example, is to frighten the judge by threats. Most popular was the move to threaten the judge with the displeasure of the Roman people or, more brutally, with prosecution for bribery.[64] Quintilian regards such threats as extreme measures which should be used only as a last resort, since in his view they lie outside of the art of oratory.[65] Such threats, a form of which must have been the curse, may have been used more often than Quintilian would like. It is significant that one of the greatest masterpieces of Greek rhetoric, Demosthenes' *De corona,* has as its *peroratio* a prayer to the gods which includes a curse upon the enemies of Athens.[66] Demosthenes has the curse in the end, in the *peroratio,* while Paul has it as part of the *exordium,* but since *exordium* and *peroratio* were considered intimately related, the difference is insignificant.[67]

The conclusion of the *exordium* is apparently reached in v. 9, while the next major section, the *narratio,* begins in v. 12. This leaves us with the question of what to do with vv. 10–11. Scholars have been divided in their opinions on whether v. 10 should be connected with the preceding or with the following, and whether the following section begins in v. 11 or v. 12. A clear decision seems impossible unless one recognizes that, according to the rhetoricians, there should be a smooth transition between the *exordium* and the *narratio.*[68]

The most extensive discussion on this point is found in Quintilian,[69] who calls this transitional part *transitus*[70] or *transgressio.*[71] The purpose of this *narratio* is to provide an end to the *exordium,* which is distinguishable but in harmony with the

---

[62] See section 4, below.

[63] Quintilian, *Inst.* 4.1.20–22.

[64] Quintilian, *Inst.* 4.1.21: "*Sed adhibendi modus alter ille frequens et favorabilis, ne male sentiat populus Romanus, ne iudicia transferantur, ulter autem asper et rarus, quo minatur corruptis accusationem.*"

[65] Quintilian, *Inst.* 4.1.22: "*Quod si necessitas exiget, non erit iam ex arte oratoria, non magis quam appellare, etiamsi id quoque saepe utile est, aut antequam pronuntiet reum facere; nam et minari et deferre etiam non orator potest.*"

[66] Demosthenes, *Cor.* 18.324 (Vince, LCL): Μὴ δῆτ', ὦ πάντες θεοί. μηδεὶς ταῦθ' ὑμῶν ἐπινεύσειεν, ἀλλὰ μάλιστα μὲν καὶ τούτοις βελτίω τινὰ νοῦν καὶ φρένας ἐνθεῖητε, εἰ δ' ἄρ' ἔχουσιν ἀνιάτως, τούτους μὲν αὐτοὺς καθ' ἑαυτοὺς ἐξώλεις καὶ προώλεις ἐν γῇ καὶ θαλάττῃ ποιήσατε, ἡμῖν δὲ τοῖς λοιποῖς τὴν ταχίστην ἀπαλλαγὴν τῶν ἐπηρτημένων φόβων δότε καὶ σωτηρίαν ἀσφαλῆ.&&&

[67] On the *peroratio* see section 2 (b) above.

[68] See Lausberg, *Handbuch,* §288.

[69] Quintilian, *Inst.* 4.1.76–79.

[70] Quintilian, *Inst.* 4.1.77.

[71] Quintilian, *Inst.* 4.1.78.

beginning of the *narratio*.[72] An abrupt change from one part to the next is to be avoided, as well as the complete smoothing out of any differences.[73] In addition, the transition should contain an announcement of the major topic of the *narratio*.[74]

Verses 10–11 meet these requirements very well. The two rhetorical questions and the assertion in v. 10 put a clear end to the *exordium*. They deny that Paul is a rhetorical "flatterer,"[75] "persuading" (ἀνθρώπους πείθω) or "pleasing" men (ἀνθρώποις ἀρέσκειν),[76] or a magician, trying to "persuade God" (πείθω τὸν θεόν).[77] Verse 11 then introduces[78] what is going to be Paul's contention in the *narratio*: γνωρίζω γὰρ ὑμῖν, ἀδελφοί, τὸ εὐαγγέλιον τὸ εὐαγγελισθὲν ὑπ᾽ ἐμοῦ ὅτι οὐκ ἔστιν κατὰ ἄνθρωπον.

(b) The Narratio (1:12–2:14)

As the Greco-Roman rhetoricians recommend, Paul's *exordium* (1:6–11) is followed by the "statement of facts" (διήγησις, *narratio*).[79] In discussing Paul's *narratio* (1:12–2:14) one must keep in mind that, as Quintilian says, "there is no single law or fixed rule governing the method of defense. We must consider what is most advantageous in the circumstances and nature of the case. . . ."[80] Consequently the handbooks contain wide-ranging discussions with room for considerable differences of opinion going back to the various schools of rhetorical theory.

Cicero's treatment of the subject in *Inv.* 1.19.27–31.30 contains what may be regarded as a summary of the *communis opinio*. He starts by providing a general definition of "narrative": "The *narrative* is an exposition of events that have occurred or are supposed to have occurred."[81] He then distinguishes between three types (*genera*) of narrative, the first of which applies to Galatians: "that form of narrative which contains an exposition of a case at law."[82] Nearly all writers of the period agree that such

---

[72] Quintilian, *Inst.* 4.1.76: " . . . *id debebit in principio postremum esse cui commodissime iungi initium sequentium poterit.*"

[73] Quintilian, *Inst.* 4.1.79: "*Quapropter, ut non abrupte cadere in narrationem, ita non obscure transcendere est optimum.*"

[74] Quintilian, *Inst.* 4.1.79: "*Si vero longior sequetur ac perplexa magis expositio, ad eam ipsam praeparandus erit iudex.*"

[75] See, e.g., Demosthenes, *Exord.* 1.3; 19; 26.2; Quintilian, *Inst.* 4.1.9, 55–60. Cf. also Quintilian's polemic against Ovid (*Inst.* 4.1.77f.): "*Illa vero frigida et puerilis est in scholis adfectatio, ut ipse transitus efficiat aliquam utique sententiam et huius velut praestigiae plausum petat. . . .*" The rejection of rhetorical tricks at the beginning of a speech was part of rhetoric. See, furthermore, Betz, *Apostel Paulus*, 15ff., 57ff.

[76] Both phrases describe the "art of rhetoric." See, e.g., Plato, *Gorg.* 452E; *Prot.* 352E; *and Lausberg, Handbuch*, §257.

[77] Cf., e.g., Plato, *Resp.* 364C; and the proverb quoted in 390E.

[78] *Rhet. Her.* 4.26.35 provides examples of *transitio*, in which what follows next is set forth; e.g.: "*Mea in istum beneficia cognoscitis; nunc quomodo iste mihi gratiam rettulerit accipite.*"

[79] On the *narratio* see Schafer, "De rhetorum praeceptis"; Loheit, "Untersuchungen"; Volkmann, *Rhetorik*, §13; Lausberg, *Handbuch*, §§289–347.

[80] Quintilian, *Inst.* 4.2.84 (Butler): "*Neque enim est una lex defensionis certumque praescriptum: pro re, pro tempore intuenda quae prosint. . . .*"

[81] Cicero, *Inv.* 1.19.27 (Hubbell): "*Narratio est rerum gestarum aut ut gestarum expositio.*" Cf. Quintilian, *Inst.* 4.2.31 (see below). See Lausberg, *Handbuch*, §289 for other definitions.

[82] Cicero, *Inv.* 1.20.28: "*Nunc de narratione ea quae causae continet expositionem dicendum videtur.*" See Lausberg, *Handbuch*, §290, 1.

a "narrative" ought to possess three necessary qualities (*virtutes necessariae*): "it should be brief, clear, and plausible."[83] In Cicero,[84] the *Rhetorica ad Herennium*,[85] and especially Quintilian[86] we find extensive discussions about how such qualities can best be achieved.

Several points in Quintilian's discussion of the *narratio* are directly relevant for Paul. The first of these points addresses the question of whether or not the *narratio* is dispensable in certain cases.[87] Contrary to others, Quintilian takes the position that the *narratio* should not be omitted even when the accused simply denies the charge.[88] Indeed, in Gal 1:11ff. we have both a strong denial (vv. 11f.) and a longer *narratio* (1:13–2:14).

Quintilian's explanation, for which he can rely on the highest authorities,[89] makes clear why the short sentence of a denial is not an adequate "statement of facts."[90] The denial must not simply contradict the charge made by the opponent. Instead, the denial should introduce the subject matter on which the defense wishes to be judged.[91] It is part of the defense strategy. The *narratio*, on the other hand, is more than simply a narrative form of the denial.[92] In fact, the *narratio* may not even explicitly mention the charge. Its purpose is to deal with the facts that have a bearing on the case, in order to make the denial plausible.[93]

If this has a bearing on Paul, one should exercise caution and not simply conclude from v. 11 that the charge against Paul was in fact that his gospel was κατὰ ἄνθρωπον. Rather, this denial is part of his defense strategy. In v. 12 the simple denial of v. 11 is made more explicit: οὐδὲ ἔστιν κατὰ ἄνθρωπον (v. 11) means negatively: οὐδὲ . . . ἐγὼ παρὰ ἀνθρώπου παρέλαβον οὔτε ἐδιδάχθην, and positively: δι' ἀποκαλύψεως Ἰησοῦ Χριστοῦ (v. 12).[94] The *narratio* proper begins in v. 13, substantiating the claims made in v. 12 by appropriate "facts." However, neither the denial nor the charge is explicitly mentioned in 1:13–2:14. The reason for this can only be that the "facts" of 1:13–2:14 serve to make the denial (1:11f.) credible in the eyes of the addressees of the letter.

Another point of relevance concerns the beginning of the *narratio*, which intends "not merely to instruct, but rather to persuade the judge."[95] Quintilian recommends

---

[83] Cicero, *Inv.* 1.20.28: "*Oportet igitur eam tres habere res: ut brevis, ut aperta, ut probabilis sit.*" See Lausberg, *Handbuch*, §§294–334.

[84] Cicero, *Inv.* 1.20.28–1.21.30.

[85] *Rhet. Her.* 1.8.12–1.10.16.

[86] Quintilian, *Inst.* 4.2.2–132.

[87] Quintilian, *Inst.* 4.2.4ff.

[88] Quintilian, *Inst.* 4.2.9: "*Sed ut has aliquando non narrandi causas puto, sic ab illis dissentio qui non existimant esse narrationem cum reus quod obicitur tantum negat.*"

[89] Quintilian, *Inst.* 4.2.9ff.

[90] Quintilian, *Inst.* 4.2.12: " '*Non occidi hominem*': nulla narratio est; convenit: . . ."

[91] Quintilian, *Inst.* 4.2.1: " . . . *res de qua pronuntiaturus est indicetur.*"

[92] Cf. Quintilian, *Inst.* 4.2.10.

[93] Quintilian, *Inst.* 4.2.11: "*Ego autem magnos alioqui secutus auctores duas esse in iudiciis narrationum species existimo, alteram ipsius causae, alteram in rerum ad causam pertinentium expositione.*" Examples are given in 4.2.12–18.

[94] Cf. Gal 1:1.

[95] Quintilian, *Inst.* 4.2.21: "*Neque enim narratio in hoc reperta est, ut tantum cognoscat iudex, sed aliquanto magis ut consentiat.*" See Lausberg, *Handbuch*, §§300–301, 308.

beginning the *narratio* with a statement, the *propositio*,[96] which will influence the judge in some way, even though he may be well informed about the case.[97] He mentions examples like these: "I know that you are aware . . ."; "You remember . . ."; "You are not ignorant of the fact . . ."; etc.[98] Which one of these one chooses depends entirely upon how one can best influence the judge.

Paul announces his *narratio* with the words γνωρίζω γὰρ ὑμῖν, ἀδελφοί (v. 11), thus conforming to Quintilian's advice. We must conclude, therefore, that the term γνωρίζειν does not simply announce information, but by pretending to tell the Galatians something new in fact reminds them of something they no doubt know, but would at this time rather forget.[99]

As to the "facts" themselves, Quintilian provides a more explicit definition than Cicero, saying that "The *statement of facts* consists in the persuasive exposition of that which either has been done, or is supposed to have been done, or, to quote the definition given by Apollodorus, is a speech instructing the audience as to the nature of the case in dispute."[100] Consequently, the facts themselves, as well as their delivery, are subjected to partisan interest.[101] The three qualities of lucidity, brevity, and plausibility serve no other purpose.[102] This does not mean that the facts are necessarily false. On the contrary, a statement that is wholly in our favor is most plausible when it is true.[103] But truth is not always credible, nor is the credible always true. In short, whether the facts are true or fictitious, the effort required to make them believable is the same.[104]

Most of the remaining discussion of the *narratio* by the rhetoricians is devoted to the explanation of the three qualities.[105] Quintilian begins with "lucidity" or "clearness."[106] This quality is ensured by first choosing "words appropriate, significant and free from meanness" and by avoiding the "farfetched or unusual"; secondly, by the "distinct account of facts, persons, times, places and causes."[107] The delivery

---

[96] Cf. Quintilian, *Inst.* 3.9.5; 4.8.7, 30; its purpose is defined 3.9.2: "*proponere quidem quae sis probaturus necesse est.*" See Lausberg, *Handbuch*, §289.

[97] Quintilian, *Inst.* 4.2.21: "*Quare etiam si non erit docendus sed aliquo modo adficiendus narrabimus, cum praeparatione quadam.*"

[98] Quintilian, *Inst.* 4.8.21–23.

[99] See also the beginning of the *narratio* in Demosthenes' *De corona* (18.17): ἔστι δ' καὶ ἀναγκαῖον, ὦ ἄνδρες Ἀθηναῖοι, καὶ προσῆκον ἴσως, ὡς κατ' ἐκείνους τοὺς χρόνους εἶχε τὰ πράγματ' ἀναμνῆσαι, ἵνα πρὸς τὸν ὑπάρχοντα καιρὸν ἕκαστα θεωρῆτε.

[100] Quintilian, *Inst.* 4.2.31 (Butler): "*Narratio est rei factae aut ut factae utilis ad persuadendum expositio, vel, ut Apollodorus finit, oratio docens auditorem quid in controversia sit.*" See on definitions Lausberg, *Handbuch*, §289.

[101] Cf. Quintilian, *Inst.* 4.2.33. See Lausberg, *Handbuch*, §§289, 308.

[102] Cf. Quintilian, *Inst.* 4.2.31–33. See Lausberg, *Handbuch*, §294.

[103] Quintilian, *Inst.* 4.2.34: " . . . *quod proposuerim eam quae sit tota pro nobis debere esse veri similem cum vera sit.*" Cf J. Sanders, " 'Autobiographical' Statements."

[104] Quintilian, *Inst.* 4.2.34: "*Sunt enim plurima vera quidem, sed parum credibilia, sicut falsa quoque frequenter veri similia. Quare non minus laborandum est ut iudex quae vere dicimus quam quae fingimus credat.*"

[105] See Lausberg, *Handbuch*, §§294–334.

[106] Quintilian, *Inst.* 4.2.31, 36. See Lausberg, *Handbuch*, §§315–321.

[107] Quintilian, *Inst.* 4.3.36: "*Erit autem narratio aperta atque dilucida si fuerit primum exposita verbis propriis et significantibus et non sordidis quidem, non tamen exquisitis et ab usu remotis, tum distincta rebus personis temporibus locis causis.*"

must conform to this quality, so that the judge will readily accept it.[108] At this point Quintilian wants to eliminate all rhetorical tricks and gimmickry normally employed to evoke the applause of the crowds.[109] It is when the speaker gives the impression of absolute truth that his rhetoric is best.[110] One would have to say that Paul's narration conforms to these requirements.[111]

The quality of "brevity"[112] will be achieved, "if in the first place we start at the point of the case at which it begins to concern the judge, secondly avoid irrelevance, and finally cut out everything the removal of which neither hampers the activities of the judge nor harms our own case."[113] As Quintilian sees it, "brevity" should not be misunderstood as the excision of necessary information: "I mean not saying less, but not saying more than occasion demands."[114] If brevity is misunderstood as excessive abridgement, the *narratio* loses its power of persuasion and becomes meaningless.[115] If the case requires a longer statement, various means of avoiding tediousness should be employed.[116] Among the measures Quintilian recommends is the division of the statement into several sections, thereby creating the impression of several short statements instead of one long one.[117]

It is apparent that Paul follows this recommendation. His case requires a long statement of facts, since he has to cover his entire history from his birth on. He begins with his birth because it is relevant to the case. Then he covers the history of the problem, which one must know in order to understand the *causa* (1:6), by subdivisions. His *narratio* has roughly three parts, a method of division which seems to have been popular.[118] The first section (1:13–24) covers a long period of time and is divided up into several subsections. The middle section is somewhat shorter, reporting on the so-called Apostolic Council (2:1–10). The final section contains just a brief episode, the conflict at Antioch (2:11–14). In this way Paul is able to cover the long history of the problem, saying all that is necessary to know for the case, while leaving out all un-related material. The account is brief, but not excessively concise. It is a lively and dramatic narrative, but there is no superfluous embellishment or ornament. The information given has no other purpose than to support the denial (1:11f.).

The most difficult task is, of course, to make the *narratio* "credible."[119] In principle Quintilian suggests that this quality will be achieved, "if in the first place we take

---

[108] Quintilian, *Inst.* 4.3.36.

[109] Quintilian, *Inst.* 4.2.37–39.

[110] Quintilian, *Inst.* 4.2.38: "*tum autem optime dicit orator cum videtur vera dicere.*"

[111] See esp. Gal 1:10 and the oath 1:20.

[112] See Lausberg, *Handbuch*, §§297–314.

[113] Quintilian, *Inst.* 4.2.40: "*Brevis erit narratio ante omnia si inde coeperimus rem exponere unde ad iudicem pertinet, deinde si nihil extra causam dixerimus, tum etiam si reciderimus omnia quibus sublatis neque cognitioni quicquam neque utilitati detrahatur.*"

[114] Quintilian, *Inst.* 4.2.43: "*Nos autem brevitatem in hoc ponimus, non ut minus sed ne plus dicatur quam oporteat.*" Cf. Lausberg, *Handbuch*, §§298–308.

[115] See Quintilian, *Inst.* 4.2.41–47.

[116] See Quintilian, *Inst.* 4.2.47–51.

[117] Quintilian, *Inst.* 4.2.49–50: "*Et partitio taedium levat: . . . ita tres potius modicae narrationes videbuntur quam una longa.*" Cf. Lausberg, *Handbuch*, §§299–307, 311.

[118] See Lausberg, *Handbuch*, §338.

[119] See Lausberg, *Handbuch*, §§322–334.

care to say nothing contrary to nature, secondly if we assign reasons and motives for the facts on which the inquiry turns (it is unnecessary to do so with the subsidiary facts as well), and if we make the characters of the actors in keeping with the facts we desire to be believed."[120] Among the specific devices Quintilian recommends, we notice that it is "useful to scatter some hints of our proofs here and there, but in such a way that it is never forgotten that we are making a *statement of facts* and not a proof."[121] Simple and brief arguments may be thrown in, but these should be taken as only preparatory for the arguments to be developed in the *probatio*.[122] Such remarks should remain part of the *narratio*, since they are most effective when they are not recognizable as arguments.[123] Again, Paul's *narratio* seems to obey the main rules of theory. Motivation and reason are provided for the major "facts" (revelations in 1:15f.; 2:1; ὅτι κατεγνωσμένος ἦν in 2:11), but not for the subsidiary ones (1:17, 18, 21). Persons are characterized in conformity with the events (the "false brothers" in 2:4; the δοκοῦντες in 2:6; the ὑπόκρισις of Cephas, Barnabas, and the "other Jews" in 2:11–14). Scattered throughout the *narratio*, but remaining subject to it, are hints of proofs and small arguments (e.g., 1:13 ἠκούσατε; 1:23 ἀκούοντες ἦσαν; 1:20 an oath; 2:3, 4, 5, 6, etc.). The entire *narratio* is so designed that it makes the introductory statement (1:11f.) credible.

Among the further points in Quintilian's discussion, two deserve special attention as far as Paul is concerned. First, Quintilian disagrees with the general rule that the order of events in the *narratio* should always follow the actual order of events.[124] He himself wants to subject the order of events in the *narratio* to the rationale of expediency, which seems logical. But his examples show that he would indicate to the judge the order in which the events occurred.[125] With this being the exception, Quintilian reaffirms the general rule, saying that "this is no reason for not following the order of events as a general rule."[126] If we apply this to Paul, he apparently follows the natural order of events in 1:13–2:14, since there is no indication that he does not.[127] The other remark pertains to the conclusion of the *narratio*. Quintilian again goes against the practice of the majority of rhetoricians. The majority rule says that the *narratio* should "end where the issue to be deter-

---

[120] Quintilian, *Inst.* 4.2.52: "*Credibilis autem erit narratio ante omnia si prius consuluerimus nostrum animum ne quid naturae dicamus adversum, deinde si causas ac rationes factis praeposuerimus, non omnibus, sed de quibus quaeritur, si personas convenientes iis quae facta credi volemus constituerimus.*" See Lausberg, *Handbuch*, §338.

[121] Quintilian, *Inst.* 4.2.54: "*Ne illud quidem fuerit inutile, semina quaedam probationum spargere, verum sic ut narrationem esse meminerimus, non probationem.*" See Lausberg, *Handbuch*, §324.

[122] Quintilian, *Inst.* 4.2.54. See Lausberg, *Handbuch*, §324.

[123] Quintilian, *Inst.* 4.2.57: "*Optimae vero praeparationes erunt quae latuerint.*" See Lausberg, *Handbuch*, §325.

[124] Quintilian, *Inst.* 4.2.83: "*Namque ne iis quidem accedo qui semper eo putant ordine quo quid actum sit esse narrandum, sed eo malo narrare quo expedit.*"

[125] Cf. Quintilian, *Inst.* 4.2.83–85.

[126] Quintilian, *Inst.* 4.2.87: "*Neque ideo tamen non saepius id facere oportebit ut rerum ordinem sequamur.*" See Lausberg, *Handbuch*, §317.

[127] This rhetorical argument goes against the hypothesis of Zahn, *Galater*, 110ff., that the Antioch episode took place before the Jerusalem meeting. Cf. Munck, *Paul*, 74f., 100ff.

mined begins."[128] It cannot be accidental that at the end of the *narratio* in Gal 2:14, when Paul formulates the dilemma Cephas has got himself into, this dilemma[129] is identical with the issue the Galatians themselves have to decide: πῶς τὰ ἔθνη ἀναγκάζεις ἰουδαΐζειν;[130]

(c) The Propositio (2:15–21)

Between the *narratio* and the *probatio* rhetoricians insert the *propositio* (the name Quintilian uses).[131] Quintilian has the fullest account of this part of the speech, but again he takes a special position in applying it. We find the general view in the *Rhetorica ad Herennium* and in Cicero's *De inventione rhetorica*, although there is also considerable difference between them. The *Rhetorica ad Herennium* provides for two kinds of statements after the *narratio*: " . . . first to make clear what we and our opponents agree upon, if there is agreement on the points useful to us, and what remains contested. . . ."[132] Then comes the *distributio* in two parts, the *enumeratio* and the *expositio*, the former announcing the number of points to be discussed, the latter setting forth these points briefly and completely.[133] The function of the *propositio* is twofold; it sums up the legal content of the *narratio* by this outline of the case and provides an easy transition to the *probatio*.[134]

Gal 2:15–21 conforms to the form, function, and requirements of the *propositio*. Placed at the end of the last episode of the *narratio* (2:11–14), it sums up the *narratio*'s material content. But it is not part of the *narratio*,[135] and it sets up the arguments to be discussed later in the *probatio* (chapters 3 and 4).[136] The points of presumable agreement are set forth first (2:15f.). Paul may use the language of the opposition in v. 15, but the summary of the doctrine of justification by faith (v. 16) is entirely Pauline; yet it is made to appear as the logical conclusion one would draw

---

[128] Quintilian, *Inst.* 4.2.132: "*De fine narrationis cum iis contentio est qui perduci expositionem volunt eo unde quaestio oritur.*" Cf. Lausberg, *Handbuch,* §307.

[129] On the dilemma (*complexio*) see Cicero, *Inv.* 1.29.45, with good examples. See also Lausberg, *Handbuch,* §393.

[130] The connection of this question with the *causa* (1:6f.) of the *exordium* and with the *peroratio* of the *postscriptum* (6:12–16) should be noted because it also conforms to rhetorical theory (cf. Lausberg, *Handbuch,* §§431–442). Cf. also 2:3 (*narratio*) and 5:2 (beginning of the *paraenesis*). Paul's own position is antithetical: cf. 1:7 (*causa*); 2:3, 5 (*narratio*); 2:15–21 (*propositio*); 4:9, 11, 19–21 (*argumentatio*); 5:1–12, esp. 6:15 (*paraenesis*); 6:15 (*recapitulatio*).

[131] Quintilian, *Inst.* 4.4.1–4.5.26; Cicero, *Inv.* 1.22.31–1.23.33 calls it *partitio*, while the *Rhet. Her.* 1.10.17 uses *divisio*. See Volkmann, *Rhetorik,* §15; Lausberg, *Handbuch,* §346; Adamietz, *Ciceros De inventione,* 36ff.

[132] *Rhet. Her.* 1.10.17: "*Causarum divisio in duas partes distributa est. Primum perorata narratione debemus aperire quid nobis conveniat cum adversariis, si ea quae utilia sunt nobis convenient, quid in controversia relictum sit.*" Cf. Cicero, *Inv.* 1.22.31.

[133] *Rhet. Her.* 1.10.17: "*Expositio est cum res quibus de rebus dicturi sumus exponimus breviter et absolute.*" Cf. Cicero, *Inv.* 1.22.32; Quintilian, *Inst.* 4.5.26–28.

[134] Cf. Quintilian, *Inst.* 4.4.1: "*Mihi autem propositio videtur omnis confirmationis initium, quod non modo in ostendenda quaestione principali, sed nonnunquam etiam in singulis argumentis poni solet.*" See Lausberg, *Handbuch,* §§343–345.

[135] This formal argument would then also decide the old controversy, whether or not vv. 15–21 must be regarded as a part of Paul's speech at Antioch. See on this problem Schlier, *Galater,* 87f.

[136] This was recognized, without the formal considerations, by Schlier, *Galater,* 87f.

from the *narratio* as a whole. Verses 17f. contain the points of disagreement, again probably using language borrowed from the opposition. Verses 19f. are an extremely concise summary of the argument to be elaborated upon later. Verse 21 concludes with a sharp denial of a charge.[137] Paul does not use *partitio* or *enumeratio* because there is only one point[138] against which a defense has to be made (2:17).[139]

(d) The Probatio (3:1–4:31)

The most decisive part of the speech is the one presenting the "proof."[140] This part determines whether or not the speech as a whole will succeed. *Exordium* and *narratio* are only preparatory steps leading up to this central part. The purpose of the *probatio* (as Quintilian calls it)[141] or the *confirmatio* (as Cicero[142] and the *Rhetorica ad Herennium*[143] call it) is to establish credibility for the defense by a system of arguments.[144] Because of the importance of the *probatio,* the Greco-Roman rhetoricians have devoted the major portions of their works to it. Understandably, there is also considerable difference of opinion in regard to the classification, distribution and effectiveness of individual forms and types of arguments.

Viewing Galatians from a rhetorical perspective suggests at once that chapters 3 and 4 must contain the *probatio* section. Admittedly, an analysis of these chapters in terms of rhetoric is extremely difficult. One might say that Paul has been very successful—as a skilled rhetorician would be expected to be—in disguising his argumentative strategy. That is to say, in spite of the apparent confusion, there is to be expected a clear flow of thought. What makes these chapters look so confusing is the frequent interruption of the argumentative sections by dialogue, examples, proverbs, quotations, etc. But this is in conformity with the requirements of Hellenistic rhetoric. In fact, for the rhetoricians of Paul's time there could be nothing more boring than a perfect product of rhetorical technology.[145] Therefore, the appearance of an argument as a "dead" system of inescapable and pre-formed syllogisms had to be avoided; instead, the arguments were to be presented in a "lively" way. Quintilian's advice is to achieve "diversity by a thousand figures."[146] Paradoxically, extremely perfected logic

---

[137] Cf. the connections with the *exordium* (1:6 f.) and the *recapitulatio* (6:12–16).

[138] Quintilian, *Inst.* 4.5.8: "*Itaque, si plura vel obicienda sunt vel diluenda, et utilis et iucunda partitio est, ut quo quaque de re dicturi sumus ordine appareat; at, si unum crimen varie defendemus, supervacua.*" See Lausberg, *Handbuch,* §347.

[139] Gal 2:17 apparently contains the "charge," as Paul phrases it: εἰ δὲ ζητοῦντες δικαιωθῆναι ἐν Χριστῷ εὑρέθημεν καὶ αὐτοὶ ἁμαρτωλοί, ἄρα Χριστὸς ἁμαρτίας διάκονος; Cf. 2:2–4, 14; 5:11; 6:12–16.

[140] On the *probatio* see esp. Volkmann, *Rhetorik,* §§16ff.; Lausberg, *Handbuch,* §§348–430.

[141] Quintilian, *Inst.* 5, prooemium 5. The Greek term is πίστις (Aristotle, *Rhet.* 3.13.4 [1414b]), which Quintilian thinks is best rendered by the Latin *probatio* (*Inst.* 5.10.8). See Lausberg, *Handbuch,* §§348–349.

[142] Cicero, *Inv.* 1.24.34.

[143] *Rhet. Her.* 1.10.18.

[144] See the definition given by Cicero, *Inv.* 1.24.34: "*Confirmatio est per quam argumentando nostrae causae fidem et auctoritatem et firmamentum adiungit oratio.*"

[145] See Quintilian, *Inst.* 5.14.27–35.

[146] Quintilian, *Inst.* 5.14.32. See Lausberg, *Handbuch,* §257.

was thought to create suspicion and boredom, not credibility, while a carefully prepared mixture of some logic, some emotional appeal, some wisdom, some beauty,
and some entertainment was thought to conform to human nature and to the ways in
which human beings accept arguments as true. Gal 3 and 4 are such a "mixture."

The beginning of the *probatio* section (3:1–5) reveals interesting aspects. The
particular "case" in which Paul is involved is constituted by two components. First,
there is agreement on the *factum* itself but disagreement on the question of whether
the *factum* is right or wrong. Therefore, the argument pertains not to the *factum* itself, but to its *qualitas*. Thus the defense must try to prove that the *factum* was legal
(*iure, recte*):[147] this includes also a defense of the *auctor* of that *factum*.[148] In the case
of the Galatians, the *factum* is not disputed because the founding of the Galatian
churches by Paul is not questioned by any of the parties.[149] The question is rather
whether this foundation was done rightfully or "in vain."[150]

Secondly, the addressees of the letter, that is, the hearers of the arguments, are
also the eye-witnesses of the evidence.[151] This situation provides the writer of the letter with the possibility of proceeding as if the eye-witnesses are "in court."[152] Paul
makes full use of this opportunity in 3:1–5: by applying the "inductive method"
which rhetoricians trace back to Socrates[153] he enters into his first argument by an
interrogatio of these witnesses.[154] In every case the answers to the questions are self-
evident and need not be recorded. Paul is not only fortunate in being able to question
the eye-witnesses themselves,[155] but he also compels them to produce the strongest of
all possible defense arguments, undeniable evidence.[156] This undeniable evidence is
the gift of the Spirit, which the Galatians themselves have experienced.

The gift of the Spirit was an ecstatic experience.[157] Together with the miracles
which are being performed at present among the Galatians,[158] this constitutes

---

[147] On the *status qualitatis* see Volkmann, *Rhetorik,* §7; Lausberg, *Handbuch,* §§89, 123–130,
134–136, 171–196.

[148] Lausberg, *Handbuch,* §§126, 175, who refers to Quintilian, *Inst.* 3.6.79: " . . . *qualitatis duplex
ratio facienda sit, altera qua et factum defenditur, altera qua tantum reus.*"

[149] See Gal 1:6–9, 11; 3:1–5; 4:13–15.

[150] See εἰκῆ Gal 3:4; 4:11; cf. also 2:2, 15–21; 5:2–12; 6:12–16.

[151] Cf. 3:1: . . . οἷς κατ' ὀφθαλμοὺς Ἰησοῦς Χριστὸς προεγράφη ἐσταυρωμένος; Also this
statement uses a rhetorical *topos;* see Lausberg, *Handbuch,* §810, and index, s.v. *oculus, conspectus.*

[152] Cf. Aristotle, *Rhet.* 1.15.15f. (1376a); Quintilian, *Inst.* 5.7.1f., and Lausberg, *Handbuch,* §354.

[153] See Cicero, *Inv.* 1.31.51: "*Inductio est oratio quae rebus non dubiis captat assensiones eius quicum
instituta est; quibus assensionibus facit ut illi dubia quaedam res propter similitudinem earum rerum quibus
assensit probetur; velut apud Socraticum Aeschinen demonstrat Socrates.*" 53: "*Hoc modo sermonis
plurimum Socrates usus est propterea quod nihil ipse afferre ad persuadendum volebat, sed ex eo quod
sibi ille dederat quicum disputabat, aliquid conficere malebat, quod ille ex eo quod iam concessisset
necessario approbare deberet.*" Cf. Quintilian, *Inst.* 5.11.3–5, and Lausberg, *Handbuch,* §§419–421.

[154] On the *interrogatio* see the treatment by Quintilian, *Inst.* 5.7.8–37, and Lausberg, *Handbuch,*
§354.

[155] Cf. Quintilian, *Inst.* 5.7.1: "*Maximus tamen patronis circa testimonia sudor est. Ea dicuntur
aut per tabulas aut a praesentibus.*"

[156] Cf. Cicero, *Inv.* 1.32.53: "*Hoc in genere praecipiendum nobis videtur primum, ut illud quod
inducemus per similitudinem eiusmodi sit ut sit necesse concedere.*"

[157] For a discussion of this point see Betz, "Spirit."

[158] Gal 3:5: . . . ἐνεργῶν δυνάμεις ἐν ὑμῖν . . .

evidence of supernatural origin and character—that is, for ancient rhetoric, evidence of the highest order.[159]

If, as Paul presumes, the evidence is accepted, his readers will have to make a necessary concession: the experience of the Spirit and the occurrence of the miracles did not come about ἐξ ἔργων νόμου but ἐκ πίστεως Χριστοῦ.[160] This is evident because at the time of this experience the Galatians had no doubt heard the proclamation of the gospel,[161] but being outside of the Torah they could not have produced "works of the Torah." This, Paul argues, proves his main point, "justification by faith" instead of "by works of the Torah" (cf. 2:16). The *interrogatio* (3:1–5) thus also prepares the ground for the next major argument, the argument from Scripture (3:6ff.).

Naturally, proof from Scripture is not a subject treated by the ancient rhetoricians. One can presuppose, however, that in a primitive Christian context such proofs were accepted with a very high degree of *auctoritas*.[162] Scripture would have to be classified as written, documentary evidence.[163] Because of its divine inspiration this evidence would come close to that of oracles or divine law.[164] In any case, it would have to be treated as equal to the "inartificial proof."[165]

In terms of rhetoric, the passage Gal 3:6–18 does not figure merely as "Scripture proof," but also as an *exemplum*.[166] Generally, *exempla* belong to the *genus artificiale*.[167] Their relationship to the *auctoritas*, which also belongs to the *genus artificiale*, was recognized.[168] The figure of Abraham would be classified as a "historical example."[169] This gives it a high rank, as far as credibility is concerned, a rank

---

[159] Cf. Quintilian, *Inst.* 5.7.35: "*His adicere si qui volet ea quae divina testimonia vocant, ex responsis oraculis ominibus, duplicem sciat esse eorum tractatum: generalem alterum, in quo inter Stoicos et Epicuri sectam secutos pugna perpetua est regaturne providentia mundus, specialem alterum circa partis divinationum, ut quaeque in quaestionem cadet.*" Quintilian has also comments about the ambiguity of such divine testimonies (5.7.36). See Lausberg, *Handbuch*, §176; Volkmann, *Rhetorik*, 239.

[160] Gal 3:2, 5.

[161] Gal 3:2, 5: ἐξ ἀκοῆς πίστεως.

[162] On this subject see esp. Quintilian, *Inst.* 5.11.36–42. Quintilian mentions among such arguments the precepts of the Seven Wise Men and lines from poets, particularly Homer, and makes this remark (5.11.39): "*Nam sententiis quidem poetarum non orationes modo sunt refertae, sed libri etiam philosophorum, qui quamquam inferiora omnia praeceptis suis ac litteris credunt, repetere tamen auctoritatem a plurimis versibus non fastidierunt.*" See also Lausberg, *Handbuch*, §426.

[163] See Quintilian, *Inst.* 5.5.1–2; 5.7.1–2. Cf. also Aristotle on συγγραφαί (*Rhet.* 1.2.2 [1355b]; 1.15.20–25 [1376b]), on ancient witness 1.15.17 (1376b).

[164] Cf. Quintilian, *Inst.* 5.11.42: "*Ponitur a quibusdam, et quidem in parte prima, deorum auctoritas, quae est ex responsis, ut 'Socraten esse sapientissimum.' Id rarum est, non sine usu tamen. . . . Quae cum propria causae sunt, divina testimonia vocantur, cum aliunde arcessuntur, argumenta.*"

[165] Cf. Quintilian, *Inst.* 5.11.43, where also the reason is stated: "*quod ea non inveniret orator, sed acciperet.*" See Lausberg, *Handbuch*, §§351–354.

[166] On *exempla* see Volkmann, *Rhetorik*, §23; Lausberg, *Handbuch*, §§410–426.

[167] Quintilian, *Inst.* 5.11.1 describes it thus: "*Tertium genus, ex iis quae extrinsecus adducuntur in causam, Graeci vocant παράδειγμα, quo nomine et generaliter usi sunt in omni similium adpositione et specialiter in iis quae rerum gestarum auctoritate nituntur.*" This definition is found in 5.11.6: "*Potentissimum autem est inter ea quae sunt huius generis quod proprie vocamus exemplum, id est rei gestae aut ut gestae utilis ad persuadendum id quod intenderis commemoratio.*" See also Lausberg, *Handbuch*, §410.

[168] See Lausberg, *Handbuch*, §§410, 426.

[169] See ibid., §§411–414.

which would be heightened even more because of the position of reverence which Abraham enjoyed in both Judaism and Christianity. Furthermore, the promise God made to Abraham[170] falls into the category of *res gesta*. Consequently, since the "sons of Abraham," for whose benefit the covenant was made, are in fact identical with the Galatians themselves,[171] the covenant amounts to a *praeiudicium*,[172] another proof of the highest degree (*genus inartificiale*). That Paul thinks not only in terms of Scripture proof but also in legal terms is underscored by the fact that he refers to an analogy from law[173] and inserts an "excursus" on the Torah (3:19–25) as a negative backdrop to the covenant of Abraham.[174]

A "definition" of the Galatians' status before God is set forth in 3:26–28. As I have tried to show in a recent article,[175] this definition shows an interesting formal structure, which resembles in some ways the "macarism." There is also reason to believe that Paul lifted the composition almost in its entirety from another, perhaps baptismal, context in order to "quote" it here. If this hypothesis is assumed, the "quotation" would function here as a "reminder."

The argument 3:6–18 is joined with the "macarism" in 3:29 and is repeated after some further explanation in 4:7. As the explanation in 4:4–6, which contains perhaps another "quotation" from earlier tradition, brings out, 3:26–28 does not introduce a new argument but merely reactivates the first argument, the evidence of the experience of the Spirit (3:1–5). Therefore, the entire section 3:26–4:7 joins together the argument from the evidence of the Spirit (3:1–5) with the argument from Scripture (3:6–18, 25). The conclusion of the second major argument occurs in 4:1–11. After stating again the religious "achievements" of the Galatians (4:8–9a), Paul returns to the *interrogatio* (cf. 3:1–5), asking, πῶς ἐπιστρέφετε πάλιν ἐπὶ τὰ ἀσθενῆ καὶ πτωχὰ στοιχεῖα, οἷς πάλιν ἄνωθεν δουλεῦσαι θέλετε; (4:9c). This question, the answer to which is self-explanatory, must be seen in juxtaposition with the earlier question in 3:3: ἐναρξάμενοι πνεύματι, νῦν σαρκὶ ἐπιτελεῖσθε; In the same way, the final warning in 4:11 (φοβοῦμαι ὑμᾶς μή πως εἰκῇ κεκοπίακα εἰς ὑμᾶς) repeats the previous warning of 3:4 (τοσαῦτα ἐπάθετε εἰκῇ; εἴ γε καὶ εἰκῇ).[176]

As all commentators point out, the interpretation of the section 4:12–20 presents considerable difficulties. In a disconnected way Paul seems to jump from one point to the next, leaving in obscurity which points he is jumping from and to.[177]

---

[170] Note the term διαθήκη, Gal 3:15, 17; 4:24

[171] Gal 3:26–4:7, 28, 31.

[172] This is Quintilian's term. See his definition of the various forms of *praeiudicia* in *Inst.* 5.2.1: "*Iam praeiudiciorum vis omnis tribus in generibus versatur: rebus quae aliquando ex paribus causis sunt iudicatae, quae exempla rectius dicuntur, ut de rescissis patrum testamentis vel contra filios confirmatis: iudiciis ad ipsam causam pertinentibus, unde etiam nomen ductum est . . . aut cum de eadem causa pronuntiatum est.*" See Lausberg, *Handbuch*, §353, for further material.

[173] Gal 3:15, 17; 4:1–3.

[174] Cf. *Rhet. Her.* 2.13.19: "*Iudicatum est id de quo sententia lata est aut decretum interpositum. Ea saepe diversa sunt, ut aliud alio iudici aut praetori aut consuli aut tribuno plebis placitum sit; et fit ut de eadem re saepe alius aliud decreverit aut iudicarit.*"

[175] See above, n. 157.

[176] Cf. also Gal 2:2, 5.

[177] Cf. Oepke, *Galater*, 140f., who makes the most of this: "Nun schlägt die Leidenschaft völlig in heißes Liebeswerben um. Durch den abgerissenen, oft überkurzen Ausdruck ist das Verständnis

However, the section becomes understandable when interpreted in the light of epistolography: 4:12–20 contains a string of *topoi* belonging to the theme of friendship, a theme which was famous in ancient literature.[178] More importantly, it was customary to use material from the *topos* περὶ φιλίας in the *probatio* section of speeches[179] as well as in letters.[180] Quintilian includes the material among the various types of *exempla*.[181] The argumentative value of such *topoi* results from the fact that their truth was to be taken for granted. Compared with the preceding arguments, however, the friendship *topos* can claim only a lower degree of persuasiveness.[182] Yet, given the rather "heavy" character of the argumentation in 3:1–4:11, this insertion of an "easier" and more emotional section is entirely in order, when one judges the matter according to the tastes of ancient rhetoric.[183]

Paul concludes the *probatio* section with the "allegory" of Sarah, Hagar and their sons (4:21–31).[184] He himself indicates by his words ἅτινά ἐστιν ἀλληγορούμενα (4:24) that he wants to interpret the Abraham tradition and the verses from Scripture according to the allegorical method.[185] In regard to the composition of the letter, this poses two questions: why does Paul insert this allegory at the end of the *probatio* section[186] and what argumentative force does he attribute to it?

Quintilian has some advice to offer in regard to the distribution of arguments in the *probatio* section.[187] He favors the opinion that the strongest argument should either come at the beginning, or should be divided between the beginning and the end. He clearly rejects an order "descending from the strongest proofs to the weakest."[188] Yet allegory does not seem to be a strong proof, if we examine what some of

---

erschwert. Rein verstandesmäßige Zergliederung führt solch einem Text gegenüber nicht zum Ziel." Burton, *Galatians*, 235, believes that Paul is "dropping argument."

[178] See for references and bibliography G. Stählin, φίλος, κτλ, 9:144ff.; Treu, "Freundschaft."

[179] Cf. e.g., Quintilian, *Inst.* 5.11.41, who quotes as the first example the proverb: "*Ubi amici, ibi opes*" (see below, n. 181). See also Steinmetz, *Freundschaftslehre*.

[180] See Koskenniemi, *Studien*, 115ff.; Brinckmann, *Begriff*; Thraede, *Grundzüge*.

[181] Quintilian, *Inst.* 5.11.41: "*Ea quoque quae vulgo recepta sunt hoc ipso, quod incertum auctorem habent, velut omnium fiunt, quale est: 'ubi amici, ibi opes' et 'conscientia mille testes,' et apud Ciceronem: 'pares autem, ut est in vetere proverbio, cum paribus maxime congregantur'; neque enim durassent haec in aeternum nisi vera omnibus viderentur.*"

[182] Cf. Quintilian's discussion, *Inst.* 5.11.43–44.

[183] See the discussion in Quintilian, *Inst.* 5.12.3ff.; and Lausberg, *Handbuch*, §413.

[184] The connection between this allegory and Hellenistic rhetoric is seen and discussed by van Stempvoort, *Allegorie*, 16ff. Cf. also the relationship between Seneca, *Ep.* 88.24–28, and Philo's allegory in *De congressu eruditionis gratia*; on this see Stuckelberger, *Senecas 88e Brief*, 60ff.

[185] Actually, Paul employs both "allegory" and "typology." For this method see Volkmann, *Rhetorik*, 429ff.; Lausberg, *Handbuch*, §§895–901; Pépin, *Mythe et Allégorie*; Buffière, *Mythes d'Homère*; Barr, *Old and New*, 103ff.

[186] Many scholars see the problem, but explain the matter psychologically by calling the passage "an afterthought" (see e.g., Burton, *Galatians*, 251; Schlier, *Galater*, 216; Luz, "Der Bund, 319; Mussner, *Galaterbrief*, 316f., or as the result of a "Diktierpause" (Oepke, *Galater*, 147; Stange, "Diktierpausen," 115.

[187] Quintilian, *Inst.* 5.12.1ff.

[188] Quintilian, *Inst.* 5.12.14: "*Quaesitum etiam potentissima argumenta primone ponenda sint loco, ut occupent animos, an summo, ut inde dimittant, an partita primo summoque, ut Homerica dispositione in medio sint infirma aut animis crescant. Quae prout ratio causae cuiusque postulabit ordinabuntur, uno (ut ego censeo) excepto, ne a potentissimis ad levissima decrescat oratio.*"

the rhetoricians have to say. Being related to the exemplum and to the metaphor, allegory is included among the *figurae per immutationem*.[189] Its argumentative force is weakened by its ambiguity.[190] One could, therefore, come to the conclusion that the allegory in 4:21–31 is the weakest of the arguments in the *probatio* section. In this case, Paul's composition would be subject to a criticism like the one offered by Quintilian.

It is interesting, however, that a more positive evaluation becomes possible, if we follow the advice of Pseudo-Demetrius.[191] This author argues that "direct" (ἁπλῶς) arguments are not always the most effective ones. "Any darkly-hinting expression is more terror-striking, and its import is variously conjectured by different hearers. On the other hand, things that are clear and plain are apt to be despised, just like men when stripped of their garments."[192] As evidence the author refers to the mysteries: "Hence the Mysteries are revealed in an allegorical form in order to inspire such shuddering and awe as are associated with darkness and night. Allegory also is not unlike darkness and night."[193] When we consider that in the Christian context the Abraham tradition holds the place which is occupied in the Mysteries by their own holy tradition, Paul's argument here becomes highly forceful.[194]

There may also be another rhetorical strategy at work. Pseudo-Demetrius follows the opinion of Theophrastus, saying "that not all possible points should be punctiliously and tediously elaborated, but some should be left to the comprehension and inference of the hearer...."[195] The effect upon the hearer is this: "... when he perceives what you have left unsaid [he] becomes not only your hearer but your witness, a very friendly witness too. For he thinks himself intelligent because you have afforded him the means of showing his intelligence. It seems like a slur on your hearer to tell him everything as though he were a simpleton."[196]

In the light of the foregoing rhetorical considerations the place and function of the allegory 4:21–31 becomes explainable. Paul had concluded the previous section in 4:20 with a confession of perplexity (... ὅτι ἀποροῦμαι ἐν ὑμῖν). Such a confession was a rhetorical device, seemingly admitting that all previous arguments have failed

---

[189] Cf. the definition in *Rhet. Her.* 4.34.46: "*Permutatio* [ἀλληγορία] *est oratio aliud verbis aliud sententia demonstrans.*" See also Lausberg, *Handbuch*, §§421, 564, 755ff., 894, 895–901.

[190] Because of its ambiguity, "allegory" can easily go over into "*aenigma.*" See Lausberg, *Handbuch*, §899.

[191] Cf. Demetrius, *Eloc.* 2.99–101, 151, 222, 243 (Roberts, LCL).

[192] Demetrius, *Eloc.* 2.100.

[193] Demetrius, *Eloc.* 2.101: Διὸ καὶ τὰ μυστήρια ἐν ἀλληγορίαις λέγεται πρὸς ἔκπληξιν καὶ φρίκην, ὥσπερ ἐν σκότῳ καὶ νυκτί. ἔοικε δὲ καὶ ἡ ἀλληγορία τῷ σκότῳ καὶ τῇ νυκτί. On allegory in connection with the mysteries see esp. Griffiths, "Allegory"; *Plutarch's De Iside*, 100f; Merkelbach, *Roman und Mysterium*, 55ff.

[194] Cf. the function of the allegory in Philo; see esp. Brandenburger, *Fleisch und Geist*, 200f.; Christiansen, *Technik*.

[195] Demetrius, *Eloc.* 4.222: ... ὅτι οὐ πάντα ἐπ' ἀκριβείας δεῖ μακρηγορεῖν, ἀλλ' ἔνια καταλιπεῖν καὶ τῷ ἀκροατῇ συνιέναι, καὶ λογίζεσθαι ἐξ αὐτοῦ.

[196] Demetrius, *Eloc.* 4.222: συνεὶς γὰρ τὸ ἐλλειφθὲν ὑπὸ σοῦ οὐκ ἀκροατὴς μόνον, ἀλλὰ καὶ μάρτυς σου γίνεται, καὶ ἅμα εὐμενέστερος. συνετὸς γὰρ ἑαυτῷ δοκεῖ διὰ σὲ τὸν ἀφορμὴν παρεσχηκότα αὐτῷ τοῦ συνιέναι, τὸ δὲ πάντα ὡς ἀνοήτῳ λέγειν καταγινώσκοντι ἔοικεν τοῦ ἀκροατοῦ.

to convince.[197] Then, in 4:21 he starts again by asking the Galatians to tell the answer themselves: Λέγετέ μοι, . . . τὸν νόμον οὐκ ἀκούετε; In other words, the allegory allows Paul to return to the *interrogatio* method used in 3:1–5 by another route.[198] There this method was employed to force the Galatians to admit as eye-witnesses that the evidence speaks for Paul, an admission that leaves them in the situation of "simpletons" (ἀνόητοι). However, people who are to be persuaded should not be left in a situation of such low regard. By his confession of perplexity in 4:20 Paul removes himself from the haughty position of one who has the total command of the arguments. Through the allegory he lets the Galatians find the "truth" for themselves, thus convincing themselves, and at the same time clearing themselves from the blame of being ἀνόητοι Γαλάται. The conclusion (4:31), now stated in the first person plural, includes the readers among those who render judgment.[199] Moreover, the conclusion of 4:31 is not only the résumé of the meaning of the allegory 4:21–31, but of the entire *probatio* section, thus anticipating that the whole argument has convinced the audience.

(e) The Paraenesis (5:1–6:10)

The last part of the "body" of the Galatian letter consists of *paraenesis* (5:1–6:10). That much can be said in spite of the difficulties arising from a discussion of the matter.[200]

It is surprising that there only exist a few investigations of the formal character and function of epistolary *paraenesis*.[201] M. Dibelius' definition is clearly too vague: "Paränese nennt man eine Aneinanderreihung verschiedener, häufig unzusammenhängender Mahnungen mit einheitlicher Adressierung."[202] H. Cancik,[203] utilizing the method of language analysis, distinguished between two forms of argument in Seneca's epistles, that of "descriptive" and that of "prescriptive" language.[204] This distinction corresponds to the two means of argument, the "rational" and the "emotive." Cancik points out that the scholarly argument is facilitated not only by "descriptive" language, but by "prescriptive" as well, so that *paraenesis* cannot be regarded as a

---

[197] For the epistolographic cliché cf., e.g., Isocrates, *Ep.* 2.24; 8.8. It is related to the rhetorical *dubitatio*, examples of which are found in Acts 25:20; Hermas *Sim.* 8.3.1; 9.2.5, 6. See Lausberg, *Handbuch*, §§776–778.

[198] Cf. my discussion of the *interrogatio*, above.

[199] διό, ἀδελφοί, οὐκ ἐσμὲν παιδίσκης τέκνα ἀλλὰ τῆς ἐλευθέρας.

[200] Differently Merk, "Der Beginn," who provides a useful survey of the various opinions in regard to the beginning of the paraenesis. However, since the conclusions are not based upon a composition analysis they are not convincing.

[201] Investigations are usually aimed at elements of paraenesis, rather than the paraenetical section of the letter; for bibliography see Doty, *Letters*, 49ff. For the larger question and bibliography see Gaiser, *Protreptik*; Rabbow, *Seelenführung*, esp. 370f.; Hadot, *Seneca*; Peter, *Der Brief*, 225ff.

[202] Dibelius, *Geschichte*, 2:65. Dibelius' treatment of the subject (65–76) is little more than a random collection of diverse material from a wide range of authors. See also his *Formgeschichte*, 234–65, esp. 239ff.

[203] Cancik, *Untersuchungen*. See the review of this important dissertation by Maurach; and Maurach, *Bau*, passim.

[204] Cancik, *Untersuchungen*, 16ff.

"Kümmerform," which is deficient of logic and merely applies the result of rational theory.[205] She also distinguishes between simple elements of *paraenesis* (series of prescriptions, prohibitions, exhortations, warnings, etc.) and combinations of these with descriptive elements. In addition we have to take into account *exempla*, comparisons, etc.[206]

It is rather puzzling to see that *paraenesis* plays only a marginal role in the ancient rhetorical handbooks, if not in rhetoric itself.[207] Consequently, modern studies of ancient rhetoric also do not pay much attention to it.[208] On the other hand, *paraenesis* was characteristic of the philosophical literature, especially of the diatribes of the Hellenistic period.[209] In this material we find that "rhetoric" is denounced with regularity as nothing but concoctions of lifeless syllogisms.[210] The philosophical letters, which are most interesting to the student of Paul's letters and of which we have a large number extant, very often have at the end a paraenetical section.[211] Striking as this phenomenon is, they have been the subject of only a few studies of these letters, none of which, to my knowledge, specifically investigates the paraenetical material. But in one of Seneca's epistles (*Ep.* 85.1) we read what may be the major reason for including *paraenesis* in the philosophical letters: "I declare again and again that I take no pleasure in such proofs [sc. the syllogisms]. I am ashamed to enter the arena and undertake battle on behalf of gods and men armed only with an awl."[212]

The paraenetical section of Galatians (5:1–6:10) can be subdivided into three parts. Each of the parts is recognizable by its restatement of the "indicative" of salvation.[213]

1. Gal 5:1–12

5:1a   A restatement of the "indicative" of salvation: τῇ ἐλευθερίᾳ ἡμᾶς Χριστὸς ἠλευθέρωσεν.

5:1b–12 A warning against taking up of the yoke of the Jewish Torah by submitting to circumcision.

---

[205] Ibid., 17.

[206] Ibid., 23.

[207] Even Quintilian has no special treatment of it, but only incidentally refers to other orators as having a related doctrine; see *Inst.* 3.6.47; 9.2.103. According to Aristotle there are two kinds of "deliberative" speech: . . . τὸ μὲν προτροπὴ τὸ δὲ ἀποτροπή (*Rhet.* 1.3.3 [1358b]). This doctrine is also found later (cf. *Rhet. Her.* 1.2.2; Quintilian, *Inst.* 9.4.130), but has no apparent connection to paraenesis.

[208] See Volkmann, *Rhetorik*, 294ff.; Lausberg, *Handbuch*, §§61, 2; 1109; 1120; Ernesti, *Graecorum rhetoricae*, s.v. προτροπή, *suasio* (παραίνεσις, etc., is not even listed).

[209] See Oltramare, *Origines;* Capelle and Marrou, "Diatribe."

[210] For further literature see Betz, *Apostel Paulus*, 57ff.

[211] See e.g., the analysis of Seneca's *Ep.* 76 by Cancik, *Untersuchungen,* 18ff.

[212] Seneca, *Ep.* 85:1 (Gummere): "*Illud totiens testor, hoc me argumentorum genere non delectari. Pudet in aciem descendere pro dis hominibusque susceptam subula armatum.*" I am indebted to the passage by Cancik, *Untersuchungen*, 22f. See also Trillitzsch, *Senecas Beweisführung*, 69ff.

[213] The restatements refer to 4:31, the conclusion of the *probatio* section and, by implication, to the result of the entire preceding argument. Cf. the κανών in 6:16 (14–15).

2. Gal 5:13–24

5:13a   A restatement of the "indicative": ὑμεῖς γὰρ ἐπ᾽ ἐλευθερίᾳ ἐκλήθητε, ἀδελφοί.

5:13b–24   A warning against corruption by the σάρξ.

3. Gal 5:25–6:10

5:25a   A restatement of the "indicative": εἰ ζῶμεν πνεύματι, . . .

5:25b–6:6   A series of gnomic sentences[214] forming the positive exhortation.

6:7–9   An eschatological warning.

6:10   A summary statement of the *paraenesis*.[215]

4. The Function of the Letter

The formal analysis of Paul's letter to the Galatians permits us to arrive at some conclusions with regard to its function. We must of course distinguish between the general functions of the letter as a means of communication, a question too difficult to go into at this point, and the specific functions of the Galatian letter.

The "apologetic letter" presupposes the real or fictitious situation of the court of law, with the jury, the accuser and the defendant. In the case of Galatians, the addressees are identical with the jury, with Paul being the defendant and his opponents the accusers. This situation makes Paul's letter a self-apology. The form of the letter is necessary, because the defendant himself is prevented from appearing in person before the jury. Therefore, the letter must serve to represent its author.[216] Serving as a substitute, the letter carries the defense speech to the jury.

If one looks at the letter from the point of view of the rhetorician, the substitute is a poor one indeed. Being simply a lifeless piece of paper, it eliminates one of the most important weapons of the rhetorician, the oral delivery. The actual delivery of the speech includes a whole range of weapons relating to modulation of voice and to gestures.[217] In his remarks in 4:18–20[218] Paul shows that he is fully aware of the disadvantages connected with writing a letter instead of making a personal appearance.[219]

---

[214] The investigation of Paul's gnomic sentences remains another desideratum of New Testament scholarship. For the form in general, see Lausberg, *Handbuch*, §§872–879; Horna, "Gnome, Gnomendichtung, Gnomologien," *RE Sup.* 6:74–87; Fritz, ibid., 87–90; Chadwick, *Sentences;* Fischel, *Rabbinic Literature.*

[215] The last words, μάλιστα δὲ πρὸς τοὺς οἰκείους τῆς πίστεως, corresponding to an epistolary cliché. See P.Oxy. 293.16; 294.31; 743.43; and Meecham, *Light*, 116.

[216] On this point see the studies by Koskenniemi, *Studien*, 88ff.; Funk, "Apostolic Parousia"; Thraede, *Grundzüge*, passim; and Karlsson, *Ideologie.*

[217] On the *pronuntiatio* see Lausberg, *Handbuch*, §1091.

[218] Gal 4:18f.: . . . καὶ μὴ μόνον ἐν τῷ παρεῖναί με πρὸς ὑμᾶς. . . . ἤθελον δὲ παρεῖναι πρὸς ὑμᾶς ἄρτι καὶ ἀλλάξαι τὴν φωνήν μου . . .

[219] I am indebted to Professor Gustav Karlsson (Uppsala and Berlin) for calling my attention to this epistolary *topos.*

Far more serious problems arise from the nature of the defense speech itself. The "apologetic letter" is by definition a part of rhetoric and, for that reason, limits its writer to the devices of the "art of persuasion."[220] In its written form, such a letter can persuade its addressees only by its rational arguments.

The "art of persuasion" has its proper place in the courts of law. As antiquity saw it, this law court rhetoric is beset with a number of unpleasant characteristics which impinge upon the very things Paul wants to accomplish. Rhetoric, as antiquity understood it, has little in common with the "truth," but it is the exercise of those skills that make people believe something to be true. For this reason, rhetoric is preoccupied with demonstrations, persuasive strategy, and psychological exploration of the audience, but it is not interested in establishing the truth itself. Consequently, people who are interested in the truth itself must be distrustful of the "art of persuasion," because they know of its capacity for intellectual manipulation, dishonesty and cynicism. The effectiveness of rhetoric depends primarily upon the naïveté of the hearer, rather than upon the soundness of the case. Rhetoric works only as long as one does not know *how* it works.

Having to use this rather suspect form of logical argumentation becomes even more questionable when one realizes that *no* kind of rational argument can possibly defend the position Paul must defend. In effect, his defense amounts to a defense of the πνεῦμα which was given to the gentile Galatians outside of the Torah.[221] How can an irrational experience like the ecstatic experience of the divine Spirit be defended as legitimate if the means of such a defense are limited to those available to the "apologetic letter"?

It is quite obvious that the methods made available through the "art of persuasion" must necessarily be insufficient. It is fascinating to see that Paul is aware of these problems and how he tries to resolve them.

There is, first, the problem of the *auctoritas* of the arguments presented in the *probatio* section of the letter. We have pointed out previously that all arguments are designed to demonstrate a supernatural *auctoritas*.

The other problem is that simple rhetoric would force Paul to leave the question of the gift of the divine Spirit—that is, a question of ultimate truth—to be decided by a jury which would ordinarily not be equipped to judge a matter of this order. Paul solves this problem by formally addressing the Galatians as οἱ πνευματικοί (Gal 6:1), a designation they probably claimed for themselves. Who could be better judges of matters concerning the πνεῦμα than οἱ πνευματικοί? There is thus an implicit connection between the presupposition that the Galatians have received the divine Spirit and the apostle's confidence that they will be able to follow and appreciate the logical arguments presented in his defense letter. The ground for such confidence is that as possessors of the Spirit they do not simply rely on common sense.

However, the apostle finally overcomes the limitations of the "apologetic letter" by yet another feature. The Galatian letter begins with a conditional curse, very

---

[220] For a more extensive discussion of this problem see Betz, "In Defense."
[221] See my discussion of Paul's defense, above.

carefully constructed, cursing every Christian who dares to preach a gospel different from that Paul had preached and still preaches, different from the gospel that the Galatians had accepted (1:8–9). At the end, the letter pronounces a corresponding conditional blessing upon those who remain loyal to the Pauline gospel (6:16).

What does this imply for the literary function of the letter? It means that as the carrier of curse and blessing the letter becomes a "magical letter," another category among ancient letters.[222] In other words, Paul does not simply rely on the "art of persuasion" and its system of rational argumentation, although this system is used to yield as much as it can. He does not leave things to be decided by the reasonableness of the Galatians, although their reason is supposedly informed by the Spirit of God. He also introduces the dimension of magic, that is, the curse and the blessing, as inescapable instruments of the Spirit, in order to confront the Galatians with the choice between salvation and condemnation. Reading the letter will automatically produce the "judgment." The readers will either go free and be acquitted, or they will be sent back to the cosmic "prison" guarded by the στοιχεῖα τοῦ κόσμου (cf. 3:23ff.; 4:8–10). By including this dimension of magic Paul repeats the Galatians' initial confrontation with the gospel (cf. 1:9). Having read the letter they see themselves transferred back into the moment when they first encountered the gospel, so that suddenly Paul's defense of the Spirit coincides with the proclamation of the gospel of the crucified Jesus Christ.

---

[222] No satisfactory investigation of the genre exists. J. Sykutris mentions it in his article "Epistolographie," 5:207; see also J. Schneider, "Brief," *RAC* 2:572f.; R. Stübe, *Der Himmelsbrief.* Both authors refer to the *Papyri graecae magicae* as examples. Actually, the oldest letter in Greek literature is a magical letter (Homer, *Il.* 6.167ff.). In a conversation with Dr Jan Bergman of Uppsala it became clear that there may be also yet unexplored connections with ancient Egyptian funerary inscriptions; see Sottas, *Preservation;* E. Otto, *Biographischen Inschriften*, 53ff. These inscriptions are like magical letters from the dead, addressing the potential visitor of the tomb, and threatening him with a curse, if he is a grave robber; for those who perform the correct ritual there is a blessing. See further, Gardiner and Sethe, *Egyptian Letters*, nos. 4, 5; Bjorck, *Der Fluch.*

2

THE RHETORICAL OUTLINE FOR GALATIANS: A RECONSIDERATION

Robert G. Hall

Ancient rhetoricians, following Aristotle, divided speeches into three species: judicial, epideictic, and deliberative. Since these species differed in time reference, goal, mode of argument, and form, any analysis of a document by the categories of ancient rhetoric must begin by determining the species of rhetoric to be applied. Hans Dieter Betz classified Galatians as judicial and therefore sought to show that Galatians was in form an apologetic letter.[1] In his recent article James D. Hester followed Betz in analyzing Galatians according to the judicial mode.[2] Even the modifications Hester proposed to Betz's outline assumed that Galatians was judicial. I hope to show that Galatians fits the deliberative species of rhetoric better than the judicial. Since a deliberative speech customarily follows an outline different from a judicial one, I will also present an alternative rhetorical outline for Galatians.[3] Because deliberative oratory has a different goal from judicial, in the course of my argument an alternative understanding of Paul's purpose and of the way his various arguments support that purpose will appear. If judicial, the argument in Galatians must seek predominantly to defend Paul against the accusations of his opponents. If deliberative, it seeks predominantly to urge the Galatians to cleave to Paul and his gospel and to repudiate his opponents and their false gospel.

Although modern rhetorical theory has advanced beyond ancient rhetoric,[4] I have employed only the classical categories. Throughout the Roman Empire the study of rhetoric formed a major part of education. Boys were trained in rhetorical

---

[1] Betz, *Galatians.*

[2] Hester, "Rhetorical Structure."

[3] See Kennedy, *New Testament Interpretation,* 144–52. I owe many thanks to Dr. Kennedy, Paddison Professor of Classics, University of North Carolina, Chapel Hill, for whom this paper was first written.

[4] Notably in the concept of "rhetorical situation." See Bitzer, "Rhetorical Situation." For a comprehensive modern elaboration of rhetorical theory, see Perelman and Olbrechts-Tyteca, *New Rhetoric.*

theory and were expected to think through these categories when composing a speech. As a result, classical rhetorical theory widely influenced the way ancient writings were composed and read. Reading Galatians according to the principles of ancient rhetoric not only gives the modern reader powerful tools for understanding the text but also provides a partial entry into an important component of the world of thought in Paul's day. The pervasive influence of classical rhetoric in the first century, coupled with the power of its conceptuality, justifies an attempt to understand Galatians according to these classical categories.

The Rhetorical Species

Assigning a speech or document to one of the three species of rhetoric can prove a difficult task. The species of epideictic is less clear than the others and tends to shade into deliberative.[5] Since the special characteristics of each species (defense or accusation of judicial, exhortation of deliberative, praise or blame of epideictic) may also serve as topics for persuasion, it is not unusual for a speech of one species to employ a topic associated with another, as when a judicial orator exhorts a judge to think only of justice or praises the good character of the defendant. This overlap between characteristics of the species and topics for persuasion can cause some initial confusion in classification. Occasionally, if a work lacks unity, it may be impossible to assign it fully to one of the three species of rhetoric. Nevertheless, the classification works reasonably well for many speeches and should be abandoned only when the categories clearly do not fit. Since the three species of rhetoric can significantly clarify the purpose of the writer or speaker, they remain useful tools in the rhetorical analysis of a text.

According to Aristotle, judicial speeches accuse or defend someone (or something), considering whether a past action is just or unjust. Epideictic speeches seek to change the hearer's present attitude toward something or someone by praise or blame, considering whether something is honorable or disgraceful. Deliberative speeches exhort or dissuade to or from some future action, claiming the action is expedient or harmful (Aristotle, *Rhetoric* 1.3.3–5). A decision concerning whether Galatians is judicial, epideictic, or deliberative, then, hinges on a decision concerning just what is at stake between Paul and the Galatians. Is the letter to the Galatians primarily concerned with defending some past action of Paul? Betz and Hester answer affirmatively: the point at issue concerns whether Paul founded the Galatian churches rightly or wrongly (Betz) or whether Paul was dependent on instruction from Jerusalem and hence preaches an inferior gospel (Hester).[6]

If the letter does debate the rightness or wrongness of some past action of Paul, the letter is judicial as Betz and Hester suppose, but it is difficult to reconcile this hypothesis with the second half of the letter (Gal 3:1–6:18), where views of Paul's past actions are hardly disputed at all. Then does the letter seek merely to change a present

---

[5] Kennedy, *Classical Rhetoric,* 73–74.
[6] Betz, *Galatians,* 129; Hester, "Rhetorical Structure," 227.

attitude the Galatians have? If so the letter is epideictic, but Paul does not want the Galatians merely to approve of him and to disapprove of his opponents. The major purpose of Galatians is not to defend some past action (judicial) or to praise some and to blame others (epideictic) but to persuade the Galatians to cleave to Paul and his gospel and to reject his opponents and their gospel (Gal 1:6–9, cf. 6:12–16). The opponents have alleged that Paul's gospel is incomplete, that to be Christian one must submit to Torah, and so they urged the Galatians to be circumcised, to become Jews, to take up a way of life viewed by the Gentiles as alien. Paul vigorously attacks the opponents and their arguments, urging the Galatians to stand fast in the new thing Christ has done. Since the debate requires the Galatians to decide between two antithetical modes of life and behavior and since the participants in the debate are not primarily concerned about Paul's past action but about what future action the Galatians will take, Galatians is most naturally classified as a deliberative work.

Quintilian proposes his own taxonomy of judicial, epideictic, and deliberative oratory (*Inst.* 3.4.6–8). Every speech must concern the law courts or not. If it does it must be judicial, if not, epideictic or deliberative. Every nonjudicial speech must concern the past or the future. If the past, then it is epideictic, since we praise or denounce past actions. If the future, it is deliberative, since we deliberate about the future. Everything about which we speak must be either certain or doubtful. We praise or blame what is certain; where doubt exists we deliberate about what to do. Although the distinctions by which Quintilian defines deliberative oratory may not be satisfactory, even his definition locates Galatians as a deliberative work.[7] Galatians does not concern a court. Its central question does not concern the past. It does not consider what is certain. It must be deliberative. Other features of the letter go far to confirm this judgment.

Quintilian, in a passage deploring the excesses of declaimers, describes popular deliberative style. Declaimers on deliberative themes "affect abrupt openings, impetuous style, generous embellishment" (*Inst.* 3.8.58 [Butler, LCL]). They "open with a wild and exclamatory manner" (3.8.59). They "assume a torrential style of eloquence at a high level of violence" (3.8.60). "Declaimers fall into coarse abuse of those who hold opposite opinions when in deliberative themes and show a tendency to assume that the speaker's views oppose those who seek his advice. Consequently their aim appears to be invective rather than persuasion" (3.8.58; cf. *Rhet. Her.* 3.8.15). Galatians shows marked conformity with this summary of popular deliberative style. Paul certainly opens with a "wild exclamatory manner" (Gal 1:6–9), as commentators have noticed for centuries. He employs "a torrential style of eloquence at a high level of violence" and shows a great deal of impetuousness. Indeed, he pursues his argument with such vigor that many have assumed he labored under some powerful emotion. At times Paul's aim does seem to be invective rather than persuasion—such is his "coarse abuse of those who hold opposite opinions" (see esp. Gal 1:8–9; 5:7–12; 6:12–13). Paul's conformity with deliberative declamatory style confirms the view that Galatians is a deliberative work.

---

[7] Quintilian's definition, though easier to grasp than Aristotle's and in essential agreement with it, is not as scientifically complete. Must every speech of defense occur in a court of law? Might it not be possible to praise something expected in the future?

Paul's particular use of narrative suits a deliberative speech. A judicial narration recounts the circumstances surrounding the crime that the defendant is accused of committing. It is not part of the proof but seeks to remind the judge of the facts of the case. A deliberative speech, however, does not debate the rightness of a past action but the expediency of a future action. Therefore, Aristotle supposes that narrative rarely appears in deliberative speeches because no one can narrate things to come (*Rhet.* 3.16.11). Quintilian, in essential agreement with Aristotle, permits a narration in deliberative speaking only with the following qualification. Whereas a narration in a judicial speech states the facts central to the case, a narration in a deliberative speech introduces relevant matters external to the case (*Inst.* 3.8.10). That is, a narration in a deliberative speech functions as part of the proof, advancing reasons why some future action should be taken. In Galatians, the narration of events from Paul's past life offers three proofs supporting Paul's contention that the Galatians should cleave to him and to his gospel and should reject his opponents. (1) It acquires for Paul an authoritative ethos. Paul is authorized by God and the church for the Gentile mission. Of course, the Galatians should cleave to him rather than to his adversaries. (2) It shows that Paul's gospel is from God and was confirmed by the church. Of course, the Galatians should hold firmly to it. (3) The final part of the narration introduces a line of argument against the doctrine of Paul's opponents (Gal 2:1–21). Since in Galatians the narration does not state the past action that the letter as a whole debates but functions as part of the proof, Galatians must be deliberative.

The rhetoricians emphasize that deliberative oratory deals with choices between options. "Deliberative speeches are either of the kind in which the question concerns a choice between two courses of action or the kind in which a choice among several is considered" (*Rhet. Her.* 3.2.2 [Caplan, LCL]). The letter to the Galatians presupposes just such a choice: the Galatians must choose the route offered by Paul and his gospel or by the opponents and theirs.

Paul seeks to move the Galatians primarily by an appeal to their own advantage. It is to the Galatians' advantage to stand fast in Paul's true gospel and to reject that of his opponents (see Gal 5:2, where this is explicitly stated). To stand with Paul is to live in the new age, free from the *stoicheia,* identified with the heavenly Jerusalem. To go back under the law is to be enslaved to the *stoicheia* with the earthly Jerusalem; to be circumcised is to fall from grace. Clearly, it is to the Galatians' advantage to stand with Paul embracing his gospel. Such an appeal to advantage is in itself sufficient to distinguish the deliberative speech from the epideictic and the judicial. Quintilian characterizes the epideictic speech as one that aims at praise pure and simple, not at the acquisition of any advantage (*Inst.* 3.8.7). The judicial speech seeks to move its audience not by what is to its advantage but by what is just (Aristotle, *Rhet.* 1.3.3–5).[8] In that Paul seeks an advantage for the Galatians, the letter must be a deliberative work.

Betz had difficulty handling the exhortations sprinkled about in the latter part of the letter. He frankly states that in solving the problem by labeling Gal 5:1–6:10 the

---

[8] See also *Rhet. Her.* 3.2.3; Cicero, *Inv.* 2.51.156; and Quintilian, *Inst.* 3.8.1, 22, 30, 39.

exhortatio, he acts without rhetorical authority.[9] Betz cannot analyze this section of Galatians as judicial. Exhortation plays no part in judicial rhetoric, but is especially characteristic of deliberative. Aristotle defines deliberative speeches as either hortatory (*protropē*) or dissuasive (*apotropē:* Aristotle, *Rhet.* 1.3.3). *Rhetorica ad Herennium* makes a similar division, defining deliberative oratory as being concerned with persuasion (*suasionem*) or dissuasion (*dissuasionem,* 1.2.2). Quintilian refers with disapproval to Athenaeus, who attempted to define a stasis for deliberative themes calling it *protreptikē stasis* or hortative stasis (*Inst.* 3.6.47).[10] Elsewhere, when discussing various types of proof, he speaks of arguments that belong to the hortative genus of oratory—that is, to the deliberative species of rhetoric (*Inst.* 5.10.83). The important part exhortation plays in Galatians, rhetorically inexplicable if Galatians is judicial, is precisely what one expects in a deliberative speech. Galatians must be deliberative.

Probably Betz classified Galatians as judicial because of a defensive tone in the early portions of the letter. Is such defense consistent with the classification of Galatians as deliberative? Aristotle defines three kinds of rhetorical proof: ethos, pathos, and logos (*Rhet.* 1.2.3–6). A speech utilizes ethos when seeking to persuade by confidence in the speaker, pathos when seeking to persuade the audience by moving their emotions, and logos when seeking to persuade by giving reasons. Ethical proofs (that is, proofs from ethos) move the audience by increasing the speaker's credibility (see Quintilian, *Inst.* 4.2.18). Paul's opponents had apparently sought to undermine his credibility with the Galatians (a tactic Paul adroitly employs in turn against his adversaries!), which requires Paul to reestablish his credibility by answering charges or insinuations brought against him. In answering these charges, Paul seeks to increase his credibility with the Galatians, to reestablish their confidence in him, so that they will more readily cleave to him and to his gospel and repudiate his opponents and their gospel. Therefore, these defensive elements in the letter do not imply that Galatians is judicial or that it is partially judicial and partially deliberative. Instead they form one mode of ethical proof supporting the deliberative intent of the letter. Galatians is one of those works in which a characteristic of one species of rhetoric serves as a topic for persuasion in another. Those defensive elements of Galatians that might at first suggest assigning Galatians to the judicial species of rhetoric fit well the analysis of Galatians as deliberative. Galatians belongs to the deliberative species of rhetoric.

A Rhetorical Outline

Since opportunities in the ancient world for judicial speaking far outnumbered opportunities for deliberative speaking, rhetoricians carefully defined judicial oratory but devoted only short sections to deliberative. The various parts of any speech were usually discussed in their judicial order and function, and brief notes were

---

[9] Betz, *Galatians,* 254.

[10] Like much of rhetorical theory, stasis originated in the judicial sphere of rhetoric, where it classified various ways of making a defense. Stasis theory does not really fit deliberative oratory—hence Athenaeus's definition of a special hortative stasis. Quintilian, recognizing that giving a name to the problem does not solve it, rejects Athenaeus's suggestion.

appended showing how these elements might be used in deliberative or epideictic speeches. As a result, the order of these elements for a judicial speech was relatively fixed: *exordium*, narration, proposition, proof, epilogue (Quintilian, *Inst.* 3.9.1; *Rhet. Her.* 1.3.4)—the outline reproduced by Betz for Galatians, without the *exhortatio*. Although a certain flexibility was allowed even to judicial speakers, a deliberative speaker enjoyed even greater freedom in the use and order of these various parts of a speech. Recognizing that Galatians is deliberative frees us from the rhetorical outline for a judicial speech.

Salutation/Exordium

In a letter influenced by rhetoric, the "speech" in the author's mind usually begins after the salutation. The salutation, as an epistolary form rather than a rhetorical one, is merely appended before the rhetorical body of the letter. Ordinarily, then, the rhetorical outline of the letter ought to begin after the salutation.

In his discussion of the salutation, Betz notices that Paul has modified his usual prescript by two additions (Gal 1:1 and 1:4).[11] The insertion after *apostle* (Gal 1:1) anticipates the line of argument developed in the narration to follow (Gal 1:10–2:21). Paul asserts a powerful ethos as the one chosen by God. The insertion after *Jesus Christ* (Gal 1:4) anticipates a second major line of argument in the letter. What is expressed as deliverance from this present evil age in Gal 1:4 is expressed as freedom from slavery to the *stoicheia* in 4:1–11 and as being free children of the heavenly Jerusalem in the Hagar-Sarah allegory (Gal 4:21–5:1). By anticipating two major lines of argument that he will later develop in the letter, Paul has added to his salutation features expected in an *exordium*. Aristotle, Quintilian, and the author of *Rhetorica ad Herennium* all suggest such anticipation in the *exordium* if the case permits (Aristotle, *Rhet.* 3.14.6; Quintilian, *Inst.* 4.1.23; *Rhet. Her.* 1.4.6–7). Quintilian emphasizes that the points selected for the *exordium* should be those most apt to win the judges' favor. In Gal 1:4 Paul had expressed only that part of his argument likely to appeal to the Galatians' sense of praise and thanksgiving. Later he reasons that if we are delivered from this present evil age we are no longer under the law and consequently circumcision is unnecessary—both points contrary to what the Galatians or their teachers presently hold (for the full argument see Gal 6:12–15). In Gal 1:4 Paul is content, following sound rhetorical principles, to state only the attractive premise to his argument. Thus, although Betz correctly identifies Gal 1:1–5 by form as the salutation, Paul has placed within it features expected in an *exordium*. However, the epistolary form still has the upper hand; Gal 1:6 reads much more like the opening of a speech than does 1:1. Gal 1:1–5 is really a salutation rather than an *exordium*. Yet in the outline I have labeled it Salutation/*Exordium* to call attention to the rhetorical features in this salutation. Perhaps Paul was moved to this novel use of the salutation by his sensitivity to the abrupt opening he was about to employ in the next section, where the "speech" in the author's mind seems really to begin.

---

[11] Betz, *Galatians*, 38.

Proposition

The purpose of a proposition is to make clear what the letter or speech as a whole wants to prove. Galatians urges its readers to cleave to Paul and to his gospel and to repudiate his opponents and their false gospel. That Paul's gospel comes from God (Gal 1:10–12), that Abraham received a covenant by promise (Gal 3:15–29), that Christ has delivered us from under the *stoicheia* to freedom (Gal 4:1–11), and the rest of Paul's arguments are reasons why the Galatians should cleave to Paul's gospel and forsake his opponents'. Gal 1:6–9 succinctly states this antithesis between Paul and his opponents and implies that the Galatians must choose to cleave to Paul's gospel. It therefore functions as the proposition to the letter. But Gal 1:6–9 also shows features that fit naturally in an *exordium*. An attack against opponents such as Paul here mounts is cited by the rhetoricians as one means of developing an *exordium* of the type known as the direct approach. The mighty boost the section gives to Paul's ethos lies closer to the function of an *exordium* than to that of a proposition. Whether it is better to call it an *exordium* of the direct type which states the proposition of the letter or to call it a proposition with certain features of an *exordium* is debatable. Probably the rhetoricians would allow either designation. Since deliberative speeches frequently lack an *exordium* and since Paul incorporated features of an *exordium* into the salutation, it seems better to call it a proposition. The presence of features characteristic of an *exordium* in a proposition may be understood to confirm this conclusion. Paul simply agrees with Quintilian that the commencement of a deliberative speech, even if it lacks an *exordium,* must bear some resemblance to an *exordium* (Quintilian, *Inst.* 3.8.6). Therefore, the rhetorical body of Galatians lacks an *exordium* altogether and begins directly with the proposition. Paul recognized the abruptness of this beginning and sought to soften it by placing features expected in the *exordium* in both the salutation and in the proposition.

Proof

The rhetoricians give the title proof (called by Betz by its Latin name, *probatio*) to that portion of a speech which gives reasons why the audience should accept the proposition. We have already seen how the narration (Gal 1:10–2:21) supports the proposition as part of the proof. It remains to show how the material in Betz's *exhortatio* also supports the proposition of the letter.

Galatians as a whole is an exhortation, as every deliberative speech is. Paul exhorts the Galatians to hold his gospel fast and to reject his opponents with their false gospel. He supports this hortatory intent of the letter by two basic lines of argument, first by his powerful ethos as the chosen bearer of the gospel of God (Gal 1:1; 1:10–2:21), then by his various arguments showing that in Christ the Galatians have been freed from the old age and put in the new (Gal 1:4). This second line of argument is initially developed without exhortation. Paul argues that to stand with him in his gospel is freedom and to stand with his opponents under the law is slavery (Gal 3:21–4:11; 4:21–31). To stand with him is to walk by the Spirit; to stand with them is to walk by the flesh (Gal 3:1–14; 5:4–5). Such arguments support the proposition by disposing reason and emotion (logos and pathos) to heed the summons to cleave to Paul and his gospel and to repudiate his opponents. The summons is not long in coming: "Stand fast in the freedom in which Christ has set you free and do not again be held by the yoke of bondage" (Gal 5:1). Do not walk in the flesh, the principle of the old age, but walk in the Spirit, the principle of the new (Gal 5:16–26; 6:7–10). Such exhortations are direct descendants of the hortatory proposition of the letter: cleave to me and to my gospel (Gal 1:6–9). In them, the hortatory proposition is re-phrased to take advantage of the imagery Paul has been using to show the contrast be-tween his own gospel and that of his opponents. In this way the exhortations gather the logical and pathetic power of his earlier arguments squarely behind the proposi-tion. In the process, as the content of Paul's gospel is fleshed out by the new imagery, the basic hortatory proposition gains much in moral force, making it all the more at-tractive to cleave to Paul and his gospel. Such exhortation is not found only at the end of the letter (cf. Gal 4:12), but its concentration there is to be expected in a work whose primary goal from the beginning is exhortation. Since the exhortations seek to persuade the Galatians to adopt the proposition of the letter, considered rhetorically they are part of the proof. The proof includes both Betz's *narratio* and his *exhortatio* and extends from Gal 1:10 to 6:10.

Some confusion still reigns in the discussion of the narration. Hester rightly claims that Gal 1:11–12 (I would prefer to add verse 10 as well) stands as a thesis for the narration.[12] Quintilian, who holds that propositions may be scattered through-out the proof preceding the arguments that support them (*Inst.* 4.4.7), would probably call these verses the proposition for the narration. But to call them the sta-sis[13] shows some confusion in the use of terms. Stasis, as used by ancient rhetori-cians, was not part of a speech but a tool for classifying how the defense was related to the accusation.[14] Hester also incorrectly labels Gal 2:11–14 a digression.[15] Paul, in the proposition for the narration, advances two theses he hopes to prove in the narration. He wants to show that his gospel did not come from human beings but from God (Gal 1:11–12) and that he does not seek human approval but divine (Gal 1:10). Both of these theses develop Paul's ethos, the overriding purpose of the narration in Galatians. Gal 1:13–2:10 proves the second part of the narration's proposition: Paul's gospel is from God. The section beginning with Gal 2:11 proves the first part of the narration's proposition: Paul (in contrast to Peter!) does not seek to please human beings but God. If Gal 2:11–14 seeks to prove part of the proposition for the narration it must be part of the narration, not a "digression

---

[12] Hester, "Rhetorical Structure," 223.

[13] Ibid.

[14] In Galatians the point at issue concerns the future. Will the Galatians cleave to Paul's gospel or that of his opponents? Since this question requires a deliberative response, stasis theory does not readily apply (see above, n. 10). If we must assign a stasis to Galatians, it is necessary to rephrase the question at issue: Whose gospel is right? This question implies a stasis of fact but does not fully cap-ture Paul's argument in Galatians.

[15] Hester, "Rhetorical Structure," 231–33.

from the logical order of our speech" as Quintilian defines an egressus or digression (*Inst.* 4.3.12–14).

Betz identifies Gal 2:15–21 as the proposition for the letter as a whole.[16] Even assuming with Betz that the letter seeks to prove that Paul founded the Galatian churches rightly, it is hard to see this section as the letter's proposition. The proposition ought to assert what the letter as a whole seeks to prove, and Gal 2:15–21 does not assert that Paul founded the Galatian church rightly. Only the form expected of a judicial speech—*exordium*, narration, proposition, proof, epilogue—supports identifying Gal 2:15–21 as a proposition, but if Galatians is deliberative even this fragile support fails. Paul's address to Peter (Gal 2:14b–21) does introduce something, however; perhaps this is why Betz wants to view it as a proposition. It inaugurates that line of argument that Paul develops in the following chapters, that line of argument first hinted at in 1:4. It is formally part of Paul's admonition to Cephas and hence part of the narration, but, in accordance with sound rhetorical practice, it contains also an argument addressed to Paul's present audience, the Galatians, and as such smoothes the transition from the narration to the next heading in the proof.

Epilogue

Betz has rightly identified the epilogue (*conclusio*) as Gal 6:11–18.[17] The epilogue restates, as it should, the contrast between Paul and his opponents first expressed in the proposition (Gal 1:6–9). "They wish to boast in your flesh, I want only to boast in Christ" (Gal 6:13–14). It summarizes the various arguments addressed in the letter. Paul first puts the capstone on his abuse of the opponents (Gal 6:12–13). He next summarizes the line of argument first stated in Gal 1:4 and expressed subsequently under many different images (Gal 6:14–16). Whatever Gal 6:17 means, it surely expresses a final time that powerful authoritative ethos first presented in Gal 1:1. This epilogue, then, is to be classified as one of fact according to Quintilian's scheme (*Inst.* 6.1.1–2).

An Outline

Thus, Galatians has a salutation that has taken on some of the functions of an *exordium* (Gal 1:1–5), a proposition (Gal 1:6–9, also with some elements of an *exordium*), the proof (Gal 1:10–6:10), and an epilogue (Gal 6:11–18). The proof in deliberative speeches ordinarily is made up of a series of headings that support the proposition in various ways.[18] Galatians is no exception. Most ancient rhetoricians would probably prefer to call the first heading (Gal 1:10–2:21) a narration, even if it does contribute to the argument rather than state the case. Galatians may be outlined as follows:

---

[16] Betz, *Galatians*, 114.
[17] Ibid., 313.
[18] Kennedy, *New Testament Interpretation*, 24.

I. Salutation/*Exordium* (1:1–5)
II. Proposition (1:6–9)
III. Proof (1:10–6:10)
    A. Narration (1:10–2:21)
    B. Further Headings (3:1–6:10)
IV. Epilogue (6:11–18)[19]

Conclusion

Analyzing Galatians as deliberative permits a unified grasp of Paul's purpose in writing the letter: he writes to persuade the Galatians to cleave to him and his gospel and to repudiate his opponents and their gospel. The various parts of the letter all cohere around this purpose. The salutation introduces the lines of argument to be followed. The proposition succinctly and forcefully states what Paul wants the Galatians to do: to repudiate his opponents or anyone who preaches a gospel other than the one Paul preached to them. The proof offers various headings in support of this purpose. The narration, the first heading, acquires for Paul an authoritative ethos and advances the first argument in the proof. Paul and his gospel are from God; of course, the Galatians should heed him and embrace his message. Further headings, which show the excellence of standing in Christ and the foolishness of returning to the law, prepare for the strong exhortation to stand with Paul in Christ with which the proof concludes. The epilogue briefly recapitulates the earlier arguments and presents a last appeal to cleave to Paul and his gospel and to repudiate his opponents. This unified understanding of the letter serves as final confirmation that Galatians fits squarely in the deliberative species of classical rhetoric.

---

[19] Compare the outline given by Betz, *Galatians*, 16–23:
    I.   Epistolary Prescript (1:1–5)
    II.   *Exordium* (1:6–11)
    III. *Narratio* (1:12–2:14)
    IV. *Propositio* (2:15–21)
    V.   *Probatio* (3:1–4:31)
    VI. *Exhortatio* (5:1–6:10)
    VII. Epistolary Postscript (*Conclusio*, 6:11–18).

3

THE LETTER OF PAUL TO THE GALATIANS: A DELIBERATIVE SPEECH

Joop Smit

This study's point of departure is the important article of H. D. Betz, "The Literary Composition and Function of Paul's Letter to the Galatians."[1] In that article the author suggests a new approach to the letter to the Galatians, by using the generative rules of Greco-Roman rhetoric to analyze the structure of the letter. A rigorous examination leads him to the conclusion that the form of the various parts and the order in which they are arranged completely conform to the classical rules of rhetoric for a judicial speech *(genus iudiciale)*. Paul is under accusation by opponents. The Galatians play the role of judges. The letter contains a speech in which Paul, following all the rules of the art, defends himself before the jury.[2]

Betz's article has convinced me that classical rhetoric is an important instrument for the analysis of the letter to the Galatians and leads to a better understanding of its character and coherence. I am less enthusiastic about the actual analysis he provides. The inherent difficulties are so numerous and incisive that, after a number of preliminary studies, I dare to submit a new proposal.[3]

In this study a critical discussion of Betz's analysis and its results is followed by an elucidation of some presuppositions which appear to undermine seriously the validity of his analysis and which should therefore be replaced by more adequate ones. The whole letter is then analyzed anew in terms of classical rhetoric and in accordance with the new perspectives we have gained. By way of conclusion we return to two of the presuppositions from which we started.

---

[1] Betz, "Literary Composition." This article served as the basis for the commentary on the letter which the same author published some years later *(Galatians)*. It is incorporated in the commentary, divided in parts but otherwise almost unaltered.

[2] Betz, "Literary Composition," 26: "In the case of Galatians, the addressees are identical with the jury, with Paul being the defendant and his opponents the accusers. . . . Serving as a substitute the letter carries the defense speech to the jury."

[3] This study incorporates the results of four articles which I published earlier, viz. Smit, "Naar een nieuwe benadering"; "Hoe kun"; "Paulus"; and "Redactie."

Critical Remarks about the Analysis of H. D. Betz

In his article Betz offers a rather detailed analysis of each part of the letter. Within the bounds of this study it is impossible and also unnecessary to go into all the details. I will therefore give only the most important objections to his analysis of each part of the text.

(a) Gal 1:6–11 is defined by Betz as an *exordium*, the introduction of a speech, in which the speaker tries to make his audience well-disposed, attentive and receptive. To elucidate the curse of vv. 8–9 he appeals to Quintilian, who states that the prejudice of a judge can be effectively countered by frightening him with threats.[4] This appeal, however, is misplaced because here Paul is not threatening the judges, i.e., the Galatians but the accusers, i.e., his opponents.

The delimitation of this part is also problematic. Betz characterizes vv. 10–11 as a transition and has the next part, the narration, start at v. 12. Later on, however, he designates v. 13 as the beginning of the narration proper.[5] This later designation seems to me to be the correct one. It is evident that with the words, "You have heard of my former way of life in Judaism that I . . ." Paul shifts from addressing his audience to telling them his life-story and thereby begins the narration.

(b) Betz considers Gal 1:12–2:14 to be the narration, the part of a speech in which the facts relevant for the case are being stated. He demonstrates that Paul's narration conforms to the precepts by being brief, clear and plausible. The analysis of this part of the letter also gives rise to several objections.

Betz suggests that it is a normal construction for a *narratio* like this one to begin with a thesis or *propositio* (v. 12). The texts of Quintilian to which he refers do not corroborate this view. They treat the issue of whether or not, in case the facts are well known, the *narratio* can be left out and be replaced by a *propositio*.[6]

Furthermore, the *narratio*, as Betz delimitates it, has a very abrupt ending. The conflict in Antioch cannot be solved by a single rhetorical question addressed by Paul to Cephas. That is not compatible with the demand for plausibility to which a *narratio* should respond.

Finally it can be asked whether this narration is presenting facts about which the Galatians as a judicial body have to pronounce judgment. The story does not confront them with a precise legal question, but rather proposes two courses of action from which they should choose. Paul recounts the facts from the past to recommend his own course of conduct and to discourage them from introducing the changes his opponents are urging upon them. This would mean that the speech Paul sent

---

[4] Quintilian, *Inst.* 4.1.20–22.

[5] Betz, "Literary Composition," 13: "The *narratio* proper begins in v. 13."

[6] Betz, "Literary Composition," 13–14: "Quintilian recommends beginning the *narratio* with a statement, the *propositio*, which will influence the judge in some way, though he may be well informed about the case." For this he refers to Quintilian, *Inst.* 3.9.5; 4.2.7, 30. The said recommendation, however, cannot be found there, nor elsewhere.

to the Galatians more probably belongs to the *genus deliberativum* than to the *genus iudiciale*.[7]

(c) Gal 2:15–21 forms, according to Betz, the *propositio*. In rhetorical theory this refers to a passage following the *narratio* in which the points of agreement and disagreement between the parties are first summed up, and then followed by an enumeration and brief explanation of the points to be dealt with in the argumentation. The purpose of such a *propositio* is to make the organization of the entire speech transparent.[8] Here Betz's interpretation is forced. Gal 2:15–21 misses the formal characteristics proper to a *propositio*. It is not at all a point by point summary giving a survey of the whole speech.

(d) According to Betz, Gal 3:1–4:31 is the *probatio*, the part of a speech in which a speaker strengthens his position with arguments. In his opinion the letter belongs to the *genus iudiciale*, and in analyzing its argumentation he consequently uses the instruments a lawyer has at his disposal to compose a judicial speech. It is my conviction that these instruments are poorly suited for the text. The beginning of the *probatio* offers a good opportunity to corroborate this assertion.

Paul begins his argumentation with a series of rhetorical questions. Betz interprets this as the interrogation of the witnesses and refers to the passage of Quintilian on this subject. It is more probable, however, to interpret the questions as a rhetorical device Paul is using to strengthen his assertions to the Galatians.[9]

Besides, Paul does not confront the Galatians here with the question whether a certain course of action is legitimate or not, but he makes the reproach that they would be acting foolishly and harming themselves if they change their behavior. Honor and advantage, or shame and disadvantage, however, are at stake in the *genus deliberativum*. An argumentation starting with the exclamation, "O foolish Galatians," almost certainly belongs to that genre.[10]

Although Betz himself notes that Gal 3:1–5 and Gal 4:8–11 form an inclusion, he tries very hard to show that Gal 4:12–20 and 4:21–31 are parts of the *probatio*. In neither of these cases are his arguments, in my view, convincing.

In discussing Gal 4:12–20 he remarks that the theme of friendship was customary in the argumentation of speeches. Quintilian quotes the proverb, "*Ubi amici, ibi opes*," but that is not enough by far to prove this assertion. The emotional appeal that

---

[7] Kennedy, *New Testament Interpretation*, 145, reaches the same conclusion, though with a different argumentation: "All species of rhetoric make use of narrative, but they use it for different purposes and in different ways. The function of judicial narrative is to set forth the facts at issue from the point of view of the speaker. Quintilian (4.2.66–68) clearly recognizes this. But the narrative of the first and second chapters of Galatians is not an account of facts at issue. It is supporting evidence for Paul's claim in 1:11 that the gospel he preached was not from man, but from God, a topic which had been enunciated in the first verse of the salutation. Galatians is probably best viewed as deliberative rhetoric, a point to which we will return."

[8] Cicero, *Inv.* 1.22.31, writes on the *propositio*, which he calls *partitio*: "*Recte habita in causa partitio illustrem et perspicuam totam efficit orationem.*"

[9] Quintilian, *Inst.* 5.7, has a detailed discussion of the interrogation of witnesses in court. *Inst.* 9.2.6–32 consists entirely of a treatment of the rhetorical question as a figure of speech.

[10] *Rhet. Her.* 3.3.4 remarks in discussing the *genus deliberativum*: "*Prudentiae partibus utemur in dicendo si commoda cum incommodis conferemus, cum alterum sequi, vitare alterum cohortemur.*" We will return to this point at length later on.

Paul addresses to the Galatians here, according to the standards of the same Quintilian, is better suited to the *peroratio*.[11]

For Gal 4:21–31 Betz offers a very ingenious solution.[12] This, however, does not overcome the difficulty he himself mentions that in the general opinion of the rhetoricians, a *probatio* should never end with such a weak argument.[13]

(e) Gal 5:1–6:10 is considered by Betz as the *paraenesis*. This part creates, as he himself remarks, a serious problem for his rhetorical analysis. In classical rhetoric an exhortative passage such as this is completely unknown as a separate part of a normal speech.[14]

(f) Gal 6:11–18 is in Betz's opinion the *peroratio* of the speech. According to rhetorical theory this part serves two purposes. It refreshes the memory of the audience and it appeals to their emotions. Normally the *peroratio* consisted of three parts: the *recapitulatio* or summing-up, the *indignatio* or arousal of anger and hostility, and the *conquestio* or appeal to pity. Betz argues that Gal 6:12–17 is primarily a *recapitulatio*, while the *indignatio* and the *conquestio* in vv. 12–13 and v. 17 are only present in principle. This analysis is doubtful for two reasons.

According to the prevailing rules, a *recapitulatio* should sum up once again the main points of the *probatio*. It is evident however that Gal 6.12–17 does not conform to this rule.

It is also a fact that *indignatio* and *conquestio* as separate parts are missing. To explain this Betz gives an extensive quotation of Quintilian. This author reports that especially the philosophers objected to an appeal to the emotions at the end of a speech. Paul could have been moved by a similar restraint in the name of truth.[15] However the manner in which earlier in his letter Paul appealed to the emotions of his audience makes such philosophical restraint on his part at the end of the letter highly improbable.[16]

Points of View

The problems raised by a critical examination of Betz's analysis do not form a set of arbitrary incidents. They can be reduced to four general points of view or assumptions from which they spring. To solve the problems these points of view should be revised. We shall now first determine what these four points of view are and why and in what sense they should be revised. In that way the points of view for a fresh analysis of the letter will simultaneously become visible.

---

[11] For the proverb see Quintilian, *Inst.* 5.11.41. On the *peroratio* as the place where all floodgates of eloquence should be opened and all emotions should be unchained see Quintilian, *Inst.* 6.1.51–52; 4.1.27–28; 6.1.9–11.

[12] Betz, referring to Pseudo-Demetrius, argues that Paul in using the allegory leaves something for his listeners to figure out and that they regard this as proof of their intelligence.

[13] Quintilian, *Inst.* 5.12.14; *Rhet. Her.* 3.10.18.

[14] Betz, "Literary Composition," 25: "It is rather puzzling to see that *paraenesis* plays only a marginal role in the ancient rhetorical handbooks, if not in rhetoric itself." Cf. also n. 207, where he remarks that even Quintilian has no special treatment of the *paraenesis*.

[15] Betz, "Literary Composition," 8: "Paul's restraint at this point with regard to the emotional appeal may reflect the same kind of caution which, according to Quintilian, was characteristic of philosophers."

[16] Cf. Gal 1:6–12; 2:4, 12–13; 3:1–6; 4:12–20; 5:7–12.

(a) Witnesses

Greco-Roman rhetoric has a long history, running approximately from 475 B.C.E. to 275 C.E.[17] Although especially the views on the organization of a speech were very stable, naturally a considerable development took place in this period of time. Therefore it is incorrect to relate to Paul indiscriminately every publication on rhetorical theory originating in antiquity. We have to decide which authors are closest to rhetorical practice as Paul presumably knew it.

Betz chooses as his main witness Quintilian who wrote about 90 C.E. in Rome the twelve books of his *Institutio oratoria*. This choice, however, involves two difficulties. Rhetoric which was introduced from Greece into Rome from the second century B.C.E. onwards had at the time of Quintilian already undergone a particular Roman development.[18] Moreover, the work of Quintilian is encyclopedic in character, so that some view relating to Paul can always be found. Eclecticism is therefore a threatening danger. In my opinion Betz has succumbed to that danger. The problems that arise during his analysis are regularly solved by means of incidental remarks by Quintilian which in more than one case are also interpreted in a strange way.

Cicero's *De inventione* and the anonymous *Rhetorica ad Herennium* do not involve these inconveniences. Both works, which are very similar to each other, were written about 85 B.C.E. They are handbooks without much personal input, are close to a Greek source and, because of that, reflect Hellenistic rhetoric in a reliable way.[19] For a rhetorical analysis of the letter to the Galatians it is therefore preferable to give up the use of Quintilian and to start first of all from *De inventione* and the *Rhetorica ad Herennium*.

(b) The Genre

Classical rhetoric distinguishes three kinds of speeches: the judicial plea which belongs in the court-room *(genus iudiciale)*, the political speech which has its place in parliament *(genus deliberativum)* and the speech of praise and censure which is held at special occasions *(genus demonstrativum)*. In the handbooks each of these three genres receives separate treatment.[20]

---

[17] In *Art of Persuasion* and *Art of Rhetoric*, Kennedy gives a comprehensive survey of the history of classical rhetoric. He begins with Corax and Tisias in the second quarter of the fifth century B.C.E. and ends with Cassius Longinus, who died about 273 C.E.

[18] The *declamationes*, school-exercises which became very popular in the first century C.E., played an important role in this development. Cf. Kennedy, *Art of Rhetoric*, 312–29.

[19] Current opinion holds that Cicero and the author of *Rhetorica ad Herennium* had the same teacher and had both been using their college notes. This teacher is seen as a representative of the school of Rhodes, an important center of rhetorical studies at the time. See Kennedy, *Art of Rhetoric*, 103–48; Caplan, *Rhetorica ad Herennium*, vii–xxxiv. Other opinions in Adamietz, *Ciceros De inventione*. On the points relevant for us there exists a general consensus. It is also significant for the traditional character of *De inventione* that later on in *De or.* 1.2.5 Cicero distances himself from this juvenile work. He reviews it there as "*inchoata ac rudia*" and not in accordance with the dignity and experience he had meanwhile obtained.

[20] *Rhet. Her.* 1.2.2, e.g., defines the three genres thus: "*Tria genera sunt causarum quae recipere debet orator: demonstrativum, deliberativum, iudiciale. Demonstrativum est quod tribuitur in alicuius*

According to Betz, the speech Paul addresses by letter to the Galatians belongs to the *genus iudiciale*. It is a defense speech and is analyzed following the model of such a speech. The discussion of Betz's article, however, has shown that such important parts as the *narratio* and the *probatio* are assigned more appropriately to the *genus deliberativum*. Therefore it is better to analyze Paul's speech according to the rules designed for that genre.[21]

In the Hellenistic period the *genus iudiciale* obtained a dominant position in the handbooks. In the *Rhetorica ad Alexandrum,* an anonymous Greek handbook from about 300 B.C.E., that is not yet the case. Therefore it is probably a good thing not to lose sight of this work when analyzing Paul's speech.

(c) The Theological Perspective

In the commentaries the letter to the Galatians is, as if this were self-evident, placed within a Lutheran framework and read in answer to the question, "How does man find a gracious God?" This interpretation exhibits a fixed pattern. The emphasis on Paul's declaration of independence (1:12), the special status of justification by faith (2:15–21), the ahistorical interpretation of the law as legalism (chs. 3–4) and the problem of the relation between the indicative and the imperative of faith (chs. 5–6) are part of this pattern. Although Betz is using a new method, his analysis of the letter remains fully within this dogmatic perspective.[22]

At present the conviction is growing that Paul's main concern was the position of Christians with a Gentile background.[23] When the letter is read in answer to the question, "On what conditions do Christians from the Gentiles partake together with the Christians from the Jews in the promises of Israel?" the customary pattern gives way to very different accents. Previous research had convinced me that it is not justification by faith, but the fact that in Christ the Jews are called to unity with the Gentiles, that is the real issue of the letter. The following analysis, then, builds further on that foundation.[24]

---

certae personae laudem vel vituperationem. Deliberativum est in consultatione, quo habet in se suasionem et dissuasionem. Iudiciale est quod positum est in controversia, et quod habet accusationem aut petitionem cum defensione." Cf. Cicero, *Inv.* 1.5.7; Aristotle, *[Rhet. Alex.]* 1.

[21] In his brief analysis of the letter to the Galatians Kennedy, *New Testament Interpretation,* 146, reaches the same point of view: "The basic argument of deliberative oratory is that an action is in the self-interest of the audience. . . . That is the pervasive argument of Galatians. . . . The letter looks to the immediate future, not to judgment of the past, and the question to be decided by the Galatians was not whether Paul had been right in what he had said or done, but what they themselves were going to believe and to do."

[22] In this respect it is significant that Betz began his commentary with the following maxim of Luther: *"Nec de politica libertate agimus, sed de alia quadam, quam diabolus maxime odit et impugnat. Ea est, qua Christus nos liberavit, non e servitute aliqua humana aut vi tyrannorum, sed ira dei aeterna. Ubi? in conscientia."*

[23] A seminal work on this issue is Stendahl, *Paul.* Also important are E. Sanders, *Paul, the Law;* and F. Watson, *Paul.*

[24] See the articles mentioned above, n. 3.

(d) The Unity of the Letter

The unity of the letter to the Galatians is not in dispute.[25] Betz does not question it either, although he is faced with an unsolvable problem; namely, his *paraenesis* (Gal 5:1–6:10) has no place within the compass of classical rhetoric.[26] From the rhetorical perspective the question arises whether this exhortation could be a later addition to the letter. Once that question has been admitted, more positive indications in that direction become visible.[27]

Gal 5:13–6:10 forms a coherent unit *(sarx* vs. *pneuma),* breaking the unmistakable connection between Gal 5:7–12 and 6:11–18. While elsewhere in the letter the relation in Christ between the Jews and the Gentiles is at stake, in this passage it is shown how Christians in general should behave towards each other. While in the other parts of the letter Christ and the law exclude each other, here they are brought together in "fulfilling the law of Christ." Moreover, the aggressive tone, which Paul uses before and after, is here suddenly interrupted by a plea for mutual affection and meekness and for an all-encompassing respect. These oppositions in the statement of the problem, in outlook and in tone reflect the same motive that plays an important role in the redaction of other pauline letters: the original particularity of the letters had to be adapted in view of their more general use.[28] Therefore it is probable that Gal 5:13–6:10 was added at a somewhat later time to the letter. In the rhetorical analysis that follows we will pass by this passage without discussing it as a kind of test of this hypothesis.[29]

Rhetorical Analysis of Paul's Speech

(a) Exordium (Gal 1:6–12)

For the first part of a speech, the *exordium,* Cicero's *De inventione,* the *Rhetorica ad Herennium* and the *Rhetorica ad Alexandrum* give the following rules.[30]

---

[25] To my knowledge the only exception to this is the extreme proposal of O'Neill, *Recovery.* This work has rightly received little attention.

[26] In his commentary Betz somewhat conceals this under the notion of "*exhortatio*" which, however, is nowhere used in classical rhetoric to denote a distinct part of the speech. Kennedy, *New Testament Interpretation,* 146, who regards the *exhortatio* of Gal 5–6 as the goal the entire letter is aiming at, does not solve this problem either.

[27] I am summarizing here the conclusions of my article "Redactie."

[28] See Dahl, "Particularity"; Gnilka, *Philipperbrief,* 5–18; Schenke, "Weiterwirken"; Sand, "Überlieferung." Kennedy, *New Testament Interpretation,* 147, has correctly sensed this when he writes: "As Paul's defense, Galatians would be chiefly of historical interest for its picture of the early church filled with acrimonious dissension and of his personal insecurities and apprehensions; as Paul's exhortation it continues to speak to Christians who are tempted to substitute the form of religious observance for its essence."

[29] With this I do not intend to deny that Gal 5:13–6:10 was written by Paul and that we should read the letter in its present form as a unity. The question, however, how this should be done is focused more sharply and clearly by my proposal.

[30] Cicero, *Inv.* 1.15.20–1.18.26; *Rhet. Her.* 1.3.5–1.7.11; Aristotle, *[Rhet. Alex.]* 29.

The purpose of the *exordium* is to make the listeners well disposed, attentive and receptive.[31] If the case is honorable and is certain to meet with the sympathy of the audience, then a direct approach is appropriate. A difficult case, provoking the aversion of the public, should be introduced indirectly by way of *insinuatio*.[32]

A speaker can win the goodwill of his listeners by referring to his own acts and services without arrogance. He can also arouse hostility against his opponents by accusing them of criminal activities. Further, he can praise the wisdom and courage of his audience without excessive flattery.[33] The attention of the audience is raised by emphasizing the great weight of the case. The willingness to listen is won by briefly and clearly explaining the essence of the case.

An *exordium* should not be too general, but should be adapted to the occasion and be clearly connected with the other parts of the speech, first of all with the *narratio*, which immediately follows.

Gal 1:6–12 consists of three parts which comply precisely with the rules prescribed for the *exordium*.

In vv. 6–7a Paul first brings his audience in a state of alarm by informing them that they are deserting God. At the same time he states his subject, the gospel, and underlines this by the use of a *correctio*.

In vv. 7b–9 Paul arouses hostility against his opponents by accusing them of subverting the gospel of Christ. He further specifies his subject in a negative way by saying that their preaching runs counter to the true gospel and underlines the importance of this with a double curse.[34]

In vv. 10–12 Paul tries to win sympathy for himself by presenting himself as a servant of God and Christ. Thereafter he specifies his subject in a positive way by stating that he is preaching a gospel which he has received from God. He underlines this by explicitly addressing his audience again.[35]

The introduction of Paul's speech ties in very well with the actual situation. Without knowing it the Galatians are moving in the wrong direction. Paul immediately puts an end to this confusion. This introduction also shows a close connection with the following parts of the speech. The *narratio*, which comes next, further develops the theme "gospel." The question of the origin of Paul's gospel, which is the subject of 1:10–12, reappears in Gal 1:15–24, while the thesis that his opponents are countering the true gospel which is put forward in 1:7–9 comes back in 2:1–10 and 2:11–21.[36] This *exordium* is further taken up again by way of inclusion

---

[31] Cicero, *Inv.* 1.15.20: "*Exordium est oratio animum auditoris idonee comparans ad reliquam dictionem, quod eveniet si eum benivolum, attentum, docilem confecerit.*"

[32] Cicero, *Inv.* 1.15.20: "*Insinuatio est oratio quadam dissimulatione et circumitione obscure subiens auditoris animum.*"

[33] *Rhet. Her.* 1.4.8: "*Benivolos auditores facere quattuor modis possumus: ab nostra, ab adversariorum nostrorum, ab auditorum persona, et ab rebus ipsis.*"

[34] Parallelism, hyperbole and epiphora are the figures supporting this. For the figures of speech and thought see *Rhet. Her.* 4; Lausberg, *Handbuch.*

[35] *Figura etymologica (derivatio), inversio* and *antithesis* further strengthen this.

[36] Gal 1:10–12 and 1:15–24 have the opposition, men vs. God, in common. Gal 1:7b–9; 2:1–10, 11–21 hinge on "the truth of the gospel" (2:5, 14).

in Gal 5:7–12 at the end of the speech. There, however, Paul is less direct and chooses the *insinuatio*.[37]

Finally, it should be noted that this *exordium* contains some evidence that the speech belongs to the *genus deliberativum*. Significant in this respect is the fact that immediately at the start of this speech Paul uses such political terms as "deserting," "disturbing" and "subverting."[38] Also the way in which he lines up the parties points in that direction. The Galatians are departing from the religious practice they learned from Paul. Paul advises them not to follow his opponents and the changes they are promoting and urgently advises the Galatians to remain true to him and the course of action for which he stands.

(b) Narratio (Gal 1:13–2:21)

The *exordium* is usually followed by a *narratio,* an exposition of the facts.[39] The three rhetorical handbooks which we are using as our guides sketch something like the following picture of this part of the speech.[40]

The statement of the facts should be brief, clear and plausible.[41] A narration is brief if it mentions just the facts that are indispensable for the case, not more and not less. The speaker should not go back further in the past than the case requires, he should eliminate everything not related to the question and he should not carry his story further on than needed. So the *narratio* should be, first of all, to the point. Clarity of statement is gained by preserving the chronological sequence in which the events happened. Plausibility of statement is gained by presenting the course of time, the location of the events and the characters of the actors in a realistic way.

In addition the speaker should bend everything to the advantage of his case by omitting everything to his disadvantage that can be omitted, by touching lightly on what must be mentioned and by telling his own side of the story carefully and clearly.[42]

Paul tells a rather detailed story. Nevertheless it is brief in the sense that he limits himself to the events that in the actual situation are important for the decision the Galatians have to take. First he brings up the subject of Judaism, the point on which his listeners have to define their position (1:13–14). Next he positively indicates the direction they should choose: God himself has sent him to preach the gospel among the Gentiles (1:15–24). After that he recounts two incidents which clarify in an exemplary way which direction they should reject: Christians from the Jews cannot force

---

[37] It is remarkable that Paul, unlike in the *exordium*, does address the Galatians in 5:7–12 with a captivating *concessio:* "You were running so well."

[38] Cf. Betz, *Galatians*, 47–50.

[39] Cicero, *Inv.* 1.19.27: "*Narratio est rerum gestarum aut ut gestarum expositio.*"

[40] Cicero, *Inv.* 1.19.27–1.21.30; *Rhet. Her.* 1.8.12–1.9.16; Aristotle, *[Rhet. Alex.]* 30–31.

[41] Cicero, *Inv.* 1.20.28: "*Oportet igitur eam tres habere res: ut brevis, ut aperta, ut probabilis sit.*" *Rhet. Her.* 1.9.14: "*Tres res convenit habere narrationem: ut brevis, ut dilucida, ut verisimilis sit.*"

[42] Cicero, *Inv.* 1.21.30: "*Quare, ut hoc vitium vitetur, omnia torquenda sunt ad commodum suae causae, contraria quae praeteriri poterunt praetereundo, quae dicenda erunt leviter attingendo sua diligenter et enodate narrando.*"

their non-Jewish fellow-Christians to accept circumcision and to observe the Torah (2:1–10, 11–21). Thereby the whole question is clear. Precisely as prescribed in the rhetorical handbooks the story is not carried on any further.

Because Paul is telling the events from the past only as far as they are relevant to the actual discussion, his story shows several gaps if regarded as autobiography. His stay in Arabia (1:17), his long sojourn in Syria and Cilicia (1:21–24) and the time between the agreement in Jerusalem and the quarrel in Antioch (2:10–11) are hardly filled in at all.

The story has a clear design. The sequence of events is divided into four episodes; they are clearly distinguished from one another and follow one another chronologically.[43] Paul also paid due attention to the plausibility of his story. In each of the four episodes he underlined the reality of the events in a particular way. His zeal for Judaism becomes more true to life because he mentions his activity as a persecutor of the church (1:13–14). That God, and not the apostles in Jerusalem, has sent him to preach the gospel is documented with numerous chronological and topographical data (1:15–24). The plausibility of the agreement in Jerusalem is strengthened by enlarging on the role of the "men of eminence" (2:1–10), while the behavior of Paul in Antioch gets a more realistic character by presenting his words as direct speech (2:11–21).

Finally Paul unmistakably reports the events as advantageously as he can. His story is prejudiced. His all-surpassing zeal for Judaism (1:14), the negative picture of the pseudo-brothers who give occasion to the consultation in Jerusalem (2:4–5), and the equally negative presentation of Cephas, the other Jews and Barnabas in Antioch (2:12–13) are clear evidence of that. The way in which he on oath belittles his first visit to Jerusalem (1:18–20) and his complete silence about the outcome of the conflict in Antioch strikingly illustrate that Paul's presentation of the facts is as advantageous as possible. The entire story is told in view of the situation in Galatia and all its parts are designed to persuade the Galatians to take the decision Paul wishes.

(c) Confirmatio (Gal 3:1–4:11)

According to the *Rhetorica ad Alexandrum*, in a deliberative speech the *narratio* is followed by the confirmation by proof.[44] In *De inventione* and the *Rhetorica ad Herennium*, more interested as they are in the judicial plea, a *partitio* or *divisio* is placed between the *narratio* and the *confirmatio*. This part renders an account of the earlier stated facts by first defining the points of agreement between the parties and by subsequently stating the exact point on which judgment is asked.[45] But as we have

---

[43] The division in episodes is mainly determined by topographical and semantic data. Gal 1:13–14, place: Judaism; opposition: Jews vs. Gentiles. Gal 1:15–24, place: not-Jerusalem; opposition: God vs. men. Gal 2:1–10, place: Jerusalem; opposition: Jews vs. Gentiles viz. the circumcised vs. the uncircumcised. Gal 2:11–21, place: Antioch; opposition: Jews vs. Gentiles viz. the righteous observing the Torah vs. the lawless sinners.

[44] Aristotle, [*Rhet. Alex.*] 31–32.

[45] *Rhet. Her.* 1.10.17: "*Primum perorata narratione debemus aperire quid nobis conveniat cum adversariis, si ea quae utilia sunt nobis convenient, quid in controversia relictum sit, hoc modo: 'Interfectam esse ab Oreste matrem convenit mihi cum adversariis. Iure fecerit et licueritne facere, id est in controversia.'*" *Rhet. Her.* 1.10.17 is dealing with the *divisio*. Cicero speaks of *partitio* and discusses this, Cicero, *Inv.* 1.22.31–1.23.34.

seen Paul's *narratio* is marked by recommending and dissuading and thus does not lend itself to such a legal definition. It is therefore understandable that a *divisio* or *partitio* is missing in Paul's speech and that he passes on directly from the *narratio* to the *confirmatio,* the part in which a speaker supports his position with arguments.[46]

A deliberative speech deals with the issue of what course of action should be followed.[47] To persuade his audience to follow or not to follow a certain course of action the speaker bases his argumentation on honor and advantage or on baseness and disadvantage.[48] To "honor" belong considerations of wisdom, justice, courage and temperance.[49] By means of these virtues or their opposites the speaker tries to persuade his audience to choose the course of action he advocates.

The purpose of a deliberative speech is to induce acceptance of a certain course of action. To reach that goal it relies on the following arguments: a sign *(signum)*, i.e., something perceived by one of the senses that points to something else that the sign seems logically to imply; an accepted premise *(credibile)* i.e., a conviction which is shared by the audience and which does not need corroborating evidence; a judgment *(iudicatum)* i.e., the approval of an act by the assent or authority or judicial decision of some person or persons; comparison *(comparabile)*, i.e., a certain principle of similarity exhibited in diverse material.[50]

It is not sufficient to discover arguments. They should also be elaborated in an attractive and orderly manner.[51] In particular *Rhetorica ad Alexandrum* notes that the *confirmatio* preferably ought to be set up in different rounds of argument which are clearly distinguished from one another. The beginning as well as the end of each round ought to be specially marked; the last by means of recapitulation or conclusion. After having gone in an orderly manner through all the considerations supporting the recommended course of action, it is once again stated briefly and with due *pathos,* that it is unjust, inexpedient, disgraceful and unpleasant not to follow the advocated course of action and that it is just, expedient, honorable and pleasant to do so.[52]

Gal 3:1–4:11 exhibits a clear articulation. An introduction (3:1–5) is followed by three rounds of argument (3:6–14; 3:15–29; 4:1–7), after which this passage is

---

[46] Cicero, *Inv.* 1.24.34: "*Confirmatio est per quam argumentando nostrae causae fidem et auctoritatem et firmamentum adiungit oratio.*" Cf. *Rhet. Her.* 1.10.18; Aristotle, *[Rhet. Alex.]* 3.2.

[47] *Rhet. Her.* 3.2.2: "*Deliberationes partim sunt eiusmodi ut quaeratur utrum potius faciendum sit, partim eiusmodi ut quid potissimum faciendum sit consideretur*"; 1.2.2: "*Deliberativum est in consultatione, quod habet in se suasionem et dissuasionem.*" Specifically dealing with the *genus deliberativum* are Cicero, *Inv.* 2.51.155–2.58.176; *Rhet. Her.* 3.2.2–3.5.9; Aristotle, *[Rhet. Alex.]* 1.29–34.

[48] Cicero, *Inv.* 2.52.158: "*Ex his illud conficitur ut petendarum rerum partes sint honestas et utilitas, vitandarum turpitudo et inutilitas.*"

[49] Cicero, *Inv.* 2.53.159: "*Nam virtus est animi habitus naturae modo atque rationi consentaneus. Quamobrem omnibus eius partibus cognitis tota vis erit simplicis honestatis considerata. Habet igitur partes quattuor: prudentiam, iustitiam, fortitudinem, temperantiam.*" Cf. *Rhet. Her.* 3.23; Aristotle, *[Rhet. Alex.]* 1.

[50] Cicero, *Inv.* 1.30.47: "*Omne autem . . . probabile quod sumitur ad argumentationem aut signum est aut credibile aut iudicatum aut comparabile.*" Cf. Aristotle, *[Rhet. Alex.]* 7–12; 32.

[51] Cicero, *Inv.* 1.30.50: "*Atque inveniri quidem omnis ex his locis argumentatio poterit; inventa exornari et certas in partes distingui et suavissimum est et summe necessarium et ab artis scriptoribus maxime neglectum.*" Cf. *Rhet. Her.* 2.18.27.

[52] Aristotle, *[Rhet. Alex.]* 32.10–40.

rounded off by a conclusion (4:8–11). This division is further confirmed and elaborated by the following analysis.

The considerations in this passage are unmistakably founded on the characteristic virtues of the deliberative genre. In the opening (3:1–5) and conclusion (4:8–11) Paul states negatively that the Galatians are acting foolishly and contrary to their self-interest if they change their present religious practice. In the intermediate rounds of argument Paul demonstrates positively that the Galatians should cling to the practice he taught them. At the beginning of each of the three rounds he suggests that his version of the matter is "according to the law" (3:6; 3:15; 4:1–2). At the end of them he mentions the honor and advantage acquired by the Galatians in the manner he describes: they have received the blessing of Abraham (3:14); they belong to the seed of Abraham and partake in the inheritance (3:29); they are sons of God and heirs (4:7).

The nature of the arguments also conforms to the rules of rhetoric. In the introduction (3:1–5) Paul states the fact that the Galatians have received the Spirit as a sign *(signum)* that they should not start observing the Torah. Each of the three rounds of argument begins with a comparison *(comparabile,* 3:6; 3:15; 4:1–2) and ends with the receiving of the Spirit as a sign confirming the correctness of Paul's version of the matter (3:14; 3:26–28; 4:6). In addition, the three rounds of argument are clearly distinguished from one another while each of them is supported by a particular argument. The first round is founded on an argument of authority *(iudicatum)* consisting almost completely of quotations from Scripture (3:6–14). The second round is founded on the confession of the oneness of God, a conviction Paul shares with his Jewish and Christian audience *(credibile,* 3:15–29). The third round, finally, is founded on the faith that God, by sending his Son, has achieved the eschatological revolution; a conviction Paul shares with his Christian audience *(credibile,* 4:1–7).

Paul elaborated his argumentation in an attractive and orderly way. Because of the *exclamatio,* the rhetorical questions and the *amplificatio,* the introduction has a very emotional character *(pathos).* The three rounds of argument are based on history and demonstrate great formal similarity. The first round (3:6–14) starts with a comparison; three periods of time follow: Abraham (6–9), the Torah (10–12) and Christ (13–14); it ends with a summarising conclusion (14). The second round (3:15–29) is clearly separated from the preceding one by the renewed address to the audience and the appearance of the speaker through the first person singular. This round also starts with a comparison; once again three periods of time follow: Abraham (15–18), the Torah (19–25) and Christ (26–29); it also ends with a summarising conclusion (29). The third round (4:1–7) is, in its turn, clearly separated from the preceding one by the appearance of the speaker through the first person singular. The beginning again consists of a comparison; this time history has been divided in two periods: the former time (1–3) and the fullness of time (4–6); once again a summarising conclusion comes at the end (7). Like the introduction the conclusion of the entire passage (4:8–11) has a very emotional character *(pathos)* because of the *correctio,* the rhetorical question and the *dubitatio,* the more so because it is also marked by biting sarcasm.

Just as in the *narratio* Paul is dealing in this *confirmatio* with the question of whether the Galatians should submit to Judaism. On the one hand he adjures them to abandon the idea. On the other hand, on the basis of convictions collectively held among Christians, he tries to make plausible to them that, even without observing the Torah, by their faith in Christ they belong to the offspring of Abraham and partake in his inheritance.

(d) Conclusio, Part 1: Conquestio (Gal 4:12–20)

According to the three handbooks guiding us, a speech should end with a *conclusio* consisting of three parts: *enumeratio, indignatio, conquestio*.[53]

For the *conquestio*, an appeal to pity, they note a number of commonplaces by which a speaker can arouse the pity of his audience.[54] Of the sixteen loci Cicero mentions in this regard the following are the most important in the present context.[55] First the power of fate and the weakness of the human race should be set forth.[56] Once the mood has been set in this way the following ideas may be useful.

- To show the prosperity and happiness once enjoyed and the misery of the present situation.
- To recount shameful, mean and ignoble acts and the unworthy treatment one has suffered.
- To ask the audience to think of their parents, children or someone else dear to them.
- To reveal helplessness, weakness and loneliness.
- To deplore the separation from a person one loves.
- To implore the audience in humble and submissive language to have mercy.

Paul begins this passage by openly begging the Galatians (12a). Subsequently he reminds them of the freak of fate that led him to preach the gospel to them "because of the weakness of the flesh" (13). At the same time he ascribes the success of his mission completely to them. He gives a glowing account of the excellent relations of former times, but by means of two rhetorical questions he opposes this happy past to the miserable present, their friendship now being deeply disturbed (12b–16).

Paul mentions next the shameless behavior of his opponents and the unworthy treatment he has suffered because of them (17–18).[57] Then he addresses his audience

---

[53] Cicero, *Inv.* 1.52.98: "*Conclusio est exitus et determinatio totius orationis. Haec habet partes tres: enumerationem, indignationem, conquestionem.*" Cf. *Rhet. Her.* 2.30.47.

[54] Cicero, *Inv.* 1.55.106: "*Conquestio est oratio auditoris misericordiam captans.*" See for more information, *Inv.* 1.55.106–1.56.109; *Rhet. Her.* 2.31.50; Aristotle, *[Rhet. Alex.]* 34; 36.

[55] The loci enumerated here are 1, 4, 7, 10, 12, 14 in Cicero, *Inv.* 1.55.

[56] Cicero, *Inv.* 1.55.106: "*In hac primum animum auditoris mitem et misericordem conficere oportet, quo facilius conquestione commoveri possit. Id locis communibus efficere oportebit, per quos fortunae vis in omnes et hominum infirmitas ostenditur.*"

[57] The threefold καλός in vv. 17–18 is significant.

as "my children" and attributes to himself the role of their mother going through the pain of giving birth to them all over again (19). Having expressed his wish to be with them, Paul ends this passage by openly avowing his helplessness.

This passage, starting with a supplication and ending with a confession of helplessness, undoubtedly forms the *conquestio* of the speech Paul is addressing by letter to the Galatians.

(e) Conclusio, Part 2: Enumeratio (Gal 4:21–5:6)

Regarding the *enumeratio* the three handbooks give (among others) the following precepts.[58] An *enumeratio* is a summing-up at the end of the speech meant to refresh the memory of the listeners. This summing-up must be brief and should not extend to the *exordium* and *narratio* but limit itself to a recapitulation of the *divisio* and *confirmatio*.

The *enumeratio* may be constructed in different ways. The most obvious and usual one consists of the speaker running over his arguments in the order in which he previously discussed them.[59] Cicero indicates in particular two possibilities for the presentation. The speaker can pronounce the recapitulation in his own person. By means of personification however he can also put it in the mouth of another person or thing, as for instance the lawgiver, the law, a place, a city, a monument.[60] Personification moreover is the obvious means to enliven the conclusion of a speech.[61]

The *enumeratio* of Paul's speech consists of two parts, which we shall discuss separately. First Gal 4:21–5:1 contains a summary of the *confirmatio* that was elaborated in Gal 3:1–4:11: Its line of thought is closely followed.

Gal 4:21 corresponds with Gal 3:1–5, the beginning of the argumentation. In both instances the Galatians are being addressed as people planning to fulfill the law. An apparently informative question, but actually a reproach, urges them to abandon the observance of the law (νόμος).

Gal 4:22–23 is in accordance with Gal 3:6–14: Paul suddenly introduces Abraham and reproduces the text of Scripture in a particular way (γέγραπται). Both passages end with a reference to the promise (ἐπαγγελία) regarding the Spirit.

Gal 4:24–28 concurs with Gal 3:15–29. In both instances Paul explains the Scripture passages he reproduced a moment ago and opposes the covenant God

---

[58] Cicero, *Inv.* 1.52.98–100; *Rhet. Her.* 2.30.47; Aristotle, *[Rhet. Alex.]* 36.

[59] *Rhet. Her.* 2.30.47: "Enumeratio est per quam colligimus et commonemus quibus de rebus verba fecerimus, breviter, ut renovetur, non redintegretur oratio; et ordine ut quicquid erit dictum referemus, ut auditor, si memoriae mandaverit, ad idem quod ipse meminerit reducatur. Item curandum est ne aut ab exordio aut narratione repetatur orationis enumeratio."

[60] Cicero, *Inv.* 1.52.99–100: "Nam tum ex tua persona enumerare possis, ut quid et quo quidque loco dixeris admoneas; tum vero personam aut rem aliquam inducere et enumerationem ei totam attribuere. . . . Res autem inducetur, si alicui rei huiusmodi legi, loco, urbi, monumento oratio attribuetur per enumerationem, hoc modo: 'Quid si leges loqui possent? Nonne haec apud vos quererentur? Quidnam amplius desideratis, iudices, cum vobis hoc et hoc planum factum sit?' "

[61] Cf. *Rhet. Her.* 4.53.66.

made with Abraham to the Sinai-covenant (διαθήκη). The conclusion he subsequently draws in the *enumeratio:* "But you, brothers, are like Isaac children of the promise" (4:28) practically coincides with the previous conclusion in the *confirmatio:* "If however you belong to Christ, then you are Abraham's offspring, heirs according to the promise" (3:29).

Gal 4:29–31 conforms with Gal 4:1–7. In both instances the point is that, not the slave, but the free son is the heir (κληρονόμος). The conclusions drawn coincide with each other: "Therefore, brothers, we are not children of a slave woman, but of the free woman" (4:31) is a variation of "Therefore, you are no longer a slave but a son, and if a son then also heir through God" (4:7).

Gal 5:1 finally clearly echoes Gal 4:8–11. Just as at the end of the *confirmatio,* Paul here also adjures the Galatians with biting sarcasm not to submit themselves again to the slavery of the law (πάλιν δουλεύειν).

Paul has given this part of his summing-up a lively and attractive character by personifying a number of data. To begin with he personifies the law (4:21) and at the end he introduces Scripture as speaking in person (4:30). The allegorical interpretation of Scripture also includes a series of personifications. Hagar, the Sinai-covenant and the present Jerusalem depicted as three slave women with their children, are opposed to Sara, the Abraham-covenant and Jerusalem from above depicted as free mothers with their children. The choice Paul previously describes in conceptual language in the *confirmatio* is now put before the eyes of his audience in the form of a tableau-vivant. The three slave women impersonate the practice to be rejected, whereas the three free women stand for the course of action to be followed.

This pictorial summing-up of the *confirmatio* is followed in Gal 5:2–6 by a second summing-up in which Paul undisguisedly and very emphatically clarifies what is at stake. To this end he briefly enumerates the most important conclusions of his entire argument. In doing so he understandably refers back to the *narratio,* because it is characterized by recommending and dissuading and is not primarily a statement of the facts for a judicial case. Again, in this summing-up, the order of the previous argument is kept.

That the Galatians should not have themselves circumcised (5:2) is a message stated earlier in Gal 2:1–10. That they should not start observing the law (5:3) was made clear earlier in Gal 2:11–21. That Christ and grace on the one hand and the law on the other hand exclude each other as far as justification is concerned (5:4) is a conclusion reached earlier in Gal 2:21. That "we" Christians through faith partake in the Spirit and the promise (5:5) was met earlier as a conclusion in Gal 3:14. That in Christ the Jews are called to unite with the Gentiles (5:6) takes up a conclusion expressed earlier in Gal 3:26–28.

It is typical for the entire speech that this last summing-up so clearly shows the imprint of the *genus deliberativum.* Paul is weighing advantage and disadvantage against each other *(utilitas).* The Galatians have derived benefit from Christ now. If however they join Judaism by having themselves circumcised and by adopting the observance of the law, they annul that advantage.

(f) Conclusio, Part 3: Indignatio (Gal 5:7–12)

According to the rhetorical handbooks, the *indignatio*, a regular part of the *conclusio*, is intended to incite the listeners to great hatred of some persons.[62] Cicero sums up fifteen loci, and the *Rhetorica ad Herennium* ten which can be of help to reach this goal. The first seven, appearing in both works, are relevant in the present context. To incite indignation the following data may be successfully used.

- The gravity of the crime, as it appears from the attention that authorities like the gods, ancestors, the state and the law have given to the matter under discussion.
- The victims of the crime.
- The rejection of tolerance and indifference because in this case that amounts to a dangerous precedent.
- The danger that the crime will spread if not checked now.
- The irrevocability of the impending decision. It cannot be revised later on and the harm done cannot be remedied.
- The intention of the guilty person or persons. The crime was committed on purpose and with premeditation.
- The cruel and sacrilegious character of the crime.

In Gal 5:7–12 Paul seemingly touches on each of these typical points of the *indignatio*, lightly and in the indicated order.

First Paul represents the Galatians as victims of deceivers who are leading them away from the true gospel (v. 7). Subsequently he stresses the gravity of the crime, because it annuls God's call (v. 8). By means of a proverb he then calls attention to the danger that the evil will spread if it is not checked now (v. 9). Thereafter he states that God is certain to condemn the troublemakers and that the only thing the Galatians should do is to join in this condemnation (v. 11).[63] Paul obliquely remarks next that his opponents advocate circumcision in order to avoid persecution and that in so doing they commit an offence against the cross of Christ (v. 11). With a sacrilegious sneer Paul stresses their scandalous behavior and therewith rounds off this part (v. 12).

It is noteworthy that Gal 5:7–12 shows many points of contact with the *exordium* (Gal 1:6–12). In both passages the Galatians are depicted as people abandoning the true gospel; God is described as the one calling them; the opponents are represented as troublemakers certain to be struck by God's condemnation and Paul himself ap-

---

[62] Cicero, *Inv.* 1.53.100: "*Indignatio est oratio per quam conficitur ut in aliquem hominem magnum odium aut in rem gravis offensio concitetur.*" For the *indignatio* see Cicero, *Inv.* 1.53.100–1.54.105; *Rhet. Her.* 2.30.48–49; Aristotle, *[Rhet. Alex.]* 34.

[63] *Rhet. Her.* 2.30.48: "*Quintus locus est cum ostendimus, si semel aliter iudicatum sit, nullam rem fore quae incommodo mederi aut erratum iudicum corrigere possit.*" The similarity between "*si semel aliter iudicatum sit*" and "οὐδὲν ἄλλο φρονεῖν" is striking.

pears as the pre-eminent servant of Christ. The *indignatio* and *exordium* were adapted to one another and clearly form an *inclusio*.

A comparison of both passages further shows that the overt reproaches and accusations of the beginning were replaced at the end by the oblique terms of *insinuatio*. According to the handbooks, this suggestive approach should be followed primarily when the opposition seems to have won the favor of the public.[64] Paul is clearly taking some care not to alienate the Galatians by too much vehemence.

Within the *conclusio* this *indignatio* is the counterpart of the *conquestio* (Gal 4:12–20). Together they clearly state the choice Paul is asking his listeners to make: they should cling to the practice they learned from him and not adopt the changes proposed by his opponents.

(g) Amplificatio (Gal 6:11–18)

The end of Paul's letter confronts us with a difficulty. According to the handbooks we follow, the *conclusio* of a speech consists of three parts: *enumeratio*, *indignatio*, *conquestio*. At Gal 5:12, thus, we have apparently reached the end of the speech and consequently Gal 6:11–18 has to be considered as a transgression of the generally accepted pattern. This transgression calls for an explanation.

The motive for this transgression of the approved pattern is the fact that Paul sent his speech in the form of a letter, for this obliged him to add the usual subscription in his own handwriting.[65] The ideas Paul introduced in this addition are drawn from the remark he had just made in the *indignatio*. For it is evident that he largely elaborated the line of thought of Gal 5:11 in Gal 6:12–16 by means of antithesis (*amplificatio*).[66] That in both cases a reference to bodily marks resulted, is a further confirmation of this (5:12; 6:17).

That Paul with Gal 6:11–18 transgresses the prescribed pattern does not mean that he is now working fully outside of the framework set by the handbooks. The way in which he shaped this extra passage fits in nicely with the *genus deliberativum* which he had, until now, closely followed. The following data confirm this.[67]

---

[64] Cicero, *Inv.* 1.17.23–25; *Rhet. Her.* 1.6.9–1.7.11. Paul is using here at the end of his speech a form which according to the theory is designed for its beginning. The close connection which links *exordium* and *indignatio* suggests the transfer here.

[65] Cf. 1 Cor 16:21; Col 4:18; 2 Thess 3:17; Phlm 19.

[66] *Amplificatio* (αὔξησις) designates an increase, which comprehends an horizontal enlargement as well as a vertical heightening. The last part of a speech was the regular place for this, cf. Cicero, *Part. or.* 15.52–17.58; Quintilian, *Inst.* 8.4. The term can have a lot of different meanings. *Rhet. Her.* 2.30.47 uses it to indicate the *indignatio*.

[67] Cf. especially *Rhet. Her.* 3.4.7; Cicero, *Inv.* 2.55.166. I suspect that a passage like Gal 6:12–17 was considered to be a normal part of the *conclusio*. Aristotle, *Rhet.* 3.10 mentions praise and censure as a regular part of the *peroratio*. *Rhet. Her.* 3.8.15 notices that praise and censure should not be confined to the *genus demonstrativum*, but can be useful also in the other genres. My point of departure however is the rhetorical theory as it is presented in *De inventione rhetorica, Rhetorica ad Herennium*, and *Rhetorica ad Alexandrum* and viewed in that light Gal 6:12–18 must be described as a transgression of the normal pattern.

The *genus deliberativum* consists of the consideration of what course of action should be followed. In this process advantage *(utilitas)* and honor *(honestas)* carry the most weight. With regard to honor a distinction is made between the right *(rectum)* viz. wisdom, justice, courage and temperance and the praiseworthy *(laudabile)*. These two aspects however are not isolated from each other. The desire to strive after the right is intensified if praise accrues. Therefore a speaker should not omit to mention that the right way he is describing is also highly esteemed.

In Gal 6:12–16 Paul elaborates a sharp antithesis between the opponents and himself. The main point of comparison for the two parties is courage and the consequent reputation. First he ascribes cowardice and half-heartedness to his opponents (12–13). They are not really choosing Christ, because they do not fully accept their uncircumcised fellow-believers for fear of persecution. They are however not really choosing Judaism either, because they are still making demands on their uncircumcised fellow-Christians. Their boasting is nothing more than a pretense to conceal their cowardice and self-interest. Subsequently Paul ascribes unselfish courage to himself, sacrificing everything for the highest values and true gain: the cross of the Lord Jesus Christ, the new creation, peace, mercy and the Israel of God, which unites Jews and Gentiles within itself. This courage truly merits praise.[68] He then also mentions the scars which bear witness to his courage and thereby rounds off his argument in style.[69]

In this way, fully in terms of the *genus deliberativum,* and for the last time, Paul clearly tells the Galatians which decision they should take. The practice of his opponents is undesirable and should be rejected. The way advocated by Paul himself leads to the greatest values, the highest dignity and the real glory. They should continue to follow that attractive and promising path. In this way Paul provides his speech, which he is sending by letter to the Galatians, with a fitting end.

A Deliberative Speech

The speech contained in the letter to the Galatians follows an approved pattern. *Exordium, narratio, confirmatio* and *conclusio* succeed each other just as prescribed by the handbooks.[70] It is true that a *divisio* is missing and an *amplificatio* has been added, but in view of the circumstances that is easily understood. The theory for that matter allows room for such adaptation.[71]

---

[68] *Rhet. Her.* 3.2.3: "*Fortitudo est rerum magnarum appetitio et rerum humilium contemptio et laboris cum utilitatis ratione perpessio.*" Cicero, *Inv.* 2.54.163: "*Fortitudo est considerata periculorum susceptio et laborum perpessio. Eius partes magnificentia, fidentia, patientia, perseverantia.*"

[69] Showing wounds and scars was a well-known device, readily used at the end of a speech. See Cicero, *De or.* 2.28.124; Josephus, *J.W.* 1.197; Quintilian, *Inst.* 6.1.21, 30.

[70] *Rhet. Her.* 1.3.4: "*Inventio in sex partes orationis consumitur: in exordium, narrationem, divisionem, confirmationem, refutationem, conclusionem.*"

[71] *Rhet. Her.* 3.9.17: "*Est autem alia dispositio quae, cum ab ordine artificioso recedendum est, oratoris iudicio ad tempus adcommodatur.*"

Force of habit was not the only reason for Paul to conform to the familiar model. Everything shows that he thoroughly understood its intention. The model is devised to marshal the support of the listeners and thereby to win them over to the point of view of the speaker.[72] That is also the way it functions here with Paul. After an alarming start he first vividly recounts a number of personal memories which throw light on the question under discussion but which are not directly connected to it. In that way the listeners become informed about the question but not directly involved in it themselves. Then Paul directly discusses the problem at hand in a matter-of-fact tone. The listeners are now led to reflect on their own situation. Finally Paul introduces the human side of the question in an emotional tone: the relations that link the parties, the motives that inspire them, the ideals they hold before themselves. The listeners now become emotionally involved in the issue and are put under pressure to remain true to Paul and to share his convictions.[73]

Paul's speech further responds entirely to the norms the handbooks of rhetoric set for the deliberative genre. The question whether rites of religion should be changed or not, is explicitly listed by the *Rhetorica ad Alexandrum* among the subjects proper for the deliberative genre and, in that context, amply discussed.[74] It is precisely with that question that Paul's speech deals. The Galatians must decide whether they should cling to the religious practice they learned from Paul or whether they should make the changes advocated by the opponents.

By means of recommending and dissuading Paul tries to make the Galatians decide this question to his advantage. In each part of the letter, starting with the *exordium* and up to, and including, the *amplificatio* he contrasts his opponents and their practice on the one hand, and himself and his practice on the other hand in sharp antithesis, black and white. In this manner, each part of the letter repeatedly dissuades the Galatians to adopt the changes advocated by the opponents and positively advises them to remain true to Paul and not to deviate from the way he had shown them.

This recommending and dissuading which determines and pervades Paul's entire speech is based, as is customary in the *genus deliberativum,* on two values: advantage *(utilitas)* and honor *(honestas).* It is noteworthy that in important moments in the speech these values are explicitly mentioned. The foolishness at the beginning of the *confirmatio* (3:1), the advantage dominating the brief summing-up of the entire speech (5:2) and the glory in the center of the *amplificatio* at the end (6:12 -13) indicate that in this speech the attraction of advantage and honor and the repulsion of detriment and shame are constantly being used to influence the listeners.

The conclusion of all this is obvious: the letter Paul sent to the churches of Galatia contains a speech that exactly corresponds to the model that Hellenistic rhetoric drew up for the *genus deliberativum.*

---

[72] *Rhet. Her.* 1.2.2: "*Oratoris officium est de iis rebus posse dicere quae res ad usum civilem moribus et legibus constitutae sunt, cum adsensione auditorum quoad eius fieri poterit.*" Cicero, *Inv.* 1.5.6: "*Officium autem eius facultatis videtur esse dicere apposite ad persuasionem; finis persuadere dictione.*"

[73] According to *Rhet. Her.* 3.13.23, in delivering his speech the speaker has the disposal of three keys: *sermo, contentio, amplificatio.*

[74] Aristotle, *[Rhet. Alex.]* 2.

Rhetoric at the Service of Unity

The speech Paul addressed to the Galatians bears witness to his professional skill as a rhetorician. Above we have primarily examined how the game of recommending and dissuading is played by him and have given less attention to what is at stake. Now that we have analyzed the technical aspect of his rhetoric we will briefly entertain the question for what purpose he actually employed his eloquence.

In the *narratio* we can conclude from Paul's personal history how he visualizes his own vocation. At first he was completely devoted to Judaism, zealously championing the ancestral traditions of circumcision and Torah, and in doing so carefully maintained the separation between Jews and Gentiles. God, however, called him to preach his Son among the Gentiles. For him this meant that he crossed the bounds of Judaism by, in the name of Christ, freely associating with Titus, an uncircumcised Greek and by eating together with non-Jewish fellow-Christians who did not observe the Torah. Paul, in imitation of Isaiah and Jeremiah, is convinced that he has been called for this union of Jews and Gentiles in Christ.[75]

In the *confirmatio* we can conclude from the history of the Jewish people how Paul conceived the call of Israel. God already promised Abraham that the Gentiles would also partake by faith in his blessing. The Torah has been a hindrance to the realization of this promise for some time by separating the Jews, on penalty of sin and curse, from the Gentiles. Christ opens up the possibility for the Jews to leave the hedge of the Torah and to make non-Jews participants in the blessing of Abraham. The one God has realized the oneness of Jews and Gentiles that he already had in mind with Abraham in the one Christ. The Jews, the preferred sons and heirs of the father, are called in Christ to make the Gentiles share in the sonship and the inheritance. If Paul therefore devotes himself to uniting Jews and Gentiles in Christ, he is thereby according to his own conviction fulfilling the calling of Israel.

The *enumeratio* and the *amplificatio* both lead to the conclusion that in Christ the Jews are called to unity with the Gentiles (5:6; 6:15). The unity of the Christian community twice forms the end and goal of Paul's entire line of thought. In the end the highest ideal he aims at is "the Israel of God" (6:16). God's purpose with his people has now been realized in Christ as "the Israel of God" uniting Jews and Gentiles within itself.[76] Paul's eloquence is at the service of that goal.

Conclusion

At the end of this study it is worth returning for a moment to the hypothesis that Gal 5:13–6:10 contains a rounded off fragment of Paul added to the letter at a somewhat later time. The clear structure and line of thought shown by the text without this passage support the legitimacy of this hypothesis. Nevertheless, because of the

---

[75] Compare Gal 1:15–16 with Isa 49:1–6; Jer 1:4–5.
[76] See Dahl, "Name Israel."

presence of Gal 5:13–6:10 the structure that we discovered has a provisional character, for the addition of this passage has created a new center of gravity within the letter and makes it necessary to reorient the proposed structure and line of thought. In its present form the letter should ultimately be read within the more general perspective that Gal 5:13–6:10 introduces. Generations of readers of the letter have been wrestling with this difficult problem. Much has already been gained if this study has succeeded in improving our understanding of the nature and content of this problem.

4

GALATIANS (1:1–5): PAUL AND GRECO-ROMAN RHETORIC[1]

Robert M. Berchman

I

In this essay I shall attempt to clarify some issues concerning New Testament interpretation through rhetorical criticism.[2] My approach will be based on the assumption, shared by many students of the New Testament, that to see how a text is formed and to assess how it functions, we must view it from the vantage point of Greco-Roman rhetoric.[3] Two of the better known exponents of this approach to the study of the New Testament are Hans Dieter Betz[4] and George Kennedy.[5]

On a very general level rhetorical critics begin with the assumption that the forms of Greco-Roman rhetoric are employed by New Testament writers.[6] Identifying these forms is a simple task. They are extant in the rhetorical handbooks and doxographies of Aristotle, Anaximenes, Cicero, Quintilian, and Theon of Smyrna.[7] Once the topics *(topoi, loci)*, genres *(genê, genera)*, parts of speech *(moria logou, partes orationis)*, and syllogisms *(enthymêmê, epicheirêmê, epagôgê)* are identified, the more difficult task begins. Working as a form-critic, the rhetorical critic describes the form and defines its function in a New Testament text.[8] A good example of this method is its application to the letters of Paul, specifically Galatians.[9]

---

[1] Versions of this paper were read before the New England Regional SBL, the University of Minnesota's Classics faculty, the Religious Studies Section of the Michigan Academy of Arts and Sciences, and the Early Christianity Colloquium at the University of Virginia. I am grateful for helpful discussion on these occasions, especially to Karen King, Stanley Stowers, John Tracey Greene, Robert Anderson, Harry Gamble, and Robert Wilken.

[2] These issues are raised by Kennedy, *New Testament Interpretation*, 3–38.

[3] Cf. e.g., Wilder, *Language;* Koenig, *Stilistik;* Mullins, "*Topos.*"

[4] Betz, *Galatians.*

[5] Kennedy, *New Testament Interpretation.*

[6] Cf. e.g., Church, "Rhetorical Structure"; and J. Weiss, "Beiträge."

[7] For a description of rhetorical theory in antiquity, cf. Volkman, *Rhetorik;* Kennedy, *Art of Rhetoric* and *Greek Rhetoric;* Lausberg, *Handbuch;* J. Martin, *Antike Rhetorik.*

[8] Cf. e.g., Wuellner, "Paul's Rhetoric"; Bradley, "TOPOS"; Brunt, "More on the TOPOS."

[9] Cf. Betz, *Galatians;* Kennedy, *New Testament Interpretation*, 144–52.

Although this type of rhetorical criticism is theoretically sound, it does exhibit exegetical shortcomings. This is clear from the results of rhetorical criticism on Galatians. According to Betz's interpretation, Paul's letter is forensic.[10] It is composed according to the forms of forensic rhetoric and functions to defend Paul's character and defame his opponent's character. Kennedy, on the other hand, tries to show that Paul's letter is deliberative and exhortatory.[11] The letter functions not to defend Paul's character, but to exhort the Galatians to specific actions.

The problem exemplified in these interpretations of Galatians is that if it is not clear what genre of rhetoric Paul employed, then surely the more complex aspects of rhetorical criticism such as the definition of Paul's mode of topical arrangement, his forms of syllogistic argumentation, and the speech parts employed to frame his speech act, appear beyond description and definition. Furthermore, if these questions cannot be answered, then those concerning the meaning of the speech act and its function cannot be addressed at all.

An inability to settle such basic questions does not beset the literary critic in an analysis of Paul's epistolography.[12] Indeed, a healthy skepticism concerning the applicability of rhetorical criticism to an analysis of Paul is warranted. Its application to Galatians appears wrecked on the shoals of formal description.[13] This suggests either some flaws in the method of rhetorical criticism, or a mistake in the claim that Paul was a rhetorician.

This negative conclusion leads directly to the central issue of this essay: How ought we understand the relationship between Greco-Roman rhetorical forms and the rhetorical composition of Galatians? I will try to show that there are important formal parallels between Greco-Roman and Pauline rhetoric. However, it is confusing to suggest that these forms exist in pure form in Galatians.[14]

The confusion arises from the assumption by rhetorical critics of a mimetic relationship between the theory and practice of rhetoric.[15] According to the handbooks, rhetorical forms are self-contained constructs that are employed in a regular, indeed almost mechanistic, way. Functionally, these forms fit strictly defined persuasive situations. Certain topics are associated with specific genres of rhetoric. There are forensic, deliberative, and laudatory places of argument. A rhetorical composition is framed in one genre and its corresponding parts of speech. Never is there a mixture of genres, topics, and parts of speech in a single speech act. Finally, specific topics and types of syllogism are associated. Deductive proofs complement certain topics, inductive proofs others.[16]

---

[10] Betz, *Galatians*, ch. 1.

[11] Kennedy, *New Testament Interpretation,* 144–52.

[12] Cf. e.g., Bultmann, *Stil;* Stowers, *Diatribe;* Jewett, "Romans."

[13] This criticism is raised by Lund, *Chiasmus,* esp. 8, 23. New Testament texts do not display any of the formal characteristics common to Attic rhetoric.

[14] Following Kennedy, *New Testament Interpretation,* 12.

[15] This is particularly true in regard to New Testament composition. This is partially due to the logography of its rhetoric, cf. Burke, *Rhetoric of Religion;* Funk, *Language.* It is also due to the distinct nature of the *koinê* rhetoric found in the New Testament, cf. Brunt, "More on the TOPOS."

[16] The basic theoretical concepts underlying classical rhetoric are enunciated by Aristotle in his *Rhetoric,* in the *Rhetoric to Alexander,* and in Cicero's and Quintilian's handbooks on rhetoric. For a complete portrayal of ancient rhetorical theory see the works by Kennedy, Lausberg, and Martin, cf. n. 6.

Although these rhetorical forms had the meaning ascribed to them by the theoreticians for Paul, they had a quite different application. His art of rhetoric is not stereotyped.[17] He moves between different genres of rhetoric and topics in a single speech act. His parts of speech are equally flexible and his mode of syllogistic argumentation is connected with a wide range of commonplaces. As Paul sees it, rhetorical forms are adjusted to fit the persuasive context his letter(s) address. Thus the inventive and not the mimetic aspects of rhetoric are what interest him.[18]

This gap between rhetorical *theôria and praxis* explains why rhetorical critics dispute the genre of Galatians, argue over its parts of speech, disagree on its topical arrangement, and contest its syllogistic structure.[19] Paul combines elements of forensic and deliberative oratory in Galatians, and occasionally complements both with the use of the epideictic genre. He moves from judicial narrative to *paraenesis* and back again without breaking stride, and often amplifies both with a panegyric *lalia.*

Adaptability and flexibility are the hallmarks of Pauline rhetoric. The recognition of this basic fact forces the rhetorical critic to align handbook a prioris with Pauline *praxis.* There are profound discontinuities between the accounts of how rhetoric ought to be practiced and how Paul practices rhetoric. Therefore, to undertake a rhetorical exegesis of Galatians requires one to bracket theoretical assumptions and observe rhetoric in practice.

Assuming this is the correct way of approaching and understanding Pauline rhetoric, we have a basis for examining how it works in Galatians. I now want to turn to the purely formal dimensions of rhetorical patterning characteristic of persuasive composition.[20]

We can recognize the structure of Paul's rhetoric at least in Galatians by reference to its (1) logic, (2) topic, and (3) genre. These three aspects of the speech act, when combined, provide the foundations for a rhetorical exegesis of Galatians.[21]

(1) A speech is built upon external and internal proofs. The first type of proof relies on facts while the second is the product of invention. These proofs refer to a series of basic issues that are fact, definition, quality, and jurisdiction. Proofs are formed logically. There is the deductive proof *(enthymêmê* or *epicheirêmê)*, which takes the form of a statement with a supporting reason. The statement can be categorical, hypothetical, conjunctive, or disjunctive. It is often supported by a maxim. There is also the inductive

---

[17] This is clear from his use of the *topos*, cf. Brunt, "More on the TOPOS."

[18] This is brought out well by Mullins, "*Topos.*"

[19] Cf. e.g., Bradley, "TOPOS"; Furnish, *Love Command,* 90; Crouch, *Colossian Haustafel,* 10 n. 1. This debate on *topos* circles on the issue whether rhetorical topics in Paul have any relation to the problems and needs the apostle is facing. The genre issue is debated by Betz, *Galatians,* and Kennedy, *New Testament Interpretation.*

[20] This entails a description of rhetorical theory alone. Once the forms of rhetoric are identified, the exegete has a form-critical apparatus which can be applied to the exegesis of a text. This process of formal description and identification brackets the question whether or not these forms appear in their pure form in the text to be exegeted. This form-critical method of rhetorical exegesis has been applied to Origen of Alexandria's *Periarchon* and to *t. Teharot;* cf. Berchman, *From Philo to Origen,* 215–93; "Rabbinic Syllogistic."

[21] For a description and definition of these forms of rhetoric, see n. 6.

proof *(paradeigma)*, which uses a series of examples to demonstrate a general conclusion. Examples are drawn from the sources of external and internal proofs.

(2) In constructing a speech, topics are used. These are places of argument. Topics of *enthymēmēs* may be opposites, comparisons, considerations of time, different meanings of a word, consequences, advantages and disadvantages, to mention but a few. They function as places from which exhortation, dissuasion, praise, and blame arise and end. They touch on things possible and impossible, past and future fact, and degree. There are material and strategic headings under which these topics are arranged.

(3) A speech is composed according to three modes of internal or artistic proof. There is the character that inheres in the speaker, the emotion that inheres in the audience, and the logic that inheres within the discourse. Once the proof is introduced, it is argued through one or more of the three rhetorical genres. In the genre of forensic oratory, the aim is to defend one's character by manipulating the emotions of the audience through discourse. In deliberative rhetoric, the aim is to exhort an audience to particular actions. This is done through an appeal to the emotions of the audience through the speech act. With epideictic oratory, the aim is to extol virtues the rhetor wishes to cultivate. This strengthening of audience adherence to values is effected through an emotional appeal to the audience on behalf of these values.

With these general rules in hand we move to the prologue or proem of Galatians (1:1–5). The goal of this section of the essay is to see how Paul crafts the opening of his letter. First, the logical, topical, and generic characteristics of the proem will be outlined. This will permit a rhetorical exegesis of the pericope.

The goal of form-critical exegesis is to identify the formal structure of Paul's proem. This description of the proem's rhetoric permits us to reconstruct the strategy of composition reflected in a text, and the rhetorical situation it reflects. No claim is made that these forms appear in pure form in Galatians. Thus the rhetorical exegesis that follows functions as a hermeneutical experiment.[22]

II

The proem (1:1–5) is a linear speech that exhibits the characteristics of the topical and inductive syllogism. The syllogistic structure of Galatians (1:1–5) is:

(1) *Pisteis*

A. Proem

1:1 *lysis, ergasia*	1:1 *paradeigma*, conclusion
1:2 *ergasia*	1:2 *auxêsis* (amplification)
1:3 *ergasia*	1:3 *paradeigma*
1:4 *epicheirêmê*	1:4 conclusion
1:5 *epenthymêmê*	1:5 *auxêsis* (amplification)

---

[22] I carried out this type of rhetorical exegesis on Origen, *Princ.* praef. 1–4 and *De Deo* 1.1–9, in Berchman, *From Philo to Origen*, 215–93. For a description of this method and its limitations, see 320–21 n. 14.

Each of the topics within a part of speech is logically arranged to make an intelligible sentence. A series of sentences constitutes a proposition. (1:1–5) is the initial subproposition of the proem (1:1–10).

In this pericope, the common topics are fact, and the impossible; the material topic is the question of apostleship; and the strategic topics are from opposites, from authority, from relation, from the more and the less, and from parallel cases.

The topical arrangement of Galatians (1:1–5) is:

(2) *Topoi (Loci)*

A. Proem: *Common Topic,* Past Fact, the Impossible; *Material Topic, Apostle*

    1:1   from opposites *(ek tôn enantiôn)*; from authority *(ek kriseôs)*

    1:2   from relation *(ek tôn pros allêla)*; from the more and the less *(mallon kai êtton)*

    1:3   from authority *(ek kriseôs)*; from relation *(ek tôn pros allêla)*

    1:4   from parallel cases *(ex epagôgê)*; from authority *(ek kriseôs)*

    1:5   from authority *(ek kriseôs)*

From an examination of the topics used in a speech, it is possible to define the species of rhetoric employed in composition. The internal evidence of (1:1–5) suggests that the pericope was composed under the genres of forensic, deliberative, and epideictic oratory. The genres of (1:1–5) are:

(3) *Genera Causarum*

A. Proem	Topics	Genre
1:1	From opposites; from authority	forensic
1:2	from relation; from the more and less	forensic
1:3	from authority; from relation	deliberative
1:4	from parallel cases; from authority	deliberative
1:5	from authority (panegyric)	epideictic

This outline, in short, suggests that the proem of Galatians reflects an adaptation by Paul of Greco-Roman rhetorical forms. In the remainder of the essay I will try to illustrate in greater detail what is involved in this suggestion, and at the same time attempt to give it the sort of exegetical support it needs.

Let us look at (1:1–5) moving from its logical to its topical and general aspects.

1:1

> **Paul an apostle,** not from men nor through man, but through Jesus Christ and God the Father having raised him from the dead.

The syllogistic structure of the pericope is the following. The bold words are the statement *(lysis)* and the remainder of the pericope is the initial working out *(ergasia)* of this statement. Paul argues inductively. He begins with an example *(paradeigma)*:

Paul an apostle

The conclusion from this example is:

> Not from men nor through men, but through Jesus Christ and God the Father having raised him from the dead.

The example results in a conclusion which makes an intelligible sentence. This sentence is the initial building block of Paul's proposition that his apostolic claim is sound.

The topics make up the smallest unit of rhetorical discourse. The topical arrangement is twofold. The boldfaced words constitute the topic from authority *(ek kriseôs)*. The other words make up the topic from opposites *(ek tôn enantiôn)*.[23]

This topical sentence is a rhetorical argument. First, Paul establishes his authority as an apostle. Second, he bases it upon the opposites of:

> not from men nor through man

and:

> but through Jesus Christ and God the Father having raised him from the dead.

Paul's apostolic claim is valid because it stands in opposition to any anthropological origin, but in connection with a divine origin. The truth of his claim is sound, at least rhetorically, because of the topical arrangement and logical structure of his argument.

Colpe states:

> in the thesis *ek tôn enantiôn* . . . see if the contrary of the one follows from the contrary of the other, either directly or conversely, both when you are establishing or demolishing a view.[24]

Since Paul has the authority of an apostle on divine grounds, it is contrary to argue that his apostleship rests on anthropological bases. It would be contrary if Paul's authority as an apostle came from men or through man. Hence it comes from God the Father and Jesus Christ. This is clear from the example and its conclusion.

(1:1) establishes the fact of his apostolic claims. It establishes Paul's view that he is a true apostle. Paul amplifies this fact topically and syllogistically. His rhetorical argument leaves little room for either his opponents in Galatia, or the Galatians themselves, to reject his claims, or as Paul will argue later, to ignore the course of conduct he advocates. Since Paul argues from the topics of authority and opposites, the species of rhetoric is either forensic or deliberative. These topics are commonly used for defense and attack as well as for advice. In this pericope it appears that Paul employs judicial oratory. There are two grounds for this assessment. First, he argues from a past fact to establish a present fact. This means that he wants to defend his authority as an

---

[23] Cf. Aristotle, *Rhet.* 2.23.12; 2.23.1.
[24] Cf. Aristotle, *Top.* 2.8 (Colpe).

apostle, and refute the charge that it is invalid. Second, he establishes this fact by illustrating that which is impossible. Once he has established his claim, he can advise a course of action, but not before.

1:2

And all the brothers with me, to the churches of Galatia.

This pericope is a continuation of the *ergasia* that supports the *lysis* of (1:1). It is an amplification *(auxêsis)* of the *paradeigma* of (1:1). Logically, Paul adds to the sentence which began his speech. This extended sentence has the following syllogistic structure:

lysis: paradeigma	Paul an apostle,
ergasia:	not from men nor through man, but through Jesus Christ and God the Father having raised him from
auxêsis	the dead. And all the brothers with me to the churches of Galatia.

The word "and" *(kai)* ties together the topics which make up the working out *(ergasia)* of Paul's argument. This addition is called an amplification *(auxêsis),* and constitutes another building block of the first subproposition (1:1–5).

The topical arrangement of (1:2) is bipartite. The words in bold are the topic from relation *(ek tôn pros allêla)* and the other words constitute the argument from the more and the less *(mallon kai êtton).*[25]

The topic from relation identifies the attributes of a doer and his deed and holds each party responsible for a transaction. The topic from the more and the less is a critique that establishes a view.

The argument from relation permits Paul to assert that all the brothers (fellow Christians) accept the apostolic claim he postulates in (1:1). Using the construct *(tais ekklêsiais galatias)* he argues comparatively. This permits him to place the Galatians in relation to their brothers. This suggests they have broken with Paul and his Christian community, are in opposition to the authority of Jesus Christ and God the Father, and are less in their eyes.

This topical arrangement functions to isolate the Galatians emotionally and strengthen Paul's character *(ethos).* By manipulating the emotions of his audience, Paul's argument has an ethical end. The argument from relation identifies the attributes of the Galatians as less than Paul and the brothers. Since each party is responsible for their actions, the inference is the Galatians by their actions place themselves in opposition to divine authority.

The species of rhetoric is forensic. Paul's use of topics suggests this genre of composition. He argues from relation to defend his apostolic claim, and from comparison to criticize his opponents in the churches of Galatia.

---

[25] Aristotle, *Rhet.* 2.23.3; 2.23.4.

In (1:1) Paul established the fact of his apostleship. In (1:2) he establishes the fact of opposition to his apostleship among the Galatians. Once he has established this second datum he can advocate a course of action the Galatians should follow. Since his apostolic claims were authoritatively demonstrated from contraries, and their brothers accept this claim, Paul opens the issue, why not the Galatians?

1:3

Grace to you and peace from our God the Father and from the Lord Jesus Christ.

Topically, this pericope is a continuation of the *ergasia* which supports the *lysis* postulated at (1:1). Paul is adding to the *auxêsis* concluded at (1:2). (1:3) is also the beginning of a second inductive syllogism. It is the example *(paradeigma)* whose conclusion unfolds at (1:4).

(1:3) is an addition to the extended sentence (1:1–2). This sentence has the following syllogistic structure:

lysis: paradeigma	Paul an apostle,
ergasia:	not from men nor through man, but through Jesus Christ and God the Father having raised
auxêsis:	him from the dead. And all the brothers with
ergasia:	me to the churches of Galatia. Grace to you
paradeigma:	and peace from our God the Father and from the Lord Jesus Christ.

The new argument constitutes another building block of the subproposition (1:1–5).

The topical scheme of (1:3) is twofold. Paul argues from the topics of authority *(ek kriseôs)* and relation *(ek tôn pros allêla)*.[26] Since this sentence is a salutation in the form of a prayer, it is authoritative. Paul, as the sender of this salutation-prayer, strengthens his relation to Jesus Christ and God the Father and establishes his jurisdiction as an apostle. He is mediator for the Galatians to Jesus Christ and God the Father. That is, Paul opens a new issue *(stasis)*.[27] The first issue was one of fact. This issue is one of jurisdiction. Paul rejects the right of the Galatians to make a judgment on the validity of his apostolic claims.

Paul sets up the conditions for the re-establishment of a correct relationship between the Galatians and divine authority. He is the bridge for the Galatians to their savior and God. In order to be associated with Jesus Christ and God the Father the Galatians must accept Paul as their apostle. The key word in (1:3) is "our" *(hêmôn)*.

---

[26] Aristotle, *Rhet.* 2.23.12; 2.23.3.

[27] A *stasis* is the basic issue of a case. There are four main issues that can be addressed. They are fact, definition, quality, and jurisdiction, cf. Quintilian, *Inst.* 3.6. Classical theorists thought that *stasis* theory was applicable to deliberative rhetoric, although its categories had their origin for use in forensic oratory in the law courts.

When Paul used these topics in (1:1–2), he argued forensically to establish a *stasis* of fact. In this pericope he employs them to argue deliberatively to establish a *stasis* of jurisdiction. Paul reminds them of the fact of his apostleship, and then advises them to follow a definite course of action. They cannot be the judges of his authority.

This genre shift is self-conscious. Under a new issue, Paul advises the Galatians of their correct relationship to him and divine authority, and of the advantages (viz., grace and peace) which come with their recognition of his jurisdiction.

1:4

> The one having given himself on behalf of our sins so that he might deliver us out of this present evil age according to the will of our God and Father.

The logical structure of (1:4) is manifold. Paul's formula is an amplification *(auxêsis)* of the salutation at (1:3). As an amplification of an example, the pericope is the working out *(ergasia)* of the topical argument of the preceding verse. It is a conclusion inferred from an example. (1:3–4) has the following syllogistic structure:

paradeigma	Grace and peace to you from God our Father and the Lord Jesus Christ
auxêsis	having given himself on behalf of our sins so as he might deliver us out of the present evil age according to the will of our God and Father.

(1:4) is also the authoritative statement which concludes the topical argument of (1:1–3). (1:1–4) constitutes a topical syllogism, or an *epicheirêmê*.[28] It is a list of topics worked out *(ergasia)* to support a statement *(lysis)*. The syllogistic structure of this extended argument is:

lysis: (1:1)	Statement
ergasia: (1:1–3)	Apostolic Formula, Salutation, Prayer
epicheirêmê: (1:4)	Supporting Statement

Paul attaches this authoritative christological formula to the salutation that preceded it in order to conclude the initial subproposition of his proem. This extended subproposition has the following architectonic:

lysis: paradeigma:	Paul an apostle,
ergasia:	not from men nor through man, but through Jesus Christ and God the Father having raised

---

[28] The ancient rhetoricians maintained that topics were the source of a rhetorical system, cf. *Rhetores graeci,* 1:447. According to this definition, a rhetorical syllogism *(epicheirêmê)* is a list of topics with a concluding authoritative statement. Hermogenes places the rhetorical syllogism under the category of *stasis*. A syllogism *(epicheirêmê)* is a topically ordered statement that supports a speaker's answer to what an opponent claims. An *epicheirêmê* is a supporting statement to a *lysis,* cf. *De inventione* (Rabe), 140–154.

auxêsis:	him from the dead. And all the brothers with me
ergasia:	to the churches of Galatia. Grace to you and
paradeigma:	peace from our God the Father and from the Lord
ergasia:	Jesus Christ. The one having given himself on behalf of our sins so that he might deliver us
auxêsis:	out of this present evil age according to the will of our God and Father.

The topical arrangement of (1:4) is bipartite. Paul argues from parallel cases *(ex epagôgê)* and from authority *(ek kriseôs)*.[29] The topic from parallel cases works in the following manner. In the salutation-prayer of (1:3) Paul proclaims that grace and peace come from God the Father and the Lord Jesus Christ. This example is Paul's general case. From this general statement he infers a particular case. The particular statement is (1:4), "The one having given himself on behalf of our sins so that he might deliver us out of this present evil age." The topic from authority begins with the clause, "according to the will of our God and Father." The *kata*-clause validates Paul's argument from parallel cases.

The argument is from the general to the particular. Paul's goal is to outline to the Galatians the advantages gained if they are in an association with Paul. The content of the good is told in order that he may advise them on how they should act.

Logically and topically (1:4) is linked to (1:3). The species of rhetoric in the specific example is identical to the species of rhetoric in the general example. That is to say, the genre of oratory in (1:4) is deliberative or advisory. Arguing from authority, Paul reminds the Galatians of his *stasis* of fact. Arguing from parallel cases, he reminds them of his *stasis* of jurisdiction. In continuing in the advisory stance he assumed in (1:3), Paul can reaffirm the juridical stance he assumed in (1:1–2).

1:5

To whom the glory unto the ages of the ages, amen.[30]

The syllogistic structure of (1:5) is twofold. It is the concluding statement *(epenthymêmê)* of the subproposition (1:1-5).[31] It functions to clinch the argument of the first half of the proem. It is also an amplification of the inductive syllogism (1:3–4). In both cases it is the concluding sentence of the extended set of sentences that run from (1:1) to (1:4).

| *lysis: paradeigma* | Paul an apostle, |
| *ergasia:* | not from men nor through man, but through Jesus Christ and God the Father having raised |

---

[29] Aristotle, *Rhetoric*, 2.23.11; 2.23.12.

[30] For the background to this doxology, see Betz, *Galatians*, 43.

[31] The *epenthymêmê* is an extension of an *epicheirêmê*. It is an addition to the supporting statement that clinches the argument, cf. Hermogenes, *De inventione* (Rabe), 140–154.

auxêsis:	him from the dead. And all the brothers with me
ergasia:	to the churches of Galatia. Grace to you and
paradeigma:	peace from our God the Father and from the Lord
ergasia:	Jesus Christ. The one having given himself on behalf of our sins so that he
auxêsis:	might deliver us out of this present evil age according to the will of our God and
epenthymêmê:	Father to whom the glory unto the ages of
auxêsis:	the ages, amen.

(1:1–5) constitutes a series of topical arguments in support of two issues *(stasis).* The first issue addressed the fact of Paul's apostleship. The second issue focused on the jurisdiction of the Galatians to judge the efficacy of Paul's apostleship. Paul clinches the arguments in support of each issue by invoking a doxology. (1:5) functions to clinch the topical syllogism in support of Paul's apostolic statement (1:1–4).

(1:5) is formed topically as an argument from authority *(ek kriseôs).*[32] This argument from authority serves as a strengthening of audience adherence to a value, as the basis for a general policy of action. It strengthens Christian belief and induces the Galatians to follow Paul as their apostle.

Paul composed this doxological hymn[33] in the species of epideictic oratory. Since epideictic passages regularly occur in other genres of oratory (1:5) secures a favorable hearing for Paul's argument and moves the audience to take a course of action. The doxology is a bit of epideictic color added to Paul's juridical and advisory speech. Paul's shift into laudatory rhetoric at (1:5) is self-conscious. This hymn of praise gives attention to a belief which supports the argument of (1:1–4). The doxology is intended to be persuasive because it implies support of Paul's argument in the first part of the proem.

III

Thus we conclude that, in the initial subproposition of his proem, Paul utilizes all three species of rhetoric. The determination of the species brings out the emphases of the speech and the intent of the author. Paul argues judicially around the truth of his character, deliberatively concerning the self-interest and future benefits of the Galatians, and epideictically to deepen the values of his audience concerning Christian faith and belief.

Paul arranges his speech topically. A determination of topical strategy informs us about the context of a speech. In (1:1–5) Paul seeks to obtain the good will and

---

[32] Aristotle, *Rhet.* 2.23.12.
[33] For an excellent synopsis of these formulae, see Betz, *Galatians,* 37–43.

sympathy of the Galatians. He accomplishes this goal by arguing from authority, opposites, relation, and difference. Through the topics he amplifies his thesis, states the evidence for it, and develops his basic idea by relating it to the experience of the audience. The proem (1:1–5) is the working out *(ergasia)* of a series of inventional topics. Here Paul develops his authoritative ethos and lays an authoritative basis for his subsequent admonitions to the Galatians. Defense and advice are laid out syllogistically through examples. Paul's character is affirmed in two inductive arguments and the emotions of the audience are played with in his use of example and conclusion.

Paul organizes his speech through the three modes of artistic proof. His speech is argued in the three genres of rhetoric through common, material, and strategic topics that are arranged logically. The results of rhetorical criticism suggest that our view of the historical and religious situation in Galatia is Paul's inventive view. Nonetheless, working from Paul's speech we can mine some important information.

Since Paul argues forensically in (1:1–2), the central issue is the validity of Paul's apostleship and the allegiance of the Galatians to Paul. We do not know if (1:1) is the actual charge made against Paul by his opponents, but we do know that the Galatians have deserted him (1:2). We base these conclusions on the evidence of forensic rhetoric in these pericopae. Paul's character was at issue. This is clear from the fact that Paul opens his letter in defense of his apostleship and in attack against those no longer with him. The situation was serious in Galatia. Paul would not argue so forcefully if anything less than his credibility were at stake.

Paul argues deliberatively in (1:3–4). The issue is the right of the Galatians to judge the validity of Paul's apostleship. Since advisory rhetoric suggests a relationship between speaker and audience, we assume that although Paul's character was at issue, he was convinced the situation was redeemable. This is clear from the fact that he advises the Galatians on a future course of action. The situation was serious in Galatia, but Paul and his church (or at least a part of it) were in a relationship that had not irrevocably broken down.

Paul's use of the prayer in salutation under the species of deliberative rhetoric is significant. It tells us that both Paul and the Galatians agree on the benefits and the significance of being Christian and following the gospel of Christ. Paul and the Galatians shared a common christological and soteriological matrix. Paul would not advise the Galatians from this position if this were not the case. He employs these ideas so that he can work on the emotions of his audience and persuade them to accept his two issues *(stasis)*.

Paul argues epideictically in (1:5). The doxology is introduced in support of his forensic and deliberative arguments. Since laudatory rhetoric suggests complete agreement between speaker and audience, we assume that Paul is reminding his audience of a past fact in order to affect their emotions. He argues epideictically in support of forensic and deliberative arguments. The situation may be grave in Galatia, but Paul and the Galatians share a common world-view expressed in praise of a God they believe in. He would not use the hymn if this were not the case. Paul argues epideictically to produce an impression concerning the ethos of both himself and the

Galatians. This rhetorical device strengthens his character, disarms dissent, and permits him to introduce the *causa* (1:6–10).

The strategy of Paul's rhetoric is clear. Paul moves from confrontation (1:1–2), to advice (1:3–4), to praise (1:5). He scolds, advises, and then reminds the Galatians of the values they hold dear. Once he has manipulated their emotions in such a thorough manner, he can introduce the cause *(causa),* which is the second part of the proem (1:6–10).

What all this shows is that, formally at least, Paul exhibits a knowledge and use of Greco-Roman rhetoric. He employs rhetorical forms independently of their prescribed use, but in practicing his own art of rhetoric he adapts these forms to suit his particular persuasive needs. He moves beyond handbook stereotypes and applications of rhetoric. He applies them to the persuasive situation that confronted him in Galatia.

Much more needs to be done on the study of Paul's rhetoric.[34] But perhaps we have at least shown that in this introductory section of Galatians, as in others, Paul owes much to sophistic. His debts are deep even though the study of Pauline rhetoric in this stage of expression remains fragmentary if not illusive. Given the nature of the sources and the problems they raise, this is not surprising. It is hoped that this study makes an obscure and difficult field of New Testament studies less obscure and difficult.

---

[34] Especially on the weak link in rhetorical criticism of the New Testament writings, i.e., the connection between the forms of Greco-Roman *haut-rhétorique* and the practice of rhetoric as exemplified in New Testament *bas-rhétorique.* Lund's challenge to rhetorical criticism still presents a formidable one, cf. *Chiasmus,* 8.

5

APOSTASY TO PAGANISM: THE RHETORICAL STASIS OF THE GALATIAN CONTROVERSY

Troy Martin

The rhetorician faces a monumental task in reconstructing a controversy from a single letter written by only one of the disputing parties.[1] Nevertheless, a reconstruction of the controversy is absolutely necessary for the recovery of at least part of the original context. The elder Seneca begins each of his *controversiae* with a short description of the situation causing the controversy. His practice demonstrates the difficulty of reading a response of one participant in a debate without knowing the context of the dispute.

Paul's letter to the Galatians poses just such a situation for the rhetorician. Although the task is formidable, rhetorical theory provides important tools for reconstructing this controversy. In particular, stasis theory furnishes a means for moving from Paul's accusations and arguments to his understanding of the basic issue of the dispute. In addition, the theory of argumentation permits identification of the positions Paul thinks the Galatians are taking or may take in response to his accusations. Both stasis and argumentative theory are important tools for understanding Paul's controversy with the Galatians.[2]

The following essay will investigate the Galatian controversy by using rhetorical theory. Following a short summary of stasis and argumentative theory, this essay will determine the principal and secondary stases of the controversy and then will classify the principal stasis. Next, a detailed explanation of how the stases generate the

---

[1] I am grateful to George Lyons for reading an early draft of this essay and for offering several helpful suggestions.

[2] Several different methods have been employed in reconstructing the situation in Galatia. Tyson, among others, extracts the opponents' charges leveled against Paul from his responses to these troublemakers ("Opponents"). For a summary and critique of this method, see Lyons, *Pauline Autobiography*, and Howard, *Crisis*, 7–11. Other scholars rely on certain "key" words or phrases, but determining the criteria for identifying these "key" passages is problematic for this approach. The present article avoids these defects in method by relying on ancient stasis and argumentative theory to ascertain the "key" passages and how these passages relate to one another. This theory accords primary significance to Paul's accusations against the Galatians, and these accusations occur in the text of Galatians itself.

arguments of the letter will follow. Finally, this essay will offer some brief remarks concerning the species of rhetoric to which Galatians belongs.[3]

I. Stasis and Argumentative Theory

The Greek term στάσις comes from the root STA and means "a standing still." In Aristotelian physics, stasis refers to the pause between the end of one motion and the beginning of another.[4] A stasis must necessarily exist between opposite or contrary movements since an immobility or station must be established before a change in direction can occur.[5] Not every cessation of motion, however, is a stasis. If the "standing still" following a motion endures or continues, the "standing still" is a rest (ἠρεμία), not a stasis.

In rhetoric, a stasis refers to the pause following an affirmation or accusation (κατάφασις) and preceding a response or answer (ἀπόφασις) to that affirmation or charge. The response or answer determines whether or not a stasis exists. If the response agrees completely with the initial affirmation or accusation, then a rest (ἠρεμία) or agreement occurs instead of a stasis. Only when the response takes some issue with the κατάφασις does a stasis arise. Thus, a stasis is determined by joining the κατάφασις with its ἀπόφασις.[6]

The development of a stasis produces a controversy in which two parties disagree. The stasis of the disagreement is determined by joining the accusing statement made by the first party with the defensive response of the second party. When the conflicting statements of both parties are conjoined, the basis or stasis of the disagreement becomes evident. This principal stasis *(prima conflictio)* produces a controversy *(secunda controversia)* when the first party formulates a new charge in reaction to the defending party's response, and the defending party composes an appropriate rejoinder.[7] This process of accusation and defense generates secondary stases that represent subsequent contrary positions taken by both parties in the debate. This process continues until the controversy is resolved or until the parties despair of resolution.

The principal stasis, formed by the initial accusation and response, limits the scope of the controversy and controls the arguments advanced by the conflicting parties.[8] The initial accusation (κατάφασις) reveals the cause (αἰτία) of the dispute, while the initial response (ἀπόφασις) provides the containment (συνέχον) of the controversy

---

[3] Hall argues that the application of stasis theory to Galatians prejudices the determination of the species of rhetoric ("Rhetorical Outline," 33 n. 10; 36 n. 14). Since several ancient rhetoricians include deliberative as well as forensic rhetoric in their stasis theory, applying this theory to Galatians does not prejudice the case as Hall contends. See Nadeau, "Classical Systems," 59, 65; "Hermogenes," 377, 381, 384–86, 411–13.

[4] Modern stasis theorists understand Aristotelian physics as the basis for rhetorical stasis theory. See Dieter, "Stasis," 349–51; and Nadeau, "Hermogenes," 370–72. For a discussion of stasis theory, see Kennedy, *Art of Rhetoric*, 623; *Art of Persuasion*, 306–12.

[5] Dieter, "Stasis," 349–51.

[6] Cicero, *Rhet. Her.* 1.11; Nadeau, "Hermogenes," 374; Quintilian, *Inst.* 7.1.6.

[7] Dieter, "Stasis," 355, 362–67; Nadeau, "Classical Systems," 54–55; idem, "Hermogenes," 369.

[8] Dieter, "Stasis," 355.

by identifying the chief issue to be decided. For example, in a stasis of conjecture an accuser alleges, "You did this." The accused responds, "I did not do this." The alleged action is the cause of the dispute, and the denial indicates the chief issue to be decided—in this case, whether or not the accused performed the alleged action. This chief issue represents the principal stasis of the entire controversy. All countercharges and defensive statements must flow from this principal stasis to be pertinent to the dispute and useful for advancing the arguments of the accuser or accused.

The principal stasis falls into one of four classifications.[9] The stasis of conjecture (στοχασμός) arises when the performance of an alleged act is denied by the accused. For example, an accused murderer may deny participation in the murder. If the accused admits the act but then redefines it, a stasis of definition (ὅρος) occurs. The accused murderer may accept responsibility for the death of the victim but plead self-defense or manslaughter. If both the act and the definition of the act are accepted by the accused, the accused may appeal to some mitigating circumstances such as the victim deserved death, some benefit accrued from the victim's death, someone else is really to blame, or leniency should be shown in this case. This appeal to extenuating circumstances represents a stasis of quality (ποιότης).[10] When a defendant does not pursue any of the preceding options but objects to the entire proceedings because of a technicality, the case rests on a stasis of objection (μετάληψις). According to the rhetoricians, the principal stasis in every controversy assumes one of these four classifications.

The classification of the principal stasis determines the purpose and controls the development of the arguments. According to the theory of argumentation, arguments either prove one's claims or refute the claims of another.[11] Thus, arguments become important indicators of both parties' positions in a debate. Nevertheless, arguments may not always describe the actual positions taken by participants since arguments are sometimes constructed hypothetically. Carefully ascertaining the positions that arguments intend to prove or refute illuminates the positions both parties are taking or may take in a debate.

This brief discussion of stasis and argumentative theory describes the rhetorical tools needed to reconstruct the Galatian controversy from Paul's perspective. The primary and secondary stases of the dispute will now be determined.

II. Determining and Classifying the Stases

To determine the principal and secondary stases of the Galatian controversy, Paul's accusations must be joined to the anticipated responses of the Galatians.[12] The former

---

[9] Nadeau, "Hermogenes," 370, 372–73, 382–86; "Classical Systems," 53–54; and Dieter, "Stasis," 356–58. Some identify only three stases by omitting the stasis of objection (Nadeau, "Hermogenes," 34.

[10] A stasis of quality is the most complicated of the four types. See Nadeau, "Classical Systems," 55–56; "Hermogenes," 393–94, 406–9.

[11] Cicero, *Rhet. Her.* 1.3.4; 1.10.18; Quintilian, *Inst.* 5 Prooemium 2 and 5.13.53.

[12] Quintilian discusses both the role and dangers of anticipation (*Inst.* 5.13.44–49).

are explicitly expressed in the text of Galatians itself; the latter must be reconstructed from both the accusations Paul makes against the Galatians and the arguments Paul develops in the letter. Since arguments may visualize hypothetical as well as actual situations, Paul's accusations take precedence over his arguments in reconstructing the responses he anticipates from the Galatians. The joining of Paul's accusations and the anticipated Galatian responses permits the stases of the controversy to emerge.

Although previous studies identify only one accusation against the Galatians, there are actually two.[13] The first occurs in Gal 1:6–9; the second in 4:8–11.[14] In Gal 1:6–9, Paul charges the Galatians with exchanging his gospel for a different gospel, which requires circumcision and observance of the Jewish law. In 4:8–11, Paul accuses the Galatians of apostatizing to paganism. Since these two charges appear irreconcilable, traditional scholarship dismisses the latter in favor of the former.[15] However, recognizing both these charges is necessary for determining the principal and secondary stases of the controversy.

It is possible for both charges to stand as stated because the Galatians' decision relative to the valid Christian gospel must be distinguished from their decision to live or not live according to this gospel. The Galatians could accept the circumcision gospel as the legitimate Christian gospel and still reject its claims upon their lives. In such a case, they agree with Paul's opponents that circumcision and observance of the Jewish law are proper requirements of the gospel.[16] Nevertheless, they decline to submit to circumcision and decide to return to paganism instead. Several considerations indicate that Paul simultaneously accuses the Galatians both of exchanging his gospel for the circumcision gospel and of returning to paganism.

First, Paul does not consider any of the Galatians to have submitted to circumcision even though he accuses them of accepting the circumcision gospel (Gal 1:6; 3:1–5; 5:7).[17] If they had already become circumcised, Paul's argument against this practice would be pointless because the process cannot be reversed (Gal 5:2–12).[18] Paul's argument in Gal 3:5 presupposes that the Galatians have not submitted to cir-

---

[13] Proponents of the two-front hypothesis such as Lütgert (*Gesetz*) and Ropes (*Problem*) are exceptions. Their "two-front" hypothesis does not, however, rely on an analysis of the rhetorical stases of Gal 1:6–9 and 4:8–11. Instead, it relies on a misunderstanding of the purpose of Gal 5:7–6:10.

[14] Hester locates the stasis in Gal 1:11–12, but this passage is a proof to establish the proposition in Gal 1:10 and not an accusation ("Rhetorical Structure," 223).

[15] Betz, *Galatians*, 46–47; Bonnard, *L'épître*, 22; Burton, *Galatians*, 18; Bruce, *Commentary*, 19–20; Dunn, *Theology*, 29; Lührmann, *Galatians*, 12, 83; Mussner, *Galaterbrief*, 53–54, 290; Räisänen, *Paul and the Law*, 169; Ridderbos, *Epistle*, 46, 160; Schlier, *Galater*, 36, 201–3; and Sieffert, *Galater*, 41, 254. For other attempts to subsume 4:8–11 to 1:6–9, see the survey by Howard (*Crisis*, 66–76). In contrast to traditional scholarship, the two-front hypothesis more clearly emphasizes the pagan dimension of 4:8–11.

[16] These opponents are traditionally called judaizers, but Dunn appropriately criticizes this label (*Theology*, 10). The present study avoids this term in favor of designations such as "troublemakers," "agitators," "opponents," or "other missionaries." The term *opponent* is used even though it too may be inappropriate. See Lyons, *Pauline Autobiography*, 78–79.

[17] Lyons provides several arguments proving the Galatians have not yet submitted to circumcision (*Pauline Autobiography*, 126–27).

[18] Oepke, *Galater*, 118. The surgery cannot be reversed, but it can be masked by a procedure called epispasm.

cumcision or the law.[19] Furthermore, the opponents' desire to shut out the Galatians dissipates when the Galatians submit to circumcision (4:17). Consequently, the opponents' desire indicates that the Galatians have not yet submitted to circumcision (6:13). Since the operation requires only a few minutes, the Galatians' uncircumcised state even after they accept the circumcision gospel as valid demonstrates a reticence rather than an eagerness to submit to circumcision.

Second, the willingness of the Gentile Galatians to submit to circumcision when they recognize the circumcision gospel as legitimate should not be assumed.[20] Judaism had long provided the Galatians with the option of circumcision and submission to the law; however, they had refused to take such steps.[21] The Gentile abhorrence of circumcision prevented the widespread acceptance of this Jewish practice.[22] Among Gentiles, the adult circumcision of entire social groups is not attested except in rare instances of military compulsion. Unless the Galatian situation is a phenomenon unique to the Greco-Roman world, the Galatian churches are not contemplating circumcision even though they accept the circumcision gospel as the true Christian gospel.

Finally, the social structure of the Galatian churches contests their submission to circumcision. The Galatian churches were preexisting household units before conversion to Paul's gospel.[23] The decision of the head of the household determined the religious status of that household. Paul does not address individuals within the churches that are causing disruption. Instead, he addresses the churches as a whole, and he treats them homogeneously.[24] Even if a few of the Galatian churches accept circumcision, the unanimous acceptance of this practice by all of these autonomous Gentile units is extremely unlikely. Paul's argument suggests either that they have all agreed to submit to circumcision or none of them has. Among a diverse group of Gentiles, the latter is much more probable than the former. Consequently, it is unlikely that the Galatian churches have unanimously agreed to circumcision in spite of their recognizing circumcision as a requirement of the Christian gospel.[25]

Since both of these accusations in 1:6–9 and 4:8–11 are possible, the rhetorician should seriously consider both in reconstructing the Galatian controversy. Either 1:6–9 or 4:8–11 functions as the principal stasis of the controversy. Traditional scholarship identifies the accusation in 1:6–9 as the accusation (κατάφασις) of the principal stasis.[26] Two factors deny that this accusation provides the κατάφασις of the

---

[19] Betz, *Galatians*, 136.

[20] Lull examines three external arguments to explain the Galatians' eagerness to be circumcised; none is convincing (*Spirit in Galatia*, 29–39).

[21] Eckert discusses the barrier circumcision posed for Jewish proselytization (*Verkündigung*, 57).

[22] R. Meyer, "περιτέμνω," 6:78–79. See also Eckert, *Verkündigung*, 56–57.

[23] Meeks, *First Urban Christians*, 75–77.

[24] Brinsmead, *Galatians*, 187.

[25] Barclay perceives the improbability of a group of Gentiles voluntarily submitting to circumcision (*Obeying the Truth*, 46–47).

[26] Brinsmead, *Galatians*, 49; Lyons, *Pauline Autobiography*, 173–74; and Lategan, "Argumentative Situation," 394–95.

principal stasis. On the one hand, locating the principal stasis in 1:6–9 places Paul's accusation in 4:8–11 outside the containment (συνέχον) of the controversy.[27] Hence, scholars who identify 1:6–9 as the central issue must dismiss the accusation in 4:8–11 in one way or another. On the other hand, recognizing 4:8–11 as the accusation of the principal stasis permits the accusation in 1:6–9 to fit appropriately into the containment of the controversy. Paul seeks to discredit the circumcision gospel and those who proclaim it because the Galatians' acceptance of this gospel excuses both their apostasy to paganism and their failure to honor their initial agreement with Paul and, ultimately, God. Thus, 4:8–11 is the accusation of the principal stasis of the controversy.

This principal stasis is a stasis of quality (ποιότης), since the charge is neither denied (στάσις στοχασμός) nor redefined (ὅρος) nor rejected on technical grounds (μετάληψις).[28] This class of stasis investigates the seriousness of the alleged action "from the standpoint of its non-essential attributes and attendant circumstances."[29] The stasis of quality subdivides into four types, based on whether or not the nonessential attributes and circumstances relate to a person (epideictic, περὶ προσώπου), to the future (deliberative, περὶ αἱρετῶν καὶ φευκτῶν), to the past (forensic, δικαιολογική) or to legal questions (pragmatic, πραγματική).[30]

Since the principal stasis of Galatians pertains to the past act of the Galatians' apostasy (4:8–11) and the secondary stasis to their prior exchange of Paul's gospel for the circumcision gospel (1:6–9), the qualitative stasis of the Galatian controversy is forensic (δικαιολογική). The forensic type subdivides into actions forbidden (ἀντίθεσις) and not forbidden (ἀντίληψις). The past actions of the Galatians fall into the former category, which further subdivides into countercharge (ἀντέγκλημα), counterplea (ἀντίστασις), shifting of blame (μετάστασις), and plea for leniency (συγγνώμη). Paul's response to the Galatians' actions indicates that shifting of blame (μετάστασις) is the specific sub-stasis of the Galatian controversy.[31] The blame for the Galatians' apostasy rests squarely on the proponents of the circumcision gospel (1:7–9; 4:17; 5:8, 10, 12). Thus, the stasis of the Galatian controversy is a qualitative stasis of the forensic type, subdivided into a sub-stasis of actions forbidden and further subdivided into a sub-stasis of shifting of blame.

This classification of the stasis and the identification of 4:8–11 as the accusation of the principal stasis, as well as the joining of Paul's accusations with his anticipated

---

[27] For a discussion of containment in stasis theory, see Dieter ("Stasis," 355) and Nadeau ("Classical Systems," 54.

[28] Even though he considers the stasis differently, Betz correctly understands Paul's arguments as a response to an issue of quality (*Galatians*, 129). Hall dismisses the idea of a stasis in Galatians but admits that a stasis of fact would be the most appropriate stasis for Galatians ("Rhetorical Outline," 36 n. 14). Hall's confusion about the stasis arises from his assumption that the stasis, if there is one, must arise from accusations against Paul instead of Paul's accusations against the Galatians.

[29] Nadeau, "Classical Systems," 54; see also Nadeau, "Hermogenes," 370, 372–73, 406–13; and Dieter, "Stasis," 355–58.

[30] Nadeau, "Classical Systems," 56; "Hermogenes," 375, 383–86.

[31] For a treatment of this specific substasis, see Nadeau, "Hermogenes," 394. For definitions of these rhetorical terms, see Nadeau's index (ibid., 419–20).

responses from the Galatians, permit a reconstruction of the Galatian controversy.[32] Paul accuses the Galatians of abrogating their initial agreement with him by apostatizing from Christianity to paganism (4:8–11). He anticipates that the Galatians will agree with the charge but will contend that they were innocent in taking this course of action because the true Christian gospel requires circumcision and observance of the Jewish law (3:1–5; 6:12–13), two requirements Paul had failed to mention.[33] Paul levels a new charge that they are then guilty of altering the original agreement because the true Christian gospel does not require circumcision and observance of the Jewish law (1:6–9; 2:3, 7–9, 14, 21; 3:2, 5, 10–12; 4:21; 5:2–6, 11; 6:12–15). To this charge, he expects the Galatians will respond that they are blameless in accepting this gospel because some people have arrived and told them the truth about the actual requirements of the gospel (1:7–9; 4:16–17; 5:8–12; 6:12–13).[34] Paul's letter to the Galatians is dispatched at this stage of the controversy and attempts to nullify both excuses. Consequently, the letter begins at this point in the *secunda controversia* (1:6–9) and then moves to the *prima conflictio* (4:8–11). If the Galatians persist in their present course of action, they will behave unjustly toward Paul (οὐδέν με ἠδικήσατε, Gal 4:12) since Paul's arguments have removed both of their actual or anticipated excuses.[35] After they receive this letter, the Galatians will be without excuse and must bear the consequences for their breach of contract if they continue in their apostasy.

This identification and classification of the stases produce a reconstruction of the controversy that differs at several points from traditional interpretations of Galatians.[36] First, this reconstruction seriously considers both of Paul's accusations and not only Gal 1:6–9. Second, the accusation in 4:8–11 represents the basic accusation (κατάφασις) and along with the Galatians' anticipated response constitutes the principal stasis of the controversy. Third, Paul's accusations, not his arguments, determine the actual issues of the debate. Paul's strong argument against circumcision leads exegetes to conclude that the Galatians are seeking circumcision.[37] However, the

---

[32] This process of reconstruction yields rhetorical data, not historical data. Paul's arguments reveal only the responses he thinks the Galatians are making or will make to his accusations, and Paul could be misinformed or even mistaken. Establishing the historicity of the situation is a separate issue from determining the rhetorical stasis.

[33] Barclay says the opponents "may even have argued that Paul, himself a circumcised Jew, normally circumcised his converts but had left them in Galatia with an inadequate initiation" (*Obeying the Truth,* 59). On this issue, see Howard, *Crisis,* 44–45; and Borgen, "Paul Preaches."

[34] Paul's report that even Peter and Barnabas were persuaded by a similar group of people at Antioch implies that the Galatians should not be severely blamed for not withstanding these people either (2:12–13).

[35] In Gal 4:12, Paul states that the Galatians have not yet wronged him. Thus, he recognizes the validity of their excuses for their actions. Once these excuses are removed, however, the Galatians must act differently to avoid mistreating Paul.

[36] If this reconstruction of the controversy is accepted, then Paul's theology must be reconsidered since Galatians represents a significant source. It is beyond the scope of the present article to determine how this reconstruction affects "the new perspective on Paul" that Sanders introduced (*Paul and Palestinian Judaism*) and Dunn explicated ("New Perspective"). See the evaluation of Sanders's and Dunn's positions by Räisänen ("Galatians 2.16").

[37] Dunn, *Theology,* 9.

present reconstruction, which considers Paul's accusations to be more reliable than his arguments, concludes that the Galatians have not and never intend to let themselves be circumcised.

III. Arguing the Stasis

Epistolary Prescript

Paul responds to the Galatian controversy by dispatching a letter to the churches of Galatia. He begins this letter affirming his apostleship through Jesus Christ and through God the Father (1:1).[38] This affirmation, introduced in the prescript, is repeatedly mentioned throughout the letter. Paul mentions his divinely ordained mission (1:10–12, 15–16; 2:9; 5:11; 6:17) and reminds the Galatians that when he first arrived in Galatia, they recognized his apostleship by receiving him as a messenger from God and as Christ Jesus himself (4:14). At the end of the letter, Paul asserts his legitimacy because he bears in his own body the marks of Jesus Christ (6:17).[39] Thus, beginning with the prescript and continuing throughout the letter, Paul establishes as a matter of record that he is the authorized representative of the deity the Galatians reject in their return to paganism. Consequently, he can accuse the Galatians of abrogating their initial agreement with him and the deity he represents (4:8–11). He can then summon them to fulfill the terms of this original agreement (5:7–8; 6:14–16) and avoid an unpleasant face-to-face confrontation (4:20).

Body-Opening

Paul proceeds directly from the epistolary prescript to the body-opening (1:6–9), where he outlines the topics treated in the letter.[40] He expresses astonishment that the Galatians have rejected the validity of his gospel in favor of another gospel (1:6) that is dependent on circumcision and observance of the law (2:3–5, 12, 15–17; 3:2–5, 10–12; 4:21; 5:2–4; 6:12–13).[41] He anathematizes those who proclaim such a gospel and disrupt the Galatian churches (1:7–9). In the body-opening, Paul appropriately introduces the topics he intends to discuss with the Galatians, and he treats these topics in the order in which they are introduced. Paul begins by arguing for the validity of his gospel over against the other gospel proclaimed by the agitators (1:10–4:20). He then refutes the troublemakers themselves (4:21–5:10) and reaffirms the essential requirements of his own gospel (5:11–6:10).

---

[38] In spite of the general assumption that these affirmations respond to attacks on Paul, Paul's gospel, and not his apostleship, provides the focus of the controversy. See Cosgrove, *Cross and the Spirit*, 25; and Lategan, "Defending," 411.

[39] Eckert, *Verkündigung*, 38.

[40] For a discussion of the nature and function of the body-opening in letters, see White, *Form and Function*, 33–41. See also the works cited by Aune, *Literary Environment*, 180–82, 222–25.

[41] White lists expressions of astonishment as a way of introducing the body-opening ("Introductory Formulae").

These topics introduced in the body-opening coherently develop from the primary stasis described above. Paul already knows that the Galatians have apostatized from Christianity to paganism. He anticipates that they will defend their action by shifting blame to his failure to tell them the truth that circumcision and observance of the Jewish law are requirements of the true Christian gospel. In his letter, Paul reaffirms the truth of his initial proclamation and rejects these added requirements as perversions of the true gospel (1:10–4:20). Furthermore, he shifts the blame for the Galatians' apostasy to those who insist on the practice of circumcision. According to Paul, these troublemakers pervert the true gospel and actually place themselves outside the Christian community of grace (4:21–5:10). Finally, Paul reiterates the essential requirements of his gospel of freedom as a reminder to the Galatians of the original agreement made between themselves on the one hand and himself and the deity he represents on the other (5:11–6:10).[42] He desires for the Galatians to honor this agreement, reject the validity of the circumcision gospel, reverse their return to paganism, and live in peace as Christians according to his gospel of freedom (6:11–17).

Body-Middle

Following the body-opening, the various sections of the body-middle treat each of these topics in detail. Paul moves to each section of the body-middle by posing a question (1:10; 3:1–4; 4:8–9, 21; 5:7, 11). These questions introduce the topic for the section and set up the argumentative situation. Each of these questions, the topics they introduce, and Paul's argument must be investigated more thoroughly.

(a) 1:10: First Transitional Question

At the beginning of the body-middle, Paul asks the Galatians in 1:10, "Am I now persuading humans or God, or am I still seeking to please humans?"[43] This question considers Paul's two available options; either circumcision is or is not a requirement of his gospel. The latter portion of this question asks if Paul is still (ἔτι) seeking to please humans by advocating circumcision as he once did (1:13–14; 5:11). Paul curtly dismisses this option by stating that if he were still advocating circumcision, he would not be the slave of Christ (1:10d).

---

[42] For a discussion of the various ways the function of Gal 5:11–6:10 has been understood, see Barclay, *Obeying the Truth*, 9–26; and Howard, *Crisis*, 11–14. The present article understands this section neither as an attack by the opponents nor as a defense of Paul's own gospel but as a rearticulation of Paul's original agreement with the Galatians.

[43] Oepke correctly notes the role this question plays in this section of the epistle (*Galater*, 26–27). Usually scholars consider the two portions of this question parallel and interpret the former by the latter. However, this approach disregards the meaning of πείθω in the active voice and ignores the disjunctive ἤ that connects the two portions of the question. Further, the adverb ἄρτι in the first portion indicates an action in which Paul is now engaged, whereas the adverb ἔτι, associated with the latter portion, implies an activity in which Paul was once engaged but is no longer. Therefore, the latter portion is not parallel to the first. See Bultmann, "πείθω," 6:2.

Having dismissed the circumcision option, Paul now considers in more detail the validity of his current (ἄρτι) rejection of circumcision, which the former portion of his question in 1:10a raises.[44] Paul asks, "Am I persuading humans to accept my gospel or God?" If Paul is trying to persuade God to accept his gospel and to relinquish the requirements of circumcision and law-keeping, then the validity of Paul's gospel is questionable. If Paul is trying to persuade humans, however, then the validity of his gospel should not be impugned. Paul answers this portion of the question with an emphatic denial of his attempt to persuade God (1:11). On the contrary, God gave him this gospel through revelation (1:12), and Paul narrates his call to demonstrate that he does not persuade God (1:13–17).[45] Since God entrusted him with this gospel (1:15–16), it is absurd to think that Paul now must persuade God of its validity.[46]

Instead of God, it is humans who require convincing, and Paul illustrates this point by recounting three journeys in which he interacts with other Christians (1:18–2:10).[47] Paul briefly describes a trip he made to Jerusalem to visit (ἱστορῆσαι) Cephas (1:18a). He spent two weeks with him and also saw James, the Lord's brother (1:18b–19). This brief account tacitly suggests Paul's acceptance by certain important figures in Jerusalem. Paul then narrates his journey to Syria and Cilicia but only to explain his absence from Judea, where a report about him circulated (1:21–23). This report implies the acceptance of Paul's gospel as valid among the churches of Judea (1:23–24). Even though these two journeys are only briefly summarized, they illustrate Paul's efforts to associate with Jewish Christianity and imply initial success. Paul narrates in greater detail a third journey, where he seeks explicit validation for his gospel in Jerusalem (2:1–10).[48] Even though he encountered stiff opposition from some who operate from devious motives (2:4–5), he successfully convinced James, Cephas, and John, who were the pillars of the community (2:9).[49] These three journeys illustrate Paul's attempts to commend his gospel to humans. From these reports, therefore, the Galatians should conclude that Paul directs his persuasive efforts toward humans and not toward God.

Paul's argument concerning his persuasive efforts culminates in his report of an incident at Antioch. In contrast to the positive results of his overtures to the churches in Jerusalem and Judea, the arrival in Antioch of Cephas and later of some others

---

[44] The traditional view of 1:13–2:14 holds that Paul's autobiographical remarks establish his independence from Jerusalem. This view does not adequately assess the significance of the question Paul poses in 1:10. Gal 2:2 substantiates that Paul's autobiographical remarks demonstrate his attempt to persuade other church leaders of the validity of his gospel, not his independence from them, as Lührmann (*Galatians,* 12) and Howard (*Crisis,* 21–45) correctly observe.

[45] Paul's oath in 1:20 has a rhetorical function (Quintilian, *Inst.* 5.6.1–2).

[46] Even though Dunn considers independence an important goal of Paul's argument, he correctly perceives that the argument intends to safeguard Paul's claim for the divine origin of his gospel ("Relationship," 465). Dunn sees the validity of Paul's gospel as the primary issue in Paul's visit to Jerusalem (468).

[47] The adverb "then" (ἔπειτα) introduces each example (1:18, 21; 2:1).

[48] Paul's need to persuade others of the validity of his gospel, not the needs of the Jerusalem community, occasioned his visit. See Sieffert, *Galater,* 91–92; Schlier, *Galater,* 66–69; and Dunn, "Relationship," 466–68. For a contrary position, see Schmithals, *Paul and James,* 43.

[49] Dunn, *Theology,* 70.

from Jerusalem had disastrous results. Paul was compelled to champion the implications of his gospel before the hypocrisy of Cephas, Barnabas, and the rest of the Jews, who practiced the distinctions of circumcision and rejected the effectiveness of Paul's gospel to place the Gentiles on equal standing with themselves (2:11–21).[50] Paul's summary of his position in 2:15–21 insinuates that he was successful, but he gives no clear statement of the final outcome.[51] Perhaps Paul leaves the outcome in question because the problem the Galatians now face proves that Paul has not been completely successful in convincing everyone that his understanding of the circumcision-free gospel is valid. Nevertheless, Paul implies that he was at least partially successful, and his summary of the incident should convince the Galatians his position is correct.

(b) 3:1: Second Transitional Question

Following his argument that he persuades humans rather than God, Paul continues to establish the validity of his gospel by appealing to the Galatians' experience and to scripture (3:1–4:7).[52] Paul asks the Galatians who has maligned (ἐβάσκανεν) them into denying their own sense experience (3:1).[53] He queries them as to whether they received the Spirit by the observance of the law or by the hearing of faith (3:2). He questions their intelligence if they think they mature by the flesh after beginning by the spirit (3:3).[54] Finally, he asks whether their supply of spirit and miracles comes

---

[50] Commentators recognize the difficulty of explaining the actions of Cephas, Barnabas, and the emissaries of James in Gal 2:11–21. If the chronological sequence of 2:1–21 follows the narrative sequence, then the accord reached at the Jerusalem Assembly reported in 2:1–10 appears to contradict their actions. However, the Jerusalem accord only recognized the acceptance of uncircumcised Gentiles into the Christian community (2:3) on the basis of faith in Christ (2:16). The distinctions of circumcision still remained (2:9). The incident at Antioch addresses the issue of how this distinction is to be maintained. Under pressure from James's emissaries, Cephas and Barnabas shift their position from the complete equality of Jew and Gentile to a position of inequality. This issue was not decided at Jerusalem. See Dunn, *Theology*, 69–80; "Incident at Antioch," 225–30.

[51] Dunn concludes from Paul's silence about the outcome that Paul lost this confrontation (*Theology*, 13–14; "Incident at Antioch," 232). If Paul were defeated at Antioch as Dunn and others conclude, however, Paul should have suppressed this incident and focused on the Jerusalem accord instead. Indeed, O'Neill proposes that Paul does not report a victory over Cephas because "the victory had already been reported in the favorable judicial decision at Jerusalem" (*Recovery*, 44). See Cohn-Sherbok's critique of Dunn's position ("Reflections," 72–73).

[52] According to Betz, the argumentative section of the letter begins here (*Galatians*, 130).

[53] The verb βασκαίνω, used to describe the opposition's persuasive methods, can mean either "bewitch" or "malign." The better translation is "malign" since these methods are described in 4:17 as "shutting out," in 6:12 as pride, and possibly in 4:29 as persecution.

[54] Interpreters equate the Galatians' "finishing up in the flesh" in Gal 3:3 with their desire to be under law (Dunn, *Theology*, 103–4) or to submit to circumcision (Betz, *Galatians*, 134; Eckert, *Verkündigung*, 75). In addition to lacking proof that the Galatians desired to be under law or to submit to circumcision, this interpretation renders unintelligible the statement in 3:4 that such a shift from spirit to flesh makes their prior suffering vain. If 4:8–9 describes the Galatians' reversion to their pagan lifestyle, then "finishing up in the flesh" in 3:3 describes the Galatians' return to paganism, and Gal 3:4 becomes intelligible. When the Galatians accepted Paul's gospel and renounced their paganism, they probably suffered the social pressures associated with such a conversion and renunciation as Barclay notes (*Obeying the Truth*, 58). The Galatians' return to their former lifestyle renders vain whatever trials they experienced as a result of their brief trek into Christianity. Thus, Gal 3:3 does not refer to the Galatians' intention to submit to circumcision or the law.

from works of law or the hearing of faith (3:5). Of course, the Galatians' experiences are sufficient to answer all these questions.[55] Nevertheless, Paul proceeds to substantiate their experiences by detailed scriptural exegesis (3:7–4:7). The scriptures prove that the covenant with Abraham was based on faith in God's promise (3:7–20), and the imposition of the law does not nullify the promise (3:21–4:5).[56] The Galatians' experiences engendered by Paul's circumcision-free gospel are valid (4:6–7); consequently, Paul's gospel is also valid.

(c) 4:8: Third Transitional Question

In Gal 4:8–20, Paul applies his preceding demonstration of the validity of his gospel (1:10–4:7) to the Galatians' behavior. He asks the Galatians for the reason they are returning to their paganism (4:9), as evidenced by their renewed observance of their former pagan time-keeping scheme (4:10).[57] Paul reminds them of their original just treatment of him (4:12b–15), but he implies by his present concern and perplexity for them that they currently are injuring him by rendering his labor in vain and by forcing him to repeat tasks he had already performed (4:11, 19–20).[58] He questions their steadfastness (4:15a) and asks if he is now their enemy in spite of his continued faithfulness to them (4:16). Paul's preceding demonstration of the validity of his gospel removes the one excuse the Galatians could have offered for the unjust actions they are now taking toward Paul (4:11–20) and toward God (4:8–10).

(d) 4:21: Fourth Transitional Question

Having dismantled the Galatians' excuse for the abrogation of their initial agreement, Paul now addresses their excuse for preferring the circumcision gospel over his own. In the concluding section of 1:10–4:20, Paul abruptly introduces the proponents of the circumcision-law gospel (4:17–18). He questions their sincerity in *shutting out* or excluding the Gentile Galatians. In the next section (4:21–5:6) of the body-middle, Paul summons these troublemakers to account for their misrepresentation of the true gospel of Jesus Christ. He refutes them by scripture (4:21–5:1) and by his own understanding of the gospel (5:2–6). Paul's dismissal of these proponents of circumcision removes any excuse the Galatians might make for recognizing the circumcision gospel as the true Christian gospel.

The identification of the addressees is the most significant exegetical problem in 4:21–5:6. Paul either addresses the Galatians as a whole, a group of Galatians who are

---

[55] Dunn discusses the various aspects of the Galatians' experiences (*Theology*, 52–63); he also observes the dual argument Paul makes from the Galatians' experience and scripture ("Works of the Law," 533).

[56] For an explanation of Paul's use of scripture to discount the law in favor of faith, see E. Sanders, *Paul, the Law*, 160–62.

[57] For substantiation of the pagan nature of this list, see T. Martin, "Pagan and Judeo-Christian."

[58] Cronje, "Stratagem," 417–24.

prepared to follow a Judaizing line, or the proponents of the circumcision gospel.[59] Although this problem is difficult for later interpreters, the Galatians would have known immediately to whom Paul was speaking. According to the present essay, the stasis of the controversy specifies that the Galatians as a whole had no intentions of submitting to circumcision or keeping the Jewish law. Consequently, Paul addresses the proponents of the circumcision gospel in this section, not the Galatians either in whole or in part.[60] However, this problem of the addressees must be resolved without appeal to the hypothesis of the present essay to avoid circular reasoning.

Several considerations indicate that Paul addresses the troublemakers in 4:21–5:6 instead of the Galatians themselves.[61] The most important clues occur in the references to circumcision in this section. The verb περιτέμνω and the noun περιτομή refer either to an act, a state, or a practice.[62] An as act, circumcision relates to the physical operation itself. Following this surgery, a person then lives in a state of circumcision.[63] Even though circumcised persons have no choice but to live in a circumcised state, they still must decide if they will practice the distinctions associated with the covenant of circumcision (Gen 17:14). The author of Maccabees describes those who have been circumcised and live in a circumcised state but erase the distinction between themselves and the Gentiles (1 Macc 1:11–15, 52). Paul uses all three of these meanings in his discussion of circumcision in 1 Cor 7:18–20. For Paul, the act and the state of circumcision pose no hindrance for Christianity; however, the new community established by Jesus Christ excludes the practice of distinguishing between circumcised and uncircumcised members. Paul's succinct statements in 1 Cor

---

[59] Almost all commentators identify the Galatians as the addressees of this section. See Bonnard, *L'épître*, 95; Burton, *Galatians*, 252; Lührmann, *Galatians*, 89; Mussner, *Galaterbrief*, 317; Oepke, *Galater*, 110; and Schlier, *Galater*, 216. Lütgert (*Gesetz*, 11, 88) and Sieffert (*Galater*, 278), however, argue that only a portion of the Galatians who are prepared to follow a Judaizing line are addressed. Schmithals holds that Gal 3:6–4:7, 21–31 addresses neither the Galatians nor the opponents since it is drawn from Paul's debates with the Jews (*Paul and the Gnostics*, 41). As the following discussion demonstrates, Ulonska correctly perceives that Paul addresses the opponents in 4:21–27 ("Funktion," 65). Ulonska begins by arguing that the phrase "those under the law" (4:21) refers to the opponents whom Paul polemically asks, "Do you not understand the law?" (p. 65). Paul then develops the argument by using an authority accepted by the opponents—namely, the OT (65–66). Ulonska contends that Paul uses the pronoun ἡμῶν in 4:26 to associate himself with his Jewish opponents and then shifts the pronoun to ὑμεῖς in 4:28 to address again the entire community as brothers (68–71). Ulonska's first argument is convincing, but his second argument is inconclusive since the Galatians as well as the agitators respected the OT. His third argument is not persuasive because it rests on the dubious assumption that Paul could not shift pronouns without changing his addressees. In Gal 2:14–15, Paul shifts from a second personal pronoun to a first personal pronoun in his conversation with Peter. Even though Ulonska recognizes that the opponents are addressed in 4:21–27, he has presented neither sufficient argumentation nor correct identification of the extent of Paul's address to the opponents.

[60] Paul addresses the proponents of the circumcision gospel as brothers and includes them within the Christian community since they were Jewish Christians. Nevertheless, he attempts to demonstrate the defects in their understanding of faith in Christ. See E. Sanders, *Paul, the Law*, 19; and Dunn, "Echoes."

[61] Oepke (*Galater*, 110) and Ridderbos (*Epistle*, 173), among others, note a distinct break in the letter between 4:20 and 4:21.

[62] Eckert discusses all these meanings (*Verkündigung*, 49–53).

[63] Tyson, "Works of the Law,'" 428.

7:18–20 accurately describe his position in Galatians as well. Each reference to circumcision in Galatians must be carefully scrutinized to determine which meaning Paul intends.

Paul uses the participle περιτεμνόμενοι in 6:13a to describe the agitators in Galatia.[64] Because they are already circumcised, the participle cannot mean *become circumcised* or *let yourself be circumcised*.[65] Thus, this participle cannot refer to the act of circumcision. Neither can it designate the state of circumcision since Paul would then be including himself among the opponents of the Galatians.[66] Consequently, only the meaning of circumcision as the practice of distinguishing between circumcised and uncircumcised makes sense in Gal 6:13a. Even the present tense of this participle emphasizes the ongoing, continuous nature of this action.[67] Therefore, the best translation of the participle in 6:13a is *those who practice the distinctions of circumcision*.[68]

The reference to circumcision in Gal 2:12 must also refer to practicing the distinctions of circumcision since any other meaning does not differentiate between the agitators at Antioch on the one hand and Paul, Peter, and Barnabas on the other.[69] This reference indicates that the practice of circumcision includes more than simply performing the physical act itself. Practicing circumcision also means maintaining distinctions between the circumcised and the uncircumcised (Gen 17:14) especially by refusing to engage in table fellowship. Paul states that before some of James's people arrived, Peter and the other Jews were not observing the distinction of circumcision by excluding the Gentiles. Out of fear for those who practice circumcision (τοὺς ἐκ περιτομῆς, 2:12), however, Peter and the other Jews separate themselves

---

[64] Schlier, *Galater*, 281; Eckert, *Verkündigung*, 34 n. 4; and Bruce, *Commentary*, 269–70. Burton's contention that this participle refers to the Galatians and not the agitators requires a change of subject in the passage without a corresponding grammatical marker (*Galatians*, 352–54). His suggestion is not convincing. Hirsch concludes that the participle designates the Gentile converts of the Judaizers. These converts compensated for their inability to keep the law by convincing other Gentiles to submit to circumcision ("Zwei Fragen"). Hirsch's position is superior to Burton's because it does not require a shift in the subject of this verse. However, Hirsch's position requires different groups among the Galatian churches, and this idea is rejected by the majority of scholars.

[65] Dunn argues along with the majority of scholars that the troublemakers are Jewish Christians (*Theology*, 8–12). However, Munck contends that the agitators are Gentiles since the present middle participle always means "those who receive circumcision" (*Paul*, 87–89). Munck's proposal has been adequately critiqued by Howard (*Crisis*, 17). Furthermore, Munck's argument is refuted by Gal 5:3, where this participle does not mean "those who receive circumcision."

[66] Jewett astutely formulates this argument against understanding circumcision in Gal 6:13 as a state ("Agitators," 338). Nevertheless, his suggestion of congruity in the meaning of circumcision in 6:13a and 6:13b is misleading. Circumcision in 6:13a relates to the agitators, while circumcision in 6:13b pertains to the Galatians. The subject of the participle περιτεμνόμενοι is not the same as the subject of the infinitive περιτέμνεσθαι. This shift in subject indicates that the meaning of this verb also shifts between its first and second occurrences.

[67] Some manuscripts place this participle in the perfect tense to emphasize the past definite action of circumcision and its continuous results. The textual evidence, however, favors the present tense.

[68] Even though the agitators are primarily in view, this meaning of the participle would not exclude any Jew who practices the distinctions of circumcision. See Oepke, *Galater*, 160.

[69] See Dunn, *Theology*, 73–74; "Incident at Antioch"; "New Perspective," 198, 200.

from the uncircumcised.[70] Paul views this separation as hypocrisy (2:13–14) since both circumcised and uncircumcised are justified by faith in Christ and not from observance of the law (2:16). Therefore, the practice of circumcision that requires separation from the uncircumcised is contrary to the true, inclusive Gospel of Jesus Christ (2:14).[71]

This understanding of the practice of circumcision explains Paul's use of περιτέμνω in 5:2–3. In 5:2 Paul says, "If you practice circumcision, Christ will be of no benefit to you." In 5:3 he says, "Every man who practices circumcision is obligated to observe the whole law." Many commentators understand the middle voice of these verbal forms in 5:2–3 as causative or permissive middles and understand περιτέμνω as a reference to the surgical operation. They then translate the finite verb περιτέμνησθε as "you become circumcised" or "you permit yourself to become circumcised."[72] Correspondingly, they translate the participle περιτεμνομένῳ as "one who becomes circumcised" or "one who lets himself be circumcised." These commentators then apply these circumcision references in 5:2–3 to the Galatians and not the agitators in spite of the participle's use in 6:13 as a clear reference to the troublemakers. These commentators' explanation fails to explain why the Galatians would be excluded from Christ's benefit if they become circumcised while Paul, as a circumcised person, enjoys these same benefits.[73] After all, the Galatians' submission to circumcision really should not matter since in Christ neither circumcision nor uncircumcision makes any difference (5:6). Thus, the references here cannot refer to the act or state of circumcision as almost all commentators assume because Paul receives Christ's benefits and does not consider himself obligated to observe the whole law even though he is circumcised.

Rather, the references to circumcision in 5:2–3 designate the practice of circumcision.[74] In v. 2, Paul addresses those who practice circumcision as a means of determining the members of the covenant.[75] For Paul, the benefit of circumcision excludes the benefit of Christ and vice versa (cf. Rom 4:14).[76] In v. 3, Paul restates his contention that those who practice circumcision in this way are obligated to observe the entire law (Gal 3:10).[77] Because circumcision is only of benefit if the entire law is

---

[70] Schmithals's suggestion that circumcision in Gal 2:12 refers only to Jews and not Jewish Christians should be rejected (*Paul and James,* 66–68). For the association between the positions of the agitators at Antioch and Galatia, see Schlier, *Galater,* 84; and Bachmann, *Sünder oder Übertreter,* 110. See also the similar perspective of the party in Acts 11:2–3.

[71] Dunn, "Incident at Antioch," 222–30.

[72] Bonnard, *L'épître,* 103; Burton, *Galatians,* 272–74; Bruce, *Commentary,* 228–29; Lührmann, *Galatians,* 94–96; and Lightfoot, *Galatians,* 203–4.

[73] Räisänen, *Paul and the Law,* 190.

[74] Oepke, *Galater,* 118; Mussner, *Galaterbrief,* 346; and Ridderbos, *Epistle,* 187.

[75] Betz, *Galatians,* 258.

[76] Eckert, *Verkündigung,* 41, cf. 33, 39–40. Eckert views circumcision as the primary issue between Paul and his opponents (31).

[77] Schlier notes that πάλιν in 5:3 is omitted in some manuscripts because Paul's statement lacks a prior referent (*Galater,* 231). πάλιν could indicate a prior communication of Paul to the Galatians, or it could refer loosely to the previous verse. The least problematic explanation, however, is that it alludes to Paul's quotation in Gal 3:10.

observed (cf. Rom 2:25), circumcision is nullified if the law is broken.[78] Therefore, Paul warns that those who practice circumcision as a sign of the covenant are abolished from Christ and fallen from grace (Gal 5:4).[79]

This practice of circumcision is a distinguishing characteristic of the agitators (6:13; 2:12) and indicates that Paul addresses the agitators in 5:2–3, not the Galatians. If Paul addresses the agitators in 5:2–3, as these references to circumcision indicate, then the agitators are probably also addressed in the entire section of 4:21–5:6. Indeed, two other considerations support this interpretation. Paul's exhortation in 5:1 and his description of the addressees in 4:21 pertain to the agitators more than to the Galatians.

According to context, Paul's exhortation in 5:1 to avoid submitting again to a yoke of slavery describes the agitators' pre-Christian state, not the Galatians'. Even though Oepke astutely notes that both were in a state of slavery, the yoke metaphor in this passage relates only to those enslaved under the law—namely, Jews.[80] This type of slavery does not pertain to the Galatians, who were enslaved to false deities and not the law (4:8–10).[81] The pre-Christian slavery of Jews is different from that of Gentiles (Acts 15:10). Jews were under the tutelage of the law; they were under a *paidagōgos* until the Father's appointed time (Gal 3:23–25).[82] Their slavery thus served some purpose in the plan of salvation.[83] The slavery of the Gentiles on the other hand was

---

[78] Many understand individual transgressions as constitutive of breaking the law. See Räisänen, *Paul and the Law,* 94–96; and Hübner, *Law,* 18–19. Since the law provides a means of addressing individual transgressions, Dunn argues that breaking the law refers to the breach of the covenant upon which the law is based since living from the law (Gal 3:10) excludes living from faith (*Theology,* 83–87). Either interpretation serves the argument of the present essay. However, Dunn's understanding is preferred. See the debate between Cranfield (" 'Works of the Law' ") and Dunn ("Yet Once More").

[79] Dunn, *Theology,* 86; "New Perspective," 196–200.

[80] Oepke, *Galater,* 101–3. See also Betz, *Galatians,* 204; and Hahn, "Gesetzes-Verständnis," 59. According to Hahn, the discussion of the law in Galatians primarily pertains to Jews, not Gentiles (pp. 51–53). Hahn admits that the law is not completely irrelevant to Gentiles, but the law pertains differently to Gentiles, who do not possess it, than to Jews, who do (34–35). Thus, he understands Gal 2:16 and 3:22, which place all under sin and deny the law the ability to justify anyone, as the only passages in Galatians that relate the law to the Gentiles (52). On this issue of the relationship of Gentiles to the law, see E. Sanders, *Paul, the Law,* 81–82; and Earth, "Stellung," 508–11.

[81] E. Sanders, *Paul, the Law,* 69. Sanders, however, obscures this distinction. Dunn cogently argues that the phrase ὑπὸ νόμον includes Jews but not Gentiles ("Works of the Law," 529). See also Donaldson, " 'Curse of the Law.' "

[82] To include the Gentiles under the *paidagōgos* metaphor, Sanders must ignore the shift in pronouns throughout this passage (*Paul, the Law,* 68–69). He concurs with Reicke that the first and second personal pronouns in this section do not refer to different groups (Reicke, "Law and this World"). Paul's argument in this section rests on his statement in 3:13–14 and depends on the first personal pronouns referring to Jews and the second personal pronouns to the Gentile Galatians. Christ redeemed the Jews from the curse of the law so that the blessing of Abraham might come upon the Gentiles. Paul uses sudden shifts in the person of the pronouns to make this point explicit. Since Jews as well as Gentiles are saved by faith in God's promises and not by the observance of the law, there can be no distinction between the two groups in the church (Gal 3:28). Paul uses pronouns to make a similar contrast between Jews and Gentiles in Gal 2:15. This contrast does not apply to every section of Galatians, however, and the antecedents of the personal pronouns in each section must be carefully considered from the standpoint of the flow of thought.

[83] Hahn, "Gesetzes-Verstandnis," 56; see also Dunn, *Theology,* 88–90; and R. Longenecker, "Pedagogical Nature."

vain and led to no positive results.[84] The yoke metaphor in 5:1 can only be applied to the Galatians' pre-conversion state if important distinctions between the slavery of Jews and Gentiles are ignored.[85] According to Paul's gospel of freedom, the agitators were under the yoke of the law before becoming Christian; the Galatians, however, were not. Thus, 5:1 refers to the agitators, not the Galatians.

Paul's description of his addressees in 4:21 as those who desire to be under law also specifies the agitators, not the Galatians.[86] Throughout the letter, Paul describes the agitators as those who desire to be under law (2:4–5, 12; 3:1–2; 5:1, 4, 12; 6:12–13). In contrast, this desire is never attributed to the Galatians.[87] Interpreters usually cite the observance of the days, months, seasons, and years in Gal 4:10 as evidence for the Galatians' intention to live under law.[88] However, this passage designates a pagan temporal scheme, not a Jewish one.[89] There is simply no evidence in the letter to prove the Galatians desired to live according to the Jewish law. Indeed, the argument in Gal 3:5 presupposes that the Galatians have not yet begun to live "under law."[90] Thus, this description in 4:21 is more apropos to the agitators than the Galatians. Furthermore, Paul's use of this descriptive phrase is necessary to denote a shift of subject from the preceding verse, where the Galatians are addressed, to v. 21, where the agitators are addressed in diatribe style.[91]

These arguments provide substantial warrant for viewing the agitators as those whom Paul addresses in 4:21–5:6. This understanding explains why the scriptural argument here is separated from the scriptural arguments in the previous section (3:7–4:7), where Paul validated his gospel over that of the agitators.[92] In 4:21–5:6,

---

[84] Lightfoot, however, argues that both Judaism and paganism had a salvific purpose (Galatians, 173).

[85] See Oepke, Galater, 102; and Rengstorf, "ζυγός," 2:899.

[86] The determination of the addressees in 4:21 relates to the discussion of those under law in 3:21–4:11, where Paul describes Jews and not Gentiles as those under law as Donaldson has demonstrated (" 'Curse of the Law' "). Paul's use of the pronouns we and you suggests that he does not confuse the two groups. Belleville argues that the first person pronouns in 3:21–25 and 4:1–5 "refer specifically to pre-Christian, Jewish life under the law" (" 'Under Law,' " 68). In contrast, Paul uses second person pronouns in 3:26–29 and 4:6–11 to address his Gentile readers. Older commentators adopt a similar point of view. However, Schlier (Galatians, 193), Bruce (Commentary, 181), and Betz (Galatians, 204) take the alternative view that Paul refers to the pre-Christian state of both Jew and Gentile in 4:1–5. For a list of commentators on both sides of this issue, see Betz, Galatians, 204 n. 25. See also the excellent discussion by Duncan, Galatians, 129–30.

[87] Commentators who argue that the Galatians desire to be under law usually cite 4:21. See Burton, Galatians, 252; Mussner, Galaterbrief, 317; Oepke, Galater, 110; Ridderbos, Epistle, 173; and Schlier, Galater, 216. Of course, these commentators' argument dissipates if 4:21 addresses the agitators and not the Galatians.

[88] For example, see Bonnard, L'épître, 90–91; Bruce, Commentary, 205; Burton, Galatians, 232–33; Dunn, Theology, 94; Ridderbos, Epistle, 161–62, 173; and Schlier, Galater, 204. Betz (Galatians, 217) and Mussner (Galaterbrief, 303) agree that this temporal scheme relates to life under the law, but they do not think the Galatians are yet practicing this scheme.

[89] See T. Martin, "Pagan and Judeo-Christian," passim.

[90] Betz, Galatians, 136.

[91] Donaldson, " 'Curse of the Law,' " 97.

[92] For other solutions to this problem, see Betz, Galatians, 239 nn. 4, 5. The usual criticisms are that the scriptural argument is superfluous or misplaced.

Paul invalidates the agitators themselves.[93] He calls the agitators to account for their desire to be under law after the coming of Christ (4:21) and constructs an allegory from Abraham's two sons, Ishmael and Isaac, to erode the agitators' claim of being Abraham's elect offspring.

A most important yet unstated assumption for this allegory is that both Ishmael and Isaac were circumcised (Gen 17:23–26; 21:4).[94] Nevertheless, only through Isaac, the son of promise, were Abraham's descendants named (Gen 21:12) even though Ishmael, the son of the slave woman, would produce a nation (Gen 21:13). Paul describes Ishmael as born completely through human design (κατὰ σάρκα, Gal 4:23, 29) from the slave woman even though he bore the mark of circumcision. Furthermore, he did not receive the inheritance (4:30) and persecuted Isaac (4:29b). The distinguishing mark of Abraham's elect son was birth from a free mother according to the promise (Gal 4:22–23). For Paul, those who desire to be under law identify with the slave Ishmael (4:25, 30–31), originate from human design (4:29a), fail to gain the inheritance (4:30), and persecute the promised heirs (4:29b). In contrast, Abraham's true heirs are free (4:26, 30–31), originate from promise (4:28) and spirit (4:29), and receive Abraham's inheritance (4:30).[95]

Paul designs this allegory to prove that those who desire to be under law and practice the distinctions of circumcision are not the elected offspring of Abraham even though they are circumcised. Paul concludes that only those who enjoy the freedom from the law provided by Christ are truly heirs of Abraham (4:30). He exhorts those who desire to be under law not to submit again to the yoke of slavery under the law (5:1). Paul's allegory from scripture excludes those who desire to be under law from the covenant of promise.[96] This allegory erodes the agitators' insistence upon law and circumcision as marks of the covenant and even places them outside of the covenant since their antagonistic behavior toward the Galatians associates the agitators with Ishmael rather than Isaac.[97]

---

[93] Betz correctly notes that Paul returns to *interrogatio* in this section (*Galatians*, 240); however, he identifies the Galatians, not the agitators, as those being addressed. Barrett connects the origin of this allegory with the opponents and their propaganda ("Allegory"). He contends, however, that 4:30 is addressed to God's eschatological agents and expresses the fate of the circumcision party (p. 13).

[94] This allegory is often understood as a continuation of the scriptural arguments begun in 3:7–4:7 that establish circumcision as an unnecessary mark of the Christian covenant. See Burton, *Galatians*, 251; Oepke, *Galater*, 110; and Betz, *Galatians*, 238. Since Ishmael and Isaac were both circumcised, however, this allegory cannot prove the irrelevancy of circumcision as the previous scriptural material does, but it can invalidate the circumcised agitators by associating them with Ishmael rather than Isaac. Paul's testimony in 5:6 and his previous arguments from scripture in 3:7–4:7 invalidate circumcision as a sign of the Christian covenant; the allegory in 4:21–5:1 invalidates the proponents of circumcision themselves.

[95] Barrett perceives this connection as the primary point of the allegory. According to Barrett, Paul constructs this analogy because the agitators use the plain meaning of the Abraham story to compel the Galatians to circumcise ("Allegory," 10). The present essay argues that the Hagar material is more important to Paul's case than the Sarah material. Cosgrove correctly observes that Paul emphasizes the agitators' connection with Ishmael rather than the Galatians' relationship to Isaac (*Cross and the Spirit*, 81–82).

[96] Dunn, *Theology*, 91.

[97] Ibid., 96–97. See also D. King, "Paul and the Tannaim," and Hansen, *Abraham in Galatians*, 146–47.

In 5:2–6, Paul sharpens his refutation of the agitators by bringing his own testimony against them. Paul testifies that those who practice circumcision as a mark of the covenant do not receive Christ's benefits (5:2), become transgressors since they do not actually keep the law (5:3; 6:13; cf. 3:10), are separated from Christ in their attempt to practice the legal distinctions between themselves and others (5:4a), and fall from grace (5:4b).[98] In contrast, he testifies that those in Christ and not under law expect the hope of righteousness through faith (5:5) and perceive the decisive distinction between themselves and others as faith operating through love (5:6).[99] For Christians, the distinction between the circumcised and uncircumcised is irrelevant (5:6a; cf. 3:28).[100] Paul's testimony, like the allegory in the previous section, excludes those who desire to be under law from those in Christ. The agitators seek to exclude the Galatians from the Christian covenant (4:17); Paul through scriptural allegory and testimony excludes the agitators.[101]

(e) 5:7: Fifth Transitional Question

In 5:7–10, Paul applies his preceding refutation of the agitators to the Galatians' behavior.[102] He asks the Galatians who has hindered them from obeying the truth (5:7). He asserts that the additional requirements advocated by the agitators were not part of the original agreement made between the Galatians and himself, acting on behalf of God (5:8). He expects the Galatians to agree with him (5:10a) that circumcision and observance of the law are not requirements of the Christian gospel. Paul concludes his refutation of the troublemakers by placing the blame for the troubles in Galatia squarely on them (5:10b).

(f) 5:11: Sixth Transitional Question

Having dismissed the circumcision gospel and those who proclaim it, Paul now proceeds in 5:11–6:10 to reiterate the requirements of his gospel as the basis for his original agreement with the Galatians.[103] He reminds them of his circumcision-free

---

[98] E. Sanders rejects the notion that human inability to keep the law is a basic assumption in Paul's argument (*Paul, the Law,* 22–25, 27), and Dunn concurs ("Yet Once More," 116). See Phil 3:6. The argument in Gal 3:10, however, requires at the very least an assumption that no one *does* observe all the law even though the argument does not address whether or not one *could* observe all the law. Thus, Paul's assumption is descriptive rather than theoretical. Paul's accusation probably addresses failure to achieve the purpose of the law rather than failure to keep individual precepts. See Barclay, *Obeying the Truth,* 139.

[99] Eckert, *Verkündigung,* 37.

[100] Dunn, *Theology,* 99.

[101] In his address to these agitators in 4:21–5:6, Paul uses inclusive language (4:26, 31; 5:1, 5) and Christian labels such as *brother* (4:28, 31) because this discussion is an intra-Christian debate. These circumcised agitators consider themselves to be the true members of the Christian community. Paul accepts them as Christians but demonstrates that by their desire to be under law they actually exclude themselves from this community.

[102] The shift in subject is marked by Paul's statement, "You were running well" (5:7a). This statement pertains only to the Galatians, not the agitators.

[103] Barclay surveys the various ways Gal 5:13–6:10 has been related or unrelated to the preceding material (*Obeying the Truth,* 9–26).

gospel (5:11) and its sharp contrast with the "other gospel" advocated by his opponents (5:12). Paul's gospel summons the Galatians to live a life of freedom in loving service (δουλεύετε) to one another (5:13). Their love for one another fulfills the entire law (5:14; cf. 6:2). As they are led by the spirit and not by the law, they produce the fruit of the spirit in their lives and shun the works of the flesh (5:15–26). Their community life is characterized by relationships arising from the spirit and not the flesh (6:1–10). Paul encourages the Galatians to continue in his gospel by effecting the good for all and especially for the household of faith until the coming of the Lord (6:9–10).

Body-Closing

In the body-closing (6:11–17), which precedes the farewell (6:18), Paul reviews the points he has made in the body-middle. The agitators should be ignored because they possess impure motives and are transgressors of the law (6:12–13).[104] Paul's circumcision-free gospel, which produces a new creation, is the valid Christian gospel since in Christ circumcision and uncircumcision do not matter (6:14–15). Only those who continue in this new creation and do not return to the old pagan life-style are blessed with peace and mercy; it is these who constitute the Israel of God (6:16). Paul summons the Galatians not to furnish him with labors by continuing their apostasy (6:17a; cf. 4:11, 19). He reminds the Galatians that he is the legitimate representative of Jesus Christ and has the right to dispatch this letter to them (6:17b). He certifies that this letter is not a forgery by affixing his own hand (6:11).[105] This body-closing concludes the body of the letter and Paul's argumentation as well.

IV. Identifying the Species of Rhetoric

The preceding investigation has applied rhetorical theory to the Galatian controversy. The stasis of this controversy was identified as a stasis of quality. Paul charges the Galatians with apostasy from Christianity to paganism. The Galatians do not deny this charge but claim justification because the valid Christian gospel requires circumcision and observance of the law, neither of which is acceptable to them. Paul objects that the true gospel does not contain these requirements. The Galatians respond that it does require circumcision because some individuals have told them the truth. Paul's letter dismisses both of the Galatians' justifications by refuting the circumcision gospel as well as its proponents. Paul shifts the blame for the Galatians' apostasy to the agitators. If the Galatians continue in their apostasy after receiving

---

[104] Howard rejects the view that the agitators taught only part of the law (*Crisis*, 15). Instead, he argues that the function of Gal 6:13 is to damage the influence of the troublemakers by asserting that they do not keep the law perfectly. Eckert discusses the possible relationships of the agitators to the law (*Verkündigung*, 41–42).

[105] Quintilian's discussion of these practices may explain why Paul signs his name in such large letters and calls the Galatians to witness his signature (*Inst.* 5.5.1; 5.7.1). Their witness verifies the genuineness of the letter.

this letter, however, they will be without excuse and will receive Paul's blame when he is again present with them (4:20).

This reconstruction of the Galatian controversy enables identification of the species of rhetoric to which Galatians belongs. H. D. Betz originally placed Galatians in the category of forensic rhetoric, but subsequent scholars increasingly prefer the deliberative category.[106] This disagreement arises both from misunderstanding the stases of the Galatian controversy and from ambiguity in the determining criteria for each of these rhetorical species.[107] Since Paul is not in a court of law and he is seeking to persuade the Galatians to alter their behavior, several scholars conclude that Galatians cannot pertain to forensic rhetoric.[108] However, forensic rhetoric was often practiced outside the courtroom as the numerous classroom examples illustrate. In addition, forensic rhetoric sometimes seeks to persuade someone to adopt a different course of action. For example, a plaintiff may seek the aid of the court to force a defendant in breach of contract to fulfill the original agreement or pay damages. Thus, the distinguishing criteria used by scholars in identifying the species of rhetoric are inadequate.

A much more promising approach is that of Seneca the Elder. He distinguishes *controversiae*, which are issues that may be argued in a court of law, from *suasoriae*, which cannot.[109] According to this approach, Galatians is a *controversia*, not a *suasoria*. The breach of the original agreement between Paul and the Galatians represents an issue that could be tried in a court of law. Of course, whether this issue would ever come to trial depends on the decision of the plaintiff in this case, namely, Paul.[110] Galatians, therefore, belongs in the category of forensic rhetoric as Betz concluded even though its initial reading occurs outside a courtroom.

Although it belongs to forensic rhetoric, Galatians is a letter and not a speech designed for the courtroom.[111] It is a pre-trial letter written to an offending party to summon that party back to the original agreement. The letter removes two legal maneuvers available to the defendants if the case should ever come to trial. The Galatians cannot shift the blame for their apostasy to a change in the original agreement since Paul verifies that the original agreement remains intact. Neither can the Galatians

---

[106] Betz, *Galatians,* 24. Hall rejects Betz's forensic identification and argues for the deliberative species instead ("Rhetorical Outline." See Bachmann (*Sünder oder Übertreter,* 15–18, esp. nn. 125–26), who prefers the deliberative species (pp. 159–60).

[107] For example, compare Aristotle (*Rhet.* 1.3.3–5) with Quintilian (*Inst.* 3.4.1–16).

[108] Hall presents the essential contours of this argument ("Rhetorical Outline").

[109] Seneca the Elder usually begins each *controversia* by quoting a law pertinent to the case as well as a short description of the actions in dispute (Winterbottom, *Seneca the Elder,* xvi). He begins his *suasoriae* with the following formula: "X, in circumstances Y, deliberates" (ibid., xx). See also Quintilian, *Inst.* 3.4.6–7; and Nadeau, "Hermogenes," 368.

[110] Lyons refutes prior identifications of Galatians as forensic (*Pauline Autobiography,* 112–21); however, the studies he dismisses only consider Paul's self-defense or his accusations against opponents. The present study identifies Galatians as forensic in that Paul accuses the Galatians. Thus, Lyons's criticisms do not pertain to the present study.

[111] Galatians should be analyzed as a letter since it is written in epistolary form. Rhetorical analyses should not indiscriminately superimpose the structure of a speech upon the epistolary structure, as Mitchell correctly notes (*Reconciliation,* 10 n. 33, 22 n. 5).

shift the blame for their acceptance of the circumcision gospel as the valid Christian gospel to the agitators, since Paul refutes these insincere troublemakers as perverters of the true gospel. If this case should ever come to trial, the letter to the Galatians is one of the documents the plaintiff, Paul, would most certainly enter as evidence against the defendants, the Galatians.[112]

It is unlikely this case would ever find its way into a Roman courtroom at Paul's instigation. At several places, however, Paul reminds the Galatians of an eschatological judgment.[113] He mentions the judgment borne by the troublemakers (5:10) and warns the Galatians that those who perform the works of the flesh will not inherit the kingdom of God (5:21). He develops the eschatological judgment metaphor of sowing and reaping in 6:7–10 and threatens more severe action than the letter when he is again present with the Galatians if they do not return to the agreement (4:20). Further, the conditional blessing in 6:16 carries an implicit threat against those who do not return to life according to Paul's gospel.[114] Paul's pre-trial letter removes the potential excuses the Galatians might offer at the eschatological judgment for their abandonment of the deity Paul proclaims. Of course, the Galatians can avoid such an eventuality by renouncing their return to paganism and resuming their life according to Paul's gospel.

Galatians is in the tradition of a divine lawsuit (רִיב). Like the prophets of old, Paul threatens the Galatians with legal proceedings for breach of contract. Paul emphasizes his apostleship to establish his right to represent the deity in the proceedings. Like the prophets, Paul continues addressing his audience as covenant partners because he refuses to ratify their apostasy by letting them go. In the Hebrew Bible, God also refused to accept the apostasy of the Israelites by concluding the legal suit. Both the prophets and Paul exert pressure on the unfaithful partner to return to covenant faithfulness. Perhaps Paul's legal action was more successful than the efforts of his prophetic counterparts, but rendering a verdict on this issue requires further investigation.[115]

---

[112] Thus, the letter functions as an inartificial proof (ἄτεχνος). See Quintilian, *Inst* 5.1.1–2.

[113] Dunn discusses other apocalyptic aspects (*Theology*, 46–52).

[114] Betz, *Galatians*, 321.

[115] If Galatians were written before 1 Cor 16:1, then the Galatians' participation in the collection for Jerusalem indicates that they renounced their apostasy and the letter achieved Paul's objective.

6

ST. PAUL'S EPISTLES AND ANCIENT GREEK AND ROMAN RHETORIC

C. Joachim Classen

In August 1974, at the 29th General Meeting of the Studiorum Novi Testamenti Societas at Sigtuna, Sweden, H. D. Betz gave a lecture on "The Literary Composition and Function of Paul's Letter to the Galatians" which seems to have initiated a new era in Biblical Studies or at least in New Testament Studies in the United States and, to a lesser degree, elsewhere. In 1979 he published "Galatians: A Commentary on Paul's Letter to the Churches in Galatia" in which he repeated the claims he had made in his paper and applied in detail the method which he had outlined five years before. And in 1988 a German translation of his commentary appeared in which he reproduced the original text without noticeable changes; only in the introduction Betz shows some awareness of the criticism and doubts some reviewers expressed.[1]

However, on the whole the reaction to the commentary was favorable and some reviewers even hailed Betz's work as marking the beginning of a new era in New Testament Scholarship.[2] Today, numerous scholars in this field, especially in the United States of America, try to employ the same method as Betz, and the terms "rhetorical" and "rhetoric" figure more and more frequently in the titles of their books and papers.[3] The new element which Betz introduced or rather claimed to have introduced

---

[1] Betz, "Literary Composition"; *Galatians* (= *Galaterbrief*); *Second Corinthians 8 and 9* (= *Zweiter Korinther 8 und 9*); The article "Literary Composition" is reprinted in Betz, *Paulinische Studien,* 63–97 (with a Nachtrag [97] which merely lists a few more recent books and articles), together with some other of his articles on Galatians (20–45; 46–62; 98–125) and on the problem of rhetoric and theology (126–162: see below, n. 6).

[2] See the reviews by Barrett; Aletti; Davies, P. Meyer, and Aune; Meeks; Swetnam; and Hübner.

[3] See, e.g., Bünker, *Briefformular;* Jewett, *Thessalonian Correspondence,* esp. 61–87: more convincing than his pupil Hughes, *Early Christian Rhetoric;* D. Watson, *Invention;* Elliott, *Rhetoric of Romans;* more critical and discerning, Übelacker, *Untersuchungen;* W. Wuellner's pupil Thurén, *Rhetorical Strategy;* Mitchell, *Rhetoric of Reconciliation;* and especially Johanson, *To All the Brethren,* whose analyses are more convincing as they avail themselves also of the insights of modern rhetoric (see also below, n. 74). These and many other also more recent titles are now listed by D. Watson and Hauser, *Rhetorical Criticism.* See further e.g., Saw, *Paul's Rhetoric;* Morland, *Rhetoric of Curse;*

into New Testament Studies is the use of the categories of ancient Greek and Roman, that is, classical rhetoric and epistolography for the exegesis of Paul's letters.

This alone would explain and justify the interest of classicists in this development; and not surprisingly one of the leading experts in this field, George A. Kennedy, a few years later took his stand in his book *New Testament Interpretation through Rhetorical Criticism*, approving of this type of exegesis in general and applying it to various texts from the New Testament, but modifying Betz's results with regard to the letter to the Galatians.[4] However, the enthusiasm for this new instrument for the interpretation of biblical texts is not shared in all quarters, and some scholars prefer simply to ignore it or to suspend judgment, while others, clearly, feel uneasy about their uncertainty or even ask for advice or assistance from classicists.[5] A new assessment seems to be called for.

In his commentary Betz claims: "Paul's letter to the Galatians can be analyzed according to Greco-Roman rhetoric and epistolography. This possibility raises the whole question of Paul's relationship to the rhetorical and literary disciplines and culture, a question which has not as yet been adequately discussed," and he adds in a footnote to the first sentence: "This fact was apparently not recognized before."[6] Next, however, he rather oddly gives a couple of references to Luther and Melanchthon as well as to J. B. Lightfoot, thus admitting that he did have predecessors.[7] This raises a number of questions: (1) Are rhetoric and epistolography regarded by Betz as two separate disciplines, each of them separately being of service to the interpretation of the New Testament, or are they taken together by him and if so, is this justified? (2) Is Betz referring to the theory of rhetoric and/or epistolography or to their practical application or to both? (3)

Kern, *Rhetoric and Galatians*, and the bibliographies each of them provides. Today any volume of *Journal of Biblical Literature, New Testament Studies, Novum Testamentum, Theologische Zeitschrift* or *Zeitschrift für die neutestamentliche Wissenschaft und die Kunde der älteren Kirche* will furnish examples of articles on biblical "rhetoric." Interestingly some scholars seem to remain totally unaffected by this approach, see e.g., Schutter, *Hermeneutic and Composition;* Prior, *Paul the Letter-Writer.* For a brief survey see Majercik, Dozeman, and Fiore, "Rhetoric and Rhetorical Criticism."

[4] Kennedy, *New Testament Interpretation:* on Galatians, 144–52; reviews: Robbins; Patton; Fowler; Betz. See also D. Watson and Hauser, *Rhetorical Criticism,* 109–12. In appreciation of his work a Festschrift was offered to Kennedy: D. Watson, *Persuasive Artistry,* with several useful contributions.

[5] This paper grew out of a talk given on March 26th, 1990 in Einsiedeln (Switzerland) at the request of the group of Roman Catholic and Protestant Commentators on the New Testament and published as Classen, "Paulus." The English version was written afresh and presented first at the University of Helsinki on May 8th, 1991 ("Paul"), and later at the conference in Heidelberg, organized by Pepperdine University ("St. Paul's Epistles" [1993]). It was revised again for *Rhetorical Criticism.* Recent contributions to the debate are found in Porter and Olbricht, *Rhetoric and the New Testament; Rhetoric, Scripture, and Theology; Rhetorical Analysis;* Anderson, *Ancient Rhetorical Theory* and review by Classen; Porter, "Paul of Tarsus"; and see n. 3. H. Schweizer, "Bibelrhetorik," is disappointing; also G. Otto et al., "Christliche Rhetorik"; more useful is Grondin, "Hermeneutik"; see further Bormann, Schmidt, and Schenk, "Hermeneutik"; and Sternberger et al., "Schriftauslegung."

[6] Betz, *Galatians,* 14 (= *Galaterbrief,* 54); more recently Betz seems to have become more aware of his predecessors, cf. *Second Corinthians 8 and 9,* 129 n. 2 (= *Zweiter Korinther 8 und 9,* 231–32 n. 2), and his "Problem of Rhetoric" in *Paulinische Studien,* 126–62, esp. 126–31.

[7] Betz, *Galatians,* 14 n. 97 (= *Galaterbrief,* 54 n. 97). Betz mentions Luther's commentary of 1535 (for details see his bibliography, where he also lists Luther's earlier lectures and commentaries which he does not seem to have consulted) and Lightfoot, *Galatians,* and adds that G. Ebeling called his attention to Melanchthon's commentary on Romans.

What exactly is the aim of applying the ancient categories? (a) Is it to demonstrate to what extent Paul was familiar with them, with rhetoric and/or epistolography, theory and/or practice (as the second sentence seems to indicate), or (b) is it in order to help modern exegetes to arrive at a more thorough understanding of the letter(s)? (4) If this is the aim, the question arises whether one should restrict oneself to applying the categories and insights of ancient rhetoric only, or perhaps even only to rhetoric prior to and contemporary with Paul, or whether one may also employ whatever new aspects have been added since antiquity. (5) If, however, the aim is solely a more adequate appreciation of Paul himself, at least three further groups of problems come up: (a) when, where and how is Paul likely to have become familiar with ancient rhetoric and epistolography; (b) exactly which form or which aspect of rhetoric and epistolography and at which phase of their history is meant (provided it is possible to distinguish clearly several phases of the development); (c) did he deliberately draw on such knowledge of rhetorical theory and employ its categories consciously or not? (6) Finally, as Betz stresses the novelty of his method, it seems obvious to ask: why was it not discovered and used before; or, as he mentions Luther, Melanchthon and Lightfoot in a footnote, were they the first and what did they do?

In view of these questions some general observations seem to be called for. When one turns to the categories of rhetoric as tools for a more adequate and thorough appreciation of texts, their general structure and their details, one should not hesitate to use the most developed and sophisticated form, as it will offer more help than any other.[8] For there is no good reason to maintain that a text could and should be examined only according to categories known (or possibly known) to the author concerned. For rhetoric provides a system for the interpretation of all texts (as well as of oral utterances and even of other forms of communication), irrespectively of time and circumstances (except, of course, for the fact that some rules of rhetoric immediately concern the external circumstances).[9]

When one turns to the categories of rhetoric in order to appreciate more fully an author's writings, one should examine what is known about the writer himself, his background, his education and other factors that influenced him. When, however, lack of independent sources renders this impossible and one has nothing but a text or a group of texts, one has to bear in mind that in any speech or any piece of writing, elements or features occur which are found in handbooks of rhetoric and which we are inclined to classify and designate accordingly, but which may, in fact, originate from four sources: from rhetorical theory (and its deliberate application), from a successful imitation of written or spoken practice, from unconscious borrowing from the practice of others, or from a natural gift for effective speaking or writing.

In application to Paul's letters, this means that one may collect the external evidence regarding the conditions under which he grew up and the experience of interpreting the Bible which he gained later. I shall not attempt to do this here, as I am

---

[8] On this problem see Wuellner, "Where?"; hesitatingly Porter, "Ancient Rhetorical Analysis." Saw, "Paul's Rhetoric," tries at length to justify why he uses ancient rhetoric only (11–31, also 63–79); see also Brucker, "Versuche," (11–15).

[9] See Classen, "Paulus"; "Rhetorik."

not competent;[10] but I should like to add two observations: (a) Anyone who could write Greek as effectively as Paul did must have read a good many works written in Greek, thus imbibing applied rhetoric from others, even if he never heard of any rules of rhetorical theory; so that even if one could prove that Paul was not familiar with the rhetorical theory of the Greeks,[11] it could hardly be denied that he knew it in its applied form; and (b) anyone who studied the Old Testament as carefully as Paul undoubtedly did must have noticed the rhetorical qualities displayed there[12] and must have given some thought to the best way of expressing himself.

In turning to Paul's letters now, one has to emphasize a point to which Betz does not pay attention sufficiently—the difference between rhetoric and epistolography. Most ancient handbooks of rhetoric do not deal with letters, and where they do, they are content with a few remarks mostly on matters of style[13] Manuals on letter-writing on the other hand differ substantially from handbooks on rhetoric in content and structure:[14] Instead of dealing with either the *officia oratoris* ("the tasks of a speaker") or the *partes orationis* ("the parts of a speech") they list a large number of types of letters and give advice on stylistic problems. Obviously, a fundamental difference was felt in antiquity between a speech or even a poem or another type of composition on the one hand and a letter on the other, and while for example brevity, clarity or appropriateness of style are recommended for letters as for other pieces of writing or speaking,[15] as regards the "structure" of letters *(dispositio)*, no particular rule or advice seems to have been given.

I could now enter upon a detailed examination of Betz's method, the new arguments which he formulates with the aid of rhetorical theory and the insights he thus gains, or I could offer a rhetorical analysis of Paul's letter to the Galatians or at least some comments on such elements and features, the function of which one would explain with the help of rhetorical categories in any work of ancient literature. Instead, I turn to the last question raised above: To what extent ancient rhetoric was made use of for the interpretation of the Bible before 1974. I cannot, of course, deal here with

---

[10] The literature on Paul is too vast to be referred to here, see e.g., Hübner and Flusser, "Paulus" (literature: 149–53 and 159–60).

[11] It seems most likely that he was; see Classen, "Philologische Bemerkungen," an English version of which appears in Classen, *Rhetorical Criticism.*

[12] Studies on the rhetoric in the Old Testament are listed in the first part of D. Watson and Hauser, *Rhetorical Criticism*, 21–98; on possible rabbinic rhetorical elements in Paul's writings see the article by Lemmer, "Rabbinic."

[13] See the two best known examples: Radermacher, *Demetrii Phalerei*, 47–49 (223–35) with *Adnotationes* (109–10), and Giomini and Celentano, *C. Iulii Victoris*, 105–6 *(de epistolis).*

[14] Cf. Weichert, ΤΥΠΟΙ ΕΠΙΣΤΟΛΙΚΟΙ; also Foerster and Richtsteig, *Libanii Opera IX*, 27–47; for other texts on ancient epistolary theory see Hercher, *Epistolographi graeci*, 6–13 (Ps.-Proclus) and 14–16 (Philostratus and Gregory of Nazianzus); also Malherbe, *Ancient Epistolary Theorists.* On the various types of letters see Görgemanns, "Epistolographie"; Görgemanns and Zelzer, "Epistel"; and Schmidt, "Brief." On the relationship between rhetoric and epistolography, Reed, "Epistle"; and with reference to Paul, Porter, *Paul of Acts*, 98–125.

[15] Cf. e.g., the references given by Malherbe, *Ancient Epistolary Theorists*, 13–14; for these qualities in general see Lausberg, *Handbuch*, and J. Martin, *Antike Rhetorik*, 362–74, register, s.v. *brevis/brevitas, dilucidus, decorum*, etc.

the history of the exegesis of the Bible in general.[16] But even a brief glance at some arbitrarily selected earlier commentaries shows very quickly that this method is by no means new. It was practiced in antiquity and it was not totally neglected in the Middle Ages; it was frequently employed with great skill during the Renaissance, and it has never been forgotten ever since in some quarters, while others preferred to ignore it; and it was revived after the Second World War first by such Old Testament scholars as J. Muilenberg,[17] before Betz brought it back to New Testament Studies so effectively.

In this long and varied history, few have done more for the study of ancient rhetoric, for its development and its application to the needs and requirements of his own time and for its use for the interpretation of the Bible than Philip Melanchthon;[18] and yet, few have experienced a more complete neglect later. Betz refers to him in a footnote, but not in the bibliography where Erasmus and Lefèvre d'Etaples, Luther, Calvin and Bullinger are listed with their commentaries; G. A. Kennedy does not mention him at all.[19] Some modern scholars seem to ignore him, because they disagree with his theological position, others because he wrote in Latin (or an old fashioned type of German).

How does he proceed? How does Melanchthon practice rhetorical criticism? To what extent does he anticipate Betz? What, if anything, can the modern scholar learn from him? In this context I can do no more here than remind the reader that Melanchthon wrote three handbooks on rhetoric and three handbooks on dialectic, the art of defining words and objects, of dividing kinds and of finding and using arguments,[20] also a large number of commentaries on books of the Old and New

---

[16] See in general Reventlow, *Epochen der Bibelauslegung;* for the Church fathers, Sieben, *Exegesis patrum;* for the Middle Ages, Lubac, *Exégèse médiévale,* and Smalley, *Study of the Bible;* for the humanists and the Renaissance, Bentley, *Humanists and Holy Writ,* and the bibliographical references given by Wengert, *Melanchthon's* Annotationes; see now also Sæbø, *Hebrew Bible/Old Testament.*

[17] Muilenberg, "Form Criticism and Beyond"; Hauser provides a brief survey of the history of rhetorical criticism of the Old Testament in D. Watson and Hauser, *Rhetorical Criticism,* 3–20; D. Watson provides a survey relating to the New Testament, ibid., 101–25; see now also Regt et al., *Literary Structure.*

[18] His works: Bretschneider and Bindseil, *Melanchthonis Opera,* with his commentaries on books of the Bible in 13:761–1472, and vols. 14 and 15. Also Stupperich, *Melanchthons Werke;* Bizer, *Texte* (to be used with the corrections by Scheible, "Review"). Melanchthon's correspondence: Scheible and Thüringer, *Melanchthons Briefwechsel: Regesten,* and Wetzel and Scheible, *Melanchthons Briefwechsel: Texte.* For his biography see Hartfelder, *Philipp Melanchthon,* with detailed though incomplete lists of his publications and lectures (577–620 and 555–66); Maurer, *Der junge Melanchthon.* Bibliography: Scheible, "Melanchthon"; on Melanchthon as interpreter of the Bible see most recently Wengert and Graham, *Philip Melanchthon,* and Classen, "Bedeutung der Rhetorik," an English version of which appears in Classen, *Rhetorical Criticism.*

[19] Betz, *Galatians,* 14 n. 97; 337 (= *Galaterbrief,* 54 n. 97; 566–67); Kennedy, *New Testament Interpretation;* N. Elliott, *Rhetoric of Romans,* grants him no more than a footnote (22 n. 1).

[20] Melanchthon, *De rhetorica libri tres; Institutiones Rhetoricae; Elementorum rhetorices libri duo* (1536 edition used here); *Compendiaria dialectices; Dialectices libri quatuor; Erotemata dialectices.* For details see Bezzel, *Verzeichnis,* 13:497–98, M4179–4185; 417–18, M3514–3527; 364–68, M3101–3136; 327–28, M2797–2809; 350–52, M2996–3021; 381–84, M3242–3273. See further Knape, *Philipp Melanchthons Rhetorik* (disappointing) and Berwald, *Philipp Melanchthons Sicht* (and my review); on his dialectic see Frank, "Melanchthons Dialektik"; and on his teaching manuals in general Leonhardt, "Melanchthon."

Testament in addition to editing numerous texts.[21] In addition I shall content myself with a few remarks on his earliest editions, lecture notes and commentaries to give some idea of the earliest stages of the development of his rhetorical criticism.

In preparation of his lectures on the letter to Titus Melanchthon published an edition of the Greek text in 1518 in Wittenberg (which was printed again with a Latin translation in 1519 in Erfurt).[22] In 1519 he contributed a preface to Luther 's commentary on the psalms as well as a preface and an epilogue to his commentary on Galatians. He lectured himself on the psalms, on the letter to the Romans and the gospel of Matthew, and wrote the "Theologica institutio . . . in epistolam Pauli ad Romanos."[23] In 1520 he delivered a "Declamatiuncula in divi Pauli doctrinam" on January 25th, the feast of Saint Paul, the patron of the Divinity Faculty in Wittenberg, and continued to lecture on the gospel of Matthew; published an edition of Erasmus' Latin translation of the letter to the Romans with a preface and some notes in the margin, and an "Ad paulinae doctrinae studium adhortatio" (also printed separately); and perhaps an edition of the Greek text with more rhetorical notes in the margin. He lectured on this letter and composed the "Artifitium epistolae Pauli ad Romanos";[24] he also edited the Greek text of the letter to the Galatians with Latin translation and lectured on that letter.[25] In 1521 he edited (perhaps) the Greek text of the letter to the Romans, certainly a Latin translation of texts of the two letters to the Corinthians and also of that to the Colossians, lectured on these four letters[26] and published his "Loci communes."[27] What do they contain, what do they teach us?

---

[21] For the editions of and commentaries on books of the Bible by Melanchthon and his contemporaries see Bezzel, *Verzeichnis* 2:401–739, B2568–5312; for Melanchthon also, ibid. 13:261–534, M2330–4425.

[22] For the lecture see Hartfelder, *Philipp Melanchthon,* 555; for the editions, Bezzel, *Verzeichnis* 2:724, B5174 and 5175.

[23] For the prefaces see Wetzel and Scheible, *Melanchthons Briefwechsel: Texte,* 1:110–13 (no. 47) and 121–24 (no. 54); for the epilogue, 1:148–49 (no. 65); for the lectures on the psalms, 1:115–17 (no. 50); on the letter to the Romans and on Matthew, 1:158–59 (no. 68); see also 1:189–97 (no. 84) with important notes on line 67 (Matthew; his *Annotationes* was published by Luther in 1522), and line 70 (Romans). For the text of the *Institutio* see Bizer, *Texte,* 90–99.

[24] For the *declamatiuncula,* printed three times in 1520, see Koehn, "Philipp Melanchthons Reden," 1323–25 (no. 51–53); and Wetzel and Scheible, *Melanchthons Briefwechsel: Texte,* 1:166–67 and 167–76 (nos. 75 and 76). For the lectures on Matthew see above, n. 23. For the edition of the Latin translation of the letter to the Romans, see Weitzel and Scheible, *Melanchthons Briefwechsel: Texte,* 1:211–12 (no. 94a), with *adhortatio,* 209–210 (no. 94); and Koehn, "Philipp Melanchthons Reden," 1325 (no. 54), separate printing: 1325–26 (no. 55). For the edition of the Greek text 1520 is assumed as the year of publication by Strohm et al., *Griechische Bibeldrucke,* 9 (C9); see also Hartfelder, *Philip Melanchthon,* 580, no. 27; 1521 is assumed by Weitzel and Scheible, *Melanchthons Briefwechsel: Texte,* 1:292–93 (no. 142). For lectures see ibid., 1:267–72 (no. 132). For the *Artifitium* and the marginal notes see Bizer, *Texte,* 20–30. On the chronology of Melanchthon's early work on Romans see R. Schäfer, "Melanchthon's Interpretation."

[25] For the edition see Bezzel, *Verzeichnis* 2:713, B5068. For the notes taken during his lecture, Bizer, *Texte,* 34–37.

[26] For the edition of the letter to the Romans see above, n. 24. For that of the letters to the Corinthians, see Wetzel and Scheibel, *Melanchthons Briefwechsel: Texte,* 1:279–80 (no. 138) and 357–58 (no. 172); of that to the Colossians, Beuttemüller, *Vorläufiges Verzeichnis,* 28 (no. 117: year uncertain), and Strohm, *Griechische Bibeldrucke,* 9 (C11: 1521). For the lectures, see Hartfelder, *Philip Melanchthon,* 556–57, and Bizer, *Texte,* 40–42, who prints, 45–85, ΡΑΨΟΔΙΑΙ [*sic!*] ΕΝ ΠΑΥΛΟΥ AD ROMANOS.

[27] For details see Bezzel, *Verzeichnis* 13:428–31 and 431–33, M3583–3613 and 3614–3632.

The notes on the epistle to the Galatians are rather elementary. However, it seems appropriate to characterize them briefly here, as Betz applied his new method in a commentary on this letter.[28] In accordance with the practice in such lectures, as we know it from contemporary lecture-notes on Ciceronian speeches,[29] Melanchthon first determines the "kind" or "type" *(genus)* to which he thinks the work should be assigned and gives a summary of its content. Rather surprisingly, he regards it as belonging to the "instructing kind" *(genus didacticum)*, a new *genus*, which he himself adds to the traditional canon of three ("judicial," "deliberative" and "epideictic": *iudiciale, deliberativum, demonstrativum*), as we learn from his manual of rhetoric in which he explains and justifies this innovation.[30] Clearly, while Melanchthon is thoroughly familiar with the rhetorical tradition, he feels free to modify it and to introduce a new element where he considers it incomplete or inadequate; and he uses it here as in his opinion it is Paul's intention in this letter after censuring the Galatians to give them a brief demonstration of what Christianity is (*epistola haec est generis Didactici qua arguit Apostolus Galatas Qui ab iis quae eos praesens docuerat declinaverunt, Paucis denuo scribens Christianismi summam Quam si excesserint iam in errorem labi demonstrat:* "This letter belongs to the instructing kind by which the apostle blames the Galatians who turned away from what he had taught them when he was there; again briefly outlining the whole of the Christian religion he shows that if they moved away from it, they would then lapse into wrong views").[31]

He characterizes the first two verses by an unusual, but appropriate term (ἐπιγραφή: "inscription," "address") and a brief description of their content and the third merely by a Latin term, *salutatio* ("greeting"), again not commonly used in ancient handbooks of rhetoric, but familiar from contemporary works on epistolography.[32]

---

[28] Not surprisingly there is a comparatively large number of recent studies on this letter. See D. Watson and Hauser, *Rhetorical Criticism*, 194–98; Morland, *Rhetoric of Curse;* Kern, *Rhetoric and Galatians;* Ciampa, *Presence and Function.*

[29] For such notes cf., e.g., *In omnes M. Tulli Ciceronis orationes;* on earlier and contemporary commentaries on Cicero see Classen, "Cicerostudien"; "Cicero, orator"; "Rhetorical Works."

[30] Cf. Bizer, *Texte,* 34; for the new *genus didacticum* see Melanchthon, *De rhetorica,* 12–47, 64–65, 91–93, esp. 13; idem, *Institutiones rhetoricae,* fol. A IIr-v *(dialecticum)* and *Elementorum rhetorices libri duo,* fol. A 8v-B 1r and B 3r-B 6r: *genus* διδακτικόν (see n. 20). The fourfold division may have been suggested to Melanchthon by the four qualities which Maximus of Tyre expected the philosophically trained orator to display in the four areas of his activity (Maximus of Tyre, *Or.* 25.6; Trapp, *Maximus of Tyre* 213; Koniaris, *Maximus Tyrius* 307); for he refers to Maximus in his Greek grammar of 1518 (see Melanchthon, *Operum,* 5:168; Maximus of Tyre, *Or.* 10.6 [Trapp, 83; Koniaris, 119]), and to his explanation of Homer's μῶλυ (*Od.* 10.305: Maximus of Tyre, *Or.* 26.9 and 29.6 [Trapp, 225 and 242; Koniaris, 352]) in 1519, in the preface to his first rhetoric, a letter to Bernard Maurus (see Wetzel and Scheible, *Melanchthons Briefwechsel: Texte,* 1:140). See also Melanchthon, *De rhetorica,* 7. For other possible sources for Melanchthon's new *genus* see Classen, "Paulus," 16–17 n. 54 (see above, n. 5) and Bullemer, *Untersuchungen,* 36–41. It deserves to be noticed that διδακτικός ("capable of teaching") occurs in 1 Tim 3:2 and 2 Tim 2:24.

[31] Cf. Bizer, *Texte,* 34. In the sense of "superscription on outside of a letter" ἐπιραφή is used in antiquity not by rhetoricians, but by others; see, e.g., Preisigke and Kießling, *Wörterbuch,* 1:547, or ἐπιγραφή, *PGL* 519.

[32] For *salutatio* cf., e.g., Erasmus' *De conscribendis epistolis* (Margolin, *Opera,* 205–579, esp. 276–95). Melanchthon's remarks should be set against the rich discussion of his time on the rules of letter-writing, see, e.g., Henderson, "Erasmus" (with references to further literature), and W. Müller, "Brief," esp. 70–72 (short bibliography: 72).

The section from 1:6 to 2:21 he regards as the "introduction" *(exordium)*, dominated by "feelings of anger" *(affectus indignationis)*, and he adds approvingly: "As elsewhere the best introductions start from emotions" *(Sicuti alias optima exordia sunt ab affectibus)*. Perhaps he has such precepts in mind as that given by Quintilian in the fourth book of his *Institutio oratoria* (4.1.33) that the audience may be made attentive by stirring its feelings. Being also aware of Quintilian's warning that such appeals to emotions should be used sparingly in introductions (4.1.14), he interprets Paul's next sentence (1:7) appreciatively as "toning down of the anger" *(mitigatio est indignationis)*, possibly because usually *indignatio* is shown with reference to the adversary (e.g., in the courts of law), not to the recipient of a letter.[33] Next Melanchthon explains the inferences Paul draws or the arguments he proposes in the following verses, sometimes expressly stating the "gist" *(summa)* of the matter in question, sometimes pointing to particular parts of an argumentation. On 1:11 he remarks: "He accounts for what he said in the introduction and shows by some inferences that his teaching is from God, and these inferences are briefly connected with each other" *(rationem reddit propositi Exordii, et demonstrat doctrinam suam esse a deo Coniecturis aliquot. Et breviter complectuntur coniecturae)*, then quoting from 1:12 and 1:16–17, and on 2:6: "Further he proves by another inference: Evidently I have thus also not learned anything from them when I was with them" *(Etiam probat alia coniectura: Nimirum ita neque cum apud eos essem aliquid ab eis dididici [sic!])*.[34] Before 3:1 *(O stulti Galatae)* he notes: "Issue or statement of the case by means of rebuke" *(Status seu propositio per obiurgationem)*, thus marking the beginning of the main part of the letter, and by adding a little later "And this he proves to be so through arguments" *(Idque probat esse Argumentis)*, he characterizes Paul's procedure here, i.e., that he is producing arguments.

There is no need to give further details of the manner in which Melanchthon comments on the syllogisms.[35] It deserves to be noticed, however, that more than once he employs terms which are not common in traditional rhetorical theory, but which he also uses in his own handbooks, e.g., *declaratio . . . per similia* instead of *locus e similibus* ("demonstration through similarities"), *inversio* ("inversion") for a

---

[33] In his *Elementorum rhetorices libri duo*, fol. C 1v, Melanchthon recommends "milder feelings" *(affectus mitiores)* for the introductions; for his views on feelings and emotions *(affectus)* in general see Berwald, *Philipp Melanchthons Sicht*, 50–56.

[34] Cf. Bizer, *Texte*, 34. On Gal 2:1 he remarks: "The gist: I have reproached Peter; therefore I have not learned anything from him, but through revelation, to which he adds the justification for his reproach" *(Summa: reprehendi Petrum; ideo nihil ab eo didici, sed per revelationem, cui subiungit rationem suae reprehensionis)*; on Gal 2:15: "The gist: The Jews need the justification, therefore they are not justified by virtue of their works" *(Summa: Judaei indigent iustificatione; ergo operibus non sunt iustificati)*; on Gal 2:17: "The gist: If we being justified through Christ are still in need of further justification through our own works, then Christ is the minister of sin" *(Summa: Si iustificati in Christo ad huc habemus opus ulteriore iustificatione per opera—ergo Christus est peccati minister)*; on Gal 2:21: "If they are justified through their works, then Christ does not contribute anything" *(Si per opera iustificantur ergo Christus nihil confert)*.

[35] On 3:10 Melanchthon remarks, "συλλογισμός est," which he then develops; Bizer, *Texte*, 35, notes the letters *Bar* and *ba* and *roi* (?) in the margin and identifies them as *Barbaroi*; clearly Melanchthon merely characterizes the syllogism in the traditional manner (*Barbara*, see also Scheible, *Melanchthon*, 418); see Melanchthon himself, *Compendiaria dialectices*, fol. E 1v; *Dialectices libri*, fol. F 6v–7v; and *Erotemata*, fol. D Vr and E.

piece of evidence brought forward against one side when turned in favor of that side, *occupatio* instead of *anteoccupatio* or *praesumptio* ("anticipation of an opponent's argument") and *paraenesis* for *exhortatio* ("admonition").[36]

Thus we find Melanchthon interested in the general structure of the letter and in the arguments: He distinguishes introduction, proposition of the subject matter, argumentation and "peroration" *(epilogus)*, he analyses a number of syllogisms and he gives labels from the manuals of rhetoric where they seem appropriate, while he adds new ones whenever the traditional system seems incomplete to him and he feels the need of supplementing it. Thereby, he assists the reader in understanding the intention of the letter as a whole, the general line of the argumentation and the structure of particular arguments. In doing so, he falls back upon the tools provided by ancient rhetoric and demonstrates that this system—even after many centuries—renders useful service in interpreting a text such as an epistle by Paul. But as he introduces new categories and new terms also, he implies that he sees no reason why the modern reader or scholar should limit himself to what tradition has to offer; rather, he encourages him to apply rhetoric in its most advanced form or even to develop it further when and where need be, thus maintaining a view which, as I have indicated, seems to require justification even today (see n. 8).

Melanchthon was by no means the only humanist who made use of ancient rhetoric in interpreting the Bible nor was he the first. Lorenzo Valla seems to have been the first to avail himself of the newly discovered resources from pagan antiquity for the exegesis of the New Testament. However, he and later Jacques Lefèvre d'Etaples and Desiderius Erasmus were primarily interested in the explanation of factual details or textual criticism.[37] But Martin Luther and Huldrych Zwingli, Martin Bucer and Johannes Brenz (who also wrote a rhetoric, however mainly with view to preaching), Heinrich Bullinger and Jean Calvin deserve more than a place in the bibliography;[38] for their works offer valuable insights to the modern exegete and are worth studying.[39] But apart from the fact that they cannot all be presented here and

---

[36] Cf. Bizer, *Texte*, 35–36. On *declaratio per similia* see Melanchthon, *De rhetorica*, 45 (*locus e similibus*: Quintilian, *Inst.* 5.10.73); on *inversio*, pp. 100–101, and *Institutiones rhetoricae*, fol. B 3v: *inversio qua docemus signum, quod contra nos producit, pro nobis facere.* On *occupatio* (instead of *anteoccupatio*: Cicero, *De or.* 3.205; *praesumptio*: Quintilian, *Inst.* 9.2.16), see Melanchthon, *Elementorum rhetorices libri duo*, fol. K 1v; on *paraenesis* (παραίνεσις) see what Melanchthon says on *exhortatio: De rhetorica*, 34–35, and *Elementorum rhetorices libri duo*, fol. D 8v.

[37] Cf. Valla, *In latinam Novi testamenti interpretationem* (written 1453–1457; the earlier version was not published till 1970: Perosa, *Collatio;* see Bentley, *Humanists and Holy Writ,* 32–69; also 112–193 on Erasmus; cf. further d'Etaples, *S. Pauli epistolae;* see on this and his other works Bedouelle, *d'Etaples;* Erasmus, *Novum instrumentum;* Reeve and Screech, *Erasmus' "Annotationes";* see Rummel, *Erasmus' Annotations;* Krüger, *Humanistische Evangelienauslegung;* M. Hoffmann, *Rhetoric and Theology.*

[38] Betz, *Galatians,* 337 (= *Galaterbrief,* 566–67): Luther, Calvin, Bullinger only; in Betz, *Second Corinthians 8 and 9,* they do not even figure in the bibliography.

[39] For Luther, see *Luthers Werke;* Bezzel, *Verzeichnis,* 12:3–557, L3306–7642; Benzing and Claus, *Lutherbibliographie.* On his exegesis see Ebeling, *Evangelische Evangelienauslegung;* Junghans, *Der junge Luther.* On Zwingli: Schuler and Schulthess, *Zwinglis Werke,* esp. vols. 5 and 6, part 1; Egli et al., *Zwinglis sämtliche Werke,* esp. 12:1 (marginal glosses), and vols. 13 and 14 (exegetical writings on the Old Testament); see further Bezzel, *Verzeichnis,* 22:626–50, Z758–938; Finsler, *Zwingli-Bibliographie;* Gäbler, *Zwingli.* There is no complete modern edition of Bucer's works: see only his

discussed at length with their respective methods and merits, it seems fair to say that no one contributed more to the development of rhetorical criticism of the Bible than Melanchthon. It is all the more surprising that later generations allowed his observations and his achievements to be virtually forgotten. Yet conscientious study of the history of biblical exegesis shows that the application of rhetorical categories was never given up completely.

In a lecture "Histoire de 'l'analyse rhétorique' en exégèse biblique," delivered at the seventh congress of the International Society for the History of Rhetoric in Göttingen in 1989 and published in 1990, Father R. Meynet describes a number of scholars and their methods from the middle of the eighteenth to the middle of the twentieth century and adds a specimen of his own manner of interpretation which shows that rhetorical analysis is still practiced today by Jesuits as it always has been since the foundation of the order.[40] The *Introductio hermeneutica in sacros Novi Testamenti libros,* published in Vienna 1777 by the Benedictine Stephan Hayd, Professor of Greek and New Testament Hermeneutics at Freiburg, shows that members of other orders also practiced rhetorical criticism of the Bible; in this case the author pays special attention to tropes and figures of style, but also to the structure of the argumentation.[41]

Before trying to assess the contribution of rhetorical criticism to the understanding of biblical texts, or rather the contribution made by individual scholars and the possibilities as well as the limits of such a procedure, I may be permitted briefly to indicate how I think the categories of ancient rhetoric and of ancient literary theory and criticism[42] may in general be exploited with profit today.

Anyone attempting to understand and appreciate a speech or a written composition will first determine the nature of the piece in a very general way: literary,

---

Opera latina and *Opera omnia,* particularly Backus, *Enarratio.* The original works are listed by Stupperich, "Bibliographia Bucerana," and in Bezzel, *Verzeichnis,* 3:447–65, B8825–8958. See also Stupperich, "Bucer" (bibliography, 269–70); further J. Müller, *Bucers Hermeneutik;* Roussel, *Martin Bucer, lecteur;* idem, "Bucer Exegete." On Brenz, see his *Opera;* this collection and the early single editions are listed in Bezzel, *Verzeichnis,* 3:261–330, B7469–8000; and by Köhler, *Bibliographia brentiana.* See further Brecht, *Frühe Theologie* (on the early commentaries) and in general Brecht, "Brenz" (bibliography, 180–81); on the later commentaries: Brandy, *Die späte Christologie;* on the rhetoric: Hermann, "Fragment" (quotation: *rhetoricam tractabimus quatenus eius usus est in rebus Ecclesiasticis,* 81). On Bullinger: there is no complete modern edition of his works, but see now Bullinger, *Werke,* part 3 (including Berg, *Exegetische Schrifte* and *Unveröffentlichte Werke*) and part 1 (Büsser, *Bibliographie,* including Staedtke, *Beschreibendes Verzeichnis,* and Herkenrath, *Beschreibendes Verzeichnis*); see further Hausammann, *Römerbriefauslegung;* Büsser, "Bullinger," bibliography, 385–87). On Calvin: Baum, Cunitz, and Reuss, *Calvini Opera* (bibliography: vols. 58 and 59, 433–44 (listed as printed in this edition); 445–54 (alphabetical order) and 455–512 (chronological order; printed also separately as Erichson, *Bibliographia calviniana,* 1–68); Armstrong et al., *Ioannis Calvini Opera omnia,* esp. volumes by Feld (vol. 11, parts 1–2, on the Gospel of John; vol. 15, 2 Corinthians; vol. 16, Galatians, Ephesians, Philippians and Colossians); and Parker (vol. 19, Hebrews); see also Parker, *Calvini Commentarius;* Girardin, *Rhétorique et théologique;* Ganoczy and Scheld, *Hermeneutik Calvins;* Pucket, *Calvin's Exegesis;* Opitz, *Calvins theologische Hermeneutik.*

[40] Meynet, "Histoire."

[41] Hayd, *Introductio,* 166–259 (sectio II, caput VII: *Tropi et figurae*); arguments are analyzed in sectio III: *Institutiones analytico-hermeneuticae in singulos Novi Testamenti libros speciales,* pp. 282–416). On Hayd see Reusch, "Hayd."

[42] On the nature and function of literary criticism in antiquity and its relationship with rhetoric see Classen, "Rhetoric and Literary Criticism."

non-literary or sub-literary, casual or serious, personal or general, poetry or prose, with emphasis on content or form, and so forth. In the case of a letter it seems advisable to take into consideration (if possible) the following facts: the writer's education and experiences, the education and experiences of the addressee or addressees (one should remember that a letter may be directed to an individual or a group,[43] but also, as in the form of a literary letter, to future generations), the circumstances of the writer, the circumstances of the addressee(s), present or future ("circumstances" meaning time, place and events which have just happened or are imminent). Moreover, one should consider the relationship between writer and addressee(s)—such as personal knowledge, earlier correspondence, views and experiences shared or not shared, opposing views—and, finally, the intention of the writer, whether he wishes to communicate information on actual facts, on events of the past or expected developments in the future, on personal feelings or on general views, or whether he hopes to give advice or encouragement, consolation or warning, to express praise or disappointment and so forth. In addition one should remember that a letter is a letter and cannot be expected to have the structure of a speech, though in parts it may be comparable.

After these general considerations I turn to Paul''s epistle to the Galatians.[44] In his first sentence the apostle makes it abundantly clear that he is writing a letter by using a formula by which letters generally were introduced.[45] But he supplements this formula, and by making additions he draws attention right from the start to what he considers important: "not from men nor through man, but through Jesus Christ and God the Father" (οὐκ ἀπ' ἀνθρώπων οὐδὲ δι' ἀνθρώπου, ἀλλὰ διὰ Ἰησοῦ Χριστοῦ καὶ θεοῦ πατρός). One could register a *polyptoton* here and an *antitheton*.[46] However, what matters is not such a classification, but the function of the figures thus labelled. Nor does it really help to assign them to the "embellishment" *(ornatus);* they are chosen to give special emphasis to what the writer is saying. And as these two figures here stress the same point, it gains considerable momentum, especially as each of the two members of the *antitheton* consists of a twofold expression: the first of a *polyptoton,* the second of the two nouns Ἰησοῦς Χριστός and θεὸς πατήρ, connected by a participle[47] which describes the unique act which God performed for Jesus and at the same time his resurrection, that is, his divinity.

The following greeting "grace and peace" (1:3: χάρις ὑμῖν καὶ εἰρήνη), also found elsewhere,[48] is expanded by the reference to God and Jesus Christ; this repetition serves to relegate the apostle, though being the writer of the letter, to the

---

[43] In antiquity this means that it will not only be read aloud by an individual, but may be read aloud to a group.

[44] Text: NA[27] 493–503. There are too many commentaries to be listed here (see also above, n. 28), and I had to refrain from consulting them except for general observations on the structure of the letter. In preparing this revised version of my paper I have throughout consulted the REB (1989).

[45] See Schnider and Stenger, *Studien,* 3–25 (with references to earlier literature).

[46] See Porter, "Paul of Tarsus," 580, but also 583; on *polyptoton* and *antitheton* in general see Lausberg, *Handbuch,* 325–329, 389–398; on Paul, N. Schneider, *Rhetorische Eigenart* (very useful).

[47] τοῦ ἐγείραντος αὐτόν: "(God the Father) who raised him from the dead."

[48] See Schnider and Stenger, *Studien,* 25–41.

background. It is God the father and Jesus Christ who are acting here; and while in the first sentence (1:1–2) God's activity (with respect to his son) is described by a participle, now in a corresponding construction Jesus Christ is characterized with respect to mankind (1:4) after God has been called πατὴρ ἡμῶν (1:3). This is even further elaborated in a subclause which repeats for the third time θεὸς (καὶ) πατήρ, again adding ἡμῶν and resorting to another *polyptoton* with three members: "from this world" (ἐκ τοῦ αἰῶνος) and "for ever and ever" (εἰς τοὺς αἰῶνας τῶν αἰώνων) in order to contrast the present world from which men will be saved (notice the parallel to Christ being resurrected) with God's eternity (1:5).[49] Attentive reading reveals that by means of additions to common formulae, by carefully construed sentences and by equally well chosen words the apostle most impressively conveys what he wants his readers to feel: That they are being addressed not so much by him, but in the name of God and together with him of Jesus Christ. The scholar familiar with the rules and categories of rhetoric who observes these details—whether he applies technical terms to them or not—cannot but register that an author is at work here who knows to select and to present his ideas and to employ the tools of language in the most effective manner possible.

Having thus used the introductory formula of greeting to manifest his own position, the apostle turns to the addressees, first expressing surprise about their change of mind, adding a clarification (1:6–9). There is no εὐαγγέλιον other than the one he preached to them, and it is merely some people who confuse them, trying to misrepresent the gospel of Christ. This he emphasizes with a curse which he repeats, placing it twice at the end of a sentence (1:8, 9). Again one notices the repetition of several words: εὐαγγέλιον twice; forms of εὐαγγελίζεσθαι three times; ἀνάθεμα ἔστω twice,[50] clearly for emphasis, and a correcting addition ("which is not another": ὃ οὐκ ἔστιν ἄλλο) with respect to one of these words, εὐαγγέλιον, for precision and emphasis of the essential term. But the repetition of the curse gives the whole an element of agitation and excitement, whereas rhetorical theory warns not to appeal to passions in a proem (and the theory of epistolography does not give any precepts for the parts of a letter). Are we coming to the end of rhetorical criticism, at least when applied to letters? It is certainly advisable at this stage to remember that Paul is not making a speech, and that rules for speeches and other types of compositions cannot be expected (as indicated) in all respects to be applicable to letters, especially as ancient theorists seem to have been aware of the very particular nature of letters. It is no less important to remember that exceptional circumstances require exceptional means, both from a speaker and from a writer of letters. Our stylistic observations

---

[49] ". . . that he might deliver us from this present evil world, according to the will of our God and Father: To whom be glory for ever and ever. Amen."

[50] Gal 1:6–9: "I marvel that you turned so soon from him who called you in the grace of Christ away to another gospel: Which is not another; except that there are some who trouble you and try to pervert the gospel of Christ. But if I or an angel from heaven preached any other gospel unto you than that which I have preached unto you, let him be accursed. As I said before, so I say now again: If any other man preaches any gospel unto you other than that which you have received, let him be accursed."

and the fact that there is no parallel for such an introduction in Paul's letters warrant the conclusion that he regards the situation as a very unusual one and that he wants to underline here that he is particularly concerned about the true nature of the εὐαγγέλιον Χριστοῦ and about the right understanding of his own position. Is he thereby preparing for and pointing to the central issue(s) of the letter?

In the next three verses (1:10–12) Paul continues to stress his concern for the correct understanding of the message he is preaching by contrasting men and God, pleasing men and serving Christ, a gospel received from men (which his is not: 1:11) and a gospel revealed by Christ. Again one notices several forms of *antitheton* no less than the elaborate expression τὸ εὐαγγέλιον τὸ εὐαγγελισθὲν ὑπ' ἐμοῦ ("the gospel preached by myself"), echoing the repeated forms from verses 1:7–9, and the *polyptoton* κατὰ ἄνθρωπον . . . παρὰ ἀνθρώπου ("according to man . . . from man"),[51] taking up the similar figure from verse 1:1. Once more the apostle makes and emphasizes the claim by which he opened his letter, a claim concerning himself as mouthpiece of God and Christ. In the following verses[52] Paul indicates that he is still uncertain whether the addressees are willing to accept him, to listen to him, whether the claim he has so far merely stated will be honored. He turns, therefore, to his own past and gives a full account, first of his zeal in persecuting the Christians and of the revelation of Christ through the grace of God in order that he may preach the gospel (1:13–16), next, a little more fully, of his journeys and activities in Arabia, in Damascus, in Jerusalem (first visit, contact with Cephas), Syria, Cilicia, Judea (1:17–24) and again in Jerusalem (2:1–10). Here the tone changes; Paul no longer simply reports, he explains, he mentions details, he justifies, he emphasizes differences and distinctions (1:17–24 and 2:1–10). For the controversy with Peter in Antiocheia (2:11–14) he chooses mostly a factual style again, culminating in a direct question which he asked Peter: "How do you force the gentiles to live the Jewish way of life?" (2:14: πῶς τὰ ἔθνη ἀναγκάζεις ἰουδαΐζειν), before he outlines at some length and with obvious emotions his own position (2:15–21).

While at the beginning of his account he prefers a matter-of-fact kind of style— once colored by a quotation from the prophets (1:15: Jer 1:5; Isa 49:1)—gradually he changes his tone, first underlining the trustworthiness of his words (1:20, later not only employing words he used before in describing his own conversion, his present activity and the revelation as the factor behind it,[53] but also resorting both to such a

---

[51] Gal 1:10–12: "For do I now try to persuade men, or God? Or do I seek to please men? For if I still tried to please men, I should not be Christ's servant. But I assure you, brethren, that the gospel which was preached by me is not according to man. For I neither received it from any man, nor was I taught it, but (I received it) through the revelation of Jesus Christ."

[52] Gal 1:13–2:14 or 2:21. Experts disagree whether this section ends at 2:14 or should be extended to 2:21, i.e., whether the last seven verses are a summary of what he said in Antioch. See, e.g., Betz, *Galatians*, 113–14 and n. 6 (= *Galaterbrief*, 212–13 n. 1). What matters, to my mind, is that Paul adopts a different style again for these verses and uses them to move from the report of his past to the message he wants to preach to the Galatians.

[53] Cf. Rahlfs, *Septuaginta*, 2:656 (Jeremiah 1:5) and 2:633 (Isaiah 49:1). Gal 1:13: "That excessively I persecuted the Church of God, and tried to destroy it" (cf. 1:23); "that I might proclaim him amongst the gentiles" (1:16; cf. 1:23; 2:2); "revelation" (1:12; cf. 1:16; 2:1).

polemical expression as "false brothers" (ψευδάδελφοι: 2:4) and to words with emotional appeal (2:4: "liberty" [ἐλευθερία] and 2:5: "truth of the gospel" [ἀλήθεια τοῦ
εὐαγγελίου]) in order to stress his own steadfastness and the reputation he enjoyed
with James, Peter and John. Again in the final section he allows emotions to gain
more and more ground: *antitheta, polyptōta* and suchlike figures as well as metaphorical and paradoxical expressions abound.[54]

Before one determines the function of this section either with the help of a rhetorical classification or on the basis of stylistic observations or otherwise, one should look
at the rest of the letter and examine how what was said so far serves as preparation for
the following chapters, how, if at all, it is related to what follows. The first words of the
next chapter may cause astonishment. Paul rebukes the addressees of his epistle: "You
stupid Galatians " (3:1: ῏Ω ἀνόητοι Γαλάται). However, such a move is not entirely
uncommon in letters (or even in speeches), when a particular effect is intended,[55] and
this is obviously the case here. After indicating at the beginning that the Galatians had
been turned away by certain people from the true gospel (i.e., that which he had
preached to them: 1:6–9), he now addresses them directly in order to lead them back to
the right path (3:1–5). Once more, the tone changes. Paul begins with a number of
questions to shake up his addressees, to make them consider and reconsider what they
are doing, what was preached to them, what is being offered to them and by whom and
wherefrom: "works of the law " (ἔργα νόμου) or "hearing of the faith" (ἀκοὴ
πίστεως), a contrast which pointedly repeated as rebuke[56] cannot easily be overheard.
This is the subject-matter of the following example: Abraham as testimony for faith,
but also as someone whose blessing even the gentiles will receive through Jesus Christ
(3:6–14). "Works of the law" and "faith" continue to dominate the next section, introduced with the address "Brethren" (ἀδελφοί: 3:15) to win the audience, a section in
which Paul first adduces the example of the last will (3:15–18) to illustrate the validity
of God's promises, and then discusses the Jewish law which had but a temporary function until the coming of the faith (3:23; that is Christ: 3:24); and to this argument he
adds several lines of promise and encouragement to the Galatians, thus emphasizing
the immediate relevance for them of the preceding arguments.

In an even more immediate manner Paul combines promise and argument at the
beginning of chapter four, where he pronounces rather than proves that through
Jesus Christ God freed those subjected to the law (4:1–7), applying this both to himself and the Galatians by using "we" and "you."[57] In the same vein he continues with
questions and requests, expressing more than once his special concern for the Galatians (4:8–20); and he adds yet another example from the Old Testament with a

---

[54] *Antitheta:* Gal 2:15, 16, 20; *polyptota:* 2:16–17, 19, 20–21; metaphorical and paradoxical expressions: 2:18, 19, 20.

[55] The theory knows the "blaming" (μεμπτικός), "reproachful" (ὀνειδιστικός), "censorious" (ἐπιτιμητικός), "vituperative" (ψεκτικός), and "accusing" (κατηγορικός) types; cf. Pseudo-
Demetrius, *Typ. epist.* praef.; 3; 4; 6; 9; 17 (Weichert, *Demetri*, pp. 2, 4–6, 9).

[56] Cf. 3:1 and 3:2; "works of the law": 3:2, 5, 10; "law": 3:10, 11, 12, 13, 18, 19, 21, 23 and 24;
"hearing of the faith": 3:2; "faith": 3:7, 8, 9, 11, 12, 14, 22, 23, 24, 25 and 26.

[57] "We": 4:3, 5, 6; "you": 4:6, 8–21.

lengthy interpretation (4:22–31) to illustrate once more the difference between slavery and freedom. Paul uses these as the key terms in the following chapters for a long series of admonitions and warnings (5:1–6:10), before he ends with an unusually long postscript in his own hand and the blessing.[58]

This brief analysis with a few remarks on Paul's style shows, I trust, sufficiently what the apostle is aiming at here. Faced with reports on activities of people in Galatia who spread some teaching different from his own, he seeks first briefly to establish his position as apostle and to draw a clear line between the εὐαγγέλιον he preaches and the message of the others, before he speaks of his past activities, obviously in view of and in response to accusations which were leveled against him. Only after establishing (or reestablishing) his authority and clearly stating his own views (as he maintained them even in opposition to Peter), he turns to the main subject of this letter, the relationship between law and faith, the function of the law in the past, the liberation through Christ, and the meaning of both freedom and faith and their vital importance for people's lives.

Anyone attempting to explain this work with the help of ancient, that is Greek and/or Roman, rhetoric and/or ancient theory of epistolography will soon discover that the function of numerous particular features in the area of "style" (elocutio) may easily be explained in terms of traditional rhetoric. Also numerous arguments can be analyzed in this manner (and this was realized centuries ago and never quite forgotten). But one will also find that the structure of this letter differs fundamentally from the "ideal" structure of a logos as recommended by rhetorical theory. The address is followed by what one might call an exordium ("introduction"); but its unusual elements must be taken as a warning that what follows is not one of the three traditional types of logos distinguished by rhetorical theory; indeed neither a judicial nor a deliberative nor a demonstrative type of speech would have been appropriate here, as Paul is neither addressing a court of law from which he expects a verdict at the end, nor an assembly which will pass a resolution, let alone praising an individual or a group.

It is not surprising that the categories of ancient rhetoric fail us with respect to the structure of this epistle, because it is an epistle, and they were not made nor meant to fit such kinds of composition. Instead, one might turn to such lists of types of letters as are provided by Pseudo-Demetrius and Pseudo-Libanius. However, whether their numerous types offer much help is another matter. For even when one decides—not without hesitation—in favor of the τύπος νουθετητικός ("admonishing") or διδασκαλικός ("didactic"),[59] such a term alone does not really assist one in understanding the letter's intention or any of its details.

However, as Betz is more optimistic with regard to the application of the categories of ancient rhetoric, we have to look briefly at his methods and results. Both in his early article and in his commentary on the letter to the Galatians he states that rhetoric and epistolography help to understand Paul's epistles, and he states that

---

[58] Gal 6:11–18: see Schnider and Stenger, Studien, 135–67, esp. 145–51.

[59] Cf. Pseudo-Demetrius, Typ. epist. 7 (Weichert, p. 6); Pseudo-Libanius, Epist. char. 27; 72 (Weichert, pp. 18, 29–30; see also 47–48).

certain sections are to be given particular labels.[60] He does not seem to offer any arguments, even though he himself complains that "despite an extensive search, I have not been able to find any consideration given to possible criteria and methods for determining such an outline" (of the epistle as often given in commentaries).[61] Moreover, Betz states as his thesis that Paul's letter to the Galatians is an example of the apologetic letter genre which, as he informs us with reference to several publications of the distinguished ancient historian A. Momigliano, arose in the fourth century B.C. and presupposes the "letter" form, as well as the genres of "autobiography" and "apologetic speech." He then shows that, apart from such features which are typical for an epistle as prescript and postscript, the traditional *partes orationis* follow, first the *exordium* in which the reasons are stated why the letter was written.[62]

Any piece of writing has a beginning, as does any kind of orderly speech, so that certain agreements and similarities between a letter and a speech are to be expected; they cannot be used to prove that Paul gave this letter the structure of a *logos*. However, the rules for *exordia* of speeches may, as was shown above, be used to appreciate particular features of epistles also, whether the writer follows the recommendations of the theory or ignores them. The section 1:12–2:14 is understood by Betz as *narratio*.[63] Kennedy has said what needs to be said to show this to be erroneous:[64] The narrative of the first and second chapters of Galatians is "not an account of the facts at issue." [65] Their real function was seen and explained by an expert on ancient rhetoric more than fifteen centuries ago, by Marius Victorinus who, in summarizing this section, says "with (the apostle's) authority having been strengthened" or "reestablished" *(confirmata igitur auctoritate)*.[66] The apostle is anxious first of all to establish or reestablish his own authority before discussing any details. Parallels for this procedure can easily be found in speeches delivered in the courts of law,[67] and in

---

[60] Cf. Betz, "Literary Composition," 9–24 (= *Paulinische Studien,* 70–91); *Galatians,* 16–22 (= *Galaterbrief,* 57–66), and context.

[61] Betz, "Literary Composition," 3 (= *Paulinische Studien,* 63).

[62] Ibid., 5–12 (= *Paulinische Studien,* 64–75); *Galatians,* 14–15, 44–46 (= *Galaterbrief,* 54–56, 98–102). I fail to see how Momigliano's works on Greek biography support Betz' thesis; see also n. 72 below.

[63] Betz, "Literary Composition," 12–17 (= *Paulinische Studien,* 75–81); *Galatians,* 16–18, 57–62 (= *Galaterbrief,* 58–60, 112–28).

[64] Kennedy, *New Testament Interpretation,* 144–46. However, his view that the epistle to the Galatians belongs to the deliberative genre (145) is not convincing either (even though it has been accepted e.g., by Smit, "Letter of Paul," and F. Vouga, "Zur rhetorischen Gattung"; for the addressees are not called upon to take a decision as a group as e.g., the Athenian assembly or the Roman senate.

[65] Cicero, *Inv.* 1.27 distinguishes three types of *narratio,* one as digression, one for pleasure *(delectationis causa)* and a third kind, "in which the case itself and the whole reason for the controversy is comprised" *(genus, in quo ipsa causa et omnis ratio controversiae continetur);* cf. also Quintilian, *Inst.* 4.2.31, who quotes amongst others the definition given by Apollodorus that *narratio* is "a speech instructing the audience as to the nature of the case in dispute" *(oratio docens auditorem, quid in controversia sit).*

[66] Cf. Locher, *Commentarii,* 1, or Gori, *Opera exegetica,* 96; on his commentaries see Souter, *Earliest Latin Commentaries,* 8–38 (also on "Ambrosiaster," 39–95; Jerome, 96–138; Augustine, 139–204; and Pelagius, 205–30); and Erdt, *Marius Victorinus Afer.*

[67] Cf. Cicero, *Mur.* 2–10; *Sull.* 3–10; 17–20; 21–29; *Dom.* 3–32; also *Rab. Perd.* 10–17; *Sest.* 36–52. See also Classen, *Recht Rhetorik Politik,* 127–34, esp. 224 n. 27.

so far one can certainly learn a good deal from oratorical practice for the interpretation of epistles.

What about the other parts of this "apologetic letter"? Betz finds 2:15–21 conforming to the form, function and requirements of the *propositio* and claims that this passage is a summary of the doctrine of justification by faith.[68] Even if one does not regard these verses as a summary of Paul's speech at Antioch, they are clearly formulated in a very personal way in the first person singular or plural, and this is not the way he talks later in the third and fourth chapter after turning to the Galatians. The difficulties Betz has in discovering the traditional pattern of a *logos* in Paul's letter become even more obvious in the second half, as he is forced to call a long section (about a third of the whole) "*paraenesis*" or "*exhortatio*" (5:1–6:10)[69] which may have a place in other types of letters, but not in an apologetic one (let alone in an apologetic *logos*). This alone should have warned Betz not to apply too rashly categories to this letter that were developed for another genre and are, therefore, not applicable except for selected aspects and features. The fact that one element (or possibly two) of the traditional ("ideal") structure seem to occur in a composition does not warrant the inference that the other parts must be discoverable there as well or that the composition as a whole conforms to such a pattern. In the epistle to the Galatians the main body is not concerned with Paul's defense, and there is no reason, therefore, to regard it as an "apologetic letter," even less so, because the examples Betz cites are quite different, and the model of an "apologetic letter," as it is found in Pseudo-Demetrius, shows no resemblance either.[70]

This takes us back to the original questions asked at the beginning, and I shall try now to combine the answers to them with an assessment of the possibilities and merits of rhetorical criticism of the epistles of the New Testament, of its limits and its dangers. It has become clear, I hope, that rhetoric (oratory) and epistolography were regarded as two different fields in antiquity; and it seems advisable, therefore, not only to keep them apart, but to ask also how and why they differed so substantially in the elaboration and presentation of their respective theory. The writers of manuals on rhetoric,[71] though aware of the great variety of speeches required by the realities

---

[68] See Betz, "Literary Composition," 17–18 (= *Paulinische Studien*, 81–82); *Galatians*, 18–19, 113–14 (= *Galaterbrief*, 60–61, 212–15); on the controversy with regard to this section see above, n. 52.

[69] On paraenesis: Betz, "Literary Composition," 24–26 (= *Paulinische Studien*, 91–93); *exhortatio: Galatians*, 22–23, 253–311 (= *Galaterbrief*, 66–68, 433–528). The corresponding type of letter is called παραινετική: Pseudo-Libanius, *Epist. char.* Praef.; 1. See also the examples: 1; 90; 91 (Weichert, pp. 14, 15, 21–22, 56–57).

[70] Betz, "Literary Composition," 4–5 (= *Paulinische Studien*, 64–65); *Galatians*, 14–15 (= *Galaterbrief*, 54–56). For the "apologetic type" of letter (ἀπολογητικός), see Pseudo-Libanius, *Epist. char.* praef.; 18 (Weichert, pp. 2, 9–10; cf. also Pseudo-Libanius, *Epist. char.* 15 [Weichert, pp. 16–17]); for some examples see Stowers, *Letter Writing*, 167–70.

[71] Editions by Kassel (Aristotle); Fuhrmann (Anaximenes); Marx *(Rhetorica ad Herennium)*; Stroebel, Kumaniecki, and Westman (all Cicero); Winterbottom (Quintilian). For the need of flexibility in applying the rules see, e.g., *Rhet. Her.* 3.17: "But there is also another form of arrangement which when one must depart from the order imposed by the rules of the art, is accommodated to circumstance in accordance with the speaker's judgment" *(est autem alia dispositio, quae cum ab ordine artificioso recedendum est, oratoris iudicio ad tempus adcommodatur).*

of life, nevertheless did venture to construe a standard structure, at the same time allowing for flexibility in its application and giving advice on particular forms. Those trying to formulate general rules for the writing of letters, on the other hand, aware of the even greater variety of letters actually written by people, did not propose an ideal structure or perhaps two—at least we have no knowledge of anything like that. They merely listed many various types together with recommendations for the appropriate style in each case. Thus for the analysis of epistles of the New Testament the theory of epistolography will be of use with regard to matters of style, while the large number of actual letters in their manifoldness will provide material for comparison.[72] The theory of rhetoric on the other hand, though developed for another area, together with practical oratory, will also render service, but again within limits, that is in the areas of *inventio* ("invention") especially for the argumentation and *elocutio* ("style"), where there is overlapping with the theory of epistolography. On *dispositio* ("structure") rhetorical theory may be consulted, but extreme caution is called for, as has been pointed out. Perhaps the most useful aspect which practical oratory can illustrate is that the best orator disguises his knowledge of the theory,[73] that he alters accepted patterns and adjusts them to the particular case and his special intention. Thus, not what conforms to the rules, but what seems at variance with them often proves most instructive for the interpretation. Correspondingly, in trying to understand a particular composition, one should always look not primarily for what is in accordance with the rules or with general practice, but for the contrary.

Secondly, as the example of Melanchthon has shown, there is no reason why one should restrict oneself to the rhetoric of the ancients in interpreting texts from antiquity, and not avail oneself of the discoveries and achievements of more recent times.[74] Thirdly, with regard to the problems raised about the person of Paul himself, his education and the form of rhetoric with which he may have been familiar, and the question whether he employed the tools of rhetoric deliberately, it is not my intention to deal with them here. I would merely like to add one or two observations:[75] (a) that Paul must have read a good deal of Greek literature and thus have come into contact with rhetoric applied, and (b) that he must have been familiar with the Rabbinic tra-

---

[72] See above, n. 14 for the theoretical works on epistolography. Recently much comparative material has been collected and analysed, e.g., by Doty, *Letters;* White, *Light;* Stowers, *Letter Writing;* and the works listed in their bibliographies (White, *Light,* 221–24; Stowers, *Letter Writing,* 177–79). To my mind it is more promising and fruitful to set Paul's epistles against the whole range of Hellenistic literature with its variety of genres, see, e.g., Berger, "Hellenistische Gattungen"; and also, of course, against the Jewish (Rabbinic) tradition.

[73] On the *dissimulatio artis* see Neumeister, *Grundsätze,* 130–55.

[74] See above, n. 8, especially Wuellner, "Where?" and his other articles, listed in Porter and Olbricht, *Rhetoric and the New Testament,* 19–20. Successful and convincing in applying modern rhetoric are, e.g., Siegert, *Argumentation bei Paulus;* with special emphasis on sociological aspects; Robbins, *Jesus the Teacher;* and even more so Petersen, *Rediscovering Paul;* see further F. Watson, *Paul.* On the other hand, in my view misguided is Kinneavey, *Greek Rhetorical Origins,* because the parallels which he points out do not prove what they are supposed to prove.

[75] It should not be overlooked that Paul at least once uses a technical term (2 Cor 3:1): συστατικαὶ ἐπιστολαί, cf. Pseudo-Demetrius, *Typ. epist.* praef.; 2 (Weichert, pp. 2–3); Pseudo-Libanius, *Epist. char.* praef.; 4; 95 (Weichert, pp. 14, 16, 22, 58).

dition of interpreting the Old Testament and thus have been sensitive to the possibilities inherent in language. As regards the stage in the development of rhetoric which he may or may not have known, it should be remembered that the essential insights, classifications and rules, once formulated by the Greeks, remained largely unchanged for centuries. Furthermore, one should not forget that the occurrence of rhetorical figures does not allow the inference that an author employed them because he was familiar with a theory; for they recommended themselves in practice long before any theory was ever developed (Quintilian, *Inst.* 2.17.5–9), and they are found in authors who were never exposed to any such theory in any form.

However, it does not follow that rhetorical theory cannot render useful service in such cases. Whether a writer or a speaker had knowledge of such a theory or not, whether he was familiar with literature written under the influence of such a theory or not, for the interpretation of texts from any period rhetorical theory offers a most helpful set of instruments which have to be used, however, with the greatest care possible.

Rhetorical and Epistolary Genre

Section B
Epistolary Approaches

7

PAUL'S LETTER TO THE GALATIANS: EPISTOLARY GENRE, CONTENT, AND STRUCTURE[1]

Nils A. Dahl

The Ironic Rebuke and Related Features

A. Form and usage

The most obvious peculiarity of Galatians in comparison with the other letters of Paul is the absence of an initial assertion of thanksgiving. As generally recognized, this is an indication of a strained relationship between sender and recipients. Second Corinthians provides a partial analogy. The opening of a letter with benediction (εὐλογία, *berakah*) may serve as a variant to the epistolary thanksgiving in the style of Jewish praise and prayer (cf. Eph 1:3; 1 Pet 1:3). But in 2 Cor 1:3–4 the benediction does not refer to what God has done to the recipients of the letter and to all Christians but to what God has done to the sender, comforting and rescuing him and thus enabling him to comfort others. At the time of writing, the relations between Paul and the Christians at Corinth were too strained to allow for the usual thanksgiving. This explanation applies even more to Galatians. At the place where we normally find an assertion of thanksgiving or a benediction, that is, immediately after the salutation, Galatians has an expression of astonishment (θαυμάζω, Gal 1:6).

---

[1] The original 1973 paper presented to the SBL Paul Seminar contained five sections, of which two have been edited for publication here (originally in the paper as "The Ironic Rebuke and Related Features," 12–36, and "Structure and Purpose," 76–101). Omitted entirely here are the introduction, "The Problem of Classification," 2–11; section 3, "Apologetic Autobiography," 36–52; section 4, "Interpretation of Scripture and Paraenesis," 52–76; and several charts and appendixes. The original endnotes were no longer attached; works of authors cited in the text as well as primary sources, however, have been reconstructed. The Greek and Latin texts have been updated and, where Dahl did not provide a translation, this has been supplied from the Loeb Classical Library or, in the case of biblical citations, the RSV. For further indications of the literature with which Dahl interacts and additional insights on epistolography, see Dahl, "Letter"; in *Studies in Ephesians:* "Benediction and Congratulation," 279–314; "Das Proömium des Epheserbriefes," 315–34. *Ed.*

Commentators have been fully aware of this peculiarity, but most of them have failed to observe that, while the opening with θαυμάζω ("I am astonished/surprised/amazed/I wonder") is unique among Paul's letters, it nevertheless accords with epistolary conventions no less than an opening with thanksgiving (εὐχαριστῶ). Some parallels from papyrus letters have been adduced by various scholars. A closer analysis of the usage was made by Terence Mullins, who pointed out that an epistolary θαυμάζω usually, but not always, introduces a reproach or a rebuke.[2] I retain the term "ironic rebuke," coined by him, even though the phrase has become such a conventional form for a rebuke that irony is not always felt. The appropriateness of the word "ironic," however, would have been confirmed if Mullins had taken greater account of letters in literary transmission and of model letters. As Wettstein had pointed out, the phraseology in Gal 1:6, θαυμάζω ὅτι οὕτως ταχέως μετατίθεσθε ἀπὸ . . . εἰς . . . ("I am astonished that you are so quickly deserting . . . turning to . . .") has a significant parallel in the model of an "ironic letter" (εἰρωνική) in the handbook of Pseudo-Libanius's *Epistolimaioi charactēres* (Ἐπιστολιμαῖοι χαρακτῆρες) (no. 56): Λίαν ἄγαμαι τὴν σὴν ἐπιείκειαν, ὅτι οὕτω ταχέως μεταβάλλη ἀπ᾽ εὐνομίας εἰς τὸ ἐναντίον ("I am greatly astonished at your sense of equity, that you have so quickly rushed from a well-ordered life to its opposite").[3] Atticism accounts for the choice of ἄγαμαι over θαυμάζω. The latter verb is used in the example of a "reproach letter" (ὀνειδιστική), which is contained in some of the manuscripts of the handbook (no. 64): Πολλὰ καλὰ πέπονθας ὑφ᾽ ἡμῶν καὶ θαυμάζω καθ᾽ ὑπερβολήν, πῶς οὐδενὸς τούτων μνείαν ποιεῖς, ἀλλὰ κακῶς ἡμᾶς λέγεις ("You have received many favors from us, and I am exceedingly amazed that you remember none of them but speak badly of us"). The affinity of the two subgenres, ironic and oneidistic letter, is obvious, as is the affinity of Galatians to both of them.

My collection of data is certainly far from complete, but it leaves no doubt that θαυμάζω used with a note of irony and/or disapproval occurs more frequently in ancient letters than does εὐχαριστῶ used to assert thanksgiving rendered to the gods. The usage extends over a period of a thousand years, ca. 400 B.C.E. to ca. 600 C.E. Like εὐχαριστῶ, θαυμάζω is often used as an opening formula, but can also occur in the middle or toward the end of a letter. From a functional point of view, an expression of astonishment is one among several epistolary phrases that are used to express the mood of the sender and his disposition toward the addressees, sentiments of joy or grief, worry, distress, concern, and so forth. It is therefore misleading simply to say that the assertion of thanksgiving has been left out in Galatians; it has been exchanged for an expression of astonishment and disapproval.

In epistolary usage, as otherwise, θαυμάζω allows for various constructions. Usually, at least in papyrus letters, the verb is followed by a subordinate clause introduced by εἰ, εἴπερ, πῶς, or ὅτι. To some extent, the conjugations are interchangeable, but usage also varies to some degree according to the context. If one really

---

[2] Mullins, "Formulas," esp. 385–86; see also White, *Form and Function,* 34–36, 80.
[3] Cf. Wettstein, *Novum Testamentum graecum* 2.216 n. 6. All citations and translations for Pseudo-Libanius are from Malherbe, *Ancient Epistolary Theorists,* 66–81.

wonders and does not know, θαυμάζω εἰ is the most natural construction. But the same construction can also express reproach and disappointment. The form θαυμάζω πῶς has connotations such as "How is it possible?" or "What is the reason that . . . ?" It is frequently used when the astonishment is caused by the recipient's failure to communicate. Θαυμάζω ὅτι would seem to be a strong expression of disapproval of some action or negligence on the part of the recipient. It is hardly accidental that Paul uses this form in Gal 1:6. Prepositional phrases also occur, but the distinctions among the various constructions are not clear.

Even in reproaches, θαυμάζω is mainly used when the relationship between sender and recipient is basically good or has been good in the past. The verb occurs in several letters that also contain philophronetic phrases, such as a health wish. In distinction from other forms of rebuke, θαυμάζω is an expression of disappointment; the sender would have expected another kind of behavior. In private papyrus letters, the ironic rebuke most frequently refers to the addressee's failure to communicate. A typical example is P.Oxy. I 123.5–9 (about third–fourth century): "I am very much surprised [πάνυ θαυμάζω], my son, that till today I have not received any letter from you, telling me about your welfare. Nevertheless, my master, reply to me promptly, for I am quite distressed [πάνυ γὰρ θλείβομαι] at having no letter from you." Comparison with another letter illustrates the degree to which personal feelings were expressed by means of conventional phrases: "But I am surprised that no one has brought a letter from you and I am distressed [ἀθυμῶ] for this reason" (P.Corn. 52.5–7; third century).

In such cases, the ironic rebuke is an indirect "expression of affection and concern" (φιλοφρόνησις) for the addressees. The sender is disappointed because he has not had any news about the recipient and his well-being or because an opportunity of being together has been missed. These stereotyped reproaches for failing to communicate are frequent in private letters from the second century C.E. onward. But both Latin and Greek evidence proves that the form is older.

The ironic rebuke is not limited to the conventional usage in private letters. It is also used, especially in private and other business letters, to rebuke a person for his negligence, his failure to comply with instructions, or for some inappropriate or foolish action of his. Thus, the recipient can be reproached because he has failed to take care of the body of his dead brother (P.Grenf. II 77; third/fourth century) or because he has not sent what the addressor had written about and was in need of (P.Oxy. I 113.20–30; second century).

B. Early Examples

Isocrates' letter to Archidemus, if genuine, contains the first epistolary use of θαυμάζω known to me: "I marvel [Θαυμάζω] also at those men who have ability in action or in speech that it has never occurred to them to take seriously to heart the conditions which effect all Greeks alike" (*Ep.* 9.8; 356 B.C.E.). Here the astonishment is caused by a third party, but in spite of the private address, the rebuke is clearly intended for the public. In Demosthenes' third letter, to "The Council and People of

Athens," the irony is directed toward the recipients: "I am amazed [Θαυμάζω . . . εἰ] if none of you thinks that it is a disgraceful thing for the people of Athens, who are supposed to be superior to all men in understanding and culture and have also maintained here for the unfortunate a common refuge in all ages, to show themselves less considerate to Philip. . . . Moreover, I am amazed [θαυμάζω . . . εἰ] if any one of you is ignorant of this fact also" (*Ep.* 3.11, 23; 324–322 B.C.E.). This "public" letter is almost a written speech, giving "advice" and seeking to "persuade" (συμβουλευτικόν, δημηγορία); it was sent by the exiled orator, who asks for clemency toward the sons of Lycurgus and for himself, too. Θαυμάζω is not used in the opening of the letter, and not in a formulaic way. But the early examples may indicate that the epistolary convention has its roots in the rhetorical use of θαυμάζω.

In any case, the formulaic use of θαυμάζω was well established before the middle of the third century B.C.E. The earliest examples occur in business letters that belong to the Zenon papyri:

P.Cair.Zen. I 59060.10 (257 B.C.E., Hierocles to Zenon):

ἔγραψας δέ μοι θαυμάζεις εἰ μὴ κατέχω ὅτι . . . ("You wrote to me that you were surprised that I did not realize . . .");[4]

PSI V 502.11–12 (257/256 B.C.E., copy of letter from Panakestor to Apollonius, sent to Zenon):

Ἐκομισάμην τὴν παρου σου ἐπιστολὴν . . . ἐν ἧι γράφεις θαυμάζω ὅτι οὐθέν σοι ἀπέσταλκα περὶ τῆς συντιμήσεως καὶ τῆς συναγωγῆς τοῦ σπόρου ("I received your letter . . . in which you express astonishment that I have sent you no word about the valuation and the gathering of the crops").[5]

The examples illustrate the two main usages of the form. In *PSI* V 502 the rebuke is caused by failing communication; in P.Cair.Zen. I 59060.10, by negligence or lack of understanding (cf. also *SB* V 8244.3–4, 10–11, Zenon to Kleitarchos). In the first two response letters, θαυμάζειν can be used even if the first writer employed another verb of rebuke, as shown by the preserved part of the letter from Apollonius to Panakestor (*PSI* V 502.8–9): Κατεπλησσόμην τὴν ὀλιγωρίαν σου ἐπὶ τῶι μηθὲν γεγραφέναι μήτε περὶ τῆσεως μήτε περὶ τῆς συναγωγῆς τοῦ σίτου ("I am astounded by your negligence in not having written either about the valuation or about the gathering of the crops").[6]

A very remarkable example of the form occurs in the collection of letters contained in P.Paris 63 (Oct. 23, 164 B.C.E.), reprinted in *UPZ* I 110.20–192, which were apparently copied by professional scribes and future administrators as a part of their training. In the letter of interest to us, Herodes, probably the royal Ptolemaic secretary of finance, writes to a local administrator, the *hypodioikētēs*, Dorion, reproaching him that he and his associates have misunderstood, objected to, and failed to enact re-

---

[4] Citation and translation from White, *Light,* 38.
[5] Ibid., 42.
[6] Ibid., 42.

peated and clear instructions concerning the drafting of laborers for cultivation of the royal estates. The letter is a school example of exquisite chancellery style, labored beyond reasonable limits. The θαυμάζω period extends over sixty-one lines, "the largest period that we know of in papyrus literature."[7] The basic structure is nevertheless that of an ironic rebuke (note lines 34–36, 78–79, 83–84, 85).[8] The space between the conjunction (εἰ of lines 34–35) and the first predicate of the subordinate clause that it introduces is filled by a series of absolute genitives, seven in all, with a number of qualifying prepositional phrases, infinitives, subordinate clauses, and so forth (lines 35–78). A reference to previous instructions and/or some other aggravating circumstance is often part of the ironic rebuke. Only the number and length of the phrases is extraordinary. The blatant irony is as obvious in Herodes' letter to Dorion as it is in Paul's letter to the churches in Galatia.

C. Latin letters

The ironic rebuke is found in Latin as well as in Greek letters. Some of Cicero's letters illustrate the combination of the formula with other expressions of disappointment, rebuke, and irony. In a letter to Trebatius, Cicero says that he was already astonished to have received no letter, when—to his even greater surprise—he learned that his friend had become an Epicurean (*Fam.* 7.12; 53 B.C.E.):

> I was wondering [*mirabar*] why it was that you had stopped writing to me. Well, my friend Pansa has let it out—you have turned Epicurean! What a marvellous camp! What would you have done had I sent you, not to Samarobriva, but to Tarentum?

Most of the letter is made up of more or less ironic questions, several of which point to aggravating factors.

In a highly agitated state of mind during April or May of 49 B.C.E., Cicero wrote a letter to his protégé M. Caelius. Caelius had written that he surmised from a previous letter of Cicero's (which is not preserved) that the latter planned to leave Italy and join Pompeius (Cicero, *Fam.* 8.16). That was in fact exactly what Cicero did on June 7. But a month or so earlier, Cicero rebukes his young friend that he should nourish any such idea (*Fam.* 2.16.1):

> I should have been deeply grieved at your letter had not my own reflection by this time stifled all sense of irritation. . . . What surprises me [*illud miror*] is that you, who ought to know my inmost heart, could ever have been induced to regard me as either so shortsighted as to desert a cause exalted to such a height for one that is tottering and all but prostrate, or so inconsistent as to forfeit in a moment all the favor I had accumulated in the eyes of one now in the heyday of his prosperity, to prove myself a

---

[7] *UPZ* I 489.
[8] Ἐθαυμάξομεν οὖν, εἰ τοσούτων καὶ τηλικούτων διαστολῶν γεγονυιῶν ὑμῖν. . . . (lines 34–36)
τούτων μὲν πάντων ἀμνηστίαν ἐσχήκατε. . . . (lines 78–79)
ἐπὶ δὲ τοσοῦτον εὐγνωμοσύνης ἐληλύθατε. . . . (lines 83–84)
ὥστε. . . . (line 85)

renegade from my own principles and—what I have always avoided from the very first—to engage in a civil war.

The letter contains a number of questions that express astonishment, not without elements of irony.

Even writing to Atticus, Cicero can adopt the style of the rebuking, ironic letter, at least in one segment of a letter (*Att.* 16.7; Aug. 19, 44 B.C.E.):

> when I read your letter, I was certainly surprised [*admiratus equidem sum*] that you had so utterly changed your opinion; but there seemed to me to be good reason for it. . . . What did astonish me beyond measure [*illud admirari satis non potui*] was that you should use the words: "A fine thing for you, who talk of a noble death [εὐθανασίαν], a fine thing! Go, desert your country."

In this, as in several other cases, the ironic rebuke is occasioned by reproach and even by irony from the side of the partner in the correspondence.

That the expression of astonishment had become a conventional formula, even in Latin letters, may be illustrated best by a dispatch from Pompeius to one of his generals, the proconsul L. Domitius, written in February 49 B.C.E., shortly before Pompeius had to leave Italy with his troops (Cicero, *Att.* 8.12b). Pompeius first expresses his "great amazement" *(Valde miror)* that Domitius has not written, with the result that he had to be informed about the political situation by others. Next, Pompeius complains that the proconsul had not, as previously arranged, started to move so that the two might join their armies but had instead changed his plan: "I wonder [*miror*] what reason there has been for your change of plan." There is not much irony in this letter, but the note is one of bad disappointment and perplexity. The structure of the letter is made up of two parts, of which the first, dominated by the rebuke, provides the background for the second, and urgent, begging request, that Domitius might after all come as soon as possible: "Wherefore again and again I entreat and exhort you—as I did in my previous letter—to come to Luceria on the first possible day, before . . ."

I have commented briefly on the historical setting and general content of some sample letters that not only contain an ironic rebuke but also other features that have counterparts in the whole of Paul's letter to the Galatians. It would be worthwhile to identify the genres, or various types, of letters of rebuke or reprimand that may or may not at the same time be ironic letters. But that would require a more systematic collection of material than I have been able to undertake. It would have to be taken into account that the ironic rebuke is a form that is not as such constitutive of any genre; there exist letters of rebuke and even ironic letters in which this form does not occur. There are also letters in which the θαυμάζω period is only one element and is not determinative for the structure. But in default of any thorough investigation of the relevant epistolary types, it is of interest to us that the θαυμάζω period in Gal 1:6 is not to be seen as an isolated formula but must be seen in conjunction with other, related features, such as direct questions, irony, reproaches, and so forth.

D. Aggravating circumstances

The constitutive elements of the ironic rebuke are a verb of astonishment, usually θαυμάζω, used as an expression of the sender's disapproval, and an indication of the action or negligence for which the addressee is rebuked. A number of related features occur more or less frequently in letters that contain an ironic rebuke. Most prominent among them is an indication of one or several aggravating circumstances that ought to have made the recipient act otherwise and give the sender additional reasons for his dissatisfaction. Such factors are often mentioned within the θαυμάζω period. The most regular construction is one or more absolute genitives. But even when the aggravating circumstance is added in an independent clause, it is so closely linked to the ironic rebuke that it must be considered an optional element of the form itself. The reasons given for sharp disapproval vary according to the nature of the basic fault and the epistolary situation in general. But several factors recur with some regularity. Here I am mostly concerned with those that can also be found in Paul's letter to the Galatians.

1. *Opportunity.* In private letters, the complaint about failing communication may be sharpened by reference to the arrival of a person who could have brought a message if the addressee had cared to send one.

2. *Prior instruction.* The addressee's failure to comply with given instructions is adduced as a reason for surprise. In letters of various kinds, the addressee may be blamed for not having written in spite of the admonitions of the sender. The long series of absolute genitives in the letter of Herodes, the secretary of finance, enumerates the explicit instructions that had been given on various occasions (cf. *UPZ* I 110.35–36; *SB* V 8244.3–4; *BGU* III 850.3; Cicero, *Fam.* 2.16.3; Gal. 1:9).

The passage from Galatians is not quite typical, since the recipient churches would not have recognized that Paul's prior statement applied to their case. But Paul has formulated his rebuke in such a way that it does. As he sees and states it, they have turned to "another gospel" (Gal 1:6–7); the anathema pronounced upon anyone who would preach a gospel that differed from the one that they had received from Paul does therefore become an aggravating circumstance in their case.

3. *Promise, better knowledge, and so forth.* More general statements—for example, that the addressee had promised to do otherwise or that he ought to have known better—can fulfil the same function as references to prior instructions (cf. P.Bad. II 35.3; P.Mert. II 80.5–6; P.Lips. 107.4–5; Cicero, *Fam.* 2.16.1; Gal 3:1; 4:9).

4. *Foolishness.* Related to complaints about the obliviousness of the addressees are also remarks that the sender would not have expected them to be so stupid (Demothenes, *Ep.* 3.11, 23; P.Cair.Zen. I 59060.10; *UPZ* I 110.83ff., 94ff.; P.Bad. II 35.10; P.Grenf. II 77:9–10; P.Gen. I 57.3; Gal 3:1, 3).

The ironic formulation in the letter of Herodes deserves special attention. But even in Gal 3:1, 3 there is more irony than commentators usually observe. The only other passage in which Paul uses the word ἀνόητος is Rom 1:14. As a synonym of "barbarian" (βάρβαρος) and an antonym of "wise" (σοφός), the word "foolish" (ἀνόητος) means uncivilized or uneducated. In Gal 3:1 Paul plays with a double meaning of the word. By his time, the Galatians had been hellenized but had not completely escaped the ancient reputation that they were barbarians, uncivilized, rude and cruel people. I suspect that the phrase "foolish Galatians" (ἀνόητοι Γαλάται) had been used in this sense by Paul's opponents, who said that he had treated the Galatians condescendingly, as unsophisticated barbarians who should not be bothered by observation of complicated ritual law. Paul picks up the phrase and gives it another twist. Whether the Galatians are civilized is no concern of his. But he would not have expected them to be so stupid that they would let themselves be bewitched to turn away from the gospel he had preached.

5. *Change of mind.* Like foolishness, change of mind, or of word, can at the same time be a cause for an ironic rebuke and an aggravating circumstance. Pseudo-Libanius's model of an ironic letter (*Epist. char.* 56) has already been mentioned as the most striking analogy to the opening of Galatians, but some other examples can be added: Cicero, *Att.* 1.17; 8.12b; 16.7; P.Bad. II 35.2–10; P.Lips. 107.2–3; Gal 1:6.

The complaint that the addressees have changed their mind or that they have not kept their word underscores the note of disappointment that is inherent in the form of an ironic rebuke.

6. *Benefactions.* In Pseudo-Libanius's model of the reproaching letter (*Epist. char.* 64), the benefits that the addressee has received from the sender are mentioned as a special reason for disapproval of oblivious and ungrateful conduct. This is also the case in an example of the same type in Pseudo-Demetrius's *Typoi epistolikoi* (Τύποι ἐπιστολικοί), in which, however, the rebuke is not stated by means of θαυμάζω (no. 4).[9] The nature of the case makes it probable that prior benefactions were often mentioned as aggravating circumstances in rebuking letters. In his letter to the Galatians, Paul stresses God's benefactions more than his own (e.g., 1:6; 3:1–5; 4:6–7, 8–9), but it is clear that he has been the mediator and has been concerned for the well-being of the addressees (cf. especially 2:5). With the phrase πολλὰ καλὰ πέπονθας ὑφ' ἡμῶν ("you have received many favors from us") in Pseudo-Libanius's model letter of reproach (*Epist. char.* 64), one can compare Paul's question in Gal 3:4: τοσαῦτα ἐπάθετε εἰκῆ ("Did you experience so many things in vain?"); in all probability, πάσχειν here means "to experience," as in ordinary epistolary usage, and not "to suffer," as in other Pauline occurrences.

7. *Friends turned foes.* In Pseudo-Libanius's model of the ironic letter (*Epist. char.* 56), the expression of marvel is followed by the clause ὡς δὲ ἔοικεν, οὐ τοὺς ἐχθροὺς φίλους ποιεῖν παρεσκεύασαι, ἀλλὰ τοὺς φίλους ἐχθρούς ("It seems that you have contrived to make, not friends out of your enemies, but enemies out of your friends"). With this, one can compare Paul's question in Gal 4:16, ὥστε ἐχθρὸς ὑμῶν γέγονα ἀληθεύων ὑμῖν ("Have I then become your enemy by telling you the truth?"). The similarity is mainly verbal. Paul's question may be an allusion to charges made against him. But the theme of friends becoming foes is also attested in other letters and is an indication of the deteriorated relationships that are often part of the general background of letters that contain ironic rebukes.

---

[9] Malherbe, *Ancient Epistolary Theorists*, 35.

The kinds of aggravating circumstances that are mentioned vary according to the behavior that prompted the letter writer to express his surprise. This is especially the case when the writer points out that an offense is more serious than the addressees have realized, as when Paul stresses that the "gospel" to which the churches of Galatian have turned is no other gospel but a distortion of the gospel of Christ (1:7). It is all the more remarkable that a number of formulations or themes that do occur in connection with an ironic rebuke, either in real letters or in model letters, can also be found in Galatians. This also applies to forms of rebuke and expressions of disapproval that have a similar function as the ironic use of θαυμάζω, whether they are used independently or in conjunction with an ironic rebuke.

E. Expressions of distress

Since the ironic rebuke strikes a note of dissatisfaction, it is natural that letters that contain this form also include more direct statements about the sad mood in which the letter is written: Cicero, *Fam.* 2.16; 7.12–14, 27; P.Mich. VIII 479.6; P.Oxy. I 123.8; 1223.16; P.Cornell 52.7; Gal 4:11, 20.

In the private papyrus letters, the reason for the sender's distress is usually the addressee's failure to report and tell that he is in good health. In the letters of Cicero, as in Galatians, the causes are more complicated. Obviously, expressions of anxiety and related emotions occur in many letters that do not contain an ironic rebuke. Yet the combination of both features may be seen as the negative counterpart to the combination of thanksgiving and expressions of joy in letters that are written under happier circumstances.

F. Rebuking and ironic questions

The note of surprise that is struck by the use of θαυμάζω or synonymous verbs can also be expressed by direct questions. In many contexts, a statement such as "I am amazed that you did this" is equivalent to questions such as "Why did you do this?" or "How could you possibly have done this?" Both the statement and the question can function as a rebuke and thus express something more than genuine wondering. The meaning depends upon the context and, in oral speech, upon the modulation of the voice. One of the many functions of interrogative clauses is to draw attention to some surprising fact or to the unreasonableness of an action. It is therefore no surprise to find direct questions of various forms and types used in letters that begin with an expression of astonishment or at least contain one. On the basis of my collection of materials, it must, however, be said that it is not usual in common letters but is fairly characteristic of those that are written in a higher style from Demosthenes onward.

I have already quoted an ironic question that follows the extended ironic rebuke in Herodes' letter to Dorion and that points out how the previous orders have been misunderstood. Some of Cicero's letters are similar to Galatians in that an expression of surprise is followed, and in some cases also preceded, by a number of more or less ironic and/or rebuking questions. A question, or several questions, can also have the same function as a θαυμάζω period and be used in the opening of a letter, that is, immediately after the salutation. This usage is attested in Greek letters, but some ex-amples in the correspondence of Cicero and the younger Pliny are the most illumi-nating among those that I have found. Pliny, in general, is really surprised when he uses *mirari* and related verbs, and often wants to get information. If he is disap-pointed, he does not use the form of the ironic rebuke but does in several cases form his rebuke as a question. Thus a letter of complaint that a friend has failed to write be-gins, "I have had no letter from you for such a long time—is it because all goes well? Or is the reason that all is well but you are too busy; or, if not actually busy, have you little or no opportunity to write a letter? Please end my anxiety—I can't bear it" (Pliny, *Ep.* 3.17). An opening question is also used to rebuke a friend for his long ab-sence from Rome in *Ep.* 7.3.1: "How much longer will you persist in dividing your time between Lucania and Compania?" In this letter there are several questions, some of which are ironic: "How much longer will you be your own master, stay up when you feel inclined, and sleep as long as you like?" (*Ep.* 7.3.2).

In the examples just quoted, Pliny's questions have the same function as the con-ventional θαυμάζω formula that is used to rebuke a person who has failed to write or to appear. It is equally clear that Paul's question in Gal 4:9, πῶς ἐπιστρέφετε πάλιν ("how can you turn back again"), is a variation of the opening rebuke in 1:6. Even some of Paul's other questions function as reproaches, as do some of Cicero's and Pliny's.

A note of irony is more prominent in questions that ask for information that both sender and addressee already know, in order to remind the latter of something to which he has not paid sufficient attention, since he acts as if it were not the case. In Gal 3:2 a question of this type is even introduced by the phrase τοῦτο μόνον θέλω μαθεῖν ἀφ᾽ ὑμῶν ("Let me ask you only this"). A simpler introductory phrase is used by Cicero: "Come now, do you really think you ought to publish without my orders? . . . Do you really think . . . ?" (*Att.* 13.21a).

Rebuking, ironic, and other uses of direct questions might be the subject for a special study of style. Here it is sufficient to point out that the use of direct questions in the Pauline Letters illustrates what may be more characteristic of ancient than of modern writings, namely, that the style may reflect the genre of writing more than the personality of the writer. The letters to Philemon, the Thessalonians, and the Philippians contain few, if any, direct questions. The great majority of the many ques-tions in Romans are rhetorical and are used for purposes of argumentation and in-struction, sometimes in dialogue with an imaginary partner. Only the letters to the Galatians and the Corinthians (mainly 1 Cor and 2 Cor 10–13) contain a number of unpleasant questions addressed to the recipients. In other respects, too, the Corin-thian letters come close to the apologetic, rebuking, and, to some extent, ironic char-acter of Galatians. The parallels from other writers, especially Cicero and Pliny, show that this is not a mere coincidence but reflects a certain type of epistolary style.

The recognition that rebuking and ironic questions can have the same function as expressions of astonishment and statements of disapproval and distress helps to clarify the structure of Galatians. The clusters of questions and statements in Gal 3:1–5 and 4:8–11 elaborate the opening ironic rebuke in 1:6–7, and even later passages, such as 4:15–16, 20 and 5:7, echo Paul's reaction to the change of attitude that caused the rebuke.

G. Retorts

An expression of astonishment became a conventional form for complaint about lack of communication. But the same form could be used in response to letters and news if a person were offended by something that his correspondent had said or done. The form of the ironic response is found in some letters that are defensive, accusatory, or filled with retorts and countercharges. In his third letter, Demosthenes is accusing the Athenians for their unfair treatment of the sons of Lycurgus but is at the same time, though more indirectly, pleading his own cause before those who had exiled him (*Ep.* 3). Herodes' astonishment, rebukes, and irony in the letter to Dorion are conditioned by the charge of his subordinates that his instructions were unreasonable and impracticable (*UPZ* I 110.20–192).

An element of retort is present in the models of ironic letters, most clearly in the example given by Pseudo-Demetrius *Epist. char.* 20), which, in contrast to that of Pseudo-Libanius (*Epist. char.* 69), does not contain an expression of astonishment. The addressee is here said to have attributed his own attitude to the sender: τὸ κατὰ σαυτὸν μέρος ἀνήρηκας ἡμᾶς ("as far as you are concerned, you have ruined us"). Pseudo-Libanius lists the "retort" or "counteraccusation letter"(ἀντεγκληματική) as a special type (*Epist. char.* 69). The letter opens with a rebuking question, and the content shows an affinity of this letter type to the rebuking and ironic letters.

Some "real" letters of retort are preserved among the letters of Cicero. The best example is a reply letter from Brutus and Cassius to M. Antonius (Cicero, *Fam.* 11.3). They are surprised at his surprise, and they reply to reproach with reproach and to charges with countercharges. But even in Cicero's own letters, an ironic rebuke is used in reaction to rebuking and disapproving letters that he had received. Thus a letter to Gallus begins by saying, "I wonder *[Miror]* why you find fault with me, when you have no right to do so; and even if you had the right, you had no business to do so" (*Fam.* 7.17). In the letter to M. Caelius, to which I have already referred, Cicero's amazement is caused by the reproaches of his friend: "What then is that 'gloomy resolve' of mine?" (*Fam.* 2.16.2, cf. 8.16).

In his *Life* Josephus retorts the charges made by Justus from Tiberias in a section in which he addresses his antagonist as if he were present (ὡς παρόντα, *Life* 340). The countercharges are summarized in the form of an ironic rebuke: "I cannot, however, but marvel [θαυμάζειν] at your impudence in daring to assert that your narrative is to be preferred to that of all who have written on this subject, when you neither knew what happened in Galilee, nor . . . , nor . . ." (*Life* 357). The style of the particular passage comes close to that of a letter, but it also shows that the form may have had its setting in retorting and accusing pamphlets and speeches as well as in letters.

When he opens his letter to the churches of Galatia with an ironic rebuke, Paul reacts to a report that he had received. The appended remark in Gal 1:10 leaves little room for doubt that he, too, is retorting charges leveled against him: "Do I now persuade men . . . ?" or "Do I seek to please men?" The remark is an aside that must be occasioned by what had been alleged. The somewhat similar aside in 5:11 makes it likely that the charge was that Paul either preached or kept silent about circumcision for tactical reasons. Thus even the hypothetical self-curse in 1:8 seems to allude to a charge that was actually made, namely, that elsewhere Paul preached a gospel that was different from what he had preached in Galatia. This is his retort. Paul is in effect saying, "I am no turncoat, but you have turned around" (cf. 1:10; 4:19).

While Paul rebukes the Galatian churches, he puts the blame for their change of attitude on a third party. This is not usual in rebuking letters and corresponds more to the style of letters of accusation or denunciation. Combining rebuke and accusation, Paul directs his retorts against those who have defamed him. Paul has not withheld the truth; they have hindered the Galatians from obeying the truth. They, not he, have been motivated by concern for human success and approval. They insist upon circumcision in order to avoid persecution for the sake of the cross of Christ. Apparently, Paul was alleged to have kept silent about circumcision in order to avoid trouble and persecution in Galatia. But he claims quite the contrary, that his being persecuted shows he no longer proclaims circumcision. Both the reminder about Paul's own past in 1:13f. and the inserted remark in 4:29 make zeal for the law appear as the reason for persecution of the church.

H. Irony

According to the handbook of Pseudo-Demetrius, the ironic letter is characterized by the use of words to denote the opposite of what they normally mean (*Typ. epist.* 20). Thus, evil persons are called good. The handbook ascribed to Pseudo-Libanius (also to Proclus), *Epistolimaioi charactēres*, is more specific and defines the ironic letter as one in which we begin by pretending to praise somebody but at the end make our real intention clear (no. 56). These definitions correspond to the sense in which the word "irony" is used when a rhetorical figure of speech is meant. But both in antiquity and today the words "irony" and "ironic" are also used in less precise meanings, which are often difficult to define or to distinguish from sarcasm, persiflage, and related moods of speech. What I, adopting Mullins's term, have called the ironic rebuke is in general ironic in the wider sense of the term. But in some letters, mostly the same in which retort charges are made, the more or less ironic expression of astonishment is combined with other traces of irony.

I take it to be irony in the broad sense when Demosthenes praises Philip at the expense of the Athenians (*Ep.* 3.11–13). A nice example of irony as a rhetorical figure is found in *UPZ* I 110.83–84, where Herodes speaks of the sagacity (εὐγνωμοσύνης) of his subordinates, meaning their stupidity. Cicero is ironic when he exclaims, "What a marvellous camp!" (*O castra praeclara!*) with reference to the effects of military life upon Trebatius (*Fam.* 7.12) or when he adds, "I only wish you were a permanent tribune!" (*Fam.* 7.27). He is half serious, half ironic, when he praises the *ingenium* of Caelius. Half ironic, half serious is also Paul when he addresses his readers with the words ὑμεῖς οἱ πνευματικοί ("you who are spiritual"; Gal 6:1).

We have already pointed to Paul's ironic use of a question for information and his play upon the double meaning of the phrase "foolish Galatians" (ἀνόητοι Γαλάται). The question of 3:3b, ἐναρξάμενοι πνεύματι νῦν σαρκὶ ἐπιστελεῖσθε, is clearly ironic; but the irony is lost by the RSV when translated, "Having begun with the Spirit, are you now ending with the flesh?" The verb carries the connotation of seeking and obtaining perfection. The Galatians churches had obviously been told that they had to be circumcised so that even their members' bodies might become perfect. The word "flesh" (σάρξ) can refer to the organ that was to be circumcised, as in 6:13, but for Paul σάρξ is the sphere and the mood of human existence in this evil age and thus is opposed to the Spirit that has been given to those who have heard and believed the gospel.

The questions in 3:1–5 play upon the meaning of words, but they are also ironic in another and deeper sense; they point out an amazing, unreasonable, even ludicrous contrast between aspiration and result, pretense and reality. This more objective irony is present even in questions that do not twist the meaning of words, especially in 4:9 and 21. What was meant to complete the conversion from the false gods of paganism is by Paul branded as a return to slavery under the *stoicheia*, the heavenly bodies and other powers of mythologized nature.

Several passages are explained best on the assumption that Paul picks up phrases that were coined by his opponents and that he uses them to say the opposite or at least something different. Already the "body opening" is probably an example of this. The Judaizers are likely to have said that observation of the law was required by those who would fully turn from paganism to "Him who called you." The interpreter of Galatians has to look out for other passages in which Paul gives an ironical twist to what was said by the other side in the controversy.

The wish that those who insist upon circumcision would go further and castrate themselves (5:12) is sarcasm. Paul is also sarcastic when he asks his readers to take care that they are not in the end consumed by one another. But the contrast between this warning and the apostrophe "you the spirituals" (5:26; 6:1) is irony.

I. Conclusion

The comparative material surveyed shows that the Epistle to the Galatians is a type of letter that was written when the cordial relationship between addressor and addressees was somehow disturbed. If the disturbance was caused by failure to communicate, the ironic rebuke is in general the main element that this kind of letter has in common with Galatians. But if the troubles are more serious, the letter may well have several other features in common with Galatians. The investigation has on the whole been limited to letters that do contain the ironic rebuke, but it has become clear that features such as expressions of distress, rebuking questions, and irony also occur in letters that do not. What we have established is a kind of family relation between a group of letters that have one, two, or more features in common, and these in a variety of combinations. There may be other features of family similarity that are not to be found in Galatians and, for that reason, have not been taken into account.

The ironic rebuke is a form but not a constitutive element of a specific type or genre of letters. It does not occur in all rebuking or ironic letters, and it occurs in letters that cannot be described as letters of rebuke and that contain little or no irony. Parts of Paul's letter to the Galatians have affinity with various types of letters, such as the apologetic and the paraenetic. Such observations raise the general question, to what extent did pure genres exist in practice? It is clearly easier to find typical examples of the letter of rebuke than of the ironic letter. But the pure example of a genre may be the exception as much as the rule, and a group of letters with several, but not always the same, family features in common may be all that we should expect to find.

One conclusion is clear: more or less similar constellations of identical or related features of form and style occur in letters that differ not only with respect to author, time, and language but also with respect to subject matter, situation, literary level, and private or official character. The common element is a mood of disappointment and a note of reproach. A letter characterized by an ironic rebuke and related features differs from a normal letter of friendship much in the same way as Galatians differs from the normal form of a Pauline letter.

The opening of Galatians, with its expression of astonishment, states the theme and strikes the mood of the whole letter. The features that are related to the ironic rebuke are found mostly in the particular passages that speak most directly to the situation in Galatia (3:1–5; 4:8–11, 12–20; 5:2–12; 6:11–15). These sections are clearly written in epistolary style. Conventional epistolary formulas cluster within and around them. They, along with the opening and conclusion, provide the framework into which more general, somewhat self-contained units have been inserted: Paul's apology for his conduct (1:11–2:21), interpretation of Scripture (3:6–4:7 and 4:31–5:1), and general *paraenesis* (5:13–6:10).

Structure and Purpose

Most standard commentaries and introductions to the New Testament propose outlines that are based mainly on content, if not on the traditional chapter division. One often finds a distinction made between a historical, a dogmatic or refutatory, and a hortative part of the Letter to the Galatians, coinciding roughly with chapters 1–2, 3–4, and 5–6. Any disagreement concerns the section 5:1–12, which is held to belong to the preceding rather than to the following part of the letter.[10]

A. *Situational and more general sections*

Galatians consists of four sections that are all integral parts of the letter but that also form self-contained units: the apologetic autobiography (1:12–2:21),

---

[10] Dahl's discussion of the weaknesses of previous views, which served as an introduction to this section, has been omitted here. Also, Dahl builds on some of the background material in the omitted sections dealing with apostolic autobiography and the interpretation of scripture and paraenesis, which followed the section on ironic rebuke and preceded this section. *Ed.*

the two expositions of Scripture (3:4–29 and 4:1–7; 4:21–31 and 5:1), and the general *paraenesis* (5:13–6:10). These sections are interspersed between passages that are more directly addressed to the epistolary situation (1:1–5, 6–10; 3:1–5; 4:8–11, 12, 13–20; 5:2–12; 6:11–16, 17, 18). These situational passages have the "I—you" or the "I—you—they" style and contain all the explicit references to the troublemakers. The expressions of astonishment and distress also occur here, as do the rebuking questions. It is remarkable that the epistolary formulas and conventional phraseology also cluster within or around the same passages, often introducing the more general sections (cf. 1:11, 13; 3:2; 4:20, 21). The dividing line between epistolary and more general thematic sections is not always sharp. Transitional or thematic statements link both together (cf. 1:10, 11–12; 3:2–5; [4:1–7?]; 5:1, 10–13).

The more general sections take off from the epistolary context and return to it. The result is a back-and-forth movement of thought that makes it easy to find examples of double or triple enclosement *(inclusio)* or even extensive chiastic patterns. Similar oscillation between epistolary and situational passages and more general, often theological, statements occurs in other Pauline letters. In Ephesians and Colossians it is almost stereotyped.

The alternation of situation-related and more general sections is illustrated by chart 1, which is intended as a descriptive outline that does not beg the further questions of structure, function, and interpretation. I have included a survey of epistolary formulas and phrases that directly address the recipients.

Chart 1

Situational	General	Formulas/Phrases
1:1–5 Salutation		1:3 Grace to you and peace
1:6–9/10 Ironic rebuke		1:6 I am astonished that . . . 1:9 As we said have said before, so now I say again
	1:11–2:21 Apologetic autobiography	1:11 For I would have you know, brethren/sisters 1:13 For you have heard
3:1–5 Rebuking questions		3:1 O foolish Galatians 3:2 Let me ask you only this
	3:5–4:7 Argument from Scripture	3:7 So you see that 3:15 brethren/sisters 3:17; 4:1 I mean
4:8–11 Rebuking question		4:11 I am afraid
4:12 Request		4:12 Brethren/sisters, I beseech you

4:13–20		4:13 but you know
Paul's presence		4:15 For I bear you witness
remembered/desired		4:19 My little children
		4:20 I could wish . . . I am perplexed
	4:21–5:1	4:21 Tell me
	Scriptural	4:28 Now we, brethren/sisters
	exposition/appeal	4:31 So, brethren/sisters
5:2–12		5:2 Now I, Paul, say unto you
Pronouncements		5:3 I testify again to every man
		5:10 I have confidence in you
		5:11 But if I, brethren/sisters
		5:12 I wish
	5:13–6:10	5:13 For you
	Paraenesis	5:16 But I say
		6:1 Brethren/sisters
		6:7 Do not be deceived
6:11–16		6:11 See . . . I am writing
Autographic epilogue		6:16 Peace and mercy
6:17		6:17 Henceforth
Final pronouncement		
6:18		6:18 The grace . . . brethren/sisters
Final greeting		

B. The background section (1:6–4:11)

The opening ironic rebuke (1:6–9) is restated in the form of ironic and rebuking questions in 3:1–5 and 4:8–10. The reason for Paul's dissatisfaction is stated with increasing precision. He first speaks in general terms about turning to another gospel (1:6), then about works of the law (3:2, 5) and finally about observation of days and months, festival seasons and years (4:10). Paul's reaction is summarized in the statement that he fears that his labor for the Galatian churches may have been in vain (4:11).

The historical and theological arguments in 1:11–2:21 and 3:6–4:7 have given the letter a permanent importance. But within the epistolary structure, they are subordinate to the framework provided by the statements of Paul's dissatisfaction and fear. Both unfold the thematic statement that the gospel that Paul preached, but from which the churches in Galatia are turning away, is not a gospel "according to men" (1:11). It is the gospel of Christ and was entrusted to Paul by a revelation that completely changed the course of his life and his attitude to the law and the traditions of his ancestors (1:12–16a; 2:15–21). This is confirmed by the experience of the recipients who received the Spirit when they heard the gospel preached, without any works of the law (3:2–5; 4:6–7; cf. 3:26–27). The arguments become complicated because Paul has to add backing on controversial points. His preaching in Galatia is not compromised by his relationship with Christians in Jerusalem and Judaea (cf.

1:16b–2:14). Properly understood, Scripture proves the legitimacy of what the recipients themselves have experienced (cf. 3:6–12). The rehearsal of past events in 1:11–4:7 represents aggravating circumstances that motivate the sharpness of Paul's rebukes and the seriousness of his fear.

With the question in 4:8f., Paul returns to the present situation. His fear is clearly caused by possible future developments as much as by what has already happened (4:11; cf. 5:2–4, 7–12). In this respect, 4:11 is not only a concluding but also a transitional statement. Beginning with the request in 4:12, Paul addresses the present state of affairs, attempting to shape the future of the Galatian churches. Reminders of the past and rebuking questions are found also in 4:13–16 and 5:7, but here they no longer function as framework for the whole movement of thought.

The entire argument in 1:6–4:11 forms one structural unit in which Paul states and gives motivation for his reaction to the recent development in the Galatian churches. At controversial points, he elaborates his reasons in detail, but the whole section deals with what has happened in the past and thus provides the background for the following part of the letter, which is introduced by the request in 4:12. Galatians 1:6–4:11 has a function similar to that of background sections in petitions and letters of request.

In spite of the difference in mood, the section 1:6–4:11 corresponds to the sections that provide background for the first request in other letters (cf. esp. Phlm 4–7; 1 Cor 1:4–9; 1 Thess 1:2–3:13). The θαυμάζω period in Galatians expresses the attitude of the sender to the recipients, sets the tone, and introduces the main theme, just as the εὐχαριστῶ period does in other letters. The concluding—and transitional—statement of fear in Gal 4:11 corresponds to the report of joy in Phlm 6 or to climatic, intercessory, or doxological passages in 1 Cor 1:8–9 and 1 Thess 3:11–13.

The structural similarity between the background sections in Galatians and 1 Thessalonians deserves special attention. In Galatians, the ironic rebuke is restated in the form of rebuking questions and concluded by a statement of fear (1:6–9; 3:1–5; 4:8–10, 11). In 1 Thessalonians, repeated assertions of thanksgiving are concluded by prayer wishes (1:2; 2:13; 3:10–11, 12–14). In both letters, the statements about Paul's attitude to the recipients provide the framework for information, in part reminders, concerning experiences and actions of the sender and the recipients. It is remarkable that the same pattern recurs in the epistles to the Ephesians and Colossians, in which repeated assertions of thanksgiving and intercession, and in Col 2:5 rejoicing, frame reminders and information. The peculiarity of these letters is the absence, or in Colossians the sparseness, of specific historical information. The addressees are reminded of what God has done for them in Christ and of the commission given to Paul.

The pattern in Galatians differs from that of 1 Thessalonians in that the recollection of previous good relations during the apostle's first visit follows after the first request (Gal 4:12b–20 in contrast to 1 Thess 1:4–2:13). But this is natural enough. In 1 Thessalonians, the good relationship in the past is a reason for Paul's thanksgiving. In Galatians, it motivates the request in 4:12 more than the rebuking and disappointed tenor of the background section. In 1 Corinthians, reminders about Paul's ministry and what happened during his first visit to Corinth follow after the request period in 1:10. In Philippians, information about Paul is inserted between assertions of thanksgiving and intercession in 1:3–11 and the exhortations beginning in 1:27. Information about Paul and his relations to the recipients also follows immediately after the opening thanksgiving in Romans and the eulogy in 2 Corinthians.

C. The pleading section (4:12–6:10)

1. *First request (4:12).* With the expression of fear in Gal 4:11, Paul has concluded the background section. With the request in Gal 4:12, he shifts to the imperative mood, which has not been used in the earlier parts of the letter but recurs in 5:1 and 5:13ff. Even this second part of Galatians includes information and arguments, but they support Paul's appeals and no longer his rebukes. As in petitions, letters of request, and other letters that contain the ironic rebuke, the background section is followed by a section in which the sender states what he asks for and what he hopes to achieve through his letter.

Paul normally introduces his basic requests with παρακαλῶ, a verb commonly used for urgent but polite requests.[11] In 4:12 the request formula follows after the request itself: ἀδελφοί, δέομαι ὑμῶν. Δέομαι is normally used in petitions to sovereigns and other persons who have decision-making power. When used among equals or by a person in a superior position, the word takes on a different color; the petitioner has to ask for help, beg, and implore. Paul uses the verb only when the success or failure of his work depends upon the reaction to his request, as in Galatians and 2 Cor 5:20; 10:2.

The basic request is very personal: "Become as I am, for I also have become as you are!" (Gal 4:12). Paul asks the recipients to overcome their mistrust so that there can be mutual identification and solidarity and so that his fear would prove unnecessary. But something more is involved. The request in 4:12 is another way of saying, "Become imitators of me!" Such exhortations regularly receive their specific content from preceding statements about Paul. The request in 4:12 has to be seen against the background of the autobiographical statements in Gal 1–2, especially the report about Paul's past conduct "in Judaism," his later identification with Gentile sinners, and his death to the law (1:13–16; 2:14–21; cf. also 2:5). This is confirmed by the following parts of the letter, especially by the concluding statements in 6:14, 15 (cf. also 5:1, 5, 27).

On closer reading, the request in 4:12 does therefore make the appeal that the churches in Galatia should, like Paul, uphold the freedom given in Christ, who has rendered the distinction between circumcised Jews and uncircumcised Gentiles obsolete (cf. 3:27–28; 5:6; 6:15). In content, if not in form, the request in 4:12 does therefore correspond to the ironic rebuke in 1:6. The structure of Galatians is similar to that of letters in which an ironic rebuke is followed by the request that the recipients

---

[11] Bjerkelund, *Parakalô.*

(or recipient) should do what they have so far neglected. Most often a person who has not written is asked to do it. But rebuke and request can also refer to matters of business or general conduct.

The request is followed by a disclaimer that is inserted to avoid a false impression of what Paul has written. Paul does not feel offended but makes his request because he remembers how he was once received in Galatia, regrets the deterioration of the relationship, and puts the blame upon the intruding agitators (4:13–17).

2. *Supporting information (4:13–20).* It is quite normal that a request is followed by supporting information that supplements the preceding background section if there is any. Thus in Philemon the thanksgiving and rejoicing periods provide a general background, but the more specific motivation is inserted between the παρακαλῶ period in vv. 8–10 and the restatement of the request in v. 17. There are also analogies to a disclosure immediately after a request formula, as in Gal 4:12, 13. In 1 Thess 4:1–2 the formula, Λοιπὸν οὖν, ἀδελφοί, ἐρωτῶμεν ὑμᾶς καὶ παρακαλοῦμεν ("Finally, brethren, we beseech and exhort you"), is followed by οἴδατε γάρ ("For you know"). In P.Mich. 209.6, 9, 11, we find the sequence θαυμάζω ἄδελφε . . . Ἐρωτηθείς ἄδελφε οὖν . . . οἴδας γὰρ ἄδελφε . . . ("I am astonished, brother . . . I ask you, therefore, brother . . . For you know, brother . . .").

In spite of obvious differences, the section Gal 4:12–20 may be compared to the section that is introduced by the first παρακαλῶ period in 1 Corinthians (1:10–4:21). In both cases, the reasons given for the request include recollection of the time when Paul first preached the gospel and ironic comments about the later developments and the present situations (Gal 4:13–16; 1 Cor 1:13–2:5; 3:1–4; 3:18–4:13). Paul represents himself as the founder and father, or as the mother who is once more in travail with her children (1 Cor 3:10–11; 4:15; Gal 4:19). He admonishes them to become his imitators, or to become as he is (1 Cor 4:16; Gal 4:12). Both sections are concluded by the theme of "the apostolic Parousia" (1 Cor 4:17–21; Gal 4:18–20).

The similarities in detail are due to a similarity of function. In 1 Corinthians, the opening section is brief and dominated by assertions of Paul's thanksgiving and God's faithfulness (1 Cor 1:4–9). The fundamental request is spelled out at length and supported by profound theological arguments (1:10–4:21). In Galatians, in contrast, there is an extended background section that is dominated by expressions of astonishment and fear and that comprises detailed information and theological arguments (Gal 1:6–4:11). The reasons for the basic request are stated briefly and in personal terms (4:12–20). But in spite of differences of length and mood, the basic structure is the same.

In both cases, the relationship between the recipient churches and Christ and his apostle is at stake. In 1 Corinthians, it is in need of correction. The fragmentation of the church has to be overcome (1 Cor 1:10–12; 3:3–4). If Paul's answers to questions, which were raised by letter and by oral report, were heard as the advice of the protagonist of one party, then they might make a bad situation worse. They will avail only if the Corinthians comply with his basic requests and recognize that he speaks as the messenger of the crucified Christ, the one founder and father of the church in Corinth.

The problems in Galatia were even more severe for Paul. He fears that his whole work has been in vain. His children need to be reborn so that Christ can again take shape among them (cf. Gal 4:19). The credibility gap, which was created by the intrusion of a third party, has to be overcome. He therefore asks them to identify with himself as he has identified himself with them. Their compliance would set the relationship aright and make them willing to listen to his reply to the question that was set before him by a report from Galatia. In Gal 4:12–15, as in 1 Cor 1:10–11, the request and its motivation serve as an introduction to, and a preparation for, more specific advice that is given in the remaining parts of the letter.

The references to Paul's anticipated and desired presence form a transition to the following, as well as a conclusion to the preceding, part of the letter (Gal 4:18–20; 1 Cor 4:18–21). In 1 Corinthians, the point is that Paul's conduct when he arrives will depend upon the reactions to his instructions that are mediated both by Timothy and by the letter itself (cf. 2 Cor 10:2; 13:10). Thus, the importance of the instructions in 1 Cor 5–16 is emphasized. In the setting of Galatians, the wish that Paul were present cannot be fulfilled and no emissary is mentioned. This gives all the more weight to the letter itself as the medium of Paul's apostolic presence. From Gal 4:21 onward, Paul spells out what he would have said had he been able to be present and "change his voice" in order to persuade his perplexing children.

3. *Solemn declarations (5:2–6).* The first modulation of Paul's voice is a hortatory exposition of Scripture that concludes with the exhortation in 5:1. It is followed by a series of solemn pronouncements that motivate the appeal to stand firm in the freedom in Christ and not submit to a yoke of slavery (5:2–6).

Only at this point does Paul explicitly mention what has been on his mind all the time, namely, the possibility that the churches of Galatia might proceed from eclectic observation of some rites to acceptance of circumcision and thereby to an obligation to keep the entire law. Since the phrase "Now I, Paul, say to you" introduces a new subject matter, it cannot be understood as a variant of formulas used to introduce a "body conclusion," which give a summary review of what has already been said.

Within the historical setting, the appeal in 5:1 and the declarations beginning in 5:2 form the crucial section. Paul here comes to the heart of the matter. This has been recognized by M. Luther Stirewalt, who assumes that representatives of the Galatian churches have asked Paul whether they ought to undergo circumcision.[12] I find this convincing. The recipients may well have wondered why Paul delayed his reply and wrote an ironic and rebuking type of letter.

Stirewalt's further suggestion, that 5:1–12 is to be considered the "decision" in an official letter, is interesting and deserves careful consideration. So far I have not been convinced. The "apostolic decree" in Acts 15:23–29 is a typical example of a letter that communicates an official decision. But the form used in Galatians does not seem to be characteristic of legal or administrative decisions. An appeal is followed by a declaration, an attestation, and a new declaration with motivation (Gal 5:1, 2, 3, 4–6). In 1 Cor 5 Paul asks the recipients to execute what he has already decided. In Galatians he simply curses the offenders (Gal 5:8, 10b, 12; cf. 1:8–9).

---

[12] Stirewalt, "Official Letter-Writing."

In general, Paul tries to convince and prefers to make requests rather than give orders. In the heat of the controversy, the Galatian churches would hardly recognize that he had any decision-making power. They are likely to have asked for his advice rather than for his decision. The emphatic "I, Paul" does not need to be taken as a reference to Paul's apostolic authority alone. If Paul's reply is understood as "advice" or "counsel" (συμβουλή), then the reference may just as well be to Paul's expertise and personal experience in matters of the law, possibly also to the high esteem in which he was once held.

The symbouleutic, deliberative, advising speech was a major genre in ancient rhetoric. Correspondingly, the letter of advice was considered a standard type, represented in the handbook of Demetrius and by letters of Demosthenes. The symbouleutic genre of speeches and letters were primarily used for legal and political advice. But the genre could also get a wider application, and it is difficult to make a clear distinction between symbouleutic and paraenetic letters.

Since Aristotle it was generally accepted that the symbouleutic genre of speech (or letter) combined two elements, counsels about what to do and counsels about what not to do, "persuasion" (προτροπή) and "dissuasion" (ἀποτροπή). The letter to the Galatians contains both elements. Throughout the letter, most directly from 4:21 onward, Paul does his utmost to dissuade the recipients from submission to the law and circumcision. The uncompromising pronouncements beginning in 5:2 form the climactic conclusion to the apotreptic part of the letter. The positive, protreptic part follows in the paraenetic section, that is, from 5:13 onward.

The negative and the positive counsels correspond fairly closely to one another. The Galatian churches should not give up their freedom, but they should use it in the right way (5:1, 13). They should not submit to circumcision and be obliged to observe the entire law; if they did, they would be severed from Christ, fall out of grace, and lose the hope and the new existence that are granted through the Spirit (5:2, 4–6). But they should serve one another in love and thus keep the commandment in which the whole law is fulfilled (5:13–14). The law has nothing to bring up against those who walk by the Spirit and bear its fruits (5:18, 23b). The statement in 5:6, that in Christ Jesus neither circumcision nor uncircumcision counts, but only faith working through love, marks the transition from negative to positive counsels about the proper fulfillment of the law.

4. *Appended remarks (5:7–12)*. Before he proceeds to his positive advice, Paul inserts a number of passionate, abrupt remarks (5:7–12). Once more he expresses his disappointment and is ironic and sarcastic. He returns to the claims and charges made by his opponents. He denies what they claimed, that the "persuasion" (πεισμονή) of submission to the law came from the God whose call had reached the Galatians through Paul's preaching. Their persuasion, not Paul's, runs contrary to the truth. The persecution that Paul suffers is a final proof that he no longer "preaches circumcision." They are accursed.

These passionate remarks bring the whole argument from 1:6 onward to a preliminary conclusion; the final conclusion follows in the autobiographic epilogue (6:11ff.). The sharp either-or that was stated in 5:2–6 is applied in specific terms to the situation in Galatia. Even the proverbial saying in 5:9 serves in this context to make it clear that either dough is unleavened or it will be leavened throughout. No compromise is possible.

Paul puts the whole blame for the troubles in Galatia upon the intruding advocates of circumcision and observation of the law. After the earlier expressions of fear and perplexity (4:11, 20), it may seem strange that Paul at this point states his confidence in the addressees (5:10a). But the function of the remarks in 5:7–12 is to draw a sharp line of separation between the troublemakers and the churches of Galatia. To state it in very simple terms, the purpose of the whole letter is to make these churches dissociate themselves from the intruders and again follow the apostle and his gospel.

The phrase used in 5:10, "I have confidence in you," has been identified by John White as a "formula of confidence."[13] It should be added, however, that stereotyped statements of confidence do occur in non-Christian letters. Statements of hope are more common. The wording is open to variation in expressions of confidence (or hope), just as in request and disclosure formulas.

More or less stereotyped phrases that state that the sender is confident, does not doubt, hopes, and so forth, can have several epistolary functions. They can express a confident disposition and mood. They can express hope for, or confidence in, a future reunion. The sender's confidence in the recipients can also be a reason for the content and form of his letter. But the sender can also, as in 5:10, express his confidence that the recipients will comply with what he has written. Examples of this usage are found in the letters of Cicero: "I should write more to this effect, were I not assured that you are eager enough on your own account" (*Fam.* 2.4.2); "but you too, I am sure, will do what you discover to be most to my advantage" (*Fam.* 3.3.2).

This variant of the formula of confidence usually occurs in the conclusion of a letter. In Gal 5:10 Paul says that he is confident that the preceding parts of his letter will have the intended effect: in the future, the Galatian churches will dissociate themselves from the troublemakers and agree to what Paul has written. The phrase "that you will take no other view than mine" refers especially to the rule that was stated in 5:10 (cf. 6:14–15). The remarks about the intruders in 5:7–9 are therefore parenthetical, and the further remarks about the intruders and Paul himself in 5:10b-12 are half parenthetical. The main line of thought moves from the pronouncement in 5:6 through the statement of confidence in 5:10a to the exhortations that begin in 5:13.

5. *General observations.* There is a clear progression from Paul's expression of fear (4:11) through perplexed uncertainty (4:20) to confidence (5:10). There is a similar progression in the key admonitions—to identify with Paul (4:12), not to submit to slavery (5:1), and to use freedom in the right way (5:13). The fundamental relationship between the Galatians and the apostle has to be set aright before he can proceed to his specific advice (4:12–20). They have to give heed to his warnings and dissociate themselves from the intruders before he can proceed to exhortations that presuppose that they are indeed set free by Christ and are alive in the Spirit

---

[13] White, *Form and Function,* 99–100, 104–6.

(4:21–5:12, 13–26). Some elements of irony and sarcasm are present even in the paraenetic section, especially if it contains a tacit allusion to the Galatians' failure to contribute to the collection for Jerusalem. But apart from the concluding remarks in 6:12–13, the discussion of the controversial issue that was introduced by the ironic rebuke has come to an end in 5:12. Confident that his letter will have the intended effect, Paul can move on to give advice about the right use of Christian freedom. In this respect, the structure of Galatians is similar to that of letters in which an ironic rebuke and, in some cases, a corresponding request are followed by "business as usual."

To a considerable extent, the pleading section runs parallel to the background section. The initial appeal corresponds to the opening rebuke (4:12; 1:6–9). The supporting statements about the reception of Paul in Galatia and the relationship between himself and the recipients of his letter supplement what was said about his gospel and the conduct of his ministry (4:13–20; 1:11–2:21). The hortatory exposition of Scripture in 4:21–5:1 is based upon the argument from Scripture in Gal 3. The contrast between spirit and flesh is stressed in both sections. It is also possible to relate the declarations and advice that begin in 5:2 to the concluding parts of the background section, which already link the end of slavery to the gift of the Spirit (4:1–7; cf. 4:8–11). At the same time, however, the statements of principle that were made on the occasion of the conflict in Antioch are restated with specific application to the Galatians controversy (5:2–6; cf. 2:15–21). But even if the movement of thought within the background and the pleading sections is not completely parallel, the analogy that does exist confirms our result, that the request in 4:12 marks the decisive turning point of the letter.

The purpose of the letter in its historical setting is indeed very simple. Paul tries to convince the Galatian churches that they have no reason to lose confidence in him and the gospel that he preached. They should radically separate themselves from the advocates of the law, return to the gospel that was proclaimed by the apostle, and fulfill the law by serving one another in love and bearing the fruits of the Spirit, not by means of circumcision and other external observations. In order to achieve this goal, Paul displays his mastery of epistolary style and of midrashic interpretation.

D. Salutation and conclusion

1. *Salutation.* The salutation in 1:1–5 follows the usual Pauline pattern. The address in 1:2b is very brief. The two other items, the name of the sender (1:1–2b) and the greeting (1:3–5), have been expanded in such a way that the salutation forms a prelude to the letter (cf. esp. Rom 1:1–7). The expansion of a greeting by means of a christological relative clause and a doxology is without analogy. It brings in the doxological element that normally is expressed by the thanksgiving and may also be a substitute for a theological qualification of the address.

2. *Conclusion.* The remark about Paul's handwriting in Gal 6:11 probably introduces the autobiographic epilogue and draws attention to its importance. In a concluding summary, Paul for the last time contrasts the advocates of circumcision with himself. They want to boast of the "flesh," that is, of the circumcision of the Galatians

Christians, and to avoid persecution (6:12–13). He will only boast of the cross of Christ, which has made an end to his life in the world (6:14). Paul's personal attitude corresponds to the general rule that the distinction between circumcised and uncircumcised has become obsolete; there is a new creation (cf. 1:4; 3:27–28; 5:5–6).

The concluding wish of peace is formulated in accordance with Jewish conventions, both liturgical and epistolary (6:16). It might therefore be seen as part of the "letter conclusion" (if the *paraenesis* is part of the body, the summary is 6:11–15 is the body conclusion). The prayer wish in 6:16, however, is still closely linked to the preceding context, as are wishes of the type "But the God of Peace," and such, of other letters. Paul makes his benediction contingent upon compliance with the rule that was stated in 6:15 as a summary of the theological content of his letter. Instead of the second-person pronoun, he uses a substantival relative clause (καὶ ὅσοι), which is reassumed by ἐπ' αὐτούς. The unusual third-person form probably is chosen to make clear that the wish is conditional, so that one may paraphrase, "If you will (in the future) walk by this rule, then peace upon you—and upon the (whole) of Israel." If that is the meaning, the "Israel of God" would be the totality of which the churches of Galatia are a part, insofar as they follow Paul's rule.

The conclusion of Galatians has no greetings to or from special groups or persons. There is no remark about a letter carrier or the sending of an emissary, no request for intercession, and no final statement about rejoicing or hope. Only a stern pronouncement is inserted between the peace wish and the closing greeting. If the recipients do not follow Paul's advice, future communication will be of no avail; the letter will be his last word. He bears the stigmata of Jesus upon his body. That is, he has written the letter as Christ's slave, not as an apostle of men or as a turncoat who tries to please and persuade (cf. 1:1, 10). If Paul alludes to marks inflicted by persecution for Christ's sake, the image would be even more powerful (cf. 5:11 and 6:14, contrasted with 6:12).

The wording of the closing wish of grace is almost identical with the form used in Phil 4:23 and Phlm 25. But only in the Letter to the Galatians does Paul add ἀδελφοί ("brethren/sisters") at the end. The manuscript evidence seems to indicate that even the confirming "Amen" is an original part of the text of Galatians, and of Galatians alone. In spite of rebukes, irony, and sternness, the letter ends with a note of brotherhood and confidence that the recipients will follow the apostle's advice so that the grace of our Lord Jesus Christ will in fact be with them.

A last observation. At several points, the autobiographic conclusion is linked to the opening of the letter, both to the salutation in 1:1–5 and to the body opening in 1:6–10. I would like to draw special attention to one of these points. In the expanded salutation, Paul refers to Jesus Christ, "who gave himself for our sins to deliver us from the present evil age" (1:4). The positive correlate is "a new creation" (6:15). The statement in 1:4 is uncontroversial in the setting of the letter. But later statements have made it clear that for Paul deliverance from the present evil age equals deliverance from the law. Thus, the concluding rule can contrast the new creation with the distinction, caused by the law, between circumcision and uncircumcision.

In the salutation, Paul introduces himself as an apostle of Jesus Christ and God the Father, "who raised him from the dead" (1:1). There is no other explicit statement about the resurrection of Jesus, and there are relatively few references to the risen Christ. The stress is put almost exclusively upon redemption through the death of Christ. This is not accidental. A theology of the resurrection and pneumatic enthusiasm could easily be combined with Judaizing tendencies and even with circumcision of Gentiles believers. Paul's exclusive either-or is a consequence of his faith in the Christ who died upon the cross, under the curse of the law, and in that way delivered us from the present evil age.

Chart 2

Structure and Context of the Letter

1:1–5 *Salutation* (with prelude statements and doxology)
1:6–4:11 *Background section*
> 1:6–10 *Opening expression of astonishment:* Reason for the ironic rebuke and preliminary comments
> 1:11–2:21 *Aggravating circumstances I:* Nature and origin of Paul's gospel; his vocation and conduct
> > 1:11–12 Disclosure: Thematic statements about Paul's gospel
> > 1:13–2:21 Autobiographical statements
> > > 1:13–14 Reminder: Paul's former life as a Jew
> > > 1:15–16 The revelation of Christ, the cause of a radical change (continued in 2:15ff.)
> > > 1:17–2:10 Refutation of the charge that Paul's conduct elsewhere discredited his preaching in Galatia
> > > > 1:17–24 Early contacts in Jerusalem and Judea
> > > > 2:1–10 The conference in Jerusalem
> > > 2:11–21 The conflict in Antioch as a precedent
> > > > 2:11–14 What happened
> > > > 2:15–21 The reasons for Paul's reaction: Justification by faith in Christ without works of the law. Conclusion and transition
> 3:1–4:7 *Aggravating circumstances II:* The experiences of the Galatians and the testimony of Scripture
> > 3:1–5 Introduction: Rebuking and ironic questions; the Spirit
> > 3:6–29 Supporting arguments from Scripture
> > > 3:6–9 Warrant: Abraham's faith and the promise given to him
> > > 3:10–22 Refutation of possible objections: Unconditional validity of the promise and the function of the law
> > > 3:23–29 Application and conclusion
> > 4:1–7 Restatement: Not slaves, but sons and heirs; the Spirit
> 4:8–11 *Conclusion:* Rebuking questions; statement of fear
4:12–6:10 *Pleading section*
> 4:12–20 *Introduction*
> > 4:12 Basic request for identification with Paul. Disclaimer

4:13–17 Recollection of previous relationship and its deterioration

4:18–20 Conclusion and transition to specific pleas: Paul wishes that he
were present; his perplexity

4:21–5:12 *Apotreptic:* Freedom in Christ should not be surrendered

4:21–31 Scriptural basis for the appeal: The allegory of Abraham's two
sons

5:1 Application: The decisive appeal

5:2–6 Solemn pronouncements and warnings

5:7–12 Conclusion and transition: Appended remarks make a sharp
distinction between the troublemakers and the recipients

5:13–6:10 *Protreptic:* The freedom should be used in the right way

5:13–14 Thematic appeal with warrant from Scripture

5:15–26 Admonition to walk in the Spirit

5:15 Transitional warning against strife

5:16–25 The Spirit and the flesh

5:26 Restatement of warning; transition

6:1–10 Rules of conduct, with motivation

6:1–4 Mutual correction, etc.

6:6–9 Sharing of goods

6:10 Concluding admonition

6:11–18 *Autographic conclusion*

6:11–15 *Summary review:* Introduction, remarks about the advocates of
circumcision and Paul; restatement of his "canon"

6:16 *Conditional wish of peace*

6:17–18 *Final pronouncement and greeting*

8

A PARADIGM OF THE APOCALYPSE: THE GOSPEL IN THE LIGHT OF EPISTOLARY ANALYSIS

G. Walter Hansen

Adistinctive contribution of Richard Longenecker's commentary on Galatians is his outline of Paul's letter on the basis of its rebuke-request letter structure.[1] Even though many have observed Hellenistic epistolary conventions in the letter,[2] most major commentaries have offered some variant of an outline that divides the letter into three parts: autobiographical explanation (chs. 1–2); theological exposition (chs. 3–4); ethical exhortation (chs. 5–6).[3] Professor Longenecker is the first commentator on the letter to show how the common rebuke-request letter form in Greek papyrus letters provides the basic framew?ork for Paul's letter to the Galatians.[4] This revolutionary perspective on the structure of Galatians deserves careful examination. I wish to honor my mentor by exploring some of the implications of this new perspective for our understanding of Paul's exposition of the gospel in Galatians. Four prominent features of the rebuke-request letter form in Galatians which I examine here are: (1) the initial request in 4:12, (2) the subscription in 6:11–18, (3) the salutation in 1:1–5, and (4) the disclosure statement in 1:11–12.

The Initial Request in 4:12

After Paul's opening salutation (1:1–5), his use of the θαυμάζω rebuke formula (1:6) introduces an extended rebuke of the Galatians for their defection from the true

---

[1] R. Longenecker, *Galatians*, c–cix.

[2] See White, *Form and Function;* Mullins, "Formulas," 380–90; Doty, *Letters,* 27–47.

[3] There are many variations of this outline; for example, Betz *(Galatians,* 16–23) derives his outline from rhetorical analysis: Epistolary Prescript (1:1–5); Exordium (1:6–11); Narratio (1:12–2:14); Propositio (2:15–21); Probatio (3:1–4:31); Exhortatio (5:1–6:10); Epistolary Postscript (6:11–18). But even here the threefold division is still basically intact.

[4] Longenecker built on the previous work of Dahl, "Paul's Letter," and on my doctoral dissertation published as *Abraham in Galatians.* I have now followed Longenecker's lead by using the rebuke-request structure as the basis of the outline in my commentary *(Galatians,* 29–30).

gospel (1:6–4:11). Although an expression of rebuke after his salutation differs from his usual practice of expressing thanksgiving after his salutation,[5] research on the use of θαυμάζω ("I am astonished") in common Greek letters of Paul's era demonstrates that this phrase had the same function as the Εὐχαριστῶ ("I give thanks") phrase: it states the theme and the mood of the whole letter.[6] Greek letters which contain this common expression of rebuke often include other features which are also found in Galatians[7]—thus we find the following:

Rebuke Elements	Galatians
1. a statement of the cause for the astonishment-rebuke	(1:6)
2. a reminder of previous instructions	(1:9)
3. a rebuke for foolishness	(3:1, 3)
4. a rebuke for negligence	(4:9)
5. a rebuke for a change of mind	(1:6)
6. an expression of distress	(4:9)
7. rebuking questions	(3:1–5; 4:9)
8. an expression of request	(4:12)
9. an appeal to a change of direction	(5:1–6:10)

This correspondence of characteristic elements in the letters of rebuke with similar elements in Paul's letter to the Galatians confirms the extent to which Paul's letter reflects the mood and structure of rebuke-request letters of his day. Of course, Paul's letter of rebuke differs from the extant papyrus letters of rebuke in some respects: most of them are relatively short letters to another individual, often a member of the family;[8] Paul's letter is extended by his autobiographical and theological excursions and is addressed to churches. Nevertheless, the basic form is the same.

The request section of Paul's letter (4:12–6:10) opens with the initial expression of request and the first imperative of the letter—Γίνεσθε ὡς ἐγώ, ὅτι κἀγὼ ὡς ὑμεῖς, ἀδελφοί, δέομαι ὑμῶν (4:12). This request is the decisive turning point in the letter. From this point on Paul's primary purpose is not to rebuke the Galatian Christians for their desertion from the gospel but to appeal to them to live according to the truth of the gospel. His appeal includes his autobiographical account of his relationship with the Galatians (4:12–20), his allegorical interpretation of the Sarah-

---

[5] See 1 Thess 1:2; 2 Thess 1:3; 1 Cor 1:4; Rom 1:8; Phlm 4; Col 1:4.

[6] Hansen, *Abraham in Galatians*, 33; Paul Schubert states that "the function of the epistolary thanksgiving in the papyrus letters is to focus the epistolary situation, i.e., to introduce the vital theme of the letter" *(Form and Function,* 180). Funk says that the thanksgiving sections in Paul's letters "tend to 'telegraph' the content of the letter" *(Language,* 257).

[7] See twelve examples of θαυμάζω letters (rebuke-request letters) in Hansen, *Abraham in Galatians,* 33–42.

[8] See G. N. Stanton's criticism of the use of the rebuke-request structure for the outline of Galatians in his *Review* of *Abraham in Galatians,* 615.

Hagar story (4:21–31), and his ethical instructions (5:1–6:10). Paul closes the letter with a subscription in his own hand (6:11–18).

The epistolary structure of Galatians is presented by Longenecker as follows:[9]

1:1–5	Salutation;
1:6–4:11	Rebuke Section, with the inclusion of autobiographical details and theological arguments;
4:12–6:10	Request Section, with the inclusion of personal, scriptural, and ethical appeals;
6:11–18	Subscription.

Longenecker's outline of the epistolary structure of Galatians turns a high-wattage spotlight on the major turning point of the letter at 4:12 where Paul moves from his rebuke section to his initial request: Γίνεσθε ὡς ἐγώ—"Become as I am." Most commentaries view 4:12–20 as a subsidiary argument in a long chain of arguments stretching from 3:1–4:31 or as a parenthetical digression.[10] But when we view the request in 4:12 as the major turning point in the letter, then we are given a new perspective on the entire first half of the body of the letter (1:6–4:11). C. J. Bjerkelund's extensive analysis of request formulae in Paul's letters indicates that Paul's requests are prefaced by a background section which prepares the way for the request.[11] He discerns what he calls the εὐχαριστῶ παρακαλῶ structure in Paul's letters. In this "thanksgiving-request" letter structure, the thanksgiving section serves as a background section for the request. Similarly, in Galatians, the rebuke section is a background for the request in 4:12.

Paul's autobiography (1:11–2:21) has generally been interpreted as Paul's defence of his apostleship against accusations and misunderstandings which can only be conjured up by speculative mirror-reading of the text.[12] And Paul's exposition of scriptural texts in ch. 3 has been viewed as his response to his opponents' use of the same texts.[13] In other words, the interpretation has to a large extent been dependent on the validity of the speculation about the case against Paul. But when we view the first half of the letter as the background for his request in 4:12, we can redirect our attention from imaginary opponents to a more fundamental question of interpretation: how did Paul prepare the way for his request in 4:12 by telling his own story (1:11–2:21) and the story of Abraham (3:6–4:11)?

After his rebuke for desertion from the gospel (1:6–10), Paul intensifies his rebuke by setting forth the story of his own experience of the truth of the gospel (1:11–2:21). His story of his conversion highlights the dramatic reversal in his life when he received the revelation of Christ (1:11–16). In his account of his pre-Christian life, Paul refers twice to his past life as his life "in Judaism" (1:13–14). Even though Paul always

---

[9] R. Longenecker, *Galatians*, cix.
[10] See Betz, *Galatians*, 220–21.
[11] Bjerkelund, *Parakalô*, 139.
[12] See the analysis of the pitfalls of mirror-reading in Barclay, "Mirror-Reading."
[13] Barrett, "Allegory," 158.

identified himself as a Jew ("I am an Israelite myself, a descendant of Abraham, from the tribe of Benjamin"; Rom 11:1), he used the phrase "in Judaism" as a way of describing his life before he was "in Christ." Judaism was the distinctive Jewish way of life. Before his conversion the Jewish identity markers such as circumcision, kosher food, and Sabbath observance were Paul's frame of reference for his own identity; but they were no longer significant for Paul when he found his new identity in Christ. In his conversion experience, God commissioned him to call Gentiles to believe in Christ (Gal 1:15–16). Even under pressure by leaders in the church to compromise the truth of the gospel by demanding Gentiles to live like Jews, Paul remained true to the gospel and defended the freedom of Gentiles from those demands (2:1–14). In his own personal experience of the significance of the gospel story, Paul was set free from the law to live for God: "for through the law I died to the law, so that I might live to God, I have been crucified with Christ; and it is no longer I who live, but it is Christ who lives in me" (2:19–20). As a Jewish Christian, Paul had turned from seeking to destroy the church of God in his devotion to traditions within Judaism (1:13–14) to "running" in his mission to the Gentiles (2:2) and living "by faith in the Son of God" (2:20).

The irony of the Galatian crisis was that the Gentile Christians' commitment to Christ was eclipsed by their attempts to observe the distinctive Jewish way of life. Under pressure from the teachers of the law, they were moving in the opposite direction from Paul's conversion process: whereas Paul moved from life in Judaism to life in Christ, they were moving from life in Christ to life in Judaism. G. Lyons is right when he concludes that "Paul presents his autobiography as a paradigm of the gospel of Christian freedom which he seeks to persuade his readers to reaffirm in the face of the threat presented by the troublemakers."[14] Lyons' conclusion is supported by our recognition of the rebuke-request structure of Paul's letter. Paul presented his own story to the Galatian believers as a background to his request—"become like me." By looking at his story they could see how to find their identity in Christ rather than in Judaism.

Paul's rebuke for foolishness about the gospel (3:1–5) is followed by a detailed scriptural exposition of the meaning of the gospel in terms of the promise given to Abraham (3:6–4:11). Paul retells the story of Abraham to prove that the blessing for Gentiles promised to Abraham is not obtained by keeping the law of Moses in order to establish a Jewish identity. The unity of all heirs of the promise—Jewish and Gentile—could not be accomplished by observance of the law because the law imprisoned all under sin and separated Jews from Gentiles.[15] The promised blessing for Gentiles is received by faith in Christ and experienced by the presence of the Spirit who witnesses to the believers' true identity as children of God.

Paul's story (1:11–21) and the Abraham story (3:6–4:11) present parallel paradigms to prepare the way for the request in 4:12. As Paul's life was transformed by his faith in the gospel, so Abraham was characterized by his faith in the gospel given to him in the promise (3:6–9). In both stories the same features of the gospel are disclosed: the revelatory origin of the gospel, the blessing for Gentiles in the gospel, and the exclusion

---

[14] See Lyons, *Pauline Autobiography*, 171.
[15] See Wright, *Climax*, 170–72.

of Jewishness as the basis for the inclusion of Gentiles. At the center of both Paul's own story (1:11–2:21) and the story of Abraham (3:6–4:11) is the story of Christ. As R. Hays says, "the Abraham story is for Paul taken up into the Christ story, and the Christ story is understood, with the hindsight of narrative logic, as the fit sequel to the Abraham story."[16] Consequently, not only do we see Paul presenting himself as a paradigm for the church (2:18–21), but we also see him "discovering in the story of Abraham a prefiguration of the church."[17] Abraham had offspring among the Gentiles who believed in the gospel (3:7, 29); so did Paul (4:19). Paul's story leads to the conclusion that when the ego—self-centeredness—is crucified there will be a release from bondage to the law and an experience of new life in Christ which unites Jewish and Gentile Christians (2:15–21). The Abraham story leads to the same conclusion: baptism into Christ unites Jews and Gentiles, slave and free, male and female (3:27–29).

So when Paul is requesting Christians to become like him (4:12) he is urging them to center their lives in Christ, just as he centered his life in Christ by faith in Christ and as Abraham centered his life in Christ by faith in the promise of Christ. Egocentricity and ethnocentricity must be crucified with Christ because they do not reflect the gospel.

Immediately after his request in 4:12, the first reason Paul gives to his readers to identify with him is his identification with them: "for I became like you." As a Pharisee Paul was trained to practise a kind of second degree separation: he would not even associate with a Jew who associated with Gentiles. A major theme in the Jewish literature of Paul's era was devoted to separation from Gentiles.[18] The book of *Jubilees* demanded separation: "Separate yourself from the nations, and eat not with them . . . for their works are unclean, and all their ways are a pollution and an abomination and an uncleanness" (22:16). According to the *Letter of Aristeas,* Moses "fenced us round with impregnable ramparts and walls of iron, that we might not mingle at all with any of the other nations, but remain pure in body and soul . . . he hedged us round on all sides by rules of purity, affecting alike what we eat, or drink, or touch, or hear, or see" (139, 142). And yet Paul's new identity in Christ gave him the capacity to transcend his racial identity as a Jew and to stand with Gentile brothers and sisters in Christ. He became as they were: he ate with them; he was one with them. On that basis he calls for them to become as he is: one who no longer seeks to define his identity primarily on racial, national, or social grounds, but one whose identity is determined by union with Christ and all who belong to Christ. After all, if Paul as a Jewish Christian was willing and able to be one with Gentiles, then it was clear that living like a Jew or like a Gentile was not what mattered. What mattered was living by faith in Christ.

Paul illustrated his identification with Gentile believers by his account of his confrontation with Peter and the rest of the Jewish believers for violating the truth of the gospel by withdrawing from table-fellowship with Gentile believers (2:11–21). They were more influenced by their common racial identity as Jews than by their new

---

[16] Hays, *Faith,* 226.
[17] Hays, *Echoes,* 105.
[18] See Dunn, *Commentary,* 119–20.

experience of unity with all believers in Christ. From Paul's perspective, Peter's separation from table-fellowship with Gentile Christians implied that the relationship of
Gentile believers with God and with Jewish Christians depended on identification with
the Jewish nation.[19] When Paul saw that Peter and the rest of the Jewish believers were
not walking in accord with the truth of the gospel (οὐκ ὀρθοποδοῦσιν πρὸς τὴν
ἀλήθειαν τοῦ εὐαγγελίου, 2:14), he rebuked Peter for trying to force Gentile believers
to become Jews (πῶς τὰ ἔθνη ἀναγκάζεις Ἰουδαΐζειν;). The oneness of believers in
Christ had been destroyed and the truth of the gospel had been negated because Christians had been more deeply influenced by their racial identity than by their identity and
unity in Christ.

The social crisis in the church of Antioch was exactly the same as the crisis faced
by the churches in Galatia: Gentile believers were being forced to live like Jews as the
basis of unity in the church. Paul's solution to the social problem was his exposition
of the gospel as seen in his own paradigmatic experience. If Paul and other Jewish
Christians who were seeking to be justified in Christ were found to be sinners on the
basis of the law for their practice of table-fellowship with Gentiles, that did not make
Christ the agent of sin (2:17).[20] For the real transgression would be the reconstruction of the barrier of the law between Jews and Gentiles which had been removed in
Christ (2:18).[21] But Paul refused to reconstruct the barrier of the law between Jews
and Gentiles because he had died to the law in his experience of the cross of Christ
(2:19). The only way to maintain the unity of all believers in Christ is to declare with
Paul Χριστῷ συνεσταύρωμαι! ("I am crucified with Christ!"). Only when believers
become like Paul in his experience of the cross will they know what it is to die to the
law so that they can then live to God (2:19) by the presence of the indwelling Christ
(2:20). So Paul's initial request is simple: "Become like me!"

The Subscription in 6:11–18

Epistolary analysis has highlighted the importance of the conclusions of letters.
From his survey of subscriptions in common Hellenistic letters, G. Bahr concludes
that the subscription served as an opportunity for the signatory to recapitulate the
cardinal points of the letter.[22] By giving the summary in his own hand, the signatory
made the contents of the document his own. According to Betz, Paul's conclusion in
6:11–18 "contains the interpretive clues to the understanding of Paul's major concerns in the letter as a whole and should be employed as the hermeneutical key to the
intentions of the Apostle."[23] Paul himself draws attention to the significance of his
concluding paragraph by writing it with large letters in his own hand (6:11).

---

[19] Richardson defends Peter's application of Paul's own principle of accommodation ("Pauline
Inconsistency").
[20] See Lambrecht, "Line of Thought."
[21] See Ziesler, *Righteousness*, 173: "The real sin is not the infringing the law, but in disloyalty to
Christ and to the new way of acceptability in and through him."
[22] Bahr, "Subscriptions," 35.
[23] Betz, *Galatians*, 313.

If Paul's initial request in 4:12 ("Become like me!") is a major concern of Paul, then we should expect that Paul would conclude the letter by presenting his own experience as a paradigm for the Galatians to follow. In fact, that is just what we find. Paul's paradigmatic experience of the gospel is recapitulated in his conclusion: ἐμοὶ δὲ μὴ γένοιτο καυχᾶσθαι εἰ μὴ ἐν τῷ σταυρῷ τοῦ κυρίου ἡμῶν Ἰησοῦ Χρισοῦ, δι' οὗ ἐμοὶ κόσμος ἐσταύρωται κἀγὼ κόσμῳ ("But may it never be that I should boast except in the cross of our Lord Jesus Christ, through which the world has been crucified to me and I to the world," 6:14). For Paul the experience of the gospel was conceived in apocalyptic terms: it was the end of the world for him. The end of the world, Paul explains in 6:15, means an end of the significance of circumcision and uncircumcision, for now there is a new creation. The old world order was structured by the opposition of circumcised and uncircumcised, slave and free, male and female. But that world was overthrown by the cross of Christ. In the new creation there is no longer the opposition of Jew and Gentile, slave and free, male and female, for all are one in Christ (3:28).[24]

Paul's use of apocalyptic language here about the death of the cosmos obviously does not refer to the end of the space-time universe. N. T. Wright has cogently argued that "there is no justification for seeing 'apocalyptic' as necessarily speaking of the 'end of the world' in a literally cosmic sense. . . . An end to the present world order, yes. . . . The end of the space-time world, no. . . . We must read most apocalyptic literature, both Jewish and Christian, as a complex metaphor-system which invests space-time reality with its full, that is, its theological, significance."[25] Paul's apocalyptic metaphor of the crucifixion of the world expressed the reality of his own experience of the cross of Christ. His personal reference, ἐμοί ("to me") points to a radical change in his own person. He no longer identified himself on the basis of racial or social polarities such as circumcision or uncircumcision. He contrasted himself to those in the old world order who placed such supreme importance on racial distinctive (6:13–14).

But we should not infer from Paul's personal reference to his own experience of the cross that he was using apocalyptic language only to describe his own individual, private world. Certainly his own worldview changed. But his language speaks of more than simply a change of his personal perspective. Paul speaks of three crosses: he boasts in "the cross of our Lord Jesus Christ"; the crucifixion of the world to Paul and the crucifixion of Paul to the world are derivative consequences of the cross of Christ.[26] Paul's focus is on the apocalyptic event of the cross of Christ. Through his participation in that apocalyptic event, the world has been crucified to Paul. The perfect tense of the verb ἐσταύρωται ("has been crucified") points to a permanent change: the crucifixion of the world cannot be reversed for Paul; he no longer lives in the world where the distinctions of race—circumcision and uncircumcision—are of supreme importance and where boasting in the flesh (vv. 13–14) is the primary preoccupation; from now he lives in the "new creation" (v. 15) where there is a whole

---

[24] Martyn, "Apocalyptic Antinomies."
[25] See Wright, New Testament, 298–99.
[26] Minear, "Crucified World."

new order of relationships. No wonder Richard Hays hears "echoes" of Isa 65:17 in Paul's reference to the new creation.[27] "For behold, I create new heavens and a new earth; and the former things shall not be remembered or come to mind" (Isa 65:17). Through the cross of Christ, Paul was separated from the old world by the death of that world and by his own death. And through the cross of Christ, Paul was ushered into the new world, the new creation. Martyn observes that "the motif of the triple crucifixion—that of Christ, that of the cosmos, and that of Paul—reflects the fact that through the whole of Galatians the focus of Paul's apocalyptic lies not on Christ's parousia, but rather on his death."[28] Despite Beker's claim that "the Christocentric focus of Galatians pushes Paul's theocentric apocalyptic theme to the periphery,"[29] the cross appears throughout Galatians as the apocalyptic event where the cosmic triumph of God has already taken place.

Paul's personal experience of the end of the world through the cross and of the new creation is set forth as a paradigm, a "rule" for the whole community of believers. "Whoever will walk by this rule" (καὶ ὅσοι τῷ κανόνι τούτῳ στοιχήσουσιν) will be blessed with peace and mercy (6:16).

From the vantage point of Paul's initial request in 4:12 we can see that Paul's first person expression of his own experience of the gospel in his concluding paragraph of the letter (6:14–16) is a final restatement of his original request—"Become like me!" Paul has presented his experience of the apocalypse as a paradigm for all believers to imitate. Here we have an "interpretative clue" to give us help in understanding Paul's apocalyptic conception of the gospel in the rest of his letter.

The Salutation (1:1–5)

Paul expands the standard form (sender, addressee, greetings) in his letter to the Galatians with strong statements regarding his commission as an apostle (1:1) and the death of Christ (1:4). His unusual interruption of the opening greetings and departure from the normal form with these two statements highlights their importance. In his assertion that he was commissioned as an apostle by "Jesus Christ and God the Father who raised him from the dead" (1:1), Paul expresses his new understanding of God, in contrast to his pre-Christian beliefs, as the God who raised Jesus from the dead. Of course, the Jewish apocalyptic worldview anticipated that the present age would end in death and the new age would begin with resurrection. But now in the resurrection of Jesus Christ, the triumph over death has already begun; the new age has dawned.[30] "By implication," Dunn comments, "those to whom the resurrected Christ revealed himself could share of the power of that new age, some of the life which had defeated death."[31] Paul's commission by Jesus Christ whom God the

---

[27] Hays, *Echoes*, 159.
[28] Martyn, "Apocalyptic Antinomies," 420.
[29] Beker, *Paul*, 58.
[30] Dunn, *Theology*, 47.
[31] Dunn, *Commentary*, 29.

Father had raised from the dead brought Paul into a personal experience of the life and the power of the new creation.

In his description of the purpose of the death of Jesus (1:4), Paul employs an apocalyptic metaphor: ὅπως ἐξέληται ἡμᾶς ἐκ τοῦ αἰῶνος τοῦ ἐνεστῶτος πονηροῦ ("that he might rescue us from the present evil age"). From the perspective of the Jewish apocalyptic framework the present age dominated by evil would be followed by the future age under the rule of God. In Paul's experience, the rescue operation from the present evil age began in the death of Jesus and continues in the participation of believers in the benefits of that death.

Paul's expansion of his opening greetings with references to his appointment to apostleship by Jesus, whom God the Father raised from the dead, and his deliverance from the present evil age by Jesus, who gave himself for our sins, introduces the major theme of the entire letter: Paul's personal participation in the gospel—the death and resurrection of Jesus—was a participation in the apocalypse, the intervention of God within history which brought to an end the old world order and brought into being the new creation.

It is helpful to sketch out how the theme of the gospel as found in the salutation is developed in the letter. The spotlight is kept on the gospel in the section immediately after the salutation. Although Paul asserts his divine appointment in 1:1, the opening expression of rebuke (1:6–10) is not, as might have been expected, a direct development of his claim to apostolic authority. Paul moves instead to rebuke the Galatian believers for defection from the true gospel and pronounces an anathema on all who pervert the gospel. Paul includes himself under the curse against those who pervert the gospel (1:8). The gospel takes precedence over the apostle. Schütz correctly asserts that "because the gospel is singular and takes precedence, both Paul and the community can be subordinated to it. Paul can preach only what he has already preached, and the community can receive only what it has already received. The gospel is thus a double-sided norm—for preaching and for receiving. It is the norm for faith and the norm for apostleship. By virtue of their dependence on, and the need for their obedience to, the one gospel, faith and apostleship are brought into the closest possible relationship."[32] It was precisely Paul's subordination to the standard of the gospel that validated his own apostleship and inspired the faith of the community.

The main theme of Paul's autobiography is not primarily a defence of apostolic authority as many have supposed, but a defence of the ultimate authority of the gospel. Lategan is at least partly right when he concludes that "far from focusing on Paul, his apostleship and authority, Galatians has as subject the remarkable gospel. . . . Both the experience of Paul and the Galatians conform to the unexpected and liberating nature of the gospel and it is to this gospel οὐ κατὰ ἄνθρωπον to which he wants them to return."[33] Lategan is not right when he says that Paul does not focus on himself. Paul does focus on himself to a considerable extent in his autobiography, but only as a way of demonstrating his conformity to the gospel. In 1:1–12, the gospel

---

[32] Schütz, *Paul*, 123.
[33] Lategan, "Defending," 430.

(εὐαγγέλιον) is the main topic (1:6; 1:7 [2x]; 1:9; 1:11 [2x]), while the title ἀπόστολος is used only in 1:1. In the entire letter, "apostle" is mentioned only four times,[34] while the word "gospel" and its derivatives occurs fourteen times.[35] Paul set forth the gospel as the authority to which an angel from heaven and he himself (1:8), the false brothers (2:4–5), the "pillars" of the church (2:9), and even Peter himself (2:14) are all to be subordinated and held accountable. Whoever perverts the gospel by word or action is under a curse (1:8–9), must be resisted (2:5) and rebuked (2:11–14).

After establishing the "truth of the gospel" as the touchstone of genuine authority in his autobiography, Paul sets forth his scriptural exposition of the nature of the gospel. He interprets the Abraham story in such a way as to undergird the gospel which he received and preached, and so provides a biblical basis for his own authority. Only after his authority is firmly grounded in his autobiographical account of his own loyalty to the gospel and in his exposition of the Abraham story does Paul then make his appeal for the allegiance of the Galatian believers (4:12–20). Even then, however, Paul first gives an allegorical interpretation of the Hagar story (4:21–31) before finally announcing in a clear, authoritative tone his decision regarding their case: "Behold, I, Paul, say to you . . ." (5:2).

If Paul's appeal for his converts' allegiance (4:12) and his apostolic decree (5:2) had followed directly after his salutation, it would have been clear that Paul based his authority on his apostolic appointment (1:1). Such a basis, however, would have left him at a severe disadvantage with respect to those whose priority and popularity could not be challenged. Paul, therefore, responds to the conflict between authorities by arguing that the gospel is the only final standard of authority. In his autobiography and in his interpretation of the Abraham story, he seeks to demonstrate his faithfulness to this standard, in contrast to those who deviated from it. Paul's personal participation in the apocalyptic events of the gospel provides the foundation for all his appeals and decrees.

The Disclosure Statement at 1:11–12

Some kind of disclosure statement often serves as a transition from the opening of the letter into the body of the letter (1 Thess 1:5; 1 Cor 1:11; 2 Cor 1:8; Rom 1:13; Phil 1:12).[36] After his opening rebuke of 1:6–10, Paul moves into the body of the letter with a disclosure formula: "For I want you to know, brothers . . ." (Γνωρίζω γὰρ ὑμῖν, ἀδελφοί, 1:11). In Paul's disclosure of the nature and origin of the gospel he uses the same "not . . . nor, but" structure as he used in his affirmation of his apostolic commission in 1:1. His denial of any human origin for the gospel he preached (1:11–12) is parallel to his denial of any human origin of his apostleship (1:1). Yet an-

---

[34] Gal 1:1; 1:17; 1:19; 2:8.
[35] Gal 1:6; 1:7; 1:8 [2x]; 1:9; 1:11 [2x]; 1:16; 1:23; 2:2; 2:5; 2:7; 2:14; 4:13.
[36] J. Sanders, "Transition"; Mullins, "Disclosure."

other double denial of dependence on human direction and an affirmation of a reve-latory call to his Gentile mission is found in 1:15–17. As Betz notes, there are parallels to this "not . . . nor, but" construction in Jewish traditions of the call of a prophet.[37] Amos affirmed his prophetic appointment in similar terms: "I am not a prophet, nor am I the son of a prophet; for I am a herdsman and a grower of sycamore figs. But the Lord took me from following the flock and the Lord said to me, 'Go and prophesy to my people Israel'" (Amos 7:14–15). Even the denial of a prophetic call is expressed in a similar form: "Then the Lord said to me, 'The prophets are prophesying in my name. I have neither sent them nor commanded them nor spoken to them' (Jer 14:14). 'I did not send these prophets, but they ran. I did not speak to them but they prophesied'" (Jer 23:21). Paul's sense of his prophetic call is clarified when we com-pare his description of his own call to his Gentile mission and the call of the Hebrew prophets:

| But when God, who had set me apart before I was born and called me though his grace, was pleased to reveal his Son to me, so that I might proclaim him among the Gentiles . . . (1:15–16) | "The Lord called me from the womb; from the body of my mother he named me . . ." (Isa 49:1). "Now the word of the Lord came to me saying, 'Before I formed you in the womb, I knew you, and before you were born I consecrated you; I have appointed you a prophet to the nations.'" (Jer 1:4–5) |

Paul's references to his experience of "revelation" (1:12, 16; 2:2) also draws atten-tion to his prophetic stance. His gospel message was not received by human tradition but through "the revelation of Jesus Christ" (δι' ἀποκαλύψεως Ἰησοῦ Χριστοῦ). As a prophet spoke with revelational immediacy when he said, "The Lord says," so Paul spoke out of his personal encounter with the risen Lord. Paul's expression in 1:12 "describes Jesus Christ as the one who has revealed Himself and made him His apostle, this revelation being an act of God's grace."[38]

Paul places the revelation of Jesus Christ within the perspective of salvation-his-tory in 3:23: "Now before faith came, we were imprisoned and guarded under law until faith would be revealed." Paul's point here is that the faith of Christians radically altered their relation to the law. Since "Christ's coming actualises faith"[39] which re-leases believers from imprisonment under the law, Paul can speak of the coincidence of the revealing of faith and the coming of Christ. The parallel phrases "until faith would be revealed" (εἰς τὴν μέλλουσαν πίστιν ἀποκαλυφθῆναι, 3:23) and "until Christ" (εἰς Χριστόν, 3:24) point to the same event in history: the revelation of Christ and as a result the revelation of faith. Paul's use of the verb ἀποκαλυ-φθῆναι("to be revealed") borrows from the language of "technical apocalyptic ter-minology" and has "the sense both of heavenly unveiling and climactic turning point in the divine purpose."[40] Paul's participation in that apocalyptic event occurred when "God was pleased to reveal (ἀποκαλύψαι) his son" in him (1:16). The revelation Paul

---

[37] Betz, *Galatians*, 38 n. 19.
[38] Grundmann, "χρίω, κτλ," 9.551.
[39] Beker, *Paul*, 56.
[40] Dunn, *Theology*, 48.

received was more than the revelation received by the prophets of old. They were given the promise; Paul was given the revelation of the Son "in the fullness of time" (4:4). They looked forward to the end; Paul experienced the end of the world and the new creation—the eschatological climax of God's purpose in history. He became a paradigm of the apocalypse for the church to follow.

Conclusion

When we use the most prominent points of the rebuke-request structure of Paul's letter to the Galatians as vantage points from which to view the rest of the letter, we are given a fresh perspective of the purpose that each part of the letter serves to accomplish Paul's objectives. Most significant of all is the way Paul constructs the rebuke section of the letter (1:6–4:11) to prepare the way for his initial request for the Galatian believers to imitate his example (4:12). Both Paul's story (1:11–21) and the Abraham story (3:6–4:11) establish a pattern of faith in Christ for Gentile believers to follow so that they can participate in the promised blessing. The focus of the subscription (6:11–18) on Paul's end-of-the-world and new-creation experience by his identification with the cross of Christ shows us that Paul's example for the Galatian believers is a demonstration of the way to bring about the abolition of the old world order of divisions between races ("circumcision and uncircumcision") and the inauguration of the new creation of unity in Christ through the personal appropriation of the cross of Christ. The salutation (1:1–5) places special emphasis on Paul's participation in the resurrection power of Christ (1:1) and Christ's rescue operation from the "present evil age" through his cross (1:4). This theme is developed in Paul's story of his defence of the "truth of the gospel" (2:5, 14) to protect the freedom of Gentile believers from the obligations of the law. The disclosure statement which introduces Paul's autobiography asserts that the origin of the gospel is the revelation of Jesus Christ (1:11–12), a revelation given by God to Paul so that he would preach the gospel of Christ to the Gentiles (1:16).

All of these elements of the rebuke-request structure of Galatians point in the same direction: they feature Paul's participation in the apocalypse of Jesus Christ which guarantees the inclusion of Gentile believers in the people of God. The emphasis on the apocalyptic event of the cross has a social purpose: to protect the freedom and unity of all believers in the new creation in Christ. Paul presents himself as a paradigm of the apocalypse.

PART II

Autobiographical Narratives

Section A
Rhetorical Approaches

9

RHETORICAL IDENTIFICATION IN PAUL'S AUTOBIOGRAPHICAL NARRATIVE: GALATIANS 1:13–2:14

Paul E. Koptak

W hile most studies of Paul's autobiography in Galatians 1:13–2:14 acknowledge the importance of Paul's relationship with the Christians of Galatia, little attention has been given to the language Paul uses to describe relationships within the autobiographical narrative itself. This study will examine the relationships that Paul portrays and creates with the Jerusalem apostles, his opponents, and the Galatians as a means to depict symbolically the issues at stake in Galatia. The literary-rhetorical method of Kenneth Burke will be employed to this end, with special focus on Burke's idea of identification.

Introduction

Until very recently, most studies of Galatians have followed the suggestion of Martin Luther that Paul's autobiographical remarks in Galatians 1 and 2 were "boasting and glorying" that followed out of his divine calling. Paul defended himself in order to defend the gospel.[1]

H. D. Betz took this tradition[2] one step further when he compared Paul's letter with the rhetorical handbooks of the time and concluded that the whole of Galatians took the form of an apologetic letter.[3] Betz's commentary has not failed to attract criticism.[4] New methods of rhetorical and literary study have challenged the apologetic model and have suggested alternative understandings. Three examples follow.

---

[1] Luther, *Galatians,* 35, 87.

[2] Calvin, *Epistles,* 4–5: See also Lighfoot, *Galatians,* 64, 71; Burton, *Galatians,* 72; Bruce, "Further Thoughts," 22; Oepke, *Galater,* 29, 53–54; Sampley, "Before God."

[3] Betz, *Galatians,* 14–15. Betz designates Gal 1:12–2:14 as the *narratio,* a statement of the facts that serves as the basis for later argument (58–62).

[4] Fung, *Galatians,* 28–32, surveys the reviews that are critical of Betz's approach and concludes that "*apologia* is *not* the most appropriate category to apply to the letter as a whole." However, against Fung's assertion that no examples of apologetic letters exist (quoting Meeks and

George Kennedy has argued that the presence of a hortatory section (5:1–6:10) indicates that Galatians as a whole functions as deliberative rhetoric (that which deals with future courses of action) and not as the forensic rhetoric *of apologia*.[5] Kennedy understands the narrative of 1:13–2:14 to be proof of Paul's statement of the *proem* (1:6–10) that there is no other gospel; it is therefore not part of an apology. Kennedy also does not use the term autobiography for this narrative. It is rather a proof, a building block of Paul's argument.

Another rhetorical approach was taken by George Lyons, who found parallels between Galatians and Greco-Roman autobiographies (Cicero, Isocrates, and Demosthenes).[6] Lyons claims that Paul's comments should be explained as an effort to demonstrate his *ēthos* (character) to his readers.[7]

Beverly Roberts Gaventa presented a third challenge to the apologetic model. Gaventa concluded that Paul's reference to the "revelation of Jesus Christ" in 1:15–17 is central to the text and places its focus on the manner in which Paul received his gospel.[8] She thus argues that Galatians 1 and 2 cannot be confined to the category of apology. Further, Galatians is closer in form and purpose to the letters of Seneca and Pliny than to the autobiographical narratives cited by Lyons and the advice of Quintilian cited by Betz. Seneca and Pliny wrote with the purposes of moral exhortation and instruction in view. In a similar manner, Paul used his narrative to offer himself as a paradigm of the power of the gospel (Gal 4:12).[9]

These new studies give some additional attention to Paul's orientation toward the Galatian audience and thus follow the advice of the classical writers.[10] Emphases on Pauline exhortation, *ēthos,* and example do turn the focus of study toward Paul's relation to the Galatians and away from Paul's answer to the charges of his opponents.[11]

Yet these studies also cast Paul as an individual communicator who addresses his audience by means of a letter. Comparisons with classical examples and prescriptions

---

Russel, 30), see Berger, "Hellenistische Gattungen." Berger upholds Betz's decision and also cites Plato's *Seventh Letter* as an example that merged the forms of letter, autobiography, and apologetic speech.

[5] Kennedy, *New Testament Interpretation,* 146–48. See Aristotle, *Rhet.* 1.3.1–20 (1358b), for the distinction between three types of rhetoric: forensic, political, and ceremonial.

[6] Lyons, *Pauline Autobiography,* 135: These autobiographies all recount the subject's ἀνα-στροφή (conduct), πράξεις (deeds), λόγοι (words), and make a σύγκρισις (comparison) of the subject's character with that of another.

[7] Lyons, *Pauline Autobiography,* 102–4, 61: See also the similar comments by Aune, *Literary Environment,* 189–90. Aristotle distinguished the ethical, logical, and emotional modes of persuasion (*Rhet.* 1.2.1356a, 1377b–1378).

[8] Gaventa, *From Darkness,* 28.

[9] Gaventa, "Galatians 1 and 2," 326.

[10] Roberts (*Greek Rhetoric,* 50) held that the focus of the entire second book of Aristotle's *Rhetoric* was on the audience. See also Cicero, *De or.* 1.51: "That no man can, by speaking, excite the passions of his audience, or calm them when excited . . . unless (he is) one who has gained a thorough insight into the nature of all things, and the dispositions and motives of mankind . . ."

[11] See Lyons's critique of the "mirror method" reconstruction of the opponent's charges, *Pauline Autobiography,* 96–104.

only strengthen the emphasis on Paul's references to himself and overlook the statements he makes about others.[12] To date, no study has paid particular attention to Paul's depiction of his relationships *within* the autobiographical narrative as a means to enhance further his relationship with the Galatians and to urge them away from circumcision.[13]

In addition, no study has examined the narrative as a dramatization of the issues confronting the Galatians. Above all else, the autobiography is a story with a distinct rhetorical component. As Paul tells his story, he draws a number of symbolic parallels between his own past and the present situation at Galatia. In particular, Paul means to point out the exact parallel between those persons who opposed him by attempting to compromise the gospel and those who were putting pressure on the Galatians to be circumcised. By drawing clear lines between those who stood against him and those who stood with him, Paul intends to show the Galatians the results that their choice will bring. As he draws a narrative portrait of his past relationships, he at the same time invites them to affirm their present relationship with him by resisting circumcision. In order to study these relationships, a summary of Kenneth Burke's rhetorical-literary concept of identification will be outlined below.

Kenneth Burke and Identification

Kenneth Burke began his career as a poet, a writer of fiction, and a literary critic. In the course of his thinking about literature, he noted that imbedded within all literary form was a rhetorical component. In time, he expanded his idea of rhetoric to embrace all of human communication. "Wherever there is persuasion, there is rhetoric. And wherever there is 'meaning' there is 'persuasion.'"[14]

A central idea in Burke's approach to rhetoric is the principle of identification, which may be understood as the attempt to overcome human division through the establishment of some common ground. His description of human division often makes use of biblical terminology, as for example, his "problem of Babel":

> The theologian's concerns with Eden and the "fall" come close to the heart of the rhetorical problem. For, behind the theology, there is the perception of generic divisiveness which, being common to all men, is a universal fact about them, prior to any divisiveness caused by social classes. Here is the basis of rhetoric.[15]

---

[12] Studies on Greco-Roman biography and autobiography often single out a focus on the individual as the constituting feature of the genre. See the articles "Biography, Greek," and "Biography, Roman," *OCD* 136; "Biographie," *KlPauly* 1:902–3; Misch, *Autobiographhy,* vii, 69; Stuart, *Epochs,* 39. This approach has been criticized by Momigliano, *Development,* 11–18.

[13] Although Betz does note Paul's use of the friendship motif to enhance his relationship with the Galatians in Gal 4:12–20, he does not treat Paul's depiction of relationships in Gal 1–2 (*Galatians,* 220–37).

[14] Burke, *Rhetoric of Motives,* 172.

[15] Ibid., 146.

Traditional approaches to rhetoric have described the attempt to overcome division as "persuasion."[16] In this view, a communicator seeks to persuade an audience by winning it over to a given position so that the situation becomes, in effect, a contest of opinions and wills. Through identification, however, a communicator seeks to elicit consensus and cooperation by demonstrating what Burke calls a "consubstantiality" between communicator and audience. The depiction of consubstantiality points out where persons "stand together" (from the etymology of the word) and shows how they share a similar concern or interest.[17]

Although Burke himself has said that the difference between persuasion and identification distinguishes traditional rhetoric from the "New Rhetoric,"[18] he adds that in his mind, the two are not in conflict.

> As for the relation between "identification" and "persuasion": we might well keep it in mind that a speaker persuades an audience by the use of stylistic identifications; his act of persuasion may be for the purpose of causing the audience to identify itself with the speaker's interests; and the speaker draws on identification of interests to establish rapport between himself and his audience. So, there is no chance of our keeping apart the meanings of persuasion, identification ("consubstantiality") and communication.[19]

Identification is a two way process. As the communicator establishes rapport by identifying with the audience's concerns, the audience begins to identify with those of the communicator. The sharing of opinion in one area works as a fulcrum to move opinion in another.[20]

A Burkean approach to the study of Paul's autobiographical narrative seeks to discover both the ways in which Paul sought to identify with the Galatians and the ways in which he asked them directly and indirectly, to identify with him and his message. One also watches for evidence of Paul's attempts to highlight relationships that are based upon a common understanding of the circumcision-free gospel. By depicting these relationships, Paul creates a consubstantiality (a standing together) that he asks his hearers, the Galatians, to join by rejecting circumcision. Similarly, Paul also creates relational distance between himself and those who do not share that common understanding of the gospel. As the Galatians hear Paul tell his story of his past relationships, they are forced to decide whether they will stand with Paul and his understanding of the gospel, or with those who are urging them to be circumcised. What Paul makes clear to them is that they cannot have it both ways. In addition, the narrative also shows that Paul is really concerned for their welfare, while those urging circumcision are not.

---

[16] Aristotle gave this idea its clearest expression when he defined rhetoric as "the faculty of observing in any given case the available means of persuasion" (*Rhet.* 1.2.25 [1355b]).

[17] Burke, *Rhetoric of Motives,* 62; *Grammar,* 57.

[18] Burke, "Rhetoric Old and New," 203.

[19] Burke, *Rhetoric of Motives,* 46.

[20] Ibid.

Identification in Galatians 1:13–2:14

Galatians 1:1–12

Burke recommends that the analysis of any written work should begin with the "principle of the concordance."[21] The critic builds an index of significant terms: terms that recur in changing contexts, terms that occur at significant points in the narrative, terms that seem heavy with symbolic meaning. One also looks for oppositions, beginnings and endings of sections and subsections, and indications of hierarchies.[22]

One of Paul's most significant terms and oppositions occurs three times prior to his narration of his past life that begins in 1:13: After the opening introduction of his name and title "apostle" in 1:1, he states that his apostleship is not from or through any human agency (ἄνθρωπος). Rather, its source is Christ and God.

The same opposition between human terms and Christ/God terms occurs in vv. 10 and 11–12. In the questions and answer of v. 10, Paul seeks to win God over, not humans (ἄρτι γὰρ ἀνθρώπους πείθω ἢ τὸν θεόν;) and wants to please (ἀρέσκειν) Christ, not humans (ἀνθρώποις). The use of ἔτι ("still") in v. 10 suggests that Paul here refers to a human pleasing desire that was part of his own past.[23] In vv. 11–12 Paul asserts that his gospel (like his apostleship in v. 1) is not a human gospel nor was it taught to him by any human (ἄνθρωπος). Rather it came by a revelation from Christ.

Here then, a pattern of opposition appears three times in the course of the first dozen verses of the epistle. The opposition of the divine and human terms and the orientations they represent structures Paul's thoughts about his apostleship, his motives, and his message.[24]

In addition, this opposition also gives shape to Paul's narrative, particularly as it aids him in his depiction of his relationships. Paul stands (identifies) with those who identify with the divine principle and stands against those who do not, claiming that they have embraced a human principle. The repetition of ἄνθρωπος (seven times in vv. 1–12, four of them plural) highlights the contrast.[25] In other words, Paul has introduced his narrative by stating simply and plainly, "I did not receive my apostleship

---

[21] Burke, "Fact," 283.

[22] Ibid., 299–306.

[23] Gaventa, "Galatians 1 and 2," 314.

[24] Gaventa has noted a similar antithesis between "Christ–new creation" and "the cosmos," based upon Paul's crucifixion to the world in 6:14. This antithesis subsumes a number of minor anthitheses which appear throughout the letter (Christ-law, cross-circumcision) ("Singularity," 324). However, the sevenfold repetition of ἄνθρωπος indicates that a primary antithesis exists between Christ on the one hand, and human motives and sources on the other.

[25] Lyons (*Pauline Autobiography*, 152–56) appreciates the twofold function of the human-divine contrast; Paul asserts both the divinely revealed character of the gospel as well as his own intention to remain loyal to it. However, Lyons believes that Paul's chief purpose was to show that his message was revealed and possessed divine authority, even while he holds that his report of the Antioch incident was meant to show "how easy it was to set aside the grace of God and pervert the gospel" (163). This study argues that the matter of human allegiance to the revealed gospel is equally prominent with Paul's assertion of its divine origin, and that the former follows from the latter.

or my gospel from any human source, and I do not want to please any humans. I received my apostleship and gospel from God and Christ and God and Christ are the ones I want to please." Every action and motive that follows is measured against Paul's basic statement, and Paul relates to every person as friend or foe for that same reason.

Galatians 1:13–24

The structure of opposition continues throughout Paul's retelling of his past life in Judaism. He states that he advanced beyond his contemporaries and was zealous for his father's traditions (1:14), thus describing his experience of Judaism in human, not divine terms. The divine motive enters in when God chooses to reveal his Son and Paul's mission (vv. 15–16). Paul adds that he did not consult human authorities (flesh and blood, apostles) about this, but went away to Arabia.

The above summary suggests that a large part of the motivation that Paul reveals in his narrative up to this point centers in his repudiation of his former way of life.[26] The opposition between his old life and the new is patterned after the opposition between human and divine authority seen in vv. 1–12. There Paul defined his new life as a striving for God's pleasure over that of other men. Here he contrasts God's revelation of his Son with the traditions of his fathers.

As for the apostles, he neither competed with them nor inquired[27] of them (as compared with his relations within Judaism), but rather ignored them. His move away from the apostles to Arabia, therefore, signified his break from a bondage to human tradition and authority. The contrast between Paul's old and new relationships is clear. Whereas Paul described his former life in Judaism as focused on human relationships with his contemporaries and predecessors, his depiction of his new life is so centered on his relation to God that he as yet has no relationship to the other apostles.

Paul then goes on to report that he did finally visit the apostles Cephas and James after three years (1:18). The only indication of his purpose for the visit is given in the verb ἱστορέω, which carries the sense of "visit to inquire of or get information from."[28] Paul stresses the brevity of the visit and the fact that he met with only two of the apostles. After his visit he returned to Gentile territory (1:21, Syria and Cilicia; in 1:17 he goes to Arabia and Damascus). Paul seems determined to emphasize that he was a stranger to Judea, for he adds that even the churches did not know him by sight (1:22).

Yet even while Paul establishes this physical distance between himself and the apostles and churches, he declares a common purpose; the churches hear that Paul now preaches the faith he tried to destroy. Even while many miles separate him from the churches of Judea, he has become one with them through a common faith in the gospel. Paul has established a relationship, a consubstantiality, with Christians throughout Judea. Their praise of God on his account (1:24) indicates that Paul has become a success in his new vocation of pleasing God.

---

[26] Becker, *Galater*, 14–15. Becker maintains that the contrast between Paul's old and new life is the point of narrative, and thus places the "not from men, but from God" idea in the foreground.

[27] "Inquire" may be understood in the sense of "submit for judgment" (Behm, "ἀνατίθημι").

[28] BAGD 383.

The climax of the first portion of Paul's narrative does establish that he did not receive his gospel from a human source, but it does not imply that Paul worked apart from the Jerusalem authorities because he was a rebel or did not agree with them. In fact no reason is given for the departure to Arabia apart from the ongoing opposition of the divine and human motives. In reaction to his prior life, it seems he did not wish to be taught by humans any longer. The churches hear the report (perhaps through Cephas and James) that Paul preached the faith that he once persecuted among the Gentiles, the same faith that the apostles preach.

The chapter ends in a scene of harmony, the division between the old Paul and the church having been overcome through God's revelation of Christ to the persecutor. The source of division between Paul and the church (Christ and the gospel) has now become the source of a consubstantiality. Although Paul states that he has never met the people of these churches, he has used the principle of identification to build a relationship with them within the narrative.

Paul has done much the same with the Jerusalem apostles. He shows that he is one in purpose with the apostles, although he is separate (but not independent) of them. They are joined in allegiance to the purpose of God, whom Paul is anxious to please (1:10). It is Christ, however, whom he serves, not the apostles.

Issues of circumcision and the inclusion of the Gentiles have not yet surfaced in the narrative; therefore, the Galatians are not yet drawn into the story. As they hear this portion, they may simply observe the contrast between Paul's old and new life and notice the harmony created by a common commitment to the faith (1:23). Most of all, they would see the contrast, drawn by Paul, between a commitment to the human traditions of Judaism and faith in the divinely revealed gospel.

Galatians 2:1–10

Paul established that his mission to the Gentiles was greeted with favor in the first section of the narrative (1:1–24). In the second section (2:1–10) Paul adds that the gospel he preached to the Gentiles was circumcision-free. He reports that he went to Jerusalem and met with the apostles, but he laid out before them the message he brought with him; this was not a time for them to instruct him. The mention of revelation in 2:2, whatever else its purpose, clarifies that Paul's ultimate allegiance is to God, not the Jerusalem apostles. Yet Paul also states that he needed to lay out his gospel before the apostles for evaluation in order to forestall some problem, which he believed might cause his work to be in vain, or without lasting effect.[29]

Here within the narrative Paul has defined his relationship with the Jerusalem apostles as a relationship between equals, not that of a subordinate to superiors.[30] The meeting was intended to secure a common understanding of the gospel as

---

[29] Dunn, "Relationship," 468: "what he sought was not so much their approval (without which his gospel would have no validity) as their recognition of his gospel's validity (without which his gospel would have lost its effectiveness)."

[30] Ibid., 466–68. Dunn argues that contemporary uses of ἀνατίθημι do not indicate a distinction in status between Paul and the apostles.

circumcision-free. Therefore Paul is not seeking to invoke apostolic authority by appealing to Jerusalem; he has already established that he speaks with apostolic authority himself. Rather, Paul intends to show that the Jerusalem apostles stood with him in his understanding of the circumcision-free gospel and with God who revealed it to him.

Paul notes two major results of the meeting: Titus was not compelled to be circumcised and Paul's mission to the Gentiles was received warmly. Although the sentences of 2:2–5 appear to be incomplete and do not follow grammatical convention, the use of διά with the accusative in v. 4 suggests that the false brothers were behind the push to circumcise the Gentile Christian. Paul's response was firm; Titus was not compelled (2:3) and Paul and his companions did not submit for a moment (2:5) because he saw that the false brothers wanted to bring them into bondage.

The use of the term "bring into bondage" or "enslave" (καταδουλόω) also appears in 2 Cor 11:20 in the context of false teachers. Here in the immediate context of Galatians 2, the term is set in contrast with "freedom in Christ." In the larger context of the epistle, it is also set in contrast with Paul's servant-bondage to Christ (δοῦλος) in 1:10. If the οἷς οὐδέ is accepted as the original reading,[31] Paul here claims that he did not submit to those who would enslave them. Paul uses the first person plural in 2:4 to indicate that enslavement of the Gentiles would mean enslavement to the principle of bondage for the Jewish Christians as well.

With this assertion Paul has set up another opposition between human and divine authority. Paul knew that he could only submit to one authority. If he submitted to the false brothers he would betray his loyalty to Christ and compromise freedom in Christ. The false brothers stand in relation to Paul as did his old life; they are both rejected as "still pleasing humans" (1:10). No consubstantiality exists, therefore Paul stands against them rather than with them.

When Paul speaks of preserving the gospel for the Galatians in v. 5, he stands against the false brothers for the sake of the Galatians. In other words, the struggle at the Jerusalem meeting not only resisted the enslavement of Paul and his company, but, by extension, the enslavement of the Galatian believers as well. However, the Galatians are not enjoying their freedom, but are fighting the same battle with those who are urging them to undergo circumcision. The advocates of circumcision are like the false brothers who opposed Paul, and they too will bring the Galatians under bondage to human authority. Paul, on the other hand, represents a commitment to God's authority as revealed in the circumcision-free gospel.

The scene, as Paul depicts it, shows the two principles and parties in conflict in parallel situations. The same issue is at stake now in Galatia as it was then in Jerusalem. The Galatians cannot have it both ways; they must choose to identify with one principle or the other. If the Galatians stand with Paul they will stand with one who has fought for their freedom as well as the truth of the gospel (2:5). If they choose to undergo circumcision they will not only be trying to please humans; they will be enslaved to them.

---

[31] Betz, *Galatians*, 91.

The Galatians are also encouraged to identify with Titus, who, with Paul's help, responded to the circumcision-free gospel of Christ instead of the human desires of the false brothers. Like Titus, the Galatians have been affirmed as believers without the requirement of circumcision, and have avoided the enslavement of those who would require it. Finally, to identify with Titus, Paul, and the apostles is to identify with Christ who revealed the circumcision-free message that resists the threat of bondage. These are relationships of freedom.

When Paul turns again to the apostles (those reputed to be something), he states that their evaluation of his message suggested no revisions or additions (2:6). The major implication of Paul's statement is that there is a basic relationship of equality between himself and the Jerusalem apostles in the sight of God.[32] This is given explicit statement in 2:7–8; both Paul and Peter have been entrusted with the gospel. This recognition of grace led the "pillars" to offer the right hand of fellowship so that the missions to the circumcised and to the uncircumcised are given equal standing. There is no submission to human authority, nor is there any of the competition that characterized Paul's former life (1:14). Rather, those who have been entrusted with the truth of the gospel submit together as equals under the authority of the one who entrusted it to them (2:7) and gave Paul grace (2:9). The apostles have joined Paul in a common desire to please God rather than any human authority (1:10).

Paul's second section of the narrative, like the first, ends in harmony. For the second time a source of division has been dealt with through a realization of the grace of God that was at work in Paul (2:8–9; compare with 1:24). Once again divine action has brought about a consubstantiality as it is perceived by the church. The narrative does not establish Paul's independence from Jerusalem, but rather a relationship of cooperative interdependence based on the truth of the gospel that embraces Jew and Greek. The circumcision-free gospel that Paul brought to Jerusalem now stands in consubstantial unity with the gospel preached by the Jerusalem apostles; therefore Paul's relationship with the apostles is also one of consubstantial unity.

In addition, the Galatians are welcomed with Paul in the narrative through his identification with the Gentiles. As Paul is granted the right hand of fellowship, the Gentiles he represents are welcomed into the fellowship of believers as Gentiles, not converts to Judaism. They will be treated as equals with the Jewish Christians and, like Paul's friend Titus, they will not be required to be circumcised. They can trust that in heeding Paul's apostolic authority, they are also in accord with the authority of the Jerusalem apostles.

In opposition to this decision stand the false brothers who do not have apostolic authority based on the truth of the gospel, and would not grant equality to the Gentile believers. Instead, they would require circumcision, a status of bondage to their will. Paul has used his narrative thus far to force the Galatians to see the consequences

---

[32] The similarities of "God shows no partiality" (2:6, πρόσωπον [ὁ] θεὸς ἀνθρώπου οὐ λαμβάνει) with 1 Sam 16:7, 1 Esd 4:39, Sir 4:22, 27, and Luke 20:21 suggest that Paul is using an idiom to state that God does not judge by appearances, or in this case, titles and offices. Cf. Hay, "Paul's Indifference."

of a decision to submit to circumcision by identifying the false brothers of 2:4 with those who are urging circumcision upon the Galatians. To choose their position over that of Paul, Titus, and the other apostles would be equal to pleasing humans and, worse yet, a relationship of bondage.

Galatians 2:11–14

The final portion of Paul's narrative does introduce division between himself and the apostles. As the climax of the narrative it demonstrates how the consubstantial principles of unity and equality are betrayed when one chooses to base one's actions on the desire to please humans rather than God. It is not, as James Hester argues, a digression from the narrative that brings the reader back to the conflict that might have gotten lost in the irenic settlement of 2:9–10.[33] The conflict is a negative illustration following what has up to this point been a positive illustration of unity in the circumcision-free gospel. As relations break down between Cephas, Paul, and the Gentile Christians at Antioch, the Galatians are given another picture of what lies before them should they choose to undergo circumcision.

Whatever the number and purpose of the party sent from James, its presence led Cephas to abandon the example of inclusion he had set by eating with the Gentiles. Paul interpreted his action according to the same opposition between the divine and human will that he has set up throughout the narrative. He states that Cephas withdrew because he feared the circumcised (περιτομῆς, 2:12; compare with 2:7 and 2:9) and was not walking straight according to the truth of the gospel (compare with 2:5). In fearing the circumcised (περιτομῆς), Peter was seeking to please these men rather than God. As a result, his relationship with the Gentiles was broken.

Again, the revealed circumcision-free gospel is set in opposition to human authority. The choice of the human will over the divine suddenly brings division where there was once unity. In Paul's interpretation of the events, there is only unity in the gospel, which is both revealed and circumcision-free. Once that gospel is compromised, there will be no place for Gentiles and, by implication, the Galatians in the church unless they also circumcise.

Should the Galatians choose to enter the fellowship through what Paul calls the human principle of circumcision, there will be no equality either. In confronting Peter, he charged him with compelling the Gentiles to Judaize (live like a Jew, be circumcised). To Paul, Peter was doing the same as the false brothers tried to do in Jerusalem (the word for compel, ἀναγκάζω, is used in both 2:14 and 2:3).[34] Therefore, if the Galatians choose circumcision, they will no longer be servants of Christ; they will be servants of a human authority, namely those who require circumcision. They will be living as Paul did in his former life, trying to please humans instead of God.

---

[33] Hester, "Rhetorical Structure," 231–32. Hester, following Betz's outline of Galatians, suggests that 2:11–14 is structurally and functionally separate from 1:15–2:10 and makes the *narratio* shorter, thus better meeting the criterion of brevity.

[34] Betz, *Galatians*, 112.

Only here has Paul placed real relational distance between himself and the apostles in his retelling of the story, for only here has any apostle (Peter and perhaps James)[35] chosen a human principle. If the Galatians had any concerns about Paul's relationship to the Jerusalem church, he has shown them that the apostles, Paul included, had been in harmony and equality until the revealed, circumcision-free gospel ceased to be the basis for fellowship.

For this reason the narrative portrait of Paul's relationship with the apostles is not simply meant to show that Paul was not taught by them; it is also meant to model the unity that is only possible in the fear of God and the revelation of Christ in the gospel. The incident at Antioch shows that any other principle of fellowship, based on subservience to human authority and distinctions, ultimately brings division.[36]

In contrast to his opposition to Peter, Paul continued his relationship of identification with the Gentiles in the Antioch incident by standing alone with them when all the Jewish Christians had withdrawn. As the Galatians heard this, they were still in a relationship of identification with Paul and the Gentiles that began back at the meeting with the Jerusalem apostles (2:1–10). Once again, they see Paul fighting for the right of the Gentiles (including the Galatians) to be included in the fellowship without the requirement of circumcision. Paul has shown them that the decision whether or not to be circumcised is not only a matter of freedom but is also a matter of community. The community of Christ and his circumcision-free gospel is inclusive and egalitarian; the community of circumcision is no community at all.[37]

The Galatians must therefore choose, not only whether to be circumcised, but whether or not they will continue to identify with Paul who has identified with them. Will they choose to continue a relationship of identification with Paul, begun when they first believed and continued in Paul's narrative? Or, will they choose to please humans rather than God and withdraw themselves from Paul as Peter withdrew from them? Having placed the choice before them, Paul says, "Brethren, I beseech you, become as I am, for I also have become as you are" (4:12).

Summary and Conclusion

The antithesis between pleasing God and pleasing humans in Gal. 1:10 and the corresponding antithesis between the gospel of Christ and that of humans in 1:11–12 are dramatized by Paul in his autobiographical narrative. While he demonstrates that his message was not taught to him by the Jerusalem apostles, this is not the sole purpose of his narrative. A Burkean approach has shown that Paul also depicts a

---

[35] Paul does not make explicit whether the arrival of the party signified a change in James's policy regarding circumcision. In any case, Paul's argument depends on the priority of the Jerusalem meeting and considers any departure from its conclusion to be an aberration.

[36] Dunn ("Incident at Antioch," 229–30) argues that the Antioch incident caused Paul to see the incompatibility of a system that called Gentiles "sinners" (Gal 2:15) with the gospel of Christ.

[37] Gordon, "Problem," argues that Paul replaces the exclusive identity symbol of Torah with an inclusive symbol of faith in Christ.

community created by a common response to the gospel. The community remains intact as long as its members seek to please God on the basis of the revealed, circumcision-free gospel rather than seeking to please other humans. The community also is inclusive and egalitarian when the same principle is kept, since the gospel itself becomes the sole ground for consubstantiality. Circumcision, which Paul identifies as a desire to please human authority, divides.[38]

A Burkean approach also shows how the narrative forces the Galatians to decide with whom they will stand on this issue. If the Galatians wish to be in relationship with the larger church and the Jerusalem apostles, they must identify with Paul, for all the apostles are of the same fellowship in the gospel, the Antioch incident notwithstanding. The circumcision-free gospel and apostolic authority both come from God, not from any human standing. Therefore, in order for the Galatians to please God, they must continue in a relationship of identification with Paul and the other apostles (as portrayed in 2:1–10), and not enter a new relationship with those who tell them to be circumcised. To choose circumcision is to please human authority; indeed, it is to become enslaved to it.

Finally, a Burkean approach demonstrates that Paul also uses the principle of identification to enhance his relationship with the Galatians. He depicts himself as a defender of their interests, fighting for their freedom and their right to enter the fellowship without any requirement but faith in Christ. He brings the Gentiles into fellowship with the Jewish church and he alone stands with them when all other Jewish Christians withdraw. He has been an advocate for the Galatians and all Gentiles in the past; certainly his present stormings and pleadings have their interests at heart now.

No one model can appreciate the richness of Paul's autobiographical narrative. The model proposed here, based upon Kenneth Burke's literary-rhetorical method, is offered to show that Paul not only sought to strengthen his relationship with the Galatians through his autobiographical narrative, but that he used the depictions of relationships within the narrative to create a rhetorical community that the Galatians were forced either to join or reject. Thus to reject circumcision was to identify with the community of Paul and the Christ who sent him.[39]

---

[38] Cousar (*Galatians*, 28) has stated that Paul's first purpose in the autobiography was to assert that his gospel was from no human source, and his second purpose was to state clearly that the unity of the church was based on one gospel of grace. This study asserts that the former purpose serves the latter.

[39] The author wishes to thank Professors Robert Jewett and W. Richard Stegner for their help in reading earlier versions of this essay.

10

PAUL'S ARGUMENTATION IN GALATIANS 1–2[1]

Johan S. Vos

The Gospel of the Rival Missionaries

In the Epistle to the Galatians, Paul directly addresses only the Galatian churches; through them, however, he is engaged in a polemic against rival missionaries who had influenced the churches with another gospel. If one intends to analyze Paul's argumentation in Galatians 1–2, it is necessary first to ask about the characteristics of these missionaries and their gospel. In the history of research, many different pictures of the opponents and their gospel have been drawn.[2] These reconstructions result partly from the method of so-called mirror reading; this method infers the position of the opponents by reversing the negations and affirmations in Paul's argumentation. Recently and with good reason this method has been criticized.[3] In my analysis I confine myself to what can be said with certainty about the opponents: First, the opponents shared with Paul the belief in Jesus as the messiah; otherwise Paul could not have termed their message a "gospel" (Gal 1:6). Second, for the opponents the gospel of Paul was incomplete, because it lacked part of the commandments of the covenant, particularly the commandment of circumcision as a prerequisite for full membership among the people of God (Gal 5:3 4; 6:12–13). Although Paul himself did not mention it, we can safely assume that on this point the opponents referred to scripture. Gen 17:10–11, for example, states clearly that without circumcision no one can be a member of the covenant.

---

[1] This article is an abridged version of a paper presented at the 13th Colloquium Oecumenicum Paulinum in Rome in Septermber 1992.

[2] Surveys of the history of research can be found in, for example, Mussner, *Galaterbrief,* 11–29; Hawkins, "Opponents," 5–85, 279–309; Brinsmead, *Galatians,* 9–22.

[3] See Betz, *Galatians,* 6, 56 n. 115; Martyn, "Law-Observant Mission"; Lyons, *Pauline Autobiography,* 96–105; Suhl, "Galaterbrief," esp. 3089; Barclay, "Mirror-Reading"; Hall, "Historical Inference," esp. 319.

We cannot say more about the opponents with any certainty. In the history of research, however, scholars have often tried to reconstruct from Paul's argumentation the accusations made by the opponents with regard either to the relation of Paul to the authorities in Jerusalem or to his credentials as an apostle. To some extent, these reconstructions are mutually contradictory. On the one hand, from Gal 1:1, 11–12 some scholars have reconstructed the charge that Paul was dependent on humans: the apostles in Jerusalem or other authorities. On the other hand, it is inferred from Gal 1:10 that the opponents blamed Paul because he acted too independently of Jerusalem by adapting his gospel to human needs. Some even attempt to combine both arguments into a charge that although Paul was at first dependent on Jerusalem, he later deserted.[4] The weaknesses of these hypotheses have been demonstrated more than once. In the case of the charge of dependence, it is not clear what the point of such a charge could be within the framework of the opponents' argument about circumcision.[5] In both cases—the charge of dependence and that of independence—Paul's argument as a whole would be inappropriate because he repeatedly laid himself open to attack.[6]

Apart from the contention that the gospel of Paul concerning circumcision was not according to scripture, we do not know what the opponents[7] may have said about Paul. In this article, I wish to demonstrate that it is possible to understand the argumentation in the first two chapters of the Epistle to the Galatians in every detail as an answer to the sole demand of circumcision or obedience to the law of Moses and that it is unnecessary to reconstruct other charges.

Purpose and Structure of Paul's Argumentation

Gal 1:1–5: Epistolary Prescript

The direction of the subsequent argument is indicated in the epistolary prescript. Here as in the other prescripts Paul called himself an apostle sent by God. Through this phrase he established his authority: he was not speaking as a private person, but as an envoy of God. In Gal 1:1, the twofold *correctio* οὐκ ἀπ᾽ ἀνθρώπων

---

[4] For the history of research, see Hawkins, "Opponents," 279–342; Lyons, *Pauline Autobiography*, 79–82; Schoon-Janssen, *Umstrittene "Apologien,"* 94–96.

[5] See Fridrichsen, "Apologie," 56; Bornkamm, *Paulus*, 41–42; Georgi, *Geschichte der Kollekte*, 36 n. 113; Suhl, *Paulus*, 20–21; idem, "Galaterbrief," 3094.

[6] See Fridrichsen, "Apologie," 56; Howard, *Crisis*, 20–45; Lyons, *Pauline Autobiography*, 83–95; Hübner, "Galaterbrief," esp. 7; Lategan, "Defending," esp. 421; Hall, "Historical Inference," 316–17; Hawkins, "Opponents," 287–89.

[7] The problematic aspect of the word "opponents" in this context has been pointed out in recent literature with good reason; it may carry the unproven connotation that the rival missionaries had intruded into the missionary field of Paul with the specific purpose of combating him; see Martyn, "Law-Observant Mission," 349; and Lyons, *Pauline Autobiography*, 79, 104, 120. In my opinion, however, the word "opponents" can be used meaningfully in this context: first, from the perspective of Paul, who described the other missionaries explicitly as the adversaries of the true gospel; second, from the perspective of other missionaries, who, given their own presuppositions, had to combat Paul as soon as they were confronted with his gospel.

οὐδὲ δι' ἀνθρώπου underlines this claim to authority. The only function of this *correctio* is to accentuate the positive part of the statement ἀλλὰ διὰ Ἰησοῦ Χριστοῦ καὶ θεοῦ πατρός. When one realizes how often Paul used this rhetorical figure,[8] it appears unadvisable to interpret it as a refutation of a specific charge made by the opponents.[9] This special accent on the apostolic authority in the epistolary prescript anticipates the core of the argumentation in the first two chapters. The divine authorization of the apostle is the decisive argument against the other gospel. Paul's self-presentation in Gal 1:1 is the starting point not of a defensive but of an offensive sort of argument: he first strengthened his position as an envoy of God before he launched his attack on the opponents.

Gal 1:6–9: Propositio

In Gal 1:6–9 Paul presented his most important point: he rebuked[10] the Galatians for having exchanged the true gospel for a false one, and he repeated his previous thesis that anyone who proclaims a gospel other than the one he had proclaimed is accursed. Interpreters who, in their attempt to determine the structure of the Epistle to the Galatians, make use of the classical rhetorical pattern of the parts of a discourse usually term Gal 1:6–9 (or Gal 1:6–10/11/12) an *exordium* or *prooemium*.[11] In doing so, however, one should realize that this term is used in such a broad sense as to be almost meaningless. If one adheres to the standard description of the proem in the rhetorical handbooks, the term is hardly applicable to these verses. Quintilian warned his readers not to label the beginning of every discourse a proem.[12] Only if the beginning has specific characteristics should the term be used. According to the rhetorical handbooks, the *exordium* has the function of making the readers well disposed, attentive, and ready to receive instruction. As such the function of the *exordium* is preparatory. The accent lies on the psychological aspect: the purpose of the *exordium* is to make the hearts of the hearers well disposed.[13] The manner in which Paul used

---

[8] See N. Schneider, *Rhetorische Eigenart.*

[9] Fridrichsen, *Apostle,* 21 n. 20; Betz, *Galatians,* 38; Lyons, *Pauline Autobiography,* 80–82, 97.

[10] Θαυμάζω is here—as often in Greek letters—less an expression of real astonishment than of irritation and rebuke; the word is equivalent to μέμφομαι. See Koskenniemi, *Studien,* 66–67; White, "Introductory Formulae," esp. 96; idem, *Body,* 106 n. 38; Mullins, "Formulas," esp. 385–86; Betz, *Galatians,* 46–47; Smiga, *Language,* 127 (including a reference to Dahl, "Paul's Letter"); Stowers, *Letter Writing,* 87; Hansen, *Abraham in Galatians,* 33–44.

[11] This was noted already by Bullinger, *Commentarii,* 342–46. In recent times, see Betz, "Literary Composition," esp. 9–12; *Galatians,* 44–46; Lüdemann, *Studien,* 65–73; Ebeling, *Wahrheit,* 55–56; Brinsmead, *Galatians,* 48–49, 67–69; Kennedy, *New Testament Interpretation,* 148; Hester, "Rhetorical Structure," esp. 233; Baarda, "Openbaring," 152–67, esp. 155–57; Smit, *Brief,* 35–37; Hansen, *Abraham in Galatians,* 67; Jegher-Bucher, *Galaterbrief,* 203; Pitta, *Disposizione,* 85–88; Bachmann, *Sünder oder Übertreter,* 157–58.

[12] Quintilian, *Inst.* 4.1.53.

[13] See, for example, Quintilian, *Inst.* 4.1.5: "*Causa principii nulla alia est, quam ut auditorem, quo sit nobis in ceteris partibus accommodatior, praeparemus*" ("The sole purpose of the *exordium* is to prepare our audience in such a way that they will be disposed to lend a ready ear to the rest of our speech"). Compare the speech of Antonius in Cicero, *De or.* 2.317; according to Antonius, to begin in the proem not in a fierce, but in a gentle way corresponds to a law of nature. That rhetorical

psychological means so to dispose the hearts of his readers is familiar from his other letters, in which the introductory thanksgiving serves as a *captatio benevolentiae* and thus has the function of the proem of a discourse. This strategy, however, is quite absent from Galatians.

Hans Dieter Betz[14] mentions several elements of Gal 1:6–9 that, according to the rhetorical handbooks, may constitute parts of an *exordium:* summarizing the *causa,* discrediting the adversaries, blaming the audience, expressing astonishment, and frightening the judges by threats. Although most of these elements may occur within the frame of an *exordium,* none, however, is constitutive of it. A summary of the *causa* can occur within an *exordium,* but normally only as part of the whole psychological strategy of making the audience well disposed.[15] Such a strategy, however, is absent from this pericope.[16] As is obvious from Galatians itself, discrediting the adversaries and blaming the readers can occur within all parts of the letter (Gal 3:1; 4:17; 5:7–12; 6:12–13). If an expression of astonishment is used within an *exordium,* it is normally employed more with a view to gaining the goodwill of the audience than as a means of rebuking it.[17] Concerning the last element—frightening the judges—we must simply deny that Paul was here doing something comparable to what is meant by this in the rhetorical handbooks.[18] In order to term Gal 1:6–9 an *exordium* as it was understood in the mainstream of classical rhetorical theory, it is necessary to show that this pericope as a whole and the particular *topoi* have merely a preparatory function and that the essential part comes afterwards. Indeed, interpreters have often explained the text in this way. They have differed, however, in their determination of the place where the main argument begins. On the one hand, there is a tendency to regard Gal 1:11(-12) as the *propositio.* Heinrich Bullinger, for example, remarked of verse 11: "Up to this point he prepared the minds of his audience through the *exordium . . . ,* now, however, he comes to the point."[19] Whereas for Bullinger verse 11 is the *propositio* only for the first part of the argumentation (Gal 1:11–2:14), in recent times there has been a tendency to regard Gal 1:11–12 as the principal proposition of the

---

theory does not always correspond to rhetorical praxis is to be seen in the *Exordia* of Demosthenes. This collection contains various texts in which it is hard to recognize the characteristics of the proem as described in the handbooks. See Clavaud, *Démosthène,* 5–9.

[14] Betz, "Literary Composition," 9–12; *Galatians,* 44–46.

[15] See Aristotle, *[Rhet. Alex.]* 29 (1436a–1438a); *Rhet. Her.* 1.6–11; Cicero, *Inv.* 1.20–26; Quintilian, *Inst.* 3.8.6–9; 4.1.1–79. Only Aristotle (*Rhet.* 3.14 [1414b–1416a]) would minimize the psychological preparation. For him, the specific function of the *prooemium* is to make clear for what "end" (τέλος) the speech is being made.

[16] See Aune, "Review of Betz, *Galatians.*" Aune writes, "Since the ordinary function of forensic *exordia* is threefold (securing the good will of the audience, securing their attentiveness, and disposing them to receive instruction), it is difficult to find anything characteristic of a normal forensic *exordium* in Gal 1:6–11" (326).

[17] See also the criticism by Classen, "Paulus," esp. 10 n. 23.

[18] See Kennedy, *New Testament Interpretation,* 148.

[19] Bullinger, *Commentarii,* 346: "*Hactenus paravit auditorum animos exordio . . . , nunc vero aggreditur ipsum negotium.*"

whole letter.[20] Betz, on the other hand, presented a different model, according to which the essential element follows in the *propositio* (Gal 2:15–21), after the *exordium* (Gal 1:6–9) and the *narratio* (Gal 1:13–2:14).[21] This model has considerable influence at present. A third variant of this structure is that proposed by Melanchthon, who regarded Gal 3:1 as the *propositio* of the letter.[22] The question, however, is whether this interpretation was inspired mainly by knowledge of the classical rhetorical pattern or by an analysis of the text itself.

Another model of interpretation, however, does more justice to the development of the argument. Concerning the *dispositio* of the whole letter I agree with George A. Kennedy[23] and Robert G. Hall[24] that Gal 1:6–9 relates to what follows—at least to Gal 1:10–5:12—as the main thesis to the explication or, in rhetorical categories, as the *propositio* to the *confirmatio*.[25] In Gal 1:6–9 Paul directly formulated the main thesis of the letter in the form of a rebuke and a conditional curse: the true gospel is not the gospel of the opponents, but only that of Paul.[26] He used the next part of the letter to undergird his thesis with various proofs and to draw conclusions from it. The thesis that for the Galatians there is no other gospel than the one proclaimed by Paul encompasses the whole content of the letter, which can be outlined as follows:

(1) The argument introduced by θαυμάζω is the first of several passages in which Paul rebuked the Galatians for their imminent desertion of the true gospel (Gal 3:1–5; 4:8–11; 5:7–10).[27]

(2) The Galatians' change of mind, expressed by the words μετατίθεσθε ἀπὸ ... εἰς recurs in several variants of the texts mentioned (Gal 3:3, ἐναρξάμενοι ... ἐπιτελεῖσθε; Gal 4:9, νῦν δὲ γνόντες ... πῶς ἐπιστρέφετε πάλιν ...; Gal 5:7, ἐτρέχετε καλῶς ... τίς ὑμᾶς ἐνέκοψεν ...).

(3) Although in Gal 1:6–9 Paul indicated only that a ἕτερον εὐαγγέλιον is at stake, the reader learns at various places in the rest of the letter what the content of this other gospel is (Gal 3:1–5; 4:21; 5:2; 6:12; etc.).

---

[20] Pitta, *Disposizione*, 149; see also the discussion on this subject in Lambrecht, *Truth*, 45, 47–48, 50–51, 53–56.

[21] Betz, "Literary Composition," 17–18; *Galatians*, 113–14; similar positions can be found in Brinsmead, *Galatians*, 50–51; Hübner, "Galaterbrief," 5–6; Vouga, "Zur rhetorischen Gattung," 291–92; Hansen, *Abraham in Galatians*, 69, 100–101.

[22] Melanchthon, "Ἐξήγησις," 34–37, esp. 34–35; for an analysis of this commentary, see Classen, "Paulus," 17–18. A more recent example of this approach is that of Standaert, "Rhétorique," 78–92, esp. 84–85.

[23] Kennedy remarks (*New Testament Interpretation*, 148), "The central idea of the proem, that there is no other gospel, is a general statement of the proposition of the letter, which will be taken up and given specific meaning in the headings which follow." Kennedy regards Gal 1:11–5:1 as the "proof" divided into several "headings" (148–51).

[24] Hall, "Rhetorical Outline," structures the letter as follows: (1) Salutation/*Exordium* (Gal 1:1–5); (2) Proposition (Gal 1:6–9); (3) Proof (Gal 1:10–6:10); (3a) Narration (Gal 1:10–2:21); (3b) Further Headings (Gal 3:1–6:10); (4) Epilogue (Gal 6:11–18).

[25] For the placing of a *propositio* at the beginning of a speech, see Aristotle, *Rhet.* 3.13 (1414a); Hermogenes, *Inv.* 3.2 (Rabe). For the history of the *propositio* in rhetorical theory and praxis, see Classen, "Cicero 'Pro Cluentio,' " esp. 126–37. For various forms of a *propositio* in the letters of Paul, see Aletti, " 'Dispositio,' " esp. 397–98.

[26] For the various forms a proposition can take, see Quintilian, *Inst.* 4.4.8.

[27] Smiga, *Language*, 455–59.

(4) Verbal reminiscences of the phrase ἀπὸ τοῦ καλέσαντος ὑμᾶς ἐν χάριτι are found in Gal 1:15; 2:21; 5:4, 8.

(5) An allusion to the phrase τινές εἰσιν οἱ ταράσσοντες ὑμᾶς recurs in Gal 5:10 and, in other words, in 5:12.

(6) Θέλοντες μεταστρέψαι τὸ εὐαγγέλιον τοῦ Χριστοῦ recurs in texts in which Paul defended the ἀλήθεια τοῦ εὐαγγελίου (Gal 2:5, 14; 5:7) or stated that the doctrine of his adversaries is opposed to the true gospel (for example, Gal 2:21; 3:2–5; 4:8–11; 5:2, 4).

(7) The curse pronounced on the messengers of the other gospel recurs in another form in Gal 5:10 (see also Gal 5:4). Together with the blessing at the end of the letter (Gal 6:16), this curse makes an antithetic *inclusio*.

Whereas Gal 1:6–9 covers the whole content of the letter, Gal 1:11–12 and 3:1–5 are to be understood as *subpropositiones,* that is, theses of the separate proofs, Gal 1:13–2:14(21) and 3:6–4:7 respectively. Because of its mainly argumentative character Gal 2:15–21 can hardly be termed a *propositio.*[28] Although Kennedy takes Gal 1:6–9 to be the *propositio* of the letter, he nevertheless terms these verses a *prooemium.* Because the term *prooemium* in this case is used in a sense that is much broader than is usual in the rhetorical handbooks, I would prefer to avoid it here.

Gal 1:10–12: Enthymematic Confirmatio

The question about the rhetorical categories and functions is not merely a matter of names. Only if one interprets the relation of Gal 1:6–9 to what follows in the way proposed here will it be possible to do justice to the fourfold γάρ in Gal 1:10–13 and to give Gal 1:10 a clear function within the argumentation as a whole. It is a controversial point whether Gal 1:10 belongs logically to Gal 1:6–9 or Gal 1:11–12, or whether it is separate from both parts as a kind of emotional outburst.[29] According to Betz, Gal 1:10–11 constitutes, in keeping with the rhetorical handbooks, the *transitus* or *transgressio* between the *exordium* and the *narratio.*[30] To make this interpretation acceptable, however, he must state that "the two rhetorical questions and the assertion in v. 10 put a clear end to the *exordium,*" which I fail to see. I find more evidence of John Calvin's interpretation of Gal 1:10: after he had so confidently extolled his own preaching Paul demonstrated in verses 10ff. "that he was entitled to do so" *(se id iure fecisse).*[31] For this purpose, according to Calvin, he used two arguments. The first is an argument *ab affectu animi,* that is, derived from the disposition of his mind: Paul had not the disposition to adapt himself to people to flatter them (Gal 1:10). The second argument is much stronger: he had handed over the gospel exactly in the form he had received it from God himself (Gal 1:11–12). The interpretation of Gal 1:10–13 must begin from the insight that each time γάρ occurs in these sentences it has a

[28] Kennedy, *New Testament Interpretation,* 148–49.
[29] For a partial history of research, see R. Longenecker, *Galatians,* 18; see also the survey of the history of research regarding the structure of the letter as a whole in Pitta, *Disposizione,* 13–41.
[30] Betz, "Literary Composition," 11–12; *Galatians,* 46.
[31] Calvin, *Commentarius,* 50.175, on Gal 1:10.

causal meaning.[32] These sentences build a causal chain. That γάρ has a causal meaning here four times has often been challenged.[33] It should be taken into account, however, that in sentences introduced by γάρ the phrase that has to be supported is not always fully expressed and should be supplied from the context.[34] In this case, following Calvin, the sentence "I am entitled to do so" should be inserted.[35] The reason adduced by Paul here is an amplification of Gal 1:1. There he had maintained that he was an apostle sent not by humans but by God; here in Gal 1:10 he demonstrated from the content and tone of Gal 1:6–9[36] that he really was not a slave of humans, but a servant of God and Christ.[37] This argument in its turn functions as a confirmation of his authority as the author of Gal 1:6–9. Behind these short sentences lies the following syllogism:

la. The gospel is true if it is proclaimed by a true servant of God and Christ.

1b. The gospel is false if it is proclaimed by a flatterer and a servant of humans.

2. The content and the tone of Gal 1:6–9 demonstrate that I am not a flatterer and a servant of humans but a true servant of God and Christ.

3. Consequently, the gospel I proclaimed to you is true.

Basically, Paul used a circular argument: he undergirded the truth of his gospel with his ethos as an apostle. He derived this ethos, however, from the character of the gospel.

To understand Gal 1:10 it is not necessary to assume that Paul was responding to a charge of being a flatterer.[38] In rhetorical praxis it was common for rhetors to legitimize the content of their speech by referring to their ethos. In doing so they often fell

---

[32] See also B. Weiss, *Die Paulinischen Briefe*, 320–21.

[33] Γάρ is often taken to be a confirmative adverb with the force of making the question more urgent; see, for example, Zahn, *Galater*, 54–55; Oepke, *Galater*, 26; Schlier, *Galater*, 41 n. 2; according to Betz *(Galatians*, 54 n. 100), γάρ is used not so much to connect with what precedes as to introduce another topic. Insofar as interpreters hold to the causal meaning and the argumentative force of γάρ, they mostly consider Gal 1:10 to be an attempt to justify the harsh language of Gal 1:6(8)-9; see, for example, H. Meyer, *Handbuch*, 25; Burton, *Galatians*, 31; Lyons, *Pauline Autobiography*, 137. A different approach is taken by Ellicott, *Galatians*, 11, who does not connect the argumentative aspect of γάρ with the harsh tone of Gal 1:6–9, but with the "*unquestionable truth*, the best proof of which lay in his [Paul's] being one who was making God his friend, and not men."

[34] BAG 152e s.v. "γάρ" gives Matt 2:2; Mark 8:35//Luke 9:24; and Mark 8:38 as further examples from the New Testament.

[35] For a similar interpretation in later commentaries, see Ruckert, *Commentar*, 27–28.

[36] With ἄρτι in Gal 1:10, Paul resumes the same word from the preceding verse.

[37] Like most interpreters, I assume ἀνθρώπους πείθειν and ζητεῖν ἀνθρώποις ἀρέσκειν to be synonymous and the answer to the question of Gal 1:10a to be "God." Since, even with the meaning "through the art of persuasion to make well disposed," πείθω does not in this context really fit the object τὸν θεόν, the sentence is to be considered a zeugma. See Oepke, *Galater*, 26; Mussner, *Galaterbrief*, 63; Baarda, "Openbaring," 165 n. 20. For a critical review of the differing interpretations of Rudolf Bultmann and Hans Dieter Betz, see Lyons, *Pauline Autobiography*, 141–43.

[38] See also Sieffert, *Galater*, 50; Betz, *Galatians*, 55–56; Lüdemann, *Studien*, 68–72; Lyons, *Pauline Autobiography*, 143–44; Aune, *Literary Environment*, 189–90.

back on the standard distinction between true and false rhetors. The following variants of this distinction occur:

(a) Opposed to the rhetor who only flatters and tries to please humans is the one who for the sake of the truth does not spare his audience.[39]

(b) Opposed to the rhetor who with all possible rhetorical means tries to convince his audience is the rhetorically incompetent one, who is concerned only about the truth.[40]

(c) Opposed to the rhetor who seeks his own profit, whether glory or money, by corrupt means is the one who unselfishly and with honorable motives acts only for the sake of the truth.[41]

In employing such antitheses, rhetors sometimes had concrete rivals in mind. At other times, however, stereotypical pictures were used, and the contrasts functioned merely as rhetorical antitheses. Paul used all three variants of this *topos* (1 Thess 2:1–11; 1 Cor 1:17; 2:4–5; 2 Cor 2:17; 4:1–2); in Gal 1:10 he used the first.[42] It is not always easy to decide when Paul was defending himself against concrete charges, but texts such as 1 Thess 2:4–5 and Gal 1:10 can be understood well without such an assumption.[43]

Gal 1:11 is first of all an underpinning of Gal 1:10.[44] With the words κατὰ ἄνθρωπον Paul repeated the word "human being," which occurred three times in verse 10.[45] He thus proved his contention that he is not a flatterer and a slave of humans with the fundamental thesis that his gospel is not κατὰ ἄνθρωπον, in other words, not meeting human norms and expectations and thus by no means serving to please humans. In underpinning Gal 1:10, verse 11 at the same time supports Gal 1:6–9.[46] Interpreters have often argued from the use of the "disclosure formula"[47] γνωρίζω γὰρ ὑμῖν that Gal 1:11 is the beginning of a new paragraph. 1 Cor 12:3, however, shows that this is by no means necessary. Within the causal chain this formula has a clear function, namely, to accentuate the fundamental character of his argument. Here in Galatians Paul used the first variant of the above-mentioned criterion—the true rhetor does not spare his audience—in order to distinguish be-

---

[39] For example, Plato, *Gorg.* 462b–466a; 500e–503d; 521a–b; Demosthenes, *Exord.* 1.3; 9.2; 19; 26.2; 28.1; 41; 44.1; Dio Chrysostom, *Alex.* 11; *1 Tars.* 1–16; see also Ribbeck, *Kolax,* 11–12, 16–18.

[40] For example, Plato, *Apol.* 17a–18a; Dio Chrysostom, *Dei cogn.* 1–20; *Cel. Phryg.* 1.

[41] Demosthenes, *Exord.* 32.1–2; 36; 53; *[4] Philip.* 75–76.

[42] Betz, *Galatians,* 54–56.

[43] For 1 Thessalonians 2, see Dibelius, *An die Thessalonicher,* 7–11; Malherbe, " 'Gentle as a Nurse.' "

[44] The evidence of the manuscripts does not permit a clear decision between γάρ and δέ. The arguments for γάρ as the original reading have been clearly formulated by Sieffert *(Galater,* 52), who writes, "It is not probable that γάρ has 'come into the text mechanically from the context' (Meyer); rather it is the original text and—with a view to avoiding the fourfold γάρ and because of its apparent intrinsic difficulty—has been partly changed into δέ (in accordance with 1 Cor 15:1; 2 Cor 8:1) and partly . . . omitted." See also Zahn, *Galater,* 55 n. 55.

[45] Even if one reads δέ instead of γάρ, it is important to see the close intrinsic connection between Gal 1:10 and 1:11. Ruckert interprets the text otherwise *(Commentar,* 30), defending the reading δέ with the argument that there is no intrinsic connection between Gal 1:10 and 1:11.

[46] See also Sieffert, *Galater, 52;* and Zahn, *Galater,* 55.

[47] On this formula, see White, *Body,* 2–5, 50–51; Schnider and Stenger, *Studien,* 171–72.

tween true and false. This criterion was familiar not only in the Greco-Roman world, where it could be applied to public figures such as rhetors and statesmen, as well as to private contacts such as friends, but also in the biblical world, where it was used to distinguish true and false prophets. In contrast to false prophecy, weak leadership, flattering rhetorics, or servile friendship, the speech of the true prophet, statesman, rhetor, or friend is uncompromising; the content is not what people normally like to hear. In the words of Paul, it is not κατὰ ἄνθρωπον.[48] With the fundamental thesis that the gospel is not κατὰ ἄνθρωπον Paul legitimized his ethos as described in Gal 1:10 and demonstrated in Gal 1:6–9. That Paul formulated such a fundamental thesis here only in a negative form has to do with the fact that here and in Gal 1:10 he did no more than support the polemical proposition of Gal 1:6–9.

In Gal 1:12 Paul undergirded this fundamental thesis with a statement about the origin of the gospel: he had not received it from human beings, but directly by a revelation from God or Jesus Christ. The logical presupposition of this argument is the thesis that the origin of a matter determines its essence.[49] Gal 1:11–12 are based on the following syllogistic argument:

la. A true gospel is not of a human nature.

1b. A gospel that does not have a human origin cannot be of a human nature.

2. The origin of my gospel is not human but divine.

3. Consequently, my gospel is true.[50]

In the religious tradition of Paul, this reference to divine revelation in order to legitimize a contentious message is an argument that is as common as it is controversial. The argument is fully understandable without the hypothesis that Paul was responding to a charge of the opponents.[51]

Thus, in summary, by means of an amplification of Gal 1:1 Paul proved the truth of Gal 1:6–9 in that he showed that his behavior (Gal 1:10) was in accordance with the character (Gal 1:11) and the origin (Gal 1:12) of his gospel. First, from his practical behavior he proved that he was not a slave of humans but a servant of God. Then, he proved that as matter of principle he could not be a slave of humans because his gospel was not κατὰ ἄνθρωπον. Finally, he proved that his gospel is not κατὰ ἄνθρωπον because he had received it by a heavenly revelation. The proof exists in a

---

[48] On rhetors, see above, n. 38; on statesmen, see Philo, *Ios.* 73–78; on friends, see Cicero, *Amic.* 89–92; Plutarch, *Adul. am.* 54d–55e; on prophets, see Jer 23:16–17; 1 Kgs 22:13–18; Luke 6:26. See also Sandnes, *Paul,* 56–57.

[49] Compare John 3:6, 31; 1 Cor 15:47–49; Gal 6:8.

[50] For the logic of the argumentation, see also R. Longenecker, *Galatians,* cxv–cxvi.

[51] It is not necessary to understand οὐδὲ γὰρ ἐγώ in a polemical way as "I as little as the twelve." Such an antithesis is not reflected in the context. With ἐγώ Paul picks up ὑπ᾽ ἐμοῦ from Gal 1:11, where the implied antithesis is with the rival missionaries in Galatia. Οὐδέ accentuates not so much ἐγώ in Gal 1:12 as the denial in Gal 1:11. See Lightfoot, *Galatians,* 80; Rückert, *Commentar,* 32; Zahn, *Galater,* 56 n. 57; Oepke, *Galater,* 28–29; Baarda, "Openbaring," 157–58; Rohde, *Galater,* 51.

series of enthymemes, or statements with a supporting reason, behind which stand logical syllogisms based on specific presuppositions. It is important to bring into focus the relation between the statements about the gospel and what is said about the apostolate. When in Gal 1:6–9 Paul explicitly established the *causa,* he spoke only about the gospel; the statements about his apostolate have their place within the proof of the truth of the gospel. The same is true for the rest of the letter: wherever Paul explicitly formulated the *causa,* he was talking only about the truth of the gospel (Gal 4:10; 5:2–4, 7; 6:12–13). In contrast to the letters to the Corinthians, for example, nowhere in the letter to the Galatians did Paul explicitly present the legitimacy of his apostolate as the controversial point. Insofar as he spoke about his apostolate, he did so in order to prove the truth of his gospel against that of the opponents, never to defend himself against an explicit charge.[52] In Gal 1:6–9 Paul acted more as an accuser than as the accused. Correspondingly, the supporting statements about his ethos as an apostle and the heavenly origin of his apostolate have more an offensive than a defensive function.

Gal 1:13–2:14(21): Narrative Confirmatio

In Gal 1:13–2:14 Paul related the history of his vocation and his contacts with the authorities in Jerusalem. With good reason this paragraph is often labeled a *narratio.* More important, however, than the term as such is the question of the function of this *narratio* as part of the entire argument. The rhetorical handbooks distinguished various forms of *narratio:* the *narratio* can expound the facts of the case itself, or it can present facts that are related to the case in a broader sense. This second type can be used, for example, as a means of winning belief or incriminating the adversaries.[53] An analysis of the *narratio* in Galatians will make clear that in this case it has more than one function.[54] The argument can be divided into three parts.

(1) The function of the first part, Gal 1:13–24, is obvious: it serves only as a confirmation of Paul's way of *legitimizing* himself in Gal 1:12. Paul adduced the historical evidence that he really had not received his gospel from any human being.

(2) The function of the second part, Gal 2:1–10, is threefold: (a) Paul demonstrated that the Jerusalem authorities had endorsed the *truth* of his specific gospel; the reader learns that the freedom of gentile believers with regard to circumcision is at stake (Gal 2:3, 6, 9–10). With this point Paul touched directly upon the *causa* of the letter. (b) Paul demonstrated that the Jerusalem authorities had confirmed his way of *legitimizing* his gospel: they had recognized its divine origin (Gal 2:7–10). As in Gal 1:10–12, here too the legitimization on the basis of the divine origin of the gospel has the function of supporting argument: the participles ἰδόντες and γνόντες in Gal

---

[52] For a similar position, see Lategan, "Defending," 416–26. See also Eckert, *Verkündigung,* 201; J. Smit, *Opbouw,* 66–92.

[53] Cicero, *Inv.* 1.19.27; *Rhet. Her.* 1.8.12; Quintilian, *Inst.* 4.2.11.

[54] According to Betz ("Literary Composition," 12–17; *Galatians,* 58–59), the *narratio* in Galatians 1–2 belongs to the first type; Kennedy *(New Testament Interpretation,* 145, 148), however, regards this text as belonging to the second type.

2:7–10 have the same function as the particle γάρ in the causal chain in Gal 1:10–13. They have a causal connotation and give the reason why the Jerusalem leaders had accepted the mission and gospel of Paul and Barnabas. (c) Paul gave an example of the *ethos* he had described in Gal 1:10. In the face of the false brethren in Jerusalem he had not tried to please humans, but had shown himself to be a true servant of Christ by fighting unswervingly for the truth of the gospel.

(3) In the third part, Gal 2:11–14(21), two aspects of Gal 1:6–12 are touched upon: (a) Paul gave a new example of his *ethos* as an apostle: not only before the Galatians (Gal 1:6–9) or the false brethren in Jerusalem (Gal 2:4–5), but even before Peter Paul had demonstrated publicly that as an apostle he did not seek to please humans. Unlike Peter, Barnabas, and the others who, for fear of the Jews, had played the hypocrite,[55] Paul showed himself to be the embodiment of the principle that his gospel is not κατὰ ἄνθρωπον. (b) In this section Paul's ethos is also subservient to the *truth* of the gospel. Concerning the content of this truth, the reader learns that not only circumcision is at stake, but also the halakhic rules governing purity. The *narratio* results in a fundamental theological argument about the relationship between the gospel and the law and thus about the fundamental aspect of the *causa* of the Galatian conflict.

To summarize, in the *narratio* Paul confirmed and illuminated the three points of Gal 1:6–12: he began with a confirmation of Gal 1:12 concerning the divine origin of his gospel; he then gave two examples of his ethos that he had described practically in Gal 1:10 and fundamentally in Gal 1:11. These two elements are subservient to a third, the "truth of the gospel" and thus to the *causa* of the letter described in Gal 1:6–9. With regard to the function of the *narratio*, we should say that Paul started with facts that are related to the *causa* in a broad sense, but then to an increasing extent he related the argumentation back to the *causa* itself.

We can term the *narratio* apologetic in the sense that Paul was defending the truth of his gospel. It is not apologetic, however, if by apologetic we mean that Paul was arguing mainly from a defensive position and was being urged to respond to charges concerning the legitimacy of his apostolate or his relationship to the Jerusalem apostles. Just as in Gal 1:6–9 the starting point is a charge against the Galatians concerning the content of the gospel, so in Gal 2:11–14(21) the *narratio* culminates in a charge concerning the truth of the gospel.

Recently, interpreters who share the opinion that in the *narratio* Paul was not taking a defensive position have put forward an alternative thesis that the key to the interpretation of Paul's autobiographical narrative is to be found in Gal 4:12 and that its function is mainly paradigmatic.[56] Against this view speaks not only the fact that Gal 4:12 belongs to a different context, but above all that only a few elements in Gal 1:13–2:14 really have paradigmatic force; a great deal of the information in this

---

[55] Hypocrisy is a conventional characteristic of the flatterer; see Plutarch, *Adul. am.* 53e; Philo, *Prob.* 99; *Legat.* 162; *Ios.* 67–68.

[56] Lyons, *Pauline Autobiography*; Gaventa, "Galatians 1 and 2"; Stowers, *Letter Writing*, 100–102, 109; Gaventa does not rule out an apologetic function alongside the paradigmatic one.

pericope—for example, the details concerning the journeys of Paul and his relation to the pillars—would be irrelevant from this perspective.[57]

If one shares the view that Paul's argumentation in Galatians 1–2 is not defensive, one must explain why Paul gave such a detailed account of his relationship with the Jerusalem authorities. In my opinion, it is possible to explain the argumentation in Gal 1:13–2:21 without having to resort to the hypothesis of a response to concrete charges concerning his apostolate. The argumentation here should be compared with that in 1 Cor 15:1–11. There also the true form of the gospel is at stake. Paul used the apostolic consensus as a fundamental argument to defend his gospel. This apostolic consensus in its turn is based on a uniform apostolic history: on the point of the revelation of the resurrected Christ, Paul demonstrated that he stood in the same line as Peter, the Twelve, and James. In Galatians an equally fundamental question is at stake. This time, however, Paul realized that he could not refer to a uniform apostolic consensus and a continuous apostolic history. For this reason, he adapted his method of persuasion to the situation: he demonstrated that his authority as an apostle holds good (1) *before* the existence of a consensus with the pillars, (2) *according to* an existing apostolic consensus, and (3) *in spite of* a later dissension with the Jerusalem authorities. As in 1 Corinthians 15, in Galatians 1–2 the relationship of the gospel of Paul to that of the pillars in Jerusalem is of the greatest importance because of its persuasive force.

The purpose of the *narratio* is primarily orthodidactic or orthopractical. For Paul, "acting in line with the truth of the gospel" (Gal 2:14) was at stake. I summarize the arguments for this thesis: First, the *narratio* is a part of the causal chain that has the function of supporting the thesis about the truth of Paul's gospel in Gal 1:6–9. Second, twice within the *narratio* Paul emphasized that his actions had only one purpose: the defense of "the truth of the gospel." Third, the *narratio* results in a theological argument concerning the content of the true gospel.

In Galatians 1–2 as a whole Paul defended the truth of his gospel in the face of a contrary gospel and gave instruction as to its nature. He did so in various ways: by rebuking, threatening, arguing, and narrating. Melanchthon did not consider the letter as a whole as one of the well-known rhetorical genres—forensic, deliberative, or epideictic—but used the category *genus didacticum* ("didactic genre").[58] As far as the first two chapters are concerned, this category seems to me to be preferable to any of the three derived from the rhetorical handbooks.

---

[57] For a criticism of Lyon's thesis, see Barclay, "Mirror-Reading," 379 n. 44; Lategan, "Defending," 423–24; Sandnes, *Paul*, 49–50 n. 4; Schoon-Janssen, *Apologien*, 110–11.

[58] Melanchthon, "Ἐξήγησις," 34; compare Classen, "Paulus," 16.

11

EPIDEICTIC RHETORIC AND PERSONA IN GALATIANS 1 AND 2

James D. Hester

Introduction

In an article written in 1984, I followed Hans Dieter Betz in identifying Galatians as an apologetic letter cast in the form of a defensive or forensic speech.[1] I also argued for an outline of Gal 1:11–2:14 that identified 2:11–14 as a digression (a *digressio* or *egressus*) that should not be understood as part of the narrative but instead as a bridge to the *propositio,* which Betz claims makes up 2:15–21. My effort to find a digression in the structure of 1:11–2:21 was due primarily to my acceptance of the forensic type. But by the time I wrote my essay for the Kennedy Festschrift, I had come to believe that Galatians could not be easily assigned to any one of the three genera of ancient rhetoric but contained a number of genres that reflect the topography of argumentation going on in the letter.[2]

Abandonment of my belief in the forensic genre for Galatians undermined my earlier arguments for 2:11–14 as a digression.[3] As I argued in the Kennedy essay, I now believe that Gal 2:11–14 is a response chreia, slightly expanded by Paul, and that 2:15–21 represents the elaboration of the chreia.[4] Furthermore, as I shall argue below, the chreia elaboration also serves as the statement of the rhetorical vision of the letter.

In that same 1984 article, I identified 1:11–12 as the stasis statement for the letter as a whole and the narrative in particular.[5] In the Kennedy essay, I expanded the scope

---

[1] Hester, "Rhetorical Structure."

[2] Hester, "Placing the Blame."

[3] See also Hester, " Use and Influence," 404.

[4] I have changed my identification of the type of chreia from the "mixed" type I used, ibid., 406. A response chreia is a subclass of sayings chreia; it responds to a question or remark. Aelius Theon defined the chreia as "a brief statement or action with pointedness attributed to a definite person or something analogous to a person" (cited in Mack and Robbins, *Patterns of Persuasion,* 11). For a full discussion of classes of chreia, see Hock and O'Neill, *Progymnasmata,* 28–35.

[5] Stasis refers to the issue under dispute, as, e.g., whether the accused person did what is alleged; or admitting she did it, the accused may argue that the act was justified or forgivable. A helpful

of my identification of the influence of the stasis statement. There I argued that the issue of quality underlies the whole letter, not just the narrative. Moreover, the stasis of quality is the stasis that is associated with the epideictic genre,[6] a fact that also illuminates the rhetorical situation.[7] In that paper I also argued that the narrative (1:13–2:14) is made up of a self-referent encomium,[8] imbedded in a letter that is primarily epideictic in function, in which Paul attempts to remind the Galatians of the character of the gospel that was revealed to him and preached by him to them; he is its model and therefore theirs. Moreover, both the chreia and its elaboration, as the final two topics in the encomium, serve to focus the point of the encomium, which is an illustration of the pragmatic application of Paul's rhetorical vision.

In the Kennedy essay, I made one further introductory observation. Until recently scholars tended to ignore or discount the fact that much of what was written in the ancient world was to be read out loud.[9] It was common for letters to be read out loud, even by a lone recipient who read in a low voice to himself.[10] Letter composition was a part of rhetorical education and could be understood as a kind of subset of oratory.

Having made that point, however, I failed to elaborate it with another. The selection of the letter genre was an inventional choice by Paul, dictated, presumably, by the distances between him and the communities he was addressing. Although he could have written speeches and have had them read by someone else, he chose to write a new kind of letter. Therefore, my presupposition is that Paul wrote rhetorical discourse set in epistolary conventions and that those mentioned in the opening salutation were not coauthors but letter carriers, readers, and interpreters. Having said that, however, I must emphasize that the only claim I want to make is that, generally speaking, Paul adapted epistolary forms and some of the canons of rhetoric (invention, arrangement, style, memory, and delivery) in order to meet the needs of communicating his rhetorical vision to Christian communities experiencing a variety of exigences. Paul made some use of elements of the art of rhetoric that he either learned or acquired from the culture, but it would be overstating things to say he was an orator.

---

review of stasis theory is provided by Kennedy, *Greek Rhetoric,* 73–86. See also Dieter, "Stasis"; Morland, *Rhetoric of Curse,* 120–27. Recently T. Martin, "Apostasy to Paganism," has argued that "the stasis of the Galatian letter is a qualitative stasis of the forensic type, subdivided into a substasis of actions forbidden and further subdivided into a substasis of shifting of blame" (p. 78). He bases this analysis on the identification of 4:8–11 as the principal accusation made in the letter. I do not find this identification persuasive.

[6] Perelman and Olbrechts-Tyteca, *New Rhetoric,* 47–54. The argument for the epideictic nature of Galatians has been further elaborated by Sullivan and Anible, "Epideictic Dimension."

[7] Within the scope of this paper, I cannot review the discussions of rhetorical, audience, and argumentative situations. The reader is directed to Bitzer, "Rhetorical Situation," 1–4, and subsequent reactions to that article in the journal *Philosophy and Rhetoric.* The best discussion of audience and argumentative situations can be found in Perelman and Olbrechts-Tyteca, *New Rhetoric,* 89–104.

[8] Although Forbes, "Comparison," does not deal with Galatians 1 and 2, he is able to show, in his analysis of 2 Corinthians 10–12, that Paul did use "self-praise" as an argumentative tactic. By implication, then, one can argue that Paul could make use of it in other letters as well.

[9] See Kennedy, *New Testament Interpretation,* 37, for an excellent discussion of the implications of this. See also Achtemeier, "Omne verbum"; Botha, "Letter Writing," 21–25; Loubser, "Orality."

[10] McGuire, "Letters."

Methodological Considerations

Rhetorical Criticism

Over the last decade or more, a series of arguments have been made by various scholars to the effect that the use of ancient rhetorical handbooks and other artifacts of classical rhetoric are not appropriate to the analysis of Pauline letters.[11] The point is made that the handbooks reflect models for creating speeches and are derived from educational practices of the time but do not address rhetorical theory and were not intended for analysis of speeches. For modern scholars to make use of them in this fashion results in their misuse as well as in identifying elements of rhetoric where other explanations may be as warranted.[12] The problem lies in confusing rhetorical analysis with rhetorical criticism.[13]

Rhetorical criticism is more than identifying rhetorical forms and analyzing their function in the literature of the New Testament; these activities constitute the bulk of the work of rhetorical analysis. Over time, aided by the reading of Lloyd Bitzer, Chaim Perelman, and Ernest Bormann, I have come to understand that, in its fullest operation, rhetorical criticism analyzes the historical setting of a particular speaker and audience, the rhetorical situation and the exigence, the argumentative structures and forms the speaker uses to persuade or convince the particular and universal audience, and the development of the argumentative situation along the trajectory of particular to universal. It also should identify the rhetorical vision of the author and how it is elaborated and applied by the argument being made.[14] I have also relied on the general theory of rhetoric formulated by Ernest Bormann, symbolic convergence theory, and its analytical method, fantasy theme analysis.[15] Elements of these will appear in the critical analysis that follows.

---

[11] The literature on this is fairly extensive by now. Good examples of such arguments can be found in Kern, *Rhetoric and Galatians;* Anderson, *Ancient Rhetorical Theory;* and essays by Weima, "Function"; Porter, "Theoretical Justification"; Stamps, "Rhetorical Criticism"; Classen, "St. Paul's Epistles."

[12] Cooper, *"Narratio,"* makes the point that while Victorinus drew on some aspects of rhetorical theory to analyze Paul's letters, he never treated them as though they were speeches. Therefore, says Cooper, modern interpreters can make legitimate use of some aspects of ancient rhetorical theory but must be careful not to find in the letters more than evidences of one who was a "persuasive and flexible pleader" (135).

[13] For an elaboration of this point, see Hester, "Speaker."

[14] There is not space in this paper to do a full rhetorical critical analysis of Galatians 1 and 2. I will deal mainly with structures and forms and with the movement of the argument along a particular trajectory in which Paul proves himself to be the representative of the universal values of the gospel. I will also point out evidences of his rhetorical vision.

[15] Symbolic Convergence Theory is a general theory of communication that attempts to offer an explanation for the presence of a common consciousness on the part of members of a group. It posits that the sharing of group fantasies and the chaining out of those fantasies is responsible for that consciousness and group cohesiveness. As fantasies are "dramatized," a convergence of symbols on which participants agree occurs, and fantasy themes and fantasy types help the group understand unexpected, confusing, or even chaotic events or experiences. The process of convergence creates social reality for the group until new exigences cause new fantasies and moments of sharing, which in turn produce new group realities. These realities provide the underlying assumptions used by

Epistolary Theory

Paul's response to the rhetorical situations he faced was to write letters, but these situations called for more than ordinary letters. His letters had to function as his rhetorical presence. Therefore, they do not easily map onto the conventions of the common letter tradition.

Typically the literary study of Paul's letters begins with an investigation of form and style. Epistolary conventions are identified and their purposes described in general and in the context of a particular letter. Forms characteristic of a particular letter or argumentative style are identified and analyzed. Work is also done on placing Paul's letters within certain broad classifications, for example, private letter versus public or official letters.[16] Studies concerned with analysis of type for purposes of classification attempt to provide analogies or models from the common letter tradition that could be shown to be illustrative of the Pauline letter type. Some studies attempt to analyze Paul's letters using one or more of the types that were enumerated by early epistolary theorists. [17]

One of the pitfalls to be avoided in using epistolary theory to identify a letter type is the temptation to apply, more or less literally, a description of a type from one of the handbooks. As is true for the use of the rhetorical handbooks, so here it must be emphasized that epistolary handbooks were for the use of professional letter writers. The models described in them were just that, models to be used as the basis for writing letters suited to the situation.[18] The letter writer was to keep in mind the complex of things surrounding the sender, receiver, and situation and shape the letter accordingly.

"Epistolary theory was never able to assimilate or control the practice of letter writing. The ancient theorists acknowledged the difference between ideal and practice."[19] This is almost certainly due to the fact that letters were to be written as though they were one-half of a conversation. The letter was to be a suitable substitute for one's presence. Given the fact that the letter writer could not explain himself or answer questions that might be raised by his letter, it seems likely that the sender would try to anticipate the impact of what he said and adjust the trajectory of his comments to his construction of the audience response.[20] In some situations, more than one re-

---

the group in discursive argumentation. The reader can consult the following monographs and the bibliographies found in them for descriptions and examples of the theory and method: Bormann, *Communication Theory; Small Group Communications; Force of Fantasy.* See also below, n. 60.

[16] A survey has been done by Dahl in "Paul's Letter," 2–11. See also Stirewalt, "Official Letter-Writing"; *Studies,* 6–10.

[17] See, e.g., Betz, *Galatians,* 14–15; Dahl, "Galatians"; Malherbe, "I Thessalonians" (Malherbe gives other examples of paranetic letters in *Moral Exhortation,* 124–25); Jewett, "Romans"; Chapa, "Letter of Consolation." See also Stowers, *Letter Writing,* 49–152.

[18] Poster makes this argument quite forcefully in "Conversation Halved"; "Economy of Letter Writing."

[19] White, *Light,* 190. This observation has been made by many; see, e.g., Stowers, *Letter Writing,* 86, and "Education, Art, and Professional Letter Writing," ibid., 32–35.

[20] An interesting early example in a literary letter (as opposed to a papyrus letter) can be found in Isocrates, *Ep.* 1.2 (to Dionysius).

lated type could be used to strengthen the overall rhetorical impact of the letter. This practice of mixing letter types within one letter is permitted by the ancient theorists, but the fact is not often enough acknowledged by modern interpreters.[21]

Epideictic

Epideictic was one of the three genera of rhetoric identified by Aristotle (*Rhet.* 1.3.3); it had as its major function the giving of praise or the placing of blame. Its purpose was educational, urging the honorable, and although it is often described as being concerned with the present, it is also widely recognized by ancient and modern commentators that it is allied with the deliberative and therefore has an interest in the future behavior of an audience.[22] Aristotle says that rather than using enthymeme or example in argumentation, epideictic rhetoric makes use of amplification that takes into account both the object being praised or blamed and the situation of the audience (*Rhet.* 1.9.30; 1.9.40).

Aristotle said that epideictic was the genre best suited to writing because its ability to affect the audience depended as much on style as on anything else (*Rhet.* 3.1.7; 3.12.6). It could be read and used on more than one occasion, presumably even read to audiences by someone other than the author. The inclusion of elementary exercises in epideictic style in rhetorical education makes it clear that such training was seen to contribute to judicial eloquence.[23]

Important categories of epideictic speeches included funeral orations and speeches in the praise of a king or very important person. The latter is an important representative of the most characteristic type of epideictic literature, the encomium; we shall return to it later. In republican Rome, the most important epideictic type was the funeral oration,[24] but many other forms existed, including panegyrics, marriage and birthday addresses, and even a speech for the arrival of a bride at her new home.[25]

In the lists of letter types in the handbooks, there are a number of styles associated with the epideictic genre.[26] Keeping in the mind that epideictic is the rhetoric of praise (ἔπαινος) and/or blame (ψόγος), one finds in Demetrius the following blaming types: blaming, reproachful, rebuking or censorious, admonishing, vituperative. Praising types include praising, commendatory, and congratulatory. Libanius has

---

[21] Stowers, *Letter Writing*, illustrates this mixing of types repeatedly in part 2, "Types of Letters," 49–173.

[22] Quintilian, *Inst.* 3.7.28. Burgess, "Epideictic Literature," 101, says that Isocrates saw the ideal speech as a mixture of epideictic and deliberative. See also Kennedy, *Art of Persuasion*, 188–90; and Perelman and Olbrechts-Tyteca, *New Rhetoric*, 47–51.

[23] Parks, *Roman Rhetorical Schools*, 114; Quintilian, *Inst.* 2.10.12. Quintilian makes the point that panegyrics have a suasive form. Burgess, "Epideictic Literature," 95, argues that Quintilian was not troubled by moral inconsistencies found in oratory and yet defended the "higher" interpretation of epideictic.

[24] For a survey of the funeral oration in ancient rhetoric, see Hester, "Invention."

[25] Kennedy, *Art of Rhetoric*, 21–22, 428–29, 634–37.

[26] Stowers, *Letter Writing*, 27–28.

four blaming types (blaming, reproaching, reproving, and maligning) and two praising types (commending and praising).[27]

It is possible to fit letters of exhortation and advice into the genre of epideictic. According to Stanley Stowers, certain types of letters may be seen as epideictic when advice seeks to "increase adherence to a value or to cultivate a character trait."[28] Exhortation and advice are the positive side of admonition and rebuke, letter types identified by both Demetrius and Libanius. Admonition is a form of blame intended to encourage change in a person's character, whereas rebuke is a kind of shaming designed to confront the reader with the writer's knowledge of the recipient's deeds together with exhortation to change them. Therefore, these types must be seen as epideictic as well.

C. Perelman and L. Olbrechts-Tyteca point out that in the ancient world the epideictic genre has nothing to do with the presentation of a debate in which opponents would try to win favorable judgment from an audience: "The purpose of epidictic [sic] speech is to increase the intensity of adherence to values held in common by the audience and speaker. The epidictic speech has an important role to play, for without such common values, upon what foundation could deliberative and legal speeches rest?"[29] Because the epideictic is concerned with recognizing values, the speaker's aim is often to gain and enhance adherence to these values. He is asking them, at least implicitly, to decide for what is beautiful or good or true over their opposites, and because these values are usually of a universal nature, the speaker becomes an educator.[30] It is important to note that because the speaker does not need to defend a set of values as much as increase adherence to those already accepted, epideictic discourse is not designed to change value systems. The speaker can be understood as one who responds to the exigence of an occasion for promoting the community's value system, no matter how that occasion arises.

Another modern theorist, Dale Sullivan, has a different understanding of epideictic. He admits that, historically, epideictic discourse is understood to help "create and to maintain a society's value system."[31] But he also points out that the genre has been described by modern theorists as having the following functions: conservative, educational, celebratory, and literary. Given these descriptions, he argues that epideictic rhetoric is determined by "a constellation of purposes: preservation, education, celebration, and aesthetic creation."[32] In other words, for Sullivan, any description of epideictic has to move beyond the identification of forms to the larger issues of function or purpose.

---

[27] Stowers, ibid., 85, claims five types but lists only four, unless he intended to include the ironic. He refers to the ironic, however, as "mock praise."

[28] Ibid., 107.

[29] Perelman and Olbrechts-Tyteca, *New Rhetoric*, 47–49.

[30] Ibid., 51–53.

[31] Sullivan, "Epideictic Discourse," 229.

[32] Sullivan, "Ethos," 115–16.

Epideictic in Galatians 1 and 2

As I have said, I believe that Galatians exhibits the functions and/or dimensions of epideictic and that it can be categorized as a letter of blame. Stowers identifies the fundamental elements of the letter of blame as follows: 1) the writer is the recipient's benefactor; 2) the recipient has wronged the benefactor; 3) the writer attempts to criticize and/or shame the recipient in such a way that he does not destroy their relationship.[33] These characteristics seem to describe the general situation of Paul and the Galatian churches. Beyond this general identification, however, there are elements in the letter that suggest that it be further classified as rebuking or censorious in that it accuses the Galatians of being involved with beliefs and behavior they know to be wrong (1:8–9; 4:8–11, 21; 5:2, 13, 17). It has elements of vituperation (5:2–12) and irony (1:6–7 and 3:1–5, if one allows for sarcasm as a subset of irony).[34] And there is the presence of paraenetic material (5:16–6:10).[35]

It also seems to me, however, that the overall spirit of the letter is one of reproach, a more particular style or type of blame. Demetrius says, "It is the reproachful type when we once more reproach, with accusations, someone whom we had earlier benefited for what he has done."[36] This is a refinement of the idea of blame. In general, blame, as a type, allowed the writer to take someone to task for an attitude that threatened to alter the nature of the relationship between the writer and the recipient. Reproach focused that blame on the issue of forgetting the debt of gratitude owed.

Galatians exhibits several stylistic and topical elements of epideictic. The θαυμάζω period is a feature of epideictic address; see, for example, Isocrates, who, in *Ep.* 1.9 (to Dionysius), exhorts Dionysius not to be amazed that Isocrates is trying to defend Greece and give counsel in the same letter. When describing the exordium in Galatians, Betz notes that it has the character of the epideictic because of Paul's expressions of disapproval of the Galatians' activities.[37] Letters with this feature can be classified as letters of reproach, an epideictic type. As we have seen above, the stasis of quality clearly represents the epideictic. But even the narrative contains such elements, even though it has been widely identified as an autobiographical statement of facts,[38] more likely to be found in forensic literature than in panegyrics or funeral orations.

In a section entitled "The Form and Structure of Paul's Autobiographical Narrative," George Lyons says that the autobiography proper starts with 1:13 and the

---

[33] Stowers, *Letter Writing*, 87.

[34] Nanos, *Irony*, argues for an extensive presence of irony in Galatians, including 3:1–5, which he sees as a form of Socratic irony, in which the speaker feigns ignorance and a wish to be educated. That stance may be present in 3:1–5, but the tone of the passage still seems sarcastic to me.

[35] Betz, *Galatians*, 22, labeled 5:1–6:10 the *exhortatio* division. He laments the fact that there have been few studies of the "formal character and function of epistolary paranesis" (253). His footnotes reference studies of rhetorical handbooks and philosophical letters; see 253 nn. 6, 8, 12, 13.

[36] Malherbe, *Moral Exhortation*, 30–31, 64–65, 72–73.

[37] Ibid., 45 n. 16. Malherbe cites Aristotle, *Rhet.* 3.14.2, 4

[38] See, e.g., J. Sanders, " 'Autobiographical' Statements"; Lyons, *Pauline Autobiography*, esp. ch. 3; Gaventa, "Galatians 1 and 2"; and the literature cited in them. These studies and others are usually concerned with the function of the "autobiography" as apologetic, polemic, or paradigmatic. Cf. Schütz, *Paul*, 133–34.

reference to Paul's former life in Judaism (ἠκούσατε γάρ τὴν ἐμὴν ἀναστροφήν). The use of ἀναστροφήν is associated with an emphasis on one's ethos and suggests that "the following autobiographical remarks should be understood as in the philosophical lives to be more interested in ethics than history."[39] Because he rejects the notion that Paul faces "opponents" in Galatia,[40] Lyons argues that the narrative is not apologetic per se but instead functions to portray Paul as "an ideal representative of the gospel" or as "a paradigm of the gospel of Christian freedom, which he seeks to persuade his readers to reaffirm in the face of the threat presented by the troublemakers."[41] I agree with Lyons's understanding of the function of the narrative but not with his reconstruction of its divisions or his identification of the genre of Galatians. As I argued in the Kennedy essay, it seems to me possible to identify in the narrative discourse of Gal 1:13–2:14 the topics of an encomium.[42]

According to Burgess, "No single term represents the aim and scope of epideictic literature so completely as the word ἐγκώμιον."[43] Although the word "encomium" can be synonymous with epideictic literature as a whole, it can also be a subordinate feature in other forms. In general, it is a statement of praise of the good qualities of a person or thing and can refer to a style or point of view, or a composition produced as a result of involvement in one of the elementary exercises.

The authors of handbooks on elementary exercises provide details on the rules of how one composes an encomium.[44] Topics were to be developed in the following order:

Prologue	προοίμιον
Race and origins	γένος
Education	ἀνατροφή
Achievements	πράξεις
Comparison	σύγκρισις
Epilogue	ἐπίλογος

The essential features of the major topics were these:

Προοίμιον—a statement that indicates the importance of the person or thing being praised, often with reference to the fact that the speaker feels inadequate to the task.

Γένος and Γένεσις—a reference to the ancestry and origins of the one being praised and a reference to the circumstances of the person's birth, especially to any noteworthy fact or event associated with it.

[39] Lyons, *Pauline Autobiography*, 132–33.
[40] Ibid.; see esp. ch. 2, "Existing Approaches."
[41] Ibid., 170–71.
[42] Stowers, *Letter Writing*, 46: "Epideictic forms such as encomia and consolations are frequently adapted to letters."
[43] In what follows I will be summarizing relevant points from Burgess, "Epideictic Literature," 113–31.
[44] Translations for the elementary exercises of Hermogenes can be found in Baldwin, *Medieval Rhetoric*, 23–38; and for Aphthonius in Nadeau, "Progymnasmata."

'Ανατροφή—a review of the circumstances of the person's youth, particularly those that give an early indication of character. An important subcategory of this division was ἐπιτηδεύματα—deeds that illustrate choice guided by character.

Πράξεις—activities or achievements that illustrate the person's virtues.

Σύγκρισις—comparison with others to highlight character. This was also one of the elementary exercises.

'Επίλογος—a recapitulation and appeal to others to imitate virtues of the one being praised; the contents of the epilogue are dependent on the subject and circumstances, just as in the προοίμιον.

There were subcategories associated with race, education, and activities, but the presence of any topic was to be determined in part by the circumstances of the speech setting and the audience situation.[45]

The stasis statement should be seen as the προοίμιον to the encomium. Γνωρίζω (1:11) indicates the beginning of a disclosure statement.[46] Such statements often opened the body of the letter,[47] and their presence signals a division point. In 1:11–12, the subject is Paul's gospel, which has as its unusual feature the fact that it was given not naturally, through human agency but, if you will, supernaturally, through revelation. Its importance derives from the fact that it revealed to Paul Jesus Christ.

Despite the occurrence of ἀνατροφήν in 1:13, the content of vv. 13–14 suggests the presence of a γένος-γένεσις topic. The reference to his former life in Judaism and his zeal for the traditions that he inherited have more to do with origins than the circumstances of his youth. His former life in Judaism exists in a past as distant as though it had been another life. His use of ἀνατροφήν obliges the reader to see that former life as γένος.

If we understand that, for the sake of the argument that he is making to the Galatians, Paul's "real" birth occurs at his conversion and calling (1:15), it means that the essential feature of the ἀνατροφήν topic is found in 1:15–17. As noted above, one of the subcategories of that topic is ἐπιτηδεύματα. What deed was guided by his character? The "youthful" Paul did not seek an authoritative source to interpret his revelation, nor did he go to Jerusalem but instead to Gentile territory (Gal 1: 16–17)!

The chief topic in the encomium was πράξεις.[48] In describing the activities or achievements of the one being praised, it was important to illustrate the underlying principles and moral purposes enabling these achievements. This attempt can be seen in 1:18–24. Three years after his conversion, Paul went to Jerusalem for fifteen days of conversations with Cephas and James, then on to Syria and Cilicia. The testimony in Judea concerning his change of character caused the churches to glorify God despite

---

[45] Baldwin, *Medieval Rhetoric*, 31 n. 60, compares in translation the encomiastic topics of Aphthonius and Menander.

[46] Mullins, "Disclosure," 45–50.

[47] White, *Light*, 207; "Structural Analysis," 22. See also his "Introductory Formulae."

[48] Burgess, "Epideictic Literature," 123.

the fact that they had never seen him and that he seemed to prefer Gentile contact over Judean. Clearly this contact did not weaken the impact of his ethos.

The comparison of character (σύγκρισις) "is regarded as the most important division but in application it is left to circumstances and the judgment of the writer."[49] There were two distinct kinds, minor and general, the latter allowing for a fuller comparison to be made. Lyons says that the chief comparison is with Cephas and Paul in 2:11–21,[50] but he seems to overlook the nature of the meeting in Jerusalem and the comparison Paul makes in reporting that incident between himself, the "false brethren," and the "pillars." The presence of two different temporal particles, ἔπειτα in 2:1, and ὅτε δέ in 2:11, signals two different incidents unrelated to one another in time, but there is no inherent reason to see ὅτε δέ as the sign for a new division. Therefore, the σύγκρισις topic is found in 2:1–14.

The relationship between the two incidents lies in the fact that they both illustrate Paul's character in defense of his gospel and the value system derived from it and his defense of the character of the gospel itself. In the first incident, Paul went up to Jerusalem in defense of his gospel (2:1),[51] and his character and that of his gospel are compared with those of the false brethren and pillar apostles. In the second, both are compared to Cephas.

Quite obviously that leaves 2:15–21 as the ἐπίλογος. Admittedly, this is a somewhat lengthy epilogue, but its length can be accounted for by the fact that it is also a chreia elaboration. The elaboration and encomium are completed by the epilogue for the elaboration, "I do not nullify the grace of God, for if righteousness were through the law, then Christ died to no purpose" (2:21).

It is important to recognize that the narrative section is fashioned as an encomium because of the ability of the encomium to express character and because of its usefulness in fulfilling the argumentative purpose of character contrast. Moreover, the encomium allows Paul to begin to shift the trajectory of blame exactly at 2:14.[52] Normally one would expect encomiastic narrative to be carried out in the third person. Obviously that cannot be the case in this narrative. Paul as narrator is also participant in the events and situations he describes. From the point of view of the Galatians, they are observers, watching the imitation of the events being carried through. But for effective mimesis to occur, that is, for the Galatians to become again what Paul is, to imitate him once more, Paul has to change the situation of his audience from observer to participant. This is the function of the chreia in 2:14.

As long as Paul is narrating the demonstration of the power of the gospel to change character, the audience can avoid the argumentative situation; they can see and hear but not understand. When the chreia is read, however, nothing is being demonstrated. As discourse, it can be heard as though addressed to them. This is its power. Although the narrative suggests that Peter or those associated with withdrawal from

---

[49] Ibid., 125.
[50] Lyons, *Pauline Autobiography*, 134–35.
[51] See Hester, "Use and Influence," 397, for my exegesis of κατὰ ἀποκάλυψιν.
[52] Ibid., 403–4.

table fellowship at Antioch are the intended hearers of the chreia, the chreia is not part of the narrative discourse; it is pragmatic and pedagogical. It asks the question of the teachers of the other gospel, "How can you compel Gentiles to live like Jews?"

Once spoken, the chreia sets the stage for further discourse, the elaboration, in which Paul can use the inclusive "we," to imply the condition and behavior of Peter, Barnabas, the Antiochenes, himself, and the Galatians (2:15–17), and the exclusive "I," as the one whose character should be imitated (2:18–21). The Galatian reader/hearers are drawn into a new argumentative situation in which they are charged, in the implied contrast with Paul, with misrepresenting the gospel, building up the things that have been torn down, forgetting the fact that they have been crucified with Christ. Given this new situation, Paul can confront them directly with the rhetorical questions of 3:1–4 and enter into the task, in 3:5–6:9, of amplifying why they are to blame and what they must do to correct that situation. Finally, in 6:17, he can lay claim to the highest status of all, providing an almost perfect model to be imitated, the position of one who bears τὰ στίγματα τοῦ ᾽Ιησοῦ.

If I am correct in understanding the stasis of the letter to be that of quality, both the quality of the gospel and the quality of the relationship between Paul and the Galatians, then Galatians should be understood as a reproachful letter aimed at a group of people who once shared a set of commonly held values but, under the influence of some from among them, have abandoned those values. By accepting an alternate interpretation of the gospel, they have in fact reverted to old values and practices. Paul confronts them with the seriousness of what they have done with his opening rebuke (θαυμάζω ὅτι οὕτως ταχέως μετατίθεσθε) and, having established the issue (stasis), launches into an encomiastic narrative to illustrate the legitimacy of his gospel. Its character was so superior to anything the Galatians might have encountered subsequently that because of it he triumphed over his unnamed enemies in Jerusalem and shamed Peter in Antioch.

The Rhetoric of Persona in Galatians 1 and 2[53]

Dale Sullivan and Christian Anible point out that "much of what we now understand epideictic theory to be is not explicit in the ancient treatises; rather, it had been coaxed out of classical rhetoric by synthesizing it with modern social and critical theory and by testing the resulting new insights in a number of case studies."[54] Elaborating on Sullivan's earlier work, they point out that one of the functions of epideictic is to allow the speaker to create "a representative ethos, a persona that reflects the values of the community being addressed."[55]

---

[53] A very useful exegetical analysis of Paul's allusion to authority in these chapters can be found in ch. 5, "Tradition, Gospel, and Ego: Gal. 1 and 2," of Schütz, Paul, 114–58.

[54] Sullivan and Anible, "Epideictic Dimension," 121. They list these functions of epideictic: establishing legitimacy and authority, invoking communion, instilling perspective, inscribing status, enforcing exclusion, and cultivating virtue.

[55] Ibid., 124.

It is widely recognized that chs. 1 and 2 represent one of the places in Paul's letters where self-portrayal and personal example are used for argumentative purposes. Rhetorically speaking, they can function as ethical proofs.[56] Recently Brian Dodd has surveyed what he calls examples of the "paradigmatic 'I'" in Paul to show that Paul uses personal example as literary strategy for both pedagogical and argumentative purposes.[57] Dodd's analysis clearly illustrates the nature of the argument from ethos contained in the letter opening and narrative discourse.

K. K. Campbell and K. H. Jamieson call attention to another function of the kind of argument Paul is making in these chapters. In analyzing the keynote address by Barbara Jordan at the 1976 Democratic convention, they say this: "She herself *was* the proof of the argument she was making. . . . Many critics who watched and heard her speak will have recognized a recurrent rhetorical form, a reflexive form, a form called 'enactment' in which the speaker incarnates the argument, is the proof of what is said."[58] While much argument in chs. 4 and 5 of Galatians is based on "enactment," it is in 1:1–2:21 that enactment as proof dominates.

The opening greeting and narrative discourse in Galatians 1 and 2 elaborate what the Galatians know of Paul's "persona."[59] Persona can be defined as (a) an individual's social facade that reflects the role in life the individual is playing or (b) the personality that a person (as an actor or politician) projects in public. The persona is also a person's representation that has been created by a community, based on fantasy chaining[60] that has occurred in the community. In the case of an important religious or political figure, for example, the fantasies created by a smaller group—a circle of advisors or a group of disciples—may have been chained out into a larger group to produce a public persona. Persona is largely a rhetorical creation. This is true even for a god persona to which religious groups appeal.[61]

The opening greeting (1:1–5) focuses on Paul's apostolic persona in two ways. On the one hand, the title "apostle" is immediately qualified as to its legitimacy; it came from "Jesus Christ and God the Father." On the other, he does not include the names of any coworkers or letter carriers in the address or indeed make mention of any other such persons in the entire letter. Paul claims to have received a special apostleship, and it follows from this that Jesus Christ and God the Father

---

[56] Cf. S. Elliott, "Paul," 128.

[57] Dodd, *Paul's Paradigmatic "I."* I showed above that epideictic functioned pedagogically.

[58] Campbell and Jamieson, "Form and Genre," 9.

[59] In using this term, I am not implying a definition of persona typically associated with Booth, *Rhetoric of Fiction*, 73, 83. Booth speaks of the implied author, or "second self" of a discourse, an artificially created persona who is nonetheless a reflection of the real author (71–76, 211). See also Black, "Second Persona," who argues that the implied auditors ought to be thought of as the "second" persona in the discourse.

[60] Fantasy "chains" are created when a group member tells about an experience or event, and others who shared in that experience add their view of it until it becomes the experience of the group. Fantasy sharing is a means whereby groups establish identity and set boundary conditions for identifying insiders from outsiders. It is also a way in which group history and traditions are developed, thus enabling the group to think of itself as unique. See Bormann, *Small Group Communication*, 104, 115. See also above, n. 15.

[61] Bormann, Cragan, and Shields, "Defense," 279.

are the source of authority for his rhetorical vision. This point is made fully clear in 1:11–12.

In the exordium (1:6–10), the lack of any personal deictic other than his own reinforces Paul's claim that he is the only source of the rhetorical vision the Galatians should follow, the Christian paideia he taught to the Galatians. The first person plural in the verb, "we . . . preached," in 1:8 is an example of the "epistolary plural," used when the author is implying a formal statement of authority and is thereby excluding the audience.[62] Paul wants to be the center of attention in order to reassert his definition of both his credentials and his teaching.

As Sullivan and Anible show, Paul is able to argue, by disassociating it from concepts of authority held in Jerusalem and reassociating it with divine authority and inspiration, that the actions he took in his dealings with Jerusalem establish his authority.[63] Paul clearly states this in 1:1 and 1:12 and in the narrative shows how he used this authority in his relations with the other apostles. By doing so, he invited comparison with the teachers of the "other" gospel. This comparison has not only to do with the source of their authority but also their function as teachers. In narrating his negotiations with the pillar apostles in Jerusalem and his confrontation with Peter in Antioch, Paul teaches the Galatians by example. Paul is the pragmatic example of the superiority of the gospel that he has been given. Faithful Christians such as Paul insist on the observation of sound doctrine, which creates a communion of believers who practice virtues derived from Christian paideia and excludes those whose doctrine is faulty and whose behavior is questionable.[64] According to Paul, at least, the other teachers do not teach sound doctrine or model proper behavior. They are to blame for the situation in which the Galatians find themselves, potentially alienated from the charismatic leader who was responsible for their becoming sons of God and heirs of Abraham (3:12–20; 6:12–13).

The chreia and its context (2:11–14, with the "response" chreia coming at v. 14)[65] illustrate the defense of doctrine and the insistence on behavior based on that doctrine. The change in the temporal particle in 2:11 suggests that the trajectory of the narrative of Paul's relationship with Jerusalem is replaced by a move into another region in the topography of the argument of these chapters. Antioch is a different setting altogether, a different rhetorical situation. Peter is the outsider, not Paul, and the men whose appearance unsettles Peter have not come "by revelation" but "from James." They are guilty of advocating false doctrine, and Peter and Barnabas are guilty of abdicating to them through the agency of abandoning table fellowship. The argument goes beyond a simple comparison of character or an illustration of Paul's character. The paradigm implied in the report of the rhetorical situation in Antioch is the authority of Paul's apostolic persona. Of the two

---

[62] Wallace, *Greek Grammar*, 394–96.

[63] Dodd, *Paul's Paradigmatic "I,"* 134–35.

[64] See Sullivan and Anible, "Epideictic Dimension," 135–43, for an elaboration of these points.

[65] Jegher-Bucher, "Formgeschichtliche Betrachtung," argues that while I am correct in understanding 2:11–14 as being a chreia, the "highpoint" of the chreia comes in vv. 15–16. See also her dissertation, *Galaterbrief*, 150–79.

apostles, Peter and Paul, only Paul was both correct in his doctrine and honorable in his behavior.

The chreia elaboration (2:15–21) is also an elaboration of the rhetorical vision first given to the Galatians by Paul. It is crowded with cue words and insider references: Jews, Gentile "sinners," "works of the law," "faith in [Jesus] Christ," "justified," "justification," "law," "sin," "crucified," "Son of God." It makes use of the fantasy type[66] "justification by faith" and contains the fantasy themes[67] of "Christians need not be concerned with works of the law" and "Christians live in faith in Christ."

The paraphrase (2:15–16a) and rationale (2:16b–d) of the chreia contain the heart of Paul's rhetorical vision, that justification is by faith and not by works of the law. The paraphrase makes an assertion that can be argued: Jewish Christians know that believers are justified by faith. How do they know this? Because they themselves believed in Christ and not in works of the law in order to be justified.[68]

That, in turn, is elaborated by the contrast (2:17) and the comparison (2:18). The argumentation in these verses is complex and therefore has been the subject of a variety of analyses.[69] For our purposes, however, it is enough to point out that the contrast concerns the behavior outlined in the chreia. Compelling Gentiles to live like Jews would be in contrast to the core teaching in Paul's rhetorical vision. For Paul, and perhaps Peter as well,[70] to be viewed by others as sinful because of table fellowship with Gentile Christians is not only a challenge to his vision but also to his apostolic persona. It would be sinful to insist on behavior based on values derived from the Law, which is unable to justify. Thus Paul cannot make Christ an agent of sin because Paul's behavior is based on values derived from being in Christ by virtue of his belief in Christ. This assertion is worked out further in the comparison. Having abandoned belief in the Law as the agent of justification, it would be transgression for him to return to cooperation in compelling Gentiles to live like Jews. Such activity would undermine the legitimacy of both his rhetorical vision and his apostolic persona as apostle to the Gentiles, a persona that had been accepted by James, Peter, and Cephas in Jerusalem.

Finally, the example (2:19–20) is almost a textbook model of a reflexive form of argumentation. Up to this point in the elaboration, the deictic form has been the first

---

[66] Fantasy type is a general scenario that covers several concrete fantasy themes. This scenario may be repeated with similar characters and may take the same form. It can be generalized so that characters become personae who act in predictable fashion. Rhetors simply make use of a familiar type, and the audience fills in the particulars. "Fantasy types allow a group to fit new events or experiences into familiar patterns." See Foss, *Rhetorical Criticism*, 292. An example of a fantasy type is "the American dream" or "family values."

[67] Fantasy themes become part of the group consciousness; are artistic and organized; and are slanted, ordered, and interpretive. As a result, they provide a way for two or more groups of people to explain an event in different ways. An illustration of a fantasy theme is, "Illegal immigrants consume more in social services than they contribute in taxes."

[68] Note that these elements of the elaboration are structured chiastically; cf. Martyn, *Galatians*, 250.

[69] See, e.g., Burton, *Galatians*, 124–32; R. Longenecker, *Galatians*, 88–91; Martyn, *Galatians*, 253–56, 260–74.

[70] See Martyn, *Galatians*, 255.

person plural. In 2:18, it shifts to the singular.[71] He draws attention away from Peter's inclusion in the charges made by the emissaries from Jerusalem and focuses on his activities. At Antioch Peter was tried and found wanting. He cannot serve as an example for the Galatians. Paul is the enactment of his own vision; he is proof of his own argument and an example of one who is led by his rhetorical vision.[72]

In chs. 1 and 2 Paul is doing more than making an argument from character or offering himself as a paradigm. Those rhetorical moves are made to reassert his persona and, in doing so, to reassert the authority of his gospel. While he may be expecting the Galatians to imitate his character, he is also expecting them to obey his persona as their apostolic leader.

Conclusion

In formulating a modern definition of genre, Campbell and Jamieson write,

> If the recurrence of similar forms establishes a genre, then genres are groups of discourses which share substantive, stylistic and situational characteristics. . . . A genre is a group of acts unified by a constellation of forms that recurs in each of its members. These forms, *in isolation*, appear in other discourses. What is distinctive about the acts in a genre is the recurrence of the forms *together* in constellation. . . . In others words, a genre does not consist merely of a series of acts in which certain rhetorical forms recur; for example, it is conceivable that parallelism and antithesis might recur jointly without establishing a generic similarity. Instead, a genre is composed of a constellation of recognizable forms bound together by an internal dynamic.[73]

It is my contention that I have demonstrated, at least superficially, that a "constellation" of forms related to the epideictic are found in Galatians 1 and 2. If this is true, then it would follow that it can be argued that the genre of these chapters is epideictic.

On the other hand, Sullivan and Anible have argued that attempts to define epideictic as a genre ought to be abandoned in favor of understanding what they call the "epideictic dimension" of rhetoric, its functionality, its role in "creating a persona that reflects the values of the community being addressed."[74] The analysis above also brings out that functionality. It would appear that the first two chapters of Galatians contain a fairly carefully crafted narrative discourse that fulfills a number of epideictic functions, including providing a fuller illustration of Paul's apostolic persona.

---

[71] Cf., however, Lührmann, *Galatians*, 48; and Martyn, *Galatians*, 258, who understand the shift as (a) refuting a charge made against Paul by the teachers, and (b) Paul presenting himself as the paradigm of the eschatological human made alive by God.

[72] Dodd, *Paul's Paradigmatic "I,"* 136–61, argues that Paul's "self-portrayal" in these chapters lacks explicit indicators of a literary strategy of the kind found in 1 Corinthians. If this is the case, it may be so because in these chapters "self-portrayal" has been couched rhetorically as "persona," a different kind of "proof."

[73] Campbell and Jamieson, "Form and Genre," 20–21. See also an interesting elaboration of their definition of genre by Miller, "Genre."

[74] Sullivan and Anible, "Epideictic Dimension," 124.

Furthermore, by elaborating on Paul's rhetorical vision, the narrative lays the foundation for a more direct discussion, in chs. 4 and 5, of the values commonly held by Paul and the Galatians but being neglected by the Galatians as a result of some in their midst arguing for other value systems that Paul chose to call "another gospel."[75]

It is the constellation of forms, their function in reasserting the authoritative persona of Paul and his gospel, and the kinds of action that follow from the argument that ought to guide the identification of the genre of the letter, and not issues of arrangement and style. In other words, close analysis of the pattern of argumentation and the use of epistolary formulas may satisfy form-critical requirements, but in order to serve a rhetorical critical function, they must be supplemented by analysis of the larger questions of the context of invention and the "internal dynamic" of the argumentation and then by an attempt to describe the meaning that is in the message of the argument. Doing this moves the interpreter from rhetorical analysis to rhetorical criticism.

---

[75] Cf. Gaventa, "Galatians 1 and 2"; and Dodd, "Christ's Slave."

Autobiographical Narratives

Section B
Socio-Historical Approaches

12

THE INCIDENT AT ANTIOCH (GAL 2:11–18)[1]

James D. G. Dunn

The incident at Antioch, briefly described by Paul in Gal 2, has long been a source of some perplexity to students of the NT. In the patristic period the embarrassment of an account where Paul openly condemned Peter for hypocrisy was avoided by such devious exegesis as that of Clement of Alexandria who maintained that a *different* Cephas was in view, or that of Origen who argued that the whole dispute between Peter and Paul was simulated.[2] On the whole however this ceased to be a problem when churchmen found they could cope with the incident within the framework of Petrine and papal supremacy by presenting it as a noble example of Peter's humility. Inevitably it was this aspect which also caught attention in Reformation exegesis, with Paul's rebuke of Peter giving those wishing to protest against the authority of the Papacy just the precedent they needed.[3]

In more recent decades the issues have become more historical than ecclesiastical, with the earlier exegetical assumptions being regularly and sharply questioned. In particular, can we assume that Peter accepted Paul's rebuke and amended his conduct? If he did not, what does that tell us about the development of Paul's missionary work, about his subsequent relations with Jerusalem and Peter, about factions within first century Christianity (Peter and Paul parties, etc.)?[4] Again, where does the Antioch incident fit within the history of that period? Can we assume that it formed the sequel to the Jerusalem council recounted by Luke in Acts 15? Or is the issue more complex, with the historicity of Acts being called in question in part at least by Paul's account?[5]

---

[1] This paper was delivered in briefer form at the New Testament Conference in the University of Glasgow, September 1980, and to a seminar at the University of Aarhus, Denmark, in March 1981.

[2] See further Lightfoot, *Galatians,* 128–32; Overbeck, *Auffassung;* Mussner, *Galaterbrief,* 146–54.

[3] See, e.g., commentaries by Luther and Calvin.

[4] These issues were first raised in their present sharp form by the work of Baur, *Paul,* 1:133–36, and *Church History,*1:54–55.

[5] See, e.g., the history of discussion reviewed by Gasque, *History,* index: "Gal 2" and "Gal 2:1–10." The most recent attempt to reconstruct a Pauline chronology solely on the basis of the Pauline corre-

For all that the significance of the Antioch incident has been recognized in such discussions, there has been remarkably little detailed work done on the incident itself. The question of whether or not Acts 15 = Gal 2:1–10 often seems largely to have exhausted the debate. And when commentators or historians have moved on to the Antioch incident they have not paused long over what must on any reckoning be a crucial question: *What was the nature of the table-fellowship that Peter enjoyed with the Gentile believers? What was involved in it? What precisely did he withdraw from when the men from James arrived?* The ready assumption lay close to hand that it was all simply a matter of the Jewish food laws and little more need be said.[6] But was it quite so simple? Is this not another exegetical assumption which ought to be examined more closely? Without some clearer idea of what table-fellowship at Antioch involved prior to Peter's withdrawal, our grasp of what was at stake is seriously defective, and consequently also our ability to assess the significance of Peter's and Paul's conduct.

It is on this area and aspect that I wish to focus in what follows. My belief that such an investigation is necessary is the product of reflection on several overlapping and wider issues, a reflection stimulated by various items of recent scholarship. The overlapping and wider issues inform us of the broader historical context within which we must attempt to assess the Antioch incident and will engage our attention next. In the light of our findings there we will attempt some exegesis of Gal 2:11–18 in the hope of clarifying the incident itself, including the reasons for Peter's conduct and the force of Paul's response. Finally, we shall consider possible implications for some of the more familiar questions connected with this passage.

The Historical Context

The Antioch incident is usually dated in the late 40s of the first century, depending of course on such questions as the date of the Jerusalem council (Acts 15) and the relation between Gal 2 and Acts 15.[7] Since the crisis at Antioch was provoked by the

---

spondence, with consequent considerable manipulation of the Acts data, is that of Lüdemann, *Studien,* who also argues unnecessarily and implausibly that the Antioch incident preceded the second Jerusalem visit of Gal 2:1–10 (pp. 77–79, 101–5; for earlier bibliography see Eckert, *Verkündigung,* 193 n. 3). But see already Dupont, "Pierre et Paul," and see n. 7 below.

[6] See, e.g., Burton, *Galatians,* 104; Bonnard, *L'épître,* 51; Oepke, *Galater,* 56; Filson, *History,* 224–25; Bruce, *Paul,* 176; Betz, *Galatians,* 107 and n. 448.

[7] The Jerusalem council has been dated as early as 43 C.E. (e.g., Hahn, *Mission,* 91), and as late as 51 (e.g., Knox, *Chapters,* ch. 5), but the majority prefer 48 or 49 as most probable in view of other chronological data available to us (see the brief summary in Jewett, *Dating Paul's Life,* 1–2). For the various alternative correlations of Gal 2 with the Jerusalem visits recorded in Acts (Acts 11:30; 15; 18:22) see also Jewett, *Dating Paul's Life,* ch. 4, and further below, n. 96. The Antioch incident is usually thought to have taken place a few months after the second Jerusalem visit. Suhl however argues for an interval of four years between the two, the first missionary journey intervening (*Paulus,* 70, 322–23, 340; cf. Hahn, *Mission,* 82; Haenchen, *Acts,* 439; Wedderburn, "Chronologies," 103–8), and Reicke for an interval of five years, the "second missionary journey" intervening ("Hintergrund," 175–76, 183; also *New Testament Era,* 214). But since Paul takes such care to itemize the intervals between his contacts with the Jerusalem leadership he would hardly have passed over such an interval with a mere ὅτε δέ (Gal 2:11); contrast the use of the same linking phrase in Gal 1:15, 2:12 and 4:4.

arrival of "certain individuals from James" (Gal 2:12), that is, from Jerusalem, it is important to clarify the relationship between the church in Jerusalem and the church in Antioch at that time, and to examine possible influences on these churches from the broader social and political situation within Palestine and within Palestinian and Diaspora Judaism.

The Relationship between the Church in Jerusalem and the Church in Antioch

One of the major weaknesses in many reconstructions of Christian origins and NT theology has been the failure to grasp the full racial and nationalistic dimensions of the early disputes within Christianity. As K. Stendahl pointed out in a famous essay,[8] Paul's teaching on justification through faith was not intended as an answer to a Luther-like agonizing after personal assurance of salvation. Paul's concern was rather with the relation between Jew and Gentile. His question was not, How can I be saved? but, How can Gentiles be included within the messianic community of Israel?[9] This essentially racial or nationalistic concept of righteousness as a consequence of God's election of and covenant with Israel has received fresh illumination from the major study by E. P. Sanders with his characterization of Palestinian Judaism in terms of "covenantal nomism."[10]

The point is that earliest Christianity was not yet seen as something separate and distinct from Judaism. It was a sect, like other sects within first century Judaism. The first Christians had some distinct and peculiar beliefs about Jesus; but their religion was the religion of the Jews.[11] So that when Gentiles began to embrace these particular beliefs about Jesus the question raised was still only in terms of what requirements were necessary for the Gentile to join himself to the people who worshipped the one God and to whom God had sent his Messiah, Jesus. The fact that Paul's main argument in Galatians is about how one becomes Abraham's offspring, heir of his blessing (Gal 3–4), is sufficient indication of the limits within which both sides had carried on the earlier debate.[12] As we shall see below, circumcision was only one aspect of that debate, and it was probably the incident at Antioch which helped sharpen the issues for Paul.

---

[8] Stendahl, "Apostle Paul."

[9] Stendahl, *Paul*, including a reprint of "Apostle Paul": "The doctrine of justification by faith was hammered out by Paul for the very specific and limited purpose of defending the rights of Gentile converts to be full and genuine heirs to the promises of God to Israel."

[10] E. Sanders, *Paul and Palestinian Judaism*. Sanders defines "covenantal nomism" as "the view that one's place in God's plan is established on the basis of the covenant and that the covenant requires as the proper response of man his obedience to its commandments, while providing means of atonement for transgression" (75). "The overall pattern of Rabbinic religion as it applied to Israelites . . . is this: God has chosen Israel and Israel has accepted the election. . . . As long as he (the Israelite) maintains his desire to stay in the covenant, he has a share in God's covenantal promises, including life in the world to come. The intention and effort to be obedient constitutes the *condition for remaining in the covenant,* but they do not *earn* it" (180).

[11] See further Dunn, *Unity and Diversity,* §54.1; Schiffman, "At the Crossroads."

[12] The debate continues after Galatians in the same terms, particularly in Romans; see, e.g., Munck, *Christ and Israel;* Davies, "Paul."

This nationalistic dimension to the earliest development of Christianity within Judaism also helps us to recognize that the church at Antioch would not have seen itself as an entity independent of the Jews or of the Jewish believers in Palestine. It was simply the believing Jewish community at Antioch embracing more and more God-fearing Gentiles.[13] Almost certainly the majority at heart would simply think of themselves as part of the Diaspora, with Jerusalem still serving as a source of pride and inspiration and a focus for faith and aspiration[14]—despite the persecution which had forced many of the founding members to flee from the capital city (Acts 11:19–20).[15] This would also involve the church at Antioch recognizing the church at Jerusalem as the fountainhead of their distinctive faith (cf. Rom 15:27) and probably also as the authoritative interpreter of it.

Most significant here is the degree to which Paul's treatment of his own relations with Jerusalem prior to the Antioch incident reinforces the impression that *up until that time he too had taken it for granted that Jerusalem had this primacy and authority.* I refer to the character of Paul's self-defense in Gal 1–2. As has been recently pointed out, "the dialectic between being independent of and being acknowledged by Jerusalem is the keynote of this important text and must not be forgotten."[16] In Galatians Paul is writing *after* the incident at Antioch and his exposition is heavily colored by that later viewpoint. But in trying to assert his independence from Jerusalem, and the directness of his apostleship and gospel from Christ, he cannot escape the fact that previously he had readily acknowledged the authority of the Jerusalem apostles.[17] His use of προσανατίθεσθαι ("to consult in order to be given an authoritative interpretation") in 1:16 is probably an implicit acknowledgement that the Jerusalem apostles were recognized by him at that time as the appropriate authorities to consult on the interpretation of the revelation given him at Damascus—the point (as he *now* insists) being that he had *not* consulted them (1:16–17). He does not disguise the fact that his first visit to Jerusalem had been "to get information from Cephas" (ἱστορῆσαι Κηφᾶν—1:18),[18] though the information was evidently something different from the gospel already received three years earlier through the revelation of Christ (1:12). The purpose of his second visit to Jerusalem was to consult (ἀνεθέμην) the Jerusalem leadership about

---

[13] The fact that the new movement was first given a distinctive name in Antioch ("Christians"—Acts 11:26) need not imply a distinction between the new movement and the synagogue, but only a distinction *within* Judaism (like Josephus' three sects—*J.W.* 2.8.2, etc.). The absence of any mention of hostility from synagogue authorities in Antioch against the "Christians" in any of our sources may well be significant here (see further below).

[14] Note, e.g., how Paul takes up and adapts the Jewish theme of the heavenly Jerusalem (Gal 4:25–26), as also Heb 12:22 and Rev 3:12; 21:2, 10. Apocalyptic and rabbinic references in Str.-B 3.573, 796.

[15] Stephen's views as represented in Acts 7 should not be understood as calling for an abandoning of Judaism. On the contrary they can be readily understood as a recall to a more primitive and purified form of Judaism (see particularly Simon, *St. Stephen*). Paul of course presses still further back behind Moses the lawgiver to Abraham the man of faith.

[16] Holmberg, *Paul and Power,* 15.

[17] For what follows see more fully Dunn, "Relationship."

[18] Kilpatrick, "Galatians 1:18."

his gospel, but he does not hide the fact that what they thought or decided about his gospel would make all the difference to the success or failure of his mission to the Gentiles.[19] The language he uses in 2:2, 6 indicates a certain embarrassment at this admission. He calls the Jerusalem apostles "the men of repute," a phrase familiar in political rhetoric where it was used both positively and negatively (derogatively or ironically).[20] The parenthesis of v. 6, with its noticeable change of tense—"what they were (then) is (now) a matter of indifference to me; God shows no partiality"—is all aimed at *relativizing* the authority of the Jerusalem apostles in the *current* situation in Galatia and at reducing the significance of his *earlier* acceptance of that authority.[21] Likewise, when he says "those of repute added (προσανέθεντο) nothing to me" (2:6),[22] where again the language probably indicates an acknowledgement on his part at that time of Jerusalem's "right" to instruct or give directives to its daughter churches. So too, it can plausibly be argued that Paul's convoluted statement in vv. 7–10 is a further attempt to obscure the degree to which Paul had been willing to accept Jerusalem's authority at that time—the authority clearly expressed in the pillar apostles' recognition of Paul's and Barnabas's missionary success and their approval of a future division of labor.[23] All this points strongly to the conclusion that while Paul *defended a position* at Jerusalem, the three "pillar" apostles *delivered a verdict*.

Moreover, there is a growing agreement on the view that when Paul went up to Jerusalem this second time it was not as an independent missionary or apostle, but as a delegate from the church at Antioch (so Acts 15:2; cf. 14:4, 14–"apostles," that is, of the church at Antioch, 13:2–3).[24] The question discussed at the meeting in Jerusalem was not primarily whether Paul (and Barnabas) were apostles, but whether as apostles of Antioch their practice of not circumcising their converts should continue—that is, whether the church at Antioch's practice of according full acceptance to uncircumcised Gentile believers should continue without modification. The victory, or rather, concession won by the Antioch delegation did not call in question the authority of the Jerusalem apostles to make this concession. The point is that the church at Antioch could not make this decision by themselves and readily referred it to Jerusalem. And when subsequently the delegation came from James, the majority of believers in Antioch just as readily accepted the authority of this further ruling regarding the practice of table-fellowship at Antioch.

This nationalistic dimension to the Antioch incident becomes still more significant in the light of the second feature of the broader historical context, to which we now turn.

---

[19] The point is not that Paul's gospel might be judged invalid, but that its effect among Gentiles might be nullified (see further my "Relationship").

[20] See particularly Barrett, " 'Pillar' Apostles," 1–4, 17–18; Betz, *Galatians,* 86–87, 92.

[21] Cf. Hay, "Paul's Indifference"; Betz, *Galatians,* 94–95.

[22] Cf. Burton, *Galatians,* 89–91; Oepke, *Galater,* 48–49.

[23] Cf. Bruce, *Paul,* 154, and the fuller discussion in Betz, *Galatians,* 96–103.

[24] See Holmberg, *Paul and Power,* 18, and those cited by him in n. 37; also Hengel, "Ursprunge," 18; Betz, *Galatians,* 84.

The Socio-Political Situation Confronting Judaism in the Middle of the First Century

During the period which concerns us, many Jews, no doubt a growing proportion within the Jewish territories, must have believed their distinctive religious and national prerogatives were under increasing threat. The long, drawn out crisis provoked by Caligula's insistence that a statue of himself be set up in the Jerusalem temple is well known (40 C.E.).[25] And latterly, after the death of Agrippa in 44 C.E., the situation deteriorated rapidly under a succession of weak Roman procurators.[26] Cuspius Fadus (44–?46 C.E.) demanded that the vestments of the High Priest be returned to the Romans for safe-keeping (Josephus, *Ant.* 20.1.1), and had to act against the threatened rebellion led by the self-styled prophet Theudas *(Ant.* 20.5.1). Tiberius Julius Alexander (?46–48 C.E.) crucified James and Simon, the sons of Judas the Galilean, presumably because like their father they were engaged in fomenting unrest against Roman rule on account of its threat to their faith *(Ant.* 20.5.2).[27] Under Cumanus (48–52 C.E.), things went from bad to worse, with a near riot in Jerusalem resulting in thousands of deaths (20,000 or 30,000 according to Josephus—*J.W.* 2.12.1; *Ant.* 20.5.3), and a succession of disorders involving zealot bands in Samaria and elsewhere *(J.W.* 2.12.2–5; *Ant.* 20.5.4–6). Josephus reports that "from that time the whole of Judea was infested with bands of brigands" *(Ant.* 20.6.1)—"brigands" (λῃσταί) being Josephus's way of describing the Zealots.[28]

The followers of Jesus within Palestine would not have been unaffected by these mounting pressures. The death of Stephen and the subsequent persecution (early or middle 30s) presumably had the effect of ensuring that those followers of the Nazarene who had been exempted from the persecution, or who had returned to Jerusalem thereafter, would take care to show themselves good Jews, loyal to their religious and national heritage.[29] Agrippa's execution of James (brother of John) in or before 44 C.E. is presumably also to be explained against this background; Luke notes that "it pleased the Jews" and encouraged Agrippa to move against Peter (Acts 12:1–3).

Furthermore we should bear in mind that such pressures towards conformity with the mainstream of nationalistic Judaism were experienced as much *within* the infant Christian communities as from without. It is not simply a matter of coincidence that in the preceding episode involving Peter prior to his arrest, Peter had been criticized by "the circumcision party" for eating with an uncircumcised Gentile (Acts

---

[25] Philo, *Legat.* 184–338; Josephus, *J.W.* 2.10.1–5; *Ant.* 18.8.2–9; Tacitus, *Hist.* 5.9.

[26] "It might be thought, from the record of the Roman procurators . . . that they all, as if by secret arrangement, systematically and deliberately set out to drive the people to revolt. Even the best of them . . . had no idea that a nation like the Jews required above all consideration for their religious customs" (Schürer, *History*, 1.455).

[27] The cause of Judas' rebellion had been the census ordered by Quirinius in 6 C.E. (Josephus, *Ant.*18.1.1).

[28] See the discussion in Hengel, *Zeloten*, 42–47.

[29] It may not be without significance that Paul describes himself as ζηλωτής (Acts 22:3; Gal 1:14) when speaking of his persecution of the followers of Jesus (Reicke, "Hintergrund," 178).

11:2–3). The subsequent controversy over the necessity of circumcision clearly indicates that many Jewish believers took it as axiomatic that Gentiles must be circumcised if they were to have a share in the Jewish heritage, and were prepared to exercise considerable advocacy and missionary endeavor to ensure that that heritage was neither diluted nor endangered (Gal 2:4–5; 5:2–12; Acts 15:1–5; Phil 3:2). Here too, we may note the evidence of history of traditions analysis of Matthew which seems to indicate that an earlier reshaping of the Jesus tradition took place in a conservative direction vis-à-vis the law and Israel (Matt 5:17–20; 10:5–6, 23; 15:17–20, 24; 23:3, 23; 28:18–20)[30]—a tendency which no doubt reflects the same sort of pressures within the Palestinian churches. Wholly consistent with all this, and not at all surprising in view of it, is Luke's account of Paul's last visit to Jerusalem (probably in 57 C.E.), where James describes the church in Jerusalem (and Palestine?) as consisting of "many thousands . . . who are all zealous for the law" and who know of Paul only that he is a renegade and menace to their Jewish faith and inheritance (Acts 21:20–21).

The threat to Jewish prerogatives was, of course, not confined to Palestine, nor were Jewish exertions to defend them. Philo gives a clear account of the riots in Alexandria in 38 C.E., provoked by deliberate attacks on the religious and civic rights of the considerable Jewish population resident there (*In Flaccum,* particularly 41–54; also *Legat.* 132–37).[31] Delegations to the Emperor, the first led by Philo himself, resulted in a reassertion of these rights by Claudius in 41 C.E. In the same year, according to Dio Cassius (*Hist.* 60.6.6), Claudius deprived the Jews resident in Rome of their right of assembly, and eight years later, according to Suetonius, he expelled the Jews altogether because they were "constantly rioting at the instigation of Chrestus" (Suetonius, *Claud.* 25.4; cf. Acts 18:2).[32] Since all the other Jewish unrest of this period largely centered on Jewish response to what they perceived as threats to their unique racial and religious status, it may well be that the trouble in Rome was caused by similar Jewish reaction to the success of evangelism in the name of Jesus, like that against Stephen and that against Paul (Acts 6:9–14; 21:27–36; cf. 13:50; 14:2–5, 19; 17:5–7, 13; 18:12–15).[33]

The Jewish *politeuma* in Antioch, the third largest city in the Empire, was not exempt from such unrest. The Byzantine chronicler Malalas (6th century) reports an anti-Jewish riot there in 39–40 C.E. (John Malalas, *Chron.* 10.315). And although Josephus does not mention it, the fact that in 41 Claudius sent to Syria an edict identical to that which secured Jewish rights in Alexandria, strongly suggests that Jewish rights in Syria had been similarly threatened—one of the repercussions, no doubt,

---

[30] Cf. the essays of Bornkamm and Barth in Bornkamm, Barth, and Held, *Tradition;* Hahn, *Mission,* 54–59, 63–68, 120–28; D. Hill, *Matthew,* 66–72; Hubbard, *Matthean Redaction;* Guelich, *Sermon,* 161–74.

[31] Philo describes it as an "attack against our laws by seizing the meeting houses (synagogues) . . . (and) the destruction of our citizenship . . ." (*Flacc.* 53).

[32] There is some dispute as to whether there were in fact two separate incidents in 41 and 49 C.E. (see below, n. 78).

[33] Acts 6:13: "This man never ceases to speak words against this holy place and the law . . . [he] will change the customs which Moses delivered to us"; Acts 21:28: "This is the man who is teaching men everywhere *against the people* and the law and this place."

either of Alexandria riots in 38, or of Caligula's threatened desecration of the Jerusalem temple in 40.[34] Josephus does, however, tell us of trouble in Antioch in 67 when Antiochus, an apostate Jew, denounced his father and "the other (Jews)" for plotting to set fire to the city. These unfortunates were burned to death on the spot. Antiochus then attempted to compel other Jews to offer pagan sacrifice "since the (remaining) conspirators would be exposed by their refusal." A few submitted and the rest were massacred (*J.W.* 7.3.3). Smallwood justifiably argues that only a section of the large Jewish community would have been involved, since a considerable number of "orthodox" Jews would surely have refused such sacrifice.[35] The charge of arson, she notes, is similar to that laid against the Christians in Rome less than three years earlier, and may well suggest that it was the Christian Jews who were the object of Antiochus's attack. "The mainspring of Antiochus' malice against the Christians," she concludes not implausibly, "may have been resentment, possibly even heightened by his own apostasy, against his father's conversion from orthodox Judaism to a despised schismatic sect."[36]

Whatever the precise details of these various incidents the overall picture is clear enough. During the period in which the Antioch incident took place Jews had to be on their guard against what were or were seen to be repeated threats to their national and religious rights. Whenever such a threat was perceived their reaction was immediate and vigorous. In Palestine itself more and more were resorting to open violence and guerilla warfare. The infant Christian sect was not exempt from this unrest. Indeed we may generalize a fairly firm conclusion from the above review of evidence: *wherever this new Jewish sect's belief or practice was perceived to be a threat to Jewish institutions and traditions, its members would almost certainly come under pressure from their fellow Jews to remain loyal to their unique Jewish heritage.*

The question which such a conclusion leaves us is obvious: To what extent was the Antioch incident the result of such pressures operating upon the infant communities in Palestine and Syria, pressures from Jews loyal to their heritage both without *and* within the sect itself? Against this background the hypothesis becomes rather compelling that the open table-fellowship practiced at Antioch was perceived by the Jerusalem church (and perhaps by other Jews) as such a threat. The mission of the men from James would then have been their reaction to that threat.[37] And the danger of diluting or abandoning Israel's heritage with its converse and powerful appeal to national and religious loyalty would have weighed heavily with Peter, Barnabas and the rest.

Thus already a fair amount of light has been shed on the Antioch incident from the broader background. We may summarize these preliminary observations thus:

---

[34] Cf. Kraeling, "Jewish Community." See further Meeks and Wilken, *Jews and Christians,* 4.

[35] Kraeling reckoned a Jewish population of at least 45,000 Jews out of a total population of roughly 300,000 in Antioch in the days of Augustine ("Jewish Community," 136); but see also Meeks and Wilken, *Jews and Christians,* 8.

[36] Smallwood, *The Jews,* 362. Other details in Meeks and Wilken, *Jews and Christians,* 4–5, who also refer (18) to the suggestion of Farmer, "Jesus and the Gospels," that the decisive break between Jews and Christians in Antioch came in the aftermath of the Jewish revolt (66–70 C.E.).

[37] So particularly Reicke, "Hintergrund," 172–187; Jewett, "Agitators," 340–42: "My hypothesis therefore is that Jewish Christians in Judea were stimulated by Zealotic pressure into a nomistic campaign among their fellow Christians in the late forties and early fifties" (205).

a) At this stage of its growth, the new movement of Jesus' followers would almost certainly still think of themselves as a development *of* and *within* the religion of the Jews (a form of eschatological, messianic Judaism)—not yet a distinct faith or separate religion.

b) Within this movement, the primacy and authority of the Jerusalem apostles in matters of dispute, specifically over what requirements should be laid on Gentiles who wished to associate with the new movement, would be generally acknowledged, and in fact had already been acknowledged by the church at Antioch and by Paul, the delegate/apostle of the Antioch church.

c) The increasing threat to Judaism, especially from the deteriorating political situation in Palestine, and the increasingly polemical response of the Jews themselves, would increase the pressures on those involved in the new movement to show themselves as faithful and loyal Jews. In short, the probability is strong that all the main participants in the Antioch incident would naturally think of themselves as first and foremost Jews (a probability confirmed by Gal 2:15); as such they would naturally look to Jerusalem for direction; and as such they would inevitably feel themselves moved by the mounting groundswell of Jewish nationalistic and religious sentiment.

With the broader background thus clarified we can now dig more deeply into that which most concerns us—the table-fellowship at Antioch. What was at stake in the Antioch church's practice of table-fellowship? Within the context of Palestinian and Diaspora Judaism in the middle of the first century C.E. how would the table-fellowship at Antioch have appeared?—as something unexceptional, as something very unusual, as a breach of Jewish practice and covenantal loyalty which posed a threat, or what? We are accustomed to seeing the issue through the eyes of Paul (Gal 2:11–18). But how was it seen through the eyes of "the men from James"? This brings us to the next stage of our analysis.

The Limits of Table-Fellowship in the Judaism of the Late Second Temple Period

The significance of table-fellowship in the east is well known. In Judaism particularly the *religious* significance of a shared meal was central. "In Judaism," as Jeremias notes, "table-fellowship means fellowship before God, for the eating of a piece of broken bread by everyone who shares in the meal brings out the fact that they all have a share in the blessing which the master of the house has spoken over the unbroken bread."[38] The added significance for the rabbis and their pupils is well characterized in a saying of R. Simeon (ca. 100–160 or 170):

> If three have eaten at one table and have not spoken over it words of the Law, it is as though they had eaten of the sacrifices of the dead (Ps 106:28), for it is written, "For all tables are full of vomit and filthiness without God" (Isa 28:8—"place" taken as a designation for God). But if three have eaten at one table and have spoken over it

---

[38] Jeremias, *Proclamation,* 115.

words of the Law, it is as if they had eaten from the table of God, for it is written, "And he said unto me, This is the table that is before the Lord" (Ezek 41:22). (*m. ʾAbot* 3:3).[39]

No devout Jew could engage in an act of such religious significance casually, and the question of who was and who was not an acceptable table companion must have greatly exercised the minds of such Jews during the period which concerns us, as the Antioch incident itself demonstrates (cf. Acts 11:2–3; 1 Cor 8–10). To put it another way, part of the pressure on a devout Jew in the 40s and 50s of the first century C.E. would have been the constraint to observe the limits of acceptable table-fellowship. These limits would be determined partly by the explicit laws in the Torah, particularly concerning unclean foods (Lev 11:1–23; Deut 14:3–21), and in differing degrees by the multiplying *halakhoth* of the oral tradition concerning tithes and ritual purity.

Unclean Foods

Obedience to *the law on unclean foods* had been one of the make or break issues in the Maccabean rebellion. "Many in Israel stood firm and were resolved in their hearts not to eat unclean food. They chose to die rather than to be defiled by food or to profane the holy covenant; and they did die" (1 Macc 1:62–63).[40] No one who cherished the memory of the Maccabees would even dream of eating unclean food. The typical Jewish attitude at the time with which we are concerned is probably well caught by Luke's account of Peter's reaction to the vision given him in Joppa: "I have never eaten anything that is common or unclean" (Acts 10:14). Jewish devotion on this point was particularly expressed in their abhorrence of pigs and of *pork*. The height of Antiochus Epiphanes' abomination had been his sacrifice of swine on the altar(s) of the temple.[41] Continuing Jewish antipathy to the pig is illustrated by the Mishna's refusal to allow Jews(?) to rear swine *anywhere* (in Israel) (*m. B. Qam.* 7:7). And Jewish rejection of pork was well known and often commented on in Greek and Roman society. For example, Philo reports Caligula as interrupting his hearing of the Alexandrian delegations with the abrupt question, "Why do you refuse to eat pork?" (*Legat.* 361), and Plutarch devotes one of his *Quaestiones conviviales* to discussion of why Jews abstain from pork (4.5).[42] Clearly abstention from pork was thoroughly characteristic, we may even say universally characteristic, of Jewish conduct both in Palestine and in the Diaspora.

Equally abhorrent to the devout Jew was food tainted by the abomination of *idolatry*, although the extra-biblical documentation is thinner in this case. In addition

---

[39] Abrahams records (*Studies*, 56) the report that at the feast held on the circumcision of Elisha b. Abuyah (ca. 65 C.E.), while the other guests were partaking of meat and wine, Eleazar b. Hyrkanos and Joshua b. Hananiah sat "stringing together" the words of the scriptures like pearls on a card.

[40] Cf. Josephus' characterization of the situation following Alexander's death: "Whenever anyone was accused by the people of Jerusalem of eating unclean food or violating the Sabbath or committing any other such sin, he would flee to the Shechemites . . ." (*Ant.* 11.8.7).

[41] Josephus, *Ant.* 13.8.2; cf. Diodorus Siculus, *Bib. hist.* 34.1.1–35.1.4. See also 1 Macc 1:47; 2 Macc 6:18–23.

[42] See also Petronius, frg. 37; Seneca, *Ep.* 108.22; Epictetus in Arrian, *Epict. diss.* 1.22.4; Tacitus, *Hist.* 5.4; Juvenal, *Sat.* 14.98; Sextus Empiricus 3.223.

to 1 Cor 8–10 and Acts 15:20, 29, we may mention Josephus' report of how in 64 he sought to aid certain priests of his acquaintance who had been taken prisoner in Rome and who "even in affliction had not forgotten the pious practices of religion, and supported themselves on figs and nuts" (*Life* 3), presumably in part at least to avoid meat left over from pagan sacrifices (see also 4 Macc 5:2).[43]

Likewise with meat (of clean animals) from which the *blood* had not been drained, in accordance with the clear and repeated commandments of Moses (Lev 3:17; 7:26–27; 17:10–14; Deut 12:16, 23–24; 15:23)—note again Acts 15:20, 29. What constituted a proper slaughtering of a clean animal for food is well defined in rabbinic Judaism by the time of the Mishna (tractate *m. Ḥullin;* also *Ker.* 5:1), but we can gain some idea of how far the *halakhoth* had developed by the middle of the first century from *Ḥul.* 1:2, which reports the debate between the school of Shammai and the school of Hillel on what precisely was allowed by the (presumably) earlier ruling that slaughter with a handsickle was valid.[44]

Obedience to these commands so clearly set out in the Torah was obviously fundamental to devout Jews in our period; it belonged to the distinctiveness of their race and religion and marked them out as Yahweh's chosen people. Such fundamental laws were a limiting factor of considerable consequence for the devout Jew's practice of table-fellowship. They did not, we should note, inhibit a Jew's own entertainment of others, where one was responsible for what was served up and for the manner of its preparation. But they would largely prevent a Jew from accepting with an easy conscience invitations from others who might ignore them in whole or in part—hence it is the case of an invitation to someone else's house which Paul discusses in 1 Cor 10:27–29.

Ritual Purity

One of the most striking features about the Pharisees in Palestine prior to the Jewish revolt was their preoccupation with defining the limits of table-fellowship more scrupulously. J. Neusner has concluded from his meticulously detailed study of rabbinical traditions about the Pharisees that of the 341 individual rulings from our period, "no fewer than 229 directly or indirectly pertain to table-fellowship, approximately 67% of the whole."[45] Within these the major concerns were quite clearly ritual purity and tithing.

As to *ritual purity,* the Pharisees quite simply sought to apply the purity laws governing the temple ritual to their everyday lives. Others might quite properly conclude that these laws referred only to the priests when performing their temple

---

[43] For Jewish abhorrence of idolatry see Schürer, *History,* 2.81–83. See further Moore, *Judaism,* 1.325; Str.-B 3.54–55; 4.366–72. The *halakhah* forbidding meat from pagan temples is attributed to Akiva (*m. ʿAbod. Zar.* 2:3); see also *b. ʿAbod. Zar.* 8a–b.

[44] See Neusner, *Rabbinic Traditions,* 2.242. For rabbinic Judaism's further rulings on the command against the eating of blood see Str.-B 2.734–39.

[45] Neusner, *Rabbinic Traditions,* 3.297 (the rulings itemized on pp. 291–94); also Neusner, *From Politics,* 86. For the broader background see Neusner, *Idea of Purity,* particularly ch. 2: "nearly 25% of Mishnaic law in quantity concerns purity" (8).

service and to themselves only when they went to the temple; outside the temple the laws of ritual purity need not be observed.

> But the Pharisees held that even outside the temple, in one's own home, the laws of ritual purity were to be followed in the only circumstances in which they might apply, namely, at the table. Therefore, one must eat secular food (ordinary, everyday meals) in a state of ritual purity *as if one were a temple priest.*[46]

The detail with which the schools' debates were already concerned, as to the precise circumstances in which foods and food containers would be rendered unclean, indicates clearly the importance of such matters for the Pharisees and their conscientiousness in trying to maintain their purity (cf. Matt 23:25–26).[47] Particularly important here was the cleansing of the hands which were always liable to uncleanness through an unintentional touching. A complete tractate of the Mishna was to be devoted to the purity of hands *(Yadayim),* and the ramifications must already have been the subject of debate at our time, as our own Gospel traditions also testify (Mark 7:2–5/Matt 15:2; Luke 11:38).[48]

Tithing was important according to the same logic, since only food which had properly been tithed was ritually acceptable. That is to say, tithing was as much concerned with table-fellowship as ritual washing.[49] Here too it is significant that a whole tractate of the Mishna was to be devoted to rulings about produce not certainly tithed *(m. Demai),* that is to guidance for the devout Jew in his dealings with Jews whose devotion to the law could not be presumed (particularly the *am ha-arets).* And again there can be little doubt that scrupulous tithing must have formed an important element in the Pharisaic *halakhoth* of pre-70 C.E. Palestine, as our own Gospel traditions again confirm (Matt 23:23; Luke 18:12).[50]

We should not confine the influence of such Pharisaic rulings and practice to their own ranks (the *haberim).* For the well attested Pharisaic criticisms of Jesus' table-fellowship as an eating with "tax collectors and sinners" (Mark 2:16 pars.; Matt 11:19/Luke 7:34; Luke 15:2) and of his eating with unwashed hands (Mark 7:2–5/ Matt 15:2; Luke 11:38) were precisely criticisms of a devout Jew *outside* the Pharisaic circle for not observing the Pharisaic *halakhoth*—"Why do your disciples not live according to the tradition of the elders . . . ?" (Mark 7:5/Matt 15:2).[51]

---

[46] Neusner, *From Politics,* 83; also "Fellowship"; R. Meyer, "φαρισαῖος," 9.15, 18; though Alon (*Jews,* 190–234) argues that one of the disputes among the Pharisees was over the question of how far the laws of purity extended—to the sphere of the temple and priests or to the whole of Israel.

[47] Neusner, "First Cleanse," sees in Matt 23:25–26 evidence of a stage in Pharisaic thinking at which the purity of the inside of a vessel was not determinative for cleanness ("the Shammaite rule"). But see Maccoby, "Washing," who however ignores the implication of the saying that the practice of cleansing cups and plates has particular reference to the Pharisees (Matt 23:16–26: "you say . . . you tithe . . . you cleanse . . .").

[48] See Schürer, *History,* 2.475–78; Oppenheimer, *Am Ha-aretz,* 121–24; Safran and Stern, *Jewish People,* 2.802, 829–31; Bowker, *Jesus,* 70–71; Parkes, *Foundations,* 134, 141–43. See further Str.-B 1.695–704, and the analysis of *Yadayim* in Neusner, *History,* vol. 19.

[49] "Tithing was a dietary law" (Neusner, *From Politics,* 80, 83).

[50] See particularly Oppenheimer, *Am Ha-aretz,* 69–79. See further Safrai and Stern, *Jewish People,* 818–25. Examples of rabbinic references have been cited by Bowker, *Jesus,* index: "tithe."

[51] See also the discussion in Alon, *Jews,* 205–11 (and below, n. 56).

Nor can we assume that such influence was limited to Palestine. It is true that some halakhic sources ruled that the law of tithes did not apply "outside the Land" (e.g., *m. Hal.* 2:2; *m. Qidd.* 1:9). But already in Tobit we read of tithes being scrupulously observed from a home in Nineveh (Tob 1:6–8).[52] Josephus mentions an edict issued by the proconsul of Asia Minor to the people of Miletus in the days of Caesar, permitting the Jews to "perform their native rites and manage their produce (τοὺς καρποὺς μεταχειρίζεσθαι) in accordance with their customs" *(Ant.* 14.10.21), which presumably indicates that the practice of tithing was well established among the Jews of Asia Minor in the first century B.C.E. And Philo tells us that tithing was observed by the Jewish community in Rome *(Legat.* 156) and implies that the Alexandrian Jews did the same *(Spec.* 1.153).[53] As to the purity ritual we may simply note that the practice of Jewish ritual cleansing outside Palestine is presumed by the *Letter of Aristeas* (305–306), and that such purifications are described as characteristic of Jews as a people by the *Sibylline Oracles* (3:592–93) and Josephus, *Ag. Ap.* 2.23, 24. Philo also testifies to a more general concern in Diaspora Judaism for a punctilious observance of the law *(Migr.* 89–93). Here too we should note Paul's own testimony, that though he came from the Diaspora, nevertheless he "advanced in Judaism beyond many of my own age among my people, so extremely zealous was I for the traditions of my fathers" (Gal 1:14; cf. Phil 3:6). It is this pharisaic striving for a rectitude beyond what was written which is probably in view in the fierce condemnation of Matt 23:15—a proselytizing zeal on the part of the Pharisees is elsewhere unattested, but they may indeed have been more than willing to "traverse sea and land" to ensure that those who became proselytes properly understood the full extent of their obligations under the law ("when he becomes a proselyte, you make him twice as much a child of hell as yourselves").

We may justifiably infer then that *wherever Pharisaic influence was strong during the middle decades of the first century of our era,* both within Palestine and among strong concentrations of Jews in the Diaspora, *there would be pressure on those who thought of themselves as good Jews to observe the halakhic clarifications of the laws on tithes and purity*—that is to say, *pressure on devout Jews (including proselytes) to observe strict limits in their practice of table-fellowship.*

On the other hand we should not assume that this pressure would be constant and consistent. The Pharisees were not the only ones with views on these matters. For a start, the Sadducees denied that the laws of purity were applicable outside the temple.[54] At the other end of the spectrum, the Essenes observed rules of ritual purity even stricter than those of the Pharisees (1QS 3:4–5, 8–9; 5:13; 6:16–17, 25; 7:3, 16; 1QSa 2:3–9; CD 10:10–13; Josephus, *J.W.* 2.8.5, 9–10).[55] And we know that within the

---

[52] Parkes, *Foundations,* 141–42.

[53] See further Oppenheimer, *Am Ha-aretz,* 49–51.

[54] Safrai, *Jewish People,* 828, and Alon, *Jews,* 233–34, both referring to Geiger, *Urschrift,* 223; Schürer, *History,* 2.409–10.

[55] See further Schürer, *History,* 2.569, 582, and Riches, *Jesus,* 117–28, with further bibliography in their notes. Cf. the Sabbath *halakhot* at Qumran (Schiffman, *Halakhah at Qumran;* Sigal, *Emergence,* 297–302), whose comparative severity confirms the Synoptics' picture of the extent to which the Torah was already being elaborated in the pre-70 period. See also Hengel, *Zeloten,* ch. 4.

ranks of the Pharisees there were many debates between the schools of Shammai and Hillel about particular details, where the concern in effect was to define the precise limits of table-fellowship.[56] We also know that the Pharisees of our period already distinguished several degrees of purity. Thus the ancient Mishna, Ḥag. 2:7:

> The garments of an *am ha-arets* are a source of *midras*-impurity to Pharisees; the garments of Pharisees are a source of *midras*-impurity to those who eat *terumah* (i.e., priests); the garments of those who eat *terumah* are a source of *midras*-impurity to those who eat holy things; the garments of those who eat holy things are a source of *midras*-impurity to those who attend to the water of purification (Num 19:17–18). Jose b. Joezer was the most pious of the priests and (yet) his apron was a source of *midras*-impurity to those who ate holy things. All his life Johanan b. Gudgada ate secular food at the degree of ritual purity required for holy things, and (yet) his apron was a source of *midras*-impurity to those who attended to the water of purification.[57]

Similarly with the Essenes: according to Josephus the novice had to pass through several stages of purification before participating in the common food (*J.W.* 2.8.7), and a senior member could be rendered impure by the touch of a junior member of the community (*J.W.* 2.8.10). Once the concept of differing degrees of purity within the temple ritual was translated into rules governing everyday table-fellowship it inevitably meant that different degrees of association were possible—he who lived at a stricter level of purity could not eat with one who observed a less strict discipline.

We may conclude that in the Palestine of our period there was a wide spectrum of teaching and practice on this precise issue—from the *am ha-arets* who knew not the law (cf. John 7:49) and Jesus who flouted it at one end, to the stricter Pharisees and "the many" of the Essenes at the other, with varying degrees of scrupulousness and disagreement about particular details in between.[58] *Insofar as the new sect of followers of Jesus was to any extent influenced by Pharisaic views, its members were bound to be caught up in these debates and cross-currents about the acceptable limits of table-fellowship.* We need simply note here that it is precisely an issue of this sort, and the disagreements between Christians concerning it, which is reflected in the different emphases drawn by Mark and Matthew from Jesus' words about true cleanliness (Mark 7:19; Matt 15:17, 20).

Interaction with Gentiles

Of particular interest for us is what all this would have meant for *the devout Jew* (including the devout Nazarene) *in his social intercourse with Gentiles.* The dominant

---

[56] Neusner, *Rabbinic Traditions*, 2.

[57] See ibid., 63–64; Oppenheimer, *Am Ha-aretz*, 60 n. 119. I follow Oppenheimer's translation. Those mentioned came from the period before the destruction of the second temple. *Midras*-impurity = "impurity contracted by an object on which one with a discharge (see Lev 12:2; 15:2, 25) sits, treads, lies or leans. . . . The impurity is conveyed to anyone who carries, or is carried on, the object" (Oppenheimer, *Am Ha-aretz*, 60).

[58] See further Oppenheimer, *Am Ha-aretz*, 61–62; Freyne, *Galilee*, 306–7.

tendency within Judaism in the century or so around our period seems to have been to avoid such intercourse as much as possible. The stories of Daniel, of Tobit and of Judith were all held forth as examples of the faithfulness and success of Jews who refused to eat "the food of Gentiles" (Dan 1:8–16; Tob 1:10–13; Jdt 10:5; 12:1–20; see also 3 Macc 3:4; *Jos. Asen.* 7:1). The fear of idolatry and of impurity was a considerable limiting factor, since by definition a Gentile was an idolater and certainly ritual impurity had to be assumed rather than the reverse.[59] Thus the Mishnaic tractate on idolatry is mainly concerned with defining the permissable relationships with Gentiles (*m. ʿAbodah Zarah*). And in several rabbinic sayings the uncleanness of the Gentile is axiomatic: Gentiles are simply "unclean persons" (*Mak.* 2:3); "the dwelling places of Gentiles are unclean" (*ʾOhal.* 18:7);[60] "a Gentile is in every respect like to a man who suffers a flux" (*S. Eli. Rab.* 10).[61] Such sayings cannot be dismissed as the later utterances of rabbinic Judaism subsequent to our period. The prohibition on Gentiles entering the temple sanctuary was already well established by our time (cf., e.g., Josephus, *Ant.* 12.3.4), and must have been based on the belief that Gentiles were unclean.[62] Already in *Jubilees* the same attitude is clearly expressed and the line firmly drawn:

> "Separate yourself from the nations,
> And eat not with them,
>
> . . . .
>
> For their works are unclean,
> And all their ways are a pollution and an abomination
> and an uncleanness . . ." (22:16).

According to the *Letter of Aristeas*, Moses

> fenced us round with impregnable ramparts and walls of iron, that we might not mingle at all with any of the other nations, but remain pure in body and soul . . . he hedged us round on all sides by rules of purity, affecting alike what we eat, or drink, or touch, or hear, or see (139, 142; cf. 106).

And Tacitus scornfully describes the Jewish hatred for the rest of the world: "they eat separately, they sleep separately . . ." (*separati epulis, discreti cubilibus*) (*Hist.* 5.5).

If such views were consistently and rigorously applied, no devout Jew could even have considered participating in table-fellowship with a Gentile.[63] But that is by no means the whole story. For there were Gentiles towards whom even the rabbis could maintain a very positive and welcoming attitude—Gentile converts to Judaism and Gentiles who showed themselves sympathetic to the religion of the Jews. How were

---

[59] Alon, *Jews*, 170–74; Schürer, *History*, 2.81–84. See also n. 68 below.

[60] Similar rabbinic material is collected by Neusner, *History*, 4.340–45.

[61] Cited by Danby, *Mishnah*, appendix 4. Other references in Str.-B 1.449–50; Alon, *Jews*, 149–59.

[62] Alon, *Jews*, 165–67. See the whole chapter, "The Levitical Uncleanness of Gentiles," ibid., 146–89; against Büchler, "Impurity."

[63] See further Str.-B 4.374–78.

they affected by the limits observed by devout Jews in their table-fellowship? Discussion in this area usually works with a three-fold distinction—the proselyte, the resident alien and the God-fearer (sometimes misleadingly called the "half-proselyte").[64]

a) The Proselyte, or Full Convert

Israelite religion had always inculcated a positive attitude towards the non-Jewish stranger *(ger)* who lived within the borders of Israel (Exod 20:10; 22:21; 23:9, 12; Deut 1:16; 5:14; etc.). However, by the first century C.E. these commands concerning the *ger* had been referred almost completely to the proselyte: already in the LXX the regular translation of *ger* is προσήλυτος; and in rabbinic Judaism *ger* always means a Gentile won over to Judaism.[65] A positive approach to proselytization is likewise indicated by such stories as those of Ruth finding shelter under Yahweh's wings (Ruth 2:12) and Achior in Jdt 14:10, by Isa 56:1–8 addressed to "the foreigners who join themselves to the Lord," by Matt 23:15, by the accounts in Josephus of the forceable conversion of the Idumeans by Hyrcanus and of the Itureans by Aristobulus *(Ant.* 13.9.1; 13.11.3), and by various other accounts and references in both Jewish and non-Jewish sources (e.g., Josephus, *Life* 23; *Ant.* 18.3.5; Horace, *Sat.* 1.4.142–43— "we, like the Jews, will compel you to make one of our throng").[66]

As a proselyte the Gentile had undertaken to observe the law, including circumcision, and was more or less a full Israelite (see, e.g., Exod 12:49; Philo, *Spec.* 1.51–52; *b. Yebam.* 47b).[67] Despite the stigma of being a proselyte (cf. *m. Qidd.* 4:1), and the suspicion harbored by some rabbis that he was always liable to fall back into his old ways (e.g., *m. Nid.* 7:3; *b. B. Meṣ͑ia* 59b),[68] the proselyte once his initiation was complete came within the same limits of table-fellowship that applied to the native born Jew.[69] Of particular interest to us, however, is the fact that there seems to have been some debate among the rabbis at our period over the degree of uncleanness attaching to the Gentile proselyte at his conversion and over the length of time it took before his uncleanness could be washed away by ritual purification (*m. Pesaḥ.* 8:8; *m. ͑Ed.* 5:2).[70]

---

[64] Str.-B 2.715–23; R. Meyer, "πάροικος," 5.850; Lerle, *Proselytenwerbung*, 24–39. On the inappropriateness of the title "half-proselyte" see Moore, *Judaism*, 1.326–27, 339; Kuhn, "προσήλυτος," 6.731 n. 31. See also below, n. 74.

[65] See Lake, *Acts*, 5.82–84; Kuhn, "προσήλυτος," 6.736–37.

[66] See Bamberger, *Proselytism*, 15–16, 267ff.; Safrai and Stern, *Jewish People*, 622–23.

[67] Josephus, *Ant.* 20.2.4, describes the would-be proselyte Izates as "a Jew." See further Kuhn, "προσήλυτος," 6.732–33; Schiffman, "At the Crossroads," 124–25.

[68] Other references in Moore, *Judaism*, 1.341 and notes; Kuhn, "προσήλυτος," 6.737; *EncJud* 13.1185.

[69] See further Moore, *Judaism*, 1.329–35, 342–45; Bamberger, *Proselytism*; Jeremias, *Jerusalem*, 320–34; Kuhn, "προσήλυτος," 6.736–40, who deduces from CD 14:3–6 and 1QS 2:19–23; 6:8–9 that *gerim* existed in branch establishments of the Essene order, but not at Qumran itself (735).

[70] See particularly Alon, *Jews*, 172–74. The modern debate has concentrated on the origin of proselyte baptism. Most now agree that proselyte baptism had already become an accepted practice by the middle of the first century C.E. In addition to Alon see, e.g., Str.-B 1.102–8; Rowley, "Proselyte Baptism"; Jeremias, *Infant Baptism*, 24–29; Schiffman, "At the Crossroads," 127–36; against Lerle, *Proselytenwerbung* 52–60; Zeitlin, "Proselytes," 413; Bamberger, *Proselytism,* xxi–xxii.

b) The Resident Alien

Although it understood the biblical *ger* to refer to the proselyte, rabbinic Judaism also recognized a different category of Gentile, the *ger toshav*, the resident alien. He too lived within the borders of Israel, but unlike the proselyte he accepted only some of the commandments of the Torah.

Just how much he had to accept before being recognized as a *ger toshav* was a subject of dispute among the rabbis. According to R. Meir (ca. 150) a sufficient requirement was that the Gentile in question undertook in the presence of three haberim to renounce idolatry.[71] Others defined a *ger toshav* as "a *ger* who eats of animals not ritually slaughtered, that is, he took upon himself to observe all the precepts mentioned in the Torah apart from the prohibition of (eating the flesh of) animals not ritually slaughtered" (*b. ʿAbod. Zar.* 64b). This exemption of the *ger toshav* from the prohibition against animals not ritually slaughtered was determined by Deut 14:21—"You shall not eat of anything that dies of itself; you may give it to the alien *(ger)* who is within your towns, that he may eat it . . ."—a law which could properly be held to exempt the *ger toshav* from at least some of the restrictions governing the eating of meat, and which thus provided sanction for slackening one of the limits of acceptable table-fellowship. But the *halakhah* which gained greatest support and decided the matter was that a *ger toshav* was any Gentile who takes upon himself the seven Noahic laws—that is, he holds himself subject to the established courts of justice, and refrains from blasphemy, idolatry, adultery, bloodshed, robbery, and eating flesh cut from a living animal *(b. ʿAbod. Zar.* 64b; cf. *b. Sanh.* 56a).[72]

Clearly, then, there was some debate among the rabbis in the period before the consensus view was established regarding the definition of a *ger toshav*, a debate in effect as to the terms on which social intercourse with Gentiles living locally might be acceptable. This strongly suggests that there were already during the first century period diverse views among the rabbis regarding the limits of table-fellowship as they applied to the resident alien.[73] Here we should note also that, despite such rabbinic characterizations of Gentile uncleanness as were cited above (*m. Mak.* 2:3; *m. ʾOhal.* 18:7), the Mishna contains at least two rulings which presuppose situations at the mcal table where a Gentile (not a *ger*) was present (*m. Ber.* 7:1; *m. ʿAbod. Zar.* 5:5), and the Babylonian Talmud contains discussion of the conditions on which Jews might accept invitations to and participate in Gentile banquets (*b. ʿAbod. Zar.* 8a–b). We can only conclude that, in all probability, in the Palestine of our period there was also a diversity among devout Jews in their practice of table-fellowship so far as Gentiles were involved—a diversity similar in extent to or indeed continuous with the spectrum of permissible table-fellowship as determined by the various grades of purity among Jews themselves.

---

[71] See also Moore, *Judaism*, 1.325 and n. 1.
[72] See further Moore, *Judaism*, 1.339; Str-B 2.729–39; 3.37–38; Kuhn, "προσήλυτος," 6.740–41.
[73] Cf. Str-B 2.722–23.

c) The God-Fearer

A third group of more acceptable Gentiles were those usually called "God-fearers" or "pious Gentiles"—those who showed themselves sympathetic towards Judaism—though whether "God-fearers" (οἱ φοβούμενοι τὸν θεόν, οἱ σεβόμενοι τὸν θεόν) was a technical term for such may be doubted.[74] However they should be designated, there were certainly many Gentiles (we are talking here particularly of the Diaspora) who were attracted to Judaism and who signified their interest by attaching themselves to Jewish practices in differing degrees. How diverse such attachments were is a question more easily posed than answered. We know from Acts that such Gentiles attended the synagogue or Jewish meetings for worship (Acts 13:16, 26, 50; 16:14; 17:4, 17). Cornelius, in one of the passages in which the phrase φοβούμενος τὸν θεόν most nearly approaches a technical sense (the other is the description of Titius Justus as σεβόμενος τὸν θεόν in 18:7), is described as "a devout man who feared God, gave alms liberally to the people, and prayed constantly to God" (10:2). We should also recall that pious Gentiles were welcome to worship in the temple (John 12:20; Acts 8:27; also Josephus, *J.W.* 4.4.4), within, of course, well defined limits (namely, the court of the Gentiles).[75]

The central question for us, however, is the extent to which such God-fearing Gentiles were expected to keep the law (including the oral traditions) concerning tithing and ritual purity. Josephus' claims in *Against Apion* confirm the attractiveness of Judaism for many Gentiles: many Greeks "have agreed to adopt (εἰσελθεῖν) our laws" (2.10); our laws "have to an ever increasing extent excited the emulation of the world at large" (2.38; cf. 2.28). Philo speaks in similar and similarly vague terms in *Mos.* 2.17–20.[76] But Josephus becomes more helpfully explicit a little further on in *Against Apion*:

> The masses have long since shown a keen desire to adopt our religious observances (εὐσεβείας); and there is not one city, Greek or barbarian, not a single nation, to which our custom of abstaining from work on the sabbath day has not spread, and where the fasts and the lighting of lamps and many of our prohibitions in the matter of food (πολλὰ τῶν εἰς βρῶσιν ἡμῖν οὐ νενομισμένων) are not observed (*Ag. Ap.* 2.38).

Equally interesting is the succession of notices that demonstrate how attractive the Jewish way of life was for many Gentiles in Rome itself and how alarmed the authorities were in consequence. Plutarch (in a passage which relates to the middle of the first century B.C.E.) speaks of a freedman named Caecilius "who was accused of

---

[74] See particularly Lake, *Acts*, 5.84–88; Siegert, "Gottesfürchtige"; McEleney, "Conversion"; Smallwood, *Jews*, 206 n. 15; Wilcox, " 'God-Fearers' "; though see also Stern, *Authors*, 2.103–6. On the significance of Josephus' description of Poppaea, wife of Nero, as θεοσεβής see Siegert, "Gottesfürchtige," 151–61, particularly 160–61; Smallwood, *Jews*, 278 n.79 and 281 n. 84. Rabbinic references in Str-B 2.719–20; Balz, "φοβέω," 9.207.

[75] On the much quoted Josephus, *Ant.* 14.7.2, see however Lake, *Acts*, 5.85.

[76] Cf. one of the occasional rabbinic sayings which recognize that non-Jews can be righteous and acceptable to God, attributed again to R. Meier: "A *goy* who keeps the Torah is of much greater value in God's sight than even the high-priest himself" (*Sipre* on Lev 18:5, cited by Kuhn, "προσήλυτος," 6.741)—though we have already noted how liberal R. Meir was in his definition of a *ger toshav*.

Jewish practices (ἔνοχος τῷ ἰουδαίζειν) (*Cic.* 7.6). Seneca mentions autobiographically that in his youth he began to abstain from animal food, but that he abandoned the practice because "some foreign rites were at that time being inaugurated, and abstinence from certain kinds of animal food was set down as proof of interest in the strange cult" (*Ep.* 108.22). He refers most probably to the persecution of Jewish and Egyptian rites under Tiberius in 19 C.E. (Tacitus, *Ann.* 2.85).[77] Perhaps significant here too is the report of Dio Cassius already cited, that in 41 Claudius forbade the Jews in Rome to hold meetings because they had increased so greatly in number (*Hist.* 60.6.6).[78] Better known is the persecution by Domitian of "those who followed the Jewish way of life *(vitam)* without formally professing Judaism" (Suetonius, *Dom.* 12.2); Dio Cassius, also writing of the late first century C.E., speaks of "many who were drifting into Jewish ways" (τὰ τῶν Ἰουδαίων ἔθη) being condemned for atheism (*Hist.* 67.14.1–3).[79] And Juvenal confirms the attractiveness which Judaism obviously exercised for many at this period when he attacks contemporaries who "learn and practice and revere the Jewish law" and who get themselves circumcised, under the influence of a Sabbath-reverencing, pork-abstaining father (*Sat.* 14.96–106). As evidence of Judaism's continuing influence at the other end of the second century C.E. we may simply note Tertullian's report that many Gentiles in his day observed Jewish feasts and ceremonies and Jewish practice in prayers *(Nat.* 1.13). It would not be unjust to deduce from all this that *many God-fearers attracted by the Jewish law quite naturally would have observed the law in the way native born Jews did—that is, in the way that the developed customs and developing tradition dictated.*

Still more interesting for us, not least because the incident described took place within a few years of the Antioch incident, is the well known story of the conversion of Izates, king of Adiabene, recounted by Josephus (*Ant.* 20.2.4). Izates was initially told that he need not be circumcised—"he could worship God, even without circumcision, if he had fully decided to emulate the hereditary customs of the Jews" (ζηλοῦν τὰ πάτρια τῶν Ἰουδαίων) (*Ant.* 20.2.4). Since the sticking point was circumcision, we may take it that Izates was prepared to go the whole way apart from that, and "zeal for hereditary customs" suggests that his devotion would have embraced much at least of the oral law as well as the written Torah (cf. *Ant.* 20.2.3, 4).[80] This may well be

---

[77] For more detail see Smallwood, *Jews,* 201–10.

[78] On the relations of Dio's note to Suetonius' report of Claudius' expulsion of the Jews in 49 (Suetonius, *Claud.* 25.4) see Smallwood, *Jews,* 210–16; and cf. Stern, *Authors,* 2.114–16.

[79] Dio refers particularly to Flavius Clemens, cousin of Domitian and consul, and father of the nominated heirs to the throne; see the discussion in Smallwood, *Jews,* 376–83; Stern, *Authors,* 2.380–84; on *Deut. Rab.* 2:24 see also Siegert, "Gottesfürchtige," 110–11.

[80] Τὰ πάτρια (ἔθη) (or τὰ πατρῷα ἔθη) is regularly used of hereditary customs stretching beyond those written down or codified, and sometimes of the unwritten tradition in distinction from the written—as in Philo, *Ebr.* 193; *Somn.* 2.78; *Mos.* 1.31; *Praem.* 106; *Flacc.* 52; cf. 3 Macc 1:3; Gal 1:14. Note particularly Philo, *Spec.* 4.150—"Children ought to inherit from their parents . . . ancestral customs (ἔθη πάτρια) which they were reared in and have lived with even from the cradle, and not despise them because they have been handed down without written record. Praise cannot be given to one who obeys the written laws. . . . But he who faithfully observes the unwritten deserves commendation. . . ." Josephus, *Ant.* 13.16.2, speaks of the "regulations introduced by the Pharisees in accordance with the tradition of their fathers" (κατὰ τὴν πατρῴαν παράδοσιν). See further *LSJ,* πάτριος.

confirmed by the fact that when Eleazar came upon the scene from Galilee, described by Josephus as a Jew "who had a reputation for being extremely strict concerning the hereditary customs" (τὰ πάτρια), the only further step he required of Izates was circumcision (Ant. 20.2.4).

Most interesting of all, however, is Josephus' description of the Jewish politeuma in Antioch in the period prior to the Jewish revolt: "they grew in numbers . . . and were constantly attracting to their religious ceremonies multitudes of the Greeks, and these they had in some measure incorporated with themselves" (κἀκείνους τρόπῳ τινὶ μοῖραν αὐτῶν πεποίηντο) (J.W. 7.3.3).[81] Whatever degree of devotion to the Torah, written and unwritten, on the part of the God-fearing Greeks is implied by this statement, it must denote a considerable measure of acceptance by the Antiochene Jews of these Greeks,[82] and so also a considerable measure of social intercourse between circumcised Jew and uncircumcised Gentile.[83]

We may conclude from all this that there was a broad range of attachments to Judaism and Jewish ways wherever Diaspora settlements had made any impact on the surrounding community—from occasional visits to the synagogue, to total commitment apart from circumcision, with such matters as the sabbath and dietary laws being observed in varying degrees in between. *Pari passu* there would be a *broad range of social intercourse between faithful Jew and God-fearing Gentile, with strict Jews avoiding table-fellowship as far as possible, and those less scrupulous in matters of tithing and purity willingly extending and accepting invitations to meals where such Gentiles would be present.*

We can also see that the attitude and practice of openness to the Gentile would not have been static. It would depend upon the influence of particular rabbis and of particular rulings in matters of dispute. We may compare, for example, the famous pericope contrasting the response of Shammai and that of Hillel to the Gentile who asked both to teach him the whole Torah while he stood on one foot (b. Šabb. 31a). It would depend on the mood of the surrounding populace and local authorities at the time—particularly in Rome, Alexandria and Antioch, where the Jews were strong in numbers and undue influence on their part could be construed as a threat to the state. And at the period which concerns us it would depend not least on the Jews' sense of the mounting threat to their religion and nation which we sketched out earlier and which must have expressed itself in an increasingly hostile attitude to the Gentiles. This last is illustrated by the sequence of events described in Acts 21, which depicts Jerusalem Jews in the late 50s giving ready credence to the rumor that Paul had taken a Gentile into the temple (Acts 21:27–36). Another instance is the report of Josephus that at the beginning of the revolt in 66 Eleazar "persuaded those who officiated in the temple services to accept no gift or sacrifice from a foreigner" (J.W. 2.17.2). Here

---

[81] Note also his earlier description of the people of Damascus "whose wives with a few exceptions had become captivated (ὑπηγμένας) by the Jewish religion" (Josephus, J.W. 2.20.2).

[82] We may recall also that the proselyte, Nicolaus, one of the seven in Acts 6:5, came from Antioch.

[83] In the violence which marked relations between Jews and non-Jews in Syria in 66 C.E., Antioch was one of only three cities which spared their Jewish inhabitants (Josephus, J.W. 2.18.5).

too we may mention again the episode of Izates' conversion, which among other things shows that the attitude of the Palestinian Jew was stricter than that of the Diaspora Jew on the question of how far a Gentile had to go to be acceptable (Josephus, *Ant.* 20.2.4), and which thus provides an interesting parallel to the Antioch incident.

Before moving on, it is worth noting once more, if it is not already clear, that the issue in all this would have been issues for the earliest Christians too, particularly as the circle of Jesus' discipleship began to embrace more and more Gentiles. The extent to which the spectrum of attitude and practice mirrored that within the rest of Judaism is indicated by Paul's advice to the believers in Corinth (including Jews) at one end (1 Cor 8–10), and at the other by the reaction of the Judean brothers to Peter's eating with a Gentile, even though he was a pious God-fearer and presumably already observed the dietary laws (Acts 11:2–3). At the latter end of the same spectrum we should note also the untypical saying of Jesus preserved for us not surprisingly only by Matthew—"if he (the brother at fault) refuses to listen even to the church, let him be to you as a Gentile and a tax collector" (Matt 18:17).[84] The question for us, of course, is where the Antioch incident, not to mention Acts 15:20, 29, fits into this spectrum. It is to this question that we can now at last turn.

The Issue at Antioch

Against the background sketched out in the preceding sections, the exegetical alternatives in Gal 2:11–18 become clearer. The leading question can be posed thus: What did the table-fellowship at Antioch involve *prior* to the coming of the men from James? And what would have been required of the Gentile believers if the table-fellowship was to be resumed after the initial disruption caused by the withdrawal of Peter and the others? To put it another way, what was it that the men from James objected to or found fault with in the table-fellowship at Antioch? And how could that defect be remedied, if at all?

Key Phrases

The exegetical alternatives focus particularly on the key phrases of Paul's challenge, " 'If you, a Jew, *live like a Gentile and not like a Jew* (ἐθνικῶς καὶ οὐχὶ Ἰουδαϊκῶς ζῆς), how can you compel the Gentiles to *judaize* (Ἰουδαΐζειν)?' We are Jews by birth and not *Gentile sinners* (οὐκ ἐξ ἐθνῶν ἁμαρτωλοί …" (Gal 2:14–15).[85]

a) The Antithesis ἐθνικῶς/Ἰουδαϊκῶς

This antithesis is not precise enough to give us much help, since it could embrace a wide range of contrasts between practices typically Gentile and those typically Jewish. "To live like a Gentile" must exclude any detailed observance of the law; but

---

[84] The verse probably reflects the attitude of Jewish Christian churches rather than that of Jesus during his ministry in Palestine (see, e.g., McNeile, *Matthew,* 266–67; Goguel, *Primitive Church,* 39 n. 1, 526; Gaechter, *Matthäus,* 600–601; Grundmann, *Matthäus,* 419).

[85] There is no break in thought between v. 14 and v. 15: see below, n. 117.

need it exclude a more limited observance, such as many Gentiles attracted by Judaism obviously maintained? In particular, since the Noahic rules were thought by
many Jews to apply to all mankind, we cannot exclude the possibility that the
ἐθνικῶς /ἰουδαϊκῶς antithesis here is the antithesis between what we may call a
Noahic life-style and a Sinaitic life-style, the one being characteristic of God-fearing
Gentiles, the other of loyal Jews.[86] The one instance from our other sources which
might shed some light comes from Eusebius, where he describes Symmachus as an
Ebionite, that is, as one who strongly maintained "that the law ought to be kept in a
more strictly Jewish fashion" (ἰουδαϊκώτερον) (*Hist. eccl.* 6.17). What "a more strictly
Jewish fashion" means is presumably indicated by Eusebius's earlier description of
the Ebionites as those who "insisted on the complete observation of the law," and
who "were zealous to insist on the literal observance of the law" (*Hist. eccl.* 3.27.2, 3).
This simply serves to confirm that "to live in a Jewish fashion" was a relative term and
did not imply a pattern of behavior precisely defined or widely agreed among Jews.

b) Ἰουδαΐζειν

This is for us the most intriguing word. What was it that Paul accused Peter of requiring from the Gentile believers? Some of the usages elsewhere are as unspecific as
the ἐθνικῶς/ἰουδαϊκῶς antithesis—including the reference in Plutarch already cited
(*Cic.* 7.6; cf. also Ign. *Magn.* 10.3; *Acts Pil.* [A] 2:1). But three others offer some illumination. In the LXX of Esther we read that "many of the Gentiles were circumcised and
judaized (καὶ ἰουδαΐζον) for fear of the Jews" (8:17 LXX). In Josephus we read a similar characterization of one Metilius, the commander of the Roman garrison in Jerusalem, who "saved his life by entreaties and promises to judaize and even to be
circumcised" (καὶ μέχρι περιτομῆς ἰουδαΐζειν) (*J.W.* 2.17.10). In both instances
"judaizing" is obviously not the same as being circumcised: it denotes rather the
range of possible degrees of assimilation to Jewish customs, with circumcision as the
end-point of judaizing; but evidently one could "judaize" without going the whole
way (circumcision).[87] It must therefore describe that range of conduct covered by the
term "God-fearer" (or within Palestine also the term "resident alien") and signify an
embracing of much that characterized the Jewish way of life, enough at any rate for
the judaizing individual to be acceptable to devout Jews.

Still more interesting is the passage a little later in the *Jewish War*, not least because it describes the situation in Syria in the mid-60s:

> The whole of Syria was a scene of frightful disorder; every city was divided into
> two camps, and the safety of one party lay in their anticipating the other. . . . For,
> though believing that they had rid themselves of the Jews, still each city had its
> Judaizers (τοὺς ἰουδαΐζοντας), who aroused suspicion; and while they shrank from
> killing offhand this equivocal element in their midst, they feared these neutrals
> (μεμιγμένον) as much as pronounced aliens (*J.W.* 2.18.2 [Thackeray, LCL]).

---

[86] Schechter, *Aspects*, 206–7; Str-B 3.37–38; E. Sanders, *Paul and Palestinian Judaism*, 210–11. See
also nn. 90, 93 below.

[87] Note also Origen, frg. 8, on John 1:13: οὗτοι προτίθενται τὴν σάρκα περιτεμνόμενοι καὶ
ἐν τῷ προφανεῖ ἰουδάζειν θέλοντες.

Here we have confirmation that a considerable number of Gentiles in Syrian cities (including of course Antioch) were attracted sufficiently to Judaism as to have identified or associated themselves in some marked degree with it. Moreover, these Gentiles are further described as μεμιγμένοι, which we might colloquially translate as "those who had become mixed up with the Jews," and which elsewhere in such a context denotes social intercourse including guest friendship, living with, and sexual intercourse.[88] This strongly suggests that ἰουδαΐζειν can denote a degree of affiliation to Judaism which made possible a high level of social intercourse between Jew and Gentile, including not least unrestricted table-fellowship. Moreover, when taken together with Josephus' testimony in *J.W.* 7.3.3 (discussed above), it clearly implies that the Jewish community at Antioch in the 50s and early 60s had attracted large numbers of Gentiles and that many of these Gentiles were sufficiently ready to conform to Jewish practices as to make possible regular social intercourse including at least guest friendship and table-fellowship.[89]

c) Ἁμαρτωλοί

This is not a surprising word to find at this point (Gal 2:14) in view of the context so far outlined. Ἁμαρτωλός was a word which had by this time in Jewish circles developed a particularly Jewish flavor. It denoted not just a "sinner" in general terms, but a sinner determined as such precisely by his relation to the law. "Sinner" was becoming more and more a technical term for someone who either broke the law or did not know the law—the two criticisms of course often amounting to the same thing. Thus already in the LXX of the Psalms the link between "sinner" and "lawlessness" (ἀνομία) is well established (Ps 27:3; 54:3; 91:7; 100:8; 124:3; 128:3—LXX); the sinner is defined as one who forsakes the law, who does not seek God's statutes (Ps 118:53, 155—LXX). And in 1 Maccabees "sinners" and "lawless men" are parallel terms (1 Macc 1:34; 2:44). More striking is the way in which "sinner" becomes synonymous with "Gentile"—already in Ps. 9:17, and again in 1 Macc 2:48; also *Pss. Sol.* 1:1; 2:1–2 (cf. Tob 13:8; *Jub.* 23:23–24; *4 Ezra* 4:23). It was evidently a well established usage by the time of the first Christians: "sinners" and "Gentiles" stand as variant versions of the same Q saying (Luke 6:33—"even sinners do the same"; Matt 5:47—"even Gentiles do the same"); and the same equivalence is probably implied in the saying of Jesus, "the Son of Man is betrayed into the hands of sinners" (Mark 14:41/Matt 26:45; Luke 24:7), as the parallel with Mark 10:33 also suggests. Gentiles are "sinners" by reason of the fact that they do not have the law and are disqualified by the law from covenant righteousness (Ps.-Clem. *H.* 2.16).[90]

---

[88] See *LSJ*, μείγνυμι, B.

[89] "What Paul brands 'judaizing'—circumcision and dietary laws for Gentiles—was not a barrier to Christianity but quite attractive to Gentiles, who were enamored of what was Oriental" (Stendahl, *Paul,* 70); true of dietary laws; not so of circumcision. On the question of whether circumcision was always required of the would-be proselyte see also McEleney, "Conversion," 328–33; and n. 109 below.

[90] Cf. Str.-B 3.36, 41–43, 126–28; Rengstorf, "ἁμαρτωλός," 1.324–26; Schlier, *Galater,* 89; Kümmel, " 'Individualgeschichte,' " 159–60; also n. 93 below.

Still more striking for us is the evidence of how the word was used in relation to Jesus' ministry, as a description of those within Israel whose way of life should have debarred them from the table-fellowship of the devout Jew. It applied not just to those who had abused the written Torah (Luke 7:37, 39—a prostitute?; cf. Matt 21:32), but to tax collectors (Luke 19:7; cf. Matt 5:46 with Luke 6:32), and it would seem also to other trades which put the practitioner beyond the pale of what was deemed acceptable (Mark 2:15–17 pars.; Matt 11:19/Luke 7:34; Luke 15:1–2). Here we are evidently once again back in an area where the limits of acceptability were being determined by the multiplying *halakhoth* of the Pharisaic rabbis.[91] That is to say, not just disobedience to the Torah but disregard for the rabbinic rulings on what obedience to the Torah entailed, that was what showed a person to be a sinner. This has become more explicit in the Mishna: a sinner *(rasa)* is one who treats halakhic rulings lightly (*m. ʿEd.* 5:6; *m. ʾAbot* 4:7; 5:14).[92]

Given that so much of the Pharisaic teaching of our period was concerned with the limits of acceptable table-fellowship (see above), and given that the context of Gal 2:15 is a dispute precisely about whether and under what circumstances a devout Jew could have table-fellowship with Gentiles, the presumption becomes compellingly strong that ἁμαρτωλός in v. 15 belongs to the same range of usage. That is, *it was probably a word used of the Gentile believers by the men from James to express their disagreement or dismay at the table-fellowship being practiced by Peter and the other Jewish believers.* And it probably had the connotation of "unclean" (= Gentile = sinner), one who by his very race was legally disqualified from participating in the table-fellowship of a faithful Jew: "How could you Peter, a true-born Jew, have table-fellowship with a Gentile sinner?"[93]

Exegetical Alternatives

Our examination of these key phrases in Gal 2:14–15 against the background outlined earlier thus clarifies the exegetical alternatives open to us. What was involved in the table-fellowship at Antioch before the men from James appeared? How strict was the discipline of diet or ritual purity into which Peter and the others withdrew? On what terms could the table-fellowship have been resumed thereafter?[94] There are basically three alternatives open to us.

a) The table-fellowship at Antioch practiced by the whole community, including Peter and the other Jewish believers, had completely abandoned the laws governing

---

[91] See particularly Rengstorf, "ἁμαρτωλός," 1.327–28; Jeremias, *Jerusalem,* 303–12; cf. H. Braun, *Radikalismus,* 2.38 n. 1.

[92] Rengstorf, "ἁμαρτωλός," 1.322–23.

[93] Cf. Betz, *Galatians,* 115; and above, n. 90.

[94] It is not necessary to argue that the Lord's Supper was specifically in Paul's mind at this point (see particularly Lietzmann, *Galater,* 14, and Schlier, *Galater,* 83–84), in view of the importance we have now seen was attached to *all* table-fellowship (cf. Acts 11:3). In any case the bread and the wine had probably not yet been distinguished from the meal itself at this stage (see Dunn, *Unity and Diversity,* §40). Commentators usually note that the imperfect συνήσθιεν (Gal 2:12) implies a regular rather than occasional pattern of table-fellowship.

table-fellowship. They no longer observed even the laws of unclean foods; they did not insist on animals being properly killed; they did not hold back over idol food. What the men from James insisted on was a greater observance of the law, perhaps no more than the laws explicitly set out in the Torah. Indeed it can be argued with plausibility that what the men from James brought was the decree of Acts 15:29, which had been agreed in Jerusalem following the Jerusalem conference (Paul's first missionary journey having intervened): "the demands laid down in Antioch are none other than the demands of the Decree."[95]

This alternative would give the most obvious sense to two of the phrases examined above—they were living like Gentiles, like Gentile sinners, showing no knowledge of or regard for the principal gift of God to the Jew, the Torah. We may note also that it would fit with Luke's account in Acts 10–11 of Peter's vision at Joppa and his subsequent encounter with Cornelius at Caesarea, where the lesson could have been drawn that the law of clean and unclean no longer applied to the Jewish believer. It could also fit with the hypothesis that the Antioch incident preceded the Jerusalem council (Gal 2:1–10 = Acts 11:30), and that the Jerusalem council was called to resolve the problem posed by the Antioch incident.[96]

The weakness of this alternative is that it does not fit well into the background illuminated above. (1) It is unlikely that the Jewish believers at Antioch had abandoned the law so completely. So far as we know, such a complete abandoning of the law without protest from within the ranks of the local Jewish Christians themselves is without parallel. Both in Corinth and at Rome a substantial proportion of the Jewish believers clearly felt unable to go so far (Rom 14:1–2; 1 Cor 8). We should not, of course, assume a regularity of practice throughout the Diaspora churches over this period. Nevertheless, it must be doubted whether so many Jewish believers at Antioch would have given up the law so unreservedly without it becoming an issue among themselves even before Peter and the men from James arrived. (2) We know from Josephus that the Jewish *politeuma* at Antioch had attracted many Gentiles who evidently showed themselves willing to adopt Jewish customs, at least in some measure. It is likely that the Gentile converts to faith in the Christ Jesus came initially, perhaps even almost exclusively, from the ranks of these God-fearers (cf. Acts 6:5). That would mean that the Gentile believers were already accustomed to observe the Jewish dietary laws in some measure and the table-fellowship of the new sect probably continued in the same fashion. (3) It must be doubted whether Paul would have reacted quite so sharply as he did to a requirement from the Jerusalem delegation merely that

---

[95] Catchpole, "Paul"; cf. earlier McGiffert, *History*, 211–17, who notes that Ritschl suggested that the decree stemmed from the church of Jerusalem at a time other than that designated by Acts, in the first edition of his *Entstehung*, but that he abandoned the view in the second edition (213 and n. 4); Robinson, "Circumcision," 40–41.

[96] So, e.g., Ramsay, *Paul the Traveller*, 48–60; Geyser, "Paul"; Bruce, *New Testament History*, ch. 22; Suhl, *Paulus*, 46–70; other references in Jewett, *Dating*, 69–75 and 144 n. 36. Others argue more plausibly that the accounts of a second and third visit to Jerusalem in Acts 11 and Acts 15 stem from different traditions of the same event—i.e., Acts 11:27–30 = Gal 2:1–10 = Acts 15: see, e.g., Lake, *Acts*, 5.203–4, who follows Weizsäcker, McGiffert, and Schwarz (201–2); Jeremias, "Quellenproblem"; Benoit, "Deuxième visite"; Catchpole, "Paul," 432–38.

the Gentiles should observe the most basic laws of the Torah—the Noahic laws. Later on, he saw such scruples as a threat to Christian liberty, but nevertheless advised his fellow "liberals" to observe them for the sake of "the weaker brother" (Rom 14:13–15:3; 1 Cor 8:7–13), so he did not regard them as a threat to the gospel in these circumstances. We must allow of course that Paul "cooled down" somewhat after the Antioch incident and the Galatian letter, but even at the earlier period, would he have seen an acceptance of the Noahic rules as a building up once again of the edifice of Torah righteousness over which he had labored as a Pharisee (Gal 2:18)? I think it unlikely: the Noahic requirements were hardly the same as "the traditions of his fathers" for which he had previously been so zealous (1:14).[97]

b) At the other end of the scale of possibilities, it is possible that the table-fellowship at Antioch had involved a fair degree of observance of the dietary laws, including even some of the halakhic elaborations concerning tithes and ritual purity. In such a case the men from James were in effect insisting that these God-fearing Gentile believers go the whole way and become proselytes by being circumcised, and Peter and the other Jewish believers who followed him were giving their demand added force by their actions.[98]

This interpretation would certainly fit with the background of considerable numbers of Gentiles at Antioch showing themselves willing to "judaize." It would also provide an even closer match with the story of Izates' conversion, in the contrast there between the Diaspora Jews with a laxer view of what conversion required, and the Jews from Palestine with their insistence on circumcision (cf. Josephus, *Ant.* 20.2.4). And again it would fit with the hypothesis that the Jerusalem council was called to resolve the issue raised by the Antioch incident, with an exact match being provided between Gal 2:12 ("certain men came from James . . .") and Acts 15:1 ("And certain men came down from Judea and were teaching the brethren, 'Unless you are circumcised according to the custom of Moses you cannot be saved' ").

The weaknesses of this second alternative are, however, even more compelling. (1) It does not square with the language used by Paul. Peter's conduct in such a case could hardly be called "living like a Gentile" (Gal 2:14). Ἰουδαΐζειν denotes a Gentile's adopting the Jewish customs which made social intercourse possible and is elsewhere distinguished from circumcision, with the latter seen as the crucial final step by which the "judaizer" became a proselyte. It would be somewhat surprising then if Paul used ἰουδαΐζειν to denote that final step, if they had already been judaizing to such an extent.[99] And ἁμαρτωλός would also be a surprising word to use of Gentiles who were al-

---

[97] Catchpole argues that the decree was something of a *volte-face* on the part of the Jerusalem leaders ("a thoroughgoing, not a mediating, proposal": "Paul," 431, also 441–43); but he does not allow for the possibility that Paul's own position vis-à-vis Jerusalem was also undergoing change in the period prior to the Antioch incident (see above), and that the Antioch incident itself was a significant crisis in Paul's own theological development (see below).

[98] So Suhl, *Paulus*, 71; Howard, *Crisis*, 25; Betz, *Galatians*, 112; cf. Schlier, *Galater*, 86.

[99] Cf. Mussner, *Galaterbrief*, 145 n. 53: "In das ἰουδαΐζειν ist zwar bei den antiochenischen Heidenchristen nicht die Beschneidung eingeschlossen, aber das Leben nach den jüdischen Speisegesetzen." Note also the distinction between adopting Jewish customs and circumcision in Juvenal and Josephus (discussed above).

ready judaizing to such a degree—that is, showing their knowledge of and regard for the law. (2) Even more difficult is it to see the Antioch incident thus interpreted as the sequel to the Jerusalem agreement recorded in Gal 2:1–10.[100] According to Paul, the pillar apostles, including James and Peter, had agreed that Gentile believers need not be circumcised. It is not inconceivable that James subsequently succumbed to the growing pressures within Palestine for a more clear-cut loyalty to the religion of Israel (cf. n. 96 above). But it is doubtful whether Peter would have abandoned in Antioch an agreement made in Jerusalem, an agreement reached in the face of already strong pressure from those Paul calls "false brothers," "sham believers" (2:4). It is doubtful too that the Jewish believers, particularly the Hellenists, should succumb so completely to pressure of this sort from the Jerusalem which had expelled them.

c) The third alternative is the intermediate interpretation. The Gentile believers were already observing the basic food laws prescribed by the Torah; in their table-fellowship with the Jewish believers, in particular pork was not used, and when meat was served care had been taken to ensure the beast had been properly slaughtered.[101] In this case what the men from James would have called for was a much more scrupulous observance of the rulings on what the dietary laws involved, especially with regard to ritual purity and tithing (see above).

This interpretation fits well with the language of Gal 2:14–15. It certainly makes sense of Paul's charge that Peter by his action was compelling the Gentile believers to judaize.[102] For as we have seen, ἰουδαΐζειν elsewhere denotes the adoption of Jewish customs in full measure, though not necessarily circumcision itself: men and women could be said to have "judaized" without the former having been circumcised (see above). Paul's charge against Peter, then, is most likely that by his action he had raised the ritual barriers surrounding their table-fellowship, thereby excluding the Gentile believers unless they "judaized," that is, embraced a far more demanding discipline of ritual purity than hitherto. The reason why Peter had withdrawn (ἀφώριζεν) from the table-fellowship in the first place was because the purity status of the Gentile believers had been called in question (Gal 2:12; cf. 2 Cor 6:17 with its reference to Isa 52:11).[103] So too, Paul's description of Peter as previously having lived "like a Gentile and not as a Jew" could describe a practice of table-fellowship which fell within the limits of the Noahic laws, since already no doubt the view was current that the commandments given to Noah (Gen 9) applied to all the nations (descendants of Noah) and not just the Jews (cf. *Jub.* 7:20).[104] Probably this was the level of table-fellowship

---

[100] For the view that the Antioch incident *preceded* the second Jerusalem visit see above, n. 5.

[101] Cf. J. Weiss, *Earliest Christianity*, 264: "Hitherto the converted Gentiles in Antioch . . . had been treated in the same way as the so-called 'God-fearing' Gentiles in the Jewish communities of the Dispersion: they were admitted to the religious services without being circumcised and observed only a part of the ceremonial commands."

[102] That "compel" here (2:14) denotes indirect pressure rather than an explicit demand is generally recognized by commentators. It is supported by the imperfect tenses of ὑπέστελλεν and ἀφώριζεν, which imply a somewhat drawn out process rather than a clean and sharp break.

[103] Betz, *Galatians*, 108.

[104] Lake, *Acts*, 5.209, cites *Sib. Or.* 4:24–34 (probably late first century C.E.) as a parallel. I disagree with Catchpole when he argues that "it would be quite impossible to describe existence under the Decree as living ἐθνικῶς" ("Paul," 441).

which Peter had previously learned to practice in his encounter with the God-fearing Cornelius (Acts 10–11), and which the "circumcision party" had criticized on that earlier occasion (Acts 11:2–3; though see also below n. 110). Moreover, in the phrase "Gentile sinners," ἁμαρτωλοί will not here be simply a synonym for "Gentiles" who know not the law, but could have more the connotation of its use within Palestine for Jews who disregarded the law by their mode of life (see above). That is to say, "Gentile sinners" could mean Gentiles who knew the law but whose regard for it was seriously defective in practice.

This interpretation also fits into the background of Palestine at that time—particularly the increasing nationalism as Israel's position and religious prerogatives were seen to be under a mounting threat. The pressure would be on the good Jew to withdraw more and more into a stricter definition and practice of his national religion. Here we may recall the debate between the schools of Shammai and Hillel as to the seriousness of the Gentile proselyte's uncleanness (*m. Pesaḥ.* 8:8; *m.* ʿ*Ed.* 5:2); also the probability that the stricter school of Shammai gained the ascendancy in the pre-70 period.[105] Palestinian Jews who believed in Jesus would experience the same pressures, as the Gospel of Matthew in particular confirms. Not only do the Gospels testify that Christians too were caught up in a debate about true cleanliness, where the meaning of Jesus' definition of cleanliness was at issue, and where Matthew's emphasis is distinctly more conservative than Mark's (Mark 7:19; Matt 15:17, 20). But Matthew also gives evidence of an even more conservative *Christian* tradition behind Matt 5:19 and 23:3, 23, where the *Christian* respect for the Pharisaic *halakhoth* cannot have been very different from (and may have been very close to) the views postulated here for the men from James.[106] Against this background the third alternative for our interpretation of the Antioch incident makes excellent sense. As Eleazar coming from Palestine made a higher demand on the would-be proselyte Izates than the Diaspora Jew Ananias (Josephus, *Ant.* 20.2.4), so the men from James made a higher demand on the God-fearing Gentile believers than the Jewish believers in Antioch itself.

Finally, we can say that this interpretation of Gal 2:11–18 also fits well into the preceding context in Galatians. When the pillar apostles in Jerusalem accepted Paul's gospel (2:5–7) and agreed to the division of missionary labor (2:7–9), what had been at dispute and what was agreed were the requirements laid by the gospel *upon the Gentiles.* The requirements laid upon the Jews had not been at issue. What about table-fellowship? Nothing seems to have been said (Gal 2:6d, 10).[107] Why so? Possibly because the parties to the agreement did not think about table-fellowship or consider whether it would be affected by the agreement. Or possibly because they assumed that Gentile believer and Jewish believer would avoid social intercourse. Yet neither of these possibilities can be rated very highly, since social intercourse including table-

---

[105] See Neusner, *Rabbinic Traditions,* particularly 3.315, 318; also "First Cleanse," 494–95; cf. Davies, *Paul,* 9; R. Meyer, "φαρισαῖος," 9.27–28, 31; Finkel, *Pharisees,* 134–43.

[106] Cf. Haenchen, "Matthäus 23," 30–31, 39–40; E. Schweizer, *Matthäus,* 281, 283, 285; Guelich, *Sermon,* 169.

[107] "The right hand of fellowship" (2:9) did not of itself specify what kind of fellowship (cf. Betz, *Galatians,* 100).

fellowship was evidently quite normal, though carefully regulated, both within Palestine between the devout Jew and the *ger toshav* and in the Diaspora between the devout Jew and the God-fearer, and since the issue must have arisen for the new sect as soon as Gentiles began to believe in Jesus without undergoing circumcision, as again the Cornelius episode confirms. It would be hardly likely, for example, that Titus ate his meals in splendid isolation when he visited Jerusalem with Paul and Barnabas (Gal 2:3). On the contrary, the fact that table-fellowship was not at issue on that occasion strongly suggests that Titus observed a high standard of ritual purity during that visit.[108]

Much the greater probability lies with the further suggestion that the pillar apostles simply assumed that the devout Jewish believer would continue to observe the hereditary customs already surrounding the meal table (even if not all the refinements currently under debate among the Pharisees). In which case they would have assumed also that the table-fellowship between believing Jew and believing Gentile in Antioch involved a considerable regard for the religious scruples of the devout Jew and so was maintained at a fairly high level of ritual purity.[109] This would be in line with the degree of scrupulosity earlier attributed to the Jerusalem brothers in Acts 11:2–3, where an uncircumcised Gentile *per se* was an improper table companion, because of his Gentile uncleanness (cf. Acts 10:14–15; 11:8–9). It would fit with the probability that Titus observed a high standard of table purity while in Jerusalem with Paul and Barnabas: many of the local Jewish believers would then be more likely to assume that this was the accepted practice in the more mixed communities of the Diaspora. And it would certainly explain the reaction of the men from James when they arrived from Jerusalem: they were surprised and shocked by the minimal level of law observance in Antioch; to them it would appear as though the whole heritage distinctive of Israel and most prized by Judaism, the law of Moses, was being abandoned.[110] In the same way Paul's language probably echoes the surprise he felt that the Jerusalem believers were still thinking of the Gentile believers as "sinners" (Gal 2:15, 17), still categorizing them in terms of their relation to the law.

The reasoning behind Peter's withdrawal from table-fellowship is still harder to elucidate. But given the fuller context we have now reconstructed, the most likely interpretation is along these lines. (1) He could not deny the logic of Jerusalem's demand, that a Jew live like a Jew. Nothing in the Jerusalem agreement had altered that, whatever freedom it had given to the Gentile believers.[111] (2) As a native of Palestine,

---

[108] The "false brothers" were evidently suspicious of the freedom claimed by Paul (2:4), but in this instance their suspicions and opposition focused only on the question of circumcision.

[109] It may well be significant here that the Jerusalem leadership thought it necessary to urge only the importance of almsgiving on the mission to the uncircumcised (Gal 2:10), since there is some evidence that "alms for Israel" were regarded as the appropriate expression of conversion to the God of Israel for God-fearers who were not willing to be circumcised (see Berger, "Almosen"). In the case of such a convert a high level of judaizing could be taken for granted.

[110] Cf. particularly Bousset, "Galater," in *Schriften*, 2:46.

[111] What significance would the Cornelius episode have had for Peter? If Cornelius was a "judaizing" God-fearer before he met Peter, he may even have been already maintaining a fairly high level of ritual purity. In which case the clear signs of God's acceptance of him (Acts 10:10–16, 34–35,

indeed a Galilean, he could feel the pressure of the steadily mounting threat against Judaism, and so the strong attractiveness of the call to hold loyal to the hereditary customs (see above). (3) In particular he would appreciate the counter threat felt by the Palestine believers from the more rigorous and more fanatically loyal of their fellow religionists. For Jewish believers to appear to be abandoning their national and religious heritage, or for a rumor to that effect to get about, was to invite retribution and even death (cf. again Acts 6:11–14; 8:1–3; 21:20–21, 27–36; 23:12–15).[112] Not only so, but many of his fellow Jewish believers evidently shared these more rigorist views, and Peter may indeed have "feared the circumcision party" (Gal 2:12)—that is, feared if not for his life, at least for his authority and effectiveness within the Jewish Christian communities of Palestine.[113] (4) Moreover, as one who had been specifically designated as a missionary to his fellow Jews (Gal 2:7–9), Peter would recognize the importance of retaining a good standing in Jewish eyes, or at least of not needlessly offending those who were formulating Jewish attitudes and reactions in such threatening times. To become known himself as a "sinner" would at once cut him off from the bulk of faithful Jews.[114] (5) Again a delegation from James, if that is a correct designation, was not to be lightly ignored. As we have seen, the church at Antioch, including Paul and not unnaturally Barnabas, had in effect already acknowledged Jerusalem's authority in judging matters of controversy, when they submitted the issue of circumcising Gentile believers to the pillar apostles (Gal 2:2, 9). Moreover, of the pillar apostles, James had already established himself as the leading figure in Jerusalem (Gal 2:9). Consequently a group who came from Jerusalem with the explicit (or claimed) backing of James could expect the church at Antioch to fall in line with their judgment. And Peter acted accordingly. (6) At least one other consideration may well have influenced Peter. Since so many Gentiles outside the new sect, in Antioch and elsewhere, seemed very ready to declare their attraction to Judaism by judaizing as far as circumcision, it was not unreasonable to expect that the Gentile believers in Antioch would be willing to subject themselves to a similar degree of halakhic observance for the sake of their Jewish brothers. The issue of whether the Gentile believers need be circumcised had been settled in favor of Gentile liberty of action. The issue was now of Jewish believers remaining loyal to their ancestral faith, and in return they might expect the Gentile believers to conform to the sensibilities of their Jewish brothers, in

---

44–46) would have counted only towards a resolution of the circumcision issue itself (cf. Acts 11:3 and Peter's response). That is to say, Cornelius would have been a precedent on Paul's side in the Jerusalem debate (Gal 2:1–10; cf. Acts 15:7–11), but may not have provided a sufficiently close parallel to guide Peter in the incident at Antioch. In any case the agreement at Jerusalem (Gal 2:9) could be regarded as the agreed resolution of such anomalies as Cornelius.

[112] See my discussion above together with n. 37, and below, n. 116; also Bruce, *Men and Movements,* 35–36.

[113] The point would gain greater force if οἱ ἐκ περιτομῆς denoted Jews rather than Jewish Christians; so Dix, *Jew and Greek,* 43–44; Reicke, "Hintergrund," 176–83; Munck, *Paul,* 107; Schmithals, *Paul and James,* 66–67; Nickle, *Collection,* 65; Schütz, *Paul,* 153–54; Suhl, *Paulus,* 72. The phrase is not sufficiently explicit in itself (cf. Acts 10:45; 11:2; Rom.4:12; Col 4:11; Titus 1:10) and equally permits the thesis that a faction of Jewish Christians is indicated thereby (so Ellis, "Circumcision Party").

[114] Cf., e.g., McGiffert, *History,* 206–7; J. Weiss, *Earliest Christianity,* 265; Manson, "Problem," 180–81.

much the same way as they had been willing to "judaize" when they were "God-fearers."[115] Some such pragmatic considerations, acted out as they would see it within the spirit of the Jerusalem agreement, must presumably lie behind the actions of Peter, Barnabas and the other Jewish Christians—actions however which Paul could only see and denounce as an unprincipled compromise of the gospel (2:13–14).[116]

To conclude, the third alternative seems to provide the best solution. The table-fellowship at Antioch had not totally disregarded the law but probably had paid due heed to the basic dietary laws of the Torah. Peter, having already become less tied to the more elaborate scruples of the brothers in Judea (Acts 10–11), found no difficulty in joining in such table-fellowship, as Barnabas, more used to Diaspora ways, was already doing. The men from James however were shocked at what seemed to them a minimal level of Torah observance and a far too casual and unacceptable attitude to the Torah. They would no doubt point out that the earlier agreement made in Jerusalem had in no way changed the obligations to Torah obedience resting on the Jewish believer, and must have insisted that the Jewish believers in Antioch conduct themselves with greater discipline and greater loyalty to the Torah, more like their fellow believers in Palestine and with a similar regard for the heritage of Jewish tradition and custom. Peter, persuaded by this charge of disloyalty and out of concern for the future of the Jewish Christian assemblies and "the mission to the circumcised," withdrew into a more disciplined ritual and "the rest of the Jews" followed suit—swayed no doubt by Peter's example and authority (Gal 2:13), but also hoping, we may presume, that the Gentile believers would adapt their own life-style to this more rigorous code of conduct.

It was at this point that Paul intervened and confronted Peter. The vividness with which he recalls the scene indicates the importance of the stand that he felt he must make. Indeed it is likely that in vv. 14–18 he lives again through the line of reasoning which had forced him to the conclusion that Peter was wrong and which he had used against Peter.[117] In particular it was the use of "sinner" by the Jerusalem delegation in reference to the Gentile believers and the table-fellowship at Antioch which probably brought home to him the incompatibility of such language with the gospel agreed earlier in Jerusalem ("that a man is justified not by works of law but through faith in

---

[115] Cf. Bruce, *Paul*, 177; Koester, *Einführung*, 540.

[116] "In Paul's opinion, Cephas' action must be understood in terms of political compromise . . ." (Betz, *Galatians*, 109ff.).

[117] Most scholars agree that the thought runs on from v. 14 to vv. 15ff. (see, e.g., Lightfoot, *Galatians*, 113–14; Bousset, *Schriften*, 2:46–48; Lagrange, *Galates*, 45–46; Bultmann, "Auslegung," 394–99; Bauernfeind, "Schluss," 449–63; Munck, *Paul*, 125–27; and in the past twenty years, Schmithals, *Paul and James*, 72–76; Kertelge, "Deutung," 212; Bornkamm, *Paul*, 46; Guthrie, *Galatians*, 89; Bligh, *Galatians*, 235; Feld, " 'Christus' "; Mussner, *Galaterbrief*, 135; Schütz, *Paul*, 150–53; Ollrog, *Mitarbeiter*, 206–8; Bouwman, " 'Christus.' " The probability is greatly strengthened when the appropriateness of the word ἁμαρτωλός (vv. 15, 17) to the context of the Antioch incident is appreciated (see above). Whether vv. 14–18 (or 21) represent what Paul actually said on the occasion, or would have liked to say with the benefit of hindsight, does not affect the point. That Paul turned his back abruptly on the Antioch incident at the end of v. 14 and addressed himself solely to the Galatian situation is correspondingly less likely (against, e.g., Kümmel, " 'Individualgeschichte,' " 161–62; Betz, *Galatians*, 114; Wilckens ["Was heisst?" 86–87] even questions whether the ἀναγκάζειν ἰουδαΐζειν of 2:14 can refer to the Antioch incident, but see my discussion, above). The Gentile Galatian readership could hardly have understood the ἡμεῖς of v. 15 as other than a reference to Peter and Paul.

Jesus Christ"—2:16).[118] If Gentiles are "in Christ" (v. 17) and yet still "sinners," then we who are with them "in Christ" are thereby found to be sinners too, and Christ has become an "agent of sin" (ἁμαρτίας διάκονος).[119] But that cannot be right (v. 17). I cannot live my life "in Christ" and at the same time give the law the significance it had when I was a Pharisee (Gal 2:14; cf. Phil 3:5–6), for the law neither gives nor expresses life in Christ (Gal 3:10–11, 21–22) but simply shows me up as a transgressor (2:18; 3:19; cf. Rom 3:20; 4:15; 5:13, 20; 7:7–11).[120]

The significance of Paul's stand should not be underestimated. For the first time, probably, he had come to see that the principle of "justification through faith" applied not simply to the acceptance of the gospel in conversion, but also to the whole of the believer's life. That is to say, he saw that justification through faith was not simply a statement of how the believer entered into God's covenanted promises (the understanding of the gospel agreed at Jerusalem); it must also regulate his life as a believer. The covenantal nomism of Judaism and of the Jewish believers (life in accordance with the law within the covenant given by grace—see above, n. 9) was in fact a contradiction of that agreed understanding of justification through faith.[121] To live life "in Christ" *and* "in accordance with the law" was not possible; it involved a basic contradiction in terms and in the understanding of what made a man acceptable to God. Thus Paul began to see, as probably he had never seen before, that the principle of justification through faith meant a redefining of the relation between the believer and Israel—*not* an abandoning of that link (a flight into an individualism untouched by Jewish claims of a monopoly in the election and covenant grace of God), but a redefining of it—a redefining of how the inheritance of Abraham could embrace Gentiles apart from the law.[122] To begin with the Spirit and through faith rules out not just justification by works of law, but life lived by law (covenantal nomism) also—the very argument which he develops in the rest of Galatians.

---

[118] That Paul is citing an agreed position is probable, whether Paul was deliberately following classical rhetorical practice or not (as argued by Betz, *Galatians* 114–17). In fact w. 15–21 fit the form of the *propositio* at best awkwardly: vv. 17–18 rings oddly as a statement of the point to be discussed, and the attempt to divide vv. 19–20 into four theses to be elaborated in the rest of the letter is overscrupulous and artificial.

[119] See particularly Burton, *Galatians*, 124–30; Mussner, *Galaterbrief*, 176–77. One can recognize that Paul is echoing the language used by the men from James ("seeking to be justified," cf. Rom 10:3; "sinner," see above) without having to conclude that Paul is actually quoting his opponents (Feld, " 'Christus' ") or debating with an imaginary opponent diatribe style (Bouwman, " 'Christus' "); cf. Ollrog, *Paulus*, 209 n. 20. Lambrecht, "Line of Thought," argues oddly that "a reference to the Antioch incident is not present in vv. 15–16 nor is that incident directly alluded to by the terms ἁμαρτωλοί and ἁμαρτία of v. 17," but also that "it can hardly be doubted that with the phrase 'building up again' Paul is alluding to Peter's conduct at Antioch . . ." (493).

[120] With v. 18 we probably hear the last echo of Paul's rebuke of Peter. Betz is correct to the extent that with vv. 19–21 we move into formulations which were probably forged by his maturer reflections on the issues involved and more directly stimulated by and oriented towards the challenge confronting him in Galatia. Cf. Schlier, *Galater*, 87–88. Since there are at least some indications that Paul's view of the law developed still further after Galatians (cf. Drane, *Paul;* Hübner, *Gesetz*), we should beware of exegetical conclusions with regard to Galatians which depend too heavily on parallels in Romans.

[121] Cf. and contrast Räisänen, "Legalism."

[122] Cf. Davies, "Paul," 9–10.

Conclusions and Corollaries

If this exegesis is on the right lines, it sheds light on some of the other major issues relating to Gal 2, and the incident itself has to be seen as an important watershed
in Paul's personal development and in the development of Christian self-understanding and the missionary endeavor of the new movement. At this stage all I can do is
outline these corollaries briefly.

The Apostolic Council

We do not receive much help in resolving the problem of how to relate Acts 15 to
Paul's autobiographical account in Gal 1–2. Our understanding of the Antioch incident does however clarify what remains the single most difficult feature in Acts 15
when compared to Gal 2: in Acts 15 the Jerusalem council pronounces explicitly *both*
on the issue of circumcision as though the issue had hitherto been unresolved, *and* on
the minimal requirements necessary before table-fellowship can take place (15:20,
29); whereas Paul's account in Gal 2 shows that the circumcision issue had *already*
been resolved *before* the issue of table-fellowship became the subject of controversy. If
Gal 2 preceded Acts 15, the fact that circumcision seems still to have been an issue at
the council remains a puzzle.[123] And if Gal 2:1–10 is Paul's account of the Jerusalem
council (= Acts 15), the ruling of Acts 15:20, 29 that Gentiles should have nothing
more than the Noahic requirements laid upon them renders the Antioch incident
scarcely credible (particularly in the light of Gal 2:6d).

The most plausible solution to this dilemma is that the "Jerusalem council" settled only the circumcision issue, and that the so-called "apostolic decree" stipulating
the limits of table-fellowship reflects a later agreement, an accommodation between
Jewish and Gentile believers once the Gentile mission had become well established.
The date when the "decree" was first formulated remains uncertain. Observance of
the Noahic laws had probably been the practice in Antioch before the incident, as we
have seen. And certainly such observance had Paul's approval subsequently in the
mixed churches of the Gentile mission (1 Cor 8:7–13; Rom 14:13–15:3). At some
stage it became the rule also within the sphere of Jerusalem's continuing influence
(Antioch, Syria and Cilicia), possibly not till the late 50s (cf. Acts 21:25), but quite
probably even earlier as part of Jerusalem's response to the success of the Gentile mission.[124] Since Luke recounts only one major discussion on such issues (the Jerusalem

---

[123] It was this consideration which caused Lake to abandon his earlier advocacy of Ramsay's view
(*Acts*, 5.203–4; *Earlier Epistles*, 274–93); see *Acts*, 5.201. The puzzle cannot be resolved by arguing that
Gal 2:1–10 was only a private meeting (2:2: see n. 96 above). Verses 3–10 show that however the consultation began, it soon involved a running debate with a wider circle than "those of repute." The argument that vv. 4–5 form a parenthesis, which refers to the situation in Galatia at the time of writing
(Geyser, "Paul," 132–34; Bruce, "Galatian Problems 1," 302, 306; also idem, *Paul*, 159), only compli-
cates rather than clarifies the difficulty of the grammar at that point (see my "Relationship," 472 and n.
58), and the formal character of the agreement in 2:7–10 (ibid., 477 n. 60) implies a setting which involved a wider circle of the Jerusalem believers. See also Catchpole, "Paul," 435.

[124] The specification of Antioch, Syria and Cilicia in Acts 15:23 does not necessarily require a date
for the "decree" prior to the first missionary journey (as Catchpole argues, "Paul," 438–39, 442). The

council), and since the practice behind the "decree" was so long established in the Gentile mission (more or less from the start), Luke presumably felt at liberty to trace the agreement formally back to that crucial debate about the Gentile mission.

Peter's Position

Our findings strengthen the probability that Paul's rebuke of Peter at Antioch was unsuccessful. The most frequently adduced consideration here is that Paul would have mentioned it if Peter had given way (as he was careful to do in relating the earlier encounter in Jerusalem—Gal 2:1–10). And this is almost sufficient in itself to make the case.[125] But in addition we can now note the fuller light we have been able to shed on the reasons which probably weighed with Peter in his original decision to withdraw from the table-fellowship in Antioch. The more understandable and reasonable his decision to withdraw, the less likely was he to go back on it. Despite the fierceness of Paul's attack ("acted insincerely," etc.), Peter is unlikely to have agreed that their common belief in justification through faith (Gal 2:16) was endangered. To observe the law as a principle regulating conduct did not undermine justification through faith. Covenantal nomism was not at odds with the election of grace. Consequently Jewish believers could still remain true to their heritage, and it was not unfair to ask Gentile believers to respect that degree of discipline in their social intercourse, particularly since "judaizing" was nothing strange to God-fearers in Antioch.[126]

Paul's Subsequent Mission

It follows also that the Antioch incident had a decisive effect in shaping Paul's future. Hitherto an apostle/missionary of Antioch, he could no longer act as the Antioch church's delegate—the consequence, a breach with the church at Antioch. Hitherto a partner of Barnabas, he could no longer work easily with one whose life-style was at such odds with his own—the consequence, a breach with Barnabas (cf. Acts 15:39–40). In short, as a result of the Antioch incident, Paul became an independent missionary.

Galatian churches seem to have sided with Paul (see below), so that Jerusalem's sphere of influence (in the north and northwest), where her authority would have been unquestioned, was limited to Antioch, Syria and Cilicia (contrast 2 Cor 10:13–16). Nor is it necessary to deny that Jerusalem itself was behind the final decree (as does Haenchen, *Acts*, 470–71), since the success of the Gentile mission would have made many Gentile Christians within Jerusalem's area of authority restive under their tighter discipline (cf. J. Weiss, *Earliest Christianity*, 311–15; Goppelt, *Times*, 78), and a table-fellowship between Jew and Gentile on the basis of the Noahic rules could after all be defended as properly lawful according to the Torah (had Paul made his defense at Antioch on that basis he would probably have stood a better chance of winning). On the earliest form of the "decree" see particularly Kümmel, "Die älteste Form."

[125] This is probably the dominant view today. See, e.g., McGiffert, *History*, 208; J. Weiss, *Earliest Christianity*, 275–76; Bacon, "Paul's Triumph"; Haenchen, *Acts*, 476; Gaechter, *Petrus*, 251–54; Bornkamm, *Paul*, 47; Conzelmann, *History*, 68, 90; Bligh, *Galatians*, 233–34; Bauckham, "Barnabas," 64–65; Koester, *Einführung*, 540; other references in Holmberg, *Paul and Power*, 34 n. 117.

[126] Josephus' report of the attractiveness of Judaism to the Greeks in Antioch in the period prior to the Jewish rebellion (*J.W.* 7.3.3, quoted above, and 2.18.5, referred to above, n. 83) may reflect the situation in Antioch following Paul's defeat and the degree of assimilation between Jews, Jewish Christians and judaizing Greeks (cf. Smallwood's assessment of *J.W.* 7.3.3, also cited above).

Confirmation of this comes from Acts itself. Only on his first outreach are he and Barnabas called "apostles" (Acts 14:4, 14)—that is, apostles of Antioch. And whereas Paul's first recorded missionary endeavor can properly be designated a "missionary journey" (starting from and returning to Antioch), his subsequent work can hardly be classified as "second and third missionary journeys," since he clearly settles for lengthy periods, first at Corinth and then at Ephesus as his base of operations (Acts 18:11; 19:8–10). The Antioch incident therefore had incalculable consequences on the development of the Gentile mission, as a mission which was to a decisive degree independent of Jewish Christianity, and which from the outset was challenging and beginning to break away from the self-understanding of Jewish Christianity.[127]

The Letter's Occasion

In particular, a plausible occasion for the writing of Galatians becomes increasingly attractive. If the Galatians in question are the churches of south Galatia,[128] then we are talking about churches established by Paul and Barnabas while they were still missionaries of the church at Antioch. That is to say, we are talking of Antioch's daughter churches. In which case the decision of the church at Antioch to fall in line with the ruling or wishes of the men from James would be thought by many to apply by extension to these daughter churches. Not unnaturally then, shortly after Paul's own disgruntled departure from Antioch, a delegation probably set out from Jerusalem or from Antioch itself to visit these churches, including the churches of Galatia. Whether the more conservative members of the delegation gained control or had the control from the beginning is not clear. Either way, the demands evidently made by the delegation seem to have capitalized on the victory won at Antioch and to have pressed home the usual question of the Jewish missionary to the God-fearing Gentile: if you have come so far, why not go the whole way and become a proselyte (cf. Josephus, *Ant.* 20.2.4; Juvenal, *Sat.* 14.96–99)?[129] By this time Paul would probably already have crossed into Europe, and the news may not have reached him till he had established himself at Corinth. But when it did, his anger exploded. Precisely what he had feared would happen had happened: the failure to see the incompatibility of justification through faith and covenantal nomism was now threatening the heart of the gospel; as he had tried to point out to Peter at the time of the incident itself . . .[130]

A further element in Paul's concern would be that he saw his sphere of operations being threatened and eroded. The agreement that he should go to the uncircumcised

---

[127] Cf. Stuhlmacher, *Vorgeschichte,* 106–7; Hengel, "Ursprunge," 18; also idem, *Acts,* 122–23; Holtz, "Bedeutung"; Schütz, *Paul,* 151–52; Bauckham, "Barnabas," 67; Ollrog, *Paulus,* 16–17, 206, 213–14.

[128] As I believe to be most probable—see particularly Bruce, "Galatian Problems 2"; Ollrog, *Paulus,* 55–56; others listed by Kümmel, *Introduction,* 296 n. 3.

[129] Gal 5:11 makes plausible sense as a reference to Paul's circumcision of Timothy (as reported by Acts 16:3)—the point being that Paul's Galatian opponents would have failed to see the distinction between Titus and Timothy, which would have made all the difference in Paul's eyes. For an alternative interpretation of Gal 5:11 see Borgen, "Paul Preaches."

[130] Cf. Wainwright, "Where?"

and Peter to the circumcised (Gal 2:9) was being put in jeopardy. Hence the violence of his response in Galatians. Hence too the violence of his later response in 2 Cor 10–13 and Phil 3:2, when he saw unscrupulous apostles encroaching even more deeply on his area of responsibility (2 Cor 10:13–16). And though he lost at Antioch (lost both influence and backing), he probably managed to hold the line elsewhere. In particular, the fact that the churches of Galatia took part in the collection (1 Cor 16:1; cf. Acts 20:4) presumably means that the Galatian churches remained faithful to Paul—thus explaining why it was that Paul's letter to the Galatians was preserved for posterity.

We may perhaps speculate further that it was this victory of Paul in Galatia and the tremendous growth of Diaspora churches modeled on Pauline lines which showed James that a more moderate policy on table-fellowship in the mixed communities of the Diaspora was being called for by the Spirit (Acts 15:13–21, 23–29), and which in turn made possible the renewal of a more harmonious relationship between Paul and Barnabas (1 Cor 9:5–6; cf. Col 4:10–11). In other words, though Paul lost the debate at Antioch his subsequent success as missionary to the Gentiles ensured the victory of his views in the longer term.

Paul's Theology

Finally we might simply note that this exegesis of the Antioch incident helps to explain the problem posed for our understanding of Paul's theology by Sanders' exposition of Judaism's "covenantal nomism" (above, n. 9). Was not Judaism firmly rooted in God's electing and forgiving grace, so that justification through faith was a phrase that could describe the basis for Judaism as well as for the particular expression of faith in the Messiah Jesus? What was this Judaism that Paul was so polemical against? Why was he so polemical? The Antioch incident is probably the key to the solution. The Antioch incident convinced Paul that justification through faith and covenantal nomism were not two complementary emphases, but were in direct antithesis to each other. Justification through faith must determine the *whole* of life and not only the starting point of discovering (or being discovered) by God's grace. Consequently, it is precisely in Galatians that we find the strongest assertion that righteousness is a hope still to be realized (Gal 5:5).[131]

In short, the Antioch incident was probably one of the most significant events in the development of earliest Christianity. It shaped the future of Paul's missionary work, it sparked off a crucial insight which became one of the central emphases in Paul's subsequent teaching, and consequently it determined the whole character and future of that young movement which we now call Christianity.

---

[131] See further my "New Perspective."

13

JUDAISM, THE CIRCUMCISION OF GENTILES, AND APOCALYPTIC HOPE: ANOTHER LOOK AT GALATIANS 1 AND 2[1]

Paula Fredriksen   Memoriae Menachem Stern ל״ז sacrum.

Paul's letter to the Galatians offers us glimps?es of three precise moments in the unfolding of nascent Christianity: the negative, even hostile response to the kerygma on the part of the synagogue community in Damascus, within a few years of Jesus' execution (1:12–16); a major decision affirmed in Jerusalem concerning the halakhic status and, thus, obligations of Gentile members of the movement, ca. 49 (2:1–10); and the confusions occasioned by the close social interaction of Jewish and Gentile members within Antioch's ekklesia in the early 50s (2:11–15).[2] Paul does not review these moments neutrally. They serve as his ammunition in the battle for the allegiance of the Galatian churches that he wages, mid-century, against other Christian missionaries who preach a "different gospel" (1:6 and passim): that those male Gentiles who would be saved in Christ should be circumcised, that is, convert to Judaism (5:3).

Paul's position in this controversy—that salvation in Christ is through "grace" and not through "the works of the law"—has served for centuries as the fundamental

---

[1] I would like to thank Shaye J. D. Cohen, John Gager, Martin Goodman, A.-J. Levine, Daniel R. Schwartz, and Robert Tannenbaum, who endeavored to save me from the worst excesses of my own ignorance; and the members of the New Testament Seminar at Oxford University, who commented on an earlier version of this paper in June 1989.

During my stay at Oxford on that occasion, word came of Menachem Stern's assassination in Jerusalem. I never knew Professor Stern, but as so many others in the field of Christian origins, I have turned often and gratefully to his magisterial *Greek and Latin Authors on Jews and Judaism.* That work now stands as his monument. The present essay I offer, in sorrow, as a small token of my deepest appreciation and respect. יהי זכרו ברוך: May his memory be for a blessing.

[2] While the sequence of events is clear the chronology remains uncertain, partly because of Paul's own ambiguous phrasing, partly because the chronology implicit in Acts compounds the problem. See the relevant sections in Kümmel, *Introduction;* Betz, *Galatians;* Haenchen, *Acts,* 64–71; two recent revisionist chronologies, Jewett, *Chronology,* and Lüdemann, *Paul;* the older historiographical discussions of these problems in Rigaux, *Saint Paul,* and (esp. on using or not using Acts) Knox, *Chapters.* On Acts, Galatians, and the Antiochene community, see Meier's essay in Brown and Meier, *Antioch and Rome,* 28–44.

statement of the difference between Christianity and Judaism.[3] But the historian and theologian know something that the actors in this drama could not; namely, that Jesus Christ would *not* return to establish the Kingdom within the lifetime of the first (and, according to their convictions, the only) generation of his apostles.[4] Our interpretive context for Galatians is the birth of Christianity; theirs was scriptural—that is, Jewish—hopes and expectations in the face of the approaching End of Days. To understand the episodes, issues, and arguments related in Galatians, then, we must consider Paul's statements within his own religious context, first-century Judaism. More specifically, we must consider Judaism's views on Gentiles.

1. Jewish Views on Gentiles

Judaism, of course, did not have views on Gentiles; Jews did. Their encounter with other nations, across cultures and centuries, resulted in a jumble of perceptions, prejudices, optative descriptions, social arrangements, and daily accommodations that we can reconstruct from the various literary and epigraphical evidence only with difficulty. To draw from this synchronic and diachronic mass a coherent (and so somewhat artificial) picture of what early first-century Jews would have thought of Gentiles, I have applied a form of the criterion of multiple attestation: if an identifiable position can be seen to exist in several different strata of Jewish material (LXX, pseudepigrapha, Josephus, Mishnah, and synagogue prayers, for example) or in material of ethnically, historically, and religiously varying provenance (pre-mid-first-century Jewish and pagan, coincident with post-first-century Jewish, pagan, and Christian), then, I will argue, that position *probably* obtained, at least as one among

---

[3] This "distinction" between Christianity and Judaism, born of mid-first-century religious polemic, continues to control much of what passes for historical studies of Christian origins, the recent work of such scholars as Lloyd Gaston, John G. Gager, H. Räisänen, and E. P. Sanders notwithstanding. See esp. Sanders' analysis in *Paul and Palestinian Judaism,* 33–59 and 434–42, and his shorter synthetic study *Paul, the Law;* before him: G. F. Moore's fundamental essay, "Christian Writers."

[4] That Jesus expected the Kingdom at or as the conclusion to his own ministry has been an operating assumption of most New Testament scholarship since Schweitzer, *Quest.* The most recent full study is E. Sanders, *Jesus.* I attempt to reconstruct the ways in which the continuing expectation of the End and its continuing delay affected the earliest post-resurrection community and, consequently, the kerygma, in *From Jesus,* esp. 133–215. On the eschatology of Paul's communities in particular, esp. Meeks, *First Urban Christians,* 164–92. My use of the term "Christian" for this first, transitional generation is thus necessarily anachronistic: they expected none further.

Paul's own belief is vivid and clear: the form of this world is passing away, 1 Cor 7:31; and thus he can reasonably suggest that the Corinthians foreswear sexual activity, if they are able, in order to prepare themselves for the End, vv. 26–29; the end of the ages has come, 10:11; so soon is it expected that some of his congregations evidently were surprised by some Christians dying before Christ's return, 1 Thess 4:13; Paul suggests that such deaths might be punitive, therefore exceptional, 1 Cor 11:30; for Romans, see below. See also Davies, "Paul," esp. 133ff.; E. Sanders, *Paul and Palestinian Judaism,* 441f., 549.

We are accustomed to asserting that Paul expected the End within his own lifetime. What we fail to ask, however, and what needs to be accounted for, is why, mid-century, despite (a) the passage of time since Christ's resurrection and (b) the failure of the mission to Israel, Paul had remained convinced: *How, after a quarter-century delay, could he reasonably assert that "salvation is nearer to us now than when we first believed"?* (Rom 13:11). See below.

many, in the mid–first century as well. As with synoptic material, the burden of proof is on the claim to historical authenticity; and the coherence of the Jewish position that I identify with the early New Testament data will be one of my proofs. The material relevant to Jewish views of Gentiles falls into two categories, quotidian and eschatological.

Quotidian Situations

What, on the average, did the average Jew think of the average Gentile? I think that we can rely here on Paul who, even when addressing Gentiles and in some sense acting as their advocate, refers to them, quite unselfconsciously, as "sinners" (Gal 2:15). Their characteristic social and sexual sins—slander, insolence, deceit, malicious gossip, envy, heartlessness, disrespect of parents, homosexual and heterosexual fornication[5]—are the varied expression of a more fundamental spiritual error: they worship idols.[6]

Could there be such a thing, then, as a morally good Gentile? Josephus suggests that those pagans who respect Jews and Judaism are morally superior to those who do not. Later, the rabbis discussed the question (which is to say, there were dissenting views) and for the most part concurred: Gentiles could be righteous, and as such they would have a place in the world to come.[7] When the focus of rabbinic discussion shifts from "real Gentiles considered in principle" to the imagined circumstances of the *ger toshav* or *ben Noach,* the abandonment of idolatry seems to be the measure of such righteousness: it features prominently in the various lists of the Noachite commandments.[8] The rules for the *ger toshav* describe the ideal behavior of pagan

---

[5] Rom 1:18–31, said specifically of Gentile culture; cf. the similar list, Gal 5:19–21, there characterized simply as "the works of the flesh" (τὰ ἔργα τῆς σαρκός, Rom 13:12–13 (τὰ ἔργα τοῦ σκότους).

1 Cor 6:9–11 (personal, not abstract, nouns: "idolaters, adulterers, sexual perverts. . . . And such were some of you," i.e., his Corinthian Gentile Christians); cf. 1 Thess 4:4–6: Paul's Gentiles are to avoid not only *porneia* but also, within marriage, physical passion, "unlike the Gentiles who do not know God" (εἰδέναι . . . τὸ ἑαυτοῦ σκεῦος κτᾶσθαι ἐν ἁγιασμῷ . . . μὴ ἐν πάθει ἐπιθυμίας καθάπερ καὶ τὰ ἔθνη τὰ μὴ εἰδότα τὸν θεόν). Such lists of vices are common in Hellenistic Jewish literature: see Käsemann's discussion in *Commentary,* 49f.; in Paul's letters in particular, under *porneia,* E. Sanders, *Paul, the Law;* for such lists in Hellenistic philosophy, Betz, *Galatians,* 281–83.

[6] Hence a standard rabbinic designation for "Gentile," עובד כוכבים ומזלות or, abbreviated, *akkum* עכו״ם, "a worshipper of stars and planets," applied in talmudic literature to all idolators.

[7] On Josephus, S. Cohen, "Respect," *t. Sanh.* 13:2 gives the debate between two first-century rabbis, R. Eliezer and R. Joshua. See also E. Sanders's discussion, *Paul and Palestinian Judaism,* 206–12, further developed in *Jesus,* 212–21 (esp., on this debate, p. 215: "The point of the Rabbinic passage is to pair that saying [i.e., Eliezer's denial of Gentile righteousness and redemption] with the opposite one by R. Joshua, to the effect that there are righteous Gentiles who will share in the world to come").

[8] The Noachite commandments establish certain minimal standards of moral behavior enjoined on non-Jews, *b. Sanh.* 56–60. The seven traditional rules prohibit idolatry, blasphemy, violent bloodshed, sexual sins, theft, and eating from a living animal, and enjoin the formation of law courts, *b. Sanh.* 56b. Cf. *ʿAbod. Zar.* 8(9):4–6; *Jub.* 7:20ff.; cf. James' ruling in Acts 15:20. See Robert Tannenbaum's comments in Reynolds and Tannenbaum, *Jews and Godfearers,* 48, 59; Goodman, "Proselytising," esp. 182; S. Cohen, "Crossing," esp. 22. Novak provides a comprehensive discussion, *Image.*

residents in Palestine, to be observed or enforced (according to later rabbinic traditions) when the Jubilee year would be kept, that is, in a period of Jewish sovereignty.[9] Such "legislation," drawn up as it was after the wars with Rome, was thus in many ways a form of wistful thinking.

In real life, Gentiles had another option: they could convert. Conversion to Judaism in antiquity was a common enough phenomenon to provide the material for sarcastic or satirical remarks—Horace's on modes of persuasion; Juvenal's on the effects of parents' bad habits on children.[10] Rabbinic law specified as halakhic requirements for those who would join Israel instruction in the *mitsvot* and accompanying ritual acts: immersion; while the Temple stood, sacrifice; and finally, for the male convert, *milah*, circumcision.[11] Circumcision is likewise singled out in Hellenistic Jewish, pagan, and Christian literature as the premier mark of the Jew, and specifically of the convert to Judaism. According to both Juvenal and Josephus, the decision to receive circumcision is what distinguishes, quite precisely, the sympathizer from the convert.[12]

Philo speaks warmly of the proselyte: he is to be welcomed and esteemed as one who spiritually recapitulated the journey of Abraham, quitting his idolatrous homeland and traveling "to a better home . . . , to the worship of the one truly existing God."[13] The "true proselyte" is included as part of the community in the thirteenth

---

[9] *b. ʿArak.* 293; discussion in Tannenbaum, *Godfearers,* 48; Moore, *Judaism,* 1.339–40; Schürer, *History,* 3.171–72.

[10] Horace, *Sat.* 1.4.142–143 ("like the Jews we shall force you to join our crowd," *cogemus in hanc concedere turbam*). Nolland has argued that this jibe targets Jewish political, not religious, persuasion ("Proselytism"). Juvenal complains that the sons of Judaizing fathers actually convert fully to Judaism, *Sat.* 14.96–106 (n. 12 below). See too Gager, *Origins,* esp. 56ff.; Schürer, *History,* 3.162–65, 69; also the material cited in Stern, *Authors,* below, n. 12.

[11] *Sipre* 108 on Num 15:14; *m. Ker.* 2:1; *b. Ker.* 93; *b. Yebam.* 46a–b. Circumcision stands last in my list for rhetorical reasons; in reality, it precedes immersion. That conversion requires acceptance of the whole Torah is frequently emphasized, Schürer, *History,* 3.175 n. 93, for many references; so too Paul, Gal 5:3, "every man who receives circumcision [i.e., converts to Judaism] . . . is bound to keep the whole Law." Further primary references in Schürer, *History,* 3.170 n. 78 (Mishnah). On the phenomenon of conversion to Judaism in antiquity, the older discussions in Moore, *Judaism* 1.331ff.; Bamberger, *Proselytism;* Braude, *Jewish Proselytism;* Kuhn, "προσήλυτος"; more recently Gager, *Origins,* 55–66; Schiffman, "At the Crossroads." See too Collins, "Symbol"; S. Cohen, "Crossing"; Goodman, "Who Was a Jew?" 4–19 and notes; idem, "Proselytising." The proposal that some proselytes in some communities need not have been circumcised, put forth most recently by McEleney ("Conversion") and Borgen ("Observations," esp. 85–89) has been sufficiently refuted by Schiffman ("At the Crossroads") and Nolland ("Uncircumcised Proselytes?"). The question of female conversions is more problematic. S. Cohen has pointed out that non-rabbinic materials seem to assume the usual method to be marriage to a Jewish male, "Origins," esp. 25–29.

[12] "*Quidam sortiti metuentem sabbata patrem . . . mox et praeputia ponunt; . . . Iudaicum ediscunt et servant ac metuunt ius,*" Juvenal, *Sat.* 14.96, 99, 101; Josephus, on Izates' receiving circumcision as the final stage in his conversion, *Ant.* 20.38–42 (see too Nolland's analysis, "Uncircumcised Proselytes?"); on circumcision for conversion in other cases, *Ant.* 11.285; 13.257–258, 318–319; 15.254–255; 20.139, 145–146. See esp. S. Cohen, "Respect," 419ff., and "Crossing," 25ff. On the Christian perception of circumcision as the prime identifier of the Jew, more above; for the non-Christian outsider's perspective, the material collected in Stern, *Authors,* vol. 1, nos. 55, 56, 81, 115 (37) (Strabo wrongly construes female circumcision, i.e., excision, as well), 117 (same author, same mistake), 124 (again), 129, 146, 176, 190, 193–195, 240, 241, 243, 245; vol. 2, no. 281 (Tacitus, who comments on circumcision both of the born Jew and of the convert).

[13] Philo, *Virt.* 102–104; also, e.g., *Spec.* 1.52–54.

benediction of the chief synagogue prayer, the *Amidah* or *Shemoneh Esreh*.[14] The convert had certain legal disabilities with respect to marriage (in particular, with priestly families), but in most other respects was integrated and integrable. As such, he or she becomes irrelevant to this discussion, because the Gentile who converts is no longer a Gentile, but a Jew.[15]

Some scholars take this well-attested fact of conversion to Judaism together with other data to mean that Jews actively sponsored actual *missions* to Gentiles: Judaism, they contend, was a missionary religion. According to this line of reasoning, missions are implied by ancient demography: the Jewish population increased "vastly" from the time of the Babylonian Exile to the early Imperial period; only aggressive proselytism can account for such an increase. The significant body of Hellenistic Jewish writings supports this view: it is the literary remains of an active campaign to attract Gentiles to Judaism. The effectiveness of this campaign in turn accounts for ancient pagan anti-Semitism: pagans resented Judaism's success. And finally Matt 23:15 states what this evidence otherwise strongly implies: Jews would cross sea and land to make a single convert. They actively proselytized Gentiles.[16]

But receiving and encouraging converts is one thing; actively soliciting them is another. Do data attesting to Jewish influence or, conversely, to Jews' awareness of their wider cultural environment, require missionary enterprise as explanation? To address the data in the sequence in which I presented them above: *(a)* A supposed increase in the Jewish population over more than half a millennium should count neither as a phenomenon that needs to be explained by an appeal to massive conversions (and so, *qal vahomer*, to missions), nor as a datum supporting the missionary hypothesis. We simply cannot *know* enough about ancient populations to make the argument.[17]

---

[14] "Over the righteous and over the pious; and over the elders of thy people of the house of Israel; and over the remnant of their Torah scholars; and over the righteous proselytes; and over us [i.e., the praying community] may thy mercy shower down, Lord our God." Text from Schürer, *History*, 2.457; for the addition of proselytes to the benediction, *Meg.* 17b.

[15] See Schürer, *History*, 3.175 and nn. 93–101, for rabbinic discussion of rights, duties, and disabilities of the convert who, upon the completion of immersion (since sacrifice was no longer possible) "is in all respects like an Israelite," *b. Yebam.* 47b. Similarly Philo, *Virt.* 103; Josephus, *Ag. Ap.* 2.210, 261; also *J.W.* 2.388, where Agrippa II refers to the princes of Adiabene as ὁμόφυλοι; after Achior converts and is circumcised he is considered to be "joined to the house of Israel," Jdt 14:10; cf. Justin Martyr's lament that converts to Judaism strive in all ways to be like "native" Jews, *Dial.* 122. Isa 56:3–7 asserts that those who have joined Israel will be gathered in with them at the End. more on this prophetic verse and its relation to conversion in antiquity below, n. 38.

[16] The issue is not whether Jews encouraged admiration of their religious cult and culture—clearly they did—but whether this is tantamount to "mission" as the word is normally understood and used, implying clear ideological commitments to religious advertising and solicitation, self-conscious organization—the image drawn, in other words, from later Christian practice. Besides the older studies of Jewish proselytism cited above, also Hahn, *Mission*, esp. 21–25; the more recent work of Georgi, *Opponents*, 83–228; S. Cohen, "Conversion"; Feldman, "Jewish Proselytism" (I thank Professor Feldman for allowing me to consult and cite his manuscript). Jeremias states: "This was a wholly new phenomenon: Judaism was the first great missionary religion to make its appearance in the Mediterranean world" (*Jesus' Promise*, 11). He cites in support Moore, *Judaism*, 1.323; but Moore's view is more nuanced, see n. 24 below.

[17] See Georgi, *Opponents*, 83ff. and nn. 4–15. Reliance on so-called demographical data for this period is extremely hazardous. Harnack *(Mission)*, Juster *(Les juifs)*, and Baron *(History)* are the *loci classici* for this data; see now Schürer, *History*, 2.1–19, on Palestine; 3.3–86, on the Diaspora.

(b) Hellenistic Jewish literature of the sort that argues the superiority of Judaism to idolatry, of Jewish religious and ethical notions to their pagan counterparts,[18] reveals only one voice in the sparring of competitive middle-brow *salon* cultures. It aims to inspire respect and admiration for Judaism, presented as an ethical philosophy; its intellectual and literary pretensions indicate how small, relatively, the audience for such writings must have been.[19] *(c)* As for pagan "anti-Semitism," the supposed response of Gentile culture to Jewish missionary success, most of the writers cited in support of such are culturally xenophobic: passages satirizing circumcision and abstention from pork target not Jews or Jewish customs *per se,* but anything perceived as foreign, hence threatening.[20] Finally, *(d)* Matthew's Pharisees evidently do seek converts. But they do so in a passage of highly charged rhetoric, within a document whose social situation is difficult to reconstruct. Whether real Pharisees—or, for that matter, Jews generally—sought converts is a question that Matthew cannot help us with.[21]

---

[18] Which are usually condemned (hence the vice lists, mentioned earlier) or, at best, damned with what amounts to faint praise; i.e., where the Greeks got something right (philosophical monotheism, for example) they relied on Jewish learning and revelation. Hence the traditions that a Greek translation of Jewish scriptures existed before Ptolemy Philadelphus (285–246 B.C.E.) commissioned the LXX: Homer, Hesiod, Pythagoras, Socrates, and Plato had obviously had some access to Torah! (Aristobolus, a 3rd–2nd century B.C.E. Jewish writer, preserved in Eusebius, *Praep. ev.* 13.12.1–16). Sometimes pagans even conceded the point: "What is Plato," asked Numenius of Apamaea, "but Moses speaking Greek?" (*apud* Clement of Alexandria, *Strom.* 1.72.4).

[19] See too Tannenbaum's remarks, *Jews and Godfearers,* 60. Put differently: *Joseph and Aseneth* does indeed "argue" that conversion to Judaism is preferable to continuing in idolatry. But does that make it a "missionary" tract? Is persuasion by one literate minority directed toward another tantamount to "missionary activity"? Only in a limited sense. But scholars who maintain the existence of Jewish missions think in terms of vast numbers. To the degree that this literature had a target, that target would have been individuals rather than populations; and its primary intended audience might have been internal, its goal to affirm Jewish identity in the Diaspora. See, e.g., Tcherikover, "Jewish Apologetic Literature"; for the opposite argument, e.g., Feldman, "Jew and Gentile," 314–16 and the literature cited nn. 43–54. See too the remarks introducing "Jewish Literature composed in Greek" in Schürer, *History,* 3.470ff.; also 160, persuading Gentiles to the fundamental viewpoints of Judaism (esp. regarding ethical life) is not tantamount to converting them to Torah.

[20] Cf. Seneca's remarks, *Ep.* 108.22 (Stern, *Authors,* vol. 1, no. 189); Tacitus, *Ann.* 2.2, 85 mentions a ban on Jewish and Egyptian practices; on the cultural xenophobia of Roman literati, Gager, *Origins,* part 2.

[21] See now esp. A.-J. Levine, "Traversing." Levine conjectures that such activity was an *ad hoc* response to preceding missions by Matthew's group. Similarly Martin Goodman, on third-century rabbinic statements that seem to favor actual missions: "One new factor that might have encouraged this novel attitude is that the rabbis in Palestine were by now aware of the success of some Christians in winning pagans. . . . [T]he effectiveness of the Church's methods may have gradually changed the religious assumptions of some non-Christians in the ancient world" ("Proselytising," 185).
    Pagan evidence on Jewish proselytism is no easier to assess. Valerius Maximus suggests that Jews were expelled from Rome in 139 B.C.E. who "*Romanis tradere sacra sua conati sunt*" or "*qui Sabazi Iovis cultu Romanos inficere mores conati erunt*": Was this effective influence or active missionizing? Astrologers were likewise expelled (Stern, *Authors,* vol. 1, nos. 147 a–b; also discussion, 359f.). These passages are preserved in two epitomes drawn up some 500 years after Valerius' lifetime, well into the Christian era. Dio Cassius also says that Tiberius expelled the Jews from Rome in 19 C.E. because they were converting many Romans (τῶν τε Ἰουδαίων πολλῶν ἐς τὴν Ῥώμων συνελθόντων καὶ συχνοὺς τῶν ἐπιχωρίων ἐς τὰ σφέτερα ἔθη μεθιστάντων, τοὺς πλείονας ἐξήλασεν (*Hist.* 57.18.5a [Stern, *Authors,* vol. 1, no. 419]). They may have been; but, again, receiving converts is not necessarily synonymous with missionizing.

If the external evidence for Jewish missions is unobliging, the internal evidence is no less so. "One of the great puzzles of the proselytizing movement is how to explain the existence of a mass movement when we do not know the name of a single Jewish missionary, unless, of course, we except Paul."[22] Beyond not knowing *who* missionized, we do not know *how*. We might expect, at least from the rabbis—those Jews of antiquity evidently most concerned about categories, boundary-formation, and halakhic precision—prescriptions for and legal discussion of correct missionary practice, if missionizing were a normal and widespread Jewish activity: in fact, we find nothing. Rather, the rabbis' (perhaps idealized) accounts describe the procedure to follow once a Gentile requests conversion: by implication, the initiative is the Gentile's, not the Jewish community's.[23] Further, the earlier Jewish evidence both of Josephus on the royal house of Adiabene and the broader data of the earlier New Testament writings evinces the improvisational character of "Jewish outreach." If conversions were the result of missions—as opposed to the freelance, amateur, non-institutionally based efforts of individuals or the side-effect of unstructured contact through Diaspora synagogue communities[24]—we should be able to have a better sense of how such Jewish missions proceeded. Again, on the evidence of Paul's letters, no one, when faced with a missionary situation (which, according to this line of argument, would have to be accounted for) apparently knew quite what to do. And finally, to mention here a point that I will develop shortly, Judaism had little reason, ideologically or theologically, to solicit converts.

Between these two extremes of fornicating idolaters and full converts we find a gradient of Gentile affiliation with Judaism, especially in the Diaspora. Synagogues drew interested outsiders. Some, as the Greek Magical Papyri perhaps show, might attend out of a sort of professional interest, in order to make the acquaintance of a powerful god in whose name they could command demons.[25] Others, as

---

[22] Feldman, *Jew and Gentile*, 324, who goes on to tackle the problem. I *would* except Paul: he is Jewish, his gospel is quintessentially Jewish; but it is his anonymous competition, the circumcisers, who preach Judaism to the Gentiles, not he; see below.

[23] *B. Yebam.* 47a: "When a man comes in these times seeking to convert, he is asked, 'What is your motive? Do you not know that Israel is now afflicted, distressed, downtrodden . . . ?' If he answers, 'I know,' they accept him at once."

[24] So Moore: "[T]he belief in the future universality of the true religion, the coming of an age when 'the Lord shall be king over all the earth,' led to efforts to convert the Gentiles . . . and made Judaism the first great missionary religion of the Mediterranean world. *When it is called a missionary religion, the phrase must, however, be understood with a difference. The Jews did not send out missionaries.* . . . They were themselves settled by thousands in all the great centers and in innumerable smaller cities. . . . Their religious influence was exerted chiefly through the synagogues, which they set up for themselves, but which were open to all whom interest or curiosity drew to their services" (*Judaism*, 1.323–24, emphasis mine). This is the point that Jeremias either missed or misunderstood, above, n. 16. Izates' wives evidently become sympathizers through Ananias while at Charax; Helena's contact is unnamed; once back in Adiabene, Izates is urged to convert through contact with an itinerant Jewish merchant, Josephus, *Ant.* 20.34–35, 49–53.

[25] "Adjure demons by the god of the Hebrews . . . [and say]: 'I adjure thee by him who appeared to Israel in the pillar of light and in the cloud by day [cf. Exod. 13:21–22]. . . . I adjure thee by the seal which Solomon laid upon the tongue of Jeremiah [sic] and he spoke,' " *Paris Magical Papyri* 2.3007–85. The anonymous pagan author (third century C.E.) may well have copied out his charm from a Jewish magical handbook; but the confusions in biblical chronology incline me to suspect

Philo mentions in his *De vita Mosis,* were drawn by the public Jewish festivals, like the one held on Pharos near Alexandria to celebrate the translation into Greek of the Bible.[26] But others, well attested in literary and epigraphic data, formed an identifiable, if liminal, group of adherents. Their ancient designations vary: φοβούμενοι, σεβόμενοι or, in inscriptions, θεοσεβεῖς; in Latin, *metuentes;* in Hebrew, שמי יראי, "fearers of heaven." I am speaking of course, of the "God-fearers."[27]

Who are the God-fearers? They are Gentiles, but not proselytes; if they were proselytes, they would then be Jews. To think of them as "semi-proselytes" is unhelpful: the word suggests some sort of arrested development or objective impediment. These people were voluntary Judaizers. According to both Philo and especially Josephus, they could be found in significant numbers in any urban center where a Jewish community lived.[28] Some of these people assume—again I emphasize voluntarily—certain Jewish religious practices: ancient data speak most often of dietary restrictions, the Sabbath, and the festivals.[29] Since they are not Jews, their observance of Jewish law is not regulated by Jewish law: halakhically, they are literally anomalous.[30]

The Aphrodisias inscription presents further evidence of the God-fearers' anomaly, their Law-freeness.[31] This stone lists the names of Jews and God-fearers—contributors, perhaps, to a fund-drive for the establishment of a soup kitchen for the poor.

---

that he relied on impressions and memories from scriptural readings in a synagogue service. See now on these texts Gager, *Curse Tablets.*

[26] "Therefore, even to the present day, there is held every year a feast and general assembly on the island of Pharos, whither not only Jews but multitudes of others cross the water, both to do honor to the place where the light of that version [sc. LXX] first shone out, and to thank God for the good gift so old yet ever new," Philo, *Mos.* 2.41.

[27] For an overview of the current interpretative debate, see the articles in *BAR* 12 (1986); for further discussion and bibliography, Schürer, *History,* 3.150–76, esp. 165ff.; also the lengthy note to Juvenal in Stern, *Authors,* vol. 2, nos. 103–107.

[28] E.g., Josephus, *Ant.* 14.7.2: σεβόμενοι contribute to the Temple; *J.W.* 2.18.2, Ἰουδαΐζοντες can be found in every city in Syria; 7.3.3, Greeks attend synagogue services in Antioch and after their fashion become part of the community. Josephus, *Ag. Ap.* 2.39, is ambiguous: Josephus might refer either to adherence (hence God-fearers) or conversion (hence proselytes) when he speaks of the spread of Jewish observances in Gentile populations. See Schürer, *History,* 3.166–68, for review of this and the inscriptional data. Luke, in Acts, also refers to the ubiquity of God-fearers, 10:2, 22; 13:16, 26, 43, 50; 16:14; 17:4, 17; 18:7. Kraabel offers an astute analysis of the God-fearers' function in Acts as a theological middle term between Judaism and Christianity, but he concludes from this observation that they had no existence in fact ("Disappearance"). In light of all the other data, reports of the God-fearers' demise seem greatly exaggerated.

[29] Josephus, *Ag. Ap.* 2.39, mentions Sabbath, food laws, and festivals; similarly Tertullian, *Nat.* 1.13.3–4; Juvenal, *Sat.* 14.96–106.

[30] "The purpose of halakah is to determine whether or not a biblical passage does in fact constitute a commandment, if there can be any doubt; to establish the application of a biblical commandment; to define its precise scope and meaning; and to determine precisely what must be done in order to fulfill it," E. Sanders, *Paul and Palestinian Judaism,* 76. We should not be surprised, then, at the absence of halakah (whether rabbinic or other) on such topics as the status of God-fearers within the synagogue community, on the one hand, or on the way Gentiles would enter into the Kingdom of God, on the other. We find, rather, *ad hoc* social arrangements in the first instance, and opinions (bad Gentiles destroyed; other Gentiles liberated from the blindness of idolatry, and so participants) in the second: neither constitutes an halakhic issue. See below, n. 45.

[31] For the text of this inscription, Reynolds and Tannenbaum, *Jews and Godfearers,* 5–7; Tannenbaum's translation of the first eight lines, p. 41; for a survey of other pertinent inscriptions, 25ff.

Among the Jews are given three proselytes, who have assumed Jewish names; and, listed separately, fifty θεοσεβεῖς, that is, participating Gentiles. Two of these appear as well among the names of those belonging to the δεκανία (probably the prayer quorum); nine others are identified as βουλευταί, members of the town council.[32] This last is most intriguing, since it indicates that Gentiles whose status in the larger urban community necessitated their public idolatry (their office would require their presence at sacrifices to the gods of the πόλις and the empire) could at the same time be active (if not, perhaps, fully integrated) participants in the synagogue community and worshippers, after their fashion, of the Jewish God.

Scattered literary evidence supports this view. The centurion Cornelius, for example, described as a "fearer of God" who prays constantly and supports the poor, whether fictive or not, would have been understood by Luke's ancient audience to be a public pagan too, since as an officer he would have participated in his unit's military cultus.[33] Pagan and later Christian sources speak mockingly of Gentiles who worship in the synagogue and at traditional altars both. Tertullian in North Africa and, centuries later, Cyril of Alexandria comment bitterly on the inconsistency of such practices; while Commodian—who can be placed reasonably in either the third century or the fifth—criticizes Jews for tolerating this behavior.[34] The fogginess of rabbinical discussion of God-fearers reinforces this impression: their association with the synagogue was voluntary, their status ambiguous (since, as Gentiles—and unlike proselytes—they were not subject to the strictures of Torah), their religious allegiances various.[35] Despite the Jewish horror of idolatry, Jews evidently made room in the synagogue for those Gentiles who, like Naaman, worshipped YHWH as a god among gods.

---

[32] On the δεκανία, ibid., 28–38; the βουλευταί, 54ff.

[33] Acts 10:1–4, 22, 31; observed by Reynolds and Tannenbaum, *Jews and God-fearers*, 63. So too with Luke's centurion at Capernaum who "loves Israel" and builds a synagogue (Luke 7:5; cf. Matt 8:5–13).

[34] Tertullian, *Nat.* 1.13.3–4: Some pagans keep the sabbath and Passover, yet continue to worship at traditional altars; Cyril, *Ador.* 3.92.3. Men in Phonecia and Palestine, calling themselves θεοσεβεῖς follow consistently neither Jewish nor Greek religious custom. Commodian mocks those who "live between both ways": they rush from synagogue to pagan shrine, "*medius Iudaeus*" (*Instr.* 37.1). He adds, disapprovingly, that the Jews tolerate such behavior ("*Dicant illi tibi si iussum est deos adorare*," 37.10). On dating Commodian, Brisson, *Autonomisme,* 378–410.

Gentiles evidently continued in their Judaizing ways even after conversion to Christianity: Ign. *Magn.* 10.3 ("It is foolish to talk of Jesus Christ and to Judaize"); Ign. *Phld.* 6.1 ("If anyone should undertake to interpret Judaism to you, do not listen to him. For it is better to hear of Christianity from a man who has been circumcised [= a Jew or a convert to Judaism, become Christian] than to hear of Judaism from someone uncircumcised [= a pagan Judaizer]"). Chrysostom, in 386 C.E., delivered eight bitter sermons during the autumn High Holidays against those members of his church (πολλοί, as he says frequently) who attend synagogues and observe Jewish festivals and fasts. See discussion in Meeks and Wilken, *Jews and Christians,* 25–36; also 85–126 for translations of Sermons 1 and 8. Justin, more than two centuries earlier, discusses a number of types of Gentile Christian affiliation with Judaism, up to and including full conversion to τὴν ἔννομον πολιτείαν, asserting that even such proselytes will be saved as long as they believe fully in Christ. He frankly admits, however, that other Christians do not share his liberal views, *Dial.* 46–47.

[35] "Halakically they're easy to define. They're Gentiles. Period" (Shaye Cohen, personal correspondence). But there are Gentiles and Gentiles, and obviously a pious sympathizer would raise questions for his host community that a totally unaffiliated Gentile would not. See Martin Goodman's nuanced speculations on this issue, "Nerva," 40–44; "Who Was a Jew?"

Idolatrous pagans condemned in the abstract, ideally forbidden residence in the Holy Land, welcomed fully as Jews should they decide to convert, tolerated (and evidently solicited for *tsedakah*) should they stay in the synagogue's penumbra as affiliated outsiders. Let us consider Gentiles now in a different situation: Can they, ultimately, be redeemed? What happens to Gentiles at the End?

The idiom of Jewish restoration theology draws on the images and experience of the Babylonian captivity. "Redemption" is imaged concretely: not only from sin, and from evil, but from exile. The twelve tribes are restored, the people gathered back to the Land, the Temple and Jerusalem are renewed and made splendid, the Davidic monarchy restored: God's Kingdom is established.[36] What place, if any, do Gentiles have in such a kingdom?

We can cluster the material around two poles.[37] At the negative extreme, the nations are destroyed, defeated, or in some way subjected to Israel. Foreign monarchs lick the dust at Israel's feet (Isa 49:23; cf. Mic 7:16f.); Gentile cities are devastated, or repopulated by Israel (Isa 54:3; Zeph 2:1–3:8); God destroys the nations and their idols (Mic 5:9, 15). Many passages from the prophets and the pseudepigrapha bespeaking such destruction,[38] however, are followed closely by others describing the Gentiles' eschatological inclusion. Perhaps, then, such texts envisage the destruction of the unrighteous Gentiles alone, not of all Gentiles *tout court;* and *T. Mos.* 10:7 speaks of the destruction only of idols, not idolaters.

At the positive extreme, the nations participate in Israel's redemption. The nations will stream to Jerusalem and worship the God of Jacob together with Israel (Isa 2:2–4//Mic 4:1ff.); on God's mountain (i.e., the Temple mount), they will eat together the feast that God has prepared for them (Isa 25:6). As the Jews leave the lands of their dispersion, Gentiles will accompany them: "In those days ten men from the nations of every tongue shall take hold of the robe of a Jew, saying, 'Let us go with you, for we have heard that God is with you'" (Zech 8:23). Or the nations carry the exiles back to Jerusalem themselves (*Pss. Sol.*

---

[36] On the themes of Jewish restoration theology, E. Sanders, *Jesus,* 77–119, 222–41 (a reconstruction of Jesus' views within this traditional perspective); Schürer, *History,* 2.514–46; Fredriksen, *From Jesus,* 77–86.

[37] For other florilegia on the same theme, but organized differently, E. Sanders, *Jesus,* 214; Donaldson, " 'Curse of the Law,' " 110, nn. 43–50; Jeremias, *Jesus' Promise,* 46–75.

[38] Sir 36:1–10, a malediction against the nations ("Rouse thy anger and pour out thy wrath; destroy the adversary and wipe out the enemy"); *1 En.* 91:9, "All that which is with the heathen shall be surrendered; the towers shall be inflamed with fire and be removed from the whole earth. They shall be thrown into the judgment of fire, and perish in wrath . . ."; Bar 4:25, 31–35, "Your enemy has overtaken you, but you will soon see their destruction and will tread upon their necks. . . . Wretched will be those who afflicted you . . . fire will come upon her [the enemy city] for many days"; *Sib. Or.* 3:517–540, the nations will see themselves subject to destruction, outrages, and slavery; 3:669, God will destroy the kings ringed round Jerusalem; 3:761, God will burn with fire a race of grievous men; *Jub.* 23:30, "The Lord's servants . . . will drive out their enemies . . . and they will see all of their judgments and all of their curses among their enemies"; *Pss. Sol.* 7:30, the Messiah "will have gentile nations serving under his yoke"; 1QM 12:10–13, "Rejoice, all you cities of Judah; keep your gates ever open, that the hosts of the nations may be brought in. Their kings shall serve you; and all your oppressors shall bow down before you." Biblical passages and citations from the apocrypha are from the RSV; pseudepigrapha, from *OTP.*

7:31–41). Burying their idols, "all people shall direct their sight to the path of uprightness" (*1 En.* 91:14).

Who are these redeemed Gentiles? Are they the ones who had already *converted* to Judaism before the Kingdom came? No: such a Gentile, though a special sort of Jew (that is, a proselyte) would already "count" as a Jew. To say that a proselyte is not in the category of "Gentiles redeemed at the End" is thus a tautology. I take this to be the point of a passage often cited in support of an End-time mission to convert Gentiles, Isa 56:3–7. Given the present force of the subordinate verbs and the future action of the main verb ("those who join . . . I will save"), these verses are better construed as speaking to the place of those *quondam* Gentiles— be they foreigners or even eunuchs—who have already converted at some indeterminate time before the End. God assures them that they will be gathered together with the native-born when final redemption comes. "The foreigner who *has joined* himself to the Lord . . . the eunuchs who *keep my sabbaths and hold fast my covenant* . . . I **will** *give* them an everlasting name; . . . the foreigners who *join*, . . . every one who *keeps the sabbath and holds fast my covenant*, these I **will** *bring* to my holy mountain."[39] . . .

Are the saved Gentiles the ones R. Joshua would have had in mind, when he spoke of the righteous of the nations having a share in the world to come (*b. Sanh.* 13:2)? I think not. That context implies that Gentiles who are righteous *in this present world*, that is, who eschew the worship of idols *now*, will be redeemed *then*, in the future, at the End. The passages in the prophets, Tobit, Sirach, and the pseudepigrapha, however, imply a different sequence of events: at the End, the Lord of Israel reveals himself in glory, and it is that revelation which prompts the nations to bury their idols.[40] So too, as

---

[39] . . . ὁ ἀλλογενὴς ὁ <u>προσκείμενος</u> πρὸς κύριον . . . [αὐτοῖς] ὄνομα αἰώνιον δώσω . . . καὶ τοῖς ἀλλογενέσι τοῖς <u>προσκειμένοις</u> κυρίῳ δουλεύειν αὐτῷ . . . καὶ πάντας τοὺς <u>φυλασ-</u> <u>σομένους</u> τὰ σάββατά μου . . . καὶ <u>ἀντεχομένους</u> τῆς διαθήκης μου, εἰσάξω αὐτοὺς εἰς τὸ ὄρος τὸ ἅγιόν μου.

בן־הנכר הנלוה אל־יהוה . . .
שם עולם אתן־לו . . .
ובני הנכר הנלוים על־יהוה לשרתו
ולאהבה את־שם יהוה
להיות לו לעבדים
כל־שמר שבת מחללו
ומחזיקים בבריתי:
והביאותים אל־הר קדשי . . .

What the "historical" Isaiah might have intended by these verses I do not know. My point is that an ancient reader whether of the LXX or the Masoretic Text would have little reason to think (as New Testament scholars, to account for Paul's activity, frequently assert they did) that Isaiah here prophesies an End-time mission to the Gentiles.

[40] Isa 45:22, "Turn to me and be saved, all the ends of the earth! For I am God, there is no other"; 49:6 (and elsewhere), "I will give you [Israel] as a light to the nations, that my salvation may reach to the ends of the earth"; Zeph 3:9, "At that time I will change the speech of the peoples to a pure speech, that all of them may call upon the name of the Lord and serve him with one accord"; Zech 8:20–22, "Peoples shall yet come, even the inhabitants of many cities. The inhabitants of one

I construe it, the second paragraph of the synagogue prayer, the *Alenu:* first God's final revelation, and then the repudiation of images.[41]

Do all Gentiles then become Jews at this point? Is this not conversion, if these "eschatological Gentiles" enter the Kingdom and turn to Israel's God? Again, I think not. All the material we have reviewed—biblical and extra-biblical Jewish writings, Josephus, the rabbis, and outsiders whether pagan or Christian—emphasize circumcision as the *sine qua non* of becoming a Jew.[42]

But the (male) Gentiles' *eschatological* acknowledgement of God and consequent repudiation of idols would not (theoretically) alter their halakhic status, which can change only through conversion, hence circumcision. Zechariah 14 does envisage, peculiarly, these redeemed Gentiles' keeping Sukkot: but I have found no tradition anticipating universal ברית מילה. Given the precise focus on circumcision as the mark of the (male) convert, one would expect this. But Jews did not expect this, and so no such tradition exists.[43] They looked forward, rather, to the nations' spiritual, and hence moral, "conversion": Gentiles at the End *turn from* idolatry (and the sins associated with it) and *turn to* the living God. *But moral conversion is not halakhic conversion;* and non-idolatrous Gentiles are Gentiles nonetheless. When God establishes his Kingdom, then, these two groups will together constitute "his people": Israel, redeemed from exile, and the Gentiles, redeemed

---

shall go to another, saying, 'Let us go at once to entreat the favor of the Lord of hosts; I am going.' Many peoples and strong nations shall come to seek the Lord of hosts in Jerusalem . . ."; Tob 13:11, "Many nations will come from afar to the name of the Lord God, bearing gifts in their hands"; 14:5–6, the Temple will be rebuilt forever, "Then all the Gentiles will turn in fear to the Lord God in truth, and will bury their idols"; Sir 36:11–17 calls upon God to make good on his promises through the prophets, to restore Jerusalem and his people so that "all who are on the earth will know that you are the Lord, the God of the ages"; *Sib. Or.* 3:616, after the coming of the Great King, the nations will "bend a white knee . . . to God"; 3:715–724, the nations will send votive offerings to the Temple and process there, they will renounce their idols; 3:772, "From every land they will bring incense and gifts to the house of the great God."

[41] "We hope, therefore, Lord our God, soon to behold thy majestic glory, when the abominations shall be removed from the earth and the false gods exterminated; when the world shall be perfected under the reign of the Almighty, and all humankind (כל בני בשר) will call upon thy name. . . . May they bend knee and prostrate themselves and give honor to thy glorious name. May they all accept the yoke of thy kingdom, and do thou reign over them speedily and forever . . ." *(Siddur hashalem).*

[42] Again, the situation of female converts is harder to reconstruct, since the ritual and social acts, whatever they would have been at whatever period and place, simply do not receive the attention that circumcision does in these various texts. The much-misinterpreted episode concerning Izates, however, does conform to the principle I sketch here: Josephus does not depict Ananias "allowing" Izates to be a convert without circumcision, while Eleazar insists on it; rather, Ananias welcomes Izates as a sympathizer precisely to preserve the king's status as a Gentile, and thus lessen the risk of provoking a popular incident *(Ant.* 20.38–41); Eleazar tells him that, if he would be a Jew, he must convert, i.e., be circumcised (20.42–47).

[43] *Retractandum est:* "The tradition Paul's opponents criticize him for violating is the same one he invokes to legitimate his position: Jewish missionary practice in the face of the coming End of Days," Fredriksen, "Paul and Augustine," 29f. I knew such a tradition, because I had studied early Judaism at university; Paul and his co-religionists, deprived of my educational advantages, did not. E. Sanders errs similarly: in Paul's view, he says, the church was "not established by admitting Gentiles to Israel according to the flesh, *as standard Jewish eschatological expectation would have it*" *(Paul, the Law,* 178, my emphasis; cf. 198).

from idolatry.[44] Gentiles are saved as Gentiles: they do not, eschatologically, become Jews.

I want to emphasize this last point, because as far as I can see it has been universally missed. From the notes at the bottom of the Oxford RSV to virtually every secondary discussion in books or journal articles, interpreters routinely slip from seeing the eschatological *inclusion* of Gentiles as meaning eschatological *conversion*.[45] This is a category error. Saved Gentiles are *not* Jews. They are Gentiles; they just do not worship idols any more. The speculations in *b. Yebamot* 24b that in the Messianic age Israel will not receive proselytes shows how unselfconsciously those rabbis assumed that Gentiles, too, would be present in the Kingdom; because, of course, only a Gentile could be a candidate for conversion.

To sum up the two main points of this section: First, with respect to the quotidian situation of God-fearers in Diaspora synagogues, these Gentiles were free to observe as much or as little of Jewish custom as they chose; but, more specifically, they were not expected to abandon their ancestral observances if they chose to assume certain Jewish ones.[46] No consistent set of requirements was demanded of them; they could (and evidently some did) worship idols as well as the God of Israel, and yet still form a group within some synagogue communities. Their affiliation was completely voluntary; in Nock's terms, they were adherents, not converts.[47] Eschatological Gentiles, on the other hand, those who would gain admission to the Kingdom once it was established, would enter as Gentiles. They would worship and eat together with Israel, in Jerusalem, at the Temple. The God they worship, the God of Israel, will have redeemed them from the error of idolatry: he will have saved them—to phrase this in slightly different idiom—graciously, apart from the works of the Law.

How do these two interpretive facts help us to understand the events Paul describes in the first two chapters of Galatians?

---

[44] Thus Zech 2:11 concerns eschatological inclusion, not conversion: "Many nations [ἔθνη; גוים] shall join themselves to the Lord on that day, and they shall be my people [λαός; עם]." Isa 66:19, 21 might be taken to imply some sort of eschatological mission to the nations, and their subsequent conversion, but the passage is difficult: "I shall send survivors to the nations . . . and they shall declare my glory to the nations. . . ." The nations will carry the exiles back to Jerusalem, and "some of them also I will take for priests and Levites." The last verse in particular is extraordinary, since in the normal course of events for native Jews the status of *cohen* or *levi* is hereditary.

[45] E.g., the RSV notes on Zeph 3:8–13 and Tob 14:6. Historians who explain proselytism by asserting that Jews conducted missions to Gentiles appeal to these verses as support, claiming them as the biblical source of Judaism's supposed missionary ideal. I have not traced this interpretation back to its source in the academic literature, but the misunderstanding of these scriptural passages is at least as old as Justin Martyr, who both castigates Trypho for the Jewish failure to missionize Gentiles as Christians are doing, and argues that such missions are proof that the Church has realized the eschatological promises to Israel (and thus that the Messiah really has come) because Gentiles, through Christ, now abandon their idols (*Dial.* 122–123).

A study of the LXX's use of ἐπιστρέφω and related words (which I cannot undertake here) would go far to clear up this ambiguity: "turning to" and "converting," esp. in an apocalyptic context, are two quite different things.

[46] So too Gentiles were free to go up to the Temple and worship in Jerusalem without the expectation of an exclusive allegiance to the God of Israel: see Schürer, *History*, 1.176, 378; 2.222, 284f.

[47] Nock, *Conversion*, 6–7.

2. Paul's Persecution of the Ekklesia

Paul's general situation when writing Galatians is clear enough. Other Christian missionaries—whether Judaizing Christian Gentiles or more traditionally observant Christian Jews[48]—have come into his Gentile communities and taught that membership in the ekklesia required conversion to Judaism, that is, circumcision. In repudiating their gospel, Paul asserts the divine source of his own (ch. 1), and cryptically relates three previous occasions on which he had encountered Peter and others of the original Palestinian followers of Jesus, and come away from those encounters secure in his own interpretation of the gospel. The telescoping of his current polemical situation with his accounts of these earlier events and conversations is both obvious and difficult. The issue when he writes is circumcision; and he implies that it was the issue as well for the episodes he relates in chapters 1 and 2.[49]

Commentators are well aware that Paul frames these episodes this way for rhetorical effect, and that the historical reality behind them is more nuanced than his report allows. None the less, most continue to see some sort of direct relation between the issue at stake in this mid-century letter—Gentile circumcision—and the reason why Paul himself persecuted the ekklesia some fifteen or so years earlier. I want to argue that there was not.

Let us consider the definition of "persecution" first. Taking the evidence of the epistles over that of Acts, and drawing on the dating suggested by Paul's references in chapter 1, we distil the following: that sometime before 33 C.E. or so, the year of his call, Paul persecuted the Jewish members of the ekklesia that had formed in his synagogue community in Damascus. I follow, *inter alia*, Hultgren in construing "persecution" to mean, not "execution" (Luke's picture) but disciplinary flogging, *makkot mardut* (cf. 2 Cor 11:24). I translate Paul's καθ᾽ ὑπερβολήν as "to the utmost" (cf. the RSV's "violently"), and in this context construe him to be saying that he (as an officer of the Damascus *bet din*?) administered the maximum number of stripes permitted by the Law, namely thirty-nine lashes.[50] Those receiving this flogging would have been other Jews—as Sanders has pointed out, punishment implies inclusion[51]—and

---

[48] All commentaries treat the question of the identity of Paul's opponents; see discussion in Betz, *Galatians;* also the earlier conjectures in Schoeps, *Paul,* 74–78; Munck, *Paul,* 87–134. Again, my use of "Christian" here is anachronistic.

[49] Thus 2:14 speaks to 6:12–13; 2:20, to 6:14; see E. Sanders, *Paul, the Law,* 174.

[50] Hultgren, "Persecutions"; cf. my discussion in "Paul and Augustine," 10–14; also *From Jesus,* 142ff. While only Acts claims that Paul was acting in an official capacity (and then as an agent of the High Priest), I assume that Paul himself would not have been a free agent, "persecuting" on his own authority.

Hultgren implies that Paul received *makkot arba'im,* "*the* thirty-nine lashes," the fixed number referring to the penalty for violation of a biblical prohibition (*m. Mak.* 3): this is unlikely. *Makkot mardut,* however, is not a fixed number (except for its upper limit, thirty-nine blows), and could be assigned at the discretion of the court. On disciplinary flogging, Hare, *Jewish Persecution,* 42–6.

[51] E. Sanders, *Paul, the Law,* 192. This is perhaps the burden of ἡμᾶς in Gal 1:23: the other churches in Judea that rejoice because of Paul's change of heart ("they only heard it said, 'He who once persecuted *us* is now preaching . . .' ") would have been almost exclusively Jewish; Christian Jews in Damascus had been Paul's prime target.

in any case no synagogue court would have had a jurisdictional authority over local Gentiles. So: within three years or so of Jesus' execution, the gospel in his name had spread at least as far as Damascus, where a Christian cell formed *within* the synagogue community there. Paul participated in having Jewish members of this group flogged, to the maximum degree permitted by the Law. Why?

What can we know about the early kerygma that can explain why its apostles or adherents would have been subject to synagogue discipline? A minimal reconstruction would permit us to say that it declared that the Messiah had come, that he had been crucified and raised, and that he would shortly return (cf. 1 Cor 15:1ff.).[52] Once in the Diaspora, this message would be heard by Gentiles as well as Jews, since Gentiles were present with Jews in Diaspora synagogues. Why then the synagogue's hostile response? Scholars focusing primarily on the content of the kerygma—the message of the crucified Messiah—conjecture either that the proclamation of the arrival of the Messiah would have led to legal offence, since with the arrival of the Messiah the Law would be seen to be ended; or, second, that the proclamation of a crucified Messiah would have been religiously offensive, since such a claim presents the Messiah as having died as a criminal, a death "cursed by the law"—Deut 21:23, by way of Gal 3:13.

One sees the first explanation less frequently now. It suffers not only from lack of evidence in sufficiently early Jewish tradition,[53] but also from counter-evidence: the first generation of Jesus' original Jewish followers evidently proclaimed him Messiah while continuing to keep Torah.[54] Additionally, Paul nowhere makes the claim, when arguing that the Law is no longer valid, that it is the Messiah's coming as such that overthrows or undoes the Law.[55] If such a Jewish tradition existed, then, evidently the first generation of Jewish apostles did not know it.

The second explanation is more complicated. The "hanging" in Deuteronomy refers not to a mode of execution, but to the publication that a sentence of capital punishment has been executed: the offender's body is displayed by hanging. In the biblical text, such a person would have been perceived as "cursed" because of the crimes for which he would have been executed, presumably by stoning: blasphemy or idolatry (cf. *m. Sanh.* 6:4). The "hanging" itself is not the reason for the "curse." Paul interprets "nailed to a cross" as "hanged on a tree," and suggests, by invoking

---

[52] For my reconstruction of the content of the primitive kerygma in this period between the apostolic resurrection experiences and the composition of Paul's letters, see Fredriksen, *From Jesus*, 133–43.

[53] See esp. Levy, "Torah"; E. Sanders, *Paul and Palestinian Judaism*, 479 and n. 25, 480, 496; cf. Davies, *Torah*.

[54] On the continued Torah observance of Jesus' disciples, e.g., Acts 2:46; 3:1; 5:12, 42; 21:23–27; cf. Matt 5:23–24, on how a Christian should sacrifice at the Temple's altar. In all the Passion narratives, the caesura between Jesus' burial and the discovery of the empty tomb occurs because his (female) disciples wait until the Sabbath is over, Mark 16:1//Matt 28:1; cf. Luke 23:56, which states this explicitly. John 19:42 and 20:1, with its slightly different chronology, refers to Passover ("the day of Preparation") rather than the Sabbath in particular, but my point remains. On the strains caused by the Evangelists' commitment to present a Jesus opposed to the Law, while using traditional material attesting otherwise, Fredriksen, *From Jesus*, esp. 98–114; on Jesus' disciples, E. Sanders, *Jesus*, 323; also 245–69 (Jesus).

[55] So too E. Sanders, *Paul and Palestinian Judaism*, 479–80.

Deuteronomy, that someone (or perhaps, according to some commentators, in particular a Messiah) dying like a criminal was cursed. Such a message, so goes the argument, would be deeply offensive to religious Jews.[56]

Several observations. First, Paul is not the only ancient Jew to conflate the biblical hanging with crucifixion. 11QT 64:6–13, which paraphrases Deuteronomy, mandates execution by hanging/crucifixion as a punishment for treason or for maligning the Jewish people: the "curse" would obtain, one presumes, because of the deceased's crime of betrayal, not because of the mode of execution itself. Similarly, popular Purim celebrations in antiquity could refer to Haman's gibbet as a "tree": Haman was "cursed," however, because of his role in the Esther story, not because he died by hanging.[57] My point is that nowhere outside of Paul's snarled passage in Galatians 3 does one see the claim that death by crucifixion *eo ipso* means a death cursed by God—not in Josephus' description of the eight hundred Pharisees crucified by Alexander Janneus *(Ant.* 13.14.2), nor in his discussions of the thousands of insurrectionists (for whom he otherwise shows little sympathy) so dispatched by Rome. Further, a crucified Jew might look like a criminal to Gentiles; to other first-century Jews, Deut 21 notwithstanding, he would probably look more like a fallen hero. And finally, once again, the original apostolic community actually presents counter-evidence: it existed in Jerusalem unmolested for decades,[58] though it too proclaimed a crucified Messiah.

Nothing in first-century Judaism, in other words, seems to *require* that a crucified man *ipso facto* be seen as cursed of God, and we have no evidence of Jews having done so. Paul deploys Deut 21:23 in order to wend his way from "curse" to "blessing" in Gal 3. In this context the verse has rhetorical force.[59] But it cannot provide the grounds for a religious reason why Paul, and others in his synagogue, would have moved to discipline Jewish members of the ekklesia in their midst.

What else, then, have we got? The fact that this kerygma of the crucified Messiah was evidently heard also by the synagogue's Gentiles, who were in turn welcomed into the ekklesia. The controversy in Galatia revolves around whether to circumcise Christian Gentiles; Paul implies elsewhere that he is persecuted because he does not preach

---

[56] A ubiquitous tradition in New Testament scholarship. See discussion and bibliography in Fredriksen, "Paul and Augustine," 10–13 and n.

[57] See discussions in Bruce, "Curse of the Law," 30ff.; Thornton, "Trees," 130–31; on ξύλον/עֵץ, idem, "Crucifixion of Haman"; Wilcox, " 'Upon the Tree' "; Fitzmyer, "Crucifixion."

[58] Luke reports a flurry of activity, usually initiated by the Sanhedrin, in the period immediately following Jesus' execution (Acts 4:1–23; cf. 5:17–42, where the apostles are first "beaten" [i.e., lashed, v. 40] and then released; 6:8–8:1, charges are brought against Stephen, which culminated in his being stoned; whether this is done by order of the court or by mob action is unclear; 8:1–2, the curious "persecution" aimed at everyone "except the apostles," who remain in the city). See Haenchen's treatment of these passages, *Acts.* Thereafter, Luke reports nothing until Agrippa II executes James the son of Zebedee ca. 44 (12:1ff.; no motive provided; similarly, Peter is arrested but escapes). Finally, some fifteen years later (ca. 58?), Jews from Asia accuse Paul of defiling the Temple, and so incite a riot (21:27ff.). Josephus relates briefly that the High Priest Ananus, ca. 62, had James, Jesus' brother, arrested and executed along with unidentified others. His action offended some other Jews (perhaps Pharisees), who protested to the secular authorities; they deposed Ananus *(Ant.* 20.9.1). The point is that, from ca. 30 to the destruction of the city in 70, the church in Jerusalem by and large was left alone.

[59] E. Sanders, *Paul, the Law,* 25–27.

circumcision (Gal 5:11; cf. 6:12); where he speaks of his former activity as a persecutor of the Church, he sometimes mentions his zeal for the Law (Gal 1:13; Phil 3:6; cf. Gal 1:23 and 1 Cor 15:9). Pulling these disparate pieces of evidence together, a third explanation for Paul's pre-Christian activity emerges. Paul persecuted for the same reason he later claims to be persecuted: admission of Gentiles to the ekklesia without requiring circumcision, that is, conversion to Judaism. The Law-free mission to the Gentiles, in other words, would have existed before Paul; once its opponent, he later became its champion.[60]

Let us consider this proposal in light of the material on Jews and Gentiles with which I began our investigation. Once in the Diaspora, the gospel spread so quickly to Gentiles because Gentiles were present in synagogues to hear it. These Gentiles would demonstrate their reception of the gospel, we can suppose, by voluntarily doing something never demanded of them by the synagogue: they relinquished completely their native observances, most especially the worship of idols.[61] And the original apostles would have readily accepted these Gentiles, because such a response was consonant with a prominent (indeed predominant) strain of Jewish apocalyptic expectation with which the earliest movement—also Jewish, also apocalyptic—aligned itself. Gentile reception of the gospel of the coming Kingdom and their subsequent repudiation of idolatry, in other words, would seem one more "proof"—as Jesus' resurrection itself—that the Kingdom was, indeed, at hand.[62] The ekklesia, this mixed association of Jews and Gentiles, would then form as a subgroup *within* the synagogue. Paul then would persecute the Jewish members of this group precisely because they permitted (uncircumcised) Gentiles as members.

I do not see how this can work. The same factors that explain the early apostles' ready inclusion of Gentiles—namely standard Jewish practice toward sympathizers, on the one hand, and a strong and articulated apocalyptic tradition, on the other— make circumcision impossible as an issue between Paul and the ekklesia ca. 33. *Gentiles within Paul's own synagogue could attend services without receiving circumcision:* why then should Paul and his community persecute an internal subgroup for following exactly the same practice?

---

[60] This mission is usually associated with the Hellenists, who are then construed as somehow in opposition to the Aramaic-speaking core group of disciples—see, e.g., Hengel, *Between;* also *Acts;* Gager, "Some Notes," 700f; cf. Davies' discussion, "Jewish Christianity," 170; E. Sanders, *Paul, the Law,* 190ff.

[61] On this expectation in other Jewish literature, see above. Paul too rigorously insists that his Gentiles "in Christ" absolutely abandon their idols (and so, fornication; e.g., 1 Thess 1:9ff.; 1 Cor 5:11, 6:9f.; 10:7–22; cf. 2 Cor 6:15–7:1; Gal 4:1–11, which probably accounts for some of their confusions regarding food, e.g., 1 Cor 8:1–13, cf. 10:18). No synagogue would do this: it is an *eschatological* demand to make of Gentiles. In it we see the strength of the earliest Church's conviction that, through Jesus' resurrection, the Kingdom had in some sense already dawned, and that the community gathered in Jesus' name proleptically represented this Kingdom in the interregnum between his resurrection and parousia. See Fredriksen, *From Jesus,* 165–75 (Paul); also, on this aspect of "now/not yet" in Jesus' own preaching, 98–101.

[62] See ibid., 127ff. E. Sanders observes, "The overwhelming impression is that Jesus started a movement which *came to see the Gentile mission as a logical extension of itself*" (author's emphasis, *Jesus,* 220, and discussion, 212–21—though he conflates inclusion with conversion, 216–17).

Perhaps the higher degree of intimate social intercourse between Jews and Gentiles within the ekklesia religiously offended the larger community. During the group's eucharistic celebrations—especially if these were held in the homes of Gentile members—problems with table fellowship, or with the ritual status of food or wine, might have arisen. Three practical and historical considerations, however, compromise such a reconstruction. First, we must recall that Jews, too, belonged to their religious communities voluntarily. If they were publicly flogged by religious authorities every time they privately violated the laws of *kashrut,* zealous synagogue officials would soon have had trouble assembling a *minyan.*[63] Secondly, Gentiles and Jews in the first-century Diaspora and later would have eaten together; later rabbinic Judaism even discusses the procedure to be followed on such occasions.[64] Thirdly, if food were already the issue in Damascus in 33, it is hard to understand why, more than fifteen years later, Paul and Peter have their falling out at Antioch (Gal 2:11–14).

We return then to circumcision. Clearly by mid-century, normal Jewish practice notwithstanding, some members of the community objected strongly to the Church's admission of uncircumcised Gentiles. Why would this *not* have been the issue ca. 33? *Precisely because the question addresses the conditions for the admission of Gentiles into the ekklesia, not into the synagogue.* Gentiles could and did enter synagogues voluntarily, and as they would. And should they choose to enter *Israel,* i.e., become a Jew, the standard practice was perfectly clear, specifying, for males, circumcision. The question *whether,* at community initiative, to urge Gentiles to be circumcised arose only within the Church, and only eventually; it was, in other words, an internal problem for the churches, not for their host environment, the synagogues. Paul stood outside the Church when he persecuted it. His reasons, then, must have had to do with issues important to the larger Jewish community, not issues of membership and group identity within the small new cell.

What, finally, do we know about the ekklesia in Damascus around 33? That, on whatever conditions, it probably included Gentiles who were exposed to the Christian message through the synagogue. The content of this message was: Jesus the Messiah, crucified for the atonement of sin and raised to the right hand of God, is about to return to establish the Kingdom. We have failed to derive from these two facts any religious reason for Paul's persecution of this group. What other reason might he have had?

Here we have to consider the mood of the movement in the years immediately following Jesus' death. An intense expectation that the Kingdom was about to arrive had motivated Jesus' ministry. His disciples had shared this belief. Their faith in his

---

[63] Philo's lament in *Migr.* 16.89–93 should help to remind us that, in ancient Jewish populations as in modern ones, those Jews who troubled to think about religious legislation when they ate could be perfectly comfortable transgressing traditional prohibitions in light of "higher" modern understandings—allegory in the first century, scientific hygiene in the twentieth (cf. Hertz on Leviticus 11 in Hertz, *Chumash*).

[64] The point is that, if such intercourse is acknowledged and legislated even by that stream of Judaism explicitly concerned to articulate domestic applications of purity laws, we should expect even freer mixing in other pre- or non-rabbinic communities. See now E. Sanders, "Jewish Association."

message would have been radically challenged by the crushing disappointment of his crucifixion; just as radically, the post-resurrection appearances would have recon-firmed it. These Christophanies multiplied: first only Peter, and then the twelve, later more than five hundred brethren, and finally "all the apostles" and James saw the Risen Christ (1 Cor 15:4–7).

And still nothing happened.

At some point not long after, this group burst into sustained and energetic mis-sionary activity. The word "mission" is perhaps not quite correct, because they were Jews taking a very Jewish message—that the Kingdom approached—to other Jews. They would have fanned out through Palestine, then on into the Diaspora through the network of Jewish communities ringed round the Mediterranean, continuing Jesus' work of preparing Israel for the impending redemption.

Into Paul's synagogue in Damascus, then, sometime shortly after the year 30, came apostles enthusiastically proclaiming the imminent subjection of the present order through the (returning) Messiah to the coming Kingdom of God. If we can generalize from the picture later presented in Paul's letters and Acts, these apostles would have found opportunities at the regular Sabbath service or thereafter to speak, debate, interpret scripture, and perhaps demonstrate the authority of their message with charismatic healings and exorcisms. Normally present on such occa-sions would be Gentiles voluntarily attached to the synagogue. Their reception of this message and consequent abandonment of idols would only serve to confirm the apostles' conviction that the End was at hand. The ekklesia subsequently formed of Jews and Gentiles both would constitute a committed, energetic, and vocal sub-group *within* the larger community—meeting separately to celebrate a common meal in anticipation of the Messianic banquet; praying, prophesying, interpreting scripture.

How would the larger community respond? The belief in a Messiah known to have died must have struck many *prima facie* as odd or incredible; a Messiah without a Messianic age, irrelevant. But the enthusiastic proclamation of a Messiah executed very recently by Rome as a political troublemaker—a *crucified* Messiah—combined with a vision of the approaching End *preached also to Gentiles*—this was dangerous. News of an impending Messianic kingdom, originating from Palestine, might trickle out via the ekklesia's Gentiles to the larger urban population. It was this (by far) larger, unaffiliated group that posed a real and serious threat. Armed with such a re-port, they might readily seek to alienate the local Roman colonial government, upon which Jewish urban populations often depended for support and protection against hostile Gentile neighbors. The open dissemination of a Messianic message, in other words, put the entire Jewish community at risk.

The synagogue court would have no formal jurisdiction over Gentile sympathiz-ers. But it could discipline those Jews who seemed oblivious to the politically sensitive nature of their proclamation of a coming *christos*. The form that discipline would take was *makkot mardut*—discretionary lashing. Were Paul an officer of the court, re-sponsible for the administration of its decision, he might execute its orders *kath' hyperbolēn,* to the maximum thirty-nine lashes allowed by the Law.

This reconstruction is of course speculative. Lest it seem unduly so, we should pause to consider seriously the casualty figures of Jewish urban populations at the outbreak of the first revolt: 20,000 in Caesarea; 2,000—the entire community—in Ptolemais; in Paul's home community, Damascus, variously 10,000 or 18,000 Jews slain.[65] Alexandria's convulsions in 38–41, Antioch's in 40, and again in 66 and 70, stand as striking attestation of the Jewish community's vulnerability to the violent hostility of local populations if Rome's attention were alienated or withdrawn.[66] And the pagan urban casualties at the outbreak of the War in 66, and in later rebellions in the Diaspora, underscore the reasonableness of Gentile anxieties should they hear of news originating from Palestine, disseminated through the local synagogue, of a coming Messiah.[67]

This reconstruction can also suggest an explanation for the very different experiences of the nascent church in Jerusalem as opposed to abroad. As both Acts and Josephus attest, Jewish anti-Christian activity was fairly subdued in Jerusalem, whereas—Acts and Paul[68]—in the Diaspora it continued. Why? The answer may lie in the fact that Jerusalem, unlike Damascus or the cities in Paul's eventual itinerary, had a Jewish majority. The social situation was accordingly much less volatile. Also, in the course of the four decades until the destruction of the Second Temple, the Sanhedrin had other noisily apocalyptic popular movements and *living* messianic preachers to worry about. As long as normal conditions obtained—that is, in any situation short of outright war—Jerusalem's Jewish community was fairly

---

[65] These figures derive from Josephus, so the usual cautions obtain. Accuracy aside, their simple existence points to the indisputable fact that these communities were slaughtered. On Caesarea, Josephus, *J.W.* 2.18.1; 7.8.7; Ptolemais, 2.18.5; Damascus, 2.20.2; cf. 7.8.7. On the destruction of Jews in Gaza and Anthedon, 2.18.1; in Ascalon, 2.18.5; Hippus and Garada, 2.18.1, 5; Scythopolis, 2.18.3–4; 7.8.7; *Life* 6. See review of these data in Schürer, *History*, 2.85–183; also the following note.

[66] For the anti-Jewish riots in Alexandria, Philo, *In Flaccum* and *Legatio ad Gaium;* Josephus, *Ant.* 18.8.1; on the anti-Roman nature of this incident, see Gager, *Origins*, 46–54.

Greeks in Antioch apparently attempted to clear the way to molesting Jewish residents of the city by first alienating Roman colonial government. Their attack on Jews in 40 C.E. may relate to the Jewish reaction earlier that year to Caligula's efforts to put his statue in the Temple in Jerusalem (Josephus, *Ant.* 18.8.2; on the attack on the Jews, John Malalas, *Chron.* 50.10; see discussion in Downey, *Antioch*, 190–95). In 66, rumors that Jews were plotting to burn the city started a pogrom (Josephus, *J.W.* 7.3.3); four years later, when fire did break out, more slaughter was prevented only when the Roman deputy-governor Gnaeus Collega intervened, conducted an investigation, and cleared the Jews of all charges (7.3.4). And shortly thereafter, when Titus, then Caesar, stopped in Antioch after his successful campaign against Palestinian Jews, Greek Antiochenes demanded that Jews be stripped of their civic privileges. Titus refused (7.5.2).

[67] On Hippus, Gadara, Scythopolis and Pella, all attacked by Jewish insurgents in 66, Josephus, *J.W.* 2.18.1; Josephus attributes the revolt specifically to popular messianic expectation, 6.5.4. He further relates that Alexandrian Jews, after provocation, likewise took up arms against Greeks in 66 (2.18.7). Dio Cassius reports that Jewish rebels killed 220,000 in Cyrene and 240,000 in Cyprus during the insurrection of 115–17 *(Hist.* 68.32.1–3); the actual figures are probably no more accurate than his lurid details, but again they make the point. The deliberate destruction of pagan temples in this last insurrection may indicate a messianic enthusiasm; see discussion in Schürer, *History*, 1.529–34; also Applebaum, *Jews and Greeks;* Smallwood, *Jews*, 389–427.

[68] E.g., Acts 13:13–52 (Pisidian Antioch); 14:1–6 (Iconium); 17:1–9 (Thessalonica); 17:10–15 (Beroea); 18:1–17 (Corinth); etc. Paul both gave and received lashing, which he characterizes in both instances as "persecution" (Gal 1:13, 23; Phil 3:6; 1 Cor 15:9; 2 Cor 11:24).

secure.[69] But in the Diaspora, and in a situation of messianic agitation, things could, and ultimately did, worsen abruptly.

In brief: to understand the reasons for early first-century Jewish persecutions of Jewish Christian apostles, we should look not to supposed exegetical traditions defining theological offence (the appeal to Deut 21:23); nor should we retroject a mid-first-century ecclesiastical issue—the circumcision of Gentile Christians—back into the earliest years of the preaching to synagogues. Paul indeed invokes his past as a persecutor of Jewish Christians before his current Gentile Christian audience against other mid-century (and probably Jewish) Christian missionaries who do advocate full conversion to Judaism. Our confusions in reconstructing that past are in part the measure of his rhetorical skill. But to understand the reasons why he and other Jews "persecuted," we would do well to remove the issue from his rhetorical framework and place it where it belongs: incarnate in the mixed and often mutually hostile urban populations of the Roman Mediterranean. Ideas and ideology do provide important motivations for human actions; but in real life they are grounded in social fact—in this instance, in the politically precarious situation of urban Jewish communities in the Western Diaspora, dependent as they often were on protection from Rome.

3. Jerusalem, Antioch, and Gentiles in the Ekklesia

I have argued that, from its inception, the Christian movement admitted Gentiles without demanding that they be circumcised and observe the Law. This was so precisely because nascent Christianity was Jewish. Diaspora Jews, as we have seen, routinely permitted sympathetic Gentiles access to their synagogues on a "Law-free" basis; and those who thought in traditional ways about the Kingdom of God would have expected Gentiles too to be redeemed, again as we have seen, on a "Law-free" basis.

Neither quotidian practice nor prophetic tradition, then, can help us account for the situation Paul describes in Gal 2. Some fourteen years after his first visit (1:18), Paul again went up to Jerusalem "by revelation," together with Barnabas and a Gentile co-worker, Titus, in order to present to "those of repute the gospel which I preach among the Gentiles" (v. 2). Other Christian Jews (in Paul's view, uninvited and unwelcome, v. 4) at this point apparently urged that Titus be circumcised (ἠναγκάσθη περιτμηθῆναι, v. 3)—an idea that the "pillars" reject (vv. 6–10). Most commentators have seen these "circumcisers" as conservative Jews, backsliding into some supposedly traditional Jewish view that (Christian) Gentiles, to be saved, must be made to observe Torah.[70] In the light of our review of Jewish beliefs and practices, however, we

---

[69] The periods around the great pilgrimage festivals—Passover, Shavuot, and Sukkot—would be exceptions, both because the city would be swollen with visitors, and because the Roman government, in light of this fact, garrisoned extra troops there during the holidays (Josephus, *J.W.* 2.12.1). Crowded conditions, excited crowds, messianic fervor (esp., naturally, at Passover) and skittish Roman soldiers could and did combine to make the atmosphere in Jerusalem volatile and the Sanhedrin, accordingly, more than usually anxious to preserve peace. See Fredriksen, *From Jesus*, 110–25.

[70] So, e.g., Betz, *Galatians*, 82. See Holmberg, *Paul and Power*, 18–32, for a review of the arguments; also E. Sanders, *Paul, the Law*, 17–27.

know the opposite to be the case: *these men, the "false brethren," were actually propos-ing a startling novelty* both within Judaism and, *a fortiori,* within the Christian move-ment. For until ca. 49, evidently—that is to say, for nearly twenty years—the ekklesia had never demanded circumcision as an entry requirement for Gentiles. What had changed between ca. 30 and ca. 49, and why?

Posing the question puts the answer. By the time of this council, Paul had been a member of a movement that had been preaching the imminent establishment of the Kingdom of God for almost a generation. Certainly among the members of the Church in Jerusalem—perhaps even among the "false brethren"—were those who had followed Jesus of Nazareth in his lifetime, and so had lived with this expectation even longer. If Jesus' execution had crushed this hope, their experience of his resur-rection would have revived it. And as the Kingdom (now linked to Jesus' Parousia) tarried, these apostles continued his work of preparing Israel by taking the message out to the Israel of the dispersion. There they received another unexpected confirma-tion of their belief: Gentiles in these synagogues, finally abandoning their idols, also embraced the gospel. But still the Kingdom did not come.

Time drags when you expect it to end. Put differently: millenarian movements tend, of necessity, to have a short half-life. As the End-time recedes, reinterpretations and adjustments must reshape the original belief, else it be relinquished to unintel-ligibility or irrelevance.[71] By mid-century, surely, all these Christians must have real-ized that their expectations had not been fulfilled. Worse: the traditional prophetic scenario—from which the kergyma, in proclaiming Jesus crucified and raised, had al-ready deviated—had gone awry. Gentiles continued to join the movement in num-bers; the mission to Israel, however, had foundered. How could they interpret these facts and hold on to the gospel, continuing in their belief that Jesus' resurrection truly did signal the turning of the age and the nearness of the Kingdom?

We see in Paul's terse review of the Jerusalem council the variety of Christian re-sponses to this double disappointment of the Kingdom's delay and Israel's increasing hostility or indifference. One group, the "false brethren," evidently began to press for Gentile *conversions* to Christianity—meaning, of course, to this particular branch of first-century Judaism—rather than simple inclusion. And there the halakhah was clear: male Gentiles would have to be circumcised. Paul angrily suggests that they would have "compelled" Titus (v. 3). We have the measure of his hyperbole when we hear him speak similarly to Peter in Antioch: "How can you compel the Gentiles to adopt Jewish practices?" (πῶς τὰ ἔθνη ἀναγκάζεις ἰουδαΐζειν, 2:14). At worst, Peter was passive-aggressive: he "compelled" Gentile Christians by withdrawing (v. 12b). The coercion Paul alleges of the "false brethren" was most likely heated and passionate argument—and more likely not with Titus, but with Paul.[72]

---

[71] On the intrinsic interpretive instability of millenarian prophecy, Gager, *Kingdom and Com-munity*, 20–65, esp. 37ff.; on the paradoxical longevity and vitality of Christian millenarianism, Fredriksen, "Apocalypse and Redemption"; Landes, "Millennium."

[72] Similarly Justin Martyr, *Dial.* 47.3: "Those men of your race [i.e., the Jews, though here Justin intends Jewish Christians] who . . . compel the Gentiles who believe in this Christ to live completely by the law ordained through Moses, or do not choose to have close fellowship with them, these I do

We can speculate on their rationale. Perhaps, sizing up the movement's situation mid-century, they adduced a causal connection between the Kingdom's delay and the worsening unreadiness of Israel. Perhaps—not unreasonably—they saw the increasing prominence of Gentiles in the movement as a factor contributing to most Jews' rejecting the gospel. Perhaps they had in mind converting not all Gentiles members, but only those who, like Titus, held highly visible positions of leadership in their Diaspora communities. If Jews had to be reached, better such spokesmen be Jews; were Titus circumcised, he would be a Jew. For their conviction that Israel should be the movement's first priority, and that Gentile redemption was contingent upon Israel's, they had no further to look than the teaching of Jesus himself and, behind him, to scripture. Whatever their rationale, their motivation and their goal were, doubtless, to ensure the spread of the gospel.

But their proposal was rejected. Jews other than Paul also found the idea of an actual mission to Gentiles to convert them to Judaism too novel. We know the names of some: James, Peter, John, Barnabas. Despite the stress-points in the gospel message caused by the Kingdom's delay, the traditional Jewish apocalyptic view held: Gentiles would be admitted into the Kingdom—and so, for the (as far as they knew, brief) time being, into the Church—with only the requirement of moral, not halakhic, conversion. This meant no idols. It also meant no circumcision.

These "false brethren," caught between their faith in the gospel and its evident disconfirmation, improvised a strategy, and so devised something both awkward and new: a Jewish *mission* to the Gentiles. Caught in the same dilemma, Paul improvised too, on a much larger scale. They revised traditional practice; he revised biblical history.

We see how, most clearly, in Rom 9–11.[73] Paul's letter had built to a crescendo in chapter 8 where, overwhelmed by his vision of the imminent and universal redemption of all creation at Christ's second coming, he had burst forth in praise of the power and constancy of God's love as manifest in the sending of his son. But what

---

not accept" (ἐὰν δὲ οἱ ἀπὸ τοῦ γένους τοῦ ὑμετέρου πιστεύειν λέγοντες ἐπὶ τοῦτον τὸν Χριστόν, ᾧ Τρύφων, ἔλεγον, ἐκ παντὸς κατὰ τὸν διὰ Μωυσέως, διαταχθέντα νόμον ἀναγκάζουσι ζῆν ἐξ ἐθνῶν πιστεύοντας ἐπὶ τοῦτον τὸν Χριστὸν ἢ μὴ κοινωνεῖν αὐτοῖς . . . τούτους οὐκ ἀποδέχομαι).

In this context, ἀναγκάζειν may have the sense of "to require." Some Jews in Justin's period, feeling the force of biblical injunctions to circumcise their non-Jewish slaves (e.g., Gen 17:12, 23–27; Exod 12:44), permitted the man a year to consider the proposition. If he declined, the *tannaim* urged that he be sold to a Gentile owner. This raises the question: if Jews, at least in principle, were not to compel their own slaves to be circumcised, in what way would those in Jerusalem "compel" Titus? See Schiffman, *Who Was a Jew?* 36–37, on the *eved kena'ani;* Bamberger, *Proselytism,* 124–31. On forced conversions as part of military conquest, Josephus, *Ant.* 13.9.1 (Hyrcanus and the Edomites); cf. Ptolemy, *Historia Herodis,* in Stern, *Authors,* vol. 1, no. 146 (ἀναγκασθέντες περιτέμνεσθαι); Josephus, *Ant.* 13.11.3 (Aristobulus and the Ituraeans), but this too is confusing: unless we conjecture the existence of vigilante *mohelim,* the generations subsequent to the one conquered would have been circumcised at parental initiative. For a more plausible reconstruction, see S. Cohen, "Respect," 423; Kasher, *Jews:* circumcision was embraced as part of a voluntary federation with the Jewish kingdom in a common reaction against Seleucid Hellenistic rule.

[73] On Paul's revision of the sequence of events expected by more traditional Jewish eschatology, e.g., E. Sanders, *Paul, the Law,* 171, 192–97; Davies, "Paul," 130–33, 142–47 (Rom 9–11 a tortuous discussion that ends in paradox); Donaldson, " 'Curse of the Law,' " 100, 106f.

about God's constancy as manifest in history toward his people—Israel's election ("sonship"), God's presence (δόξα; Heb. כָּבוֹד), the covenants, the giving of the Law, the Temple cult (λατρεία; cf. RSV's much-weakened "worship") and the promises, the patriarchs and even, κατὰ σάρκα, the Messiah (9:2–5)? Was that for nothing? Would history end with God breaking his promises to Israel?

Ingeniously, tortuously, Paul integrates biblical history and his religious convictions as a Jew with precisely those discouraging facts of the Christian movement mid-century—too many Gentiles, too few Jews, and no End in sight—to formulate a solution to both dilemmas: the status of Israel in light of the gospel, and the status of the gospel in light of continuing quotidian reality. Israel did not heed the gospel? That was part of God's plan: just as in the past the elder (Esau) had served the younger (Jacob), so now Israel serves the Gentiles (vv. 11–13). And as God had once hardened Pharaoh's heart so that his own name might be proclaimed in all the earth, so now, to that same end, he hardens Israel's (vv. 17–18; 11:7). Gentiles overwhelmed the Church with their response? That too was God's plan all along: the Kingdom would come once their "full number" was brought in (11:25). The Kingdom tarried? No: rather it waited on Paul (and doubtless others, though Paul fails to keep them in mind here) to complete the work among the Gentiles, bringing their donation, and in a sense themselves, as an acceptable sacrifice to Jerusalem (15:16, 31). Then God would cease hardening Israel, then Christ would be revealed in glory, then the final events would unwind (11:7–15, 23–32; 15:8–12). Paul's very success among the Gentiles confirmed for him that the time was indeed at hand.[74] "The God of peace will soon crush Satan beneath your feet" (16:20).

Ultimately, all these issues and arguments were settled by the *force majeure* of time. The apostolic generation died away, Roman armies destroyed Jerusalem, and traditions from and about Jesus grew in increasingly Gentile milieux. As evangelical tradition evolved, Christianity distanced itself both from its apocalyptic past and from its parent religious culture. The Jesus of the canonical gospels comes less to announce the coming Kingdom than to establish the (Gentile) Church.

Yet Luke did draw, as he claims, on historical sources;[75] and thus embedded in Acts, his late first-century reshaping of these sources notwithstanding, lie nuggets of historical fact. We detect these most securely where we have convergent lines of independent evidence.[76] Luke names Diaspora synagogues as the particular loci of resistance to the gospel, and usually in this connection mentions the God-fearers' enthusiastic response; I have argued, from Josephus, Philo, and other historical sources, that there are solid social reasons to hypothesize such a link.[77] Luke's Paul

---

[74] We must take Paul to speak figuratively when he claims to have preached the gospel from Jerusalem around to Illyrium (Rom 15:19) so that he had no work left in these regions (v. 23); but his phrasing conveys his own sense of satisfaction with nearing the πλήρωμα τῶν ἐθνῶν (11:25).

[75] Luke 1:1–4, equally introductory of Acts.

[76] I stand closer to Knox than not on the issue of using Luke to reconstruct episodes in Paul's career: see "Paul and Augustine," 6–19.

[77] E.g., Acts 13:45, 50 (jealous of multitudes harkening to gospel, the Jews instigate persecution); 14:1–5 (Gentiles react positively; the unbelieving Jews dissuade them and instigate trouble); 17:1–5 (Paul persuades many God-fearers ["devout Greeks" in Thessalonica's synagogue] and lead-

avails himself of the network of Diaspora synagogue communities, and through them makes contact with Gentiles. Nothing in Paul's own letters rules this out,[78] not least his statements about his Gentiles' former idolatry (e.g., 1 Thess 1:9; Gal 4:8; 1 Cor 5:12, 10:14—apparently the Corinthians' idolatry is not entirely effaced). As we know from the scattered literary evidence, Jewish, pagan, and Christian, and most especially from the stone at Aphrodisias, idolatrous God-fearers could indeed be found in the synagogues of the Diaspora. And Luke's account of the Jerusalem council in Acts 15, chronology aside, recognizably echoes some of the voices in Gal 2. James did not require circumcision, and the Church did not sponsor missions, in this sense, to the Gentiles.

Luke further relates (and in relating, disowns) yet another tradition that Paul himself might confirm: the Asian Jews' accusation that Paul brought Gentiles past their boundary on into the Temple (Acts 21:28).[79] A trajectory that we might draw from Paul's own statements in the closing chapters of Romans could converge on Luke's report. Paul's letter revises biblical history and "rearranges the eschatological sequence so that it accords with the facts."[80] The prophets had thought that Gentiles would be redeemed from their idolatry and turn to the God of Israel only once Israel had been redeemed from exile; he, Paul, knew better. God's adoption of the Gentiles had preceded the restoration of Israel: God must have wanted it that way, and so temporarily hardened Israel until Paul could complete his mission. This reordering of traditional elements enabled Paul to confront what might otherwise seem unambiguous disconfirmation of the gospel, and feel encouraged and enthused. Thus, a generation after his experience of the Risen Christ, Paul could coherently and reasonably affirm to the Church at Rome that "salvation is nearer to us than when we first believed" (13:11).

The process begun by Christ's resurrection, Paul firmly believed, would be brought to fulfillment through his own work. In his revised scenario, the Gentiles

---

ing women; the Jews, jealous, set the city in an uproar); 17:10–15, so too in Beroea; 18:1–17, Paul speaks in Corinth's synagogue and persuades many Jews and Greeks; the Jews finally bring him before Gallio and accuse him of transgressing Jewish law, v. 12ff. Jews from the Diaspora residing in Jerusalem instigate the fatal contretemps with Stephen (6:9), and later, finally, with Paul (21:27, Jews from Asia). On this theme of the Diaspora Jews' villainy, Fredriksen, *From Jesus,* 193–94. Luke always attributes bad motivations to them; I have argued above, from the data on urban populations in Josephus et al., that their actions, triggered by the messianic enthusiasm of Gentile adherents, may have stemmed from a justifiable anxiety.

[78] Cf. E. Sanders *Paul, the Law,* 181–90, for the counterargument; I am obviously not convinced. The assumption that Paul did work through the synagogues provides a plausible social context for, e.g., 2 Cor 11:24 (receiving thirty-nine lashes five times) and 1 Cor 9:20 (becoming as a Jew to win Jews), a plausible explanation for his constant appeal to scripture (his Gentile congregations would have been even more at sea than they seem to have been in any case were the source for Paul's exhortations and arguments completely unfamiliar), and a plausible environment for Paul's circumcising opponents mid-century, who are obviously making some headway within his groups.

[79] Luke represses both in his gospel and in Acts traditions that might seem hostile to the Temple: cf. Luke 19:45–48//Mark 11:1–19; he drops the accusation at the trial scene that Jesus threatened or predicted its destruction, Luke 22:54–71//Mark 14:57–61; Stephen's prediction of the Temple's destruction is put in the mouth of false witnesses, Acts 6:13.

[80] E. Sanders, *Paul, the Law,* 185.

serve as the trip-switch of the Eschaton. What would be more like him, then—confident in God's promises, confirmed in his interpretation of events by the very success of his ministry—than to attempt to inaugurate the End-time by enacting a paradigmatic moment from the traditional scenario? Though the sequence is changed, the prophetic script remains.

I see Paul coming up to Jerusalem with the collection and, following through the logic of his own convictions, walking with his Gentile brother-in-Christ into the Temple. He knew that he lived in the very last days. And in those days, according to his tradition, God would redeem the nations from their idolatry graciously, without the works of the Law; in those days Jew and Gentile together would go up to the mountain of the Lord, to worship, together, at the house of the God of Jacob.

14

MAKING AND BREAKING AN AGREEMENT MEDITERRANEAN STYLE: A NEW READING OF GALATIANS 2:1–14

Philip F. Esler

Paul's letter to the Galatians refers to two distinct situations and chronological periods. The first is the situation in his Galatian congregations as it exists at the time of composition and which has actually stirred him to write to them; in the rhetorical terminology of L. F. Bitzer this may be termed the "exigence" of the letter.[1] The second is the evolving situation which existed in the past between himself and the leaders in Jerusalem, beginning with his first visit to Peter and James, continuing with his journey to the Holy City with Barnabas and Titus which resulted in the agreement with James, Peter and John (1:18–2:10), and culminating in his confrontation with Peter in Antioch (2:11–14).[2]

A question of pressing importance for the interpretation of Galatians is why Paul chose to recount details of his past relationship with the leaders in Jerusalem in the midst of a letter written some time later to his churches in Galatia.[3] In a general sense the earlier events bear on the question of his apostolic authority, yet in this article I wish to develop one aspect of a different and far more particular explanation for Paul's inclusion of the Jerusalem meeting and the Antioch incident in this letter. The earlier problem, after all, seemed to climax in some sort of dispute over table-fellowship, while the problem principally agitating him as far as the Galatians are concerned turns on the issue of circumcision of his Gentile converts. What is the relevance of the earlier events to his Galatian addressees? How were the two situations related? Many attempts to understand the Antioch incident are predicated upon a fairly loose relationship between the two situations.[4]

---

[1] Bitzer, "Rhetorical Situation."

[2] My reasons for rejecting the view that Gal 2:15–21 also form part of what Paul said to Peter at Antioch will be set out below.

[3] For a recent discussion which covers most of the possibilities, see Gaventa, "Galatians 1 and 2."

[4] This is seen most clearly in the view that Peter wanted the Antiochean Gentiles to adopt Jewish customs yet not to become Jews through circumcision. Dunn has been an influential exponent of

My broad answer to this problem, developed elsewhere, is that Paul raises the past situation in connection with the present because it concerned exactly the same issue, namely, whether Jews and Gentiles would be able to enjoy eucharistic table-fellowship with one another in spite of a recognized ban in the first century on Jews dining with Gentiles, in the full sense of sharing the same food, wine and vessels, which was characteristic of the eucharistic meal (1 Cor 10:16–17).[5] The problem with such a practice from a Jewish point of view was that, given the widespread Gentile habit of offering their gods a libation from any wine they drank, if Jews were to eat from the same loaf as Gentiles and drink from the same cup of wine, this involved, or (almost as bad) might appear to involve, idolatry.[6] My position, in summary, is that in Antioch, following the secession by Peter and the other Jews (2:12–13), circumcision had been demanded of the Gentile Christians before they would be permitted once again to participate in table-fellowship with the Jewish members, whereas in Galatia the Gentile Christians are being threatened with exclusion from table-fellowship unless they become circumcised. On this view Ἰουδαΐζειν in Gal 2:14 means "to become Jews (through circumcision)."

To adopt such a perspective does not entail denying that Paul's primary instincts were theological, not social. That his fundamental wish is to assert the efficacy of the redemption brought about by Christ's death and resurrection, in the face of what he perceives to be an attempt to deny it (by making the Jewish law a requirement), emerges in the statement which is the most theologically charged in the letter: εἰ γὰρ διὰ νόμου δικαιοσύνη, ἄρα Χριστὸς δωρεὰν ἀπέθανεν (2:21b). But the social aspect is inextricably intertwined with the theological, since all who believe are one in Christ Jesus (3:28) and the eucharistic meal is the pre-eminent manifestation of that unity (1 Cor 10:16–17) and a primary mode for the proclamation of Christ's death (1 Cor 11:26). The Jewish-Christian demand that there be no mixed table-fellowship unless and until the Gentiles became circumcised constituted an assault both on the social institution of the eucharistic meal and the critical theological truth which was expressed and enacted in it.

The purpose of this article is to address one significant issue bearing upon my general solution to the relationship between the Antiochean and Galatian situations.[7]

---

this view, although he has now ("Echoes"; *Commentary*) dropped his earlier suggestion ("Incident at Antioch") that the customs to be observed were Pharisaical purity requirements. Similarly, Verseput, "Paul's Gentile Mission," 53; Matera, *Galatians*, 90; and C. Hill, *Hellenists and Hebrews*, 110–11. See also my review of Hill.

[5] *Community*, 87–89, and "Sectarianism"; and see now Esler, *Galatians*, 126–40, for additional development of the argument.

[6] Exod 23:13 and 24, for example, forbid a wide range of idolatrous activities which would extend to making such a libation. For evidence as to the prohibition on mixed table-fellowship as a phenomenon, rather than as to its scriptural foundation, see Esler, *Community*, 73–84.

[7] This article develops the core of a paper delivered to the Paul Seminar at the British New Testament Conference in St. Andrews on 17 September, 1993; another version of it was delivered to a joint meeting of members of the Divinity Faculties of the University of St. Andrews and the Friedrich-Alexander Universität at Erlangen in St. Andrews on 18 October, 1993. I gratefully ac-

Had not the conference in Jerusalem, as described in Gal 2:1–10, effectively meant that Gentile Christians did not need to be circumcised, and, if so, would not an insistence by Peter on the circumcision of the Antiochean Gentiles constitute a serious breach of this agreement? Did Peter actually demand their circumcision? In my view, all these questions should be answered in the affirmative. According to Nicholas Taylor, however, who was responding to the original formulation of my position of the incident at Antioch, I am alone among recent scholars in believing circumcision was being required in Antioch.[8]

Consider how Taylor himself deals with my proposal that Peter and the other Jews were demanding circumcision:

> This would have been a complete breach of the agreement between the Jerusalem and Antiochene churches in which James had played an important role. It is most unlikely therefore that James sought reversal of the agreement, or that he believed he could enforce such a reversal, especially with Peter's being in Antioch at the time.

He continues as follows:

> The authority of the Jerusalem church in Antioch may have been entrenched by the Jerusalem conference, but James would have been jeopardizing this authority had he attempted to reverse the decision of the conference without reference to Peter, and while Peter was in Antioch. Furthermore, there is no evidence that this is what James sought to accomplish.[9]

Taylor does not explain why James would have been jeopardizing his authority if he sought to reverse the decision without reference to Peter. This is merely asserted. Presumably he believes that there was some significant group in the early church who would have frowned on James' acting in this way, even to the extent of discontinuing to acknowledge his leadership. Accordingly, underlying Taylor's only argument (unless—as seems likely—the word "therefore" in the second sentence of the first part of the quotation indicates a view that James simply would not have broken an agreement) there must be some model of how interpersonal relations operated among the early church, which, unfortunately, he fails to explicate. There are also notions of "fair play" lurking not far below the surface. The lineaments of Taylor's model and values, and whether they are ancient or modern in aspect, are left quite unstated. Taylor is not alone in running this type of argument.[10] For this is an area, like many others in New Testament criticism, where generally unstated presuppositions as to the behavior expected of the biblical characters, often flavored with modern ethics, come into

---

knowledge the helpful comments made by those present on both occasions, especially the detailed response by Dr Markus Müller of Erlangen.

[8] Taylor, *Paul, Antioch,* 129 responding to Esler, *Community,* 87–89. Perhaps I am not quite so alone; see Bauckham, "Barnabas," 64, and F. Watson, *Paul,* 50–53.

[9] Taylor, *Paul, Antioch,* 129.

[10] Among the reasons Dunn, for example, offers for rejecting the idea the Jewish Christians in Antioch were demanding circumcision is that it is not "likely that Peter and Barnabas had so completely reneged on the central point of the Jerusalem agreement" (*Commentary,* 129), yet he does not suggest a basis for this view.

operation, while the social sciences, which offer an escape route from precisely this hazard, are ignored.[11]

I am happy to march to my own drum in this regard, since it seems to me that the reason for Taylor and other critics finding unpalatable the idea of James and Peter reneging on the Jerusalem agreement lies in an unexpressed, even unrealized, adherence to modern Western values which were not those of the first-century Mediterranean world. Accordingly, in this article I propose as far as possible to jettison post-Enlightenment North American and Northern European presuppositions concerning social relations in favor of the very different ones current in the Mediterranean and recently investigated by cultural anthropologists. If one looks at the situation in the light of the actual values and social practices of Paul's cultural world, a case can be made that there were strong pressures on James and Peter to abrogate the agreement, pressures to which they eventually succumbed in Antioch. As I will indicate briefly at the end of this article, there is ancient support for a critical feature of this interpretation.

It is worth stressing at the outset that the social-scientific material to be discussed should be understood as a model, as an abstraction from empirical reality, not a description of it, and certainly not as a social law, for there are no such laws.[12] Even among modern Mediterranean cultures there is a measure of diversity with respect to the model. Moreover, there is certainly room for discussion on the question of how closely ancient Mediterranean societies illustrate the cultural patterns about to be described, although I consider that there is a growing body of evidence that they do.[13] But even if this were wrong, it is simply indisputable that the values and meanings shared by contemporary Mediterranean villagers are closer to those of the ancient Mediterranean than are those of modern North Americans or Northern Europeans.[14] Consciously to adopt a perspective based on the former rather than the latter is a sensible strategy to avoid anachronistic and ethnocentric readings. Accordingly, in what follows I will explain the model and then apply it to Galatians in order to pose new questions to the text and to situate my discussion of it in a genuinely Mediterranean framework. But this does not involve a model to plug holes in ancient data, a misconception one still occasionally encounters, since while the model may supply new questions, only the text can answer them.

The Anthropology of Challenge and Response

Research conducted into Mediterranean culture in the last thirty-five years by anthropologists such as Peristiany *(Honour and Shame)*; J. Pitt-Rivers ("Honour"; cf.

---

[11] It is unfortunate that Taylor himself, who has a commendable grasp of many of the social-scientific perspectives which are helpful in this area (including those deriving from the cultural anthropology of the Mediterranean: *Paul, Antioch,* 28–44), fails to apply them in the chapters of his book dealing with the conference in Jerusalem and the incident at Antioch (chapters 4 and 5). For an early and impressive study of Paul from a sociological perspective, especially as influenced by Max Weber, see Holmberg, *Paul and Power.*

[12] Esler, *Community,* 6.

[13] The cultural anthropology of the Mediterranean has been fruitfully applied to ancient Greek magic and religion in Faraone and Obbink, *Magika hiera.*

[14] Cf. Malina and Neyrey, "First-Century Personality," 72.

Peristiany and Pitt-Rivers, *Honour and Grace*), P. Bourdieu ("Sentiment of Honour") and J. K. Campbell *(Honour),* to name only a few, has highlighted honor as the pivotal Mediterranean value, and this research has been succinctly formulated and brilliantly applied to the New Testament by Bruce Malina *(New Testament World).* Honor means both someone's claim to worth and the public acknowledgement of the merit of that claim by a relevant social group. Its opposite is shame. Honor may be either ascribed, that is, obtained without any personal effort (for example, by being born into a noble family) or acquired, that is, gained actively, through various forms of social interaction. In Mediterranean culture relationships among people who are not kin are governed not merely by self-interest but by the objective of obtaining honor from vanquishing or even deceiving non-kin in any possible situation.[15] In this context all social interactions, including gift-giving, sporting contests, dinner invitations, commercial transactions, discussions in taverns and around wells, arranging marriages and settling agreements, offer those involved an opportunity, eagerly seized upon, to enhance their honor at someone else's expense.[16] Anthropologists refer to this culture as "agonistic" on account of its pronounced competitiveness.[17]

Pierre Bourdieu has described the process whereby honor is acquired in terms of "challenge and response."[18] This process consists of four stages, and I note that the use of non-inclusive language in what follows is determined by the fact that those involved in contests over honor in Mediterranean culture are usually male.

First there is the challenge. A basic condition of any challenge is that one's adversary is one's equal in honor;[19] getting the better of a social inferior is no way to win honor. The challenge itself consists of a claim to enter the social space of another. A person of honor is ever on the alert to issue such a challenge, in the hope of enhancing his honor and that of his group, especially his family.[20] The claim may either be positive, aimed at gaining a share in that space or at least a mutually beneficial foothold, or negative, with the aim of dislodging another from his social space. The challenge may consist of a word or deed or both. A positive challenge begins with a word of praise, a gift or a genuine request for help, while a negative challenge commences with an insult, a threat or a physical assault.

The *second stage* is how the challenge is regarded. The recipient must judge the challenge in terms of the harm it will cause to his honor if it goes unanswered.

The *third stage* is the receiver's response. There are three possibilities: first, a deliberate refusal to act, expressed in scorn or disdain; second, acceptance of the challenge, manifested in a counter-challenge, either positive or negative, possibly taking the form of physical violence; and, third, a passive refusal to act, which may involve dishonor.

The *fourth stage* is the public verdict, which may either be an award to the successful challenger of honor taken from the person who receives the challenge, or it

---

[15] J. Campbell, *Honour,* 203–12.
[16] Bourdieu, "Sentiment of Honour," 203; Malina, *New Testament World,* 32–33.
[17] Peristiany, *Honour and Shame,* 14.
[18] "Sentiment of Honour"; also see Malina, *New Testament World,* 30–39.
[19] Bourdieu, "Sentiment of Honour," 197.
[20] Ibid., 199.

may be a loss of honor by the challenger in favor of the recipient. The whole game is played out precisely to obtain such a result, for the pursuit of honor is "the basis of the moral code of an individual who sees himself always through the eyes of others, who has need of others for his existence, because the image he has of himself is indistinguishable from that presented to him by other people."[21]

In this culture the establishment of honor depends not only upon words and actions but also upon the intentions that they represent. Thus, to show a desire to run away from a battle would be dishonorable whether one succeeded or not. Honor is established or impugned by conduct because it makes manifest certain intentions. An affront may be forgiven if it was actually unintentional. More commonly perhaps, an injured party may take the view that actions speak louder than words.[22] The position has been well formulated by Pitt-Rivers as follows:

> The intention of a person is paramount in relation to his honour . . . but it is the intention evident in his actions rather than expressed in his words. A man commits his honour only through his *sincere* intentions. Giving his word of honour, he asserts sincerity and stakes his honour upon the issue, be it a promise regarding the future or an assurance regarding past events. If his true will was not behind the promise or the assertion, then he is not dishonoured if he fails to fulfil the promise or turns out to have lied.[23]

This means that a man is able to lie and deceive without forfeiting his honor. This attitude coexists with the fact that to be called a liar in public is a very serious insult. But you can only call another a liar in this culture if you are sure he has committed his honor to the statement and to know this you must be aware of his true intentions. For as long as a person remains steadfast in his intentions, it is permissible for him cleverly to misrepresent them. The victim of such misrepresentation is thereby dishonored.

One way to tie someone to the truth of a statement, to the fixity of his intentions, is to obtain an oath from him. This commits his honor to the truth of what is said. Pitt-Rivers explains what is involved when a man makes an oath as follows:

> By invoking that which is sacred to him—his God, the bones of saints, his loyalty to his sovereign, the health of his mother or simply his own honour—he activates a curse against himself in the eventuality of his failure to implement his oath or, at least, he ensures that public opinion is entitled to judge him as dishonoured.[24]

Although the honor code of this society requires that every honorable man will respond to all dishonor offered to him, it often happens that a period of time will elapse before response is possible. In the meantime the person who has been slighted will be activated by a desire to wreak vengeance upon his opponent. The reason for this is that "to leave affronts unavenged is to leave one's honour in a state of desecration."[25]

---

[21] Ibid., 211.
[22] Pitt-Rivers, "Honour," 26–27.
[23] Ibid., 32–33.
[24] Ibid., 34.
[25] Ibid., 27.

The longer the aggrieved party takes to launch some attack on his adversary, however, the less effective his response will be in restoring his damaged reputation, unless he has good reasons for delay, such as that he is injured or the other party is no longer in his proximity.[26] Oddly enough, in some parts of the Mediterranean region it is thought to be honorable for a man to have enemies who hope to be avenged on him, since this means that he must have shamed them at some time in the past.[27]

Applying the Model

Making the Agreement (Galatians 2:1–10)

In Gal 2:1 Paul states that fourteen years after his first visit he went up to Jerusalem with Barnabas and that he took Titus along. Titus, as we soon learn (2:3), was an uncircumcised Gentile. He continues: "I went up by revelation; and I laid before them (but privately before those who were of repute) the gospel which I preach among the Gentiles, lest somehow I should be running or had run in vain" (2:2).[28] Presumably, Paul would not have bothered making the trip if there were not some members of the Jerusalem church for whom there was something problematic concerning the gospel which he was preaching and had preached. Acts 15:1, moreover, mentions persons who come to Antioch from Judaea insisting upon circumcision of the Gentile Christians, which results in the Antiochean church sending Paul, in the company of Barnabas and certain others, to Jerusalem (Acts 15:2). However one seeks to correlate Paul's description of the meeting in Galatians 2 with the Apostolic Council as related in Acts 15, this particular feature of the Lucan account may well be historical.[29]

Assuming, therefore, the presence in Jerusalem of Jewish Christians who did consider that Paul was "running in vain," we must enquire how his arrival would have been perceived in the light of prevailing social values and practices. In terms of the model set out above, this visit represented a clear challenge, a claim to enter the social space of the Jerusalem church.[30] This is a game that, as noted above, can only be played between social equals, and the question of Paul's status in relation to the Jerusalem leadership is a very live issue in the letter (Gal 1:1; 1:16–17; 2:2, 6, 9). His references to "those who were of repute" (2:2, 6) and those "reputed to be pillars" (2:9) suggest that Paul is writing in a context in which others are pressing the claims of James, Peter and John to pre-eminence over him, while he is deliberately failing to concede such superiority.[31]

---

[26] J. Campbell, *Honour*, 202–3.

[27] Bourdieu, "Sentiment of Honour," 199.

[28] Unless otherwise stated, biblical translations are from the Revised Standard Version.

[29] Betz, *Galatians*, 85.

[30] Luke may have failed to mention the presence of Titus among the visitors and presented Paul as sent by the Antiochean church, rather than making the trip as a result of a personal revelation (Acts 15:2), precisely in order to disguise the confrontational nature of Paul's visit!

[31] Similarly, Barrett, " 'Pillar' Apostles."

The fact that Paul mentions that he and Barnabas brought Titus along with them suggests that the source of the problem was the relationship between Jews and uncircumcised Gentiles in the community and underlines the defiant provocation of the challenge: "They don't want Jews and Gentiles to mix together in the community or partake of the one loaf and the one cup? They demand that the Gentiles be circumcised? In that case I will bring one of my uncircumcised Gentile converts right into their midst!" Such an action would have had the result of besmirching the honor of those in favor of Gentile circumcision unless and until they could somehow respond to the challenge thrown down before them. Paul was playing the game in the ruggedly confrontational style typical of Mediterranean culture. Although he may have seen this as a positive challenge for a share in the social space of the Jerusalem church, or at least to secure a mutually beneficial foothold, those favoring circumcision would have seen it as essentially a negative challenge, an attempt to dislodge them from their social sphere. Strong corroboration for the agonistic or conflict-ridden nature of Paul's encounter with the Jerusalem church emerges in an expression Paul uses in describing its resolution, when he says that James and Cephas and John δεξιὰς ἔδωκαν ἐμοὶ καὶ Βαρναβᾷ κοινωνίας (2:9), which, as will be explained below, primarily carries the connotation of a cessation of hostilities.

It should be noted that Paul seeks to assert that he laid his gospel before "those who were of repute" *in private* (κατ᾽ ἰδίαν, 2:2). The model suggests that he did so as not to embarrass them in public. In other words, Paul is suggesting that he wanted to have his discussion with the leaders of the church away from the gaze of the wider Christian community so that their honor would not be compromised by having to concede that he was in the right. This protestation is hardly convincing, however, in the light of the fact that he does not seem to have made any effort to hide the fact of his openly traveling with Titus. The whole community must have known why he had gone into closed session with their leaders (2:4).

Moreover, we should not interpret the fact that Paul laid down his gospel before them as being in any way motivated by a concern on his part that it was in need of their accreditation or approval. Thus, although the word ἀνατίθημι, which he uses to describe his presentation of his gospel to the Jerusalem church (2:2), indicates that he was submitting it for their consideration, it tells us nothing about the relative status of the parties; it is a word he would use precisely because it did not mean he was seeking their approval.[32] Similarly, while the phrase μὴ πως εἰς κενὸν τρέχω ἢ ἔδραμον in the same verse (where τρέχω is almost certainly a subjunctive) probably expresses apprehension,[33] the apprehension in question is not his but that of his opponents.[34] The possibility that he had conducted his mission in vain in the past or was doing so in the present is completely inconsistent with what he says in Galatians 1; it is the view taken by Paul's opponents, not by Paul. In fact, Paul must have claimed that God was actively supporting his mission, since part of the resolution of the meeting was

---

[32] Dunn, "Relationship," 467–68.
[33] BDF 188.
[34] So Betz, *Galatians*, 87–88, *contra* Dunn, "Relationship," 467, and *Commentary*, 93–94.

an acknowledgement by the pillars of "the grace which had been given" to him (v. 9). Accordingly, the preferable interpretation of Gal 2:2, notably consonant with the agonistic overtones of the previous verse, is that Paul was saying, "Look, judge me by the results of my efforts!" He had not gone to Jerusalem because he was worried about the validity of his message, or because he needed any approval from the leaders there, but rather to stifle any criticism by reference to the results he had achieved. Moreover, the statement in 2:3, "But even Titus, who was with me, was not compelled to be circumcised [ἠναγκάσθη περιτμηθῆναι], though he was a Greek," most naturally suggests that Titus was not circumcised.

Gal 2:3 is sometimes taken to imply, however, that, although there was no compulsion, Titus was circumcised *voluntarily*.[35] This reading of the verse depends, accordingly, upon giving special emphasis to the word ἀναγκάζειν. The principal difficulty with this view, and it is a significant one, is that later in the letter, at 6:12, Paul also uses ἀναγκάζειν with a passive infinitive of περιτέμνειν in a situation where the notion of voluntary circumcision is not in issue. The repeated use of the two words in close relationship to one another, in relation to the compulsion that is a hallmark of opposition to Paul's gospel, constitutes one of the many ways in which Paul ties together the Antiochean and Galatian contexts. Moreover, the third instance of ἀναγκάζειν in Galatians is at 2:14 in connection with Ἰουδαίζειν to refer to the action being taken by Peter against the Gentiles. Thus, the usage of ἀναγκάζειν elsewhere in the letter strongly suggests that no special point is being made at 2:3. To take the contrary view would also mean that Paul had allowed an event to occur in Jerusalem directly inconsistent with the opposition to circumcision he expresses in 2:5; 2:21b; 5:2 and 5:11a. I conclude, therefore, that, with respect to Titus, Paul is trumpeting the fact that, having starkly challenged his opponents by bringing this uncircumcised Gentile to Jerusalem in the company of himself and Barnabas, he has got away with it.

The vigor of Paul's challenge to his opponents in Jerusalem inevitably meant that he could expect a vigorous response. The potential scale of the response in this culture can be gauged from the fact that in Acts the Jews who were affronted by the allegation that Paul had, *inter alia,* brought Gentiles into the Temple regarded assassination as the appropriate reaction (Acts 21:27–31; 23:12–15). Even if Acts is not historical in this regard, Luke's account nicely reflects Mediterranean thinking.

In Jerusalem, the response from those most antagonistic to Paul came in the form of the secret infiltration into the meeting of certain "false brothers" who Paul asserts were seeking "to spy out our freedom which we have in Christ Jesus, so that they might bring us into bondage" (καταδουλώσουσιν, Gal 2:4).[36] These persons no doubt advocated that Gentile converts must be circumcised. Paul emphatically states that he did not yield to them, so that "the truth of the gospel" might be maintained "for you" (v. 5), meaning his Galatian readers, which constitutes a striking link

---

[35] So Burkitt, *Christian Beginnings*, 118.

[36] F. Watson's suggestion (*Paul*, 50–51) that the insinuation of the false brethren took place at Antioch and not Jerusalem is an unnatural reading of v. 4.

between the two contexts.[37] In other words, Paul successfully defended his version of the gospel, involving a eucharist shared by Jews and Gentiles without the latter needing to be circumcised, against determined opponents, whose defeat meant they had been dishonored in the eyes of the Christian community in Jerusalem. The actual form of his victory came in the result of the meeting, that the pillars "added nothing" (v. 6) to Paul, the words οὐδὲν προσανέθεντο having a most emphatic position at the conclusion of an admittedly tortuous clause. This means that they did not seek to impose circumcision and the Jewish law on Paul's Gentile converts,[38] in spite of the arguments of the "false brothers" that they do just that.

Paul goes on to say that the pillars, acknowledging both that he had been entrusted with preaching the gospel "of the uncircumcision," as had Peter of the circumcision, and that grace attended his efforts (vv. 7–9a), entered into an agreement with him and Barnabas, manifested in an exchange of handshakes, a gesture to which I will return below. The agreement had two aspects: first, that Paul and Barnabas would go to the Gentiles and James, Peter and John to the circumcised and, second, that Paul and Barnabas would remember the poor (presumably in Jerusalem), which, Paul tells us, he was eager to do (v. 9–10).

There has been much discussion as to the meaning of both aspects of this arrangement. The first must have meant in practice not simply that Paul and Barnabas would be active among the Gentiles, or that the Jewish law was not necessary for the Gentile converts, but that their communities in the cities of the Diaspora would be able to include Jews and Gentiles in complete fellowship with one another without the latter having to become Jews through circumcision. Although it is sometimes suggested that perhaps the issue of Jewish-Gentile table-fellowship, which was later to rear its head in Antioch, was simply not discussed in Jerusalem, this is highly unlikely, mainly for the reason that the traveling of Titus in the company of Paul and Barnabas (with whom he no doubt ate) raised precisely this issue. The fact that Paul and Barnabas brought Titus with them to Jerusalem and that he did not have to be circumcised represents in microcosm the larger issue that was at stake. Moreover, Paul could hardly have laid before them the meaning of his mission to the Gentiles (2:2) without covering an integral part of this, namely that Jews and Gentiles were to be permitted complete fellowship with one another in the communities without circumcision being imposed on the latter.

The second commitment, by which Paul and Barnabas undertook to remember the poor (of the Jerusalem church), must have involved some undertaking to provide them with financial assistance. Yet it is most unlikely that this obligation constituted a "significant concession" to the advocates of circumcision, as claimed by Taylor,[39] since what was proposed was so different from and fell so far short of the action the "false brothers" had sought. Moreover, even if it was meant as a concession to them, they certainly did not accept it as such. This is clear from the attitude Paul expresses

---

[37] Esler, "Sectarianism," 60.
[38] Betz, *Galatians*, 95.
[39] Taylor, *Paul, Antioch*, 121.

toward this group in Gal 2:4–5 and the tone he adopts in doing so, together with his later suggestion to the Galatians that the church in Jerusalem is implicated in slavery (4:25). These features indicate a continuing animosity on Paul's part toward them which is not compatible with their having accepted the result of the meeting on the basis of promised support for poor in the city. Thus, the promise by Paul and Barnabas to support the poor should not be interpreted as a conciliatory gesture to the Jewish-Christian advocates of circumcision, but rather as a measure proposed by James, Peter and John for their own benefit, so that they could agree to the Gentile mission as conducted by Paul and Barnabas while yet preserving their honor by being able to claim before the Jerusalem church that they had extracted a valuable concession in return. That this is the correct interpretation is supported by the way in which Paul, having stated that they had agreed to remember the poor, immediately adds: "which very thing I was eager to do" (ὃ καὶ ἐσπούδασα αὐτὸ τοῦτο ποιῆσαι, 2:10). In other words, James and Peter really got nothing out of him at all in return for the agreement, since he would, in any event, have carried out the only action which they sought from him. This means he has got the better of them in the exchange and his honor is enhanced at their expense.

The manner in which the compromise was effected, with James, Peter and John, "who were reputed to be pillars," giving Paul and Barnabas the right hand of fellowship (2:9) is extremely significant and its implications have been largely unappreciated. Commentators frequently refer to a range of data involving the shaking of hands and suggest that this was a way formally to conclude an agreement.[40] More particularly, Sampley points to a handful of papyrus evidence that "across the Greco-Roman world" contracts could be entered into by "giving the right hand," and further suggests that this interpretation is confirmed by reading κοινωνία as equivalent to *societas*, the Roman legal partnership.[41] Yet Sampley's case for a connection between "giving the right hand" and the formation of Roman *societates* is weak, since they actually "arose by mere agreement *(nudo consensu)*, i.e., without the need for any form or for any physical act,"[42] as he himself acknowledges.[43] It is therefore not surprising that Sampley does not cite a single case where the "giving the right hand" and a *societas* are found together. It is also worth noting that Greek law, with which we might expect the parties to the alleged agreement to have been far more familiar, was not nearly so liberal as Roman in dispensing with the requirement of writing in contracts,[44] and this would have rendered the suggested analogy from Roman law even more inappropriate. Finally and even more fundamentally, we are speaking of an arrangement reached between five Jews in Jerusalem, and there is a context for the phrase "giving the right hand" much closer to such persons than the language of commercial law. It tends to be forgotten that the precise expression δοῦναι δεξιάς (or δεξιάν), occasionally accompanied by λαβεῖν δεξιάς (or δεξιάν), is virtually a

---

[40] Sampley, *Pauline Partnership*, 26–28; Betz, *Galatians*, 100; Dunn, *Commentary*, 110.
[41] Sampley, *Pauline Partnership*, 26–28, 29–32.
[42] Nicholas, *Roman Law*, 171.
[43] Sampley, *Pauline Partnership*, 13.
[44] Nicholas, *Roman Law*, 195.

technical one in the Septuagint and refers to the institution of peace after hostilities. We cannot assume the five Jews concerned (or Paul's readers) knew Roman law or would have been comfortable with an analogy allegedly drawn from that sphere; but we can assume that some of the five and most of Paul's audience were familiar with the Septuagint. The phrase in question occurs eleven times in the Septuagint and always with this meaning (1 Macc 6:58; 11:50, 62, 66; 13:45, 50; 2 Macc 4:34; 11:26; 12:11; 13:22; 14:19). The same expression is occasionally found elsewhere.[45] Although Burton discussed this data, he missed its precise significance and proposed the excessively general meaning "to give the right hand" as "a pledge of friendship."[46] Moreover, it is always the antagonist in the militarily superior position who "gives the right hand."[47] Often such a person is asked to "give the right (hand)" (1 Macc 11:50, 66; 13:45; 2 Macc 11:26; 12:11) and the recipients thereof, sometimes virtually suppliants, are said "to take it" (λαβεῖν, 1 Macc 11:66; 13:50; 2 Macc 12:12; 13:22; 14:19). It is not a gesture made between equals, as claimed by Betz.[48] Burton did at least appreciate this dimension of the phrase. The flavor of giving the right hand in Galatians is that the Jerusalem leaders, regarding themselves as being in a superior position, offered peace as a way of resolving a period of conflict. Yet it is hardly the case that Paul acknowledges such superiority, since immediately prior to this, he describes those who make this gesture as "(those) who were reputed to be pillars," thereby explicitly refusing to endorse such a status.[49] It is odd that Sampley, having argued against the relevance of the Septuagintal expression (as to the meaning of which he follows Burton into error) for the reason that Paul would not use a phrase suggesting his inferiority to the Jerusalem apostles, actually acknowledges that Paul is capable of irony in speaking of the status of other leaders (as at 2 Cor 11:5 and 12:11),[50] yet fails to note that such irony appears just before the clause in question in v. 9.

In addition, given the position of the word "fellowship" (κοινωνία) at the end of the phrase in Gal 2:9 (δεξιὰς ἔδωκαν ἐμοὶ καὶ Βαρναβᾷ κοινωνίας), the genitive case in which it is expressed may best be understood as appositive:[51] that is, the Jerusalem leaders offered peace "which consisted in fellowship." The use of κοινωνία as the word to describe the peace which had now been established between the parties inevitably means that its reference is to what will characterize relations in the future, not to what the pillars and Paul and Barnabas already held in common.[52] We must still determine, however, what the parties meant by κοινωνία in this context. Most of the commentators opt for some general notion of fellowship, in the sense of sharing

---

[45] For example, Josephus, *Ant.* 18.326–331, where it is used of a Parthian king offering safe conduct to two Jewish leaders who had been harrying his forces, although its military application may need to be qualified here, since Josephus states that in that region it was used generally of safe conduct.

[46] *Galatians*, 96.

[47] The only possible exception to this comes in 1 Macc 6:58, where the Seleucid monarch had military difficulties in subjugating the Jews; nevertheless, he was still in a position of political pre-eminence.

[48] *Galatians*, 100.

[49] So Barrett, " 'Pillar' Apostles."

[50] Sampley, *Pauline Partnership*, 26.

[51] See BDF 92, for examples of the appositive genitive.

[52] As suggested by Dunn, *Commentary*, 110.

or of an equal and harmonious relationship,[53] but this is not a satisfactory approach. Paul uses κοινωνία thirteen times in his letters (Rom 15:26; 1 Cor 1:9; 10:16 [twice]; 2 Cor 6:14; 8:4; 9:13; 13:13; Gal 2:9; Phil 1:5, 2:1; 3:10; Phlm 6) and there are only six other instances in the New Testament (Acts 2:42; Heb 13:16; 1 John 1:3,6 [twice] and 7). Although all examples of the word in Paul involve sharing or common participation, its particular connotations vary considerably. To determine what the word means in Gal 2:9, we must primarily consider its semantic range for Paul in the light of its context in the letter itself. First of all, it is clear that the word must mean something which James, Peter and John are capable, through their own behavior, of supplying or at least guaranteeing. For this reason we may eliminate the use of the word in connection with the Holy Spirit or with Jesus Christ, or faith in him, in any general sense (1 Cor 1:9; 2 Cor 13:13; Phil 2:1; 3:10; Phlm 6). Second, its employment by Paul in connection with the sharing of physical goods in the form of the collection (Rom 15:26; 2 Cor 8:4; 9:13) has no application here, since the Jerusalem church was offering no such thing. Third, the connotation of the word as "association" in a very broad sense found at 2 Cor 6:14 is inappropriate, since some more particular meaning is required, otherwise the offer would have been a fairly empty one, which is not the impression conveyed by Paul. The fourth possibility is the sense of κοινωνία as active cooperation in the widest sense found at Phil l:5.[54] Although it is difficult entirely to exclude the meaning in Phil 1:5, on balance it does not seem the right sense. For if the pillars were promising some form of cooperation, we must still ask what form it would take. Whereas it is clear why Paul would apply the word to the efforts of the Philippians, what cooperation would the parties to the Jerusalem agreement have envisaged once they had divided the world between them? Accordingly, one possibility remains within the Pauline semantic field for κοινωνία, its eucharistic meaning in 1 Cor 10:16. It should not be forgotten that κοινωνία was commonly employed in antiquity to denote table-fellowship, including cases where human beings enjoyed sacrificial meals with the gods.[55]

Were the pillars, therefore, offering a peace which consisted of their willingness in the future to engage in eucharistic table-fellowship with Paul and his Gentile converts? Apart from the process of elimination just conducted, three other considerations suggest that this is indeed what Paul has in mind. At a general level, as already noted, demands that Gentiles be circumcised were raised by Jewish Christians in the context of mixed communities where Jews and Gentiles were sharing the one loaf and the one cup of the eucharist. Interpreting κοινωνία as eucharistic table-fellowship has the attraction that the pillars are proposing a peace on the very issue that gave rise to the problem in the first place. Second, Paul's focus on Titus, on the fact that he actually brought him to Jerusalem and that he was not circumcised, again raises the issue of the interrelationship of Jew and Gentile in the community to which James, Peter and John would be directly responding, and in Paul's favor, on this view of

---

[53] Betz, *Galatians*, 100; Dunn, *Commentary*, 110–11; Matera, *Galatians*, 77.
[54] See O'Brien, *Philippians*, 61–62.
[55] Hauck, "κοινός." 3.798–800.

κοινωνία. Last, and most significant, the very event that rouses Paul's ire at Antioch is the termination of table-fellowship by Peter and the other Jewish Christians, an event described only three verses after the reference to κοινωνία (Gal 2:12). That is to say, Paul's anger over this rupture of fellowship is readily explicable if this was precisely what the pillars had promised to guarantee, or even become involved in themselves.

The phrase which occurs at the end of v. 9 is consistent with this interpretation: ἵνα ἡμεῖς εἰς τὰ ἔθνη, αὐτοὶ δὲ εἰς τὴν περιτομήν. Although made a little obscure by the ellipsis of the verb,[56] the point of the expression is that henceforward Paul (and Barnabas) would continue their work among the Gentiles in the Diaspora, which necessarily meant intimate fellowship between Jew and Gentile, with the previous doubts about such fellowship now removed, while the pillars would concentrate on the Jews. The function of the clause is primarily to emphasize the authority of Paul and Barnabas and the legitimacy of their gospel in one mission area, and that of the pillars in another, rather than simply to differentiate those areas. This point can be made with a colloquial translation of v. 9: "so that we might do our thing among the Gentiles, while they did theirs among the Jews." On this view, when Peter travels to the Pauline missionary zone of Antioch after the Jerusalem meeting and enters into table-fellowship with Gentiles, he is simply implementing the agreement. Since he is in Paul's area of responsibility, he puts into practice the peace which has been established between the parties by taking part in the practice which constituted its substance: κοινωνία, in the sense of table-fellowship. Perhaps this was his purpose in visiting the city. The assumption of many commentators that the concluding words of Gal 2:9 refer merely to the division of the zones of evangelism, either geographic or ethnic,[57] does not sit easily with this subsequent visit of Peter to a city where Paul was actively evangelizing, or with the existence of large numbers of Jews in virtually every Diaspora city.

It is of fundamental importance in understanding the significance of the agreement recorded in Gal 2:7–10, however, to note that Paul does not record that there was any exchange of oaths to bind the parties to this agreement. As we have already noted, in contemporary Mediterranean culture the taking of an oath is the only sure way to know that the maker of a promise is truly committed to it. A consideration of the nature of ancient Greek and Jewish oaths, as set out, for example, in J. Schneider's valuable treatment ("ὅρος"),[58] reveals that they were employed in a manner very similar to their modern use. In the ancient period the oath was also primarily a form of self-cursing, effected by calling upon a particular deity for punishment should one not be speaking the truth. Specific provision was made in the Pentateuch for oaths to be taken by the name of Yahweh (Deut 6:13; 10:20) and false swearing was an abuse of God's name (Exod 20:7; Lev 19:12). There were two broad types of oath: first, those used in judicial contexts to assert the truth of testimony and, second, promissory

---

[56] An occasional phenomenon in Paul with ἵνα (Rom 4:16; 1 Cor 1:31). Bruce (*Commentary*, 124) reasonably suggested that the missing verb may be πορεύομαι or εὐαγγελίζομαι. The ἵνα probably expresses purpose here, although it may denote result.

[57] So Betz, *Galatians*, 100; Lightfoot, *Galatians*, 110; Matera, *Galatians*, 77–78.

[58] J. Schneider, "ὅρκος."

oaths, which sealed the truth of a promise made with respect to future conduct.[59] The second type is the one relevant to Paul's situation in Jerusalem. There is a good example in Nehemiah, where an oath of this kind is used to confirm an agreement *de futuro*, in that the Israelites agree, under curse and oath (10:29), to adhere to the law of Moses.[60] Other Old Testament examples of promissory oaths can be seen in those which Rahab took from the Israelite spies to ensure the safety of herself and her family when Jericho was captured (Josh 1:12–22) and in the oaths of the Israelites not to give their daughters to the tribe of Benjamin (Judg 21:1–5). In time difficulties began to beset the giving of oaths.[61] Nevertheless, they still remained a common practice among many Jews; they appear, for example, in the *Damascus Document* (9:9–10:3), among the Pharisees and in the Mishnah.[62]

All this suggests that oaths were a characteristic Jewish way of solemnly confirming a promise as to future conduct. That Paul himself was not opposed to oaths, and, indeed, regarded them as the appropriate means of undergirding one's commitments, is evident in Gal 1:20 ("before God, I do not lie") and in the many other occasions in his correspondence where he resorts to them.[63] Accordingly, the suggestion by Verseput that the exchange of the right hand of fellowship was "an especially binding pledge of good faith often in the face of a hostile situation"[64] is correct with respect to the second aspect, but wrong as to the gesture being particularly binding. Although the proffering of the right hand was the usual method of calling hostilities to an end, to obtain a stronger guarantee from the (dominant) party making the offer it was necessary to obtain an oath, as can be seen in two of the eleven Septuagintal instances of the expression δοῦναι δεξιάς, where oaths are given as well.[65]

The possibility that Paul sought an oath from the pillars but was refused, or simply did not bother to ask for one because he knew it would be useless, is raised by certain evidence external to Galatians which suggests that James, and perhaps Peter and John, would simply have refused to give one. In Jas 5:12 there is an injunction against making oaths: "But above all, my brethren, do not swear, either by heaven or by earth, or with any other oath, but let your yes be yes and your no be no, that you may not fall under any condemnation." Even if one does not accept the traditional attribution of this letter to James, the brother of the Lord, the same person whom we meet in Galatians 2,[66] we may be reasonably confident that its author had access to traditions about James which

---

[59] Ibid., 5.458.

[60] Presumably the type of curse involved a general formulation along the lines suggested by Schneider: "Yahweh do this to me, and more also, if . . ." (ibid., 5.460).

[61] The prophets, for example, complained of the giving of false oaths (Jer 5:2; Zech 5:3–4), while false and excessive oath-taking was lambasted in the wisdom literature (Sir 23:9–14).

[62] J. Schneider, "ὅρκος," 5.461.

[63] Rom 1:9; 9:1; 1 Cor 15:31; 2 Cor 1:23; 11:23; Phil 1:8; 1 Thess 2:5, 10.

[64] Verseput, "Paul's Gentile Mission," 49–50.

[65] 1 Macc 6:61 and 2 Macc 4:34, in both of which cases the oath was promptly broken! In the latter case the relevant phrase is καὶ δεξιὰς μεθ' ὅρκων δούς, which well illustrates the supernumerary nature of the oaths. Another instance can be seen in Josephus, *Ant.* 18.326–331, where one of the two Jewish leaders at war with the Parthians accepted a proffered right hand as sufficient for the safe conduct, but the other wanted (and got) an oath as well.

[66] See the discussion on the authorship of the Epistle of James in Dibelius, *James*, 11–21.

may have been historical, such as that he had opposed swearing oaths. It is significant that a similar prohibition on oaths appears in Matt 5:33–37. This might also originate in a Jewish-Christian stratum of tradition, possibly even originating in the teaching of Jesus himself,[67] and, if so, it would be further evidence of an antipathy to oath-taking among Jewish Christians like James, Peter and John which may well have proven an insuperable obstacle to Paul's obtaining from them an oath on their intention to be bound by the agreement. Whatever the reason, the consequences of Paul's failure to obtain such an oath, the ultimate sanction on the performance of compacts in this culture, were, as we will see, extremely significant.

Breaking the Agreement (Galatians 2:11–14)

Although Paul does not say so explicitly, we may deduce from Gal 2:11–14 that immediately after the meeting in Jerusalem he returned to Antioch, no doubt accompanied by Barnabas and Titus.[68] Peter followed them there some time later (Gal 2:11). In seeking to comprehend the event in Antioch recounted in Gal 2:11–14, it is essential to ask what happened in the Jerusalem church following the departure of Paul, Barnabas and Titus. Since Paul himself supplies no information whatever on this question (except as to the fact that certain people were sent to Antioch by James, leading to Peter's suspension of table-fellowship with the Gentile members of the community, Gal 2:12), it is necessary to generate scenarios and then to test them against the evidence in the text. Although most New Testament critics engage in such an exercise, difficulties arise when the scenarios employed originate in a modern Western outlook on social relations and not in an ancient Mediterranean one. What I propose, therefore, is the stimulation of culturally appropriate possibilities or questions using the challenge and response model outlined above.

The members of the Jerusalem church who advocated the circumcision of Gentile converts had experienced a decisive defeat at the hands of Paul and Barnabas. In Gal 2:4–5 Paul denigrates these opponents and presents himself as having successfully resisted their attack. These verses offer a vignette of a Mediterranean man at his agonistic best. They had taken on Paul and lost and there is nothing to suggest that they had secured some advantage to sweeten their defeat. In the terms of the model, Paul had grievously dishonored them. As I have already explained, persons in this social context who have been so seriously shamed do not forgive or forget the insult. Bitterness and hostility will characterize their attitude towards him who has shamed them and they will seek every opportunity to obtain revenge. We may reasonably propose, therefore, that when Paul departed from Jerusalem with Barnabas and Titus, he left behind him a group in the church of that city who were actuated by powerful malice toward him and who would seek in some way to injure him or his mission. Given his absence from Jerusalem, one favored Mediterranean means of vengeance,

---

[67] The fact that Paul himself had no difficulty in giving an oath (Gal 1:20) when such a practice may have been banned by Jesus shows how far Paul may have been from historical Jesus traditions.

[68] I see nothing to recommend the view of Lüdemann (*Paul*, 75–77) that the incident at Antioch occurred before the Jerusalem conference.

physical assault, was unavailable. But this still left another course, to bring dishonor upon him by interfering with his mission or, best of all, to have the authorities in the Jerusalem church revoke the agreement they had made with him and Barnabas, in particular by insisting on circumcision for Gentile converts.

A plausible scenario to propose, accordingly, rooted in ancient Mediterranean rather than modern North Atlantic values, is that the Jewish Christians went to work on James and Peter by putting pressure on them to resile from the agreement soon after Paul's departure for Antioch. This may have started even before Peter's departure for that city, although, if so, it was unsuccessful since, upon his arrival in Antioch, Peter implemented the agreement by engaging in table-fellowship with the Gentile of the community there (Gal 2:12a). As already noted, such action was a very practical demonstration of the κοινωνία which James, Peter and John had proffered in Jerusalem as the regime to characterize relations between them now that peace had been declared. In due course, however, the position changed, for people came from James and, following their arrival, Peter broke off table-fellowship, as did all the rest of the Jews, even Barnabas. There seems little reason to doubt that James sent representatives to tell Peter and the other Jews that mixed table-fellowship must cease.[69] Some explanation is needed for this radical alteration of attitude. One socially realistic possibility is that after Peter had left Jerusalem, those favoring circumcision had intensified their campaign on James, who, with Peter out of Jerusalem, succumbed to the pressure, decided to resile from the agreement and sent word to Peter of the new position. It is clear that behind the change lay the activities of Jewish Christians, since Paul attributes Peter's withdrawal from table-fellowship in Antioch as motivated by fear of this group (Gal 2:12b). No doubt a fear which Peter could entertain in Antioch would have been just as real for James in Jerusalem. I conclude, therefore, that the strict Jewish Christians, having lost the first round when Paul and Barnabas were in Jerusalem, found an effective way of restoring this slight to their honor by bringing to bear on James (and Peter as well) some kind of threat significant enough to have them renege on the agreement they had reached with Paul. As a result, the Jews of Antioch, except Paul, would no longer share meals with the Gentiles, including the all-important eucharistic meal, which was for Paul the significant form of commensality (1 Cor 11:17–34).

There is strong confirmation for this view of how the agreement was broken in the first clause of v. 14: ἀλλ᾽ ὅτε εἶδον ὅτι οὐκ ὀρθοποδοῦσιν πρὸς τὴν ἀλήθειαν τοῦ εὐαγγελίου, εἶπον τῷ Κηφᾷ . . . "But when I saw that they were not walking straight with respect to the truth of the Gospel, I said to Cephas . . ."[70] Paul interprets their behavior as involving an illicit change of direction, and the fact that he describes their failure to keep on course as being "with respect to the truth of the Gospel" helps us identify the nature of their aberration. For Paul employs the phrase "the truth of

---

[69] So Betz, *Galatians*, 108, who suggests that it is only because of Acts 15:24 that some critics doubt that James himself was behind the men from James.

[70] My translation. The word ὀρθοποδοῦσιν does not occur before Paul; I have rendered it literally to preserve the force of the image. The possible meanings of πρός here are "towards" or "with respect to." I follow Lightfoot in favoring the latter meaning (*Galatians*, 113).

the Gospel" in only one other place in his correspondence, in Gal 2:5, where he uses it to refer to what he was protecting from the actions of the "false brothers" who had sought to replace the freedom which his Gentile converts enjoyed with slavery, undoubtedly of circumcision and the law (Gal 2:4). By specifying "the truth of the Gospel" as the reality with respect to which Peter and the other Jewish Christians in Antioch had changed direction, Paul is saying about as plainly as he could that they had adopted the views previously expressed in Jerusalem by the strict Jewish Christians. In other words, the party which had been defeated in the Holy City had now been victorious in Antioch. Having been dishonored in Jerusalem, when Paul and Barnabas managed to bring an uncircumcised Gentile into their midst and persuade the pillars to permit such association among the mixed congregations of the Diaspora, they had now got their revenge and restored their honor by bringing an end to the very practice of Jewish Gentile table-fellowship which so outraged them.

Moreover, if Paul's complaint against Peter and the other Jews is that they had now altered their position and accepted the views of the strict Jewish Christians, it follows from this that they had come to insist upon circumcision of the Gentiles as the price of the reinstitution of table-fellowship. This is yet another reason for suggesting Paul's claim that Peter was seeking to "compel the Gentiles to Judaize" (τὰ ἔθνη ἀναγκάζεις Ἰουδαΐζειν, Gal 2:14) involved circumcision. At a more general level, moreover, it is probable that circumcision was the price of fellowship, for the reasons that this was the goal of the group from fear of whom Peter withdrew from the Gentiles, that Gal 2:15–16 (where Paul is plainly drawing out the implications of his charge against Peter in v. 14) concerns the imposition of the Law (by circumcision) and that this view is required by the connections Paul draws between the Antiochean and Galatian contexts.[71] Paul uses Ἰουδαΐζειν rather than περιτμηθῆναι at 2:14 because it is the most appropriate way of making the point following Ἰουδαῖος and Ἰουδαϊκῶς earlier in the same verse.

The position of Barnabas needs consideration. In Jerusalem he stands with Paul, yet in Antioch he sides with Peter. Is this alteration of position compatible with the case presented so far? We know a little about Barnabas. There is no reason to doubt the information in Acts to the effect that he was a Jew from Cyprus who had moved to Jerusalem, joined the early community there and even sold some property for its benefit (Acts 4:38–39). The further suggestion in Acts 9:27, however, that it was Barnabas who introduced Paul to the apostles in Jerusalem runs into the difficulty that the trip to Jerusalem which Acts has Paul make after his conversion cannot be reconciled with Gal 1:17, while, on Paul's second trip to Jerusalem (Gal 1:18–24), there is no mention of Barnabas. Presumably, Barnabas met Paul in Antioch, but Barnabas must have retained links with the Jerusalem church. Plainly, for a time, Barnabas adopted Paul's approach of allowing Gentiles entrance to mixed Christian communities without their needing to be circumcised. In Jerusalem he maintained this view jointly with Paul. The only question then becomes whether it is likely that Barnabas would have abandoned such principles in Antioch. There is nothing that renders such a view im-

---

[71] See Esler, "Sectarianism."

plausible. In Jerusalem he and Paul had persuaded the leaders there to accept the legitimacy of the approach to the Gentiles. If they had been unsuccessful in Jerusalem, perhaps he would have abandoned Paul's view then and there. As long as such agreement continued, the position of Barnabas was not problematic, but, as soon as James and Peter had resiled from the agreement, his situation, as a Jew having closer links with the Jerusalem church than Paul himself had, altered. Now the choice was either the strict Jewish-Christian line newly espoused by the pillars, behind which lay some significant pressure (enough to make even Peter afraid, 2:12), or the line taken by Paul. Faced with this change of events, Barnabas, like all the other Jewish Christians except Paul himself (2:13), broke off table-fellowship (and insisted on circumcision of the Gentiles as the price of its reinstatement). The impact on Paul of this desertion by Barnabas can be discerned at a number of places in Galatians.[72]

Yet if the actions of Peter, instigated by James, did constitute a contravention of their Jerusalem agreement with Paul and Barnabas, why does Paul not charge Peter with such perfidy before the Antiochean congregation, choosing instead to tax him merely with inconsistent conduct in first living like the Gentiles (which obviously includes eating with them) and later seeking to have the Gentiles Judaize? At first sight his failure to do so might seem to be an obstacle to the view that the agreement had been breached. The answer to this apparent difficulty lies in Mediterranean attitudes to honesty and dishonesty. As noted above, those who make promises or enter into agreements commit their honor only through their sincere intentions. If their true will is not behind their words, they are not dishonored by going back on their promises. Indeed, to get the better of someone by a false statement to which one was not truly committed is actually a way of winning honor. Those who cleverly misrepresent their intentions dishonor those who are thereby misled. That is why in this milieu actions speak louder than words, since they are more likely to reflect genuine intentions. The only way to ensure that someone stands behind his or her promise is to have the arrangement sealed by an oath.

Paul's problem in Antioch, as far as criticizing Peter was concerned, lay in the fact that he had not obtained an oath from James and Peter to the effect that they would stand behind their promise. This meant that there was no way of knowing whether they had really committed their honor to the arrangement. Even worse, it meant that by going back on it they would dishonor him who had been misled by their unsupported undertaking. Accordingly, Paul cannot charge Peter with a breach of the Jerusalem agreement, since this would merely remind his readers of the shame which James and Peter had heaped upon his head. All that Paul can do is to accuse Peter of perfidy by pointing to the inconsistency in his actions in first dining with Gentiles and then breaking off such fellowship. In so doing he is relying on the fact that one's intentions are evidenced by one's actions, and Peter's actions thereby condemn him.

This analysis is also of assistance in considering the one substantial issue which remains, namely the vexed question, debate on which began in antiquity,[73] of

---

[72] As noted by Bauckham ("Barnabas").

[73] Betz, *Galatians*, 113.

whether Paul's address to Peter and the Antiochean church ends at Gal 2:14 or whether it continues until v. 21. According to Dunn, most scholars agree that the thought runs on from v. 14 to vv. 15ff. and on to v. 21.[74] Verseput, for example, takes this view for the reason that "not only does Paul give no real indication to his readers that he is abandoning the Antiochean story in v. 15, but the Pauline remark in 2:14 is in the words of O. Bauernfeind . . . 'sinnlos knapp' when divorced from the following verses."[75] Betz, on the other hand, runs a strong case on rhetorical grounds for Paul's Antiochean address ending at 2:14.[76] There are persuasive reasons, in addition to those advanced by Betz, for regarding 2:14 as the end of Paul's address. As already noted, since Paul had not obtained an oath from Peter and James, he was unable to charge Peter with breach of the agreement; all he could do was to accuse him of inconsistency of action in Antioch. He announces that Peter stands condemned in v. 11 and then provides just this rationale for the condemnation in v. 14. In other words, vv. 11 and 14 constitute an *inclusio*. In the agonistic context of Paul's relationship with the Jerusalem leaders presented above, what he says in v. 14 is his best point. It is not "sinnlos knapp" but "sinnvoll knapp"! The subject to which he proceeds in v. 15 falls outside of his confrontation with Peter in Antioch. In vv. 15–21 we find not the condemnation of Peter required by v. 11 but a generalized theological reflection on the broad issues at stake written for the benefit of his Galatian audience.

It is occasionally suggested that a Galatian readership would have understood ἡμεῖς in v. 15 as a reference to Peter and Paul.[77] Yet that would not preclude Paul's making a point of the similar position of Peter and himself for the benefit of his Galatian audience, even if no such words had passed his lips in Antioch. More significantly, the idea that ἡμεῖς in v. 15 covers Peter and Paul runs up against the problem of the change to first person singular in v. 18, especially since the parallel between the situations described in v. 17, where the first person plural is used, and v. 18 is so close as to suggest the reference is to the same person. The best explanation for the ἡμεῖς in v. 15 is that Paul is using it with respect only to himself. The "epistolary plural,"[78] or *pluralis sociativus*,[79] a usage in which the first person plural was employed with reference to the first person singular, was idiomatic in *koine* Greek. C. E. B. Cranfield recently concluded there was a high degree of probability that "Paul did sometimes use the first person plural with reference simply to himself,"[80] and Scott J. Hafemann has come to the same view on good grounds.[81] As this form is not common in Paul,[82] each case always needs to be assessed on its merits. Yet even if one were to conclude

---

[74] Dunn, *Jesus, Paul,* 172. It is difficult to see how scholars could hold this view and yet propose, as does Dunn, that Ἰουδαΐζειν in v. 14 does not mean circumcise, given that in vv. 15–21 Paul is plainly opposing the need for Gentiles to take on the law, which entailed circumcision.

[75] Verseput, "Paul's Gentile Mission," 51, citing Bauernfeind, "Schluss," 68.

[76] Betz, *Galatians,* 113–14, argues that the *narratio* ends at 2:14 and that 2:15–21 function as a *propositio.*

[77] Dunn, *Jesus, Paul,* 172.

[78] Moule, *Idiom Book,* 118.

[79] BDF 146–47.

[80] Cranfield, "Changes of Person," 286.

[81] Hafemann, *Suffering,* 12–16.

[82] Lofthouse, "Singular and Plural."

that the ἡμεῖς in v. 15 went beyond Paul himself, however, its epistolary context would point to its including Jews among his Galatian readership, rather than Peter. This would exemplify a common aspect of the epistolary plural, whereby the author identifies himself with some or all of his addressees,[83] and in this case it would mean that Paul was making a theological point which some of his readers, Galatian Jews, understood but were, by their conduct, egregiously disregarding.

Conclusion

By consciously adopting a model of social relationships rooted in the Mediterranean world, I have been able to investigate Paul's account of his interaction with the Jerusalem church in Gal 2:1–14, asking questions rather different from those posed in existing scholarship. From the abundant data in the text responsive to these questions, moreover, I have obtained answers that are quite at odds with those of many modern commentators. On the critical issue I have concluded that Peter did indeed demand circumcision of the Antiochean Gentiles and that in so doing he and James behind him were reneging on the agreement previously struck with Paul in Jerusalem. In this perspective, to interpret the meaning of Peter's attitude as requiring any other action, such as that the Gentiles "Judaize" in some lesser sense, for example, by adopting Jewish customs, underestimates the seriousness of the problem in Antioch and makes it difficult to appreciate the force of the long-standing social pressures which were the context for Paul's primary theological affirmation in Galatians: εἰ γὰρ διὰ νόμου δικαιοσύνη, ἄρα Χριστὸς δωρεὰν ἀπέθανεν (2:21).

After reaching the conclusions set out above, by deliberately trying to clear my mind of modern presuppositions, I discovered that the earliest extant commentary on Galatians, which was written sometime between 366 and 384 C.E. by an unknown author referred to as Ambrosiaster, who was possibly a former Jew and very knowledgeable concerning Judaism,[84] also supports the view that Peter had been advocating circumcision in Antioch. This commentary, a superb work of interpretation by any standard, continually seeks to bring the Antiochean and Galatian contexts into close conjunction, in ways similar to the manner I have advocated here and elsewhere.[85] Thus, after quoting Gal 6:13, Ambrosiaster writes:

> *tale est [hoc], quale et illud dictum ad apostolum Petrum: si tu cum sis Iudaeus, gentiliter vivis, quomodo compellis gentes iudaizare? ita et hi cum ipsi legem non custodirent conversantes et conviventes cum gentilibus Galatas, circumcidere semetipsos cogebant, ut placerent Iudaeis. Per hoc enim molliebant sibi animos Iudaeorum, ut etiam de ipsis non crederent, quod gentiliter viverent.[86]*

Satis dictum.

---

[83] Moule, *Idiom Book*, 117.
[84] Souter, *Earliest Latin Commentaries*, 43–49.
[85] Esler, *Community*, 87–89; and "Sectarianism."
[86] Vogels, *Ambrosiastri Commentarius*, 66.

15

WHAT WAS AT STAKE IN PETER'S "EATING WITH GENTILES" AT ANTIOCH?

Mark D. Nanos

Paul told the Galatians of a time in Antioch when he "condemned" Peter "to his face" for failing to "walk straight toward the good news."[1] He attributed Peter's change of mealtime behavior to a hypocritical effort to escape pressure from "the ones for [ἐκ] circumcision" (Gal 2:11–21).[2] For before "certain ones came from James," Peter "was eating with the Gentiles" but afterwards he "drew back and separated himself, because of fear."

This essay will focus on two interpretive elements that are central for determining what was at stake in the incident recorded and, by implication, in Galatia. Many other questions arise, granted, but the prevailing historical and theological

---

[1] Paul's characterization of the intentions and meaning of the actions of the other players in Antioch, including Peter, represent his rhetorical interests when addressing his later audience in Galatia, and would likely be challenged by each of them. We cannot know how they perceived their own motives or actions, each other's, or even Paul's. For conciseness I will not continue to state at every point that this or that way to understand the situation represents only Paul's point of view, or at least rhetorical interests. See Mitternacht, *Sprachlose;* Thurén, *Derhetorizing Paul;* and my discussion of the various perceptions of the exigence in Galatia in Nanos, *Irony,* 86–109.

[2] This translation and the decision to understand the usage of this label to signify a group advocating ("for") the circumcision of the Gentiles in question, rather than merely an interest group composed of circumcised people, will be discussed below.

The question whether to divide this narrative unit into two or more parts, and, if so, how to do so, is not of concern here. This discussion will focus on the details that emerge in vv. 11–15 but will also seek to take into account the logical implications of the argumentation in vv. 16–21. There are no clear grammatical or conceptual markers dividing this unit (see esp. Holmstrand, *Markers and Meaning,* 157–65). The many different proposals on offer (between vv. 14 and 15, between vv. 15 and 16, and so on) only serve to demonstrate the arbitrary and thus less than convincing results upon which to base any argumentation on the choice made. Is not the entire narrative constructed by Paul after the fact to serve his rhetorical purposes for the Galatian addressees, so that any evidence that may be gathered from throughout this discourse unit is useful for the purpose of constructing and testing all hypotheses of the Antioch incident?

Any effort to coordinate this narrative unit with the accounts in Acts would take us too far afield and thus will not be a matter for discussion in this essay.

constructions of "Pauline" and "Jewish" Christianity[3] depend upon the way two particular questions—which naturally touch on many of the other ones—have been answered to date:

1) What did the ones for circumcision, whom Peter feared, find so objectionable about Peter's eating with Gentiles?

2) What did Paul find so objectionable about Peter's decision to withdraw and separate from these mixed meals?

In other words, what was at stake in Peter's eating—or not—with these Gentiles? In addition, the exegete should consider what may be at stake in his or her interpretation of this event. Getting at the answers entails discussion of a thicket of associated matters that arise in this brief text and some that are brought to its interpretation.

On the one hand, although our text does not include any representation of their own voice, the exegete must make sense of the reaction of those whose disapproval Peter withdrew to avoid. To what did the ones advocating circumcision object? Was it that the food being served at these meals was inappropriate according to Jewish dietary norms? Or that Peter was eating with Gentiles? If the latter, did those whom Peter feared maintain that it was improper to eat with these Gentiles under any conditions, or was there something in particular about the way these mixed meals, to which they objected, were conducted? Could it be that the novel identity claims of these Gentiles apart from proselyte conversion were at dispute and that these were symbolized by the way the meals were served, although the food itself conformed to prevailing Jewish dietary norms and the presence of Gentiles *per se* was not objectionable? In other words, might the problem arise not from the fact that Peter ate *with* Gentiles but because of *the way* that he ate with *these* Gentiles?

On the other hand, we need to make sense of Paul's severe reaction to Peter's change of course. Here, too, we must attend to rhetorical dynamics, not least the one-sided nature of the account, its construction for the purpose of persuading the later Galatian addressees, and the interpretive tradition's investment in understanding Paul to be evaluating negatively the motives for, and results of, observing Jewish law. Paul says he immediately and publicly challenged Peter to his face because Peter stood condemned, accusing Peter of behavior that departed from the principles consistent with the good news of Christ and of hypocrisy, that is, of doing so against his own convictions. Why did Paul object so strongly to this development? What was it precisely that Paul believed was compromised by Peter's withdrawal from these mixed meals? To what kind of mealtime behavior would Paul have Peter return? And how would it reflect walking toward the truth of the gospel, as opposed to how Peter was behaving after his withdrawal, not eating with these Gentiles in the same manner that he had beforehand?

---

[3] See Paget, "Jewish Christianity," 731–75, for discussion of the phenomena and taxonomy usually associated with so-called Jewish Christianity.

Traditionally Paul has been understood to be upset because he maintained
that faith in the gospel obviated continued regard for eating according to Jewish
dietary regulations. But for Paul, did observing a Jewish diet compromise in principle "the truth of the gospel"? Or did he perhaps object instead to the degree
of Jewish dietary rigor necessary to comply with the standards of those whom
Peter feared? Or again, in a different direction, could it be that Paul understood that
Peter's withdrawal and separation undermined the identity of these Gentiles as
equals while remaining Gentiles? If so, then this might indicate that at dispute were
the identification policies of this coalition for its Gentile members, which were
made manifest by the way eating with them was conducted—as among equals instead of according to the prevailing conventions for mixed meals with either
"pagan" guests or proselytes and those engaged in completion of the rite of proselyte conversion.

I will work from the following translation of 2:11–14, and hope that the reader
finds it substantiated by the arguments offered below.

> (11)But when Cephas [Peter] came to Antioch, I [Paul] confronted [ἀντέστην] him
> to his face, because he was standing condemned (indefensibly/dishonorably)
> [ὅτι κατεγνωσμένος ἦν]. (12)For before certain ones came from James, he was eat-
> ing [συνήσθιεν] with the Gentiles; but when they came, he was drawing back
> [ὑπέστελλεν] and he was separating [ἀφώριζεν] himself, because of fear of the
> ones for [advocating] circumcision [φοβούμενος τοὺς ἐκ περιτομῆς]. (13)And
> with him the rest of the Jews were being equally two-faced [καὶ συνυπεκρίθησαν
> αὐτῷ (καὶ) οἱ λοιποὶ Ἰουδαῖοι], so that even Barnabas was being carried away by
> their hypocrisy [ὑποκρίσει: masking of their true face]. (14)But when I saw that
> they were not walking straight toward [ὀρθοποδοῦσιν πρός][4] the truth of the
> good news, I said to Cephas in front of [ἔμπροσθεν] them all, "If you, being a
> Jew [Ἰουδαῖος ὑπάρχων],[5] are living [ζῇς] in the same way as [like] a Gentile
> [ἐθνικῶς][6] and not in the same way as [like] a Jew [Ἰουδαϊκῶς],[7] how can you com-
> pel [ἀναγκάζεις] the Gentiles to become Jews [Ἰουδαΐζειν]?"

---

[4]BAGD 710 (5.d.) on πρός here (note that BDAG 875 [3. ε.δ.] moves this to "in accordance
with," but see entry for ὀρθοποδέω, where the possible sense of direction ["progress"] is acknowledged for this usage in Gal 2:14, although preferring the figurative sense of to "act rightly" or "be
straightforward about the truth of the gospel"). While the figurative sense may still capture the
meaning, a graphic quality is conveyed by the literal sense of "walking"; more important, it keeps the
focus on a halakhic issue of appropriate behavior in view of what one believes. Thus πρός is translated "toward": "walking straight toward. . . ." Another translation that would convey the meaning
would be "walking straight in the way of the truth of the good news." The idea is walking in the right
way or manner, walking on a particular path according to what one believes to be true. See also
Dunn, "Echoes," 462.

[5]Ὑπάρχων refers to being in a state or circumstance, thus expressing the fact that Peter is still a
Jewish person when Paul addresses him (cf. BDAG 1030 [2]); contrast this with v. 15, where Paul
will refer to the fact that Peter (and Paul) were born [φύσει] Jewish.

[6]Lit., "Gentilishly."

[7]Lit., Jewishly. The phrase καὶ οὐχὶ Ἰουδαϊκῶς is not in some important manuscripts, and
Tomson suggests that it should be dropped, noting that the sentence is clearer and displays a chiastic
symmetry when omitted (Paul, 229).

The Problem of Identifying the Interest Groups in Antioch

In addition to the clearly identified persons of Paul, Peter,[8] and Barnabas,[9] there are three other interest groups to whom Paul refers but in terms that can be variously defined, even translated. These groups include the "certain ones from James," "the ones for [ἐκ] circumcision," and "the rest of the Jews" who follow Peter's lead. Although a full discussion of these groups cannot be undertaken in this essay, the translation and approach adopted here should be explained.

As I have discussed elsewhere, none of these labels or identities is ever attributed to the ones influencing the Galatian addressees; any analogies they may have drawn are beyond our knowledge, and our hypotheses should follow from an investigation of the situational discourse to the Galatians and then proceed to the elements that arise in these narratives.[10] That is, although the process is inescapably circular, for we have only this letter from which to work, we run a higher risk of limiting our understanding of the situations in Galatia if we begin from these narrative units—which provide examples to support Paul's later situational purpose with the addressees—and project these events and interest groups onto the Galatian situation. In a similar vein, Paul addresses a singular exigence among several groups in Galatia, but we should not assume that before this letter's arrival—and its effect upon those addressed and, in turn, upon those influencing them—this is the way the situations would be assessed by either the addressees or those in any of these locations who were influencing them in the direction to which Paul objects. The fact that this narrative unit is autobiographical, not to mention an example of ancient rhetorical sensibilities, further obscures the direct relationship with the situational details of the Galatian addressees.[11] Moreover, we do not know what the addressees may already have learned about this incident in Antioch from Paul, if at all, or, for that matter, from anyone else.[12] Thus, we must leave largely aside here a question that is so important to the interpretation of Galatians itself: what did the Galatians make of these narra-

---

[8] I see no reason to question that this Cephas is Peter the apostle. The switch between Aramaic and Greek names may have to do with the fact that Paul is writing to Greek speakers. They might otherwise miss the ironic twist on rock/pillar, by which Paul undermines any pretension to human authority if it should fail to conform to the revelation of Jesus Christ (cf. my "Intruding Spies"). There has been some controversy over the reference to Cephas in the history of interpretation, however. For a recent discussion of the positions, see the conflicting views of Ehrman, "Cephas and Peter," and Allison, "Peter and Cephas."

[9] A helpful discussion of Barnabas is available in Bauckham, "Barnabas," 61–63.

[10] See Nanos, *Irony*, 62–72, for discussion of the structure of Paul's argument and, 143–54, for additional analysis of the autobiographical narratives. See also my "Inter- and Intra-Jewish."

[11] Cf. Dahl, "Paul's Letter," 49: "No autobiography is objective. Paul's apology for his conduct aims more at being persuasive than at providing historical details." See Lyons, *Pauline Autobiography*, 17–73; J. Sanders, "'Autobiographical' Statements"; Hall, "Historical Inference"; Most, "Stranger's Stratagem"; Momigliano, *Development*; Weintraub, *Value of the Individual*.

[12] It should not be expected that all of the elements communicated in this letter represent new information (cf. 1:9; 5:3, 21). Paul even indicates at the start that he has told the Galatian addressees about certain aspects of his life story (1:13), and on the basis of the nature of his relationship with them, it would be natural to expect this to be the case (4:11–20).

tives, given their own later circumstances, and what did they understand Paul to wish to communicate in the rest of the letter's situational argumentation?[13]

Least controversial, and less significant for the argument that will be made here, is the identification of those Paul referred to as οἱ λοιποὶ Ἰουδαῖοι, that is, "the rest of the Jews" or, alternately, "the rest of the Judeans." It is unlikely that they were involved in causing Peter's change of course; rather, it seems that they were following Peter's lead: "and with him [Peter] the rest of the Jews were being equally two-faced." In fact, since they are said by Paul to be masking their true convictions (συνυπεκρίθησαν) when they joined Peter, they are not likely outright advocates of this policy and should be assumed to compose a group different from the ones whom Paul calls "for circumcision." It is usual to assume that these people were Christ-believing Jews, and this identification seems most likely on the argument that I will make as well.[14] It is less clear whether this group consisted of Antiochenes or Judeans, or both, or how they overlapped, if at all, with any of the other groups mentioned.

The Greek phrase ἐλθεῖν τινας[15] ἀπὸ Ἰακώβου (v. 12) is fairly simple to translate as "certain/some ones came from James." But the implications are anything but clear. There is general agreement that the James with whom these people are associated is the James of Jerusalem referred to previously in Paul's autobiographical narrative, apparently James the brother of Jesus (1:19). This James was an important voice in the coalition of Christ-believers in Jerusalem (2:1–10).[16] Paul tells us that James—in concert with Cephas and John—confirmed Paul's mission to the "foreskinned" as being consistent with James's own understanding of the good news of Christ for the "circumcised." But were these "certain ones" *sent by* James, even though that is not precisely what Paul wrote?[17] And if so, did they perhaps—whether intentionally or not—misrepresent his intentions? Or did they come instead by his permission? If so, did they represent his opinions and policies? Or was James constrained to let them "interfere" because of political circumstances affecting him and his communities in Judea? This same question arises for the vaguely identified "pseudo-brethren" in the prior narrative, who sought to "spy on" or, perhaps better, to "investigate" a meeting in Jerusalem that Paul had planned to hold privately, that is, without them.[18] In a different direction, was their arrival, although ultimately consequential—at least from Paul's point of view—actually otherwise incidental and the resultant events in no way anticipated or intended? Were they perhaps simply traveling through Antioch or there for something that had nothing to do with the events that unfolded?

Identifying the third group, τοὺς ἐκ περιτομῆς, is extremely involved, and even the translation can generate controversy. But it is important to be decisive here; for it is "because of" this group that Peter is clearly said to have reacted in

---

[13] Analysis of the Galatian situation is a central topic in Nanos, *Irony*.

[14] *Pace* Richardson, *Israel*, 94–95. The "ones for circumcision" whom Peter fears seem most likely to be the ones who are not Christ-believers, as will be discussed.

[15] Some manuscripts have the singular τινα.

[16] See Bauckham, "James"; and the essays in Chilton and Evans, *James the Just*.

[17] Instead he writes ambiguously, "came from" (ἐλθεῖν ἀπό).

[18] Discussed at length in Nanos, "Intruding 'Spies.'"

"fear": φοβούμενος. Περιτομή simply means "circumcision," and it is used to designate the distinction between Jewish and non-Jewish (and thus foreskinned) males (ἀκροβυστία: cf. 2:7–8), often also referred to as ἔθνος, Gentile people, or corporately, as members of the nations, the Gentiles (τὰ ἔθνη).[19] These terms of reference are often used interchangeably, as in v. 7, where Paul writes of being entrusted with the good news "to the foreskinned," as distinguished from the other apostles who go to the "circumcised," and then in v. 8, where he writes of God working through him to reach the Gentiles/nations.[20]

There has been much debate about whether Paul used the label τοὺς ἐκ περιτομῆς here to refer exclusively to Jews who believe in Jesus[21] or only to Jews who do not,[22] each side armed with its various references and grammatical arguments. Nonetheless, it is simply not possible or logical to limit the usage of this label in either direction on purely lexical grounds. References to "the circumcised" and to "the Jews" are usually synonymous.[23] Thus, to make this distinction, one would have to maintain that when Jews believed in Jesus, they sought to reverse this surgically so that they were no longer circumcised ones, Jews. To take only the above reference to the ministries of Peter to the circumcised and of Paul to the foreskinned as an example: is not Paul still "of circumcision" himself? Certainly he so argued vehemently in this setting ("we [Peter and Paul] are Jews by birth"; v. 15) and elsewhere (Rom 9:3–5; 11:1; Phil 3:3–5; and it is a logical inference from 1 Cor 7:17–20), and this identity framed his worldview "irrevocably," witnessed, for example, by the fact that it is as Jews and Gentiles or Greeks that he knows his audiences and friends.[24] And what of the circumcised ones responding to the mission of Peter to which Paul alludes (v. 7): are they no longer "ones from/out of circumcision"? Moreover, one need not reach out of this context for a demonstration of Paul's view of Jewish believers in Jesus as simply Jews, for he refers in this context to "the rest of the Jews [οἱ λοιποὶ

---

[19] The limitations of the label "Gentiles" are demonstrated in LaGrand, " 'Gentile,' " 77–87; it is, however, common convention, and no adequate substitute has emerged. In the same vein, the label "pagan" is problematic, and since Jewish people can also be "Greeks" or "Romans," it is not always helpful to distinguish along this line either. Likewise it is difficult to settle on an emic label for referring to the non-Jews who have renounced Greek and Roman idols but have not become Jewish proselytes. "God-fearers" is a good candidate, but disputed by some, and "righteous Gentiles" is also a reasonable etic label for these non-Jews from a Jewish perspective.

[20] See also Rom 3:30; 4:9, 12; 15:8; and Rom 2:25–3:1; Phil 3:3; also Eph 2:11; Col 3:11; 4:11; Titus 1:10; Acts 10:45; 11:2.

[21] See Burton, Galatians, 108; Betz, Galatians, 109; Matera, Galatians, 86–88; Richardson, Israel, 93, esp. n 2.

[22] See Reicke, "Hintergrund," 177; Schmithals, Paul and James, 66–67; Bruce, Commentary, 131; Hawkins, Opponents, 110–11; R. Longenecker, Galatians, 73–75.

[23] Cf. J. Smith, "Fences and Neighbors," 9–15; S. Cohen, Beginnings, esp. 156–74, 219–21; Segal, Paul, 72–109; Feldman, Jew and Gentile; 153–58; Nolland, "Uncircumcised Proselytes?" 173–94; P. Schäfer, Judeophobia, 93–105.
This is not to say that this custom of identification is not attested among other ethnic or national groups of people. It appears that it was practiced by some of Israel's neighbors in ancient times—e.g., according to Herodotus, by the Egyptians, Ethiopians, and Phoenicians (Hist. 2.36, 37, 104; also Strabo, Geogr. 17.2.5). See also Josephus, Ant. 8.262; Ag. Ap. 1.168–171; 2.141–142; Philo, Spec. 1.1.2; and discussions of P. Schäfer, Judeophobia, 93–95; S. Cohen, Beginnings, 39–49.

[24] Cf. Rom 11:29; see Donaldson, "Gospel," 184–90; this is to be noted even in Rom 16.

'Ιουδαῖοι]" who join Peter in withdrawing, along with Barnabas.[25] Therefore, especially for the period under discussion, the labels "the circumcision" or "the ones
from/out of [ἐκ] circumcision" by themselves do not sufficiently distinguish between
Jews who believe in Christ and those who do not, but only between Jews and Gentiles,
the still operative labels throughout Paul's correspondence, regardless of their position on Jesus, which is itself telling.

The label "the circumcision" symbolizes a decidedly Jewish way to distinguish
among males and, by extension, human communities. "Gentiles" and "foreskinned"
are clearly not terms of comparative self-reference among Gentiles and foreskinned
males.[26] But the phrase can also be employed to distinguish among Jewish—and thus
circumcised (male)—people, as it is doing here, where Peter and "the rest of the Jews"
are circumcised yet distinguished from those Paul labels "the ones ἐκ circumcision."
This kind of comparison among a variety of interest groups suggests a salient intra-
or inter-Jewish group distinction. It is not just any Jewish group in view—and
thus the members circumcised and advocating circumcision as a norm for Jewish
people—but an interest group specifically distinguished from other groups of circumcised Jews as *advocates* of circumcision.[27] The phrase, as Dunn puts it:

> is used by a Jew in reference to another Jew and must indicate still other Jews distin-
> guished from the likes of Peter and Paul in a way analogous to the distinction be-
> tween Jew and Gentile. That is to say, they were a faction within Judaism who gave
> such emphasis to circumcision that they could even be distinguished from other Jews
> as "the circumcision."[28]

It is, however, not clear that they represent a factional or even minority view.
Since Paul represents the view that these Gentiles should not become circumcised to
be considered children of Abraham—which deviates from the Jewish communal
norms—a slightly different twist on this element of group differentiation should be
considered.

Given a rhetorical context dealing with Gentile associates, the likely connotation
of this particular advocacy is proselyte conversion. All Jewish groups of which we
have direct evidence advocated the circumcision of newborn Jewish males. But where

---

[25] So too Dunn, *Theology*, 124–25; Howard, *Crisis*, 41. Of course, the point is circular, as it de-
pends upon the interpretation that at least some of those referred to as the rest of the Jews are
Christ-believers. But if none are, then we are left with no reference to any Christ-believers in
Antioch withdrawing except Peter and Barnabas.

[26] The distinction between foreskinned/circumcised can arise in other group settings, such as
among some Egyptians, and between any one nation and other nations, but the case here is clearly in
Jewish/non-Jewish terms, as it is often among Greek and Latin authors during this period (see S.
Cohen, *Beginnings*, 39–49).

[27] *Contra* Lightfoot, *Galatians*, 112, who states as though obvious that the preposition indicates
they are "not 'Jews' but 'converts *from* Judaism.' " That view depends upon a separation of Christ-
believers from Jewish identity in personal and institutional terms that is very doubtful, and takes this
language in a direction independent of the rhetorical concern about whether *these Gentiles* ought to
undertake "circumcision." See Dunn, "Incident at Antioch," 201–2; *Partings*.

[28] Dunn, "Echoes," 460–61; see also, Dunn, *Theology*, 123, where he cites Rom 4:12; Col 4:11;
Titus 1:10; and see Cameron, "Translation," 140.

inclusion of Gentiles as full members was concerned, the prevailing view was that this could be negotiated by completing the rite of proselyte conversion, except for the coalition of Jewish believers-in-Jesus. Thus, since the point of view Paul expresses here is characteristic of those aligned with "the truth of the gospel [of Jesus Christ]," this label may indicate that the "ones for circumcision" are representatives of the dominant Jewish communal norms, even if a particular subgroup that is perhaps more aggressive about the matter or perhaps more aware of this particular situation. They advocate the proselyte conversion of Gentiles with whom Paul, Peter, and "the rest of the Jews" eat as though they should not undertake this rite, and they bring sufficient pressure to bear that Peter, along with the rest of the Jews, seek to avoid their disapproval. Therefore, the Christ-believing Jews try to mask their conviction that these Gentiles are not regarded among their subgroups as mere "pagan" guests, but at the same time not as proselyte candidates either, by withdrawing from eating with Gentiles to distance themselves from meals symbolizing this nonconforming "truth." Thus the translation adopted here: "the ones for circumcision," where "for" stands for "advocating."[29]

But many questions remain. Are they native Antiochenes or are they Judeans? When this event unfolds, are they in Antioch or in Judea? Are they Christ-believers or not? If they are, how are they related, if at all, to the ones from James, or to Judean Christ-believers in general, or to Paul and his communities? If they are not related, why have they suddenly provoked Peter's change of behavior, and how, if at all, is it related to the interests or actions of the ones from James, except for the timing of this event? What is their interest in the way these meals are conducted? What kind of pressure can they or do they bring to bear so that Peter can be said to fear them?

Traditionally, interpreters have understood both those whom Paul labels "certain ones from James" and "the ones for circumcision" to be one and the same interest group, and this approach continues in modern works, many offering little to no argumentation.[30] The significance of this decision for interpretation of this incident is profound. Although it does simplify the discussion, it also limits the hypotheses considered, for example, to those revolving around an intra- and intermural Christian crisis that imagines "Jewish" factions from James/Jerusalem pitted against Paul and "Paulinism," the dispute centered on the level of Jewish identity (circumcision) and behavior (law observance) to be retained among Christ-believers. Little or no consideration is given to the probability that the kind of tension described would be expected to emerge along newly defined intra- and inter-Jewish group boundaries resulting from this coalition's controversial challenge to a particular long-standing norm—that is, the way this norm identifies Gentiles as full members apart from completion of the rite of proselyte conversion—which was made public policy in

---

[29] Similar is Fung, *Galatians*, 108.

[30] E.g., Burton, *Galatians*, 107–8; Schlier, *Galater*, 84–85; Betz, *Galatians*, 108–9; Dunn, *Theology*, 121, 124 (clearly assumed, as in "Incident at Antioch"); Tomson, *Paul*, 226; Hansen, *Galatians*, 63; Esler, "Making," 276–78; Martyn, *Galatians*, 236–40 (more discussion than most); Tarazi, *Galatians*, 77–78; Holmberg, "Jewish *versus* Christian," 410–11; Zetterholm, *Antioch*, 210.

Jerusalem, as related in the preceding narrative unit (2:1–10). Moreover, such intra- and inter-Jewish communal tensions are suggested for Paul (1:13–16; 5:11; 6:17), and among the Galatian addressees throughout the situational-discourse units of the letter, as the result of his teaching that they are children of Abraham on a par with empirical children of Israel apart from proselyte conversion. Significantly, it is for the unique decision not to circumcise these Gentiles, rather than for his belief in Jesus as Messiah, that Paul says he has suffered at the hands of certain Jewish leaders (5:11; 2 Cor 11:25).[31]

Such developments within the Jewish communities and between the various subgroups would surely be expected if these Christ-believing groups were still Jewish groups of a time preceding the parting of the ways, before the several Jewish revolts and other conceptual, social, and institutional developments ultimately separated these siblings.[32] The Christ-believing groups would thus be, by nature, subgroups of the larger Jewish communities in which they are located, which are themselves minority groups within the dominant Roman and Greek communities of the Diaspora and suffering occupation even in Judea. Such marginalized groups must deal with any inter- and intragroup constraints that thereby obtain, such as might arise when new subgroups challenge long-standing norms in ways that appear to threaten the status quo not just of their own communities but also of the dominant communities within which they dwell and with which, to varying degrees, they share interests.[33] And surely such social-identity claims by emerging subgroups within Jewish communities of Syria in the name of a Judean martyr of the Roman regime constitute a consequential threat. But discussion of these matters here would take us too far afield; I simply want to indicate the kind of historical and political limitations inherent in the prevailing hypotheses that suggest an entirely intramural Christian dispute.[34]

---

[31] Delineating his suffering as "persecution" demonstrates that Paul does not agree with the assessment, but it is unlikely that those from whom he suffered would agree or consider that whatever measures they took were "persecution." Rather, they would likely consider such actions legitimate expressions of discipline or punishment toward one perceived to be challenging or transgressing long-standing communal norms, regardless of what justification for doing so he might have claimed.

[32] Cf. Dunn, "Incident at Antioch"; so too E. Sanders, "Jewish Association"; Fredriksen, "Judaism"; and see Segal, *Rebecca's Children;* Dunn, *Partings of the Ways,* among other recent works recognizing that the split was neither as monolithic and uniform from place to place nor usually as early as it was previously understood to be in the interpretive tradition.

[33] See Nanos, *Irony,* 253–71.

[34] Note that Dunn, "Echoes," is confined to discussion of intramural rhetoric among Christbelievers, and in that essay, as in his "Incident at Antioch," an ideological advantage is suggested. While I agree that the traditional "against the Jews" approaches, which pit Christianity against Judaism and seek to demonstrate superiority, are both inaccurate and harmful and I deeply appreciate the change of sentiment, I do not see the ideological payoff to which Dunn and others appeal. The criticism that remains is of Jews who retain the value of their Jewishness after faith in Christ, and this is made in the voice of Paul, the supposed advocate of Jewish-free Christianity. The most historically viable as well as useful approach seems to me to be one focused on the intra- and intercommunal dynamics, including the tensions that naturally arose between Jewish believers in Jesus as Messiah and their kin who did not share this conviction. Then the discussion can move from an a priori value judgment of things Jewish to a difference of conviction among Jewish groups about how to interpret and apply the several Jewish options at dispute.

In recent years a new proposal has been gaining ground. This view suggests that the "ones for circumcision" are non-Christ-believing Judeans, perhaps Zealots, who have successfully brought sufficient pressure to bear upon James and his groups that James has sent a delegation (the ones from James) to Antioch.[35] The ones for circumcision are thus not actually present in Antioch, but the interests of both of these unnamed groups from Judea are intimately connected although they remain two distinct groups. The fear Peter expresses is thus toward non-Christ-believing Judeans (ones for circumcision) on behalf of the threatened interests of the Judean believers in Christ (ones from James).

There are several problems with this construction. It assumes at this time the existence of a party in Judea that is attested later, during the revolt.[36] And it assumes that any such group, if it existed, would have had an interest in, or the ability to affect, the circumcision of Gentiles in Antioch, which would seem to be counterintuitive for Judean anti-Roman political-interest groups anyway. It would be more logical to expect them to be suspicious of Gentile guests as representatives of the dreaded enemy, and outright opposed to the inclusion of proselytes as potential informers—thus "the ones *against* circumcision." These issues prove to be even more problematic to explain the very distant Galatian situation, but the details need not detain us here.[37] The approach does allow for the kind of inter- and intra-Jewish—even Judean/Diaspora—tensions that seem to be obscured by the traditional conflation of the two groups as "Christian," yet it moves the real political tensions away from the local Antiochene context, where Paul seems to place them, and away from a conflict between rival methods for inclusion, suggesting a policy of exclusion instead. Is it not more likely that the ones whom Peter intended to appease by withdrawing are in Antioch? Do they not constitute part of the group before whom Paul confronts Peter to his face ("before them all")? And are they not open to the inclusion of these Gentiles, insisting, however, on traditional methods?

It should be clear by now that Paul's turn of phrase does not clarify how the ones for circumcision were related to the ones from James, if at all, beyond the fact that the arrival of the ones from James was somehow related to the timing of Peter's change of behavior. They may represent two distinct groups, and Paul's language might indicate that the arrival of the ones from James was merely coincidental and that those from James were not in sympathy with the ones advocating circumcision, even perhaps that they were their adversaries.[38] Or that they were there by James's permission, for whatever reason, likely as a result of his own local constraints, but they did not

---

[35] This alternative was raised in different ways by Dix, *Jew and Greek*, 42–44; Reicke, "Hintergrund," 177; Munck, *Paul*, 106; Schmithals, *Paul and James*, 66–67; idem, "Heretics," 13–17; Jewett, "Agitators," 340–41; Haacker, "Paulus," 95–111; and adopted to various degrees by, e.g., Fung, *Galatians*, 108; Bruce, *Commentary*, 131; R. Longenecker, *Galatians*, xci–xciv, 73–75; Witherington, *Grace*, 154–56.

[36] Cf. Horsley and Hanson, *Bandits*.

[37] See Nanos, *Irony*, 207–17.

[38] Many interpreters note that a pronoun reference to the ones Peter feared would be expected if they were one and the same as the certain ones from James. Note that each of these identifying labels is not repeated either in this narrative unit or elsewhere in the letter.

represent his views or even opposed his agreement, as had the "pseudo-brethren" in Jerusalem. The arrival of these certain ones from James in Antioch may have functioned as a trigger for the events that followed or merely as a time marker in Paul's retelling of the story for the Galatian addressees. It may be that they encouraged an interest group in Antioch already advocating this policy to step up the pressure brought to bear, directly or indirectly. Or perhaps instead, the ones from James also joined in these mixed meals that may have served as the last straw for the ones for circumcision, who had been opposing this behavior for some time but now saw clearly that it was even supported by the Judean leaders of this coalition.

In short, Paul does tell us not what the ones from James were advocating, or even precisely who they were or how they were or were not related to "the ones for circumcision," but only the part they played in the timing of this incident: Peter began to withdraw and separate himself from eating with these Gentiles in the way that he had been doing so because he feared the ones advocating circumcision, and this occurred after the arrival of certain ones from James. Thus, when I refer to the ones for/advocating circumcision, or the ones that Peter fears, it should be understood that I am not referring to the certain ones who came from James.

The Prevailing Views of the Issues at Stake at These Mixed Meals

Interpreters have understood the issue to turn on the nature of the food at the mixed meals: either the food did not conform to Jewish dietary regulations or the inclusion of Gentiles led to the compromise of social regulations. More recent interpretations, such as those included in this section of this volume, alter these two options slightly: either the food did not conform to the stricter Jewish dietary regulations of the faction whom Peter feared or the level of Gentile inclusion was threatening, for it was feared that it compromised—or would lead to the compromise of—such regulations, even to idolatry. In these approaches, Jewish dietary laws continue to be issue, although differently construed. The consequences are significant not only historically but theologically.

Traditional Interpretive Approaches

To arrive at the traditional conclusions—excluding discussion of the negative caricatures and stereotyping that often accompany them—it has been necessary to assume that observant Jewish people and groups, including Jewish believers-in-Jesus who were not Paulinists, objected to eating with Gentiles as a matter of course because to do so either necessitated the compromising of dietary regulations or would lead to such compromising, whether intentional or not. In addition, it has been assumed that the meal at which Peter was eating, since it was "Christian" and inclusive of Gentiles, was conducted according to Gentile rather than Jewish dietary norms and in Gentile rather than Jewish social space. This has also been assumed to be the case for the Galatian addressees, so that they would naturally draw the analogy in that direction. Thus one did not have to look very hard to find the problem at hand: these meals did not conform to Jewish dietary norms. For the ones Peter feared, the food was inappropriate, as was the inclusion of non-Jews or attending their meals. It is to such Law-free norms that Paul is assumed to be committed, so that he objects to Peter's undermining of this "truth" when he withdraws and separates himself, taking along the other Jewish members also.

In such readings, the objection raised by the circumcision advocates was to Jews such as Peter ignoring, if not outright renouncing, the value of Jewish dietary practices because of their faith in Christ. Peter's withdrawal was to avoid further transgression of Jewish dietary laws; this entailed separation both from the Gentiles with whom he had been eating and from the kind of food that he had been eating when sharing meals with them. Paul challenged Peter's change of behavior because any observance of Jewish dietary customs—indeed, any observance of the Torah and concomitant halakah by Christians—was at worst anathema or at least a matter of indifference and should not be permitted to influence church life. This understanding of the incident fits nicely with the conviction that, for example, Christianity was universalistic and inclusive but Judaism was particularistic and exclusive, or Christianity was a religion of faith and grace versus Judaism, a religion of works and law, even legalism, and so on. A few examples of this reasoning from leading commentators should suffice to support the point I am trying to make, including the ideological importance of this traditional understanding.

J. B. Lightfoot argues that before the withdrawal Peter "had no scruples about living ἐθνικῶς [like a gentile]," that is, without observing Jewish dietary restrictions ("discard Jewish customs"), for the vision of Acts 10 "taught him the worthlessness of these narrow traditions."[39] Lightfoot assumes that this change is the logical result of the desire to "mix freely with the Gentiles and thus of necessity disregard the Jewish law of meats."[40]

Ernest D. W. Burton proposes that the behavior characterizing Peter and the rest of the Jews before the arrival of these others is deduced from the Jerusalem meeting's decision, as narrated in 2:1–10:

> The brethren at Antioch might naturally seem to themselves to be only following out what was logically involved in the Jerusalem decision, when they found in the recognition of uncircumcised Gentile believers as brethren the warrant for full fellowship with them on equal terms, and, in the virtual declaration of the non-essentiality of circumcision, ground for the inference that the O. T. statutes were no longer binding, and ought not to be observed to the detriment of the unity of the Christian community.[41]

The reason for the objection of the ones for circumcision to Peter's eating with Gentiles is clear for Burton from the language of v. 12: the sharing in ordinary meals with

---

[39] Lightfoot, *Galatians*, 112–14.
[40] Ibid., 114. Note that meat is not mentioned in the text.
[41] Burton, *Galatians*, 106.

these Gentiles "exposed himself to the liability of eating food forbidden by the O. T. law of clean and unclean foods (Lev. chap. 11), and thus in effect declared it not binding upon him."[42] Burton assigns this conclusion to Peter before his withdrawal: "Peter went beyond anything which the action at Jerusalem directly called for, and in effect declared the Jew also, as well as the Gentile, to be free from the law."[43] This custom of eating non-Jewishly cannot be laid on Peter, according to Burton. Its practice in Antioch preceded his arrival, too; it "was clearly an expression of the 'freedom in Christ Jesus' which Paul advocated, but in all probability a new expression, developed since the conference at Jerusalem (vv. 1–10)."[44] Burton thus links the drive for mixed fellowship with Gentiles with the need for Jewish members of this coalition to compromise Jewish dietary customs in order to achieve this goal. For him, it follows logically that "full fellowship with them [Gentiles] on equal terms," as warranted by "the recognition of uncircumcised Gentile believers as brethren," necessitates the "non-essentiality of circumcision" and "that that the O. T. statues were no longer binding."

Hans D. Betz explains the meaning of Paul's challenge in v. 14 thus:

> In the protasis Paul defines Cephas' present religious status as being a Jew ('Ιουδαῖος ὑπάρχων) who has given up his Jewish way of life. He lives like a Gentile (ἐθνικῶς), that is, no longer in observation of Jewish customs and law (οὐχὶ Ἰουδαϊκῶς). The present tense of ζῆς ("you are living") implies much more than an act of table fellowship with Christian Gentiles. It suggests that the table fellowship was only the external symbol of Cephas' total emancipation from Judaism. The apodosis presupposes Cephas' recent change of conduct as a self-contradiction: "how can you compel the Gentiles to live like Jews?"[45]

For Betz, the issue is not as described in Paul's few words about changing the people with whom Peter mixed. Betz believes the reason is otherwise; it was "not Cephas' breaking of fellowship by first participation in and subsequent withdrawal from the meal, but his shifting attitude with regard to the Jewish dietary and purity laws."[46] But in the next sentence Betz undermines this observation, noting that the decision to eat with these Gentiles previously did not result from a belief that purity laws were no longer in force but from a new evaluation of the standing of these Gentiles: "They are not to be regarded as 'sinners out of the gentiles' (cf. 2:15). For the conscientious Jew, therefore, they could not be regarded as impure. It must have been for this reason that Cephas ate with them."

After arguing at cross-purposes, Betz moves away from the view that the Jewish participants decided to abandon the practice of purity laws for themselves as a matter of principle, instead attributing to them a new evaluation of the status of the Gentiles

---

[42] Ibid., 104.
[43] Ibid., 104. Burton does allow that Peter may not have been "prepared to apply the principle consistently to other prescriptions of the law," noting the likely exception of Peter circumcising his children (104).
[44] Ibid., 105.
[45] Betz, *Galatians*, 112.
[46] Ibid., 107.

as "pure." While the visible issue concerns the practice or nonpractice of Jewish dietary laws (not the status of the Gentiles), Paul's accusation that Peter is compelling Gentiles to Judaize "describes forcing one to become a Jewish convert obliged to keep the whole Torah (cf. 5:3)."[47] In the end, Betz understands the central issue to be a new evaluation of the *identity* of the Christ-believing Gentiles as pure, which, by his logic, leads to a change of *attitude* and *behavior* on the part of the Christ-believing Jews, namely, the decision to abandon Jewish dietary laws.

Betz may be uncertain which came first, these Christ-believing Jews' new attitude toward the value of these Gentiles or their new attitude toward the Jewish Law, but he is certain that this incident demonstrates that these Christ-believing Jews ultimately changed their attitude toward Jewish dietary laws as a part of a principle conviction that they were "totally emancipated from Judaism." Yet it should be noted that Betz introduced this behavioral element, not Paul, and then dismissed it as tangential in the course of his argumentation. Why did Betz take this circular route or introduce this nontextual element? Could it be that he knows something—along with many other interpreters—that no one in Antioch or Galatia knew, namely, that Peter and the rest of the Jews had, on principle, abandoned the practice of Jewish dietary regulations, indeed the whole of Torah, in keeping with the supposed teaching and practice of Paul? Could it be that, as a careful exegete, Betz remained close to the textual material and yet found this feature ideologically necessary to disclose, even though it was not indicated in the text, and logically undermined his conclusion?

Of particular interest here is the fact that, regardless of how the conundrum of Peter's change of behavior is resolved, these interpreters maintain that Peter's new behavior represented a return to Jewish dietary practices that were deemed to be exclusivistic and that he had supposedly until then recognized as inappropriate to guide the behavior of Jewish as well as non-Jewish people after they became believers in Jesus Christ. The ideological values that separate Jewish and Christian sensibilities are taken to fall along this line: exclusive versus inclusive, particular versus universal, traditional versus revealed, Law-bound versus Law-free.[48] Yet these judgments depend

---

[47] Ibid., 112. This point is underscored when Betz observes, "Ironically, therefore, by attempting to preserve the integrity of Jewish Christians as Jews, Cephas destroys *the integrity* of the Gentile Christians *as believers* in Christ." It is not their integrity as believers in Christ, however, as noted in the second clause, that is destroyed. They are still this. What changes is the perception of their integrity as equal in status with Jewish believers in Christ if they remain Gentiles. The identity contrast is not in Christ-believing terms—i.e., their level of Christ-believerness, if you will—but in terms of who are the members of the historical people of God, of Israel; i.e., it is their non-Jewishness at dispute. In other words, Betz's second clause would strike a balance with the point made in the first clause if his statement instead read, "by attempting to preserve the integrity of the Jewish Christians as *Jews*, Cephas destroyed the integrity of Gentile Christians as *Gentiles*."

[48] An instructive early example of this ideological concern emerges in Jerome's response to Augustine. In his rejoinder, Jerome expressed disapproval of Augustine's acceptance of this incident as real, rather than (as Origin and Chrysostom proposed, and Jerome adopted) a pretension conceived in order to permit Paul to effectively condemn the advocates of proselyte conversion by way of condemning Peter, the chief of the apostles, who graciously accepted the force of the rebuke (although he never did behave in the manner of which he was accused), thus setting an example for all to follow. The ideological motivation for adopting one approach over another is then plainly stated. Jerome objects that Augustine's approach effectively opens the door to legitimating Peter and Paul

upon interpreting Peter's new choice of meal partners as proof that the mixed meals in Antioch at which he previously ate served food that did not conform with the dietary scruples of those who have come from James or those advocating circumcision. And these basic lines of argumentation continue to prevail in recent works, even if they are sometimes nuanced differently in view of what has been learned about first-century Jewish thought and life, and with many of them also expressive of more respectful intentions toward Jewish people and ways of life.

Recent Trends in Interpretation

Traditional approaches, as exemplified in the above survey, depend upon perceptions of Jewish sensibilities that have been undermined in recent years by Christian interpreters in sympathy with the challenges that have been regularly raised by Jewish interpreters. This is especially the case for supposing that observant Jews, as a matter of course, did not participate in meals with Gentiles.

As E. P. Sanders makes exceptionally clear, there is no reason to believe that observant Jewish people and groups did not eat with Gentiles given the right conditions, and it does not follow that doing so involves the need to compromise observance or purity.[49] In Jewish social space, the meals would be conducted according to prevailing norms, and the Gentiles would be expected to behave like guests, respectful of the conventions of the host's meal. In Gentile social space, the accommodation was not quite as simple, but obstacles could be overcome, for example, by bringing along one's food and drink. Certainly there would be Jewish people and groups who would not suffer such exceptions graciously; there are always people and groups of an extremist stripe who do not exemplify the prevailing norms or sensibilities.[50]

I see no reason to recite all the evidence, but I do want to note that even more could be provided, not least the logical problem that would have to be surmounted to account for the inclusion of proselyte candidates while they were engaged in this right of passage, which would arguably be a process involving a long period of close association between at least some Jewish facilitators and Gentiles engaged in this identity transformation. In addition to the many ways in which Gentiles seeking to associate with Jewish communal life would compel solutions including mixed meals, there are the realities of the involvement of Jewish people and communal leaders in local Diaspora social life, including matters political and economic. It is becoming ever clearer that in these years Jewish Diaspora communal life was not isolated but

---

as Torah-observant Jews. If this is allowed, reasons Jerome, then the "heresy" of the Ebionites and Nazarenes—Torah observance by Christ-believers—would be justified. The ineluctable and unacceptable result would be Jews coming into the church doing "what they are accustomed to do in the synagogue of Satan": "they will not become Christians but they will make us Jews" (Jerome, "Letter 112.13," in Trigg, "Augustine/Jerome," 284–85; see Trigg's discussion, 250–57, and translation of the original correspondence, 258–95). Mussner, *Galaterbrief*, 146–57, offers a useful excursus on ancient interpreters of this incident up through Luther and, 157–67, on interpreters up into the 1970s.

[49] E. Sanders, "Jewish Association"; see too Segal, *Paul*, 230–33; Tomson, *Paul*, 230–36; Fredriksen, "Judaism."

[50] See Tomson, *Paul*, 233–36; and Esler, *Galatians*, 104–8.

intimately connected with the larger communal life of its idolatrous neighbors; even local patriotism is to be noted.[51] There is no reason to believe that many, if not most, observant Jews, certainly those living in the Diaspora, would not and did not eat with Gentiles without compromising their Jewish dietary norms to do so. The need to do so probably arose quite often in normal social life. It is thus unlikely that the issue in Antioch was of the character previously assumed.

Despite recent challenges to the traditional stereotypes of Jewish exclusiveness, the solutions offered have not changed the substantial issues considered to be at stake in Antioch.[52] These mixed meals with Gentiles either led or were feared to lead to the compromising of Jewish behavior by the eating of inappropriate food according to Jewish dietary norms, inclusive of the food and drink associated with idolatry. Consider the following conclusions, which represent some of the most recent and thoughtful work on the subject.

Dunn retains the view that food was at issue, but not because it was objectionable per se. In fact, Dunn questions the "ready assumption" of interpreters that "it was simply a matter of the Jewish food laws," suggesting instead that the issue turns around "what table-fellowship at Antioch involved prior to Peter's withdrawal."[53] Dunn notes also the importance of "the question of who was and who was not an

---

[51] Cf. Jones and Pearce, *Jewish Local Patriotism;* Trebilco, *Communities,* 167–85; de Vos, *Conflicts;* Nanos, *Irony,* 253–77.

[52] For example, here are a few brief quotes from recent commentaries that reveal the essential issue for Christian ideology if one is to follow Paul's teaching: R. Longenecker, *Galatians,* 75, takes Peter to have been eating "with Gentiles at Antioch in an unrestricted manner," for "he had no theological difficulties with such table fellowship himself," but in response to the pressure from the delegation from James, "he took a course of action that, in effect, had dire theological consequences: that there could be no real fellowship between Jewish believers and Gentile believers in Jesus unless the latter observed the dietary laws of the former. Such a tenet, of course, would have serious implications for the proclamation of the gospel to Gentiles and for a doctrine of the oneness of the body of Christ"; Matera, *Galatians,* 89, favorably cites Dunn's reading of the food issues, although taking this to mean that the pressure on Peter was to return to "all the dietary prescriptions of the Law," and on p. 91 concludes, "If he [Paul] originally viewed that gospel in terms of the Gentiles and their freedom from the Law, now he clearly sees its importance for Jewish believers as well. Christ freed them as well as the Gentiles from the need to do legal works. The freedom from the Law which Christ brought extended to all"; Williams, *Galatians,* 60, is well aware of the ideological implications: "His [Paul's] condemnation of Cephas's withdrawal amounts to a demand that Christian Jews continue to eat with Gentiles even though continued table fellowship would mean abandoning the observance of Torah laws and Jewish custom. In effect, then, Paul was insisting that Cephas and Barnabas and the other Christian Jews make themselves Gentiles. When the oneness of God's new inclusive Israel was at stake, Paul would have *everyone* be Gentile!" (emphasis his); Martyn, *Galatians,* 232, observes that, "at least by implication, the food laws were declared to be essentially a matter of no consequence in the church. By putting the verb 'ate' in the imperfect tense, Paul indicates that over a period of some length Peter was fully at home in the Antioch church, adopting its meal practice," and Martyn concludes, pp. 244–45, that Peter's decision to lead a "corporate walkout . . . had the effect of compelling the Gentile members of the Antioch church to observe the food laws, as though that form of Law observance were God's elected means of making right what had gone in the world"; Witherington, *Grace,* 158: "In Paul's view one would have to choose between Jewish purity or body unity. The church could not have both. . . . Body unity could only happen one of two ways— the Gentiles could be required to Judaize [i.e., 'to adopt Jewish customs and practices,' 159], or the Jews could be asked to recognize that observance of the Law was only optional, not required even of Jewish Christians." The few exceptions of which I am aware will be discussed below.

[53] Dunn, "Incident at Antioch," 200.

acceptable table companion."[54] The result is the most thorough discussion of the issues that arise for the interpreter of this incident.[55] Yet his conclusion still revolves around food; he even brings specific purity concerns to bear. At issue is which faction defines the dietary regulations that apply, and thus where the food practices of one group are judged objectionable according to the norms of another group looking on. The practices of the Antiochenes did not meet the stricter norms of the Judeans. The representatives from James, who practiced Torah zealously, expected "a fairly high level of ritual purity" to be maintained among the Antiochene Christ-believers; they were "surprised and shocked by the minimal level of law observance in Antioch; to them it would appear as though the whole heritage was being abandoned."[56]

The interpretation of Pauline ideology remains essentially traditional in Dunn's approach, even if the usual negative stereotyping of Jewish motives does not have a place and the conflict is defined decidedly to be among and between "Christian" groups. He suggests that at Antioch, probably for the first time, Paul clearly realized that justification by faith extended beyond acceptance of the gospel to regulating the lifestyle of the Christ-believer. Paul thus concluded that

> the covenantal nomism of Judaism and of the Jewish believers (life in accordance with the law within the covenant given by grace) was in fact a contradiction of that agreed understanding of justification through faith. To live life "in Christ" *and* "in accordance with the law" was not possible; it involved a basic contradiction in terms and in the understanding of what made someone acceptable to God. . . . To begin with the Spirit and through faith rules out not just justification by works of law, but life lived by law (covenantal nomism) also—the very argument which he develops in the rest of Galatians.[57]

Although Sanders doubts "that biblical law was actually being transgressed," he suggests that the most probable concern in general terms was that the conduct was feared to be "too close to Gentiles too much of the time," "since close association might lead to contact with idolatry or transgression of one of the biblical food laws."[58] This is applied in particular to James's concern about the reputation of Peter, lest he be "thought to be flirting with idolatry or food that the Bible calls 'abomination.'" In other words, food still defines the concern, but in this case, it is the *fear* of

---

[54] Dunn, "Incident at Antioch," 208.

[55] Note also the monographs by Kieffer, *Foi et justification*; N. Taylor, *Paul*; Wechsler, *Geschichtsbild*; and, recently, Zetterholm, *Antioch*; Cummins, *Crucified Christ*.

[56] Dunn, "Incident at Antioch" 227; see also *Theology*, 121, where the same conclusion is reached, that the James people were "shocked at the degree of laxness being shown by these Jewish believers and criticized them accordingly." But the offense is understood to be mixed meals "on less clearly defined Jewish terms," which is taken to include "welcoming Gentiles to their table" and "accepting invitations to Gentile tables without asking too many questions."

[57] Dunn, "Incident at Antioch" 230 (emphasis his). This observation clearly relies upon the traditional Reformation interpretation of justification by faith and not the view of Stendahl and others—including Dunn in later works—that justification by faith has to do with the inclusion of Gentiles. For the newer perspective, the theological conviction is inextricably tied to the social implications for association with Gentiles, and Dunn's bifurcation of these elements would be left appealing to an anachronistic (later Reformation) premise. Note that Dunn's essay first appeared in 1983; note his later view in *Theology*, 121.

[58] E. Sanders, "Jewish Association," 186.

what might develop if this kind of fraternization continued unchecked. This applies to the case of idolatry also: it is a fear that the food is being eaten or the wine drunk in a compromising manner, even if, as Esler argues, this is merely a fear of idolatrous intentions, rather than of explicit demonstrations of such dedication. The issue of mixing with Gentiles serves to bring to the fore the fear that eating meals in this fashion can lead to compromising Jewish dietary norms.[59]

For Philip Esler, the Antioch incident concerns *how* food and drink were involved, in the sense of the way they were physically shared in a mixed setting of Jewish and Gentile people.[60] Esler maintains that, because of fear of idolatry, which could be undetectable, especially at the level of mere intentions, Jews concerned with Jewish dietary regulations would not eat the same bread and drink wine from the same vessel passed around with Gentiles. Thus the issue was not precisely that the food was objectionable but how it was being eaten in the mixed social setting of Antioch: it is the Gentiles eating it who were objectionable. Thus they should get circumcised if this practice is to continue. Although this view challenges many elements of the traditional views as well as those of Sanders and Dunn, the ideological issue understood to be at stake remains unchallenged: "for Paul, in fact, the 'truth of the gospel' (2.5, 14, and nowhere else in his writings) means the freedom with which his Israelite and gentile converts can be members of the same congregation without having their 'freedom' replaced with the demands of the Mosaic law."[61]

Each of these approaches relies upon interpretation of the material available to all of them. Although there is not space to engage each argument in detail, I am convinced that in Diaspora locations such as Antioch, most Jewish people would have eaten with Gentiles given the right conditions. The mixing to which Josephus refers certainly suggests close contact was common in Antioch (e.g., *J.W.* 2.461–63; 7.41–62; *Ag. Ap.* 2.39). To the degree that the Jewish people in attendance remained Jewish and concerned to live as Jews, that is, to the degree that these groups predate the parting of the ways and the establishment of (non-Jewish) Christianity—this incident took place twenty or more years before the destruction of the temple—I see no reason to suppose that these mixed meals did not include eating food with Gentiles in conformity with prevailing Jewish norms for eating with non-Jewish guests as guests.[62]

---

[59] Although Fredriksen does not discuss the Antioch incident per se, the comments in "Judaism" 252 seem to indicate that she is drawing from the essay of Sanders ("Jewish Association") and that she regards the Antioch case to turn on the issue of food, to make the point that food was not likely the problem in Damascus fifteen years earlier.

[60] Esler, "Making"; *Galatians*, 93–116, 130–40.

[61] Esler, *Galatians*, 119.

[62] Of course, those norms varied, not only from Judea to Antioch or any other Diaspora location but within any location, including Judea, from group to group and subgroup to subgroup. But contra Dunn, there is no indication that the objection here is to Antiochenes' norms according to Judean (supposedly more rigorous) standards, especially to the degree that it is recognized as far from clear that the ones from James are the same as, or even in collusion with, the ones advocating circumcision. And circumcision is the norm that is clearly at stake. But advocacy of proselyte conversion, as far as we are aware, was the norm in all places for the inclusion of non-Jews as full members. It should also be noted that the boundaries of Judean and Syrian identity were in some ways ambiguous; see the discussions of M. Hengel, "Ἰουδαία"; Bockmuehl, "Antioch," 169–79; Scott, *Paul,* 158–59.

These Gentiles are, after all, making a significant social statement to their pagan communal networks of family, friends, neighbors, masters, and so on, as well as to the Jewish members with whom they have joined: to have turned from idols to the worship of Israel's God as the one God of all the nations.[63] Why should their intentions be doubted any more than those of Jewish people intimately involved in pagan communal affairs? And if they are, why would circumcising their foreskin be assumed to alter distrust of their intentions? The debate is not about how to exclude these Gentiles, after all, but how to include them, and the ones whom Peter fears are identified as advocates of circumcision, that is, as upholding the traditional norms for including Gentiles as full members once they have become proselytes.

It is clear that the issue at Antioch—from Paul's point of view—concerned the *eating* of Peter and the rest of the Jews *with Gentiles,* and then their *withdrawal and separation*—*because of fear of the ones advocating circumcision* of these Gentiles. And it seems that there was something objectionable about the way these meals were conducted. I propose to account for what was considered compromised while I maintain that the food conformed to the Jewish dietary norms of these advocates and that their objection was not to the inclusion of Gentiles at meals per se. There is certainly no unambiguous evidence in this text indicating either to be the problem.[64] But in deference to the diversity of opinion just surveyed, including the sharply different views of Jewish faith and practice observed in the essays included in this volume, the historical critic should exegete this text anew without privileging any one of these approaches a priori. Since I propose to challenge these interpretations, including their portrayals of Paul as living and advocating a Gentile style of life for Christ-believing Jews, it is necessary only to ask that the reader remain open to the possibility that there was nothing offensive in principle about either the food or the eating of meals with Gentiles—that is, according to the prevailing norms of those advocating circumcision.

The Identity of Gentiles as Equal Members apart from Proselyte Conversion

I propose that "the truth of the gospel" to which the ones advocating circumcision objected had nothing to do with the food being eaten or with the fact that it was being eaten with Gentiles, and it was not the threat of impurity or idolatry either. Rather, it was the way that these Gentiles were being *identified* at these meals.[65] These

---

[63] This concern is suggested in Philo's discussion of nobility, *Virt.* 108, 187–227, esp. 218–219, and *Spec.* 1.51–54, 308–310. In Josephus, *Ant.* 20.34–53, it is also one of the dynamics at work in the example of King Izates as to whether he should become a proselyte or remain a righteous Gentile. The effect upon himself, his family, and his kingdom are all matters of concern. And it is present in rabbinic tradition; cf. Porton, *Stranger.*

[64] Noted similarly by Gaston, "Paul and the Law," 43 n. 10; Howard, *Paul,* xix; Tomson, *Paul,* 227–30.

[65] Awareness of this element can be traced in the comments of certain interpreters, but it does not direct their conclusions. For example, Burton, *Galatians,* 106, notes that the mixed meals were

Jews were not "eating with" these Gentiles according to prevailing norms for eating with Gentiles: on the one hand, as pagan guests or, on the other hand, as proselyte candidates. The food was Jewish, and the Gentiles were eating it Jewishly, that is, as deemed appropriate for non-Jews to eat with Jewish people. But they were eating together as though these Gentiles and Jews were all equals, although these Gentiles were not Jews; in fact, they were—on principle—not even on their way to becoming Jews, meaning proselytes. The ones advocating the proselyte conversion of these Gentiles thus objected to circumventing the place of this rite to reidentify these Gentiles *as full and equal members* of this Jewish subgroup—which was how they were being identified at these meals, rather than as merely pagan guests. They did not accept the appeal to the good news of Christ as sufficient justification for the claim to deviate from established convention. And it was thus the undermining of this "truth" by the withdrawal and separation of Peter and the rest of the Christ-believing Jews to which Paul objects. Doing so subverted the very meaning of the grace of God in Christ for Jew and non-Jew alike.

To put this another way, this reading proposes that what was objectionable to the ones for circumcision was the way that this food was being eaten with *these* Gentiles apart from their becoming proselyte candidates, as though they were no longer merely pagan *guests* yet *also not* on the way to *becoming proselytes.* They instead were being treated as representatives of the nations to be regarded on a par with proselytes, a situation arguably to be expected when the age to come dawns.[66] But now? That defies the long-standing conventions of the present age. So when these Gentiles ate according to Jewish dietary regulations, yet did not do so identified as pagan guests but rather like equals in standing among these Jewish subgroups—as would be appropriate for proselytes and other fellow Jews—this behavior turned prevailing traditions for social identity and interaction on their head. It was not the fact that Peter ate *with* Gentiles that was at dispute but *the way* that he ate with *these* Gentiles.

These mixed meals symbolized a principle of identity at stake in the gospel of Jesus Christ. It pronounced these Gentiles full members of the people of God apart from the traditional conventions for rendering them such. Thus the pressure is specifically said to be from "advocates of circumcision." And the reaction of Peter and the other Jews was to "withdraw" and "separate" in order to "hide" their conviction with behavior that does not exemplify "the truth of the gospel," instead of dismissing the Gentiles as though they agreed in principle with those who brought the pressure

being conducted according to what might be deduced from the Jerusalem decision: "the recognition of uncircumcised Gentile believers as brethren" provided "the warrant for full fellowship with them on equal terms"; and Betz, *Galatians,* 107, somewhat similarly notes that the decision to eat with these Gentiles previously did not result from a belief that purity laws were no longer in force but from a new evaluation of the standing of these Gentiles: "They are not to be regarded as 'sinners out of the gentiles' (cf. 2:15)"; while Dunn, "Incident at Antioch," 208, observes the importance of "the question of who was and who was not an acceptable table companion," although he pursues the question of what was or what was not an acceptable way to conduct the meals; and Esler, "Making," proposes an objection not to the food but to suspicion of the intentions of the ones who share it.

[66] See Fredriksen, "Judaism," 244–47; Donaldson, *Paul,* 69–74.

to bear, thereby seeking to directly reverse the policies toward Gentiles thereafter.[67] They were but seeking temporary relief. But Paul regards them as "masking" their true convictions and thus in effect undermining the principles in which they believe.

Paul deduces that the only response thereafter available to these Gentiles—if they are to gain beyond dispute that identity which they have already been told to believe was theirs according to the gospel of Christ—is to Judaize, that is, to become Jewish proselytes. And so his challenge to Peter revolves around the theme of *justification*—legitimation really—of the identity claims of these Gentiles.[68] Although not Jews "from birth" like Peter and Paul and "the rest," they nevertheless "live" before God and with each other on equal terms, by way of "faith in/of Jesus Christ." And these Gentiles remain Gentiles instead of becoming proselytes on principle—according to the truth of the gospel—because this coalition believes that the age to come has dawned in the present age in the meaning of the death and resurrection of Jesus Christ. They, too, are *"righteous-ed"* ones of God in Christ. Thus Paul argues that "even we," that is, both "Jews by birth" and "Gentiles/sinners . . . have believed in Christ Jesus, in order to be justified by faith in/of Christ" (vv. 15–16).[69] So the differences of identity (Jew or Gentile) remain, but the discrimination according to the conventions that define who and what is appropriate in the present age (circumcision/works of law) because of these differences has been challenged (cf. 3:28).

All of this "truth" is symbolized in the way that these mixed meals are conducted within Jewish subgroups of believers in Jesus. Everyone is eating Jewish food as though everyone is a full member of the people of God celebrating the dawning of the age to come, when the righteous of the nations will join with the righteous of Israel to worship the righteous One God of all. The rub is that, in the present age, these Gentiles would continue to be regarded by the Jewish people and groups that do not share this conviction as either merely guests—and thus, even if quite welcome, not entitled to such treatment—or proselyte candidates, but neither, they are being told, is the case.

The issue is one of identifying these Gentiles, and the meal merely symbolizes the principles to which the various parties are committed, even if some may seek to avoid paying the price for belonging to the group that is challenging the prevailing view. And it is this hypocrisy, this avoidance of suffering, this undermining of the basis of their own standing with God as those belonging to Christ, as well as of that of the Gentiles in their care, that Paul attacks. For when Peter seeks to avoid the disapproval of those who do not share this conviction, he is in effect behaving as though there is still a difference of standing before God and each other on the basis of Jewish or Gentile identity among Christ-believers—even though he believes otherwise and

---

[67] If Peter intentionally reneged and taught circumcision, per Esler, then it seems that dismissal of the Gentiles or modification of the meals rather than the withdrawal of the Jewish participants would be expected, and a charge of heresy or apostasy instead of hypocrisy would be mounted.

[68] See Stendahl, *Paul,* 27.

[69] There is not space to engage the discussion of how to translate the genitive phrase as either "faith in Christ" or the "faithfulness of Christ," but in v. 16b the faith of Peter in Christ Jesus is an element of Paul's argument.

has in the past publicly demonstrated his commitment to the gospel of Christ by the way he was "eating with the [i.e., *these*] Gentiles."[70]

Paul approaches Peter as though Peter's thinking has been clouded by social anxiety, so that he has not realized the logical implications of this choice of behavior. But Paul makes it clear that such (mis)behaving must cease, that the meaning of the death of Christ is at risk. To the details of this proposed reading I now turn.

Peter's Mealtime Behavior Symbolizes a Challenge to Identity Conventions

It should be noted that in this text Paul never mentions the food itself, and he does not identify those whom Peter fears as "the ones for Jewish diet" or "for a more rigorous diet," not even, per Dunn, for example, for what might be described as "a more rigorous Noahide diet." They are instead identified by their interest in identity—specifically, transforming the standing of the (male) Gentiles with whom Peter has been eating from foreskinned to circumcised. In fact, they are labeled by Paul according to their interest in the traditional way to negotiate the inclusion—not exclusion—of Gentiles seeking full membership among Jewish communities: "the ones for circumcision."

As already noted, it is unlikely that the meaning of Paul's reference is that the ones Peter fears are circumcised; Peter, Paul, and the rest of the Jewish believers are circumcised as well. The point is that they are advocates of circumcision for these Gentiles. Naturally, this implies that the advocates are circumcised. They are responding to the ambiguity created by the way these Gentiles are being treated at these meals by encouraging a clearer discrimination of difference between Gentiles, even if welcome as guests, and proselytes, who have become full members. Their reaction exemplifies the anthropological generality that "cultural intolerance of ambiguity is expressed by avoidance, by discrimination, and by pressure to conform."[71] The issue at stake is how these Gentiles ought to be identified in the present age: it is the view of those Peter fears that they ought to become proselytes (Jews), the completion of which rite of passage is symbolized (for males) by circumcision.[72]

There is something about Peter's eating—or not eating—with Gentiles to which the advocates of circumcision, or Paul, object, but the social relations symbolized by the way this meal is conducted are emphasized in the way Paul describes the case.[73] For it is the *status* of these Gentiles that is at stake in Peter's decision to eat with them

---

[70] This is the point of Paul's rhetorical question and reply in vv. 17–18. Peter's action implies that the truth of the gospel's uplifting of these Gentiles to righteousness and thus equality with Jewish people while remaining Gentiles represents instead his stepping down to the standing of a Gentile sinner, which would make Christ the agent of this process. Instead, Peter has proven himself to be the agent of the problem at hand if he fails to continue to walk straight toward the gospel.

[71] Douglas, "Pollution," 53.

[72] On proselyte conversion, see S. Cohen, *Beginnings;* Porton, *Strangers;* L. Hoffman, *Covenant.*

[73] The pattern of social relations is encoded in the way a meal is conducted, which sends a message: "The message is about different degrees of hierarchy, inclusion and exclusion, boundaries and transactions across the boundaries" (Douglas, "Deciphering a Meal," 249).

or not. They are said by Paul to be "compelled *to Judaize*" by Peter's obsequious with-drawal from eating with these Gentiles to appease those advocating their *circumci-sion*. This social dynamic exemplifies the observation that

> in ordinary society any occasion on which people of different social levels ate to-gether was likely to become an occasion for exhibiting the distance between them.[74]

The differences might be salient in several ways—for example, by the seating arrange-ments, by the portion or kind of food served, or by the amount of water mixed with the wine. The details of this meal are not mentioned, but discrimination at meals was common according to Roman and Greek as well as Jewish social conventions, even if subject to criticism.[75] It continues in various ways in most cultures to this day; so we still speak of "the upper crust," which derives from the way bread was distributed at meals according to social rank.

The force of this point is reinforced by observing that, according to Paul, the re-action of the Gentiles from whom Peter withdraws is not to change their diet but "to Judaize," if, that is, Ἰουδαΐζειν, as Paul uses it here, has to do with changing their identity, not just their behavior. Although a change of identity would include a change of diet if they were not already eating according to Jewish conventions, it is reasonable to expect that if food were the issue, this is what Paul would say these Gen-tiles were being compelled by the force of Peter's withdrawal to alter: they would now be concerned "to eat like Jews." Positive consideration of a change of diet to gain ac-ceptance would certainly be expected to precede a change of one's identity by way of circumcision! And the topic of matters related to food would be expected to emerge somewhere in Paul's interpretation of the principles at issue in the explanation that follows in vv. 14–21. Or somewhere in his message to the Galatians! But food is never the topic of concern in this letter; rather, the issues that are raised concern the iden-tity of these (male) Gentiles as foreskinned rather than circumcised. The question at issue in Galatia is whether this identity is appropriate for these Gentiles who now claim to be children of Abraham, full members of the people of God. There is simply no explicit statement in this narrative or the whole of the letter that the meals at which Peter and the other Jewish believers in Jesus—including Paul(!)—had been "eating with Gentiles" included food that was objectionable on Jewish dietary terms.

Contributing to the direction that interpretation has taken to date, that is, the focus on an objection to behavior (food or the level of mixing) instead of identity (with whom they are mixing in this particular way), are at least two details central to

---

[74] Meeks, *Origins*, 96.
[75] Jewish sources include Prov 25:6–7; Sir 7:4; 13:8–9; 29:27; 32:1–2; Luke 14:7–11; 1 Cor 11:17–34; Josephus, *Ant.* 12.210; Philo, *Contempl.* 69; 1QS 2.20–26; *Lev. Rab.* 1; *'Abot R. Nat.* 25; Greeks include Plato, *Symp.* 177D–E, 212C–213B; Theophrastus, *Char.* 21.2; Plutarch, *Mor.* 149B; 219E; 615D–619; Epictetus, *Diatr.* 4.1, 105; Romans include Cicero, *Att.* 13.52; Lucian, *Gall.* 11; *Sat.* 17; *Symp.* 9; Horace, *Sat.* 2.8; Pliny, *Ep.* 2.6; Juvenal, *Sat.* 3.140; 5; Martial, *Epigr.* 3.60; Petronius, *Sat.* 38.14; Suetonius, *Jul.* 48. For discussions see Theissen, *Pauline Christianity*, 145–74; D. Smith, "Table Fellowship"; W. Braun, *Feasting*, 45–48, 100–31; Newton, *Deity and Diet*, 228–31, 243–44; Gowers, *Loaded Table*; Garnsey, *Food.*

our discussion. Both perhaps stem from failing to keep in view the sufficient distinction between what is symbolized by circumcision, which has to do with transformation of status that renders a non-Jew a proselyte (identity)[76]—which does have behavioral implications, since it thereby obliges them to Jewish behavior in the same way as a Jew from birth (note Paul's statement in 5:3)—and the language of Law observance (e.g., obliged to observe the whole Law), behavior that does not apply to non-Jews (although elements of "Noahide" behavior—however labeled—would apply to Gentiles deemed righteous, either in principle or, more likely in this case, because of positive association).[77] But apart from proselyte converts—and those who are engaged in the rite of passage that will result ultimately in this identity—Law observance and circumcision represent two very different matters. Interpreters of Galatians have generally conflated them, mixing discussion of circumcision and proselyte conversion (identity transformation from Gentile to Jewish standing) seamlessly with issues of Law observance (behavior for those identified as Jews or proselytes, not Gentiles, except to the increasing degree applicable for those engaged in the ritual process). As Mary Douglas puts the general principle:

> Rites of passage are not purificatory but are prophylactic. They do not redefine and restore a lost former status or purify from the effect of contamination, but they define entrance to a new status. In this way the permanence and value of the classifications embracing all sections of society are emphasized.[78]

Two examples that arise in discussions of this narrative exemplify the problems that result from overlooking the difference. One, the prevailing understanding of the meaning of Paul's logical deduction that the Gentiles are being persuaded, as a result of Peter's behavior—if not also his teaching them—"to Judaize," obscures the focus on status transformation at issue. Judaizing is usually taken to be an indication of a relative change of behavior (imitating Jews) rather than a transformation of identity (becoming Jews). The second example is the prevailing understanding of the behavior of which Peter is accused by Paul in setting up his argument, when Peter is said to be behaving hypocritically because he "is living in the same way as a Gentile." The consensus view redirects Paul's argumentative concern away from how a Jewish Christ-believer's behavior affects the self-identity of these Gentiles (compelling them to Judaize) to how it ought to exemplify Jewish Christ-believers' commitment to reidentification according to Gentile behavioral norms. That is, it is usually interpreted to mean that Peter gave up a Jewish lifestyle, or at least the rigor of observing the elements of dietary regulations thought to be at issue, because he no longer holds

---

[76] I do not mean to suggest that there might not be some hierarchical distinctions that remain, and even rabbinic discussions of whether proselytes should be referred to as Jews or Israelites testify to the issues that continue to arise when dealing with such identity transformations, that is, when members of the dominant social order (pagans) become members of these minority ethnic groups. See Porton, *Strangers*.

[77] The theoretical nature of some later rabbinic discussions of Noahides versus the issues that arise in this actual kind of socially mixed setting in Syria should be recognized.

[78] Douglas, "Pollution," 56.

them to be essential for believers in Jesus Christ. Paul is understood to object to Peter's supposed return to Jewish observance. These elements of the enthymeme of v. 14 are understood to concern behavioral modification that symbolizes commitment to a Law-free gospel, rather than identity modification in view of the gospel "righteousing" circumcised and foreskinned (men) on equal terms. Let us examine both of these examples more closely.

1. Engaging Dunn's thesis offers a good way to organize the discussion of the first matter. To what does Paul refer when employing the language of "Judaizing" ('Ιουδαΐζειν)? Dunn argues in principle—and his conclusion depends upon the case—that this is not the same thing as becoming a proselyte, that is, being circumcised. Rather, " 'judaizing' denotes a range of possible degrees of assimilation to Jewish customs, with circumcision as the end-point of judaizing; but evidently one could 'judaize' without going the whole way (circumcision)."[79] Granted, these are two different terms and denote two different things. Judaizing can refer to merely adopting one or more aspects of a Jewish manner of life or even to siding politically with the Jewish people.[80] But the evidence Dunn marshals to conclude that Paul refers to something other than proselyte conversion is far from unambiguous. In fact, much of it can be argued to subvert what Dunn contends to be the case in these contexts. Most important, the context of the interests at stake in Antioch does not support this interpretation for the case at hand.

Dunn appeals to Josephus's usage in *J. W.* 2.454, where Metilius, the Roman commander of the garrison in Jerusalem, "saved his life by entreaties and promises to turn Jew, and even to be circumcised" (Thackeray, LCL). This example could support Dunn's proposition. The terms clearly denote two different things, however they might overlap. A more literal translation of the phrase καὶ μέχρι περιτομῆς 'Ιουδαΐζειν would read, "to Judaize even to the point of [or 'as far as'] circumcision." In a context such as this, it might even be better translated, "to *Judeanize* even to the point of circumcision," emphasizing the geopolitical rather than the religious dimension of ἰουδαΐζειν.[81] In other words, Metilius was willing not only to become affiliated with the Judeans and their political cause, "to Judeanize," but even to become identified with them religiously, to complete proselyte conversion as symbolized by circumcision, "to Jewize," you might say, to become a Jew.[82] Dunn's argument would not be supported in that case. But if translated "even to Judaize to the point of cir-

---

[79] Dunn, "Incident at Antioch" 220.

[80] See the comprehensive discussion of S. Cohen, *Beginnings,* 179–97. Cohen makes clear that this is a reflexive verb, so one thing that "judaizing" does not mean is influencing others to take this step, such as in the case of missionaries, although this usage continues to be used to describe and label the influencers of the Galatians (see also Nanos, *Irony,* 115–19).

[81] Cf. S. Cohen, *Beginnings,* 69–139, for discussion of the issues surrounding translation as "Judean" or "Jewish," and 181–85 for the examples under discussion. He notes, for example, Josephus's usage in a subsequent passage of ῥωμαϊζόντων, "to romanize," where the political meaning of the phrase is clear, referring to bringing back to their side those who "were still romanizing" (*J.W.* 2.562). See also M. Smith, "Gentiles"; G. Harvey, *True Israel.*

[82] S. Cohen, *Beginnings,* 183, admits that this reference may be taken to indicate "the functional equivalent of conversion," although he concludes, like Dunn, that "judaizing" here does not mean "to become a Jew" but to "behave like a Jew."

cumcision," would that support his argument? It could, but words and phrases can be put to many uses. In this context, Josephus's turn of phrase appears designed to emphasize the extreme nature of the case: even a Roman official was so intimidated by the treachery of these Judean "brigands" that he would "judaize" to save his life, that is, change his identity—become a Jew. Melitius's pledge was urgent, he was willing to go all the way, even allowing "mutilation" of himself—for that is how a Roman would view the act of circumcision. They had nothing to fear from him in the future should they spare his life. Does this use of language by Josephus imply that he could have become a Jew or in some way "Judaize" his behavior without becoming circumcised, that is, changing his identity, or does it rather suggest that while foreigners could "Judeanize"—become Judeans, for example, move to Judea, and respect Judeans' way of life—at the extreme end of the scale they could become members of the Judean ethnos, including religious conversion, symbolized (for males) by circumcision, and thus Jews? Whichever the case might be, this reference does not provide unambiguous support for Dunn's thesis, and may in fact be argued to undermine it.

The same criticism applies to the example Dunn cites from Esth 8:17 LXX: "and many of the Gentiles were circumcised [περιετέμοντο], and became Jews [καὶ Ἰουδαΐζειν], for fear of the Jews [φόβον τῶν Ἰουδαίων]." Whether it is translated "imitating" or "becoming" "Judeans" or "Jews," these Gentiles decided to change the way they were identified, not merely some aspects of their behavior, by becoming circumcised. It could be argued in this context, however, that even if Ἰουδαΐζειν had not been mentioned, what was being communicated explicitly was what would have been implied anyway: that these Gentiles were becoming Jews/Judeans, that is, deciding to be circumcised; that the expression following καί may overlap the one preceding it, clarifying or intensifying the meaning, rather than indicating something wholly different. The context is again geopolitical, so it might imply the salience of the religious dimension in addition to the political, as argued above in the case of Metilius. Their change of identity, and thus concomitant behavior, was not understood to represent conformity but compliance, for it was motivated by intimidation. But the point of mentioning circumcision here seems to be to emphasize that their Judean or Jewish status, or both, is beyond dispute—they were circumcised. Otherwise, perhaps their identity might be questioned. This example hardly makes the case that "Judaizing" signifies the adoption of Jewish or Judean behavior apart from a change of social identity, which is signified by circumcision for males upon completion of the transformation rite.[83]

Dunn's reference to Josephus *J.W.* 2.462–563 is interesting because it relates directly to Syria, albeit slightly later, in the mid-60s, and is a part of the string of accounts that includes the example of Metilius just discussed. Again, the socio- and geopolitical context for translating Ἰουδαῖοι as "Judeans," or at least the importance

---

[83] Contra S. Cohen, who argues that in this case it is most likely that the Gentiles in view did not become proselytes, although this is implied by the Greek translation, which includes "circumcision" with their "judaizing." Since this is not indicated in the Hebrew *mityahadim,* Cohen suggests they merely "pretended to be Jews to protect themselves" (*Beginnings,* 181). But his main argument is circular, appealing to the definitions of the usage he established (182) but that are here in question.

of keeping the salience of this dimension in view when translating it as "Jews," is evident. This is indeed a most interesting reference. But does it really support Dunn's case? There is no mention of circumcision by which to measure the distinction he seeks to draw. The references to those non-Judean Syrians who have "judaized/ judeanized" (Ἰουδαΐζοντος), who are arguably also described as a "mixed" (μεμιγ-μένος) and "equivocal [ἀμφίβολον] element in their midst," are simply too vague to provide any kind of clarity on the matter at hand.[84] It is interesting to note that these Syrian Judaizers/Judeanizers are "feared as much as pronounced aliens," that is, as much as Judeans by birth; this emphasizes the geopolitical dimension of the tension Josephus sought to relate.[85] Were they circumcised, that is, proselytes, or were they merely some kind of non-Jewish or non-Judean sympathizers? We cannot say. The example is too ambiguous to draw a conclusion either way.

The other case to which Dunn appeals is a much later one found in Eusebius *Praep. ev.* 9.22.5, where we find the translation "until all the inhabitants of Shechem were circumcised and judaized [περιτεμνομένους ἰουδαΐσαι]." But there is no con-junction in the text, and although the participle can be variously understood, it clari-fies the circumstances of the verbal action. Thus it might be better translated as, "until all of the inhabitants of Shechem became Jews/Judeans by having themselves circumcised." A more literal translation, however the participle is translated, enunci-ates parallel concepts: if passive, "were Judaized/Judeanized, receiving circumcision," or if middle voice, "Judaized/Judeanized by having themselves circumcised."[86] Since the context is again one of compliance with pressure rather than conformity out of conviction, in order to accommodate the demands of Jacob if Dinah was to be joined to the sons of Shechem, the translation "to Judeanize" might be preferred. But what-ever the case, it does not support Dunn's contention that Judaizing here implies the adoption of some Jewish behavioral practices, as distinguished from becoming Jewish inclusive of circumcision. From Eusebius's point of view, it suggests the opposite to be the case.[87]

It should be noted that Josephus does not use "Judaize" or its cognates for nonproselytes in comments where that might be expected according to Dunn's argu-

---

[84] Thackeray translates μεμιγμένος as "neutrals" (LCL); Dunn suggests the colloquialism "those who had become mixed up with the Jews"; S. Cohen translates " 'mixed'—that is, of mixed ancestry" (*Beginnings,* 184–85), and argues that this reference is to the same ones as those referred to as "ambiguous [αμφίβολον] in their midst," but this group is to be distinguished from those who are referred to as having "judaized" (184 n. 38). It is not clear to me why two or more different groups are indicated by these references. Is it not a way to describe the ambiguous, mixed, non-Judean members of the Syrian people who are related somehow (in various ways?) to Jewish com-munal life as guests or friends or even members but not clearly enough linked with their political ob-jectives to be destroyed indiscriminately along with the Judeans as though outright political traitors? Does this not imply a more religious sense of affiliation?

[85] Cf. S. Cohen, *Beginnings,* 184–85.

[86] I am grateful to Carl Conrad for a helpful discussion of translation options.

[87] S. Cohen, *Beginnings,* 188–89, argues that the usage in this case means "to become a Jew," since what is at issue is "to become of the same nation (*genos*) as the Jews," although Cohen main-tains that this meaning for the term is only found later than Paul (a point I am herein seeking to challenge).

ment. For example, in *Ag. Ap.* 2.210, Josephus understands Moses' community to welcome those not only born into the family but also aliens adopting "the way of life" (τοῦ βίου νομίζων), a kind of inclusion in the "intimacies of our daily life" that is distinguished from that granted the "casual visitor." And Josephus did not refer, for example, to those "multitudes of Greeks" in Antioch who had become "in some way a part" of the Jewish community's "worship practices" (θρησκείαις) as "Judaizers" (*J.W.* 7.45). Perhaps this was because he did not understand them to have "Judaized," that is, to have become proselytes. The similarity of the Antiochene situation Josephus describes to the one we are examining is intriguing, to say the least. And consider the case of Plutarch's use of ἰουδαΐζειν and Ἰουδαῖος in *Cic.* 7.6, seemingly the only appearance of ἰουδαΐζειν in classical non-Jewish or Christian Greek. This derisive usage may indicate that this Gentile's behavior is judged to be similar to the observance of Jewish practices, or to indicate his political support of Jews.[88] But even if this is so, the point is that the irony of the judgment turns on the fact that behaving Jewishly when not a Jew meets with disapproval by Plutarch's Cicero. He may be questioning whether this Gentile has in fact "Judaized" unless he has actually become a Jew or Judean, that is, been circumcised. But it is just as plausible to understand that Cicero here explores the suspicion that this freedman was circumcised, that is, a Jew, and thus it might be thought strange for him to weigh in on the affairs of Verres directly in a way that threatened to change the course of the prosecution's case. Thus Cicero's dismissive pun might have meant, "What has a Jew [Ἰουδαίῳ = circumcised non–pork eater] to do with a verres [χοῖρον = castrated porker]?"

The most telling criticism of Dunn's proposition arises from the usage of this terminology in the context of the Antioch incident itself. The context pushes the usage of "to Judaize" in v. 14 to the extreme end of Dunn's definition of assimilation behavior, it is true, yet it falls within the limits that he allows (as inclusive of circumcision), although he does not consider circumcision to be indicated in Paul's usage here. Why would the Gentiles logically conclude from this departure of the Jewish people "to Judaize," and what does the phrase most naturally mean in this context? Peter has withdrawn because of fear of those advocating a different standing for Gentiles: he fears "the ones for circumcision." As already noted, those whom Peter fears are denoted by their advocacy not of a more Jewish or Noahic lifestyle for the Gentiles but of *circumcision*.[89] Peter's fear is not, after all, toward ones identified by Paul as "for stricter observance of Noahic commandments" or even "Sinaitic laws"! Surely his own circumcision is not at issue; as a Jew he was circumcised as a child. Moreover, Peter is not accused of compelling these Gentiles to "live like a Jew [Ἰουδαϊκῶς]," which would contrast more precisely with the charge that he is "living like a Gentile [ἐθνικῶς]," but "to Judaize" (Ἰουδαΐζειν).

In making the same case for which I am arguing, Esler perceptively notes that Paul's choice of Ἰουδαΐζειν ("to Judaize") here instead of περιτμηθῆναι ("to be circumcised") is "because it is the most appropriate way of making the point following

---

[88] Ibid., 180–81.
[89] So too Esler, "Making," 278.

Ἰουδαῖος and Ἰουδαϊκῶς earlier in the same verse."[90] This argument is strengthened to the degree that Paul's statement in v. 14 is understood to exemplify ironic inversion in an elegant though complex enthymeme, "a brief and pointed argument drawn from contraries" that could be used to expose logical inconsistencies in a ridiculing manner.[91] This enthymeme cleverly turns on the fact that Peter's behavior implies a priority for Jewish identity that drives these Gentiles to conclude they need to become Jews. But Peter's belief in Christ undermines that conclusion, since Peter, a Jew by birth, has turned to Christ "in the same way as" have these Gentiles. For, as Paul explains in the next verses, in Christ both Jews and Gentiles are legitimated (justified/righteoused) before God—and thus are indiscriminate equals with each other—on the same terms, while remaining Jews and Gentiles. There is no discrimination according to identity as Jew or Gentile in Christ, and Peter knows this—he was even there when this was confirmed at Jerusalem—yet later Peter has behaved as though there were, because of fear of the consequences threatened by those who do not share this conviction.

Thus Paul approaches Peter's behavior here as exemplifying *hypocrisy,* not apostasy or heresy, which would be the case if Peter were actually *advocating* that these Gentiles become proselytes, Judaize.[92] And that is also why Peter and the rest of the Jews have withdrawn instead of altering the way the meals exemplified this conviction or dismissing these Gentiles, a point that has been generally overlooked in the interpretive tradition.[93] Peter and the Jews who follow his lead do not advocate that for which they do not want to suffer; they merely want to avoid the outcome they fear will result if they do not *appear* to comply with the policies of the ones for circumcision.[94] Paul's ironic dig brings to the surface that Peter's attempt to behave in a manner that *masks* his true convictions, when that behavior is in conflict with his claims for the gospel, undermines the meaning of the very truth for which Christ died and for which Paul and Peter now live (vv. 15–21).

In this context, for these Gentiles "to Judaize" means for (male) non-Jews to become circumcised, to complete the rite of conversion that renders them proselytes,[95] Jews by acquisition, not birth (ascription), as were Peter, Paul, and "the rest of the

---

[90] Esler, "Making," 278.

[91] Holloway, "Enthymeme," 335–36, although I disagree with his interpretation of the verse, which is, in keeping with the prevailing view, based on understanding Peter to have departed from Jewish behavior. This insight remains the same, or is sharpened, if Tomson's suggestion to follow the manuscripts that drop the phrase "and not in the same way as a Jew" is adopted (*Paul,* 229).

[92] Peter is accused of masking his beliefs because of fear by behavior that departs from the path set down by those beliefs, but not of leaving that path to adopt a new one (apostasy) or of advocating a new path in opposition to the former one (heresy).

[93] This tells against Homberg's suggestion that what was being proposed by James and upheld by Peter's withdrawal and separation was the permanent establishment, on the basis of conviction, of two commensality groups, one for Jewish Christ-believers and another for Gentiles ("Identity," esp. 410–11).

[94] Note 2 Macc 6:24–26; 4 Macc 6:17–22.

[95] Although a minority, this interpretation does have other advocates; see Betz, *Galatians,* 112; Esler, "Making," 278; idem, *Galatians,* 137–38; Tomson, *Paul,* 229–30, translates differently ("to live like a Jew") but comes to the conclusion that it means "to become Jewish proselytes."

Jews." The Gentiles left behind at this meal would logically conclude that this was a compelling solution only if they have already *behaved* to date according to the prevailing halakic standards for inclusion of non-Jews at this coalition's Jewish meals but now find that they still somehow remain open to status discrimination within this group because they lack the *identity* required for the equality claimed, that is, because they are not proselytes. They need to become proselytes if they are to gain what they seek, indeed, what they had believed already theirs on the basis of the teaching of these Jewish members—full and equal membership with the Jewish believers in Christ, standing as children of Abraham, righteous ones among the historic people of God. In other words, these Gentiles' self-esteem—which has been to date invested in the teaching of this subgroup about who they have become by way of faith in/of Christ and which has led them to believe that proselyte conversion was inappropriate for themselves—has been dashed. They have been shamed for believing and acting in a manner that has in effect been undermined by the very ones who have created this expectation.

It is natural that those on the margins are seeking predictability by conforming to membership criteria and behavior thought appropriate, in order to overcome the ambiguity and uncertainty of their identity:

> Strong pressures encouraging conformity—with penalties attaching to deviance— may oppress most those whose membership or social identity is insecure.[96]

The identity and concomitant rights these Gentiles have been led to believe are theirs within this subgroup exist only to the degree that they are confirmed by the guardians of the communal norms.[97] The withdrawal of Peter and the rest, instead of their willingness to suffer to stand up for them, undermines the principles upon which these Gentiles' expectations have been based. It seems rather that the norms to which these Gentiles should conform are set by the ones advocating circumcision, the ones by whom Peter and the rest of the Jews are intimidated. And thus Paul felt compelled to publicly confront this hypocrisy, putting Peter, and the rest of the Jews involved, in their place. Paul thereby confirms the place of these Gentiles as Gentiles, and this point is central to the argument of the following verses of this narrative (15–21) and throughout the letter.

The question before these Gentiles, as Paul sees the matter, is one of identity, not behavior per se, although it is Peter's change of *behavior*—because of his desire to maintain the privileges of *identity* on terms that no longer should dictate the *behavior* of members of *this* coalition—that provoked the incident around which Paul constructs this case. This does not mean that Peter should not continue to behave like a Jew in the sense of observing Jewish dietary and other halakic conventions (consider here the logic of 5:3!) but that he should not behave as though the *identity* of these Gentiles in Christ as equals threatens the value of *his* identity *as a Jew,* for he too is

---

[96] Jenkins, *Social Identity,* 124. For a detailed discussion of this dynamic at work in the Galatian context, see Nanos, *Irony,* 86–109, 242–83.

[97] Jenkins, *Social Identity,* 135; Hogg and Abrams, *Identifications,* 171.

identified *in Christ,* thus *in the same way as a Gentile.* That is, because of the truth of the gospel in which they have believed, the communal norms for "eating with Gentiles" within this Jewish subgroup have been modified to include these Gentiles *as Gentiles* in the way that other Jewish groups would include proselytes, even if other—including more powerful—groups may disagree and bring pressure to bear to have such Gentiles become proselytes if this behavior is to continue. The members of this subgroup are not abandoning Jewish dietary regulations, but as we would expect to find any Jewish group doing if challenged by a new revelation, they are reinterpreting the prevailing practices to conform with the new insights—in this case, how to interact with these Gentiles at mixed meals. They are negotiating the prevailing "rulings," deciding appropriate halakic norms for this Jewish coalition of believers in Jesus as Christ.

2. When Paul confronts Peter *after* his withdrawal for behaving in a way that logically compels these Gentiles to Judaize, he turns his accusation around the observation that Peter "is living *in the same way as a Gentile,* and not in the same way as a Jew." The interpretation of the phrase, "living in the same way as [like] a Gentile," has been understood to mean *behaving* with no regard for Jewish halakhot. Longenecker's comment is representative of the traditional and still prevailing view:

> The terms ἐθνικῶς and Ἰουδαϊκῶς refer to living according to Gentile and Jewish customs, particularly here with respect to the observance of the Jewish dietary laws—the former ignoring and the latter observing them.[98]

Dunn modifies the point slightly: it is not that Peter was ignoring Jewish dietary regulations entirely; rather, he was observing to the level of a Noahide.[99] But this ingenious twist does not account for the fact that Noahide expectations are not for Jews like Peter but for Gentiles, and it fails to explain why these Gentiles are then described as being compelled by Peter's behavior not "to Gentilize" or "to Noahidize" but "to Judaize." Regardless of whether Noahide or some other terminology might better describe what would be expected of Gentiles seeking association with Jewish

---

[98] R. Longenecker, *Galatians,* 78; see also Burton, *Galatians,* 111–13; Betz, *Galatians,* 112 (cited above); or virtually any commentary.

[99] Dunn, "Incident at Antioch," 219–20, 225. Tomson, *Paul,* 228–30, goes further, challenging the traditional view that this expression indicates abrogation of Jewish food laws. He suggests that in the rhetorical context of Paul's opposition to circumcision, "it does not describe Paul's diet but the liberal attitude towards the gentile brethren," offering this paraphrase: "Before, you agreed to live and eat as a Jew together with the gentiles, and although some call that 'living like a gentile,' why do you now separate and wish to eat with them only if they become Jews?" (230). Tomson understands the expression in a way similar to Sanders and Esler, signifying a relationship with these Gentiles that is too close for comfort for the ones from James, who have an "excessive fear of idolatry." Similar to Dunn, Tomson locates the differences of view somewhat along a Judean/Antiochene line, for he suggests that like the later "Tannaic tradition supported by most Sages in post-Temple times," "the majority of Jews of first century Antioch" would have been more able to find ways to have mixed meals, as did Peter (236). Tomson, however, does seem to indicate that some compromise of food laws for Paul is implied: "The conclusion is that here Paul does not urge Peter *to join him again* in *a non-Jewish way of life*" (230; emphasis added).

communal life,[100] if the pressure was to become Noahides or to observe Noahide commandments to a more rigorous level, then the statement of v. 15 and the argument that follows it make little sense. For Paul's appeal is based on agreement with Peter in principle, that they are both Jews by birth (= righteous ones) and not therefore Gentiles (= sinners); nevertheless, they have believed in Jesus Christ *in the same way as* these Gentiles (v. 16).[101] If the point of the preceding phrase was to indicate a limitation of Peter's observance to Noahic rather than Sinaitic behavior, as Dunn argues the case to be, what would be the point of making a contrast with "works of Law," that is, with Sinaitic identity or behavior? Why set out the contrast between Jews by birth and Gentile sinners when it is in effect between levels of Noahic behavior for Jews and Gentiles alike?[102]

An interesting element in Paul's accusation is the fact that it is delivered as though Peter's living in the same way as a Gentile represents the *present* situation at the time of Paul's challenge. That is, Paul does not refer to Peter's prior behavior, when he "was" eating with these Gentiles, but to the way Peter "is living" (ζῆς), although Peter is by this time behaving in a way that complies with the norms of the advocates of circumcision. For after his withdrawal, at the time of Paul's accusation that is, Peter is no longer living like a Gentile in the sense of his dietary practice: he is surely eating Jewishly at this point, according to whatever conventions were in force at the meals to which he has separated himself. Therefore, even if Peter had been eating in a so-called Law-free (or Noahide) way (which I do not see indicated in the

---

[100] The topic as well as terminology are matters of considerable debate; my interest here is to engage Dunn's argument as it has been made. See Nanos, *Mystery*, 50–57, 166–79, for further discussion and sources.

[101] This similarity does not, however, indicate that any compromise of Torah was implied for Jewish people who became believers in Jesus as a Jewish messiah. Jews need not become Gentiles to become believers in the messiahship of Jesus or the righteousing power of God in him. Holmberg, "Jewish *versus* Christian," however, assumes that this would have been implied from the start for the first Jewish believers in Jesus, as though being "made righteous before God without the Law" would have been a salient concern (419), and that is essential to the conflict he understands to have arisen in Antioch. But Holmberg elsewhere recognizes that "the Christians of Jewish descent, of course, had not stopped being Jews by becoming baptized in the Messiah Jesus: they still thought of themselves as Jews, and observed the Law, etc." (422, and see 424: "Jewishness of the first Christians, which they never had dreamt of questioning or leaving").

[102] Dunn argues that Paul's usage of "sinners" here suggests a matter of degree from the perspective of other interest groups, such as it may for Pharisees, who might take issue with any deviation from halakhic rigor as defined among themselves. His discussion suggests behavioral "sins," that is, moral impurity, and not merely identity outside covenant righteousness. But elsewhere in his essay he considers the issue to be ritual purity, which Sanders has adequately dismissed. Dunn, however, undermines his definition when he observes that "it probably had the connotation of 'unclean' (= Gentile = sinner), one who by his very race was legally disqualified from participating in the table-fellowship of a faithful Jew" ("Incident at Antioch," 222). That would not be an issue of either ritual or moral (e.g., idolatry) impurity but of identity, concerning the status of the Gentile as profane by birth. On ritual and moral impurity as well as profane status, see Klawans, "Notions"; *Impurity and Sin*. The interpreter's decision about whether this case concerns the ritual and moral impurity or the profane status of Gentiles will turn largely on what one understands to be at dispute at the mixed table, and thus presents the problem of circularity. Nevertheless, note that the contrast in this verse is with status from birth, which is not a question of either ritual or moral purity but identity in terms of sacred/profane. Winninge, *Sinners*, offers a comprehensive examination of usage of the term "sinner/s" in Paul and other Second Temple sources, although not to the same conclusion.

text), he would no longer have been doing so when Paul confronted him. In other words, the prevailing interpretations logically turn Paul's phrase upside-down, as if he had written,

> If you, though *no longer* a Jew *[but a Christian], used to behave* like a *Gentile* (read: Law-free Christian) and not like a (Law-observant*)* Jew (and still believe that this is as it should be, but are momentarily hiding this conviction), how can you behave now in a way that compels these Gentiles to behave like [or become] Jews?[103]

The only sense in which Peter is still living *in the same way as* or *like* a Gentile when living separate from this Gentile table is in the sense of his *identity* in Christ, which is, as Paul so clearly puts the case in vv. 15–16, by being justified *in the same way as* are these Gentiles, by faith in/of Christ.[104] I propose that it does *not* indicate any kind of *Gentile-like behavior,* including Noahic, but instead signifies the way in which Peter, *like any human in Christ,* Jew or Gentile, is *identified* as a *righteous one,* that is, justified or legitimated as one of God's own, regardless of status as Gentile or Jew.[105]

Paul's challenge assumes that Peter still understands his righteous standing ("living" = justification/legitimation) to be based in Christ, and that Peter understands that he is equal in status with the Gentiles from whom he has withdrawn. Peter has not intended to nullify by his action this equal standing in Christ with these Gentiles; his discrimination has been, rather, in terms of compliance with the prevailing conventions of the present age, to which "the ones for circumcision" seek to hold him. But according to Paul, Peter's discriminatory action in the present age, which is based on his *privileging* of Jewish identity, undermines the equality of standing of non-Jewish people in Christ in the present age as taught by this coalition, by Peter himself. Thus Paul clarifies that there is no legitimate basis for such *discrimination* within this Jewish coalition without subverting "the truth of the good news"—indeed, without rendering merely gratuitous the death of Christ in which Peter and the Jews who follow his lead believe.

Paul does not introduce a new concept to Peter but appeals to the one already held by Peter and the others in Antioch, not to mention the other "pillars" of this coalition in Jerusalem with whom Paul had met earlier, James and John.[106] This usage of "living" to signify the identity of one standing righteous before God is in keeping

---

[103] Note Dunn, "Incident at Antioch," 225: "Paul's description of Peter as *previously having lived* 'like a Gentile and not as a Jew' " (emphasis added). Esler, *Galatians,* 139, observes that the use of the present tense sharpens the point that Peter's withdrawal from the Gentiles "is merely a pretence, since his adoption of Gentile ways really represents his true position." This observation, however, seems to undermine Esler's contention that Peter reneged and is now explicitly promoting proselyte conversion.

It should also be observed that Paul does not accuse Peter of moving back and forth between Jewish and Gentile behavior, as many propose when understanding the charge of hypocrisy to indicate vacillation; for then, on their interpretation, we would expect Paul to write, "are behaving [living] at the same time [or 'alternately'] as a Jew and as a Gentile."

[104] This point was also a topic of discussion in Nanos, *Mystery,* 351–54, where it is brought into conversation with the implications of Paul's instructions in Rom 14.

[105] See the interesting discussion of righteous identity in Esler, *Galatians,* 141–77.

[106] Along a similar line, see Holmberg, *Paul and Power,* 152, 200–201, although to a very different conclusion. See also Koptak, "Rhetorical Identification."

with the force of Paul's argument (vv. 15–21), which draws upon the language of Hab 2:4 ("the just [righteous ones] shall by faith live").[107] Regardless of how interpreters view the move from v. 14 to vv. 15–21—as a continuation of what Paul said to Peter, or an elaboration developed only later, perhaps specifically with the address to the Galatians in mind, or even a version of what he wished he would have said—the narrative explains the centrality of righteousness by faith of/in Jesus Christ for Jew and Gentile on equal terms. In other words, although Paul's theme of how Jew and Gentile are justified—*live* before God and with each other in Christ—is often noted by interpreters as the theme of vv. 16–21, I am simply suggesting that this same theme is present in v. 14 when Paul writes of how Peter "lives."[108] Verse 14 might be paraphrased, then, as follows:

> If you Peter, remain Jewish yet are identified now as a righteous one (justified) in the same way as are these Gentiles (by faith in/of Christ) and not by virtue of the fact that you were born a Jew, how can you decide to behave in a way that implies that these Gentiles are not your equal unless they become Jews too?

In this narrative unit Paul employs the identity language of *living* to challenge the implication that logically arises for these Gentiles from the discriminatory behavior of Peter and the other Jews who join him: it now seems that they too need to become identified as Jews, that is, by circumcision = "works of law"[109]—a privileged identity to which Peter, Paul, and the rest can appeal—if they hope to become accepted as equals within this coalition, not to mention by those who stand outside of it. That is, regardless of how appropriately these Gentiles have been eating and conducting themselves according to the Jewish norms for mixed meals, they have remained Gentiles on principle, though no longer pagan idolaters. But because of the truth of the gospel as proclaimed by Jews such as Peter and the rest, they have also not become proselyte candidates, as would be expected of pagans turning from idolatry if they seek incorporation as full members. But since this has been shown to be insufficient to avoid the results of pressure from those to whom Peter and the rest now capitulate—in fact, to be the source of such pressure—these Gentiles realize that they need to become circumcised=proselytes=Jews, that is, people of Torah, those identified by works of Law. At least Paul asserts this deduction on their behalf.

---

[107] Cf. 3:11, where association is made explicit; also Rom 1:17.

[108] Ciampa, *Presence and Function,* 210–12, notes the presence of Hab 2:4 in vv. 16–21.

[109] Jim Hester has helpfully observed that "within the context of the argument of Galatians 'works of law' can be described as an example of the figure 'antonomasia,' i.e., a descriptive phrase used for a proper name. That raises the question, what proper name? Circumcision" ("Sanders and the New Perspective"). It should be noted that, in general, the phrase "works of law" is not confined to signifying circumcision, which itself is a figure signifying proselyte conversion in this rhetorical context (circumcision representing the completion of this rite of passage). "Circumcision," like "works of law," marks out those who are the people of the Mosaic covenant, Israelites, from those who are not. In Paul's argument with Peter here, "works of law" indicates identification, not effort, since the issue is whether Peter's *identity* as a Jewish person is threatened by the policy of social interaction with Gentile Christ-believers that follows from the meaning ascribed to the death of Christ for Jew and Gentile alike.

If all of the Jewish people (including Christ-believers such as Paul, Peter, and the rest) are "living" Torah-observant lives according to prevailing Antiochene norms, and the Gentiles present in this Christ-believing subgroup are likewise "living" according to the local norms that apply for "righteous" Gentiles, then the differences at issue revolve around the claim that God in Christ is now "righteousing" Jew and Gentile "in the same way." The salient difference is the claim of this subgroup to *live* "in Christ" as equals before God and one another, as "one," whether Jew or Gentile. Claiming that the end of the ages has dawned, this coalition seeks to exemplify this "truth" by living together without discrimination according to certain prevailing conventions of the present age (cf. 1:3–4; 3:27–29; 6:14–16).

Conclusion

At Antioch the ones advocating circumcision were not objecting to what was being eaten or to the fact that these Jewish Christ-believers were eating with Gentiles per se. The food conformed to prevailing Jewish dietary practices to which they subscribed. But they did object to the assertion that the Gentile "guests" with whom these Jews were eating were not merely guests, yet at the same time not proselyte candidates, but instead social equals, righteoused ones of God on the same terms as the Jewish participants—as proselytes would be. They have learned that this behavior is considered by the participants of this group to be justified (legitimated) by way of faith of/in Jesus Christ, by whom God has righteoused Gentiles in the same way as Jewish people. While such a situation may be expected at the end of the ages, when the nations worship together with Israel the one Creator God of all humankind, to claim such to be the case now, in the present age, was unsettling, threatening the present understanding not only of identity but of appropriate behavior.

This claim was symbolized by the way that these mixed meals were conducted. This might have been witnessed by altering the way the seating was arranged, the distribution of food and drink, or some other social convention that inscribed discrimination in a way that departed from the prevailing conventions for the accommodation of Gentiles at meals. Whatever the particulars, which are not mentioned in the text, the behavior that symbolized this claim was deemed threatening to the communal interests of the ones for circumcision, whoever they were, most likely on behalf of the larger Antiochene Jewish communities. Since these Jewish communities were minority groups in Syria, after all, the probability is high that these interests include the concern not to allow standard conventions to be altered so far as to risk upsetting those of the dominant Syrian communities who might not take well to the idea that so many neighbors and kin are taking refuge from their citizen responsibilities under the umbrella of Jewish communal privileges—to, for example, abstain from the imperial cult—without having actually become full members of the Jewish communities according to the accepted norms for such transformation.[110]

---

[110] See Nanos, *Irony*, 257–71.

In response, the advocates for proselyte conversion simply wanted Peter and the other Jewish Christ-believers to bring this situation back into conformity with social conventions in place for the inclusion of Gentiles. This could be done in either of two ways. If Peter and the rest wished to continue to treat these Gentiles as social equals, they could instruct them to become proselyte candidates—hence Paul's reference to advocates of circumcision. Or presumably they could alter the way the meals were conducted so that it was plain that these Gentiles were not members of the Jewish community on a par with proselytes but merely welcome guests. But Peter, not wishing to teach these Gentiles something against the gospel of Christ, which both of these options entail, sought instead to avoid the problem. He withdrew from these mixed meals and thereby separated himself, momentarily anyway, from the need to either abandon what he believed in or suffer the consequences threatened for continued noncompliance with the prevailing norms. And the other Christ-believing Jews followed his lead.

Peter may have considered his choice of action noble, perhaps what was necessary to preserve the integrity of this Jewish subgroup, or to enable it to continue to function unimpeded within the larger Jewish or even Syrian communities, or even to protect these Gentiles. But according to Paul, he had not calculated the effect that this obsequious behavior would have on these Gentiles or on the principles on which this coalition was founded. For these Gentiles were now shamed for failing to properly assess who they are—indeed, for having believed what they had been taught by these Jewish Christ-believers about the meaning of the gospel of Christ. They find themselves left out of the all-Jewish meal, victims of discrimination who are not entitled to follow Peter's lead. They are exposed, marginalized for not conforming to the prevailing Jewish communal norms, for having believed that in Christ they have become already full members of the Jewish community, children of Abraham on equal standing with proselytes. Logically, they are thus "compelled to Judaize" to reduce this dissonance, which can be accomplished to the satisfaction, it seems, of those who advocate the prevailing norms if they will but complete the rite of proselyte conversion, thereby diffusing the threat embodied in these meals.

Thus Paul objects to the withdrawal of Peter and the rest from eating with these Gentiles on the terms dictated by the truth of the gospel of Christ. He recognizes the logical inference that has apparently escaped the thinking of Peter and the rest because they are instead reacting in fear or that, if deduced by them to some degree, has been suppressed to avoid the consequences considered by them to be more immediate. Such action Paul condemns as self-serving. And he does so publicly so that the truth at stake will not be undermined. Paul calls Peter to stand up and walk straight toward the principles of the gospel of Christ in which he has believed and for which he is a most important witness. Such obsequious behavior cannot be tolerated; the implications are far too grave. For Paul recognizes clearly that "the truth" of the gospel of Christ is symbolized in the way that these mixed meals are conducted within these Jewish subgroups. If they are to claim that the end of the ages has dawned in the present age, then they must live together as one, as social equals, Jew and Gentile living righteoused together by God in Christ.

In this reading, the incident at Antioch offers a window into the intra- and inter-Jewish as well as pagan communal tensions that were provoked by the claims of these Christ-believing subgroups when still wholly identified as members of the larger local Jewish communities. Josephus writes that there were many Syrian Gentiles mixing in Jewish social space and that this could create difficult situations, especially in times of political stress, when ambiguous politico-religious loyalties among locals could pose grave problems for those charged with protecting Syrian interests considered to be under threat from Judeans.[111] There is not space to consider the many likely constraints upon each of the Jewish people and groups at play, but it should be noted that those who find fault with the practices of these Christ-believers probably had a very different perspective on what was in anyone's and everyone's best interests. They have convictions of faith too. The incident symbolizes a conflict between Jewish groups that have different opinions about the relevance and meaning of the death of a Judean martyr of the Roman regime upon the identity of Gentiles who believe in him, and thus about how Jews who believe in him should mix in the present age, and how their choices might be considered to impose upon the interests of other Jewish people and groups who do not share this belief.

Finally, this reading of the Antioch incident offers the interpreter of the Galatian letter a different way to conceptualize what analogies would have been most likely drawn by the addressees in Galatia for their own situation. As already noted, however, it is best for the interpreter to first hypothesize the Galatian situation and then see if a reading of this narrative confirms its probability. As I have explained elsewhere, if the Galatian situation involved pressure on Gentiles claiming standing as full members apart from proselyte conversion to comply with prevailing conventions for inclusion as proselytes—regardless of whatever claims they may wish to make about some Judean martyr of the Roman regime—then the analogy these Gentiles drew would likely have been very different from what interpreters of Galatians have proposed it to be.[112]

[111] Cf. Josephus, *J.W.* 2.461–463; 7.41–62, esp. 43, 45; *Ant.* 12.119–124; *Ag. Ap.* 2.39; and see the discussions of Kraeling, "Antioch"; Downey, *Antioch;* Meeks, "Jews and Christians"; Wilken, "Jews of Antioch"; Zetterholm, *Antioch;* Pucci Ben Zeev, *Jewish Rights.*

[112] I want to thank those who commented on earlier drafts of this essay, especially Dieter Mitternacht, Loren Rosson, and Scot McKnight; naturally, any errors remain my own.

PART III

The Galatian Situation(s)

16

THE OPPOSITION TO PAUL

A. E. Harvey

The prodigious success of Paul's missionary work is sufficient proof that, for all he says about his uncertain speech and stammering tongue, he was a remarkably powerful and successful man; and perhaps it was an inevitable consequence of such a record that he should so often have provoked fierce opposition. Throughout his Christian life, Paul was a controversial figure. Indeed one could almost say that the only Paul with whom we are certainly acquainted is Paul the controversialist. There are, of course, other things besides controversy in his letters. There are sublime passages of devotion and exhortation (for instance in Colossians and Ephesians)—but these, it is often suspected, may owe more to the devotional and paraenetic tradition of the early church than to Paul himself. There are terse and powerful summaries of the faith—but these may reflect an already established liturgical formula. There are exalted passages like the Christ hymn in Philippians 2 or the praise of love in 1 Corinthians 13—but even these, by reason of their very symmetry and serenity, raise suspicions that they may not be the original work of the tumultuous Paul himself. It is only when we find him in earnest argument with his opponents, defending his own convictions against those more liberal or more conservative than himself, or boldly legislating in the face of a crisis, that we feel we can be sure of recognizing the authentic voice of Paul.

It is this factor, more than any other, which makes Paul's letters so hard for us to understand. We are continually having to reconstruct the other side of the debate. An argument is in progress; but we do not know what the opposition has been saying. An attack has been made; but we do not know exactly at what it was directed. We have to read between the lines in order to recover Paul's real motive for saying what he does say; and the danger is to read too little or too much. Take any strong and emphatic affirmation in a letter of Paul: why, we may ask, does Paul say precisely this, and with so much emphasis? Is it a proposition particularly dear to his heart, or is there some antagonist in the background who has been maintaining the opposite and whom Paul is anxious to refute? When he begins a letter, "Paul, an apostle of Jesus Christ," is this, as one might naively suppose, simply a natural way for him to begin, or should we, as some interpreters insist, be ready to overhear the malicious tones of some opponent who has been saying, "Paul is not an apostle"?

In many cases, there is probably no sure way of deciding between these alternatives. Nevertheless there are certain contexts in which it is plainly illegitimate to read too many counter-arguments and insinuations into the text. The point can be illustrated from 1 Corinthians. "How do some of you say that there is no resurrection from the dead?"[1] Here is a straight theological issue which Paul immediately tackles in theological terms, and we are entirely justified in trying to reconstruct the arguments of the opposition from the counter-arguments used by Paul. But consider another type of argument. The Corinthian Christians have become litigious, and are taking each other to law in the official courts. This was a lapse from the standards both of Jewish communities in the dispersion[2] and of some unofficial Greek societies:[3] in both, it was normal for disputes to be settled within the community, without recourse to the law. So Paul, when dealing with this lapse, first draws attention to the general impropriety of what the Corinthians are doing. But then he suddenly takes the argument on to a deeper level. Their behavior is not merely improper: it offends against basic Christian principles. "Why do you not rather suffer injustice?" he asks; and with that, what began as a simple moral issue becomes a matter of theological significance. From a Christian point of view, the Corinthians simply had not realized the seriousness of what they were doing, and Paul now brings home to them the full implications of their conduct. It is the same with the eucharist at Corinth. Behavior on these occasions was becoming such as to offend elementary decency and justice. The whole ethos of a Jewish solemn meal, or indeed of a reputable Greek reunion, was being flouted. On these grounds alone, the Corinthians' conduct was reprehensible. But Paul does not leave the matter there. Once again, he raises it to a higher, theological, level. The eucharist, as our Lord instituted it, is entirely incompatible with anything but the most serious spiritual preparation. The Corinthians have not paused to consider the implications of what they are doing; and Paul's theological treatment of the question is provoked, not by any arguments of the Corinthians, but by the fact that they clearly have not given it any serious thought at all.

In both these cases there is a clear pattern of argument. The Christians to whom Paul is writing have been behaving in a certain way that, to them, doubtless seemed harmless; but Paul sees the implications, and hastens to alert them to the seriousness of what they are doing.

In both these cases, and in others like them in Paul's correspondence, it would be pointless to try to reconstruct arguments used by the other side. Paul's quarrel with them is precisely that they have no arguments—they have been acting unreflectively, without considering the implications, from a Christian point of view, of their con-

---

[1] 1 Cor 15:2.
[2] Str-B 3.362f.
[3] Poland, *Griechische Vereinswesen,* 501: the Ἰόβακχοι.

duct. Paul's arguments are not to be understood as answering the theological objections of his opponents, but as awakening his correspondents from their theological thoughtlessness. This type of argument, therefore, needs to be distinguished from the other type, which starts from a clear difference of opinion on a theological issue, and to understand which it is necessary to look for the arguments of the other side.

In the light of this distinction, let us now consider what must have been some of the strongest opposition that Paul ever had to face—the opposition of those members of his churches whom it has become customary to call "Judaizers." At one time it was held that this form of opposition was a constant factor in all his churches. As soon as Paul's back was turned (so it was believed) a delegation would arrive from Jerusalem denouncing him as libertine in morals and renegade in convictions, and endeavoring to bring the primarily non-Jewish churches which he had founded in Greek-speaking cities to accept a more Jewish version of Christianity. This conflict was supposed to occur regularly within a very few months of Paul's founding visit, and to provide the clue to understanding his letters. Such a simple and unified view of the nature of the opposition to Paul is no longer widely held. Nevertheless, it remains true that one of the most serious types of opposition which Paul encountered was of Jewish origin, and was concerned with the relations between Jewish and Gentile Christians. No other opponents are addressed in quite such fierce language. "Dogs" he calls them in Phil 3:2; "Let them make eunuchs of themselves," he exclaims in Gal 5:12. There can be no doubt that these "Judaizers" constituted a serious source of trouble in Galatia, at Philippi, and perhaps elsewhere. But the question needs to be asked, What type of opposition did this "Judaizing" belong to? Was it a theological position, a Jewish gospel, which Paul had to combat point by point? Or was it a more practical matter, a drift towards Jewish customs and observances? Are we to attempt to reconstruct a series of arguments used by Paul's opponents, or is it once again a case of Paul alerting his converts to the theological implications of their unreflective conduct?

Let us consider first the word "Judaize" itself. The word ἰουδαΐζειν occurs once in the New Testament (Gal 2:14), and its meaning in that passage is suggested by the corresponding phrase ἰουδαϊκῶς ζῆν, to live in a Jewish manner. This meaning, of acting in a Jewish way rather than of entertaining Jewish beliefs, is indeed exactly what we should expect of a word of this formation. Ἑλληνίζειν means "to speak Greek," δωριάζειν means to behave with the indecorum of a Dorian woman, μηδίζειν means to take the (from the Greek point of view) wrong side in a notable war. These words have nothing to do with forming beliefs or opinions; they are words of conduct and behavior. And so when Josephus (our only other witness from the first century) uses the word ἰουδαΐζειν, it is no surprise to find that he uses it in exactly the same way. Ἰουδαΐζειν μέχρι περιτομῆς (J.W. 2.454) means to adopt Jewish observances up to the point of circumcision. And similarly, ἰουδαϊσμός in Maccabees and in Gal 1:13, 14 means "the Jewish way of life."

On the face of it, then, ἰουδαΐζειν in Gal 2:14 should mean, not "hold Jewish beliefs," but "adopt Jewish observances"; and in fact the context supports this interpretation. Paul has been recounting his disagreement with Peter over a question of

observance at Antioch. The trouble had evidently arisen out of the inevitable problems of social—and perhaps eucharistic—fellowship between Jews and Christians. It
is sometimes said that this episode could not have taken place if the agreement recorded in Acts 15 had already been reached in Jerusalem regulating the conduct of
Jews and Gentiles in the church. But this does not necessarily follow. The council of
Jerusalem, if it is historical at all, was convened in order to settle the fundamental
question, whether or not Gentile Christianity was a legitimate development. Were
uncircumcised Gentiles to be regarded as full members of the church, and if so, what
minimum moral and ritual requirements (in the place of the whole law, which would
have been the consequence of circumcision) should be imposed on them? But even if
Acts is correct in reporting that a generally agreed decision was reached on this question, we are not to imagine that that was the end of the matter. It was one thing to settle the principle in Jerusalem, where the great majority of Christians were Jews, and
where an uncircumcised Christian must have been something of a rarity. But how
was it going to work out in practice in a city like Antioch, where the church was already a mixed community of Jews and Gentiles? In particular, how was a common eucharist to be envisaged, in view of the strong feelings which the Jewish members had
inherited against sitting down at table with non-Jews? The solution tried at Antioch,
and cordially endorsed by Paul, was what he called "the liberty which we have in
Christ Jesus":[4] all were to sit down together regardless; and when Peter arrived, he fell
in with this, and "ate with the Gentiles."[5] But, in theory at least, another solution was
possible, and was apparently considered seriously by a party at Jerusalem. If all the
Gentiles could be persuaded to be circumcised, the practical problem would simply
disappear: the Jewish Christians could then sit down at table with them without any
scruples. The arrival of some men from Jerusalem put the matter to the test: the Jewish Christians began "separating themselves" and eating by themselves; and when
Peter also adopted the same attitude, the situation became serious. So long as he and
the others persisted in their attitude, only one way remained of re-establishing full
fellowship and a united eucharist. If the Jewish Christians would not eat with the
Gentile Christians, the Gentile Christians would have to be persuaded to receive circumcision so that they could eat with the Jews. This is what Paul means by "compelling the Gentiles to Judaize." And this is precisely the meaning which we would expect
the word ἰουδαΐζειν to bear: not "professing Jewish beliefs" but "adopting Jewish
observances." So far as I can discover, the word bore no other meaning until at least
the time of Hippolytus.

By the time the letter to the Galatians was written this episode belonged to the
past. Circumcision was still an issue in the Galatian churches, but the crisis which
had just brought this issue into the open was no longer the practical question of table-
fellowship between Jewish and Gentile Christians, but was something much more serious. It is at this point that we meet the traditional view about the Judaizing opposition
to Paul in its most persuasive form. It is commonly believed that there was by this time

---

[4] Gal 2:4.
[5] Gal 2:12.

a well organized and theologically articulate Judaizing party in Galatia who were not merely recommending certain Jewish observances, but also advocating "another gospel"—that is to say, a Jewish version of Christianity which differed, in important points of doctrine, from that originally preached by Paul. If this view is correct, then it is clear that we shall have to enlarge our definition of Judaizing to include, not merely the adoption of certain observances, but the profession of certain beliefs; and since this kind of dogmatic opposition to Paul would be something very different from what, up till now, we have understood by the word Judaizing, it is necessary to see whether this view represents a correct reading of the letter to the Galatians.

Since, in that letter, so much is in dispute, let us begin by setting out certain premises. In the first place, there can be no question that the Galatian Christians were under pressure to receive circumcision—this is the crisis which the letter is about. This means that most, if not all, of them were Gentiles. At the same time, Paul addresses to these same Gentile Christians arguments which would be readily understandable by a well educated Jew, but which could only have been followed by Gentiles who were already well grounded in the Old Testament and in Jewish methods of scriptural exegesis. But what sort of Gentiles were these, who could boast of such accomplishments? There can be only one answer: they must have been already long associated with the synagogue, and have belonged to that group of (as it were) associate members whom the Jews called "God-fearers." It was to these people, if we are to believe Acts, that Paul regularly turned after his rejection by the Jewish community. Such people were drawn to the synagogues in order to hear more about the celebrated monotheism of the Jews; and in return, certain moral standards and certain observances were probably required of them. But they do not normally seem to have been under any obligation to take the further (and to the Greek mind thoroughly uncongenial) step of full incorporation into the Jewish community by circumcision. Why those God-fearers who had become Christians in Galatia were now under pressure to do precisely this is one of the questions to which we shall have to find an answer.

In the second place, something may be said about the relations between these converted God-fearers and the synagogue at the time the letter was written. It may be assumed that when they first became Christians they had made a clean break from the Jewish community. But now, to Paul's despair, they were beginning, once again, to observe "days and months and seasons and years."[6] It is not certain exactly what is meant by this phrase; but the language is so similar to that which Justin uses[7] to refer to Jewish observances that it is difficult to believe that anything else is intended here. In other words, the Galatian Christians had already renewed their contact with the synagogue to the extent of observing the Jewish festivals and holy days, and were now contemplating the further step of accepting circumcision.

---

[6] Gal 4:10.

[7] Justin, *Dial.* 8: τὸ σάββατον καὶ τὰς ἑορτὰς καὶ τὰς νεομηνίας τοῦ θεοῦ. Cf. *Dial.* 46: τὰ ἔμμηνα φυλάσσειν. Philo, *Spec.* 2.56, gives a possible explanation of καιρός: ἔνιοι δὲ αὐτὴν (sc. ἑβδομὴν) καιρὸν προσηγόρευσαν.

In the third place, it may be asked, who was it that was putting this pressure on the Galatian churches? One would have thought, the Jews of the synagogue; but Paul explicitly refers to them as "those who get themselves circumcised," οἱ περιτεμνόμενοι,[8] and none of the evasive tactics adopted by commentators can really mitigate the force of this present participle.[9] Those who are troubling (ταράσσοντες)[10] the church are not Jews by birth, but Gentiles who have only recently become Jewish proselytes, or who are still contemplating doing so. Why it should be they, and not the Jews of the synagogue, who are exerting this pressure on their fellow Christians, is another of the difficult questions posed by this epistle.

We are now in a position to ask, what was the nature of this pressure? What kind of opposition was Paul really confronted with here? Was it "Judaizing" in the strict sense—a question of whether or not it was expedient to adopt certain Jewish observances? Or was it something more theological, a doctrinal position that may be called a Jewish version of Christianity? To this question the generally accepted answer is, not observances, but theology; and the principal basis for this view is to be found in Galatians 3. Since so much turns on the interpretation of this chapter, it is necessary to spend a little time on its elucidation.

The standard view of what is going on in Galatians 3 is clearly expressed by Burton in his commentary:[11] Paul is "refuting the contention of his opponents that only through conformity to law (i.e., by circumcision) could men become sons of Abraham." The argument of Paul's opponents is held to be as follows: it can be proved from Genesis 12 and 17 that the blessing promised to Abraham is only available to those who are circumcised; therefore it is not enough merely to be Christians; if you want to receive the blessing, you must be circumcised as well. Galatians 3, it is maintained, contains Paul's answer to this argument; indeed the chapter only becomes comprehensible when we realize what it is that he is attacking. Paul argues from the same chapters of Genesis, but draws a different conclusion: the real sons of Abraham are those who have faith; you have had faith in Christ, and your faith has been signally attested in that you have received the Holy Spirit; therefore you are already sons of Abraham, you do not need to be circumcised as well.

Now commentators are aware that this interpretation labors under considerable difficulties. There is, for example, the point made by J. H. Ropes,[12] that if Paul was trying to persuade the Galatians that they did not need to be circumcised, he went about it in an extraordinarily cumbrous way. Why bring in Abraham at all? Surely it would have been sufficient, and a considerably more cogent argument to Gentile ears, to have said, as Paul did elsewhere, that all things are yours, for you are Christ's and

---

[8] Gal 6:13.

[9] A parallel often invoked to justify the translation "those who have been circumcised" is *Acts Pet. Paul* 63: οὗτοι οἱ περιτεμνόμενοι πανοῦργοί εἰσιν. But it is doubtful whether this isolated example will bear the weight put upon it; particularly since, in his reply to the accusation, Paul is made to repeat the present tense and use it metaphorically: καὶ περιτεμνόμεθα καὶ περιτέμνομεν.

[10] Gal 1:7; 5:10.

[11] Burton, *Galatians*, 153.

[12] Ropes, "Problem."

Christ is God's. Seen in that perspective, circumcision and descent from Abraham are irrelevant. This point, I believe, can be answered in a way which renders unnecessary Ropes' awkward hypothesis of two different opposition parties in Galatia: even if the Gentile Christians had no interest in Abraham (which is perhaps unlikely, if they were capable of following Paul's argument at all) the same was certainly not true of Paul, who could only understand what God had done in Christ in terms of the original promise given to Abraham. But there are two other difficulties that are sufficiently severe to make commentators uneasy. One is that if Paul is arguing from Genesis against his opponents' contention that circumcision is essential for salvation, then it is hard to see why he does not get the worst of the argument; for an impartial reading of Genesis unequivocally supports the necessity of circumcision.[13] Secondly, if the chief point of contention in this chapter is whether or not circumcision is necessary, it is peculiar, to say the least, that there is no single reference to circumcision in the course of it. These difficulties alone ought to be sufficient to arouse one's suspicions. But there is in fact a further difficulty, this time a fatal one, which is not noticed in any modern commentary I have seen, though it was sufficiently obvious to the fathers.[14] Let me sharpen the point at issue by quoting once again Burton's summary of what Paul is doing in this chapter: Paul is "refuting the contention of his opponents that only through conformity to the law (i.e., by circumcision) could men become sons of Abraham." The fatal objection to this is that his opponents cannot have been contending any such thing. They could perhaps have said that there is an advantage in being circumcised and becoming a proselyte: it conferred a definite status (though a humble one) in the Jewish community, and it guaranteed favorable (though not first-class) treatment on the day of judgment. But one thing it could never do was to make a man who was not physically a Jew into a son of Abraham. Even after circumcision, a proselyte in the synagogue must not presume to say, with the Jews, "our father Abraham"; Abraham was not his father, therefore he must say, "your father Abraham."[15] And this conclusion does not depend merely on later Rabbinic sources; it is integral to the Jew's understanding of himself. What distinguished him from Gentiles, proselytes, indeed the rest of humanity, was his physical descent from Abraham. It was inconceivable that a Gentile, merely by being circumcised, could share in this sonship.[16]

Paul's opponents, therefore, cannot have been arguing in this way; the alleged theological position of the Judaizers turns out to be a fiction. But, if it was not theological, what was the motive that inspired those who were receiving circumcision themselves and recommending the same course to others? Paul gives us the answer to this question himself. In 6:12 he says quite clearly that the pressure to be circumcised

---

[13] Cf. Burton, *Galatians,* 157: "These chapters furnish no natural basis for a direct argument [on Paul's side] . . . but they furnish the premises for a strong argument for the position which Paul is combating."

[14] Cf. Theodore of Mopsuestia, ad loc.: *et quoniam Iudaei naturae adfinitatem proponentes plus sibi aliquid vindicari videbantur, quod nullo modo illis qui ex gentibus errant adesse poterat, ait . . .*

[15] *Bik.* 1:4. Cf. Str-B 3.558.

[16] In Philo, proselytes are always named as a class distinct from Jews, so much so that Philo has to plead for sympathetic treatment of them. Cf. *Spec.* 1.51f.

arises "only so that they may not be persecuted for the cross of Christ." And again, in 5:11, Paul asks rhetorically, "Why, if I preach circumcision, am I still being persecuted?" Evidently to be circumcised is a way of avoiding persecution. Persecution by whom? There can hardly be any doubt about that: persecution by the synagogue. And why were the Jews persecuting the Christians? There are sufficient answers to this question in the Book of Acts; and if it is true that these Christian congregations were composed mainly of people who had once been "God-fearers," then such persecution was only what was to be expected. The church had drawn away numerous supporters from the synagogue: reprisals were inevitable unless those who had defected could not merely be brought back to their former allegiance but made to commit themselves permanently by accepting circumcision and persuading their fellow-Christians to do the same.[17] There is however one interesting feature of this policy of the synagogue. It does not seem to have taken the form of stealing back members of the church and forcing them to renounce their Christian beliefs. Paul does not devote himself either to attacking the synagogue or to strengthening waverers; his arguments are all directed against those who are still within the congregation but who are endeavoring to impose a certain course on the whole church. The danger does not seem to consist in individual Christians deserting to the synagogue, but in the church as a whole taking the line of least resistance and complying with the requirements of the synagogue so far as observances are concerned, while continuing to profess their Christian beliefs. The object of the synagogue is not to wean the Christians from their new faith but to make them conform to an outward pattern of Jewish observances; and Paul's real opponents are those Christians in Galatia who are ready to yield to this pressure and are persuading others to do the same.

If this interpretation is accepted there is no longer any reason to suppose that the Judaizing opposition in Galatia represented a theological position. The issue, once again, was a matter, not of doctrine, but of observances. This conclusion may seem surprising: are we really to believe that, at this stage at least, the synagogue made no objection to the beliefs professed by Christians, and was entirely concerned with the extent to which Christians adopted Jewish observances? And yet this is in fact entirely consonant with what we know about Judaism. It is doubtless an over-simplification to say that Judaism was concerned with orthopraxy rather than orthodoxy, yet it is evident that a very wide range of beliefs (on even such important matters as whether Bar Kochba was the Messiah), and a wide latitude in the interpretation of the Scriptures, was accepted as permissible. Josephus introduces his account[18] of the three "philosophies" within Judaism without any suggestion that some were "better" Jews than others; and Philo, whose intellectual approach to religion belongs to a different world altogether from that of Jerusalem, nevertheless knows himself to be a faithful Jew, as opposed to those who allowed their freedom of exegesis to affect their attitude

---

[17] Cf. Gal 6:12–13: the Judaizers' object was εὐπροσωπῆσαι ἐν σαρκί, i.e., to make a good showing so far as outward rites were concerned, and to be able to boast of the number of Christians who had followed them to the point of circumcision (ἵνα ἐν τῇ ὑμετέρᾳ σαρκὶ καυχήσωνται).

[18] Josephus, *J.W.* 2.119ff.

to traditional observances.[19] Within certain limits, a Jew was free to understand the Old Testament as he wished. What he was not free to do was to exempt himself from Jewish observances—in particular, those relating to the keeping of sabbaths and festivals, to food, to ritual cleanness, and to the avoidance of idolatry. We have no evidence of Jews who were excluded from the community for unorthodox beliefs; but we do know, at any rate in Palestine, of Jews who lost their civil rights because their profession was held to be incompatible with observing the law. The very thing which distinguished the Jew in the eyes of others was that he consistently behaved like a Jew; and so Epictetus[20] is able to point to the Jews as an object lesson which will put to shame those pseudo-philosophers who have become adept at expounding a certain philosophy but have done nothing about bringing their lives into accordance with it.

There is therefore nothing improbable in the suggestion that, at least in early years, the quarrel between Jews and Christians was not about beliefs but about observances, and that the Judaizing opposition which Paul had to contend with represented not so much a theological position as a drift towards adopting the Jewish way of life. This is certainly the form which the struggle takes in the narratives of Acts, and the same is true right into the second century. In Justin's *Dialogus cum Tryphone,* for instance, Trypho more than once makes it clear that his ultimate complaint against the Christians, and his condition for giving serious consideration to their beliefs, is the question of observances. Indeed, so monotonous is the theme, that Justin is led to say:[21] "Do you then have no other complaint against us, than that we do not live according to the law, or accept physical circumcision, or keep the sabbath the way you do?" This is not to say that the Christians did not seek to meet this pressure with theological arguments, or that they did not quickly work out their own exegetical methods for using the Old Testament as a means of discrediting the Jews. It is simply to say that the Jews were not trying to get the Christians to change their beliefs, but only to adopt Jewish observances, and that this was the principal issue between them up to at least the middle of the second century. Indeed, much the same can be said about Jewish Christianity. It may well be true that a distinctively Jewish-Christian theology did develop in the early church, and that this theology left its traces on all subsequent Christian thinking. But on the occasions when we can document a conflict between Jewish and Gentile Christianity, the issue is always one of observances.

The Judaizing opposition, then, in Galatia was "Judaizing" in the strict sense; it was not theological but practical—it advocated, not another doctrine, but a certain course of action. It follows that it is beside the point to look for arguments on the other side; indeed Paul's own argument conforms perfectly with that other type of argument which starts, not from a theological point made by the opposition, but from a pattern of behavior which Paul finds it necessary to censure. Paul had already communicated with the Galatian churches on the subject of Judaizing, and had shown his disapproval of the direction they were moving in. But this had had no effect; it had merely caused ill

---

[19] Philo, *Migr.* 91–93.
[20] Epictetus, *Diatr.* 2.9.19ff.
[21] Justin, *Dial.* 10.

feeling towards himself and had provoked some members of the congregation to ask what authority Paul had for opposing what seemed to them such a harmless compromise. In our epistle, Paul is now returning to the attack, and endeavoring to show the Galatians the full seriousness of what they are doing. Their real motives for adopting Jewish observances are fear and expediency, and Paul's task is not so much to meet their arguments as to show them up as having no arguments, indeed as having given the matter no serious thought at all. They had not even realized the consequences from the Jewish point of view (that once they were circumcised they would have to keep the whole law), let alone from the Christian point of view: they had not realized that by accepting circumcision they would be re-erecting those barriers between men which Christ had died to remove, and denying that new sense of sonship of Abraham which faith in Christ makes possible (for this I believe to be the true bearing of the argument of chapter 3). If the Galatians thought they were merely adding a trivial matter of observance to their Christian belief, they must be shown that their actions amounted to a denial of the new unity of mankind created in Christ.

The real nature of the opposition in Galatia, then, was not theological at all, but was simply a tendency to adopt Jewish observances under threat of persecution or discrimination. Other letters from Paul show the same kind of pressure being exerted from the Jewish side, though sometimes in more subtle forms. The words in Philippians, "Look out for the dogs," are a clear indication of Jewish pressure, though Paul's answer to it ("We are the circumcision") suggests that here the pressure was accompanied less by a threat of persecution than by some insidious propaganda.[22] The Jews would say, You Christians have no temple, no priesthood, no sacrifices, no circumcision; to which the Christians would reply, We have these things, but our temple is not made with hands, we are our own priesthood, our sacrifices are spiritual, we are the true circumcision (or, as it is in Colossians, we have a περιτομὴ ἀχειροποίητος).[23] Again, the Jews would argue that unless these Gentile Christians were made to observe the law of Moses, their morals would be no better than those of the heathen idolaters by whom the Jews felt themselves to be so oppressively surrounded. This was, after all, the usual argument used in favor of trying to impose the law, or some part of it, on mankind at large; and Paul surely had this argument in mind when, in Galatians, he showed that "walking by the Spirit" entails a high standard of ethical conduct, or when, in Romans, he drew out the ethical implications of Christian baptism. But the fact that this propaganda was used, and had to be refuted by Paul, does not affect my basic contention that the issue at stake was, not doctrines and beliefs, but observances; and indeed this remained the issue between Jews and Christians at least up to the time of Justin, and the temptation for some Christians to try to get the best of both worlds by combining their Christian profession with Jewish observances lasted a great deal longer.[24] It is possible, indeed, that it is those who

---

[22] See the excellent discussion of this by Moule, "Sanctuary."

[23] Col 2:11.

[24] Cf. Origen, Hom. Lev. 10:2; Hom. Exod. 12; Eusebius, Sermones 7: καὶ οἶδά τινας ὅτι Χριστιανοὶ ὄντες ἰουδαΐζουσιν λέγοντες: σήμερον σάββατόν ἐστιν καὶ οὐχ ἔξον μοι εὐεργεσίαν ποιῆσαι.

yielded to this temptation who are referred to in that mysterious phrase in the Book of Revelation, "those who say they are Jews but are not."[25]

But alongside this sustained pressure exerted upon Christian congregations to adopt Jewish observances, there is another quite different kind of contact with things Jewish to be found in the New Testament, initiated this time from the Christian side. In the Pastorals, the Christians are warned against "Jewish fables," "myths and genealogies,"[26] and speculations about the resurrection;[27] and some of the worst offenders are evidently Christian Jews.[28] In Colossians,[29] again, "philosophy, empty deceit and the tradition of men" are referred to in the same context as some characteristic Jewish practices and the thoroughly unorthodox Jewish cult of angels. This is clearly something different from the practical ἰουδαϊσμός which we have been discussing up to now. Before, it was a question whether or not to adopt certain Jewish observances; now, it is a question of how far Christians should be free to go in speculating with ideas borrowed not only from the Hellenistic, but also from the Jewish world. Before, the question was practical; now it is speculative and theoretical. All the evidence so far suggests that is only the former of these two which it is correct to call ἰουδαϊσμός; the latter is a danger of quite a different kind, to which it is the intellectuals of the church, rather than the rank and file, who are exposed.

And yet it is not so simple. In a most puzzling way, these two categories (ἰουδαϊσμός and φιλοσοφία, observances and speculation) seem sometimes to overlap. In Colossians, philosophical speculation and fanciful exegesis (παράδοσις τῶν ἀνθρώπων) go along with a limited degree of practical ἰουδαϊσμός—and indeed with Jewish heteropraxy in the form of angel-worship; and even in Galatians there are hints of the same combination: whatever may be the precise meaning of the word στοιχεῖα, it must belong to the speculative, philosophical type of religion, and the word occurs (as in Colossians) in the immediate context of specifically Jewish observances. We can only speculate on what brings these two things together. It may be just a special case of the tendency for esoteric knowledge to involve ascetic practices; or it may be (and this is perhaps a more probable explanation) that the easiest way to acquire the scriptural materials for speculative and syncretistic thought was to attend the synagogue, and this would oblige the inquirer to observe sabbaths and festivals and certain rules of purity. But whatever the reason, it is clear that a limited amount of ἰουδαϊσμός tended to go with a search for esoteric wisdom drawn from Jewish traditions.

It seems then that the Judaizing opposition to Paul, after all, took more than one form. There was, first, the form exemplified by the crisis in the Galatian churches. Here, Judaizing meant adopting Jewish observances in order to conform to the requirements of the synagogue, and the pressure to do so came ultimately from non-Christian Jews,

---

[25] Rev 2:9; 3:9. Cf. *Acts Pet. Paul* 64: Simon was circumcised—οὐδὲ γὰρ ἄλλως ἠδύνατο ἀπατῆσαι ψυχὰς εἰ μὴ Ἰουδαῖον εἶναι ἑαυτὸν ὑπεκρίνετο.

[26] 1 Tim 1:4.

[27] 2 Tim 2:18.

[28] Titus 1:10.

[29] Col 2:8.

though it might be mediated by Jews or Gentiles within the church; this pressure, sometimes supported by powerful propaganda, sometimes by the threat of persecution, was strong enough even to lead to the drastic step of circumcision. Secondly, there was a form of Judaizing that arose spontaneously among Christians themselves, who wished, in order to enrich their religious speculations, to become acquainted with the Jewish scriptures and Jewish traditions. In this case, Judaizing was voluntary: the individual adopted Jewish practices in order to gain an entrée into the synagogue; and it is unlikely that this often led to circumcision. Any pressure that there was to Judaize will then have come, not from the synagogue, but from non-Jewish Christians. As Ignatius of Antioch put it (who clearly had quite a lot of this sort of thing to contend with), one heard about Judaizing from the uncircumcised—ἰουδαϊσμὸν ἀκούειν παρὰ ἀκροβύστου.[30] It appears, then, that when we talk of Judaizing opposition to Paul, we have to distinguish between these two different kinds of movement, one practical, and one speculative; and we have further to distinguish between the two types of argument which Paul employs to deal with them—in the first case, an argument drawing out the theological implications of a certain course of conduct, in the second an argument exposing the futility of the syncretistic speculations of his opponents.

Throughout this discussion, no mention has been made of the epistle to the Romans. Much of the argument in that letter is very similar to that in Galatians, and it is clear that relations between Jews and Gentiles are never far from the author's mind. But which type of argument does this letter exhibit? Is it again an attempt by Paul to alert the Romans to the consequences of certain kinds of conduct, or is there here, for the first and only time in the New Testament, an articulate and reasoned Jewish position, an intellectual ἰουδαϊσμός, which Paul has to counter with arguments of his own?

It has to be admitted that the task of reconstructing an alleged Jewish-Christian theological position from Paul's counter-arguments in Romans would be a peculiarly difficult one. For one thing, Paul is not likely to have been sufficiently familiar with what the Christians in Rome were saying to be able to give a point by point reply to it; and even if the letter was originally drafted for sending to some other church which Paul knew better, there is a generality and an absence of the kind of direct, personal attack which we find, say, in Galatians, which make it seem unlikely that he had any distinct opposition in mind. For another thing, the extent to which Paul makes use of the conventions and mannerisms of the diatribe in Romans makes it difficult to be sure that any opposition we may think we have detected may not be imaginary, invoked for rhetorical effect. For these reasons—and without arguing the point in detail—I would be inclined to look in a rather different direction for an explanation of the arguments used by Paul in Romans. I would suggest that his starting point is once again, not theoretical, but practical. The difficulties in Rome arose out of tension between Jewish and Gentile Christians, and this tension was a sufficiently common fea-

---

[30] Ign. *Phld.* 6.1.

ture of any church with a mixed congregation for Paul to have to address himself to it in general terms sooner or later.

From Justin Martyr we can get a vivid impression of how the tension had built up in Rome by the middle of the second century. There were some Jewish Christians, he tells us[31] (though this was by no means true of all of them) who endeavored to impose the full Mosaic law on their fellow-Christians; when they failed, they went off by themselves and refused to share anything in common with the rest of the church. This indicates a considerable hardening of their attitude, beyond anything which we read of in the New Testament: and that the non-Jewish Christians, for their part, had become equally intransigent is shown by the attitude of Justin himself, who very much doubts whether those same Jewish Christians can have any chance of being saved. Relations between the two parties had evidently deteriorated, and it was not long before Jewish Christianity ceased to exist as a distinctive part of the church. Now we clearly cannot read this situation back into the middle of the first century; yet the beginnings of tension were surely there. The time had passed when there was any danger of Jewish domination in a Gentile church; indeed the tendency was probably quite the reverse, since the Jewish Christians must have been soon outnumbered. The problem was for these two groups to learn to live together. And if we ask why Paul devotes so much of this epistle to warning Jewish Christians against a sense of superiority based on their law, to warning Gentile Christians against treating too lightly both the scruples and the heritage of their Jewish brethren, to establishing the claims of both parties to a place in the Kingdom, and even perhaps to counseling obedience to authority and a peaceable and law-abiding disposition, the answer may be that we have here another example of one of Paul's characteristic types of argument. Starting from purely practical matters—those deviations from tolerance and Christian brotherhood which tended to appear in any church where there was tension between Jew and Greek—Paul drew out the implications of such conduct, showed it to concern matters of vital Christian principle, and so raised the argument to a level of such theological significance that the epistle became, and has remained, one of the principal documents of the Christian faith.

---

[31] Justin, *Dial.* 47.

17

THE AGITATORS AND THE GALATIAN CONGREGATION

Robert Jewett

In recent years,[1] especially since the appearance of Walther Schmithals' studies,[2] the identification of Paul's opponents in Galatia has become increasingly problematic. The core of the dilemma is that the apparent presence of libertinistic tendencies in the Galatian congregation is difficult to reconcile with the main argument of the letter directed against an orthodox nomism. The F. C. Baur hypothesis, namely that Judaizers officially sponsored by the Jerusalem church were agitating in Galatia, provided no answer to this dilemma. Wilhelm Lütgert broke with the Baur tradition by arguing that there were two separate groups against which Paul struggled in Galatians—a libertinistic group and a Judaizer group claiming support from the Jerusalem pillars.[3] James H. Ropes set forth a similar hypothesis, but attributed the nomistic agitation to a curious group of Gentile Christians within Galatia itself.[4] Neither Lütgert nor Ropes could explain why Paul dealt with the congregation as a more or less homogeneous group. Furthermore, they could not make plausible the strange and sudden enthusiasm of Gentile Christians for the Torah or circumcision. Emanuel Hirsch,[5] in suggesting the agitators were Gentile Christians from Antioch who had been converted into Judaizing missionaries by the Judean Judaizers, offers nothing beyond Ropes or Lütgert to make plausible such a Gentile interest in circumcision. Johannes Munck picked up Hirsch's thesis and attempted to explain the advocacy of circumcision on the basis of a misunderstanding of Paul's message about the role of Jerusalem as well as a misinterpretation of the Septuagint.[6] But since Munck insists

---

[1] Cf. Schlier, *Galater*, 18–24; Staehlin, "Galaterbrief"; Talbert, "Again"; Bronson, "Paul."

[2] Schmithals, "Häretiker." See also the somewhat differing picture of the historical situation in Schmithals, *Paul and James*, especially 103–17.

[3] Lütgert, "Gesetz." Foerster has supported Lütgert's thesis with the reservation, based on Gal 1:18–19, that the Judaizers were also in conflict with James and Peter. See Foerster, "δοκοῦντες"; "Abfassungszeit."

[4] Ropes, *Problem.*

[5] Hirsch, "Zwei Fragen."

[6] Munck, *Paul,* 88–134; cf. the critical review by Davies, *Christian Origins,* 179–98.

that the Judean church played no role in this Judaizing campaign, even agreeing wholeheartedly with Paul in opposing it, it is difficult to imagine where the Gentile Judaizers could have received their extensive information about Paul's relations with Judea as reflected in Gal 1:11ff. or how they could have sustained their campaign.

The recent phase of the discussion was really opened by Frederic R. Crownfield.[7] In attempting to do justice to the impression that the letter does not reflect two separate factions in Galatia, he suggested that there was one group of Jewish Christian syncretists who favored circumcision for symbolic reasons. Since this identification was somewhat lacking in historical precision, it is best to turn to Schmithals' gnostic hypothesis as the most significant representation of this general viewpoint. Schmithals succeeds very well in providing a link with libertinism in Galatia by suggesting that the agitators were Gnostics whose viewpoint and behavior had tendencies in this direction.[8] But in order to account for the struggle against nomism in Galatians, Schmithals must resort to the assumption that Paul was poorly informed about the situation. Such an assumption naturally undercuts any deduction from the letter regarding the historical situation. Another difficulty with Schmithals' hypothesis is that his examples of later gnostic use of circumcision do not succeed in making plausible a gnostic missionary campaign to promote circumcision as necessary for salvation. The Gnostics such as Cerinthus seem to have been interested in circumcision as a symbol of transcendence over the fleshly sphere, but there is no conclusive evidence that they actually held this symbolic act to be essential for salvation.[9] In short, without some connection with nomism, the circumcision campaign is inexplicable.[10] Klaus Wegenast has attempted to deal with this shortcoming in Schmithals' hypothesis by identifying the Galatian agitators with the later Ebionites.[11] This would account for the nomistic demand for circumcision, but since it eliminates any possibility of linking the agitators with

---

[7] Crownfield, "Singular Problem"; Talbert, "Again," 29, accepts Crownfield's identification of the agitators as "syncretists" and suggests that their case was strengthened by the fact that Paul circumcised Timothy (Acts 16:1–4). For a critical appraisal of this questionable passage in Acts, see Haenchen, *Apostelgeschichte*, 425–28.

[8] Schmithals, "Häretiker." In *Paul and James* he suggests in contrast that the intruders at the Apostolic Conference were Jews rather than gnostic Christians. It is difficult to see how these two theories can be reconciled, for it is apparent that Paul thought the intruders in Gal 2:4–5 were related to those entering Galatia.

[9] There is considerable scholarly doubt, for example, about the historicity of Epiphanius' account which places Cerinthus clearly back in the apostolic period and pictures him as a radical nomist. See Bauer, "Cerinth." Some gnostic writings, such as the *Gospel of Thomas* (logion 53), contain explicit polemic against physical circumcision. Cf. Gartner, *Theology*, 59f.

[10] This is the gist of the critique of Schmithals by R. Wilson, "Gnostics." But he concludes with a theory that was considered and discarded in the last century: "in Galatia everything points to the fact that the trouble was the danger of reversion into Judaism." In a somewhat similar vein, A. E. Harvey, in the same volume, suggests that recent Jewish proselytes from the synagogue in Galatia are putting pressure on the Galatian church for stealing synagogue members. This theory cannot account for the Judaizers' appeal to close relationship with the Jerusalem church (Gal 1:11–2:21) or the probable location in North Galatia where no evidence of Jewish synagogues has been found. That the Judaizers therefore did not "represent a theological position" but merely a practical one does not fit with Paul's charge that they are proclaiming "a different gospel." See A. Harvey, "Opposition."

[11] Wegenast, *Verständnis*, 36–40.

libertinism, it destroys Schmithals' one-front hypothesis. Helmut Koester and Dieter Georgi probably come closer to the mark in their insistence that the agitators were Jewish Christian Judaizers with a syncretistic approach to circumcision and the law.[12] At least it is apparent, as I shall develop below, that they presented the law and circumcision in Galatia on a rather syncretistic basis. Yet even this hypothesis leaves unanswered the key question that Schmithals raised. Why would Jewish Christians suddenly lose their traditional disinterest in the Gentile mission and embark on a circumcision campaign in Galatia? This is the question I would like to attempt to answer in this study.[13] The first step is to work out a picture of the agitation in Galatia.

The Agitators and Their Programme

In the opening lines of Galatians we read that some persons had come into Galatia with the aim of stirring up the congregation and perverting the gospel (Gal 1:7). Who were these people and what was their programme? The clearest statement of their aims is provided us in Paul's "postscript" at the end of the letter (6:11–18). First and foremost they promoted circumcision of the Gentile Christians. The phrase used for this, οὗτοι ἀναγκάζουσιν ὑμᾶς περιτέμνεσθαι (6:12), refers to the "necessity" of circumcision. Apparently for the agitators it was a condition *sine qua non* for salvation. An essential link in Paul's argument was that precisely this demand had been waived in the case of Titus by the "pillars" at the time of the Apostolic Conference (2:3). Acts' account of the conflict leading to this conference throws light on the rationale of the demand.[14] The men coming from Judea to Antioch demanded circumcision, saying, "Unless you are circumcised according to the custom of Moses you cannot be saved" (Acts 15:1). Here again circumcision was viewed as indispensable for salvation. The understanding of circumcision in Judaism during this period centered on its significance as a sign of the covenant carried by those who were heirs of the promise given to Abraham.[15] In the light of the fact that Paul devoted a main portion of his argument to the question about the true sons of Abraham, it is likely that the agitators argued for circumcision on grounds that entrance into the elect spiritual community demanded prior admission into Abraham's covenant through circumcision. This fits in well with Holtzmann's suggestion that their mottos were σπέρμα Ἀβραάμ (3:16) and Ἰερουσαλήμ ἥτις ἐστὶν μήτηρ ἡμῶν (4:26).[16] Paul accuses them of wanting to change the gospel of Christ (1:7), which indicates that they were

---

[12] Georgi, *Geschichte*, 35–38; Koester, "Häretiker."

[13] Bronson pursues a similar quest ("Paul"). He suggests that "James and his group were swept into a more active nationalism" by the political situation in the years prior to the outbreak of the Jewish War (128). It is highly unlikely, however, that the Galatian agitators were actually sponsored by James.

[14] Cf. Georgi, *Geschichte*, 15–16.

[15] R. Meyer, "περιτέμνω," 6.76–77.

[16] H. Holtzmann, *Lehrbuch*, 243; A. Harvey (327 n. 15) apparently misunderstands Str-B 3.558 as implying that Gentiles could not enter the "seed of Abraham" through circumcision.

Christian believers. The reference in 6:12 to their desire to avoid persecution for the cross of Christ points conclusively to their Christian origin. The traditional view that they held an orthodox, even Pharisaic view of the law has been thrown into question by Schmithals,[17] who argues on the basis of 6:13 and 5:3 that their approach to the law was gnostic. But these two passages admit equally well to clarification on the basis of a Judaizer hypothesis which takes much better account of the antinomistic argument of the letter than Schmithals' theory does. In 5:3 we probably have an indication that the agitators contented themselves with the limited goal of circumcision, believing that obedience to the entire law would follow in due course. Such adjustment of preliminary requirements in accordance with the person being converted would follow the Jewish precedent established by Hillel, who accepted several persons as disciples on the basis of drastically limited requirements.[18]

Paul's description of the agitators in Gal 6:13 has been variously interpreted. E. Hirsch suggested that νόμον οὐ φυλάσσουσιν indicated that the agitators could not obey every single law because they were not Jews by birth and thus lacked intimate knowledge of the Torah.[19] This interpretation and most others which read 6:13 in terms of incomplete compliance with the Torah[20] are based on the assumption that νόμος for Paul was a collection of commandments whose exact observation was almost impossible for man. But when Paul thinks of "laws" he can say as in 5:3 ὅλον τὸν νόμον. Here he refers to the Torah as a whole, the concretization of God's will, which every man has opposed (Rom 3:9–20). It is not that the agitators failed to live up to the "whole law" but that they annulled grace (Gal 2:21) and rested on their boasting (Gal 6:13–14; cf. Rom 3:27). They denied and perverted the truth of the gospel which the law itself affirmed (Gal 3:6–14; 4:21–31). This provides a more substantial basis than that of Schmithals in interpreting the expression νόμον οὐ φυλάσσουσιν in Gal 6:13. His theory is that the agitators did not obey the law because they were in reality antinomians. But if Paul had wished to indicate they had made "*einen grundsätzlichen Verzicht auf den Nomos*,"[21] he would have used ἀθετέω or καταργέω instead of οὐ φυλάσσουσιν, which is never used in the sense of categorical denial.[22] Furthermore, Schmithals' position demands that one view Paul's entire argument against works-righteousness as superfluous since it would only fit in if the agitators were advocates of the law.[23] A more probable interpretation of 6:13 is that the Galatian agitators in perverting the gospel were in Paul's view rejecting God's will as revealed in the Torah. Paul's use of the law in Gal 3:6–29 and 4:21–31 shows that he believed it affirmed his gospel of faith and grace rather than the path of

---

[17] Schmithals, "Häretiker."

[18] *Šabb.* 31a; see also Daube, "Maxims," 159. Emil Schürer comments: "Der jüdischen Bekehrungseifer hat sich eben mit dem Ereichbaren begnügt" (*Geschichte*, 3.173).

[19] Hirsch, "Zwei Fragen," 193–94.

[20] Schlier, *Galater*, 204; Duncan, *Galatians*, 190.

[21] Schmithals, "Häretiker," 42–43.

[22] BAGD 876.

[23] Schmithals argues that the entire discussion about works-righteousness in 3:6–4:20 contains no direct reference to the Galatian situation and simply documents Paul's mistaken view of the cause of the circumcision problem ("Häretiker," 60 n. 108).

works-righteousness. Thus to oppose the gospel, as the agitators did, was in Paul's view an opposition against the Torah itself. Far from overtly rejecting the law, however, these agitators believed that obedience to it was necessary for salvation and that the Gentiles must submit to circumcision as the first step in this direction.

An additional puzzle about this verse pertains to the participle οἱ περιτεμνόμενοι. Hirsch, Munck and, more recently, Harvey have argued strenuously that the implications of a present passive form should be taken seriously, namely that the Judaizers are presently getting themselves circumcised. This would indicate that they were not Jewish but Gentile in background. That such implications were seen and countered in the early church is indicated by the textual variant περιτετμημένοι, which is generally recognized as a secondary correction.[24] It is easy to see why Paul did not choose this past form of the participle: that would imply that anyone who had been previously circumcised, even as a child, would be standing in opposition to the law. But Paul is not concerned here with the presence of circumcised persons—like himself—in the church; he is concerned instead with those who now demand circumcision for Gentile Christians. Thus the present tense of the participle is demanded by the argumentative situation. Moreover, it is wrong to assume that περιτεμνόμενοι must be passive; it could just as easily be a middle form, and the only way to tell the difference is to examine the context. Since οἱ περιτεμνόμενοι in Gal 6:13a specifies the subject of the verb in 13b, one would expect congruity between 13a and 13b in regard to the circumcision which appears in both. So, if a passive "those who get circumcised" were intended in 13a, it would be somewhat out of keeping with the active "desire to have you circumcised" in 13b. In this verse as in 6:12, the matter under discussion is the effort on the part of the Judaizers to circumcise the Galatians, not to circumcise themselves. Such congruity would be perfectly maintained if the participle were taken to be in the middle voice with a causative significance:[25] "for even those who cause to be circumcised do not themselves keep the law, but they desire to have you circumcised that they may glory in your flesh." A more succinct form of this translation is provided by Lightfoot— "the advocates of circumcision";[26] and Schlier—"die Beschneidungsleute."[27] Finally, it should be noted that this translation is the only one which can retain any strict sense of present tense in the participle.[28] Given the length of time required for circumcision, it is hard to visualize the present tense being used to describe the actions of the leading Judaizers in circumcising themselves, but it is natural to use the present tense to depict their current advocacy of circumcision.

Paul ascribes two subsidiary motives to their preaching of circumcision: they did so "in order that they might not be persecuted for the cross of Christ" (6:12) and

---

[24] Cf. Schlier, *Galater*, on 6:13.

[25] Cf. Goetchius, *Language*,104; Robertson, *Grammar*, 808f.

[26] Lightfoot, *Galatians*, 222.

[27] Schlier, *Galater*, ad loc.; cf. Cf. O. Holtzmann, "Zwei Fragen."

[28] Hirsch is forced to speak of οἱ περιτεμνόμενοι "als Neujuden jungen Datums" ("Zwei Fragen," 193), and A. Harvey also slips into the past tense in describing the "Gentiles who have recently become Jewish proselytes" ("Opposition," 326ff.).

"that they might glory in your flesh" (6:13). These remarks fit in with the pattern found elsewhere in Galatians, combining in a striking fashion with the unusual connection between law and circumcision on the one side and persecution on the other. In 5:11 Paul asks why he is still being persecuted if he preaches circumcision, while in 3:4 he warns that their suffering would be in vain if they took up circumcision.[29] The background for these statements is the intense Jewish opposition to Paul's work which manifested itself in almost every mission center. Just how such agitation reached the North Galatian church cannot be reconstructed except in its broad outlines. But this much is clear: Paul considered that the Galatians had suffered for the anti-circumcision gospel just as he had. Now it would not be unusual if Paul had said the Galatians themselves sought to avoid persecution by means of circumcision.[30] But he does not say this at all. Instead he says that the *agitators* sought to avoid persecution by getting the *Galatians* circumcised![31] Since the agitators were in all probability Jews by birth, they were themselves already circumcised. If they were in favor of circumcision and promoted obedience to the law in this way, how could they have been in danger from the anti-Pauline persecution? Moreover, how could they have thought to ease the persecution against their own group by getting the Galatians circumcised?

In order to deal with these questions one must first determine whether the agitators came into the Galatian church from the outside and, if so, where their headquarters could have been. That they came from outside the congregation seems to be indicated by the fact that a sudden and unexpected shift of mind came over the Galatians (1:6) and that there was a struggle for the congregation's allegiance (4:17).[32] Paul always refers to the agitators (1:8–10; 5:12; 6:12–13) as if they were separate from the Galatians themselves (3:1–5; 4:8–16; 5:7–8). Furthermore, Paul's explanation of his relations with Jerusalem indicates clearly that he is dealing with persons who had access to detailed information which the Galatians had not possessed since they would have heard about such things only from Paul himself or his associates. The fact that the agitators dwelt on Paul's alleged dependency on Jerusalem indicates they themselves had a Jerusalem-oriented viewpoint. This, along with their possession of detailed information about the Judean church, would appear to point to either Judea or Jerusalem itself as a point of origin. This fits in well with Paul's polemic against Jerusalem (4:25–31) and his reference to the Judean churches (1:22). Thus the fragments of evidence all point in the general direction of Judea as the origin of the Galatian

---

[29] Lütgert saw this clearly: "Wenn die Gemeinde die Beschneidung annimmt, so hat sie die Verfolgung vergeblich erlitten. Also ist sie verfolgt worden, weil sie nicht beschnitten war" ("Gesetz," 568). Opposing such a view are Schlier, *Galater*, 83, and Oepke, *Galater*, 68. Both Schlier and Oepke take πάσχειν in its neutral sense of "experience." But Duncan is right in rejecting this interpretation on the grounds that πάσχειν is never used with this meaning elsewhere in the Greek Bible; when it has the positive sense of "experience" it is always combined with other words which make this clear (*Galatians*, 81).

[30] Cf. Ropes, *Galatians*, 44.

[31] It is typical for Schmithals' method that such a revealing statement as this is shrugged off as "zunächst doch wohl nicht mehr als ein bissiger Vorwurf des Paulus" ("Häretiker," 47).

[32] Cf. Oepke, *Galater*, 107.

agitators. Now the quest for the historical background of this agitation can be more precisely formulated. Under what circumstances would a nomistic Christian group in Judea be in danger of anti-Pauline persecution and have an interest in converting the Gentile churches to nomism in order to save itself from such a threat?

The Political Background of the Agitation

The background of the missionary movement which touched Galatia may be found in the troubled political situation in Judea and Galilee during the period from the late forties until the outbreak of the Jewish War in 66 C.E. It was during this period that the Zealot campaign to undermine Roman control through terror tactics was increasingly effective.[33] During the procuratorship of Ventidius Cumanus (48–52 C.E.), the resistance movement felt strong enough to rob an official Roman courier on the main highway from Jerusalem to Caesarea (Josephus, *Ant.* 20.113) and shortly afterwards to arouse the whole countryside into a revenge attack against Samaria which could only be put down by use of most of Cumanus' forces *(Ant.* 20.118). The frequency of such incidents reported by Josephus makes plain that for practical purposes the countryside was in the control of the Zealot underground movement by the late forties. This meant that persons in the villages of Judea or Galilee who maintained close relationships with Gentiles or who did not zealously seek the purity of Israel were in mortal danger. The Zealots patterned themselves after Phinehas, who had averted God's wrath from Israel by lynching an Israelite sinner and his foreign wife (Num 25:6–13). Their programme was to continue the work of Judas Maccabaeus who had "destroyed the ungodly out of the land; thus he turned away wrath from Israel" (1 Macc 3:8).[34] This ideology explained the postponement of the messianic kingdom in terms of the presence of God's wrath over a sinful Israel. God's wrath could be appeased only by cleansing Israel through extermination of all impure persons. This would achieve an absolute separation from the heathen world and any uncircumcised element.[35] Here is the reason for the atoning murders committed by the Zealots against those who retained contact with uncircumcised persons. A final step in their strategy would be to cause Israel to rise as one man against the Romans so that by this single act of absolute obedience the eschatological kingdom might be brought in. Martin Hengel has provided an excellent description of this Zealot strategy and notes that it was directed specifically against such persons as Paul.[36] Concrete examples of such Zealotic murders are provided by Josephus in *J.W.* 4.335–344; 2.254–257, 264–265.[37] A clear indication that this movement considered Paul a

---

[33] Cf. Hengel, *Zeloten*, 351–86; Reicke, *New Testament Era*, 202–23.

[34] Cf. Farmer, *Maccabees*, 65–68; 125–58.

[35] Old Testament support for this policy was found in such passages as Ezek 44:9: "Therefore says the Lord God: no foreigner, uncircumcised in heart and flesh, of all the foreigners who are among the people of Israel, shall enter my sanctuary."

[36] Hengel, *Zeloten*, 231.

[37] Cf. also Joseph, *J.W.* 4.169–170, 259, 263; 5.402; 7.256–260. Hengel provides examples also from other sources in *Zeloten*, 190–95.

highly appropriate victim of its cleansing zeal is found in such incidents as the plot against his life in Jerusalem (Acts 23:12–22; cf. 20:3). Would not Christians who were connected with such a man by common allegiance be equally suspect? There was in fact during this period an anti-Christian persecution in Judea which has never been adequately explained (1 Thess 2:14–16).[38]

My hypothesis therefore is that Jewish Christians in Judea were stimulated by Zealotic pressure into a nomistic campaign among their fellow Christians in the late forties and early fifties. Their goal was to avert the suspicion that they were in communion with lawless Gentiles. It appears that the Judean Christians convinced themselves that circumcision of Gentile Christians would thwart Zealot reprisals. Very probably this belief was illusory and, as the later flight to Pella at the beginning of the Jewish War indicates, they had overcome by that time any illusions as to how Zealot control would affect them. There are other bits of historical detail that correlate with this hypothesis. Bo Reicke suggested that it was on account of Zealot pressure on the Judean Christians that they chose a man popular with that movement as the head of the church during this period—James the brother of Jesus.[39] We also know that it was during this period that the agitators first appeared in Antioch with the demand that the Gentiles be circumcised (Acts 15:1–5).[40] The agents who appeared in Galatia some time later were probably part of the same movement.[41]

The agitators' demand for circumcision in Antioch and Galatia was thus only in part motivated by the belief that it was essential for admission into the chosen people of Israel. Paul sarcastically noted that the agitators' zeal was influenced by the desire to avoid persecution for the cross of Christ. If they could succeed in circumcising the Gentile Christians, this might effectively thwart any Zealot purification campaign against the Judean church! It is in this sense, therefore, that the second subsidiary motivation ascribed to the agitators in Gal 6:13 is to be understood: "that they glory in your flesh." The clue is in the juxtaposition between "their" pride and "your" flesh. The nomistic Christians in Judea would have ample reason to boast if they could induce the Gentile churches to enter the ranks of the circumcised, for such an achievement would release them from a mortal threat leveled against all who dared to

---

[38] Furthermore, Paul's statement in 1 Thess 2:16, "but God's wrath has come upon them at last," may refer to the disturbance which occurred in Jerusalem during the Passover of 49 when twenty to thirty thousand Jews were supposed to have been killed. Cf. Josephus, *Ant.* 20.112 and *J.W.* 2.224–227. Since this disturbance was instigated by Zealots (*J.W.* 2 225), Paul could well have interpreted the massacre as punishment for the persecution against the Christians in Judea. Bammel provides a sketch of the discussion regarding the persecution mentioned in 1 Thess in "Judenverfolgung," see especially 295, 306. He favors the theory that Paul refers to the expulsion of Jews from Rome in the year 49, but this does not correspond well with Paul's clear reference in 1 Thess 2:14 to the Christians in Judea having suffered from the Jews.

[39] Reicke, "Hintergrund," 185.

[40] Cf. Jewett, *Paul's Terms*, 51–82. I place the agitation in Antioch in the late 40s, the Apostolic Conference in the summer of 51, the second visit to the North Galatian churches in 52 and the writing of Galatians in the winter of 52.

[41] This hypothesis offers an answer to Schmithals' central argument against the Judaizer theory. He notes that since the conservative group in the Judean church did not at an earlier time express interest in a Gentile mission, there would be no reason why they would suddenly have sent agitators to Galatia ("Häretiker," 28ff.).

associate themselves with the ungodly and the uncircumcised. It was this hope of
public recognition for their loyalty to the Torah which lay behind Paul's bitter words:
"they wish to put up a good show in the flesh" (6:12).

The Agitators' Tactics

I have suggested that a Zealot threat to the Judean church in the late forties and
early fifties provided the motivation for the sudden missionary enterprise. It stands
to reason that the situation placed considerable pressure on the missionaries to
achieve prompt and notable success. Their strategy, as revealed in the Galatian letter,
was cleverly designed to this end. It appears that they did not plan to oppose Paul or
his theology directly but instead to offer a completion to it. This is evident in Gal 3:3
where Paul angrily asks, "Having started out with the Spirit, are you now finishing up
with the flesh?" The word ἐπιτελεῖσθε in this sentence refers to a perfecting or completing of what was already there. In Oepke's words, "*die Irrlehrer möchten den
Galatern gesagt haben, ihr Christentum bedürfe der Ergänzung, der Vollendung—durch
das Gesetz.*"[42] There is no indication that they sought to introduce the Galatians to the
entire Torah. They were content to achieve the first visible steps—circumcision and
the observance of the cultic calendar.

It appears that circumcision was presented as a prerequisite for entering fully
into Abraham's promise, into the chosen people whom God would spare in the
parousia (Gal 3:6–18).[43] At first glance it may seem strange that a Hellenistic congregation would consider undergoing circumcision simply to enter the promised people
of Israel. It may be, however, that the contact with their own Hellenistic aspirations
was at the point of the promise of perfection which the Judaic tradition attached to
circumcision. Billerbeck writes, "*Durch die Beschneidung ist Israel so gewissermassßen
das Elitevolk der Menschheit geworden; denn erst die Beschneidung macht den Menschen
vollkommen, während die Vorhaut ihn verächtlich erscheinen läßt.*"[44] Gen 17:1 had
mentioned the promise of being τέλειος which was given to Abraham, and we know
the institution of circumcision was thereafter interpreted as bringing perfection (cf.
Gen. Rab. 46:4; *Jub.* 15:25–33). The promise of perfection would have a powerful appeal to the Hellenistic Christians of Galatia, for such was the aim of the mystery reli-
gions as well as of the classical philosophy. The commonly held assumption was that
perfection could be approached by stages and finally attained in the vision of God or
the absorption in him.[45] For those holding such assumptions, the promise of gaining
the final degree of perfection through the mysterious ceremony of circumcision

---

[42] Oepke, *Galater,* 68.
[43] Cf. Foerster, "Abfassungszeit," 139.
[44] Str-B 4.32. Cf. especially *Midr. Pss.* 2, para. 13 (Str-B 4.156); *Pesiq. Rab.* 10 (Str-B 4.350).
[45] Cf. Reitzenstein, *Mysterienreligionen,* 338–39: " 'Vollkommen,' d. h. geweiht ist ein fester
Begriff in den meisten orientalischen Religionen und der ganzen Gnosis. Die Bildung des Begriffes
geht aus von der festen sakralen Formel τελεία μυστήρια . . . und sie hängt natürlich mit der
Vorstellung zusammen, daß es einen festen Weg und daher auch ein ἄρχεσθαι und τελευτᾶν in
den Mysterien gibt, und daß der Höhepunkt, die Vollendung (τέλος), das Schauen Gottes ist." For
a recent appraisal of these concepts see Du Plessis, ΤΕΛΕΙΟΣ.

would exert a powerful attraction.[46] In order that this attraction might not be weakened, the agitators in Galatia tactfully did not mention that circumcision imposed the obligation to obey the entire range of the law (Gal 5:3).

An analysis of Paul's discussion of the Galatians' cultic observances indicates the tactic used by the agitators in this regard. The terms Paul used have always been puzzling to exegetes: ἡμέρας . . . καὶ μῆνας καὶ καιροὺς καὶ ἐνιαυτούς (4:10). The search for exact equivalents has ended in vain. If Paul meant by ἡμέρας simply "sabbath" (with Zahn, Steinmann, Bousset) or "festival" (with Burton, Oepke), why did he not use σάββατον or ἑορτή as in Col. 2:16? Why does he use the more general term μήν instead of the term used for liturgical observances like νεομηνία (Col. 2:16)? Does ἐνιαυτός refer to the sabbath year (Zahn, Bousset, Oepke) or possibly the New Year's Festival (Burton)? Although the relationship with *1 En.* 75ff. is relatively close,[47] the decisive point is that Paul uses no term here which was specifically Jewish. This indicates that the agitators had not made use of the typically Jewish terminology but sought instead to connect the Jewish festivals with ideas and terms generally prevalent in the Hellenistic world. From this a significant deduction may be drawn. The widespread assumption that the στοιχεῖα (Gal 4:9) ruled during certain periods through the stars and planets seems to have been connected by the agitators with the Jewish festivals. In celebrating the festivals at the proper times, the powers of the universe would be appeased and the success of human activity would be ensured. Thus the cultic calendar was presented to the Galatians on a basis that was far from orthodox. But the agitators were not disturbed as long as quick and observable results could be achieved. It was more important to them that the Galatians be circumcised and begin to keep the festivals than that they do so for proper reasons.

A further manifestation of their cunningly devised tactic may be seen in Paul's refutation of their slanders concerning him. It appears that they were too clever to attack him. Instead they claimed he was on their side but had trimmed the demands of the gospel in order to please his hearers. "In reality," they had said, "Paul has always preached circumcision [5:11] and been zealous for the law [1:14]. He received his gospel from the same Jerusalem authorities who support our mission [1:18–2:9; 1:11]. This is general knowledge because Paul is well known in our Judean churches on account of his many visits through the years [1:22]. In his work as the representative of the 'pillars' to the Gentiles [1:12, 15–19], he simply began a work that we have come to complete [3:3]. But in order not to offend you when you were still pagans [1:10], Paul softened some of the harder and more advanced features of the faith. Our aim is not to overthrow but simply to finish the great work he has begun by informing you of the last step which guarantees perfection—circumcision." In short, despite the pleading of Schmithals[48] and Lütgert[49] that no one would do such a thing, the agitators in effect domesticated Paul. They did so in order to win the Galatians

---

[46] However, there is no indication that the agitators presented circumcision as a gnostic "Befreiung des Pneuma-Selbst von dem Kerker dieses Leibes," as Schmithals suggests ("Häretiker," 47).
[47] Cf. Schlier, *Galater,* 144.
[48] Schmithals, "Häretiker," 35ff.
[49] Lütgert, "Gesetz," 492ff.

quickly over to their Judaizing programme. It may well be that Olof Linton was right in seeing here a primary source for the Jerusalem-oriented picture of Paul which later came to be set forth in Acts.[50]

The Galatian Congregation

I have been assuming with Lightfoot, Goguel, Oepke, Schlier and others that Paul's letter was addressed to the North Galatian congregations. However, the possibility of determining the character of the congregation on the basis of geographic criteria is limited. The one factor that coincides quite well with the North Galatian setting is that the congregation did not center in a Jewish minority which had split off from a synagogue. The only inference we can draw from Gal 4:8–9 is that the congregation was predominantly Gentile.[51] We have already noted that Paul distinguished sharply between the agitators who are accursed as false brethren and the congregation itself. The question therefore is whether Paul viewed the congregation as a homogeneous unit or as divided between a group that favored the Judaizers and one that opposed them. Lütgert and Ropes argued that the Galatian church was split between a nomistic and an antinomistic wing. Such statements as 5:15 may well refer to some sort of strife within the congregation,[52] but in general Paul refers to them as an undivided unit. Gal 1:6, 3:1–5, and 5:7 imply that all of the Galatians had accepted the propaganda and received circumcision. In contrast, 5:1 and 5:10 imply that they had not yet taken the fatal step, while 4:8–11 indicate that they are in the process of deciding to do so. It is a rather puzzling state of affairs. The same sort of perplexing unity is presupposed in 6:1 where ὑμεῖς οἱ πνευματικοί are exhorted to restore any member who might be detected in a trespass. The use of προλημφθῇ makes clear that Paul does not have in mind those who followed the Judaizers but rather the case of an individual who falls more or less fortuitously into sin. Nor does Paul consider that only a few members of the church can be called the "pneumatics."[53] He uses this term to refer to the whole church, as the parallelism with ἀδελφοί in 6:1 makes plain. Since the entire congregation has received the Spirit (3:2–5), all are pneumatics. From this evidence, it appears that Paul viewed the congregation as a more or less homogeneous unit capable of being swayed in this direction and that. Without implying the existence of firmly set parties or groups within the congregation, Paul speaks as if they were all wavering between accepting circumcision and rejecting it, between being pneumatics or being fools (3:1). Directing his argument not against party groups but towards the congregation as a whole, he argues in 3:6–4:31 against the nomistic threat to the gospel and then in 5:13–6:10 against the libertinistic threat. If we take his view of the situation seriously, the entire congregation was as much in danger from the one as from the other. The Hellenistic assumptions of this congrega-

---

[50] Linton, "Third Aspect."
[51] For an alternative interpretation of this situation, see Robinson, "Distinction."
[52] Lütgert, "Gesetz," 479.
[53] Lütgert in contrast views the pneumatics as "besonders begabten Christen," "Gesetz," 482ff.

tion were as susceptible to the propaganda of the agitators as to the lures of libertinism. Yet we must not lose sight of the fact that the first danger was imported while the second was native. In 3:6–4:31 it is clear that Paul is dealing with arguments introduced by the Judean agitators in favor of circumcision. But it is equally clear that the other threat—libertinism—was there from the very beginning. This is indicated by Paul's statement in 5:21 regarding the threat of lawlessness: "I tell you as I told you before, those doing such things [i.e. the works of the flesh] will not inherit the king-dom of God."

In delineating the shape of the libertinistic threat, therefore, one must avoid the assumption that there was a separate libertinistic group in Galatia or that certain in-dividuals particularly exhibited such tendencies. As it appears, Paul considered that libertinism was a danger for the whole congregation. Furthermore, in the anti-libertinistic section (5:13–6:10) there are answers to questions raised by the nomistic influx. In 5:14 Paul shows that Christian love replaces the law while in 5:23 he assures the Galatians that the law will not condemn the fruits that flow from the Spirit. In 6:2 he states that behavior based on love would "fulfill the law of Christ." This shows that the ethic arrayed against libertinism was phrased as a replacement of the law and was directed to the congregation as a whole just as the earlier portions of the letter were. This ethic was made necessary by several clearly related characteristics of the Galatian congregation. They may be summarized as follows.

(a) The Galatians shared the typical Hellenistic misunderstanding about the Spirit. This is reflected in 5:25 where Paul says, "If we live in the Spirit, let us also march in line with the spirit." As Oepke has shown, στοιχέω (5:25) is not a synonym for περιπατέω but refers to the order in which one fits oneself.[54] It is a military term for marching in regiment (Xenophon, *Cyr.* 6.3.34) which came to be used more gen-erally in the sense of behaving in accordance with certain principles or examples. Paul's stress on the normative function of the Spirit indicates that the Galatians had disconnected "life in the Spirit" from "life according to the Spirit." In Schmithals' words, there was in Galatia a "*prinzipielles Auseinanderfallen von 'den Geist haben' und 'im Geist wandeln.'*"[55] Both sides of the statement have ample parallels in Galatians. In 3:2–5, 14 and 4:6 we see that the content of their salvation was thought to be the reception of the Spirit. It was something they had received and thus possessed.[56] Here the goal of religion was thought of as the reception of the Spirit, and once this took place, earthly behavior became irrelevant. Spirit was understood in an enthusiastic, Hellenistic manner as divine power which takes man over and grants him immediate

---

[54] Oepke, *Galater*, 145ff.

[55] Schmithals, "Häretiker," 51ff.

[56] Schmithals wrongly asserts that τὸ πνεῦμα λαμβάνειν is exclusively gnostic terminology (ibid., 51). Actually this expression is typical for early Christian usage. Cf. Acts 2:33, 38; 8:15, 17, 19; 10:47; 19:2. It is an expression that Paul in no way avoids: Rom 8:15; 1 Cor 2:12; 2 Cor 11:4; Gal 3:14. Schmithals draws another questionable conclusion in saying that opposition between living in the Spirit and walking by the Spirit would be impossible for a Pauline-oriented congregation (ibid., 52). He tries to substantiate this by reference to Rom 8:2ff.; 1 Cor 3:1ff.; Gal 5:17 and 6:7ff., which indi-cate in reality that such was a rather constant threat to the Pauline churches.

immortality.[57] The Galatians felt that life in the Spirit was a self-sufficient circle rather than a path leading to the parousia. What counted for them was not what one did but what one had. But Paul was not willing to have them remain in the static self-sufficiency of Spirit-possession. He stressed walking in the Spirit and being led by the Spirit.

(b) These assumptions led the Galatians into a disregard for ethical distinctions. Paul found it necessary to list the differences between moral and immoral behavior (5:19–23) because their power of distinction was blurred. In this catalogue of vice and virtue, it is sexual immorality, impurity and licentiousness that lead the list. Although these features are typical for such a catalogue in the comparable Jewish literature, they probably reflect the actual behavior of the Galatians.[58] Another area of behavior that appears to have been out of order was that of interpersonal relationships. Of the fourteen vices listed in the catalogue, the middle seven are of such a character: "enmity, strife, jealousy, anger, factiousness, dissension, party spirit. . . ." The cause for this disruption of interpersonal harmony may have been the extreme individualism resulting from their belief in having possession of the divine Spirit. But Paul's intention seems to be not so much to deal with any of these vices in detail but rather to stress the point that basic moral distinctions were necessary. It appears that the Galatians regarded ethical distinctions as irrelevant for those possessing the Spirit. This is related to a third characteristic of the Galatian congregation.

(c) The Galatians apparently did not believe they would individually have to face judgment in the present or future. In a passage which contrasts undue self-confidence with the necessity of testing oneself (6:3–8) there is a solemn warning, "Each will have to bear his own load." As the future βαστάσει indicates, this is a reference to the Last Judgment (cf. 5:10). Apparently the Galatians were indulging in boasting over against each other (6:4) and needed to be reminded that it would be better for each to test oneself with the goal of successfully passing through the coming eschatological judgment. The severe words in 6:7–8 would be best understood in the same light: "Do not deceive yourselves; God is not mocked, for whatever a man sows, that will he also reap. . . ." The self-deceit which amounted to a mocking of God was characteristic of those who did not believe that reaping had to do with sowing and that the harvest was a future, eschatological event. Heretofore most interpreters have seen in μὴ πλανᾶσθε, Θεὸς οὐ μυκτηρίζεται a reference to the inconsistency of claiming to be in the kingdom when one does not produce the fruits of the kingdom.[59] But the word "mock" is too harsh for mere inconsistency. It indicates the presence of scornful rejection of the impending future judgment. Such a rejection would be understandable in a Hellenistic, enthusiastic congregation that believed it had achieved immortality by the possession of the Spirit. Judgment for them was something the spiritual man would forever transcend. This leads us to the fourth characteristic of the congregation.

---

[57] Paul, in contrast to this widespread notion, depicts with πνεῦμα in Gal 6:8 a reality which is future rather than present.

[58] Voegtle, *Tugend- und Lasterkatalogue*, 26ff.

[59] Burton, *Galatians*, 339ff.; Duncan, *Galatians*, 185ff.; Schlier, *Galater*, 203ff.

(d) The Galatians had an intensely proud spiritual self-consciousness. It has been suggested that Paul addressed them with a title the members claimed for themselves when he called them οἱ πνευματικοί (6:1).[60] This title implied the claim of having attained superhuman existence through the Spirit which one possessed. It implied that one was already released from the root of sin in the material world. That such a title led to conceit (5:26) is not at all surprising. Each was great in his own estimation (6:3) and had an unlimited self-esteem that resulted in envy (5:26) as well as provocations (5:26) and strife as vicious as the biting and devouring of wild animals (5:15). This rampant self-centeredness led quite naturally to a lack of interest and support for the established teachers in the congregation (6:6). Why should a group of superior pneumatics need a teacher?[61]

To conclude, therefore, in Galatia the congregation seems to have had an enthusiastic self-consciousness based on possession of the Spirit. This led to denial of established authority as well as to a libertinistic view of ethical questions. It led to a rejection of the doctrine of future judgment on the basis of works. The consequence that Paul seems to have feared was a dangerous indifference to ethical distinctions. Hence it would be appropriate to term this particular tendency in Galatia "pneumatic libertinism." The evidence does not justify calling the Galatians Gnostics. They have not yet moved to a radical, thoroughgoing dualism such as was characteristic of Gnosticism. Nor is there evidence that they had begun to reject the doctrine of creation. Furthermore, there is no sign that the Galatians had begun to connect σοφία and γνῶσις with πνεῦμα in a typical gnostic fashion.

It is remarkable that a group exhibiting such a marked tendency towards pneumatic libertinism would at the same time be in danger of nomism. The solution suggested for this puzzle is that the Galatians were attracted by circumcision and the cultic calendar for reasons that were not nomistic at all. It was their desire to gain the final level of perfection that led to circumcision when they heard from the agitators that such an act would ensure entrance into the mythical seed of Abraham. And it was their instinctive respect for the cosmic powers that led them to a celebration of the calendar whose mystery was revealed by the wisdom of the Old Testament.

---

[60] Lütgert, "Gesetz," 483; Schmithals, "Häretiker," 50.
[61] Lütgert, "Gesetz," 490.

18

A LAW-OBSERVANT MISSION TO GENTILES

J. Louis Martyn

A Widely Accepted Portrait of Early Christian Missions

That the early church was passionately evangelistic is clear to every reader of the New Testament. Equally clear, or so it would seem, is the scholarly consensus that when Christian evangelists—notably Paul and his co-workers—took the step of reaching beyond the borders of the Jewish people, they did so without requiring observance of the Jewish Law. The work of these evangelists, in turn, is said to have sparked a reaction on the part of firmly observant Christian Jews, who, seeing the growth of the Gentile mission, sought to require observance of the Law by its converts. Struggles ensued, and the outcome, to put the matter briefly, was victory for the mission to the Gentiles, for the Law-free theology characteristic of that mission, and for the churches produced by it.[1] In broad terms such is the standard portrait of early Christian missions. That portrait was codified at the beginning of the twentieth century by the great historian Adolf von Harnack (1851–1930).[2] However varied the Gentile mission may have been in minor regards, in respect to the Jewish Law all *primary, evangelistic* efforts toward Gentiles were the same: *The* Gentile mission was the mission loosed from observance of the Law.

This portrait is not arbitrary. Harnack and his successors drew it on the basis of primary evidence in the letters of Paul, traditions and editorial material in the Acts of the Apostles, and other traditions scattered throughout the New Testament, notably in the gospels.[3] The evidence in Paul's letters is basic, because those letters were written during the sixth decade of the first century, in the midst of what is termed the

---

[1] Instructed by my friend Paul Meyer, I have learned in the final analysis to refer to the theology characteristic of the Pauline churches as circumcision free rather than as Law free: see my *Theological Issues,* chapter 14. In the present context, however, I will stay with the standard nomenclature.

[2] Harnack, *Mission.*

[3] Regarding the testimony of Luke and the other synoptists, see Martyn, "Law-Observant Mission" (1985), 308–9.

Gentile mission. Most influential is a paragraph in Paul's letter to the churches of Galatia, in which, speaking of the leaders of the Jewish-Christian church in Jerusalem Paul says, "they saw clearly that I had been entrusted by God with the gospel as it is directed to those who are not circumcised, just as Peter had been entrusted with the gospel to those who are circumcised" (Gal 2:7). From Paul's own mouth, therefore, we have a picture that presents two distinguishable missions proceeding along two parallel lines. The context of the quotation makes it clear that one of the lines is Law observant, while the other is not: Peter pursues *the* mission to the Jews (Law observant); Paul pursues *the* mission to the Gentiles (Law free). Thus, the standard portrait of *the* unified, Law-free mission to the Gentiles is drawn on the basis of primary evidence stemming from that mission itself.

Doubt

Is that portrait also fully accurate? Reading between the lines of Paul's letters, we may be assailed by doubt. Here and there, we find hints that at least some early Christian preachers directed their evangelistic message to Gentiles without surrendering observance of the Law. Could it be, in fact, that Galatians, the major witness to the existence of a single, Pauline Law-free mission to Gentiles, proves, upon inspection, to reflect a picture rather more complex than is customarily assumed?

We have only to consider the persons whose coming into Paul's Galatian churches compelled him to write the letter. Is their work entirely secondary to Paul's labors, in the sense that they have no Gentile mission of their own? An affirmative answer is reflected in the custom of referring to these persons as Paul's "opponents," for in that usage we imply that their identity is given in their opposition to Paul.[4] True, Paul makes it clear that he views them as opponents, and there are indications that to a considerable extent they view him in the same manner. There is, however, one good reason for considering that nomenclature somewhat reductionistic. As Paul himself makes clear, he is certain that, in their basic identity, these persons are opponents of *God,* not merely of himself (Gal 1:6–9). Could he be implying that they oppose God quite fundamentally by carrying out their own Law-observant mission to Gentiles? As we focus our attention on that question, we will avoid a premature answer by referring to these persons neutrally as "the Teachers," thus taking care not to identify them solely on the basis of their relationship with Paul.[5]

---

[4] E.g., Lüdemann, *Antipaulinismus,* 144–52.

[5] Martyn, *Theological Issues,* especially chapter 2, deals with the probability that the Teachers were in touch with the False Brothers and their circumcision party in the Jerusalem church, even being to some degree sponsored by that wing of the "mother" congregation. Thus, we can assume that the Teachers were well acquainted with stories about Paul's activities, both at the Jerusalem meeting and in the Antioch incident (Gal 2:1–14). It is therefore possible that, in part, they came to Galatia in order to counter Paul's work. As we will see, however, they seem also to have had their own Law-observant mission to Gentiles, apart from their concern to correct what they took to be Paul's errors (cf. Martyn, *Theological Issues,* chapters 10 and 12).

Do the data available to us offer clues sufficient in number and clarity to enable us to draw a reliable picture of the Teachers? There are solid grounds for confidence, even though we have nothing from the hands of the Teachers themselves.

Data in Galatians Itself

Most important are several explicit and highly revealing references to the Teachers in Galatians itself: 1:6–9; 3:1–2, 5; 4:17; 5:7–12; 6:12–14. From these passages alone we can arrive at a sensible portrait. But there is also the helpful fact that, because Paul composes no sentence of the letter without thinking of the Teachers, his explicit references to them are accompanied by numerous allusions to them and to their work. As we will see below, carefully interpreted, these allusions fill out in important ways Paul's explicit references.

Pertinent Jewish and Christian-Jewish Traditions[6]

Data in Galatians show the Teachers to have connections both with Diaspora Judaism and with Palestinian, Christian Judaism. Whatever their birthplace and locale of education, the Teachers are messianic Jews, at home among Gentiles, in the sense of being able not only to live among them, but also to make effective, apologetic contact with them. Several motifs that Paul connects with the Teachers—the view that Gentiles worship the elements of the cosmos, for example—find significant parallels in the apologetic literature of Diaspora Judaism.[7] We can enrich our portrait of the Teachers, therefore, by relating some aspects of their message, as reflected in Galatians, to passages in some of the literature of Diaspora Judaism, such as Wisdom, the writings of Philo and Josephus, Aristobulus, and *Joseph and Aseneth*.[8]

---

[6] Here and elsewhere I intend some degree of distinction between the adjectival expressions "Jewish-Christian" and "Christian-Jewish" (and their corresponding nouns), the second word being the dominant one. Churches, for example, that were essentially Jewish sects would be groups of Christian Jews, rather than groups of Jewish Christians.

[7] Martyn, *Theological Issues*, chapter 8.

[8] On Wisdom, Philo, Josephus, Aristobulus and *Joseph and Aseneth*, see the relevant articles, with bibliographies, of Winston, Borgen, Feldman, Holladay, and Chesnutt in the *Anchor Bible Dictionary*. On the literature of Diaspora Judaism, as it is important for our understanding of early Christian theology and history, one can still learn by reading with care such older works as those of Dalbert, *Theologie;* Bussmann, *Missionspredigt;* and Georgi, *Opponents.* But see notably the corrective and enriching dimensions of more recent contributions: Borgen, "Judaism" (Egypt); Applebaum, "Judaism"; Walter, "Hellenistische Diaspora-Juden"; Barclay, "Paul"; idem, *Jews.* Older theories about a unified and organized Jewish *mission* to Gentiles in the first century sometimes formulated in part by taking at face value Matt 23:15 cannot be sustained. See, e.g., Walter, "Hellenistische Diaspora-Juden," 50–51; McKnight, *Light* (but also the tempering review by Westerholm); Goodman, "Jewish Proselytizing"; Feldman, *Jew and Gentile.* But the rejection of the theory of an organized Jewish mission to Gentiles does not tell us that the motif of hoped-for conversions is wholly absent from the literature of Diaspora Judaism. We can take *Joseph and Aseneth* as an example. Burchard is right both to reject the characterization of *Joseph and Aseneth* as a missionary tract—a document having no theme other than the conversion of a Gentile—and to affirm that it was written

From Galatians itself, we can also see that the Teachers are in touch with—indeed understand themselves to represent—a powerful circle of Christian Jews in the Jerusalem church, a group utterly zealous for the observance of the Law.[9] Seeking to reconstruct the Teachers' message, then, we will find pertinent data in such Palestinian Jewish traditions as those preserved in Sirach and the Dead Sea Scrolls. There are even good reasons for thinking that certain traditions current in the Jerusalem church of the first century were in fact preserved and shaped in two second-century communities of Christian Jews, known to us from the *Epistle of Peter to James* and the *Ascents of James,* not to mention Christian-Jewish traditions in the canonical epistle of James and in the gospel of Matthew.[10] With caution, then, we can further enrich our portrait of the Teachers by noting certain passages in these Christian-Jewish sources.[11]

In short, then, the picture that emerges from Paul's own references to the Teachers' work shows considerable internal coherence *and* a number of motifs for which there are significant parallels in traditions connected with Diaspora Jews, Palestinian Jews, and Christian Jews of various locales. We have reason, then, to think that a trustworthy picture can be drawn.[12]

---

for Jews, born and converted ("Joseph and Aseneth," *OTP* 2.194–95). He is also right, however, (a) to identify Gentile conversion to Judaism as the author's main focus ("Importance," 104), (b) to speak of Aseneth's re-creative transformation as "a pattern which conversion often followed" (*OTP* 2.192; note especially Joseph's prayer for Aseneth; *Jos. Asen.* 8:9), and thus (c) to characterize conversion as the subject by which the author can remind converts "of what they, or their forefathers, gained by crossing over to Judaism" (ibid., 2.195). Thus, as regards our attempts to portray the Teachers in Paul's Galatian churches, *Joseph and Aseneth*—and other Diaspora literature as well—is helpful in a role secondary to data in Galatians itself (in spite of the fact that most of this literature is Alexandrian). In the study of Diaspora literature, it is important to note two apologetic stances, and to note also their combination. *First,* there is the apologetic stance that reflects an enormous cultural and religious distance from Gentiles (see notably Barclay, "Paul"). Jewish authors express horror, for example, at their Gentile neighbors' idolatry and sexual practices, insisting on what one might call the absolute superiority of Judaism (e.g., *Jos. Asen.* 8:5). *Second,* there is also the apologetic stance that can express a loathing for polytheism and insist on the superiority of Judaism, precisely in order to extol Gentile conversion. In *Joseph and Aseneth,* insistence on the maintenance of an absolute religious distance from Gentiles serves the climactic presentation of Aseneth as the prototypical proselyte, whose conversion is dramatized—indeed celebrated—in fine detail, and who leads her entire family to embrace Judaism (*Jos. Asen.* 20:7–8; cf. Aseneth as a City of Refuge for all Gentiles who repent, 15:7; 16:16; 19:5). As we will see, an analogous combination of these two apologetic stances proves to be characteristic of the Teachers who invaded Paul's Galatian churches. Their horror at the Godless life of Gentiles does nothing other than serve their major motif: that of recommending the path of conversion to the God of Abraham.

[9] Martyn, *Theological Issues,* chapters 2 and 12.

[10] The history of the study of the *Epistle of Peter to James* and the *Ascents of James* is complex and the critical literature extensive. See notably F. S. Jones, who has recently expressed doubt about the theory of a source called the *Preaching of Peter,* of which the *Epistle of Peter to James* has been thought to be the first element (*Ancient Source,* xii). The source-critical issues will never be altogether settled. See Strecker, "Kerygmata Petrou"; Klijn and Reinink, *Evidence,* 31–32, 37, 69; Martyn, "Clementine Recognitions"; Betz, *Galatians,* 9, 331–32. On James, see L. T. Johnson, *James;* on Matthew, Davies and Allison, *Matthew,* and Luz, *Matthew* (especially 79–95); idem, *Theology.*

[11] On occasion I will even cite late rabbinic traditions, but only to amplify a point secured by other sources, or to suggest a possibility not essential to the exegetical argument.

[12] The integrity of the picture that will emerge below, added to the points of similarity with certain motifs in Jewish and Christian-Jewish traditions, suggests that Paul was himself well informed

A Sketch of the Teachers and Their Message

1. Outsiders

Paul consistently differentiates the Teachers from the members of his Galatian congregations. He addresses the Galatians quite directly as "you," whereas he always refers to the Teachers by such terms as "some persons," "they," "these people." The Teachers are outsiders who have only recently come into the Galatian churches.[13]

2. Jews

Paul almost certainly knows the Teachers' names, or at least some of the epithets by which they identify themselves (cf. 2 Cor 11:22–23). We can conclude, then, that instead of using their names and epithets, he employs such colorless expressions as "some persons" in order to indicate disdain. We also note, however, that he does employ three descriptive terms in his direct references:

(a) those who are frightening you (1:7, cf. 5:10);

(b) those who are troubling your minds (5:12);

(c) those who are circumcised (6:13).

We shall return to the first two of these below. The third almost certainly tells us that the Teachers are Jews. We thus have a group of Jews who have come into the Galatian churches from somewhere else.[14]

---

about the Teachers and their labors. In our own effort to reconstruct a picture of the Teachers, two extremes are to be avoided. On the one side lies the temptation to be overly bold in our detective work, falling unawares into massive speculation, reconstructing an entire face, so to speak, on the basis of the cut of the mustache. Some of Paul's polemical statements were doubtless formulated by him solely for the sake of rhetorical emphasis. On the other side lies the temptation to be too modest, limiting ourselves to points which can be scientifically demonstrated beyond doubt. Exegesis is more an art than a science, although it partakes of both. It is by asking at crucial points how the Galatians are likely to have understood the text in front of us that we shall acquire both the scientific control and the poetic imagination needed for our own understanding of the text. Note the cautions offered by Barclay, "Mirror Reading," and Sumney, *Opponents.*

[13] *Pace,* e.g., Munck, *Paul,* 87–90. See Hawkins, "Opponents." As we will see, the Teachers are outsiders to the Gentile communities of the Galatians, somewhat as Joseph is an outsider to the Egyptian family of Aseneth in *Joseph and Aseneth.*

[14] Both in "Paulus" (1986) and in "Hellenistische Diaspora-Juden," Walter argues that the Teachers were some of the *non-Christian* Jews who, like the pre-Christian Paul himself, persecuted the church (for Walter, they were intent on abolishing the circumcision-free Christian mission). Before making the case for his hypothesis by analyzing data in Galatians, Walter refers to Acts 20:3; 21:27–29; 22:22; 23:12–15; and Matt 23:15 ("Paulus" [1986], 351; see now "Paul"). The final result is a reading of the data that is at once provocative and productive. Had one asked the Teachers whether they were Jews, the response would almost certainly have been in the affirmative. As I will argue below, however, they were surely Christian Jews, in the sense that, employing the term "gospel" in their own mission, they confessed Jesus to have been the Messiah, whose death atoned for the sins of all peoples, thus opening the way for the taking of the Law to the Gentiles.

3. Christian-Jewish Evangelists

What, precisely, are they doing in these congregations? In his initial reference to the Teachers (1:6–9), Paul says that, under their influence, the Galatians are turning their allegiance to "another *gospel*." Then, having said that, he corrects himself by insisting that in reality there is no "other gospel." Does Paul take the route that requires self-correction only for the sake of rhetorical emphasis? Probably not. It would have been easier to avoid associating the Teachers with the term "gospel," by saying that, under their influence, the Galatians are turning *away from* the gospel, in that they are giving their allegiance to a *false teaching* (cf. "the teaching of Balaam" in Rev 2:14) or to an *impotent philosophy* (cf. "philosophy . . . according to human tradition" in Col 2:8). It seems highly probable that Paul takes the path requiring self-correction because he knows that the Teachers are in fact referring to their message as "the gospel." It follows that, no less than the Apostle himself, the Teachers are in the proper sense of the term evangelists, probably finding their basic identity not as persons who struggle against Paul, but rather as those who preach "the good news of God's Messiah." They are, then, Jews who have come into Galatia proclaiming what they call the gospel, God's good news. And what do they consider that good news to be?

4. The Law as the Good News

Although they themselves speak of the good news as the gospel of Christ, Paul repeatedly portrays them as those who find in the Law the absolute point of departure for their theology (e.g., 5:3–4). Whatever they may be saying about Christ (see below), the Law is itself both the foundation and the essence of their good news.

5. The Law as the Good News for Gentiles

For whom is the Law good news? In the Teachers' view, the Law is good news for the whole of the world, and specifically for Gentiles.[15] For that reason the Teachers' evangelistic vision is, in its scope, no less universalistic than that of Paul (3:8).[16] Just as we do well not to speak of the Teachers simply as Paul's opponents, so we shall not refer to them as "Judaizers," as has so frequently been done. For in modern parlance the term "Judaizer" usually refers to someone who wishes to hem in Gentile Christians by requiring them to live according to "narrow" Jewish practices.[17] In their own time and place, the Teachers are embarked on an ecumenical mission. They are Christian Jews

---

[15] Cf. Acts 21:20–21; Ps.-Clem. *Ep. Pet. Jas.* 2:3 (HS 2.112). The Teachers are thus first cousins, so to speak, of various Diaspora Jews who dramatically portrayed and even facilitated Gentile conversions to Judaism. See, e.g., *Joseph and Aseneth* and Wisdom, and note that in *Joseph and Aseneth* nomistic salvation "is a 'necessity' appropriate only for non-Jews" (Burchard, "Joseph and Aseneth," 2.192).

[16] On the motif of universalism in some Jewish traditions, cf., e.g., Urbach (*Sages*, 552): "The hope for conversion did not cease as long as the belief in Israel's election and in the power of the Torah was a living and dynamic faith that deemed its purpose to be the perfection and renewal *of the world*" (emphasis added).

[17] See Ign. *Magn.* 10.3; Burton, *Galatians*, liii–lxv; and note the motif of Jewish universalism in Martyn, *Theological Issues*, chapter 4.

active in the Diaspora, who preach their nomistic gospel in Greek, quote the Law in Greek, and interpret the Law in ways understandable to persons of Greek culture.[18] Moreover, the Teachers carry out their mission under the genuine conviction—shared, for example, by the author of Wisdom—that the Law of Moses is the cosmic Law, in the sense that it is the divine wisdom for *all* human beings.[19] From the vocabulary employed by Paul in Gal 4:24–25, we can surmise that, in issuing their evangelistic invitation, the Teachers spoke explicitly of "the covenantal Law of Sinai."

6. The Motivation for a Law-Observant Mission to Gentiles

Beyond indicating that the Teachers are greatly concerned to correct what they see as the Law-less evangelism of Paul, the letter shows that they are carrying out their Law-observant mission to Gentiles in order to keep on good terms with some persons of considerable power (Gal 6:12). But their concentration on the expression "descendants of Abraham" raises the additional possibility that they see their mission in thoroughly positive terms, perhaps understanding it to be the means by which God is filling out the infinite number of progeny he had promised to the patriarch. One notes the motivation for the Law-observant mission to Gentiles portrayed in the *Ascents of James:*

> It was necessary, then, that the Gentiles be called . . . so that the number of descendants which was shown to Abraham would be satisfied; thus the preaching of the kingdom of God has been sent into all the world.[20]

7. The Law as the Source of the Spirit

God's readiness to invite Gentiles into his own people is marked by the fact that God bestows his Spirit even on communities of Gentiles, if their communal life is ordered by correct exegesis of scripture and thus by true observance of his Law.[21] In Gal 3:1–5 there are several hints that Paul is contrasting the type of worship service the Galatians first knew under his direction with the type of worship service they are now experiencing at the hands of the Teachers. Both services have about them certain aspects of the theater. In his preaching, Paul clearly portrayed before the Galatians' eyes the dramatic picture of Christ, as he suffered crucifixion (3:1). Presented with this

---

[18] Note especially the Teachers' Pythagorean-like, columnar interpretation of Genesis 15–21 (Martyn, *Theological Issues,* chapter 12).

[19] Cf. Georgi, "Weisheit Salomos"; Hawkins, "Opponents"; Walter, "Hellenistische Diaspora Juden," 49. Note the claim, widespread in Diaspora Judaism, that the whole of Greek philosophy is dependent on Moses; see, e.g., Walter, *Aristobulos,* 43–51; Philo, *Mos.* 2.12–44.

[20] The Latin text of Ps.-Clem. *Recogn.* 1.42.1 (for both Latin and Syriac, see Van Voorst, *Ascents,* 57; Jones, *Ancient Source,* 72). Here and elsewhere, I cite the *Ascents of James* both by the numbering in the Pseudo-Clementine *Recognitions* and by the pages in Van Voorst, *Ascents,* and Jones, *Ancient Source.* Cf. Philo, *Somn.,* 1.173–176.

[21] Note several of the motifs in Joseph's prayer for Aseneth prior to her conversion to Judaism: "Lord God of my father Israel . . . renew her by your spirit . . . and number her among your people that you have chosen . . ." (*Jos. Asen.* 8:9); and cf. Joseph's later giving to the new convert "spirit of life," "spirit of wisdom," and "spirit of truth" (*Jos. Asen.* 19:11).

theater, the Galatians found that the message of the cross elicited their faith, and that the Spirit fell upon them.

Now a new acting company has arrived on the scene, presenting a novel and highly effective drama.[22] In the services of worship conducted by the Teachers, the Galatians see extraordinarily masterful exegetes who quote and interpret the Scriptures with the firm conviction that out of true exegesis will flow mighty manifestations of the Spirit (Gal 3:5).[23] And, indeed, developments in Galatia seem to confirm this conviction. In their dramatic services, the Teachers somehow manage to demonstrate to the Galatians the impressive connection between their interpretation of the Law and the miraculous dispensation of the Spirit.[24] It follows that God is to be known as the one who supplies the Spirit to those who are both true exegetes of his Law and faithful observers of it.

8. The Threat of Exclusion

This laying down of a strict condition for the dependable granting of the Spirit is a token for the conditional nature of the whole of the Teachers' good news. We return, then, to the fact that Paul twice characterizes the Teachers as persons who frighten the Galatians (1:7; 5:10). How are we to understand these two references? Help comes from Paul's comment in Gal 4:17, where, employing the image of a gate, he says that the Teachers threaten to shut the Galatians out of salvation. Encountering Gentiles they consider to have been badly misled by Paul, the Teachers feel they must issue a sharp warning: "*Only if* you pass through the gate of repentance into the genuine observance of God's Law, will you be included in God's people Israel, thus being saved on the day of judgment."[25]

9. The Necessity of Circumcision as the Commencement of Law Observance

How is a Gentile to pass through the gate to salvation? One of the major foci of the Teachers' preaching is the subject of circumcision (e.g., Gal 6:12). It is a subject

---

[22] Cf. the *Exagoge* of Ezekiel the Tragedian (*OTP* 2.803–19).

[23] See Sir 39:1–8; Philo, *Spec.* 1.8; 3.178 (exegetes who are more than human [*thespesioi andres*]). Cf. Georgi, *Opponents*, 112–17, 258 71; according to some Jewish traditions "the spirit portrayed and communicated itself essentially in the interpretation of the scriptures" (114); Fishbane on mantic oracles (*Biblical Interpretation*, 268–69). Note also that the dirge of *m. Soṭah* 9:15—"When ben Zoma died, there were no more interpreters," etc.—reflects the assumption of an earlier connection between exegesis and the glory of the law *(kabōd hattorah)*.

[24] The Teachers' success may have been similar to that achieved somewhat later in the Corinthian church by the pseudo-apostles. Note the portrait of Abraham in Philo, *Virt.* 217; and cf. Martyn, *Theological Issues*, chapter 6.

[25] Like the other pictures Paul paints of the Teachers, this one is decidedly negative. But the Teachers' own view of their threat was probably analogous to the harshly strict words of Joseph to Aseneth (*Jos. Asen.* 8:5). When the Teachers were not dealing with Gentiles they considered to have been misled by Paul, they may have employed the image of the gate in an essentially positive way, understanding themselves to be gatekeepers intent on ushering Gentiles through the gate into full participation in the people of God, Israel. See Joseph's prayer for Aseneth (*Jos. Asen.* 8:9).

that properly belongs to proselytizing, for, in most cases, a Gentile passes into the people of the Law by belonging to a family, the males of which submit to circumcision.[26] Circumcision is the commandment par excellence, the commandment which signifies full participation in the people of God. The Teachers, then, are circumcised, Christian Jews who preach circumcision to Gentiles as the act appropriate to the universal good news of God's Law, the observance of which is the condition for God's pouring out his Holy Spirit. They also preach the necessity of the observance of holy times (Gal 4:10) and the keeping of dietary regulations (2:11–14).

10. The Christ of the Law

We may further summarize the motifs we have mentioned thus far by asking what the Teachers say about Christ, the Messiah. However difficult it may be to answer this question with the detail we would desire, and however uncertain we remain as to how the Teachers are successfully communicating their christology to the Galatian Gentiles, five points can be stated with some degree of confidence.[27] (a) The Teachers view Christ much as do the members of the strictly observant circumcision party in the Jerusalem church, perhaps seeing him as the savior who brought to completion the ministry of Moses.[28] (b) In any case, they view God's Christ in the light of God's Law, rather than the Law in the light of Christ. This means that, in their christology, Christ is secondary to the Law. (c) Paul is emphatic, when he says that the Teachers avoid taking their theological bearings from the cross (e.g., Gal 6:12). They must be including references to Christ's death, however, presumably understanding it to have been a sacrifice for sins, perhaps emphatically for the sins of Gentiles. In short, the Teachers must see Christ's death as a redemptive sacrifice enacted in harmony with God's Law. (d) We can be sure, above all, that they consistently avoid every suggestion that God's Law and God's Christ could be even partially in conflict with one another.[29] (e) In their own terms, they are presumably certain that Christ came in order to fulfill the Law and the prophets (cf. Matt 5:17–18), perhaps even to complete Moses' ministry by bringing the Law to the Gentiles.[30] For them, the Messiah is the Messiah of the Law, deriving his identity from the fact that he confirms—and perhaps normatively interprets—the Law.[31] If Christ is explicitly involved in the Teachers' commission to preach to the Gentiles, that must be so because he has deepened their passion to take to the nations God's gift of gifts, the Spirit-dispensing Law that will guide them in their daily life.

---

[26] S. Cohen, "Crossing"; Lieu, "Circumcision."

[27] Absent from these five points is the suggestion that the Teachers' christology included dimensions of the this-worldly, political, anti-Gentile messianism we find in some of the traditions of Diaspora Judaism. See, e.g., *Syb. Or.* 3, and cf. Amir, "Die messianische Idee"; Collins, "Sybilline Oracles"; idem, "Jesus and Messiahs."

[28] Cf. Van Voorst, *Ascents*, 163; F. S. Jones, *Ancient Source*, 160.

[29] Cf. Jas 1:22–25; Ps.-Clem. *Ep. Pet. Jas.* 2:3 (HS 2.112).

[30] On the expectation that the Messiah will bring the Law to the Gentiles, see later rabbinic references, such as *Gen. Rab.* 98:9.

[31] For the Christian-Jewish conviction that Christ permanently confirmed the Law, see Matt 5:17–19; Ps.-Clem. *Ep. Pet. Jas.* 2:5 (HS 2.112).

These ten points would seem to encapsulate most of what Paul reveals about the Teachers and their gospel in his direct references. As noted earlier, however, there are other data quite revealing of the Teachers' gospel, allusions which, carefully interpreted, fill out in important ways the picture we receive of these evangelists, and especially of their gospel.

11. The Descendants of Abraham; the Blessing of Abraham

The character of Paul's argument in Gal 3:6–29 shows that he refers to "the descendants of Abraham" because the Teachers are already doing that in their own way.[32] Specifically, the Teachers are designating themselves as Abraham's descendants, and they are telling the Galatians that they can claim that identity for themselves if they submit to circumcision.[33] Indeed, the Teachers seem also to be speaking at some length about "the blessing of Abraham," indicating that when God blessed the patriarch, he did so in such a way as eventually to bless those Gentiles who, by circumcision and Law observance, become "Abraham's true descendants."[34] We thus find solid confirmation of the suggestion of Holtzmann that "descendants of Abraham" is one of the Teachers' favorite catchwords.[35]

12. "Jerusalem Is Our Mother"

There is good reason to think that, in addition to identifying themselves and their Law-observant Gentile converts as "descendants of Abraham," the Teachers speak of Jerusalem as their "mother," referring thereby to the Jerusalem church.[36] We cannot say with certainty that the Teachers have come to Galatia from Jerusalem, but there are grounds for thinking that they claim to be the true representatives of the Jerusalem church, and that, in making that claim, they are confident of the support of a powerful group in that church.[37]

---

[32] See Martyn, *Theological Issues,* chapter 10.

[33] We know that the expression "descendants of Abraham" was a significant self-designation among Christian Jews of the first century (2 Cor 11:22; John 8:33, 37). Jewish references to the proselyte as a descendant of Abraham are very numerous; see, e.g., *Tanḥ., Lekh Lekha* 32a; cf. Philo, *Virt.* 219.

[34] It is worth noting that the Christian Jew who authored the second-century *Ascents of James* portrayed true religion as the line extending from Abraham to his descendants. Similarly, as noted above, in the *Ascents,* God's blessing of Abraham provides the motivation for the Law-observant mission to Gentiles (1.42.1; Van Voorst, *Ascents,* 57; Jones, *Ancient Source,* 72).

[35] H. Holtzmann, *Lehrbuch,* 243. See now Brinsmead, *Galatians,* 107–14. With regard to the history of early Christian missions, it is important that, concerning the link between Abraham and the impulse to evangelize the Gentiles, it is the author of Galatians who is doing the reacting, not the Teachers. There is no good evidence that they have developed their interpretations of the Abraham texts simply in order to counter the effects of Paul's circumcision-free mission. On the contrary, Paul takes up the traditions about Abraham—and especially the expression "descendants of Abraham"—in his argument against the use the Teachers are already making of those traditions in their Law-observant mission.

[36] Martyn, *Theological Issues,* chapter 2. Cf. again H. Holtzmann, who advanced the thesis that the agitators spoke of Jerusalem (presumably Holtzmann meant the city) as their mother (*Lehrbuch,* 243).

[37] See again Martyn, *Theological Issues,* chapter 2, and cf. the image of the Jerusalem church in the *Ascents of James;* Van Voorst, *Ascents,* 174–80. Note the argument of Jones for locating the *Ascents* in Judea or Jerusalem (*Ancient Source,* 157–67).

13. Israel

The way in which Paul employs the word "Israel" in his final blessing (Gal 6:16) suggests that, in inviting the Galatians to claim Abraham as their father and the Jerusalem church as their mother, the Teachers are promising the Galatians that they will thereby enter the company of God's people Israel.[38] It is even conceivable that the Teachers are emphasizing the antique superiority of Israel by noting—at least in effect—that Plato and Pythagoras imitated the Law of Moses.[39]

14. Victory over the Impulsive Desire of the Flesh

Finally, horrified at the continuation of various Gentile patterns of life among the Galatian churches (cf. 5:20–21a), the Teachers are taking up the matter of the Galatians' daily behavior. Here, in addition to attacking Paul for leaving the Galatians without potent ethical guidance—an unfaithful student of the Jerusalem apostles, Paul does not teach his Gentile converts what the Law means for the church's daily life—they voice a crucial promise: "If you Galatians will become observant of the Law, we can promise you that you will not fall prey to the Impulsive Desire of the Flesh" (cf. Gal 5:16; 4 Macc 1). In this regard, as in others, the Teachers are likely to have portrayed Abraham as the model to be emulated. For, by keeping God's commandments, the patriarch was said to have avoided walking in the path of the Impulsive Desire of the Flesh.[40]

Most of these motifs can be effectively brought together if, attempting to sense the reasons for the Teachers' remarkable success among the Galatians, we allow ourselves the disciplined freedom to imagine a sermon they might have preached on the subject of the identity and blessedness of Abraham's true descendants.

The Teachers' Sermon on Abraham[41]

Listen, now![42] It all began with Abraham. Looking beyond the fascinating movements of the heavenly bodies, he was the first to discern that there is but one God. Because of that perception, he turned from the service of dumb idols to the worship of that true God.[43] Therefore God made him the father of our great people Israel. But that was only the beginning, for God blessed Abraham in a way that is coming to its

---

[38] Martyn, *Galatians*, comment 52.

[39] See, e.g., Aristobulus, frg. 3.

[40] CD 3:1–3; 16:4–6. See Martyn, *Theological Issues*, chapter 15.

[41] On the role of Abraham in the Teachers' theology see Barrett, "Allegory"; Brinsmead, Galatians; Hansen, *Abraham in Galatians;* Walter, "Paul." Rabbinic references are given for some of the motifs included in the following sermon, but usually in addition to references of early date. Regarding the scheme for referring to passages in the *Ascents of James*, see note 20 above.

[42] At numerous points in Galatians (noted here in parentheses), Paul's words reflect the message of the Teachers.

[43] Philo, *Abr.* 69–70; Josephus, *Ant.* 1.155–156; *Jub.* 11:16–17; Hebrew *T. Naph.* 9; Martyn, *Theological Issues*, chapter 8.

fulfillment only now in the messianic age. Speaking through a glorious angel, God said to Abraham:

> In you shall all nations of the world be blessed, for I shall multiply your descendants as the stars of heaven. Come outside, and look toward heaven, and number the stars, if you are able. So shall your descendants be, for I speak this blessing to you and to your descendants (cf. Gen 12:3; 15:5; 17:4; 18:18).

What is the meaning of this blessing which God gave to Abraham? Pay attention to these things: Abraham was the first proselyte. As we have said, he discerned the one true God and turned to him. God's blessing took the form, therefore, of an unshakable covenant with Abraham, and God defined the covenant as the commandment of circumcision.[44] He also revealed to Abraham the heavenly calendar, so that in his own lifetime our father was obedient to the Law, not only keeping the commandment of circumcision, but also observing the holy feasts on the correct days.[45] Later, when God handed down the Law on tablets of stone at Sinai, he spoke once again by the mouths of his glorious angels, for they passed the Law through the hand of the mediator, Moses (Gal 3:19).[46] And now the Messiah has come, confirming for eternity God's blessed Law, revealed to Abraham and spoken through Moses.[47]

And what does this mean for you Gentiles? Listen again to the scripture we have just quoted. When God said to Abraham that in him all nations of the world would be blessed, God spoke explicitly of blessing you Gentiles in Abraham. But this blessing will come to you only if you are included in the people of Israel via your legitimate incorporation into our father Abraham. For, in addition to being himself the first proselyte, Abraham was the great maker of proselytes.[48] You must become, therefore, Abraham's true descendants, his true seed, along with us.[49]

Listen yet again to scripture. It is written that Abraham had two sons: Isaac and Ishmael (Gal 4:22). On the day of the feast of the first fruits, Isaac was born of Sarah the freewoman, and through him have come we Jews, true descendants of Abraham.[50] Earlier, Ishmael was born of Hagar the slave girl, and through him have come you Gentiles. You are descendants of the patriarch! We are in fact brothers![51]

Offspring through Ishmael, however, you are descended through the son who was begotten by Abraham while, lacking in trust, he was yet ignorant of God.[52] Most important of all, you have come through the slave girl, and, failing to observe God's

---

[44] Gen 17:10.

[45] *Jub.* 16:12–28; Sir 44:19–20.

[46] Deut 33:12 (LXX); *Jub.* 1:29; Acts 7:38, 53; Davies, "Note."

[47] Matt 5:17–18; Ps.-Clem. *Ep. Pet. Jas.* 2:5 (HS 2.112).

[48] CD 16:4–6; *Tanḥ.* Lekh Lekha 32a; ʾ*Abot R. Nat.* 12:27a (Goldin, *Rabbi Nathan*, 68); *Midr. Pss.* 110:1; *Gen. Rab.* 43:7.

[49] In both Jewish and Christian-Jewish tradition, it was held that proselytes enter corpus Israel as descendants of Abraham; see, e.g., *Tanḥ.* Lekh Lekha 32a; *y. Bik.* 64a (on *m. Bik.* 1:4); *Asc. Jas.* 1.42.1 (Van Voorst, *Ascents*, 57; Jones, *Ancient Source*, 72).

[50] *Jub.* 16:13.

[51] *Jub.* 16:17; 1 Macc 12:21; *Asc. Jas.* 1.33.3; 34.1 (Van Voorst, *Ascents*, 48–49; Jones, *Ancient Source*, 60–61); *b. Sanh.* 59b.

[52] *Asc. Jas.* 1.33.3; 34.1.

covenantal Law, you are enslaved to the power of the Impulsive Desire of the Flesh (Gal 5:16). In a word, you Gentiles are not yet *true* descendants of Abraham. You have not been incorporated into Israel. In order to participate in God's blessing of Abraham, therefore, you are to make your descent legitimate.

Who are the genuine and therefore blessed descendants of Abraham, Abraham's true seed (Gal 3:7, 29)? Again the answer is given in scripture, for the Law makes clear that God has set Two Ways before human beings, the Way of death and the Way of life.[53] You can see this in the case of our father Abraham. He chose the Way of life. Turning from idols to the observance of the Law, he circumcised himself, thus avoiding walking in the deadly power of the Impulsive Desire of the Flesh.[54] It follows that Abraham's true descendants are those who choose the path of virtue, becoming faithfully obedient to the virtue-creating Law, along with faithful Abraham (Gal 3:6–9). Let us say yet again that transference to the path of true descent is precisely what we now offer to you. For, fulfilling the ancient blessing he pronounced over Abraham, God is pleased at the present holy time to extend this line of true descent to the Gentiles. To be specific, God is creating descendants of Abraham through the Law-observant mission to Gentiles approved by his church in Jerusalem, the community that lives by the Law confirmed to eternity by the Christ.[55] In our Lawful preaching to the Gentiles, we represent that church, the community of James, Cephas, and John (Gal 2:1–10).

What are you to do, therefore, as Abraham's descendants through Ishmael, the child of Hagar the slave-girl? The gate of conversion stands open (Gal 4:9, 17)![56] You are to cast off your enslavement to the Flesh by turning in repentance and conversion to God's righteous Law, as it is confirmed by his Christ.[57] Follow Abraham in the holy, liberating, and perfecting rite of circumcision (Gal 3:3; 6:13).[58] Observe the feasts at their appointed times (Gal 4:10). Keep the sacred dietary requirements (Gal 2:11–14). And abstain from idolatry and from the passions of the Impulsive Flesh (Gal 5:19–21). Then you will be perfected as true descendants of Abraham, members of the covenant people of Israel, heirs of salvation according to the blessing which God solemnly uttered to Abraham and to his descendants (Gal 3:7, 8, 16).[59] Indeed,

---

[53] E.g., Deut 30:19; Jer 21:8.

[54] Gen 6:5; CD 3:1–3; 16:4–6; Jas 1:2–4, 12–15; 4:5–6. For the motif of turning from idols, cf. *Joseph and Aseneth*. On the Impulsive Desire of the Flesh, see Martyn, *Theological Issues,* chapter 15.

[55] *Asc. Jas.* 1.33.3–1.43.3 (Van Voorst, *Ascents,* 48–59; Jones, *Ancient Source,* 60–74); Ps.-Clem. *Ep. Pet. Jas.* 2:5 (HS 2.112).

[56] Cf. Joseph's prayer for Aseneth in *Jos. Asen.* 8:9.

[57] Cf. *Jos. Asen.* 15:7.

[58] Holding Gentiles to be Ishmaelite descendants of Abraham, in spite of their being uncircumcised, the Teachers may simply have ignored—or interpreted symbolically?—the scriptural tradition according to which Abraham circumcised Ishmael (Gen 17:23). For, being yet ignorant of God's true power, Abraham did not carry out that act on Ismael's eighth day.

[59] As the Teachers offered the Galatians a religious process that leads to perfection (Gal 3:3), one may note the motif of re-creation in *Joseph and Aseneth*. In praying for Aseneth's conversion, Joseph links the image of God the creator to that of God the new creator: "Lord God . . . who gave life to all things and called them from the darkness to the light, and from the error to the truth, and from the death to the life, you, Lord, bless this virgin, and renew her by your spirit, and form her anew by your hidden hand, and make her alive again by your life . . ." (*Jos. Asen.* 8:9; cf. Stuhlmacher,

by entering the people of Israel, you will fill up the vast number of descendants God promised to Abraham.[60]

You say that you have already been converted by Paul? We say that you are still in a darkness similar to the darkness in which not long ago you were serving the elements of the cosmos, supposing them, as Abraham once did, to be gods that rule the world.[61] In fact, the fights and contentions in your communities show that you have not really been converted, that Paul did not give you the divinely ordained antidote to the Impulsive Desire of the Flesh, the guidance of God's holy Law, the perfecting observance of which is commenced in the circumcision of the flesh (Gal 5:15). Being an unfaithful student of the Law-observant apostles in the mother church of Jerusalem, Paul has allowed you to remain a group of sailors on the treacherous high seas in nothing more than a small and poorly equipped boat. He gave you no provisions for the trip, no map, no rudder, and no anchor. In a word, he failed to pass on to you God's greatest gift, the Law.[62] But that is exactly the mission to which God has called us. Through our work, the good news of God's Law is invading the world of Gentile sin.

We adjure you, therefore, to claim the inheritance of the blessing of Abraham, and thus to escape the curse of the Impulsive Desire of the Flesh and sin (Gal 1:4a; 3:18; 5:16). For, be assured, those who follow the path of the Flesh and sin will not inherit the Kingdom of God, lacking the perfection of virtue given by the Law (Gal 3:3). It is entirely possible for you to be shut out (Gal 4:17). You will do well to consider this possibility and to tremble with fear.[63] For you will certainly be shut out unless you are truly incorporated into Abraham by observing God's glorious and angelic law. Turn therefore in true repentance, and come under the wings of the Divine Presence, so that with us you shall be saved as true descendants of father Abraham.

"Erwägungen"). See also *Jos. Asen.* 15:5 ("renewed and formed anew and made alive again"); cf. 16:16; 18:9.

[60] *Asc. Jas.* 1.42.1 (Van Voorst, *Ascents,* 57; Jones, *Ancient Source,* 72).

[61] Martyn, *Theological Issues,* chapter 8.

[62] Ps.-Clem. *Ep. Pet. Jas.* 2:3 (HS 2.112).

[63] Cf. *Jos. Asen.* 10:1–3.

19

PAUL AND THE OPPONENTS OF THE CHRIST-GOSPEL IN GALATIA[1]

Nikolaus Walter

In this essay I will develop the hypothesis that Paul, in his letter to the Galatians, was striving with a Jewish countermission threatening to draw the Galatian Christians away from the gospel of Christ but that this conflict was not with a *Christian* Judaistic mission. Indeed, in Paul's letters we are used to finding Christian opponents of the Pauline mission under the direction of a non-Pauline branch of early Christianity, especially among the "Judaistic" Christians somehow connected to the Lord's brother James in Jerusalem.[2] Yet, in my opinion, some of the (unstressed) information provided by Luke in Acts (20:3; 21:27–29; 22:22; 23:12–15; cf. 21:20–24), in Matt 23:15, and not the least in the pre-Christian activities of Paul himself indicates that already in the time of early Christianity there were not only attempts by Jews to hinder the missionary work of Paul but also the development of an active Jewish countermission against the spread of the Law-free Christian (especially Pauline) gospel. How is this shown in Galatians?

The countermissionaries in Galatia proclaim "another gospel" because they want to "change the gospel of Christ into its opposite" (Gal 1:6f.). The alternative that they offer is thus not another version of the Christ proclamation but the opposite of a gospel of Christ: a gospel without Christ Jesus. In this respect, the situation here should not be confused with Corinth, where the so-called apostles of Christ actually preach "another Jesus" and in this sense proclaim "another Gospel" (2 Cor 11:13; cf. v. 4). In Galatia, on the contrary, the opponents are obviously using a missionary

---

[1] Translated from Walter, "Paulus" (1986) by Mark D. Nanos, with assistance from Peter Spitaler and Cisca Verwoerd, and revisions by the author. For a somewhat longer version of this argument (in German) see Walter, "Paulus" (1997). Ed.

[2] Because of the shortness of this article, it is impossible to describe the *communis opinio* regarding the opponents of Paul or enter the discussion of whether they might be Christian "Judaists" or early Christian "gnostics." Compare the introductions in commentaries and especially Schmithals, "Judaisten," as well as Lüdemann, *Antipaulinismus.*

trick: they use the persuasive word εὐαγγέλιον (a term that they derive from Paul) for their own message, which instead turns away from Christ.

They reprove Paul, saying that *his* gospel is not from God but, rather, from men (this accusation becomes clear from Paul's reaction from Gal 1:1 onwards). In what way is it not from God? In my opinion, it is precisely that Paul himself appeals to Jesus the Christ. Not even the Jesus-believing Jews in Jerusalem, who had acknowledged Jesus of Nazareth as the Messiah, would have called him a "Son of God" in the sense of the Christology of preexistence. Even less could the Jews who did not believe in Jesus see in him anything other than a "human being." For them, the message of Paul was, in any case, at best a "human message"; even worse, really, it was blasphemous. The message questioned the universal validity of the Torah, and at the same time it did so by appealing to Jesus, the crucified—that is, to one whom God had publicly handed over to a curse (Deut 21:23; Gal 3:13–14). To put such a human being against—indeed, even over—the Torah was a "scandal" (5:11b). Moreover, the opponents of Paul had received God's own word, the Torah, which God had given to Moses on Sinai.

Paul defends himself in the following way:

> I know the Torah very well, and thus once had—zealously, just like the opponents now—persecuted the Gospel of Christ. But my call for the Gentile mission was "revealed" to me directly from God [διὰ ἀποκαλύψεως], and this call came in such a way that God revealed to me Jesus, whom I had persecuted until then, as His Son [1:12–13]. Therefore I cannot now, for the sake of pleasing people, give up my service of Christ [1:10b]. Certainly, Jesus the Christ was crucified. But as he is the Son of God, his crucifixion was not for anything he himself had committed, but rather it was for our misdeeds that this took place [2:20b; 3:13–14]. Therefore, it is now according to God's own will that the law is no longer valid for us; or rather, that we no longer exist for the law [2:16–21]. The Torah by which these false "evangelists" try to impress you now came, on the contrary, only indirectly from God, being received by Moses through an angel [3:19]; moreover, this happened very late, long after the promise was given to Abraham [3:17]. To be sure, this too is actually mentioned in the Torah, but it was announced and valid long before the Torah was given. Yet this Torah has no saving power; in itself it could not bring life [3:21b], but could only prepare in a negative way for that which is better, for the faith which came with Jesus Christ [3:22–25].

Apparently the opponents held against Paul his alleged present dependence on both Peter and James. In other words, they depicted his dependence as something that devalued his message. Their argument does not run in the direction that one would expect from Jewish Christians (as is usually assumed, anyway). That is, the opponents do not argue, "We alone have the right connections to the original apostles; Paul does not." For, if this were the case, it would be tactically unwise for Paul to be so explicitly involved in depreciating his relations with the Jerusalem Christians by seeking to create a sense of distance between his relationship to them and the origin of his Christian identity and apostleship (1:15b–22). His assertion of truthfulness in 1:20

cannot be understood except that he was being blamed for dependence upon the original apostles rather than God.

The opponents saw Peter, James, and Paul as joined together in the same group, and they suspected them of together betraying the essentials of Judaism. Yet the most dangerous seemed to them to be Paul, the most important representative of this group, the most active practitioner of a mission to the Gentiles. Apparently they did not accuse those from Jerusalem of such a programmatic and active transgression of the boundaries of Judaism. Paul reacts to the accusations defensively, although he is not entirely comfortable with this reaction. He appeals to the sanctioning of his law-free mission to the Gentiles through the same Jerusalem apostles who are known by everyone as pious law keepers—even by the Jews of Jerusalem who did not believe in Jesus (for James, the reference in Josephus is well known, *Ant.* 20.200). It has always stood out that Paul speaks of this (before-mentioned) appreciation of the original apostles with a measure of aloofness, "reputed to be something" (δοκούντων εἶναί τι, 2:6; cf. 2:2 and 2:9). In fact, the insertion in 2:6b puts this into perspective. It is important to note that the labeling of those from Jerusalem as "pillars" (στῦλοι, 2:9) is to be interpreted with this in view. The only comparable Jewish use of this metaphor is one wherein exceptionally pious and righteous ones are being called "Light of Israel and Righteous Pillars."[3]

The way interpreters usually find the authority of James, Cephas (Peter), and John signified as leaders of the original community in Jerusalem fails to fit this context. Yet it would be hard to understand why Paul would refrain from pronouncing this kind of respect, since Paul cares enough about the validity of the agreement reached with them to reproach Peter (and Barnabas) sharply for later disregarding this agreement (2:11–14). For tactical reasons, then, Paul makes clear the faithful law keeping of the original apostles in Jerusalem to the evangelists of the Torah in Galatia: "Those who are commonly known as 'respected,' they see the law-free mission to the Gentiles not as 'betrayal' of the Torah and Judaism, but as fulfillment of the will of God newly revealed in Christ Jesus."

A recent article by J. Louis Martyn provides an important fact to add to the discussion.[4] The opponents also carry out a mission to the Gentiles; of course, in distinction from Paul, they offer this as an invitation into the people of God (by means of circumcision); that is, they promote proselyte conversion. How do they justify their activity against Paul? The answer Martyn gives brings out the point clearly: God gave the promise in Abraham, that in him "all nations" should be blessed (Gen 18:18; cf. 12:3). We must dare to recognize that the Jewish missionaries genuinely pursue a mission and that their opposition to Paul's work is not their primary purpose. One

---

[3] Cf. Str-B 1.208 (bottom), 1.581 (end), as well as 3.537. For a discussion, compare, e.g., Vielhauer, *Oikodome*, 16; U. Wilckens, "στῦλος," 7.734–35. See further Walter, "Die 'als Säulen Geltenden.' "

[4] Martyn, "Law-Observant Mission." According to Martyn the opponents (the Teachers) are representatives of a Christian Judaic mission that was at work independently from Paul but appeared in Galatia only after Paul.

has to see it from their perspective as an unavoidable side effect, as was once the case for Paul as well, *mutatis mutandis.*

It is evident that, because of the propaganda of his opponents, Paul takes up in Galatians (and then in Romans) the important theme of "Abraham as the Father of believers."[5] This subject became part of Paul's theological repertoire in the same way his opponents adopted, vice-versa, the term εὐαγγέλιον from Paul. How does Paul answer the opponents with respect to Abraham? First, he establishes through histori- cal exegesis that the Torah is more recent than the promise to Abraham (Gal 3:17) and also of inferior rank (3:19): the promise came, then—in distinction from Torah—from God directly, just as does the gospel of Christ now! Second, and closely connected to the first point, Paul concludes that Abraham's justification before God (Gen 15:6) was not on the basis of Torah but on the basis of "faith" (πίστις). Third, Paul then brings to their attention that, on the basis of Gen 22:18, the promise to Abraham was linked with a "seed" (σπέρμα) of Abraham (in the singular!)—and this seed has come in Christ Jesus, no one else (Gal 3:14–16). But if the opponents were Christians, then such an argument would not have scored the necessary point! (And Paul does not use this exegesis of Gen 22:18 again in Rom 4:13ff., referring there rather to the "descendants"—as already in Gal 3:19.) Finally, Paul denies affiliation, with the legitimate children of Abraham (from Sarah, the "free"), to any Judaism that is bound to the service of Torah. Instead Paul traces their roots back to Abraham's concubine Hagar, whom he allegorically associates with Sinai, the mountain of the Torah (4:21–31). This is an extremely discriminatory argument (which Paul does not repeat again in Rom 4 or 9–11). It is only understandable against the background of Paul's terror at the opponents breaking into the community of the Galatians, whom he had won for Christ; this polemic is hardly appropriate to use against Christian competitors.

Paul did not have Christians in view but, rather, opponents who are calling people away from faith in Jesus Christ to an adherence to the Torah in trust based on God's promise to Abraham for the Gentiles. This is finally clear from the shocking and beseeching address in Gal 3:1 (cf. 5:7): The Galatians have lost their minds, they have been bewitched! Paul has shown them "Jesus Christ as publicly portrayed as cru- cified" (3:1). Now that image of Jesus Christ should be again wiped out from the eyes of the Galatians! And thus the difference that has been dissolved in Jesus Christ be- tween Jew and Greek, between master and slave, between man and woman (3:28; cf. 6:15) would again be enforced! Paul asks the Galatian Christians,

> Do you really want to stumble into the slave-yoke of being under the Torah? Al- though you have not realized this to date, it is what the opponents recommend to you as "gospel" without telling you that it is slavery that you are taking upon your- selves [5:1ff.]. Would you want this after you have just become freed of your pagan slavery under the "elements of the world" [4:3; cf. 4:8]? After all, in Christ you have everything: you are God's children [4:1–7], you have a wonderful freedom [5:1], for you are already heirs to the salvation promises given to Abraham [3:29]. If you now

---

[5] So ibid., 357–61.

let yourselves gain entrance by the preaching of the circumcision missionaries [cf. 5:11–12!], then you do not have—as they want to make you believe—more, but rather you will have less than now. You will lose everything: Christ and the grace of God [5:4; cf. 2:20–21], freedom [5:13], the new creation that God has done among you [4:5ff.; cf. 6:15]. From God, who called you to all of this, certainly such propaganda [πεισμονή] does not come [5:8].

A final observation—which is also noted by Martyn[6]—may be useful. In his letter Paul does not speak directly with the opponents, but rather he warns the readers, the Christians, in a very strong fashion about them. They are not thought of as present, therefore, when the churches assemble. Surely Paul speaks similarly in 2 Cor 10–13 concerning the "super-apostles" in Corinth. Yet the situation there is different, and clearly so in the sense that the opposing apostles work *within* the community in order to revolutionize the situation according to their own understanding. Paul announces hard action against them insofar as the community itself can or will not turn against them. But Paul does not distance himself from the opponents to the point of cursing them as he does in Galatians (cf. Gal 1:8–9)! Must we, then, not assume that the opponents actually stand outside the churches, outside any relationship with Christ, and that they do not desire so much to specifically invade the churches as, rather, on the contrary, to undermine and eliminate the churches by means of "compelling" the Galatians away from Christ toward the Torah (cf. 6:12–13)?

The whole of Galatians can be read under the hypothesis merely sketched out here, although it is—for the sake of necessary brevity—not possible to go into every relevant passage or to prove every important point at this time. It is important to note that although a closer description of the Jewishness of the opponents remains beyond the aims of this project, if such a description were attempted, the obstacles to precision would be no greater than those faced by interpreters who identify the opponents as Jewish Christians. Moreover, it seems to me that the proposal offered here explains some issues that arise in the exegesis of Galatians better than do those which follow from the common assumption that the Galatian opponents of Paul are to be identified as Judaistic Christ-believers.

---

[6] Ibid., 349–52; the conclusions I have drawn from these observations, however, clearly differ from those of Martyn.

20

MIRROR-READING A POLEMICAL LETTER: GALATIANS AS A TEST CASE

John M. G. Barclay

1. Introduction

I recently heard Professor Christopher Evans describe the New Testament as "a bad-tempered book." He was alluding to the fact that an extraordinarily high percentage of the documents in the New Testament are steeped in polemics, arguing with opponents (real or imagined) who were perceived to be an external or internal threat to the writer's Christian community. One has only to think of Matthean attacks on the Pharisees, Johannine polemic against "the Jews" or the schismatics, and Petrine abuse of "the dogs who turn back to their own vomit" to realize the extent of the New Testament's "bad temper"; and that is without considering Paul, who is, perhaps, the most belligerent of them all.

If we are to understand such polemics, we must make every effort to clarify the origin and nature of the relevant dispute; and an indispensable ingredient of that effort will be the attempt to reconstruct the attitudes and arguments of the other side in the debate. However much we may be predisposed to *agree* with the New Testament authors' arguments, we will not *understand* their real import until we have critically reconstructed the main issues in the dispute and allowed ourselves to enter into the debate from *both* sides. But here we run up against a formidable obstacle. In most cases we have no independent witness to the arguments of those under attack in the New Testament; our only access to their thoughts and identities is via the very documents which oppose them. Hence the necessity for one of the most difficult and delicate of all New Testament critical methods: we must use the text which answers the opponents as a *mirror* in which we can see reflected the people and the arguments under attack. Like most New Testament methods, such mirror-reading is both essential and extremely problematic, and it is to some of the problems and possible solutions that I want to address myself in this article.

In what follows I will discuss mirror-reading almost entirely in relation to Galatians. One could apply the same questions and observations to any polemical part of the New Testament, but I choose Galatians partly because it has been the focus of my study for a few years and partly because it provides an excellent test case for my present exercise. Here is Paul at his most polemical, thoroughly involved in extensive argument against opponents. And Galatians itself is our only reliable source of evidence for what the opponents were saying and doing in Galatia. (Acts may, or may not, help us when it comes to Jerusalem, but it says nothing about Paul's disputes in Galatia.) We must therefore address ourselves to the general problems involved in mirror-reading Galatians and the specific pitfalls that await scholars, and then work our way towards a methodology which will help us mirror-read the text with care and accuracy.

2. The Problems

Let us consider first some of the general problems which we face in mirror-reading a letter like Galatians. Using different, but equally appropriate, imagery, Morna Hooker has described our problems in deducing the nature of the "false teaching" under attack in Colossians as "an extremely difficult task, as prone to misinterpretation as the incidental overhearing of one end of a telephone conversation."[1] We are all familiar with the problems here: it is so easy to jump to conclusions about what the conversation is about and, once we have an idea fixed in our minds, we misinterpret all the rest of the conversation. But there are three features of the conversation in Galatians which add even more to our difficulties.

1. In the first place, Paul is not directly addressing the opponents in Galatians, but he is talking to the Galatians about the opponents. This means that it is not just a question of trying to piece together what is being said at the other end of the telephone, but of listening in to one side of a dialogue (between Paul and the Galatians) about a third party (the opponents). Since Paul considers that the Galatians are being "bewitched" by the persuasion of his opponents (3:1), and since the Galatians are turning all too quickly to the "other gospel" (1:6), it may be fair to conclude that, generally speaking, in answering the Galatians Paul is in fact countering the opponents themselves and their message. But there are also points in the letter when Paul is manifestly attempting to prize the Galatians away from the opponents, so that what he says to the Galatians could not be read as a direct response to the opponents. For instance, in 5:3, Paul warns the Galatians that everyone who gets himself circumcised will be obliged to keep the whole law. Walther Schmithals leaps on this verse (together with 6:13) to argue that *the opponents* were unaware of the connection between circumcision and Torah-observance;[2] but Paul is instructing the Galatians, not the opponents! Robert Jewett and others consider that, although the opponents knew very well that circumcision involved keeping the whole law, the fact that Paul has to tell the Galatians this fact in 5:3 indicates that the opponents had craftily refrained from

---

[1] Hooker, "False Teachers," 315.
[2] Schmithals, *Paul and the Gnostics,* 32–33; the argument is repeated and expanded in "Judaisten," 51–57.

passing on this information.[3] But again this is a shaky assumption; the opponents may have made very clear the duties arising out of circumcision, but Paul may nevertheless feel it necessary to hammer home their full unpalatable implications. In other words, the Galatians may be not so much *ignorant as naive.* We must remember that Paul is not directly responding to the opponents' message, but responding to its effects on the confused Christians in Galatia.

2. The second point to remember is that this is no calm and radical conversation that we are overhearing, but a fierce piece of polemic in which Paul feels his whole identity and mission are threatened and therefore responds with all the rhetorical and theological powers at his command. We hear him not just "talking" but "shouting," letting fly with abusive remarks about the Galatians (as credulous fools, 3:1–3) and the opponents (as cowards, fit only for castration, 6:12; 5:12). Jost Eckert and Franz Mussner have done well to highlight this aspect of the letter and to point out how much more difficult this makes it to reconstruct what the opponents were really like.[4] We should never underestimate the distorting effects of polemic, particularly in a case like this, where Paul is going out of his way to show up his opponents in the worst possible light, with the hope of weaning the Galatians away from them. We must take into account, then, that Paul is likely to caricature his opponents, especially in describing their motivation: were they really *compelling* the Galatians to be circumcised? And was it really *only* in order to avoid persecution for the cross of Christ (6:12)? I suspect that Jewett has taken these charges too seriously when he proposes that the opponents are acting under the pressure of Judean Zealots;[5] and I am pretty sure that Schmithals has been far too gullible in taking at face value Paul's accusation in 6:13 that the opponents (or those who get circumcised) do not themselves keep the law.[6] This is not to say that Paul could have *wholly* misrepresented his opponents and their message. If he was attempting to persuade the Galatians to abandon the "other gospel," what he says about it must have been both recognizable and plausible in their ears. Thus the letter is likely to reflect fairly accurately what Paul saw to be the main points at issue; but his statements about the character and motivation of his opponents should be taken with a very large pinch of salt.

It is worth mentioning in this connection another possibility which has been raised by some scholars, namely that Paul may have seriously misunderstood his opponents. This is an essential assumption for Schmithals' case that Paul was actually entertaining Gnostics unawares,[7] and Willi Marxsen made it a central point in his interpretation of the letter.[8] One cannot, of course, discount this possibility altogether, but one must also face its implications. If Galatians is our only evidence for what the

---

[3] Jewett, "Agitators," 336–37; cf. E. Sanders, *Paul, the Law,* 29.

[4] Eckert, *Verkündigung,* 22–26 and 234–36; Mussner, *Galaterbrief,* 27–28.

[5] Jewett, "Agitators," 338–42.

[6] Schmithals, *Paul and the Gnostics,* 33–34 and n. 51 (wrongly claiming support from Schlier and Lightfoot).

[7] See Schmithals, *Paul and the Gnostics,* 18, 47 n. 98, 52 n. 110 and 54 n. 125; Vielhauer sharply criticizes Schmithals on this point *(Geschichte,* 121).

[8] Marxsen, *Introduction,* 50–58.

opponents believed, and if, in writing Galatians, Paul labored under a major misapprehension about them, our search for the real opponents must be abortive. It is one thing to say that Paul has caricatured his opponents: handled cautiously, the text could still yield useful information about them. It is quite another thing to say that despite the whole of Gal 2:15–5:12 the opponents had no interest in the Torah;[9] that totally destroys our confidence in the only evidence we have. Of course we do not know anything about Paul's sources of information, and we cannot be sure how much he knew about events and the confidence with which he speaks about their "change of course" probably indicates a reasonable amount of information.

3. A third complicating factor lies in the linguistic problem of knowing only one partner in a particular conversation. Since the meaning of all statements is, to a large extent, conditioned by their accepted associations within a particular language community, it is especially hard to interpret statements in isolation from their historical and linguistic contexts. In the case of Galatians, while we know a little about one partner in the dialogue, Paul, and can compare the meanings he attaches to similar statements in other contexts, his ultimate conversation partners, the opponents, are unknown to us. The very statements that most directly relate to them (and which we would like to use in order to gain information about them) are also the ones whose precise meaning is determined by the particular interchange between them and Paul. Thus a verse such as 1:10 ("am I now pleasing men or God?") remains obscure until we can hypothesize the other end of the dialogue, and yet it is also among the very verses we need to use in order to reconstruct that dialogue. Such circularity is as inevitable as it is frustrating and highlights the hermeneutical problems inherent in this mirror-reading exercise.[10]

Before we go into detail about the specific pitfalls, which lie in wait for the unwary scholar, it may be helpful to offer a comparison which illustrates the difficulties of mirror-reading polemical documents like Galatians. At his enthronement as Bishop of Durham in September 1984, David Jenkins delivered a famous sermon which concluded with a number of pointed remarks about the British miners' strike. At that point both sides in the dispute seemed to be intransigent—the miners under Arthur Scargill refusing to allow that more than the totally exhausted pits be closed, and the Coal Board, led by its American-born and tough-minded Chairman Ian MacGregor, insisting on large-scale pit closures. The Government was giving tacit support to the Coal Board, not least in providing massive resources of police to prevent miners' pickets traveling around the country. Jenkins's sermon instantly hit the headlines because he criticized the Government and referred to Ian MacGregor as an "elderly imported American." A few days later, the Secretary of State for Energy, Peter Walker, wrote a reply to Jenkins which was published in *The Times*.[11] It occurred to

---

[9] This is the weakest part of Schmithals's thesis, renounced even by those who follow his interpretation in other respects.

[10] I owe the general point here to my colleague, John Riches: see Millar and Riches, "Interpretation."

[11] Jenkins's enthronement sermon was delivered at Durham Cathedral on September 21, 1984. Peter Walker's letter was printed in *The Times* on September 25, 1984.

me to wonder how accurately Walker had answered Jenkins's arguments and, with the present methodological question in mind, how well we would do in reconstructing Jenkins's sermon on the basis of Walker's reply alone. Having obtained the full text of Jenkins's sermon I was able to run the experiment, with the following results. Taking Walker's letter, we would know that Jenkins had said that the miners should not be defeated, had implied that the Government wanted to defeat them, had pointed out the problems of a pit-community if the pit closes down, and had made some derogatory remarks about Mr. MacGregor (although, interestingly, we would not know about his specific reference to the "elderly imported American" or his suggestion that MacGregor should resign). Since Walker gives a lengthy exposition of the Government's concern for the coal industry, we might suppose that Jenkins had cited some detailed statistics to show the Government's neglect of miners. How does this compare with what Jenkins actually said in his sermon? The most striking feature of the comparison is that Jenkins's comments on the miners' strike take up less than a quarter of his sermon, so that from Walker's reply alone, one would be totally ignorant of three-quarters of the Bishop's total message. Moreover, although we were right in deducing some of the content of Jenkins's remarks, Walker's reply gave us no hint that Jenkins had also said there should be no victory for the miners on their present terms, that Arthur Scargill should climb down from his absolute demands, and that criticisms could be made of the Government's use of police and the complacent attitude of society as a whole. While Jenkins made specific suggestions about Mr. MacGregor which Walker did not pick up, he did not make detailed allegations about the Government's economic record as we might have supposed from Walker's letter. Thus this polemical reply turns out to be a response to a very limited range of issues. It takes particular care to rebut allegations which bear on the personal responsibility of the writer (as Secretary of State for Energy); and it tends to polarize the issues, playing down points on which the two antagonists actually agree. And all this in a setting where the respondent had full access to the facts of the case (he had clearly read Jenkins's sermon) and was obliged to conduct his argument with reason and restraint in an effort to win over skeptical readers of *The Times* like me!

If this situation is at all analogous to Galatians, it may be instructive. I realize there are important points of difference, which mostly induce one to have less confidence in the value of Paul's letter as accurate evidence about his opponents than one can attribute to Walker's letter. It does suggest, however, that there are many aspects of the opponents' message that we can know nothing about because Paul chose not to reply to them. There may also have been many points on which Paul and his opponents agreed but which are submerged by the polarizing effect of his polemic. Moreover, on the analogy of Walker's detailed personal defense, we must acknowledge the possibility that Paul's lengthy self-defense in Galatians 1–2 may not be a reply to a number of specific allegations (as is usually assumed), but may simply pick up almost incidental remarks about his personal credentials.

For all these reasons, the mirror we are trying to use may not be as smooth and clear as we would like. We have to reckon with the possibility that its image is distorted and hazy. Now we see "through a glass darkly"; and unfortunately we can entertain no hopes of meeting Paul's opponents face to face!

3. The Pitfalls

Thus far we have considered some of the major problems which plague any attempt to mirror-read a polemical letter like Galatians. We can now turn to look in more detail at some of the recent attempts to mirror-read Galatians which exemplify the dangerous pitfalls in such an enterprise. Four dangers are particularly noticeable in this regard:

1. The first we may call the danger of *undue selectivity*. In attempting to discern the opponents' message from the text of Galatians we have got to make some decisions as to which of Paul's statements are particularly revealing for our purpose. Tyson, who addresses himself to the methodological issues more fully than most, confines his search in Galatians to Paul's defensive statements, where Paul answers the opponents' accusations.[12] But this is surely unduly restricting, since much, perhaps most, of the opponents' message may have been entirely free of accusation against Paul; it is interesting that Tyson can make little of the arguments about Abraham and Scripture in Galatians 3–4, although here, if anywhere, Paul seems to be replying to his opponents' arguments.[13] Mussner follows a slightly different tack, isolating possible slogans and objections emanating from the opponents and now reflected in Galatians.[14] Again, while this may be of some help, we have surely got to end up with a reconstruction which can explain the whole letter as, in some sense, a response to the crisis brought about by the opponents. The problem of undue selectivity is highlighted even further by those scholars who read the letter entirely differently. Schmithals dismisses all of Galatians 3–4 as current "topoi" in Paul's debate with Jews, while the real character of the opponents is revealed in Galatians 5–6, where it can be seen that Paul is responding to pneumatic and libertine Gnostics.[15] We clearly need some criteria by which we can judge which are the most revealing of Paul's statements, while also taking seriously the need to provide an explanation for the entire letter.

2. The second pitfall is the danger of *over-interpretation*. In a polemical letter like this we are inclined to imagine that every statement by Paul is a rebuttal of an equally vigorous counter-statement by his opponents. But a moment's reflection will reveal that this need not be the case at all. In 5:11 Paul raises a forceful question: "But if I, brethren, still preach circumcision, why am I still persecuted?" We are inclined to

---

[12] Tyson, "Opponents."

[13] This has been plausibly argued by Barrett, "Allegory." See also Martyn, "Law-Observant Mission."

[14] Mussner, *Galaterbrief,* 13, listing "Schlagworte" and "Einwände."

[15] Schmithals, *Paul and the Gnostics,* 41–43, 46–55; because Paul's exhortation is directed against "ecstatic licentiousness," "it is sufficiently clear that people in Galatia were preaching circumcision but for the rest were thinking and living in libertine rather than legalistic fashion" (52).

mirror-read this as a reflection of a criticism by Paul's opponents, who *accused him* of still preaching circumcision.[16] But it could also be no more than a simple contrast between Paul and his opponents, reminding the Galatians that he, Paul, is in a totally different category from them; in this case *no explicit accusation* need be posited. Or we could even read this verse, as Peder Borgen has suggested, as Paul's reply to a claim made by the intruders in Galatia who *saw themselves as Paul's allies* and were pleased to show how much they were in accord by implying that he, like them, circumcised his converts.[17] Indeed, although I will call them "opponents" all the way through this article, we must bear in mind the possibility that they did not see themselves in opposition to Paul. It is quite possible for Paul (or anyone else) to count as his foes those who thought they were supporting him!

The same dangers of over-interpretation bedevil the use of other parts of the letter. Because Paul claims he was not dependent on the Jerusalem authorities or any other men in Galatians 1–2, Schmithals jumps to the conclusion that he was being explicitly *accused* of such dependence, and that the only people who would voice such far-reaching accusations would be Gnostics.[18] But again, there are a number of other possible explanations for Paul's line of argument in Galatians 1–2 which do not require one to posit any such Gnostic accusations.'[19] Or take Paul's argument about being children of Abraham in Galatians 3: Ropes made a quite unnecessary assumption when he took this to be directed against Gentiles who denied the value of Abraham and the Jewish tradition.[20] And how should we interpret Paul's commands in the ethical section 5:13–6:10? If Paul warns the Galatians about immorality and drunkenness in his list of "the works of the flesh," need we assume, with Lütgert and Schmithals, that there were at least some Galatians Christians who indulged in such libertine excesses in a wild pneumatic license?[21] Or if he encourages those who live by the Spirit to walk in the Spirit, need we take this, with Jewett, as an indication that the Galatians consciously denied the significance of any earthly behavior?[22] In all these cases the scholars concerned would have done well to reflect on the ambiguities of mirror-reading and to take into account a range of other less extreme possibilities.

3. A third pitfall awaits those who are guilty of *mishandling polemics*. I have already mentioned the inevitable distorting effects of polemical debate and cautioned against taking some of Paul's descriptions of his opponents too seriously. Although we can be fairly sure that they wanted the Galatians to be circumcised, we should be a lot less confident that this had anything to do with "making a good showing in the flesh" or "avoiding persecution for the cross of Christ" (6:12). Because Paul constantly pits the cross against the law and circumcision (3:1, 13; 5:11; 6:12, 14–15),

---

[16] See, e.g., Bruce, *Commentary*, 236–37; compare the more cautious approach by Betz, *Galatians*, 268–69.

[17] Borgen's interesting thesis is set out in two articles: "Observations" and "Paul Preaches." A similar argument is put forth by Howard, *Crisis*, 7–11.

[18] Schmithals, *Paul and the Gnostics*, 13–32.

[19] See the discussion of this passage by Dunn, "Relationship."

[20] Ropes, *Problem*, 4–11.

[21] Lütgert, *Gesetz.*

[22] Jewett, "Agitators," 344–47.

many scholars have concluded that the opponents, who taught the law and circumcision, must have *played down* the message of the cross.[23] But can we be so sure about this? They may have been entirely happy to talk about the cross, even emphasize its saving significance, only failing, *in Paul's view,* to see its message as excluding obedience to the law. We can be fairly certain that they would have described any disagreements with Paul in rather different terms, and that some of the issues on which Paul polarizes the two camps, they would have regarded as insignificant or even irrelevant.

Another way in which Paul's interpreters have mishandled his polemics is in unduly taking sides in the debate. Those who are inclined to admire Paul tend to portray his opponents as malicious, confused and theologically bankrupt; those who prefer to "put Paul in his place" paint a picture of men who were sincere Christians, with admirable intentions and a strong theological case to argue. There is a particular danger in the temptation to dress up Paul's opponents with the clothes of one's own theological foes. I suspect this is why, in Protestant circles, Paul's opponents have so often been described as legalistic and mean-minded Jewish Christians, with a streak of fundamentalist biblicism: in exegeting and supporting Paul one can thereby hit out at Jews, Catholics and fundamentalists all at once![24] One of the most patent examples of a scholar falling into this sort of temptation is found in an essay by Helmut Koester.[25] Latching onto Paul's reference to the observance of festivals and the στοιχεῖα τοῦ κόσμου in 4:9–10, Koester concludes that the Judaizers must have emphasized the "cosmic dimensions" of the law within a context of "a mythologizing of Old Testament covenant theology." Paul then turns out to be a theological hero pitting the "history" of the cross against the covenant "myth" of the opponents; and the opponents' basic heresy is their failure to "demythologize"![26] All this, of course, has a lot to do with Bultmann and virtually nothing to do with Paul's opponents; one is tempted to say that it is Koester who is really responsible for concocting myths!

4. The fourth pitfall is that of *latching onto particular words and phrases* as direct echoes of the opponents' vocabulary and then hanging a whole thesis on those flimsy pegs. In one sense this is a further example of "undue selectivity" but it has the added ingredient of regarding certain words as the very vocabulary of the opponents. A few examples will suffice. In 6:1, Paul addresses "you who are spiritual πνευματικοί." Lütgert seized on this word, and, with the Corinthian correspondence in mind, took it to be the self-designation of a party of Galatian libertine pneumatics (the second of the two fronts against which Paul had to write his letter).[27] Schmithals and Jewett followed suit, with some modifications, and even Kingsley Barrett uses this phrase to posit the existence of a group who called themselves "spiritual" and exulted in their

---

[23] See, e.g., Mussner, *Galaterbrief,* 412.

[24] See E. Sanders's devastating critique of the familiar Protestant caricatures of Judaism (and Catholicism), *Paul and Palestinian Judaism,* 33–59.

[25] Koester, "ΓΝΩΜΑΙ.

[26] " . . . the historicity of the event of the revelation becomes the decisive criterion for the understanding of traditional theologies and mythologies. The failure to apply this criterion, i.e., the failure to demythologize, is identical with the 'heresy' of the opponents" (ibid., 309).

[27] Lütgert, *Gesetz,* 9–21.

spiritual gifts.[28] In the next verse Paul refers to "the law of Christ," and recently several scholars have argued that this unusual phrase must derive from the opponents, who saw Christ as a law-giver.[29] Or again, back in ch. 4, Paul uses a rather obscure phrase, "τὰ στοιχεῖα τοῦ κόσμου," which means "the elementary something of the world" and occurs elsewhere in the Pauline corpus only in Colossians (2:8, 20). A chorus of scholars has confidently declared that Paul must here be using his opponents' vocabulary, and that this is an unmistakable sign of their syncretistic tendencies, merging the Torah with astrological speculation.[30] To give one more example, since in 3:3 Paul talks of "beginning in the Spirit and completing in the flesh," a number of exegetes have concluded that the opponents also talked of "beginning" (with Paul's gospel) and "completing" or "perfecting" (with their instructions).[31]

Although none of these suggestions is entirely impossible, I regard all of these attempts to mirror-read single words or phrases with some suspicion. One needs to spell out exactly what assumptions are involved here. Such an exercise depends on: (a) Paul's knowledge of the exact vocabulary used by his opponents; (b) Paul's willingness to re-use this vocabulary either ironically or in some attempt to redefine it; (c) our ability to discern where Paul is echoing his opponents' language; and (d) our ability to reconstruct the meaning that they originally gave to it. Such is our uncertainty surrounding each of these assumptions that I regard the results of any such exercise as of very limited value. They should certainly not be used as the cornerstone of any theory, as has all too often been done in recent scholarship on Galatians.

At this point I would like to make a few comments on a recent book by Bernard Brinsmead, which is the latest detailed attempt to reconstruct the character and propaganda of Paul's opponents in Galatia.[32] Despite his good intentions and his awareness of the methodological problems involved, Brinsmead manages to fall into all four pitfalls I have mentioned, and a good few more beside. To pick up an example we have just discussed, Brinsmead takes Paul's reference to beginning and completing in 3:3 as an echo of his opponents' vocabulary and then goes on to specify exactly how they used that vocabulary: ἐνάρχεσθαι, he tells us, "often has the meaning of an act of initiation," while ἐπιτελεῖν "commonly means a performance of ritual or ceremony which brings to completion or perfection."[33] This indicates that these terms "may comprise a technical formula for progress in a religious mystery from a lower to higher stage."[34] On this, very shaky, foundation Brinsmead swiftly builds the opponents' theological position: their message had "mystical connotations" and offered circumcision as a sacramental rite of perfection! Within the space of a few pages a

---

[28] Barrett, *Freedom*, 78–79. The adjective could be a perfectly innocent description of those who walk in the Spirit (5:16, 25).

[29] This suggestion was apparently first made by D. Georgi (see Betz, *Galatians*, 300; but I can find no indication of authorship in the text he cites in his n. 71). Betz supports it.

[30] See, e.g., Schlier, *Galater*, 202–7; Wegenast, *Verständnis*, 36–40.

[31] See, e.g., Jewett, "Agitators," 342–43; Oepke, *Galater*, 101.

[32] Brinsmead, *Galatians*.

[33] Ibid., 79.

[34] Ibid.

"suggestion" has become a "certainty" and a whole hypothesis has been built out of a tissue of wild guesses.

What makes Brinsmead's book so disappointing is that he thinks he has found a way of solving the problems of mirror-reading. In a genre-analysis of the text, largely dependent on Betz, he takes the epistle to follow the rules of a law-court defense-speech and to be a continual dialogue with the opponents. But this new methodology solves none of our problems and, in Brinsmead's hands, sometimes creates even more. In distinction from Betz, Brinsmead treats 5:1–6:10 as a "refutatio" (he never explains why), the part of the speech which is supposed to answer the opponents' arguments.[35] Having imposed this alien rhetorical description on what is a perfectly innocent piece of ethical exhortation, Brinsmead ransacks the material to find what Paul is answering here and concludes that where Paul uses *traditional* forms (catalogues of vices and virtues or words of the Lord), these must represent *the opponents' ethical traditions*. As if this totally unfounded assumption is not enough, Brinsmead then compares these catalogues with those in 1QS 3–4 and, noting the similarities, jumps to the conclusion that the opponents advocated an Essene theology and ethics![36] So far from unravelling the complexities involved in interpreting a dialogue, Brinsmead leaps from one incredible assumption to another. His book well deserves David Aune's wry comment that it is "justified only by faith"![37]

4. A Possible Methodology

From what I have said so far one might be tempted to conclude that I consider mirror-reading a polemical text to be an impossible undertaking; in fact, George Lyons has recently written it off as an unworkable technique.[38] Actually I think it is a good deal more difficult than is usually acknowledged, but not wholly impossible. What is needed is a carefully controlled method of working which uses logical criteria and proceeds with suitable caution. The following are what I consider to be the seven most appropriate criteria for this exercise:

1. *Type of utterance.* a. If Paul makes an *assertion,* we may assume that, *at least,* those to whom he writes may be in danger of overlooking what he asserts, and *at most,* someone has explicitly denied it; in between those two extremes there is a range of feasible suggestions, including the possibility that his audience have forgotten what he now reminds them about. b. If Paul makes a *denial,* we may assume that, *at least,* those whom he addresses may be prone to regard what he denies as true, and *at most,*

---

[35] Ibid., 44, 53–54, 163–81.

[36] Ibid., 164–78.

[37] See Aune, "Review of Brimstead, *Galatians.*"

[38] Lyons, *Pauline Autobiography,* ch. 2; see, e.g., 96: "The 'mirror reading' approach to the interpretation of Galatians may be challenged on several bases. It may be shown that the methodological presuppositions on which it rests are arbitrary, inconsistently applied, and unworkable." He is particularly, and rightly, critical of those who assume that every Pauline denial is a response to an explicit criticism from his opponents (105–112). But the paragraphs below may go some way to meeting his objection that the whole method is impossibly speculative and unscientific.

someone has explicitly asserted it; again, between these two extremes there is a range of other possibilities.[39] c. If Paul issues a *command, at least,* those who receive it may be in danger of neglecting what he commands, and *at most* they are deliberately flouting it; again their condition could also be anywhere between these two poles. d. If Paul makes a *prohibition,* there must be *at least* some perceived chance that what is prohibited may be done, and *at most,* someone has already flagrantly disobeyed him; but perhaps it is a case of action being performed in naive ignorance (or a host of other possibilities).[40] Thus each type of statement is open to a range of mirror-images, and one must beware of rash over-interpretation. One can only decide where in this range of possibilities the truth lies when some of the other criteria are brought into play.

2. *Tone.* If Paul issues a statement with emphasis and urgency (he has a variety of ways of doing so), we may conclude that he perceives this to be an important and perhaps central issue. Conversely, the casual mention of an issue probably indicates that it is not, in his view, crucial to the debate.

3. *Frequency.* If Paul repeatedly returns to the same theme it is clearly important for him; conversely, an occasional remark probably signals what he considers to be only a side-issue.

4. *Clarity.* We can only mirror-read with any confidence statements whose meaning is reasonably clear. Where interpretation hinges on an ambiguous word or phrase (or on a contested textual problem), or where we have good grounds for suspecting that Paul's "description" of his opponents is polemically distorted, we cannot employ that evidence for any important role in our hypothesis.

5. *Unfamiliarity.* While taking into account our limited knowledge of Paul's theology, we may be entitled to consider the presence of an unfamiliar motif in Paul's letter as a reflection of a particular feature in the situation he is responding to.

Most of these criteria are framed in terms of "mays" and "mights," which indicates that they need cautious handling, with all due sensitivity to the particular document under consideration. Taken together they should enable one to form some sort of hypothesis which can then be further tested by the last two criteria:

6. *Consistency.* Unless we have strong evidence to suggest that Paul is responding to more than one type of opponent or argument, we should assume that a single object is in view. Thus the results of the previous criteria may be tested to see if they amount to a consistent picture of Paul's opponents.

7. *Historical plausibility.* At this point we can bring into play what other evidence we have for contemporary men and movements which could conceivably be the object of Paul's attacks. If our results are anachronistic or historically implausible for some other reason, we will be obliged to start again.

---

[39] Betz rightly notes that "not everything that Paul denies is necessarily an accusation by his opposition" (*Galatians,* 6). Lyons, however, fails to explore the range of other possibilities when he concludes that, since Paul's denials need not be directed against specific charges, they "are often, if not always, examples of pleonastic tautology used in the interest of clarity" (*Pauline Autobiography,* 110).

[40] Hooker, "False Teachers," 317: "Exhortation to avoid a certain course of action certainly does not necessarily indicate that those addressed have already fallen prey to the temptation, as every preacher and congregation must be aware."

The conscientious application of these criteria may mean that there is only a limited number of facts which we could determine with anything like certainty. But this does not mean that they are excessively negative. New Testament scholars need to learn to be more candid in admitting the real value of their theories, and there is a good case for establishing a sliding scale of hypotheses ranging between "certain" and "incredible."

J. Louis Martyn suggests that we need to employ both "scientific control" and "poetic fantasy" in this matter.[41] I am not sure that "poetic fantasy" will help us much, but I agree that one should be able to discuss hypotheses which are not proven beyond doubt, so long as one recognizes their proper status. Ed Sanders does a useful job in this regard, constructing a range of categories into which we may assign hypotheses (in his case, about the historical Jesus). His range runs from "Certain or Virtually Certain," through "Highly Probable," "Probable," "Possible" and "Conceivable" to "Incredible."[42] Although one could quibble with the semantics, I think these would be useful categories into which one could place one's findings after mirror-reading a letter like Galatians.

5. Results

The main purpose of this discussion is to outline some of the methodological issues involved in mirror-reading Galatians. Given the limitations of space it is not possible to attempt a full-scale reconstruction of the opponents' message and identity, but it may help to clarify the application of the seven criteria just mentioned if I conclude with a brief statement of plausible results.[43]

On the basis of Paul's reference to "another gospel" (1:6–9) it seems clear that the opponents were Christians. Whether they were Jewish or Gentile Christians is slightly less certain because of the ambiguity in the phrase οἱ περιτεμνόμενοι in 6:13 (and the associated textual uncertainty). But in view of verses like 4:30 (apparently meant to apply to the opponents) it is highly probable that they were Jewish. Certainly it would be precarious to build an important thesis about their Gentile origin on 6:13 alone (as did Munck; see criterion 4). Paul associates their message with circumcision, both explicitly (6:12–13) and implicitly (5:24, 11–12), and the emphasis and frequency with which he discusses this subject make it clear that he regards this as a central issue (criteria 2 and 3; cf. 2:3–5). It is doubtful that they could or would actually *compel* the Galatians to get circumcised (6:12; cf. 2:14) but they clearly presented their argument with some persuasion (3:1) and won the esteem of many Galatians (4:17). What is more difficult to assess is why they advocated circumcision, since Paul's verdict in 6:12 is partial and probably misleading.

---

[41] Martyn, "Law-Observant Mission" (1985), 313.

[42] E. Sanders, *Jesus*, 326–27.

[43] I have set out detailed argumentation for most of the following statements in Barclay, *Obeying the Truth*.

This issue is closely bound up with another: to what extent were they serious in advocating the observance of the Torah? 4:10 indicates that the Galatians had begun to observe some of the Jewish calendrical requirements, and it is unlikely that that was as far as the opponents wanted them to go. In fact Paul's concern about "works of the law" (3:1–10) and his extended arguments to prove the temporary validity of the law (3:6–4:11), taken together with remarks like 4:21, make it highly probable that the opponents wanted the Galatians to observe the law as circumcised proselytes (criteria 2 and 3). 5:3 is open to a range of interpretations (criterion la), although those offered by Schmithals and Jewett find no support in any of the rest of the letter or from any other of our criteria; certainly 6:l3a looks very like an exaggerated polemic point. Taking the argument of the letter as a whole, there is sufficient evidence that the Galatians were informed of (and responded warmly to) the requirements of Torah-observance as the hallmark of the people of God.

This may indeed be confirmed by the evidence of the "paraenetic" section (5:13–6:10). The use of these verses to provide evidence for a libertine group or gnostic/libertine tendencies should be questioned in the light of criterion 1 (c and d) which emphasizes the range of possible reasons for a command or prohibition. There is no evidence in this section, or elsewhere in the letter, which would support taking these verses as a reply to Gnostics or libertines (see again criteria 2 and 3). In some instances Paul is explicitly reminding the Galatians of their duties (5:19–21) and in others the abuses he attacks are not specifically libertine (5:15, 26). (In any case all two-front or Gnostic theories run aground on criteria 6 and 7.) In giving his exhortation Paul appears intent on demonstrating that walking in the Spirit is a sufficient alternative to living under the law (5:14, 18, 23; 6:2). If the opponents wanted the Galatians to observe the law they probably argued that only the law could properly regulate their daily life.

It is very probable that another of the opponents' lines of argument, which we may again see reflected in Paul's reply, was an appeal to Scripture, and in particular the Abraham narratives. Paul's repeated references to Abraham (3:6–29; 4:21–31) support this suggestion (criterion 3), while his convoluted use of certain texts may indicate that he is countering their persuasive biblical exegesis (criteria 1 [a and b] and 5).

Paul's extended self-defense in Galatians 1–2 makes it virtually certain that the validity of his gospel and his apostleship was under attack. Unfortunately it is difficult to be more precise about any particular "charges" since, as we saw above, even quite detailed self-defense can be triggered off by a very few damaging innuendos. However, in the light of 1:1, 10–12 and Paul's repeated attempts to specify his relationship to the Jerusalem apostles, it is probable that the opponents considered Paul to be an unreliable delegate of the Jerusalem church (criteria la and b, taken together with criteria 2 and 3).[44] 5:11 may also reflect an accusation that Paul sometimes circumcised his converts, but as an implicit denial it is open to the range of

---

[44] I would maintain this even in the face of Lyons's vigorous argument that no apologetic motif is present here (*Pauline Autobiography,* chs. 2–3). I fail to see how Paul's detailed description of his

interpretations suggested by criterion 1b and is not elucidated by any other criteria (see Section 3 above).

The questions of the opponents' origin and motivation are even harder to answer. The prominence of Jerusalem in this letter (as well as Galatians 1–2, see 4:25–26) probably indicates that they had some links with the Jerusalem church; but they could have come from Antioch or almost any other church which included Jewish Christians. It would certainly be going beyond the evidence to identify them with the "false brethren" at Jerusalem (Gal 2:4; cf. Acts 15:1–5) or the circumcision party at Antioch (2:12). Given Paul's ironic but not wholly negative attitude to "those in repute" at Jerusalem, it is inconceivable that "the pillars" had actually commissioned Paul's opponents. It is not impossible that the opponents were acting under Zealot pressure in Palestine (so Jewett), but such a thesis hangs rather precariously from the single thread of Paul's comment in 6:12.

It is conceivable that at some points Paul echoes the exact vocabulary of his opponents: they may possibly have referred to the στοιχεῖα τοῦ κόσμου and the law of Christ and described their purpose as completing Paul's work, but at least in the first two cases we are still in the dark about what they meant by such phrases.

We may then tabulate these results as follows:

Certain or Virtually Certain

1. Paul's opponents were Christians.
2. They wanted the Galatians to be circumcised and to observe at least some of the rest of the law, including its calendrical requirements.
3. They brought into question the adequacy of Paul's gospel and his credentials as an apostle.
4. Their arguments were attractive and persuasive for many Galatians Christians.

Highly Probable

1. They were *Jewish* Christians.
2. They argued from Scripture using, in particular, the Abraham narratives.
3. They expected the Galatians to become circumcised proselytes and to observe the law, as the hallmark of the people of God.

Probable

1. They had some links with the Jerusalem church and thought that Paul was an unreliable delegate of that church.

---

movements in 1:17–24 can fit Lyons's conclusion that the only purpose of Paul's autobiography is "as a paradigm of the gospel of Christian freedom which he seeks to persuade his readers to reaffirm in the face of the threat presented by the troublemakers" (171; cf. 158–61). Lyons has not taken sufficient account of Paul's repeated emphases in these chapters, or the fact that the troublemakers must have considered Paul's work in Galatia insufficient.

2. Their scriptural arguments made reference to Genesis 17 and the Sarah-Hagar narratives.

Possible

They told the Galatians that Paul circumcised his converts in some circumstances.

Conceivable

They talked of "completing" Paul's work, made reference to the law of Christ and used the word στοιχεῖα.

Incredible

1. They were Gnostics or gnosticizing to an appreciable degree.
2. They were libertines or played on the Galatians' "Hellenistic libertine aspirations."
3. They were syncretists with cosmic or mystical notions about circumcision, the law or keeping festivals.
4. They were directly commissioned by the Jerusalem apostles.
5. Paul was fighting against two distinct groups.

I am well aware that this is not a complete list of those things that we can know about the opponents; but I hope it illustrates the role of the criteria outlined above and the value of collating material on a graduated scale of certainty. Having drawn up this list one could go on to compile a much longer one of all the things that we do *not* know about the opponents, either because we cannot see them clearly enough in Paul's mirror or because he chose not to reflect them at all. I will not indulge in such a tedious exercise, although it should perhaps be a requirement of all serious historical work.[45]

One could also draw up an interesting list of points on which Paul and his opponents would have agreed. This would include at least the following points:

1. Scripture, God's word, is now reaching its fulfillment through Christ.
2. Salvation is now available to Gentiles, in fulfillment of the promises to Abraham.
3. The Spirit has been given to the people of God who believe in the Messiah.
4. God's people should abstain from idolatry and the passions of the flesh.

Such a list would show how much Paul and his opponents had in common and thus help to correct the impression of complete disagreement which the letter to the Galatians conveys.

---

[45] I recall the late Sir Moses Finley starting his Cambridge lectures on ancient Sparta with the sobering (if somewhat exaggerated) statement, "We know nothing about ancient Sparta"!

I am aware that the results tabulated above are not particularly surprising or innovative. It is probably true that a critical methodology like this will tend to be most effective in questioning fashionable but flimsy attempts to build some new reconstruction of the opponents and their message. That is not to say, however, that interesting new things cannot be said on the basis of these results. However, my primary aim has been to discuss the methodological issues involved in mirror-reading a polemical letter. If these cautionary notes and positive suggestions are of any value, they could equally well be applied to Colossians, 2 Corinthians 10–13, the Johannine letters or indeed any other of the many polemical parts of the New Testament.

21

THE ARGUMENTATIVE SITUATION OF GALATIANS

B. C. Lategan

If I understand my assignment correctly, my task is not so much to offer a discussion of the theoretical concept "argumentative situation" as to try to describe what this situation is in the case of Galatians. However, in order to do the latter, it will first of all be necessary to clarify some basic concepts. In a second part, the ways and means whereby the argumentative situation can be established will be illustrated from the text of Galatians. In a final section, results of the exercise will be summarized in a comprehensive sketch of the argumentative situation.

The "Argumentative Situation"

What is this so-called "argumentative situation"?

No argument is necessary in a situation where matters are self-evident. It is only when questions arise or doubt exists that argumentation is called for. According to Perelman and Olbrechts-Tyteca, the domain of argumentation is that of the credible, the plausible, the probable, to the degree that the latter eludes the certainty of calculations.[1] Argumentation aims at persuasion. It presupposes the "meeting of minds." The way in which such persuasion can take place is one of intellectual contact through language. "The indispensable minimum for argumentation appears to be the existence of a common language, a technique allowing communication to take place."[2]

Argumentation therefore presupposes both an issue and a *Gegenüber*, or an audience which is to be persuaded regarding the issue in question. Issue and audience are indissolubly bound together and the one provides clues for the other. For Perelman and Olbrechts-Tyteca, it is important to distinguish between at least three

---

[1] Perelman and Olbrechts-Tyteca, *New Rhetoric*, 1.
[2] Ibid., 15.

types of audience: the universal audience, the single interlocutor and the subject him/herself.[3] For the analysis of Galatians as we shall see, these distinctions are of special importance. A member of parliament may formally be addressing the Speaker, while he or she is in fact trying to persuade fellow members, or speaking to a public audience outside parliament. For this reason, Perelman and Olbrechts-Tyteca prefer to describe the audience as "the ensemble of those whom the speaker wishes to influence by his argumentation."[4]

The next important point is that—in the process of argumentation—the audience is always *constructed* in the mind of the speaker or the writer. From reception theory we have learned that the implied reader is a literary construct, not a person of flesh and blood. However real the Galatians or Paul's opponents were as historical *personae*, when Paul is writing to them, he has an *image* of them in his mind. It is from this image or construct of who they are and what will be important to them, that he develops his argument. In order to persuade them, he has to start where they are and use arguments that will be persuasive for them. "In argumentation, the important thing is not knowing what the speaker regards as true or important, but knowing the views of those he is addressing."[5] At a banquet, the dishes are made to please the guests, not the cooks.

The audience, or rather readership, plays an important role in determining both the quality of the argument and the strategy of the writer. In this sense, the audience is an interested party in the process of communication. But in order to move the reader, there must also be a dialectic tension between the present position of the reader and where the writer would like him or her to be. If the reader is merely flattered, his position remains unaltered and no persuasion takes place. Quintilian's definition of rhetoric as *scientia bene dicendi* implies that the orator should not only be good at persuading, but should also say what is good.[6] The argumentative situation therefore implies a "battle of wits." The question is which of the two interested parties (writer or reader) will become the dominating one.

It is in the interplay between writer and audience that we find clues to the issue involved, to the disposition of the audience and the aim of the writer—all elements of the argumentative situation. Like on a record, the reverberations of the initial communication leave their imprint on the tracks, where a sensitive stylus can pick them up again.

What is the difference between the argumentative and the rhetorical situation? In essence we are dealing with the same concept, but with a difference in focus. In the rhetorical situation, attention is in the first place directed to the *strategies* used by the writer to effect persuasion. In the argumentative situation the emphasis is on the *issue* regarding which persuasion is attempted.

---

[3] Ibid., 30.
[4] Ibid., 19.
[5] Ibid., 24.
[6] Ibid., 25.

The Argumentative Situation in Galatians

What is the argumentative situation in Galatians? And how do we go about determining the contours of this situation? A wide variety of indications are to be found on different levels of the text. In this section we shall discuss some of these to illustrate how the argumentative situation can be pieced together from this information.

Audiences

The first line of enquiry to consider is the anticipated audience or readers of the letter. Gal 1:2 identifies these explicitly as ταῖς ἐκκλησίαις τῆς Γαλατίας. But who exactly are the constitutive members of these churches? As we go along, it would seem that we are dealing with at least three categories of readers:

(1) Those who are still uncircumcised and who are considering taking this step (5:2). There was a time that they did not know God and when they were slaves of gods who were no real gods (4:8). Paul takes great pains to explain that Gentiles may also share in the blessing originally bestowed on Abraham—ἵνα τὴν ἐπαγγελίαν τοῦ πνεύματος λάβωμεν διὰ τῆς πίστεως (3:14). The identification of Paul with the position of the Gentiles is significant, as we shall see presently. There can be no doubt that Gentiles are part of his audience—if not the dominant part.

(2) Those who are Jews by birth and not Gentile sinners (2:15). It is uncertain whether this statement is still part of the original conversation with Peter, or whether Paul has a wider audience in mind. The continuation of 2:16b makes it quite clear that Paul is referring to the position of Jews—with whom he again identifies himself by using the first person. Paul may be speaking to Jews who are genuine members of the Galatian churches, or he may be speaking, through them, to those who are sowing confusion and who are trying to distort the gospel (1:7).

(3) Finally, Paul may also be addressing a universal audience. In 2:17–20, he uses the first person, not in a personal, autobiographical sense, but as an "*überindividuelles ich*," which transcends the confines of a specific historical setting and which assumes a certain timeless quality. Here Paul is also addressing—by accident or design—contemporary readers of the letter.

The audience in Galatians is therefore of a complex nature. Or rather, Paul argues his case from all possible perspectives and in the process assumes different and even contrasting positions. The remarkable fact is that he can relate to each of these, as indicated by the use of the first person plural. The theological basis for the relationship is that, whatever the starting point—be it Jew or Greek, slave or free person, man or woman—the prerequisite of faith and the existence in faith remains the same (3:28).

The complexity of the audience is an indication of the complexity of the argumentative situation and serves as a warning to the interpreter to proceed with caution. John Barclay reminds us that we are dealing with a polemical work.[7] Paul is not

---

[7] Barclay, "Mirror-Reading," 369; *Obeying the Truth*, 37.

giving a comprehensive and disinterested exposé of his opponents' position, but attacks them with every weapon at his disposal. Because of the polemical nature of the text, we cannot assume that every statement Paul makes is the reverse of an accusation made by his opponents. Barclay provides the following guidelines for what he considers to be a more appropriate form of mirror-reading:[8] (1) Each type of statement (assertion, denial, demand, command, prohibition) is to be open to a range of interpretations. (2) A statement with emphasis and urgency may indicate a real bone of contention. (3) Repetition may suggest an important issue. (4) An ambiguous word or phrase is a shaky foundation on which to build. (5) An unfamiliar motif may reflect a particular feature in the situation responded to. (6) Consistency is to be maintained in drawing a picture of the opponents. (7) The results are to be historically plausible.[9]

However, these criteria cannot be applied in a mechanical way. For example, repetition often occurs without any special significance. The first priority is to uncover the main line of Paul's argument before further details can be added. In this respect it is important to settle the question whether the apostle is defending his gospel on two fronts.

One or Two Fronts?

Wilhelm Lütgert already suggested that Paul is involved in a dual defense: against legalistic Judaizers (3:1ff.) and against antinomian libertinists or pneumatics (5:13ff.).[10] Jewett does not see the latter as a separate group. According to him, libertinism existed among the Galatians right from the start of the church there, before nomism was imported by Jewish Christians under Zealot pressure.[11] Betz sees a connection between the introduction of the Torah and libertinism.[12] After a period of initial enthusiasm, the "flesh" became a problem in Galatia. This created an opening for Paul's opponents to introduce the acceptance of and adherence to the Torah as a solution to the problem.

It is clear that the two-front hypothesis hinges on an assumed connection between "flesh" and antinomism. The reference to σάρξ in 5:13, the dualism between σάρξ and πνεῦμα in 5:17 and the ἔργα τῆς σαρκός of 5:19 are understood as an indication of antinomian libertinism. But the catalogue of vices in 5:19–21, which certainly contains πορνεία and ἀκαθαρσία, includes much more than what is usually associated with libertinism, for example εἰδωλολατρία, φαρμακεία, ἔχθραι, and ἔρις. And from 5:16 and 5:18 it is clear that a "fleshly" existence is equivalent to an existence under the law. The connection between flesh and law is reinforced by the allegory of Hagar and Sarah (4:21–31). Those who are of the Sinai covenant and upholders of the law are like Ishmael who was born according to the flesh (4:19) and

---

[8] Barclay, *Obeying the Truth*, 40–41.
[9] In what follows, I make grateful use of Hong, *Law*.
[10] Lütgert, *Gesetz*, 513ff.
[11] Jewett, *Paul's Terms*, 209–12.
[12] Betz, *Galatians*, 253ff., 271ff.

who persecuted the one born through the Spirit. The rhetorical question in 3:3 puts the contrast very clearly: "You have started with the Spirit (by accepting the gospel through faith)—do you now want to end with the flesh (by fulfilling the demands of the law)?"

It would seem that in Galatians we are dealing not with two, but only one front. What is said about the flesh in chapter 5 is directly linked to the argument in the "theological" section of chapters 3 and 4. What we do very clearly have in the letter are two modes of existence—one of slavery under the law and one of freedom in Christ. These two modes, described in different ways, are the consistent feature of the letter as a whole and form a kind of backbone which runs through all the chapters. This binary structure is reminiscent of what we find elsewhere in Paul, as in 2 Cor 3:1–18. For Galatians, Hong has summarized the main elements of the antithetical structure:[13]

1:6–10	the gospel of the opponents *versus* the gospel of Christ
3:1–14	justification by the works of the law *versus* justification by faith in Christ
3:23–4:7; 4:21–31	slavery under the law *versus* freedom of sonship in Christ
5:1–12	circumcision *versus* faith
5:13–6:10	the flesh *versus* the Spirit
6:12–16	circumcision *versus* the cross of Christ

The Position of Abraham

A further important *topos* for determining the argumentative situation is the person and position of Abraham. The frequent reference to this figure in chapters 3 and 4 is an indication that he must have featured prominently in the presentation of the Galatians' opponents. Apparently his position as father of the believers was emphasized. Consequently, descent from the patriarch was a serious matter. At the same time, a close link between Abraham and the law was taken for granted, which provided further authority for the demand that the law should be kept.

This presumed argument of the opponents was not easy to counter. It was supported by a very powerful concept in the Jewish tradition, namely the importance of chronological priority. This concept is perhaps best illustrated by the position of the firstborn. Not only does the firstborn represent and characterize what is to follow, but as heir designate he is in an unassailable position. The first fruits represent the full harvest; as firstling of those raised from the dead, Christ is the guarantee that the dead will be raised (1 Cor 15:20). The "first" also retains its importance elsewhere in Paul (cf. Rom 8:23; 11:16; 16:5; 1 Cor 16:15; 2 Thess 2:3). The issue of priority in time and position is what lies behind the Adam/Christ parallels. Christ may be a new or a second Adam, but how can the new order that he brings have precedence over or replace what has been established by the first Adam? So powerful is this concept that Paul has to resort to an unusual measure by arguing from the pre-existence of Christ:

---

[13] Hong, *Law.*

Before Adam was, Christ was. Therefore, the order established by the second Adam is in reality the real order.

Possession is nine points of the law and Paul cannot ignore the opponents' argument of historical and hierarchical precedence: The law represents the very essence of Judaism and from the very beginning determined its character. How can Paul ever suggest that the law has lost its prominence and that believers no longer even have to do the works of the law?

Paul can only counter this argument by taking it seriously and following it to its logical conclusion. If the opponents set such a great store by the person of Abraham as the one with whom God made his covenant, let us take a closer look at his position. What was his *original* position? When he was called, he was uncircumcised and without law. His relationship with God rested purely on faith and he lived only by the promise of God. The law which came 430 years *later* (3:17) can alter nothing of this original order. If the Jews want Abraham as their spiritual father and model (and Paul would wholeheartedly support this!), they must take him as he was—uncircumcised, without the formalized law—in fact, a Gentile—who trusted God and his promise and acted only out of faith. In this way Paul not only turns the opponents' argument around on the basis of their own premises, but he also opens a perspective which makes it possible for Gentiles to identify with Abraham and—*mirabile dictu*—even become the legitimate heirs of his promises. This provides us with another clue to the argumentative situation.

Descendants of Abraham

The prominence of the kinship issue in Galatians 3 and 4 would seem to indicate that this was an important *topos* in the debate—the opponents could present themselves as the true descendants of Abraham. They had all the credentials for such a claim and they, as authentic Jews, were really the ones who could determine what Christian existence entailed—and that certainly included circumcision and upholding the law.

The issue of kinship forms part of a much wider complex of relationships which all deal with the status of the believer in the new existence of faith. The occurrence of σπέρμα, κληρονόμος, υἱοθεσία, νήπιος, υἱός, ἄββα, πατήρ and ἀδελφοί shows how widely this concept permeates Paul's thinking in Galatians. What we are dealing with is an involved process of "resocialisation,"[14] in which a transition between two theological positions, between two world views, between two semantic universes is effected. By means of the text, an alternative understanding of reality is articulated. But the articulation is not an end in itself. The intention is to move the reader to a new self-understanding, to establish a new conviction, to get him or her to act in a different way. The text therefore becomes an instrument of persuasion.[15]

---

[14] Petersen's term *(Rediscovering)*.
[15] Cf. Sternberg, *Poetics*, 475–81.

In the case of Galatians, kinship relations and, more specifically, the concept of the family of God is used to effect such a transition. The adoption as children of God is made possible through the redeeming action of the Son of God, but this becomes reality for the individual only when the new relationship is articulated and appropriated through the call of the Spirit of the Son of God in the heart of the believer: "*Abba!*" (Gal 4:4–6). The implication of this transcendental articulation for everyday reality is made clear when Paul addresses the Galatian believers as "brothers" (4:12; 6:1). "One becomes what one is addressed as."[16] The *salutatio* of the letter corpus is the most eloquent form of the articulation of the new status of the believers, with a constant reference to God, the (or, our) father (Rom 1:7; 1 Cor 1:3; 2 Cor 1:2; Gal 1:1–4; Eph 1:2; Phil 1:2; Col 2:1; 1 Thess 1:2; 2 Thess 1:2; 1 Tim 1:2; 2 Tim 1:2; Titus 1:4; Phlm 3).

The metaphor of the family enables Paul to set up an anti-structure as alternative to the claims of his opponents, who trace their line of ancestry directly back to Abraham. Here again Paul accepts the basic premise of their argument: Abraham is indeed the decisive figure, also for Gentile converts. But by redefining the essential relationship between God and Abraham in terms of Gen 15:6 ("He believed God and because of his faith God accepted him as righteous"), it becomes possible to redescribe the basis of descent as that of faith (3:7: "The real descendants of Abraham are the people who have faith"). Therefore Gentile believers *can* become true-blooded children of Abraham (3:8). They can share in the blessing given to Abraham by God (3:14). But the argument runs on. Because Christ is the real descendant of Abraham (3:16), believers are not only related to Abraham, but become children of God (3:26)—a status which is confirmed not only juridically by the formal adoption as children (4:5), but also existentially by the testimony of the Spirit who calls out in their hearts: *Abba!* (4:6).

This anti-structure of the real family of God is continued with logical consistency in the allegory of Hagar and Sarah, which eventually leads to the freedom motif being announced as the *topos* of the last two chapters (5–6; cf. 4:31). Paul's strategy is to develop new self-understanding in the minds of his readers. He starts off with the premise of his opponents, which is then redefined and eventually leads to totally different conclusions.

What is achieved by means of the family metaphor has consequences for a much wider set of social relations. In his argument Paul is not only dealing with the Galatians' relationship to the Jewish tradition, but also with the way in which the alternative semantic universe he is proposing affects other social relationships in their world—for example, slave and free man, man and woman, Jew and Greek.

Playing for the Gallery?

Before we look at a final set of indications which has relevance for the argumentative situation, it is important not to overlook the small but significant piece of evidence in 1:8–9. Why does Paul follow his double curse against those who preach a

---

[16] Petersen, *Rediscovering*, 165.

different gospel with the rhetorical question: "Does this sound as if I am trying to win man's approval?"

The reference to "man's approval" is not merely an introduction to the main theme of the first chapter which follows in 1:11–12, but discloses a sensitivity to what appears to be an accusation by the opponents that Paul is playing for the gallery by preaching a soft or easy gospel—one without the rigor of the law. The fact that he is willing to utter a curse—and repeat it to make sure there is no misunderstanding—is meant to disprove any thought that he is trying to curry favor with the audience or that he is not willing to offend people if necessary to protect the truth of the gospel. On this point Paul appears to be especially vulnerable.

Responsible and Creative Ethics

A final set of data we need to consider is the nature of Paul's ethical instructions in the last two chapters of the letter. The way in which he develops an alternative ethics is very instructive with regard to the argumentative situation of Galatians.

A remarkable feature of Galatians is the apparent underdeveloped nature of Paul's ethical statements. Although opinions differ on how the epistolary structure should be understood, there is general agreement that only chapters 5–6 can be classified as *paraenesis*. But even a superficial look at these chapters reveals the relative scarcity of explicit ethical commands or directions. The first definite paraenetic statements appear only in 5:13ff. But even then, specific instructions are only given in 5:13 and 16—the rest are either theological motivation for the instructions or illustrations of what is meant.

A structural analysis of the so-called paraenetic section of the letter (5:1–6:10) reveals that two pivotal commands provide the framework for the series of loose ethical injunctions in the rest of the section. The first is the command to stand firm in the freedom which Christ has made possible (5:1), the second is the command to walk in the Spirit (5:25). The two are structured in a parallel way. Both appear twice in this section: the call to freedom in 5:1 and 13, and to walk in the Spirit in 5:16 and 25. In both the indicative/imperative sequence is clear: "Christ has set us free for freedom. Stand therefore firm (in this freedom) . . ."; "If we live through the Spirit, let us walk in the Spirit." This parallelism extends to other elements in the paraenetic section, resulting in a series of binary oppositions in which *freedom, Spirit* and *fruits of the Spirit* are set against *the yoke of slavery, flesh* and *works of the flesh*.

The freedom/Spirit motif therefore forms the backbone of the ethical injunctions of the last two chapters and provides an insight into the way Paul's ethic functions. Three observations are of importance:

(1) Firstly, the strong and almost overwhelming theological basis of his ethic is clear. Everything which is said in chapters 5–6 is closely connected and flows from the preceding theological argument. This argument is even extended into the paraenetic section. After the freedom statement in 5:1, the apostle interrupts himself to recap the theological rationale for this call in 5:1–12. In a similar way, the ethical injunctions are interspersed with theological dictums (e.g., 5:14, 18, 24; 6:3, 5, 7–8).

(2) Secondly, Paul's style is very subdued, almost conciliatory. There is no attempt to "lay down the law" and there is no reference to his authority as apostle in this section. An appeal is made to what his readers already know or should know and the consequences of the two lifestyles (in the Spirit and in the flesh) are set out as something self-evident. In contrast to earlier parts of the letter where the distance and tension between Paul and his audience are underlined, inter alia, by the use of the second person, the inclusive first person sets the tone for the paraenetic section ("Christ has set *us* free . . ."; "if we live by the Spirit, let *us* . . ."; "let *us* not become boastful . . ."; "let *us* not grow weary of doing good . . ."). Although the loose collection of *sententiae* is not without some kind of structure,[17] there is no attempt to develop a rigid system of conduct or a complete set of rules that is then prescribed in an authoritarian style to the readers as a new or alternative code of law. The way in which Paul refers to the law in these chapters is very instructive. In 5:14 it is deliberately used in the form of its classic summary and not in the sense of a casuistic system. At the end of the list of virtues in 5:22–23, the cryptic comment is added: "No law is against these things." The fruits of the Spirit do not constitute a new law. They are not cast in the form of commands or instructions, but represent a summary of the self-evident results flowing from a life controlled by the Spirit. At the same time, they do not contradict any kind of law—on the contrary! Paul is describing the characteristics of the new existence in faith, which is attained without mediation of or recourse to the law. Responsible ethical conduct is possible without enablement by the law. For a proper understanding of what constitutes ethical behavior for Paul this is an important clue, to which we shall return later. Finally, the enigmatic reference to the "law of Christ" in 6:2 is probably an ironic play on the opponents' defense of the Mosaic Torah and certainly not an endorsement of the law.[18]

(3) Thirdly, when the content of the ethical instructions is considered, there is very little (if anything at all) that could be described as distinctly "Christian." In particular, the list of virtues and vices in 5:19–23 is a typical Hellenistic phenomenon. Such lists express those values and ideals which reflect the moral conventions of the time and one gets the impression that Paul, rather than developing a distinctive—qua content—Christian ethic, is demonstrating that the fruits of the Spirit are neither in conflict with Jewish custom nor with current Hellenistic morality.

Taking all these factors into consideration, one might be justified in talking of an "ethical deficit" in Galatians. In the light of the Galatians' need for practical guidelines and more concrete help in forging a new lifestyle as believers, this deficit is all the more puzzling. Why this apparent reluctance to develop a fuller and more distinctive ethic? I would like to suggest that the key to this question lies in two important theological concerns that shaped Paul's thinking in these matters. The first relates to a shift in the theological basis for Christian action and the second has to do with a new understanding of what it means to be ethically responsible.

---

[17] Betz, *Galatians*, 292.
[18] Ibid., 300–301.

In his interaction with the Galatian churches, Paul has in the first place gained a clearer understanding of the relationship between faith and action. The heart of the theological argument in his letter is that salvation does not come from the "works of the law," that is, being rewarded by God for obeying the law, but from "faith," that is, trusting God's promise of justification, made possible by the event of the cross (3:1–14). This basic shift was motivated, inter alia, by the surprisingly positive reaction to his preaching by non-Jews (including the Galatians). Because these converts initially accepted the gospel without the law, that is, without a Jewish background and without prior knowledge of the Torah, Paul was forced to rethink his understanding of the function of the law. Could it be—contrary to all that he as a Jew unquestionably accepted thus far—that the law was *not* essential for salvation? That it even could prevent believers from understanding the true nature of salvation? The fundamental shift from the dominance of the law was an experience of liberation for Paul. And this liberation at the same time became the hallmark of a new existence in faith—an existence in which the ethical conduct of the believer could also only be understood in terms of freedom (5:1, 13).

The implication of this freedom of the law for the ethical conduct of believers is twofold:

Firstly, such conduct can no longer be conceived of as motivated either by fear (punishment) or by gain (reward). It is now understood as the exercise of responsibility—a responsibility which flows from the theological self-understanding of the believer, which implies discretion and which must be executed in freedom. The change from "works" to "faith" therefore alters the essential *nature* of ethical conduct.[19] It is this change which is threatened by the message of Paul's opponents—purportedly offering practical guidelines for the everyday life of the believer, but in actual fact relieving him or her of the responsibility of independent ethical decisions. This would mean a return to the "flesh" after the Galatians had started with the Spirit (3:2).

It is for this reason that Paul avoids any misunderstanding that he is replacing the Torah with a new "law" or that the believers now only have to follow a new set of rules. There is no new "system" to be learned or to be played.[20] Despite the attractiveness of his opponents' message, Paul resists the temptation to offer a similar solution, for fear that it will merely confirm the misunderstanding he is trying to rectify. That is why he provides his readers with the barest essentials to illustrate what the nature of the new life should be. What appears to be an "ethical deficit" is in fact an "ethical minimum," which is the consequence of the theological nature of the new existence in faith.

The second implication of cutting the umbilical cord of the law is that the believer is no longer restricted to one ethical tradition. But it also implies that the theological basis of Christian ethics up to that point has fallen away and will have to be redefined.[21] This redefinition has already been given in the concentrated Christological formulation of 2:19–20. Paul uses the metaphor of death in a double sense, on the one hand, to explain the finality with which the law is left behind and, on the

---

[19] Cf. Betz, "Problem der Grundlagen," 202.
[20] Cf. Strecker, "Autonome Sittlichkeit," 871.
[21] Cf. Betz, "Problem der Grundlagen," 200.

other hand, why the cross is the start of a new existence. In this way the cross mediates between two modes of existence. This mediation concerns not only the theological basis of the transformation, but the ethical content of the new life.[22] It is a life in faith and a life for God, of which the ethical "style" is at the same time exemplified by the event of the cross. The mode is one of love and of service (2:20: ἀγαπήσαντος and παραδόντος). Theology and ethics remain inseparable in Paul's thinking.

On the one hand then, the severance from the law makes it possible in principle for Paul to consider all kinds of ethical traditions, including and especially Hellenistic codes.[23] On the other hand, the theological redefinition provides the criterion on how these traditions are to be used.

The Hellenistic context of the Galatians' churches renders it only natural that Paul will concentrate on traditions and concepts with which his audience are most familiar. But this does not mean that he takes over Hellenistic material at random and uncritically. Exactly because of his new theological *Selbstverständnis*, ethical injunctions cannot be added arbitrarily or exist as a separate body of instructions, unrelated to his theology. At the same time, the generalized dictums, metaphors, precepts and codes of his Hellenistic environment are not without their religious undertones. *"Religiös betrachtet war daher die antike Moral keineswegs neutral, sondern sie war 'heidnisch.'"*[24] The development of a responsible and functional ethical approach therefore not only requires from Paul a careful sifting of available material, but also that he should consider its compatibility with his theological principles. One of these principles, as we have seen, is that of the freedom to make responsible choices and to consider all traditions. There is a certain universality which characterizes the new Christian existence and which makes Hellenistic moral concepts a natural area for consideration—an opportunity which Paul exploits to the full.[25] But it is also crucial to place that which is compatible within a theological framework. Galatians gives clear evidence of how Paul goes about to achieve this. The list of (common Hellenistic) vices is characterized as "works of the flesh" (5:19), while the list of virtues comes under the caption "fruit of the Spirit" (5:22). In this way the link with the theological framework is made—as we have seen, "flesh" and "spirit" function as code words for the two modes of existence (5:16–18). In a similar way, the theological thread runs through all the *sententiae* which follow in 6:1–10: "those who are spiritual" (6:1); "the law of Christ" (6:2); "God" (6:7); "flesh" and "spirit" (6:8); "faith" (6:10). In this way substance is given to the freedom and universality of the new existence in faith, but understood in the context of its theological framework.[26]

The second theological concern which guides the development of Paul's ethical thinking in Galatians is the ideal of a creative and participating ethic. On the one hand, Paul is seeking to enable and empower his readers and, on the other hand, he is

---

[22] Cf. Lategan, "Defending," 429–30.

[23] Cf. Strecker, "Autonome Sittlichkeit," 871; Furnish, *Theology and Ethics,* 72.

[24] Betz, "Problem der Grundlagen," 200–220.

[25] Cf. Malherbe, "Paul," 13.

[26] For an indication of how Paul achieves a theological setting in 1 Thessalonians in the same way, see ibid., 12.

enticing them to participate and to follow a hands-on approach. It is because of the former—the issue of empowerment—that the indicative/imperative sequence is such a fundamental feature of Paul's ethical teaching.[27] Because one is free, one must exercise freedom (5:1); if one is spiritual, one must act in a spiritual way (5:25). It is part of the apostle's pastoral concern for his readers that he does not tire of reminding them who they are. They are liberated and therefore they must think and act in a liberated way. He expects of them to be responsible and independent. Then they will need neither him nor the crutches of a casuistic system.

In addition to empowerment, Paul is aiming at participation. In the context of reception theory, much attention has been devoted to the production of meaning and the role that the indeterminacy of the text plays in this process. An important concept developed by Wolfgang Izer is that of intentional "gaps" in the text.[28] These gaps usually refer to breaks in the narrative sequence when the story is approached from a different perspective or suddenly developed in another direction. The imagination and participation of the reader are required in order to fill in these gaps. Although Galatians is not a narrative text, the concept of indeterminacy is useful for explaining the peculiar strategy Paul is following in his paraenetical instructions. He restricts himself to the bare minimum and describes the duties of believers in very general terms, forcing them to fill in the details and use their imagination in doing so. Typical is his concluding exhortation: "Let us work for the common good of all, but in particular for the good of fellow-believers!" (5:10).

Instead of giving them detailed instructions which would relieve them of making independent decisions and which would encourage the drift back into the old mind-set of earning their salvation and gaining points for good ethical behavior, he deliberately leaves them with gaps and cryptic remarks which require the cooperation, imagination and creativity of his readers. Gaps in the text of Galatians are therefore more than a literary device to ensure participation. They constitute a cornerstone of what Paul considers to be the essential mental attitude and ethical orientation of converts to the gospel. By encouraging independent decisions and responsible ethical behavior, he is preparing his readers for both his absence and the future. Not only will the Galatians have to cope on their own, but future generations will also have to discern what the gospel requires from them in a particular situation and find the courage to act accordingly.

From the way in which Paul develops his ethic, much can be learned about the argumentative situation of the letter.

Conclusion

In conclusion, let us try to formulate a provisional description of the argumentative situation in Galatians, based on the information we have collected in the previous section:

---

[27] Cf. Schrage, *Ethik,* 156–61.
[28] Cf. Holub, *Reception Theory,* 92–95.

However difficult it may be to come to a full understanding of the anti-Pauline opposition in Galatia,[29] it is clear that it was very successful on at least one point. The opponents were able to convince the Galatians that they should—in addition to faith in Christ—obey the Torah and adopt a Jewish way of life. Considering the background of most of the Galatians, it is not difficult to understand why the argument proved so persuasive. Their conversion to the Christian faith implied a complete reorientation of both their value system and their lifestyle. For Jews this transition was difficult enough, but did not entail the abandonment of their own tradition—it was rather understood as its continuation and completion. For Gentiles the break was much more incisive. They found themselves at a double disadvantage—new to the Christian faith, but also unfamiliar with its Jewish roots. As Johnny-come-latelys they were in desperate need of practical advice to guide their day-to-day life in an environment not very sympathetic to or supportive of their new convictions. Thus they were easy targets for the proponents of "another gospel." For whatever reason, Paul had—at least in their own understanding of the matter—not given them enough practical guidelines to survive as believers under these circumstances.[30] That is why they were so susceptible to the argument of the opponents. Faith in Christ was—also in the opponents' view—essential, but to translate that into action and to make it workable in everyday life, one needed a set of time-tested rules for the practice of this faith. That was exactly what the Jewish way of life could offer—it had stood the test of time, it has guided the Jewish people through the most testing and adverse times of their long history. Not only did it offer a practical guide to the Galatians, but it also provided the means of becoming part of an age-old tradition, of becoming fully initiated and accepted by the central leadership in Jerusalem. In view of the psychological needs of new converts, their acceptance into the group, their self-identity and sense of security after being cut off from their natural environment, this was a very attractive and persuasive argument.

Despite the real need of the Galatians for a more coherent and directive set of instructions, Paul studiously avoids spelling out in more detail how the congregation should behave in different situations (unlike the practical advice he for example gives in 1 Corinthians). He does this to prevent any slip back into a "works of the law" mentality. Instead, he shows the way to a responsible and participatory ethic, which not only ensures the survival of Christian freedom, but which also correlates with the true nature of the gospel as being οὐ κατὰ ἄνθρωπον.[31]

---

[29] Cf. Betz, *Galatians*, 5–9.

[30] Cf. Betz, "Problem der Grundlagen," 206.

[31] The original publication of this essay included two excursuses that have not been reproduced here: "The Metaphorical Basis of the Family of God as Anti-structure"; "Social Consequences of the Believer's New Self-Understanding (Gl 3:28)" (273–76, original). *Ed.*

22

THE INTER- AND INTRA-JEWISH POLITICAL CONTEXT OF PAUL'S LETTER TO THE GALATIANS

Mark D. Nanos

Krister Stendahl suggested that inherent in Paul's language of justification by faith is his announcement that the promised day, when God would legitimate the standing of representatives of the nations alongside Israel as promised to Abraham, had dawned in the death and resurrection of Christ. Gentiles could now be counted among the righteous ones: "I would guess that the doctrine of justification originates in Paul's theological mind from his grappling with the problem of how to defend the place of the Gentiles in the Kingdom—the task with which he was charged in his call."[1] What kind of reaction would this assertion have received among Paul's fellow Jews? More to the point for a reading of Galatians: how would Jewish communities in central Anatolia have responded to *Gentiles* claiming to be full and equal members of the communities of the righteous, on the basis of faith in/of Christ, apart from proselyte conversion?

The reaction might have been a mixture of resistance and acceptance: denial of the Gentiles' claim on its own terms, but acceptance of the Gentiles *as candidates for proselytism*—as liminals, on their way from idolatry to righteousness. And the Gentiles, in turn, might have decided that they were willing to take this path in order to gain indisputable status among the righteous ones. This would allow them to escape the continuing constraints of their present ambiguous status, which still obliged them as "pagans," according to the prevailing views of the Jewish communities and the pagan communities within which they functioned, to continue to participate in such practices as the Imperial Cult, practices no longer acceptable for Pauline Gentiles after they have turned to God in Christ (cf. 4:8–10).[2]

---

[1] Stendahl, *Paul*, 27.

[2] This seems to be the kind of practice that these former pagans are returning to "again" in view of their status ambiguity, and to which Paul objects since they are already "known by God" (cf. T. Martin, "Pagan and Judeo-Christian"), although for reasons different than Martin proposes (cf. Nanos, *Irony*, 219–24, 257–71). On the relevance of this practice for understanding the socio-political dynamics of communities in Galatia, see Price, *Rituals and Power*.

This scenario, I suggest, is the background for Galatians. Paul heard from afar that his converts were considering complying with this "other" way to negotiate the problem, and this letter contains his response.

Imagine that these Gentiles, as relative newcomers to the Jewish communities, originally had gathered around the teaching of a visitor, Paul, with no reason to re- gard him as anything but a representative Jew working within representative Jewish groups. As time passed, however, they began to be aware that within the larger Jewish communities Paul's followers were regarded by other Jews as something of a sub- group. They became aware of an edge to Paul's teaching, an "us" and "them" aspect in the way Paul's group—their group—spoke. Their group did not mix as readily with other groups in the larger Jewish communities. Although they went to the larger as- sembly on the Sabbath for the reading of the Scriptures, these Gentiles were more at- tuned to the members of their own little group than to others around them; there was an emerging "us" in the midst of a larger "them."

Following Stendahl, we may suppose that during these months they internalized Paul's proclamation of their identity as righteous ones, entitled to full and equal membership within the people of God, though remaining non-Jews. They came to believe that this proposition was "real," revealed in scripture, beyond dispute.

But then Paul left. The Gentiles ventured into larger meetings of the Jewish communities, perhaps for a holiday celebration or to hear the scripture reading or in search of jobs, since their pagan kinship and patron relations were deteriorating. There they were welcomed by some proselytes, formerly non-Jewish townspeople, perhaps old friends or neighbors.

We may assume that these proselytes, as representatives of the larger communi- ties, did not share Paul's view of the status of those Gentiles apart from proselyte con- version. When Paul's Gentile converts boldly announced their new standing among the righteous, claiming for themselves the "righteousing" power of their faith in a Judean martyr of the Roman regime, they might have been treated as confused, but sincere. They might have been gently put in their place and extended a helping hand.

Imagine this "good" message: They could indeed gain the identity among the righteous that they sought, but they had not yet completed the course by which this identity was to be won. That course, the ritual process of proselyte conversion, would indeed grant them identity as children of the quintessential proselyte and righteous one, Abraham himself. They would be honored with the identity they now claimed, legitimately, however, and not as the result of some merely half-baked notion pro- claimed by some suspicious teacher who had recently passed through town. The won- derful age of which Paul had spoken was awaited, to be sure, but it had not yet come. No, they were still to be guided by the trusted and proven traditions of the fathers, to which they should now entrust themselves, and so find the acceptance they sought.

Of course, this Gentile group is disappointed, shamed really, for their claim to honor had not been publicly recognized by those who knew and represented the communal norms.[3]

---

[3] Cf. Pitt-Rivers, "Honor"; "Honour," esp. 21–24, 72; Malina, *New Testament World*, 25–50.

They faced misunderstanding at home as well, and much more among their neighbors and coworkers. For these Gentiles were intimately associating with the synagogue—with people who embraced "foreign ways," married only among themselves, refrained from participating in the imperial cult by which the competitive commercial and religious interests of the town were advanced. Their lack of enthusiasm and even withdrawal from normal and important communal activities, family and commercial gatherings—tied up, as these were, with drinking and eating to the gods— was cause for grave suspicion. Wouldn't their behavior bring down the wrath of the town elders, if not the gods?[4] Their families and friends grew uncertain, defensive, fearful: Were these no longer of us?

These "righteous" (however labeled) Gentiles might have been able to bear these suspicions earlier because of the value they had put on a new identity: they had become the children of God, and they would make a new life among those with whom they shared this identity. But now they were informed that this was not necessarily so! They were not yet the "us" that they had imagined, but still "them." They were not entitled to consider themselves free from the constraints of their pagan identities as though full members of the Jewish communities; for example, they were not yet included among those who were freed from participation in the imperial cult by way of the daily sacrifice made in Jerusalem (cf. Josephus, *Ant.* 14.185–267).[5] What were they to do?

This other message sounded good. It offered full membership in the new community according to prevailing communal, scripture-based norms. And this course had obviously worked wonderfully for the proselytes whom they had met. These proselytes were now honored among the leaders of the Jewish community.

I suggest that whatever disagreement had arisen over views concerning Jesus, the heart of the matter in the Galatian synagogues was halakhic (thus 5:11). Attention had focused on the Gentiles' apparent (mis)understanding of their status, that they were already to be counted among the righteous. These Gentiles might have deliberated, in Paul's absence, that the "good news" offered them—that is, the prospect of full membership through proselytism—was thoroughly compatible with the good news they had already accepted from Paul. They might have reasoned they did not have time to consult with Paul; perhaps, that they did not have need.

As the letter to the Galatians demonstrates, Paul found out nonetheless and responded in a way very different from what they might have anticipated.

The Letter to the Galatians and the Political Context of Paul's Response

Paul begins his response with irony: "I am surprised that you are so quickly defecting from him who called you in [the] grace [of Christ] for a different good news, which is not another, except [in the sense] that there are some who unsettle you and

---

[4] Cf. Walker-Ramisch, "Voluntary Associations," 133–34.
[5] Cf. Cotter, "Collegia."

want to turn upside-down the good news of Christ" (1:6–7). The verb *thaumazō* signals the feigned "surprise" appropriate to a formal letter of ironic rebuke, as clearly as our "Dear John" letters signal the nature of the message to come.[6] Paul feigned parental ignorance to express his disappointment, a rhetorical approach that leaves little room for escape. His words combine sharp censure for the recipients—"who do you think you are!" (1:6–7)—with a polemical curse-wish on anyone who would bring such pressures to bear upon "his" children—"who do you think they are!" (1:8–9).

The victims would have burned with shame from such exposure, caught in the act of compromising the minority principles they once embraced for the undeniably seductive promise of majority acceptance. The pain of such exposure is palpable; but so, too, is the anguish of the one who is seeking by this drastic approach to thwart a feared betrayal.

Such ironic rebuke is insider language, the language of parents with their children. It presumes the authority to correct the wrongdoer; it intends to stun quickly and to restore the offender to the family's norms. It seeks healing, not harm, of the family fabric. Irony gains its edge from shared values.[7]

Paul's response works from the assumption that the addressees should know that this "other" message is only apparent "good news," that it is really bad for them, that it subverts the good news of Christ.

Paul struggles to ensure that the authority with which he addresses his converts from afar will not be undermined by those nearby who are "unsettling" them: "Paul an apostle—not from human agents nor through a human agency, but through Jesus Christ and God the Father, who raised him from the dead ones" (1:1; cf. 1:10). How can his converts now question what he made so clear to them before (1:9; 5:3), speaking with the authority he had directly from God? Even if he himself had previously enjoyed the highest honors from similar human beings—that is, before he received a revelation of Jesus Christ—he in no way depends upon such esteem now (1:13–16).

We may wonder whether the proselytes who have so "unsettled" Paul's converts would accept the antithesis he sets out. Were they "merely" human agents? Had Paul considered himself to be merely a human agent in his "former" manner of life? One

---

[6] Correspondence is noted with the ironic type of letter in Pseudo-Libanius, *Epistolimaioi charactēres* [56], from Malherbe, *Ancient Epistolary Theorists,* 74–75: "I am greatly astonished at your sense of equity, that you have so quickly rushed from a well-ordered life to its opposite—for I hesitate to say to wickedness. It seems that you have contrived to make, not friends out of your enemies, but enemies out of your friends, for your action has shown itself to be unworthy of friends, but eminently worthy of your drunken behavior."

See also the example of a letter of reproach in Pseudo-Libanius, and Pseudo-Demetrius, *Typoi epistolikoi,* in Malherbe, *Ancient Epistolary Theorists,* 40–41. For social implications of these letter types see also Stowers, "Social Typification," 78–90.

These observations regarding the letter type include insights from the works of, for example, Dahl, "Galatians"; White, "Introductory Formulae," 96; Mullins, "Formulas," 385–86; Stowers, *Letter Writing,* 134, 139; Hansen, *Abraham in Galatians;* idem, *Galatians.*

A brief discussion of how to recognize irony in this period can be found in Quintilian, *Inst.* 8.6.54. The ironic theorists from which these insights have been informed, ancient and modern, are too many to list here; see Nanos, *Irony,* 32–61, 298–316.

[7] Hutcheon, *Irony's Edge.*

thinks in this connection of the later rabbinic story of Rabbi Eliezer who, confirmed in a particular halakhic judgment by miracles and the very voice of God from heaven, was nevertheless overruled since "in this age" such decisions were entrusted to the world of human agents and authorities—what Paul might have called "the traditions of the fathers" (*B. Meṣ ͨia* 59b). It would be anachronistic to stretch this apparent parallel, but the passage raises the issue of the authority of revelation compared with the authority of scripture, a live concern in this period.[8]

Who Are the "Influencers"?

Paul does not name the ones influencing Paul's addressees, although he variously describes them. He and the addressees know to whom he refers. Later interpreters have labeled them variously: (1) "judaizers," (2) "opponents," (3) "agitators" or "troublemakers," (4) "teachers," among others.

(1) While *judaizing* is something that Gentiles seeking Jewish status may do, it is inappropriate for describing efforts to persuade Gentiles to seek Jewish status. As a reflexive verb it is inappropriate as a label for Jews.[9]

Moreover, in view of its negative ideological valence it is inappropriate for historical critical application. (2) It is not certain that these people actually "oppose" Paul, even if he opposes them.[10]

In view of his accusations, it is likely that his defensive posture is rather in anticipation of the response to his message should the addressees heed his instruction. (3) Calling these people "agitators and troublemakers" merely mimics Paul's value judgments; it does not advance interpretation of the situation. Such labels stereotype the motives and methods of the others in a limited and polemical way; they hardly clarify the others' identity. (4) Referring to these "others" as "teachers" avoids the value judgments implied by the other choices and describes at least a significant part of their activity.[11]

But its occupational focus may be too restrictive.

I shall call these others *influencers.* We can be certain at least that they are "influencing" Paul's converts, just as Paul seeks in this letter to "influence" the addressees to resist them. Paul is worried that his addressees have already begun the alternate course of ritual proselyte conversion (*metatithesthe,* 1:6; cf. 3:1–5; 5:1–12; 6:12–13);

---

[8] Cf. 1:12; 2:2; 1 Cor 2:7–10; 2 Cor 3:18; 4:3; Acts 9:3–19; 22:6–21; 26:12–23; Rev 1:1. The role of revelation in the interpretation of Torah or Scripture in this period varies. In Sir., wisdom is in Torah and revealed through the sages (24; 39.1–8). *First Enoch* 92–105, on the other hand, emphasizes the role of revelations in validating the proper understanding of Torah. The Qumran community possessed a revealed knowledge of the interpretation of Torah not shared by other Israelites, which was entrusted to the authority of the community leaders (esp. 1QS 5; 8), and this is revealed to and through the Teacher of Righteousness, as it had been with the fathers on behalf of Israel (CD 1–3; 1QpHab 7:1–8:3). Cf. Nickelsburg, "Revealed Wisdom," 73–82; Rowland, "Parting of the Ways," 213–37; Thompson, "Social Location," 56; M. Bockmuehl, *Revelation and Mystery.*

[9] Cf. S. Cohen, *Beginnings,* 175–97.

[10] Different, but sympathetic on this point, see e.g., Jewett, "Agitators," 342–44; Howard, *Crisis,* 7–11; Lyons, *Pauline Autobiography,* 79.

[11] Martyn, *Galatians,* 118.

he anticipates that they have already accepted as "good" this "other" message. Such actions Paul attributes to the "unsettling" influence of these people (*tarassontes*, 1:7; 5:10), their casting of the "evil eye" of envy (*ebaskanen*, 3:1), their seeking to "exclude" (*ekkleisai*, 4:17),[12] their "obstructing" of the course the addressees were running (*enekopsen*, 5:7), all in all, their seeking to "compel" proselyte conversion (6:12–13; cf. 3:2–3; 5:1–4, 10–13).[13]

We must distinguish, moreover, as Paul does, between the "others" in Galatia and the individuals he mentions in autobiographical comments about events in Jerusalem or Antioch. Any analogies with the Galatian situations or influencers that may have been drawn by the addressees in view of these narrative examples are not as clear as many interpreters suppose, as they depend upon prior knowledge that we no longer share. The latter are identified as "inspecting or informant [*kataskopēsai*] pseudo-brethren" in Jerusalem (2:4);[14] "ones from James," or "ones for circumcision," in Antioch (2:12); by implication, the "persecutors" in the allegory of Abraham (4:29). These are "influencers," too, but they are not the influencers *in Galatia*. In these references, Paul is drawing on past examples of situations elsewhere, which he and the other apostles resolved in order "that the truth of the good news might be preserved for you" (2:5).

The overwhelming consensus in modern interpretation is that these shadowy figures in Galatia were, or claimed to be, representatives or associates of the Jerusalem apostles. As such they represented "Jewish," "Jerusalem-" or "Palestinian Christianity." Paul's gospel message is imagined by most modern critics-to-be at the strongest variance with theirs—his is "Law-free," theirs is "Torah-observant." They promote what Paul regards as "another gospel," and Paul's mission and gospel remain steadfastly independent of their influence.

On this view, the letter is an attack on the error of mixing Jewish identity and behavior with the confession of faith in Christ. Recent interpreters hasten to add that Paul's criticism of things Jewish is not aimed at Jews outside of the Christ movement. This is purely an *inter-* and *intra-*"Christian" affair. Galatians is thus not really anti-Jewish.

Clearly, Paul asserts that non-Jews in Christ are not to become Jews. But does he really equate freedom in Christ for Jewish people with freedom from observance of the Torah, for Jews as well as for Gentiles? That is, does he really suggest that Jews are also to become non-Jewish? Moreover, is the sectarian identity of "Christianity" really as institutionalized as such approaches assume?

Challenging the Consensus View

As I read Galatians, the central issue between Paul and the influencers within the Galatian synagogues is at once halakhic and eschatological. The question of how Gentiles are to be incorporated into the people of God receives different answers,

---

[12] Cf. C. Smith, "Ἐκκλεῖσαι."

[13] On the conversion process in antiquity see, e.g., Segal, *Paul,* 72–114; Finn, *From Death to Rebirth.*

[14] This section and the identity of the parties involved are discussed in Nanos, "Intruding 'Spies' "; *Irony,* 147–52.

determined by the way Paul and the influencers respond to a prior question: Has the age to come dawned in Jesus Christ, or not?

We should expect Paul and the Jerusalem apostles to *agree* on this prior question. To suggest that it divides Paul and the Galatian influencers means that these influencers stand at some considerable distance from the Jerusalem apostles and the "people of James" in Antioch. In contrast to the consensus view, which tends to *align* these three groups as something of a united front over against Paul's "Law-free" gospel, I consider it crucial to isolate the data bearing directly on the identity of the influencers in the Galatian situation from the narrative discourses relating prior situations in Jerusalem and Antioch.[15]

This latter narrative material provides illustrative examples to support Paul's argument. This material includes the autobiographical remarks in 1:11–2:21; the discussion of Abraham and his rightful heirs in (3:6–24(–4:7); and the allegory of Abraham's sons in 4:22–30. *Situational discourse* occupies the rest of the letter (1:1–10; 3:1–5; 4:8–21; 5:1–6:18).[16]

Special attention should be given within this material to the epistolary opening (1:1–10), wherein Paul first sets the tone of the letter in ironic rebuke, and the closing (6:11–18), where he summarizes his perspective on the influencers and reiterates the appropriate response for his addressees.

Paul's autobiographical comments in 1:11–2:21 form a self-contained narrative unit. Paul defines his own independent revelation of the good news of Christ in tandem with the independent revelation enjoyed by the Jerusalem apostles (1:11–13, 15, 18; 2:1–2, 5, 7–9). He is *not* concerned to oppose his apostleship, mission, or message to that of the Jerusalem apostles.[17]

Indeed, Paul shows his dyadic self; his confidence "toward the Galatians" now is embedded in the mutual agreement already reached in Jerusalem on the terms of the truth of the gospel for Gentiles: Paul had not, and is not, "running in vain."

That agreement was based not on the traditions of the fathers but upon revelation (1:15–16; 2:2). God has shown all of them that Gentiles who believe in Christ are to remain Gentiles, yet to be regarded as equals with Jewish believers in Jesus (2:7–9). That is the "truth of the gospel" (2:5, 14). This agreement was satisfactory to all the apostles. When outside agents unexpectedly tested this consensus, they were turned back: Titus was not circumcised.

In Antioch, even insiders such as Peter occasionally let similar intimidation detour them from consistently honoring the coalition's "freedom."[18] Note, how-

---

[15] I do not mean by this the rhetorical device common to forensic rhetoric labeled *narratio*, referring to that part of an oration which sets out the events that have brought the case to court (see the discussion by Kern, *Rhetoric*, 104–5).

[16] See also Dahl, "Galatians"; on the transitions see the linguistic approach of Holmstrand, *Markers and Meaning*, 145–216.

[17] Sympathetic with this view are the findings of Koptak, "Rhetorical Identification," 157–68.

[18] Boissevain, *Friends of Friends*, esp. 170–205, for general discussion of coalitions and group identities. His defining of coalition as "a temporary alliance of distinct parties for a limited purpose" is useful, especially the emphasis he develops on the temporariness implied in such groups in order to achieve a limited purpose, yet accumulating more tasks as time passes without yet achieving that

ever, that *this is not freedom from the Law,* but freedom for Torah-observant Jews to reconsider the halakhic implications for themselves of the inclusion of Gentiles in the people of God as full equals. With the changing of the ages, the traditions of the fathers have not been dismissed, but their *application* has been modified: from expectation to implementation, from an awaited future to the dawn of the age to come. This is the "good news" Peter failed to defend, and for this Paul confronted him (2:11–21).

The human agents to whom Paul opposes his apostleship and his gospel are not the Jerusalem apostles or their emissaries. They are rather interpreters of "the traditions of the fathers," "flesh and blood" agents with whom Paul does *not* confer (1:13–16). They thus must be distinguished from those who were apostles before Paul, with whom he did not consult immediately (1:17), but *only in due course* (1:18; 2:1–10). These human agents maintain the prevailing view that Gentile believers in Christ must become proselytes if they are to acquire standing as full members of the Jewish communities (e.g., Titus, 2:3; in Antioch, Gal 2:12–14).[19]

Paul reminds his readers of the good news in which they believe: that because of Christ the age to come has begun in the midst of the present age, and they can participate in this eschatological reality *as Gentiles.* That is "the truth of the gospel" that was at stake in the past events he narrates; it is at stake now as his Galatian converts find themselves facing the constraints imposed by the convictions of the larger Jewish communities and their controlling agents. "Titus was not circumcised, or the Antiochenes, and you must not be either!"

Paul tells his readers they should not be surprised to find their expectations at variance with those of the influencers in Galatia. What should they expect? The influencers are simply maintaining the traditional boundary definitions for full inclusion of Gentiles. Paul's readers know he used to promote these very practices (1:13), and they have already been warned to expect opposition as well (1:9). For announcing that they need not join other righteous Gentiles who pursue the normal course of proselyte conversion, Paul has been "persecuted" (5:11); what do they expect for themselves but "suffering"?

These believers have taken on an identity constructed within the subgroup communities of those believing in the gospel of Jesus Christ only to have it challenged or dismissed by other, seemingly more powerful courts of reputation. They have

---

purpose (171). "Coalitions may comprise individuals, other coalitions, and even corporate groups; and most show a concentric form of organization, with core and peripheral members" (173).

[19] One finds this view to be common, for example, as it is variously expressed: by Paul in his opposition to it for his Gentiles in Romans, Galatians; by Luke in Acts; and in other Jewish writings of the period: 1 Macc 1:15, 44–48, 60–61; 2:45–46, 2 Macc 6:10, *Jub.* 15:25–34; Josephus, *Ant.* 1.192; 13.318–319; 18.34–48; *Ag. Ap.* 2.137, 140–142; Philo, *Migr. Abr.* 92; and in Graeco-Roman literature, including Strabo, *Geogr.* 16.2.37; Diodorus Siculus, *Bib. hist.* 1.55; Petronius, *Sat.* 68.8; 102.13–14; Persius, *Sat.* 5.179–184; Martial, *Epigr.* 7.35.3–4, 82; 11.94; Tacitus, *Hist.* 5.5.2, 8–9; Juvenal, *Sat.* 14.96–106; Horace, *Sat.* 1.9.60–72; Suetonius, *Dom.* 12. It is attested also in the later rabbinic material (*y. Meg.* 3.2; *Midr. Exod. Rab.* 30:12). The governing statement is, of course, Gen 17:9–14. See also discussion in Nolland, "Uncircumcised Proselytes?" 173–94; Collins, "Symbol"; Segal, *Paul,* 72–109; Feldman, *Jew and Gentile,* 153–58; Porton, *Stranger within Your Gates,* 132–54.

experienced shame, the refusal of the larger communities to confirm the place of honor they had claimed. They may have seen this as "persecution," but the larger communities and their representatives may have intended it as education, discipline or punishment. Concern for one's reputation is honorable: failure to be concerned for honor or shame constitutes shamelessness, and it is just such "foolish" behavior of which the addressees have been accused (cf. 1:6–9; 3:1–5; 4:8–21; 5:7–12; 6:12–13).[20]

These Gentiles have apparently begun to accept the "influencers" demand to define their status according to the membership norms of the larger Jewish communities within which their subgroups operate. Paul approaches them as already having begun to defect, even as he insists they will not now complete this course (5:10). We detect here Paul's anxiety that they have internalized this other "good news," and now want to be circumcised (1:6–7; 3:1–5; 4:11, 19–21; 5:2–18). He fears that they are being "persuaded" by the majority communities' norms, by which they believe they may escape their current disputable and thus marginal status (5:7–12; 6:12–13). Their actions reveal the social dimensions of identity: "*Identification* depends upon affective powers of attraction, in intimate dyadic relationships and in more collective or public contexts. Identification, of course, is related to the desire to stay in the good graces of others." The "influencers" have made inroads with these Gentiles precisely because the latter, as marginals, seek to overcome the ambiguity and uncertainty of their identity by conforming to the larger community's behavioral membership criteria. "Strong pressures encouraging conformity—with penalties attaching to deviance—may oppress most those whose membership or social identity is insecure."[21]

We may describe these Gentiles as "outgrouped insiders," who now seek the dominant ingroup's acceptance.[22]

The influencers consider them liminals, righteous Gentile guests who need to be adopted into the family, perhaps even pre-liminals. Paul's addressees may well regard completion of the ritual process of circumcision as a small price to pay, for the "rights" of membership that they previously considered theirs exist only to the degree that they are recognized.[23]

I emphasize that Paul's appeal is not a message proclaimed against Israel, or against Torah observance by Jews who do not share faith in Christ. It is the message of Torah, the source of Wisdom; it expresses the plight of Israel in the midst of the nations, of the psalmist or the prophet in the den of his accusers. *Only in the context of*

---

[20] Calling someone or their thoughts or actions foolish *(anoêtos)* indicates that one has behaved unwisely, without properly perceiving the situation (cf. Rom 1:14; Aristotle, *Rhet* 1.10.4 (1368b): "mistaken ideas of right and wrong"). This does not mean that they do not "know," but that they do not understand the implications of what they "should" know, indicated by their inappropriate behavior. In honor and shame terms they are shameless, they do not show proper concern for their honor or the honor of their group.

[21] R. Jenkins, *Social Identity,* 120, 124.

[22] This may be described according to social identity theory as social mobility. For this approach versus the social change model (which in my view accounts for Paul's response, under the subcategory of social creativity), see the analysis of the Hogg and Abrams, *Social Identifications,* 51–61; used to argue a different conclusion by Esler, *Galatians,* 49–57.

[23] Cf. R. Jenkins, *Social Identity,* 135.

Paul's polemic against influencers who seek to conform (sub)groups of Gentile believers in Christ to the halakhic group norms of the larger Jewish communities do Paul's negative comments carry weight. Otherwise, Jewish identity and Torah observance are considered an advantage: Paul maintains the privilege of being "a Jew by nature, and not a Gentile sinner" (2:14). This assumption underscores his rhetorical approach and the addressees' interest in circumcision for themselves. If the Galatians do not know Paul as a Torah-observant Jew, then the rhetoric of 5:3 would have no bite: "I testify again to every man who receives circumcision that he is bound to keep the whole law." Otherwise, they might simply respond, "but we want only what you have: Jewish identity, without obligation to observe 'the whole law.'"

At the heart of Paul's rhetoric is the call to remain "in Christ," i.e., within the Christ-believing coalition's reference group norms. Here his readers' status has already been legitimated, albeit at the price of disapproval within the dominant communities. He capitalizes upon their dyadic situation in 3:1–5, rebuking their "foolishness," i.e., their shamelessness within the court of reputation of the Christ-believing subgroup, and their deference to the shame attributed by the influencers. They have been seduced by the dominant community's message that they can avoid being "excluded" by conforming (4:17). Paul insists, to the contrary, that the benefits held out to them necessarily subvert the foundational principles of their faith in Christ, just as had been implied earlier at Antioch, when Peter's withdrawal because of "fear" of "the ones for circumcision" there threatened to undermine the meaning of the death of Christ (2:14–21).[24]

The Implied Intra-Jewish Context of the Galatian Addressees

We see, then, that the Galatians whom Paul addresses are members of Christ-believing subgroups within larger Jewish communities (recognizing that this is a circular letter, 1:2). The "influencers" are most likely proselytes within these larger communities, but *not* members of the Christ-believing subgroups. Paul refers to the latter in 6:13 as *hoi peritemnomenoi*, either "those who receive circumcision"/"have themselves circumcised," or "those who cause to be circumcised."[25]

If proselytes, the influencers are the most natural contacts for education and social integration. Having previously been accorded the status of righteous Gentiles by the synagogue, they have a vested interest in guarding and facilitating the ritual process that negotiates hierarchical distinctions between righteous Gentiles and proselytes. Ritual circumcision defines their sense of self- and group-identity; it governs their social interaction; it defines their social reality and political worldview. They can empathize with the liminal situation of the addressees but not with their outlandish claim to have acquired already the equality of status that accords with proselyte

---

[24] See "Peter's Hypocrisy (Gal 2:11–21) in the Light of Paul's Anxiety (Rom 7)," in Nanos, *Mystery*, 337–71.

[25] See full discussion in Nanos, *Irony*, 217–42, 277–83.

conversion. Although they themselves have crossed the ritual threshold and gained new status as proselytes, they perhaps still experience the social insecurity associated with liminality.[26]

Thus Paul accuses them of agonistic rivalry in the flesh and of having cast the evil eye of envy upon his addressees (3:1). From the perspective of the influencers, who do these "Johnny-come-lately" Gentiles think they are? This presents a classic case in which envy is aroused, exacerbated to the degree that the influencers might once have shared status and kinship with the addressees.[27]

Moreover, these influencers, Paul alleges, seek to avoid any "persecution" that might be required of them if they were to represent the addressees' appeal to the meaning of "the cross of Christ" to legitimate their claim to full membership while remaining Gentiles (6:12): the influencers are invested in the larger Jewish communities' norms, but not the norms of the Christ-believing subgroups to which Paul's Gentile converts have committed themselves.

Paul appeals to his addressees to keep their "eyes" on the one "publicly portrayed as crucified," and thus to negate the force of the evil eye (3:1). Instead of seeking honor in the court of reputation of this present evil age, "biting and devouring one another" like wild animals (5:13–15), they should identify with the one who suffered the shame of crucifixion, the one who chose the seemingly weak and failing route of public shame in the interest of serving the other.[28] "If we live by the Spirit, let us also conform to [the way of] the Spirit. We should not be vainly proud, challenging one another [for honor], envying each other" (5:24–26; cf. Phil 2:3–8). They should rather serve one another, confident that God will bring justice for those who do right (6:1–10).

Instead of complying with the "influencers," Paul exhorts his readers to seek another way: to "stand fast, therefore," and "not submit" the "freedom" they have in Christ (5:1–4, 11–15); to "wait for the hope of righteousness" (5:5); to avoid being "unsettled," "obstructed," "subverted" by the influencers (5:7–12), or seeking honor

---

[26] Implied in Philo's concern to confront the problem, cf. *Virt.* 212–227, esp. 218–219, 223; *Spec.* 1.51–53, 308–310. See S. Cohen, *Beginnings,* 160–62; A. Cohen, *Self Consciousness,* 128; Esler, *Galatians,* 216–17, 223. Porton, *Stranger within Your Gates,* traces the rabbinic evidence.

[27] Aristotle, *Rhet.* 2.10, explains the dynamics of envy along these lines. He notes it is most likely among those closest in status. Likewise, the evil eye is the result of envy, and is thought to harm the one upon whom this gaze falls (cf. Plutarch, *Mor.* 8.5.7). Thus Paul's accusation (or "warning") that the addressees have been evil eyed by the influencers suggests that the addressees have something that the influencers might envy, though the addressees had failed to suspect this at work in the present circumstances they "suffer" (3:4: *epathete*), or in the motives of the influencers toward themselves. That which Paul considers enviable appears to be the presence of the Spirit and miracles in their midst (3:5), which would seem to indicate that the influencers regard such things inappropriate for those who have not completed the ritual process of proselyte conversion. Further discussion of Paul's accusation and the evil eye belief system to which it appeals is available in Nanos, " 'O foolish Galatians"; *Irony,* 186–91, 279–80.

[28] Cf. Quintilian, *Decl.* 274: "Whenever we crucify the condemned, the most crowded roads are chosen, where the most people can see and be moved by this terror. For penalties relate not so much to retribution as to their exemplary effect." This public display of shame (Philo calls it "show"; *Flacc.* 84–85) was designed to strike fear of deviance from the established norms (cf. Neyrey, *Honor and Shame,* 139–40).

and status according to the world (6:12–15). They are children of God. God's Spirit is at work among them; they should seek the other's interest (5:15–26). They should "restore" the other in gentleness (6:1); "bear one another's burdens" (6:2); "test one's own work," avoid "boasting over one's neighbor" (6:4), and "not grow weary in well-doing." They should "do good to everyone" (6:9–10) and resist the pressure of those who would "compel" them to be circumcised (6:12–13).

Paul's addressees have believed in one who bore the shame of public execution as a pretender (3:1). They heard this message from another who suffered similarly to preserve the truth of the good news of Christ for them (5:11; 6:17). What else but suffering should they expect from the social control agents of the larger communities if they stand fast in their (subgroup) identity in Christ?

Paul brings in this letter an *inter*-Jewish communal perspective (i.e., *between* this Jewish coalition and the dominant Jewish groups who do not agree on the meaning of the death of Christ, whether in Galatia or elsewhere) to bear upon the unsettling *intra*-Jewish communal circumstances developing *within* the Galatian situation in which this "other" *apparent* "message of good" is being proposed. Paul has suffered to defend their place as Gentiles in view of the meaning of the death of Christ; he thus hopes that his addressees will resist the temptation to conform to the "traditional" view in order to gain undisputed status in the present age, and instead continue on the course they had begun, walking straight toward the truth of the *good news of Christ*, whatever the price.

23

FOOLISH GALATIANS?—A RECIPIENT-ORIENTED ASSESSMENT OF PAUL'S LETTER[1]

Dieter Mitternacht

Paul is the model of the great martyr, who walks barefooted across thorns, feels them but refuses to pay attention to them, boasts about them instead, considering them a down payment for the glory, assured the law is being established that says: Weakness and dying exalt the power of God and are therefore strength and living.[2]

"Become as I, for I also as you, I beseech you brethren" (Gal 4:12). This is the first and foremost request in Paul's letter to the Galatians.[3] But what does it imply? How is Paul like the brethren in Galatia, and in what sense does he want them to become as he? As has been pointed out by Mark Nanos, it would diminish the persuasive force of 5:3 had Paul in mind that the Galatian Christ-believers should imitate him in terms of Torah compliance.

> If the Galatians did not know Paul as a Torah-obedient Jew, then the rhetoric of 5:3 would have no bite. "I testify again to every man who receives circumcision that he is bound to keep the whole law." Otherwise, they might simply respond—"but we want only what you have: Jewish identity, without obligation to observe the whole law."[4]

By implication we also learn from 5:3 that Paul did not expect the addressees to be aware that reception of circumcision brought with it the obligation to observe the

---

[1] I would like to thank my friends and colleagues, Jim Hester, Kevin Kiser, Mark Nanos, Birger Olsson, Anders Runesson, Thomas Schreiner, Runar Thorsteinsson, and Magnus Zetterholm for reading an earlier version of this article and giving me valuable suggestions and criticism.
[2] Wrede, "Paulus," 11, my translation.
[3] In my opinion Gal 4:12 resembles the petition formula of letters of petition and articulates the central concern of the letter; see Mitternacht, *Sprachlose*, 215–32. That the transition to 4:12 marks a major division in the letter has also been argued by Hansen, *Abraham in Galatians*, 47–48; and R. Longenecker, *Galatians*, 183–88. R. Longenecker calls 4:12 "the operative appeal of the entire letter" (188), albeit with different implications than I. See also Boyarin, *Radical Jew*, 155.
[4] Nanos, "Inter- and Intra-Jewish," 405.

whole law.[5] They had to be informed of these consequences. Consequently, observance of the whole law does not seem to have been part of what Paul conceived to be the addressees' concern.

The inference is supported by 6:12–13. There Paul remarks that the circumcised influencers[6] do not themselves keep the law. The rhetorical function of the remark here is evidently not to inform the addressees of what they don't know. Instead what they know is highlighted in order to accentuate the selfish motive of the influencers: they only want to avoid their own persecution. I will attend to the rhetoric of 6:12 below; at this point I just want to focus on the information provided: there were circumcised people in Galatia who were advocating circumcision of Gentiles not for the purpose of keeping the law but for the purpose of avoiding persecution.

Adding together the rhetorical bite of 5:3, the implicit information about the addressees provided by 5:3, and the implicit information about the influencers provided by 6:12–13, we learn that, according to Paul,

1. whoever is circumcised (including Paul) is obligated to observe the whole law,

2. there are people in Galatia who are circumcised and do not submit to that obligation,

3. these people are advising the Galatian Christ-believers to do the same, and the advice appeals to them.

Now, if it was not a desire to observe the whole law for salvation that motivated the addressees for circumcision, what was it? Was it an attraction to circumcision? Scarcely! There is ample evidence that circumcision as such did not appeal to Greeks.[7] Could it have been a fascination with Jewish faith in general? Not at this time. Had the addressees wished to become Jews, they could have converted before they met Paul. The desire for circumcision is linked to what happened to these people *after* they had met Paul and become Christ-believers.

As the rhetorical dynamic of the letter unfolds, it becomes apparent that Paul expects weighty opposition from the addressees. The expectation is indicated by the fact that whenever Paul appeals to the situation of the addressees, the rhetorical strategy shifts from argumentation to persuasion.[8] In addition, Paul moulds a rhetorical stage on which those whom he opposes are denigrated for their selfishness, those who are to be persuaded are ridiculed for their naiveté, and those of repute (especially Peter)

---

[5] Even though Paul is simply stating Pharisaic opinion (well documented in later Jewish sources: *m. Bik.* 1:4; *m. Šeqal.* 1:3, 6; *m. Pesaḥ.* 4:6; *Mek. Pisha* 15 on Exodus 12:49). For further references see Schürer, *History*, 3.170, 175; S. Cohen, *Beginnings*, 218–19, 324–25.

[6] The term "influencers" was coined by Mark Nanos in order to alert interpreters to the stereotypical character judgments inherent in the designations in the letter (troublemakers, agitators, etc.). I will try to demonstrate that from the point of view of the addressees they could be called "counselors" (see Mitternacht, *Sprachlose*, 320–21). To begin with, I will, however, use the neutral term suggested by Nanos.

[7] Cf. Josephus, *Ag. Ap.* 2.137; Philo, *Spec.* 1.1. For further references and discussion see Barclay, *Obeying the Truth*, 46–47; *Jews*, 438–39; Winter, *Welfare*, 137.

[8] See below and Thurén, *Argument*, 51.

are demonstrated to be inconsistent. The author himself emerges as the only reliable authority, divinely ordained and equipped.

Such stereotypical characterizations of persons and groups of persons indicate that more is at stake than a reassertion of the accepted principle: non-Jews in Christ do not have to become circumcised in order to be saved. That issue may have been a matter of dispute earlier (Acts 15:1), and Paul admits that he had advocated circumcision of Gentiles himself (Gal 5:11; see below). But at the time this letter was being composed, there was no indication of any dissent among Jewish Christ-believers regarding the principle argument. In fact, had Paul been arguing against a "no salvation without circumcision" front, why then would he have emphasized the indifference of *un*circumcision? It would have been an irrelevant point to make. But twice in Galatians Paul asserts that neither circumcision nor uncircumcision is of any avail (5:6; 6:15). Again, had Paul wanted to argue that there is something inherently wrong with circumcision of Gentiles, it would have been counterproductive to stress the indifference of circumcision.

In the same vein runs the assertion that "there is neither Jew nor Greek, neither slave nor free, neither male nor female" (3:28). It reiterates the indifference of religious, social, and gender distinctions for oneness in Christ. Being part of a pre-Pauline baptismal liturgy,[9] it is an accepted explication of the Jerusalem agreement, on which everyone involved can be expected to be agreed. But oneness in Christ is not the same as collapsing differences into sameness.[10] It implies equality of righteousness for Jews and Gentiles in Christ—no more, no less. Jews remain Jews, Gentiles may remain Gentiles. Together but distinct, Jews and Gentiles constitute the people of God.[11]

Living out the agreed-upon equality, however, generated life circumstances that posed new challenges. Indeed, in Galatia it had produced social disruption and dislocation with considerable difficulties for the addressees. As a consequence of Paul's preaching, they had committed themselves to the one God and his Christ and abandoned worship of their native deities (4:8–11). Such changes could easily result in "serious disruption in [their] relationship with family, friends, fellow club members, business associates and civic authorities."[12] The disruption would have been less acute if the Jewish community had attributed equality of status to the Gentile Christ-believers. But given the precarious state of Jewish communities as *collegia* with special rights, they had to insist on social conversion,[13] which by definition included circumcision. Exemption from certain aspects of *eusebeia/pietas* and *philotimia* (such as worship of gods other than their own) was dependent on the goodwill of local civic

---

[9] Betz, *Galatians*, 181–85; R. Longenecker, *Galatians*, 154–55.

[10] Contra Boyarin, *Radical Jew*, 32, 156, 228–32.

[11] A number of biblical and extrabiblical Jewish traditions on eschatological situations (e.g., Isa 2:2–4, 56:3–7; Mic 4:1ff.; Zech 2:11, 8:23; *Pss. Sol.* 7:31–41; Tob 13:11; 14:5–6; *Sib. Or.* 3:616, 715–724) suggest that "when God establishes his kingdom, . . . these two groups will together constitute 'his people': Israel, redeemed from exile, and the Gentiles, redeemed from idolatry" (Fredriksen, "Judaism," 246–47).

[12] Barclay, *Obeying the Truth*, 58. See also Winter, *Welfare*, 136.

[13] On the distinction between theological and social conversion, see S. Cohen, *Beginnings*, 168–74.

authorities. Thus the Jewish communities in turn were obligated to uphold the dominant social order.[14] It was their duty not only to exclude liminals from status equality
but to encourage them to continue in *their* sacred duty.[15] "To fail in this duty was
asebeia (impietas) and this could mean exile, or even death."[16]

Instead of removing burdens, then, the conversion of Gentile God-fearers[17] to
faith in Christ had increased burdens considerably. They were being marginalized[18]
from both their potential social and religious homesteads. Such a turnout may have
been avoidable among the wealthy in Corinth, but for Christ-believers in Asia Minor
it seems to have been a common experience.[19] And so questions were induced about
what are the requirements of the life of faith working through love and in the imminent expectation of the new creation (5:6; 6:15). As we shall see, Paul's reply to *these*
questions constitutes the main concern of Galatians. For him—living as one crucified
with Christ (2:19)—any attempt to circumvent confrontation with social and political power structures amounted to a rejection of Christ Jesus, who himself had confronted and suffered the sword of Rome. Redemption from this present evil age was
expected soon (1:4), but as of now righteousness is a matter of hope and its fulfillment is in the future, "for which we wait in the Spirit by faith" (5:5).[20] In anticipation
of that day, Paul asserts, "I boast only in the cross of Jesus Christ, through whom the
world is crucified to me and I to the world" (6:14).

Keeping these initial observations in mind, I shall now turn to the task of this investigation, which can be summarized in three basic questions: 1) How may the addressees have perceived Paul's plea in 4:12: "Become as I, for I also as you!"? 2) How
does 3:1–5 correspond with the first explication of the plea in 4:12c–15? 3) Can the
results of the first two questions be confirmed by the rest of the letter?

I will argue that 1) the reception of Christ brought upon the addressees
social and political difficulties that could be averted by participation in the ritual of

---

[14] Rajak, "Charter," 138 (also Rajak, "Rights," 24), has drawn attention to the fact that there
was no general or formalized Roman charter for Jewish communities to rely on (the term *religio
licita* was coined by Tertullian, *Apol.* 21.1). The legal validity of the privileges was not uniform and
had to be nurtured continuously and with political delicacy on the local level.

[15] Nanos, *Irony*, 257–65. The emphases on the drastic implications involved in proselyte conversion (Philo, *Spec.* 1.51–52, 309; *Virt.* 102, 108, 175, 178, 211–222; *Mos.* 2.44) confirm the point
made by implication. As liminals became proselytes, they were obligated to renounce previous customs and cut family and friendship ties. Indeed, it was then that their families turned against them
(*Spec.* 4.178). Before her marriage to Joseph (i.e., her social conversion), the author of *Joseph and
Aseneth* calls Aseneth an alien (ἀλλοτρία) despite her earlier theological conversion (see S. Cohen,
Beginnings, 171; Barclay, *Jews,* 409).

[16] Walker-Ramisch, "Voluntary Associations," 134.

[17] The term is many-sided. See below, n. 110.

[18] For the importance of social acknowledgment in honor-and-shame cultures, see Malina,
New Testament World, 28–54, 96–112.

[19] Cf. Barclay, *Obeying the Truth,* 58, who refers to 1 Pet 2:12, 15, 18–20; 3:1, 13–16; 4:3–5,
12–16.

[20] E. Sanders, *Paul and Palestinian Judaism,* 448, 492, 495. Note the turn of focus introduced
with the "we" in 5:5. Nobody has arrived as yet. As I shall argue, the influencers were also Christ-believers. Thus, the matter of dispute between Paul and the influencers was not whether the age to
come had actually dawned (contra Nanos, "Inter- and Intra-Jewish," 401–2). The dispute was about
the living conditions of the new creation within the prevailing evil age.

circumcision; 2) compared with the hardship they were facing, circumcision appeared to be the lesser of two "trials"; 3) Paul was well informed about these circumstances and wrote the letter in order to rebuke the addressees for not enduring the bigger trial;[21] and 4) the rebuke is motivated by the conviction that in this present evil age the Christ-like life is to be essentially marked by the cross.

Taking Rhetoric Seriously[22]

In order to be able to appreciate the effect of the letter on the addressees, one has to pay attention to how the strategy of argumentation and persuasion unfolds and discern the relationship between what is being anticipated, affirmed, and argued for. Paul seems to anticipate considerable opposition to what he is about to argue. At the same time, he seems to count on his ability to overcome the anticipated dissension by combining compelling ethos demonstration with combative persuasion.[23] In order to make the addressees positively inclined to a confrontation loaded with emotional appeal, he presents to them a self-portrait of an unfailing and divinely ordained follower and imitator of the suffering and persecuted Christ.

I agree with Lauri Thurén that there is no way of deducing real emotions with any kind of certainty from a rhetorical text.[24] I also agree that nevertheless "the apostle must be held fully responsible for what he dictated."[25] But I do not concur that the "informed" interpreter, who is not as "naive" as the Galatian addressees, should de-rhetorize Paul's arguments and make gaining access to his timeless thought his or her most important concern.[26] In my understanding, the historically and theologically relevant information has to be sought within the contingent communication situation of the letter.

For instance, the recognition of stereotyping is but one aspect of making a rhetorical strategy transparent. A thorough analysis also requires accepting the historical implausibility of stereotyping, so the interpreter must refrain from collaborating with the author's ascription of naiveté to the addressees and of selfishness to the

---

[21] By emphasizing what appears to be the focal point of this letter, I am not denying that Paul may have had additional motives, such as the eschatological scheme of Jews as Jews and Gentiles as Gentiles bringing in the consummation together. Cf. above, n. 11.

[22] I use rhetorical criticism for the purpose of argumentation and persuasion analysis (cf. Hester, "Placing the Blame," 284–49).

[23] Whenever confrontation is maximized, a sender will instinctively reckon with the possibility of rejection, i.e., a boomerang effect (Haseloff, "Wirkungsbedingungen," 161; Breuer, *Einführung*, 58), and search for rhetorical means to rule out the unwanted option.

[24] Thurén, "Was Paul Angry?" 306, 310; *Derhetorizing Paul*, 59–64. Similar assertions in J. Martin, *Antike Rhetorik*, 161; Betz, *Galatians*, 129–30, 132, 229–30, 270.

[25] Thurén, "Was Paul Angry?" 310. The carefully designed rhetorical strategy that is apparent throughout the letter contradicts the notion that Paul was emotionally out of control (contra, e.g., Räisänen, *Paul and the Law*, 133; Rohde, *Galater*, 13; Cosby, "Red Hot," 1: "He responded like an erupting volcano").

[26] Thurén, *Derhetorizing Paul*, e.g., v, 13–15, 59–64. According to Thurén, rhetorical analysis has to discern the core of the historical Paul's thought behind the contingency of advanced rhetorical argumentation.

influencers—however skillfully ingrained into the texture of the letter—and from collaborating with his demand of loyalty toward himself. As long as one accepts as incontestable Paul's authority to correct, threaten, and judge,[27] one will not come to terms with either the historical realities of the *first* communication situation or the rhetoric involved in any communication,[28] and thus with the plausible effect of the letter on the addressees.

In order to bring to the interpretive process that follows here an alertness to preconceptions and rhetorical pitfalls as well as a recipient- rather than a sender-oriented reading of Galatians, I will make a conscious effort not to submit to the demand of loyalty ingrained in the text and instead to exercise a critical appreciation of the rhetorical tendencies and the polemical attributions made in the text. Hopefully, the effect of the letter on the addressees will come into view in a way that suggests a new approach to the exigencies in Galatians.

Noting Peculiarities

Persons and groups of persons who do not stand in any direct relationship to the situation among the Galatian Christ-believes are referred to primarily, so it appears, for the purpose of reinforcing the ethos of the author, establishing its validity and affirming its unwavering integrity. Paul makes recourse to earlier conflicts with respected representatives among the Christ-believers in order to demonstrate his own endurance and document how he prevailed in every situation; they, however, did not; for some at least, this was because of fear (2:12).

The events narrated and the evaluations about the Christ-believers in Jerusalem and Antioch purport to exemplify inconsistency and declining integrity. Some may have been known before for their rectitude (as pillars), but such assertions can no longer be maintained. Granted, for practical purposes even Paul had sought their consent ("for fear that I was running or had run my race in vain," 2:2), but a tone of depreciation ("whatever they were means nothing to me," 2:6) and discord ("I opposed him to his face": 2:11) permeates the narrative.

Still, a difference in tone is palpable in Paul's appraisal of the so-called pillars in Jerusalem (James, Peter, and John) and Cephas and Barnabas at Antioch, on the one hand, and the so called false brethren in Jerusalem and those of the circumcision in

---

[27] Assumptions in this direction seem basic for most commentators. Cf., e.g., Burton, *Galatians*, lv–lvi; Rohde, *Galater*, 13; Dunn, *Theology*, 5; extremely so in Machen, *Notes*, 200.

[28] Cf. Dascal and Gross, "Marriage," 115 (elaborating on Perelman's categories): "Necessarily from the orators' point of view, the audiences they address are not actual, but ideal: they are creations of the speech" and, of course, to begin with, of the speaker (115). As the orator/author conceives his speech/letter, he may also estimate the effect of his arguments up to a certain point (e.g., the expected increase of ethos through Gal 1–2) and, on the basis of his estimation, dare the audience to accept an assertion that might have brought their immediate rejection had it been uttered in the beginning of the speech/letter. Cf. the soft and implicit accusation in 1:6–7 with the explicit ridicule in 3:1–5 and finally the uninhibited confrontation in 5:2ff. For similar observations on rhetorical strategy with regard to 1 Peter, cf. Thurén, *Rhetorical Strategy*, 40, 53.

Antioch, on the other. Whereas the former are credited with the advance of the gospel in general (2:2, 9), the latter are simply opposed and rejected. The false brethren are presented as intruders into the brotherhood in Jerusalem to whom "we did not submit . . . for one moment in order for the truth of the gospel to remain with you" (2:5). "Those of the circumcision" at Antioch are simply referred to as a threat to the community (2:12).

With regard to the people of repute, interactions are reported in considerable detail, motives are explicated, and even arguments described (especially if 2:15–21 is related, in some way, to the Antioch incident). But rhetorical insinuation and actual reference are at considerable variance in these narratives. For instance, neither the first incident referred to (2:1–5) nor the third (2:11–[14], 21) informs the reader beyond doubt of agreements reached.[29] And even though 2:6–10 purports a definite sense of agreement, the inferences about authority and commission are convincing only on a superficial level (i.e., the orality level).[30] A rereading of 2:6–10 raises doubts about what actually was achieved at the meeting referred to.[31]

In terms of rhetorical purpose, the three narratives convey the combined impression that whatever agreements were reached, these were due to the persistence and endurance of Paul (to begin with also Barnabas, but not in 2:11–14). Adding to this the presence of derogatory references to the Jerusalem authorities, ch. 2 seems designed predominantly to establish the superiority of the ethos of the author. Even if 2:11–14 refers to just a momentary relapse of Peter,[32] it contributes to the impression that Paul is the only reliable guarantor of stability.

As to the asserted agitation of the influencers, these people are treated in a stereotypical and polemical manner. Without references to the content of their ideas, they are consistently depicted as acting deceptively and selfishly. They are enraging troublemakers (1:7; 3:1[?]; 5:8, 12), proclaiming a twisted gospel that causes nothing but confusion (1:7; 5:10; but the content of the twisted gospel is never explicated!). They are accused of inciting destructive behavior (5:15[?]; 6:12–13) and depicted as cowards (6:12; cf. 5:12), as willing to obstruct the course of truth (5:7), and as all too keen on pressuring the addressees into circumcision (6:12). Twice their motives are articulated, both times suggesting selfishness (4:17; 6:12–13).[33]

Not only the "intruding" brethren in Jerusalem, those of the circumcision in Antioch, and the influencers in Galatia are stereotyped; so too are the addressees. They are pictured as unbalanced and easily deceived (1:6–7; 3:4), bewitched (3:1),

---

[29] The assertion "Even Titus was *not compelled* to be circumcised" (2:3) leaves room for two alternative readings: 1) he was not doing it, and he was not compelled to; 2) he was not compelled to, but he did it on his own initiative. For the problem, cf. Bruce, *Commentary*, 112. The latter alternative has not been argued for a while, but see Burkitt, *Christian Beginnings*; J. Weiss, *Urchristentum*, 118; Duncan, *Galatians*, 41–44.

[30] See Mitternacht, *Sprachlose*, 247–50.

[31] Cf. Lüdemann, *Antipaulinismus*, 90–93.

[32] Nanos, "Inter- and Intra-Jewish," 402–3.

[33] L. T. Johnson and A. B. Du Toit have demonstrated convincingly that Paul's accusations recall *topoi* of vilification that are used in antiquity not for the purpose of denotation but for connotation (see Johnson, "Slander," 433; DuToit, "Vilification," 411–12).

children in need of motherly protection (4:19). They are ridiculed for their naiveté (3:3) and their inability to discern evil and beguiling activities that threaten their position as Christ-believers (4:16–18, 20; 5:2–7), and are rebuked for their short memory (3:1b–3; 4:14–15). If they would recall the vivid portrayal of the suffering Christ (3:1b), if they had heeded their spiritual mother's advice (4:19), they would never have fallen prey to deception.

Contrasting himself to all other persons that surface in the letter[34]—in reverse stereotypical order—the letter author portrays his own actions and teachings as consistent, independently and divinely ordained (1:12, 15–16), and reflecting unfailing integrity and peerless commitment to God's calling (1:14; 2:19–21). He is the sole messenger of gospel truth (2:5, 14; 4:16), the embodiment of the revelation of God's Son (1:16; 2:20), taught only by divine revelation (1:16–18), unwavering and victorious in any trial and conflict. In sum, Paul is the divinely appointed messenger to the Gentiles in whom the one unwavering representation of the Christ-like life is manifest ("revealed *in* me," 1:16).

Toward the end of the autobiographical section, the establishment of ethos culminates in this assertion: "I through the law have died to the law, in order to live for God. I have been crucified with Christ. I no longer live, but Christ lives in me." (2:19–20a). Paul affirms his participation in the crucifixion of Christ to be the sustaining power of his present life in Christ. Since it is embedded in a complicated argument about the law (2:17–21), it is easy to loose sight of the fact that Paul here is asserting his present self-perception and, by implication, the self-perception he wants to confer onto the addressees.

As I shall try to demonstrate in my interpretations of 4:12–15 and 3:1–5, the affirmations of integrity and commitment from ch. 2 materialize in the presentation of the life marked by the cross before the addressees' eyes. Whereas the earlier assertions are to enhance Paul's ethos with the addressees, the later are to put the addressees on the spot for not appreciating what had been so vividly portrayed to them ("O you foolish Galatians . . ."). Ethos establishment is woven into some of the later affirmations also (cf. commitment even to the point of loss of friendship, 4:18–20, and exhaustion, 6:17; and consequences of being the closest possible to the crucified Christ, 6:17b).

Several implications for interpretation emerge. First, great care has to be exercised in the construction of the letter's exigencies. Stereotypical accusations and characterizations have to be taken for what they are. Second, the overall tendencies of stereotyping and of the rhetorical purpose behind hyperbole and polemic, especially when consistent patterns can be determined, have to be exposed and taken into account.[35] Third, the similarity of stereotyping undertaken for the so-called false brethren, those of the circumcision and the influencers, suggests that Paul perceived a closer affinity

---

[34] Possible coworkers (cf. the "we" of 1:8, 9) do not play any palpable role in the argument. The implicit reference to a secretary (6:11) is coincidental to the emphasis of the author's concluding assertions.

[35] I agree, that "[t]his caricature . . . means next to nothing in regard to the question as to who the opponents really were and what they really had in mind" (Betz, *Galatians*, 230). It does mean a lot, however, for determining what rhetorical strategy Paul had in mind.

between these groups than between the influencers and the authorities mentioned by name. Fourth, the derogatory tone used to describe the Jerusalem authorities, combined with uncertainty regarding the results of those events, suggests that there was a conflict in how the agreement was to be interpreted and that Paul perceived the Jerusalem authorities to be supportive of the influencers.[36] Fifth, the assertion of the cruciform life, which was prepared for in chs. 1–2 and reinforced in Paul's consistent self-perception throughout the letter, has to be recognized for being the prominent point of departure when one is constructing Paul's perception of the exigencies.

Priority for Discourse Units with Direct Situational Pertinence

As interpreters have tried to identify the exigencies of the addressees, they have based their constructions largely on mirror-reading the identity of the influencers.[37] Since no explicit assertions of their theological convictions are available in Galatians, extratextual presuppositions about an anti-Pauline opposition have been brought to bear on some of the theological arguments in the letter. Most interpreters have focused on ch. 3 and parts of ch. 4 and suggested different kinds of "judaizing-nomistic" activities to which the addressees were being subjected.[38] Some have made chs. 5–6 their starting point for proving "gnostic-libertine"[39] or "gnostic-judaizing" activities in Galatia.[40] A couple of attempts have been made at taking chs. 3–6 together and deducing a double front.[41] Chapters 1 and 2 have been used as historical-background material for each of the constructions.[42]

Acknowledging that different parts of the letter seem to support different and conflicting inferences, some have concluded that constructing an original communication situation is impossible.[43] Yet it cannot be denied that this letter of Paul conveys the strong impression of addressing a specific situation. Thus, instead of leading us to abandon the endeavor, the difficulties should alert us to the need not only for a critical assessment of the letters' stereotypical and polemical argumentation but also for a revision of the procedure according to which priority for construction is ascribed to

---

[36] Cf. Marxsen, *Einleitung,* 68–69.

[37] For recent overviews on the identification of the influencers, see Alvarez-Cineira, *Religionspolitik,* 295–312; Mitternacht, *Sprachlose,* 26–38; Nanos, *Irony,* 110–316; on the problems pertaining to mirror reading, see Berger, "Gegner"; Lyons, *Pauline Autobiography,* esp. 96–105; Barclay, "Mirror-Reading"; Mitternacht, *Sprachlose,* 38–49.

[38] Beginning with Baur, *Paulus,* then Lightfoot, *Galatians,* and still maintained by, e.g., Williams, *Galatians,* 27.

[39] Schmithals, "Heretics," who views the influencers in Galatia as being one of a kind with those in 1 and 2 Corinthians and Philippians.

[40] Wegenast, *Verständnis,* 36–40.

[41] Lütgert, "Gesetz"; Ropes, *Problem.*

[42] See my discussion in Mitternacht, *Sprachlose,* 235–39. For a slight shift toward identifying a socioreligious concern, see Betz, "Spirit," 153–54; Betz, *Galatians,* 9.

[43] Lyons, *Pauline Autobiography,* e.g., 97. Vouga, *Galater,* 1–5, who accepts the hypothesis of D. Trobisch (see below, n. 47). See also Vouga, "Galaterbrief," 245–46.

certain portions of the letter over others. Such a procedure needs to circumvent extratextual presuppositions[44] and take into account the nature of persuasive communication by ascribing priority to discourse units with direct pertinence for the situation of the addressees. These units are indicated where a) Paul explicitly refers to events in Galatia that have occurred up till or since the appearance of the influencers and b) Paul attempts to affect the behavior or cognition of the addressees regarding the influencers. The passages are 1:6–9; 3:1–5; 4:8–20; 5:2–12; 6:11–13.[45]

An objection against this procedure may come from the observation that, compared with other passages in the letter—for example, the narratives of chs. 1 and 2—discourse units with direct situational pertinence lack almost any background information. Thus, in chs. 1 and 2, several of the Christ-believers in Jerusalem and Antioch are mentioned by name, but we are left in the dark about who any of the influencers (or the addressees) were in person. Again, events in Jerusalem and Antioch are put into situational frameworks, such as special gatherings and activities of different parties, whereas events pertaining directly to the situation in Galatia are referred to without this kind of information. Some have suggested that this vagueness must be due to Paul's lack of firsthand knowledge surrounding the details of the enticement;[46] others, that Galatians must not have been written for a particular situation but as a circular letter or even a literary last will.[47] But a letter is "one of two sides of a dialogue."[48] The impression of a lack of backdrop information is due to the positioning of the perceiver. In fact, such a lack indicates the first recipients' familiarity with what is being articulated. Within the dialogue, neither sender nor recipient(s) need to repeat that of which both sides are well informed. Instead the sender will supply only what seems necessary for his response to be intelligible and persuasive to those addressed. Thus, if we do not attribute priority to discourse units with direct situational pertinence, we miss out on a fundamental principle of letter communication that indicates that these passages are most important for construction.

A second objection to this procedure could be raised on account of the observation that the conflation of recipient instruction with affective-threatening or affective-depreciating recipient coercion (see below) toward either the addressees or the influencers is especially prominent in discourse units with direct situational pertinence, so that it would seem plausible that these passages are especially difficult

---

[44] See, e.g., Meeks's and also Lyons's criticism of Betz's assertion—based on his reading of 2 Cor 6:14–7:1—of an anti-Pauline opposition in Galatia (Meeks, "Review," 306; Lyons, *Pauline Autobiography*, 100–101; Betz, *Galatians*, 9).

[45] For details and further differentiations, see Mitternacht, *Sprachlose*, 61–89. On 4:8–11 my position has shifted somewhat. I have been counting the verses among passages with indirect situational pertinence. In an independent study Mark Nanos has suggested a similar approach (Nanos, *Irony*, 62–72).

[46] Schmithals, "Heretics," 18; Marxsen, *Einleitung*, 63; Schmithals, "Judaisten," 29–30.

[47] Trobisch, *Entstehung*, e.g., 84–104; Trobisch, *Paulusbriefe*, 124–26, argues that Galatians has been edited and reworked into a "*Rundbrief*" in order to be included in a collection of four Pauline letters (Romans, 1 and 2 Corinthians, Galatians), wherefore identification of persons of communities has become impossible. Trobisch's analysis has been accepted by F. Vouga (see above, n. 43).

[48] Demetrius, *Eloc.* 223, referring to Artemon, the editor of Aristotle's letters. Cf. Seneca, *Ep.* 75.1–2 (texts in Malherbe, *Ancient Epistolary Theorists*, 17, 29).

to penetrate. But again, as has been emphasized by both ancient and modern rhetorical theorists, a sender who wants to instruct or provoke his recipients, especially on matters of which they are well informed, will always build his arguments on accepted points of departure. Otherwise he will not be able to convince.[49] Thus, as Paul makes recourse to common experiences, recounts circumstances in Galatia, or articulates motives of the addressees in order to influence their perception of these things, he should be expected to ground his argument in what is accepted on the other end of the communication.

In sum, the lack of backdrop information typical for discourse units with direct pertinence for the situation of the addressees enhances the reliability of theses passages; moreover, as one discerns within those passages the conflation of accepted points of departure with recipient instruction and recipient coercion, one may expect to find underneath the surface the most pertinent information for constructing the situation in Galatia.

Accepted Points of Departure, Recipient Instruction, and Recipient Coercion

A text constructed for communication should be expected to manifest argumentative and persuasive assertions that divulge some aspects of the production process.[50] Such manifestations may consist of easily identifiable performatives (commands, promises, and the like)[51] but also of recurring rhetorical tendencies, peculiarities, or (in)consistencies that transpire in clusters of arguments and throughout a letter.

A few theoretical considerations: During the communicative activity prior to an assertion, a sender determines the issues at stake and the means of argumentation or persuasion required to achieve the intended purpose. In the process, two major movements can be envisioned that determine the construction of clusters of arguments, namely, *intended* assertion efficacy and *expected* assertion efficacy.[52] The former denotes the sender's ambition to achieve a certain persuasion; the latter anticipates the addressees' receptiveness. Depending on the weight placed on either of these two movements, the sender will construct an argument that will, in his approximation, obtain maximal persuasive force. In a context of conflict, the persuasive force a sender attributes to an assertion depends on how he estimates the recipients' readi-

---

[49] Cf. Aristotle's reputable opinions (ἔνδοξα) in *Topica* 1.1.22–24. See also Perelman, *Realm*, 21; Ueding, *Rhetorik*, 34, 56; see Mitternacht, *Sprachlos* 301.

[50] Ricoeur, *Interpretation Theory*, 18: "The criterion of the noetic is the intention of communicability, the expectation of recognition in the intentional act itself. The noetic is the soul of discourse as dialogue. . . . Language is the exteriorization thanks to which an im-pression is transcended and becomes an ex-pression, or in other words, the transformation of the psychic into the noetic."

[51] Austin, *How to Do*, 52.

[52] For theoretical reflections on this dynamic in polemical exchanges and how it compares with Aristotelian categories (i.e., the determination of stases), see Dascal and Gross, "Marriage," 113–15. See also Thurén, *Argument*, 50, who suggests a similar yet not identical distinction of "speaker's opinion" and "speaker's will."

ness for revision. Instead of *expected* assertion efficacy, one could therefore speak of *expected* revision willingness. In order to achieve revision, the sender will supplement his assertion with recipient instruction and/or recipient coercion.

Recipient instruction serves the purpose of soliciting the addressees' consent. Typical for this type of assertion supplement would be the association of accepted points of departure with implications that demand, but also permit, degrees of discernment by the recipients. Recipient coercion imposes judgment or obligation on the addressees and demands their trust, assent, or submission. Whereas recipient instruction invites deliberation and allows for disagreement, recipient coercion in effect eclipses discernment polemically and otherwise. It is dependent on the recipients' acceptance of the sender's superior authority and competence, or their own inferiority.

The way in which intended and expected assertion efficacy comes to expression in the composite of accepted points of departure, recipient instruction and recipient coercion, will therefore reveal something about 1) the amount of *controversy* expected by the sender regarding an assertion, 2) the level of anticipated *authority/power* over the addressees, or, conversely, 3) the level of *revision readiness* expected from the addressees.

For instance, amplification of authority, prepared for in chs. 1 and 2, would seem to indicate that a) what is about to be argued demands a high degree of persuasion and will therefore provoke a strong amount of controversy and b) the sender does not expect his formerly accepted authority to achieve the expected effect on its own or at least is not sure the addressees are still recognizing that authority to a high enough degree. Again, if affective expressions, performative threats, repetitive language, and so forth, are included in an assertion, the recipients are expected to question, wonder at, be stunned by, resist the assertion.[53] We are now in a position to examine two of the passages with direct situational pertinence.

Galatians 4:12–15

According to some interpreters, there is no argumentative connection between the petition in 4:12 and the following verses.[54] Had Paul wanted to explicate

---

[53] J. Hester has argued that we should distinguish between the rhetorical situation and the argumentative situation. Whereas the rhetorical situation originates in an exigence, i.e., a need to modify something (cf. Bitzer, "Rhetorical Situation"), the argumentative situation is defined as "the influence of the earlier stages of the discussion on the argumentative possibilities open to the speaker" that determine the selection and order of topics to be used (Hester, "Placing the Blame," 283). In arranging his or her arguments, the speaker "tries to bring the audience from where they are in time and place to a more universal world view. As the arguments take effect, he or she must try to predict their effect and judge where the particular audience is along the trajectory from particular to universal" (284). This is a very helpful distinction. For polemical texts such as Galatians and from the point of view of the real audience, one may also want to consider that the argumentative trajectory moves in the opposite direction, namely, from universal to particular. For the Galatian addressees, Paul accentuates a universal value (circumcision is not required for Gentile Christ-believers) and imposes on it his own particular interpretation, trying to enforce it with different means of persuasion.

[54] According to Burton, *Galatians,* 235, Paul is "dropping argument." See also Betz, *Galatians,* 223.

the petition, it is argued, he would have continued his plea with something like "Hold fast to the truth of the gospel as I do, for you are children of God *without* the law." We are all sinners (2:17), saved by grace.[55] The assumption is that Paul's primary concern was ideological, or even visionary, and the issue of uncircumcised Gentile Christ-believers purely soteriological, presupposing that the circumcision of Gentile Christ-believers, in and of itself, would effect their falling out of grace. Given Paul's double affirmation in the same letter that circumcision, in and of itself, is a matter of indifference (5:6; 6:15), this assumption seems strange. In addition, the construction of the implications of the plea is based on another—as I will try to demonstrate, not very convincing—presupposition, namely, that the addressees, too, perceived of their exigency as one of soteriological uncertainty. Based on these presuppositions, the following verses have indeed little to contribute to the understanding of the plea.

For the reasons articulated, it would seem worthwhile to suspend judgment on the traditional presuppositions and take another look at 4:12–15. If the section is read as a coherent whole, with 4:12c–15 considered the first of two explications to the petition (second explication, 4:16–20), what kind of picture emerges regarding Paul's plea and the addressees' exigency?

To begin with, we have to consider the somewhat enigmatic and paradoxical character[56] of the petition itself:

a   "Become as I (am)" = content of petition

      "for I also (am) as you (are)" = affirmative motivation

b   "Brethren" = personal address

      "I beseech you" (δέομαι) = formal but involved petition verb

Except for γίνεσθε, there is no verb or other time indicator. Thus, while it is clear from the main clause of the petition that the addressees are expected to change from something that characterizes their present condition to something else that they do not embrace at the present time, for the subordinate clause ("for I also as you") there are no time references. Most translations presuppose that the subordinate clause should be supplemented with ἐγενόμην (or γέγονα)[57] and read, "Become as I am, for I *have become* as you are" (RSV). This reading suggests that Paul had changed from a Torah-obedient Jew into someone who is equivalent to Gentile Christ-believers, asking them to join in. Such a presupposition is not only contradicted by 5:3 (as already stated); it does not fit the immediate context. Two alternative verb supplements have been suggested from early on: Chrysostom, Jerome, and others supplemented ἤμην (". . . for I was as you"); and Pelagius, Augustine, and others,

---

[55] Citation from Williams, *Galatians*, 120. Similarly Rohde, *Galater*, 183; Witherington, *Grace*, 308; and others. The rhetorical question of 2:17 is misinterpreted unless it is recognized for stating an unreal case with a definite rejection added (μὴ γένοιτο). No inference concerning what actually happened can be drawn from it (Mussner, *Galaterbrief*, 176–77).

[56] Burton, *Galatians*, 236; and others.

[57] Argued for since Zahn, *Galater*, 215.

εἰμί (". . . for I am as you").[58] The first two alternatives find supporters to this day, with the first one being prominent among modern commentators.[59] Since the time references in the subordinate clause are undecided, however, there is no reason to exclude that both past *and* present are in view: "Become as I, for I (have been *then* and am *now*) as you."[60] This would agree with the two time references articulated in the following verses: their first meeting and the present circumstances. Then Paul's challenge could be reformulated: "As you know from past experience, I share your present predicament ('I as you') and I beseech you to regard your predicament as I do ('Become as I')." Let me try to substantiate this reading and elaborate its implications.

First, 4:12c ("you did me no wrong") may be taken as a cautious expression of confidence, known as an occasional addition to the epistolary petition formula, introducing the friendship theme.[61] It is cautious, since it articulates past experiences as the basis of confidence without asserting the extension of that confidence into the future. Behind the cautiousness one might suspect a soft rebuke ("How come I cannot express my confidence fully?"). As the expression of confidence is both part of the epistolary petition formula and clearly connects with what follows, it would be quite surprising if it had nothing to do with 4:12ab.

Second, 4:12c–15 directs our attention to perceptions of social circumstances, that is, the way Gentiles (Christ-believers to be) perceived their encounter with Paul in Galatia. The narrative focuses on human interaction, danger, and refuge, presented as "a string of *topoi* belonging to the theme of friendship,"[62] a standard topic in epistolary literature.[63]

Third, "the weakness of the flesh" is presented as having been involved in the advance of the gospel (δι᾿ ἀσθένειαν τῆς σαρκός). Διά with the accusative refers to cause and may in this case be taken as the "occasioning condition,"[64] including accompanying circumstances that contributed to the cause.[65]

Fourth, Paul praises the Galatian Christ-believers for not despising and rejecting him at the initial encounter[66] even though they were tempted to. The reference in οὐκ ἐξουθενήσατε οὐδὲ ἐξεπτύσατε ("you neither despised me nor spit out") accentuates the disdain and rejection that may have been imposed on Paul by a separation

---

[58] Cf. Sieffert, *Galater*, 256.

[59] For ἐγενόμην see, e.g., Lührmann, *Galatians*, 85–86; Martyn, *Galatians*, 418–19; Williams, *Galatians*, 119; for ἤμην see Vouga, *Galater*, 106–7 (somewhat unclear). Bruce, *Commentary*, 207, translates, "I am as you are," but supports his translation with γέγονα.

[60] Similarly argued by Goddard and Cummins, "Ill-Treated," 99, though with different inferences.

[61] Cf. White, "New Testament Epistolary," 1737; Betz, *Galatians*, 223.

[62] Betz, *Galatians*, 221.

[63] Koskenniemi, *Studien*, 115–27.

[64] Sieffert, *Galater*, 262 ("*veranlassender Zustand*").

[65] See Güttgemanns, *Apostel*, 175–76; Goddard and Cummins, "Ill-Treated," 103. Contra Hafemann, "Role," 169. Lightfoot, *Galatians*, 174 (followed by many), strongly opposed the Latin fathers for translating δι᾿ ἀσθένειαν τῆς σαρκός with *per* ("through") instead of *propter* ("because of") *infirmitatem* but admitted at the same time that several of the Greek fathers included circumstance.

[66] I take τὸ πρότερον, as most interpreters, to simply assert a contrast to νῦν, referring to the first encounter without necessary implications of further visits; e.g., R. Longenecker, *Galatians*, 190.

curse[67] but in which the addressees did not participate. Even though spitting is considered one of the strategies to guard against the evil eye, inferring demonological connotations from ἐξεπτύσατε may go a little to far.[68] Yet the context of envy and moral defectiveness (4:17–18), which are also connected with evil-eye imagery,[69] and the parallels between this passage and 3:1–5 (ἐβάσκανεν, 3:1), suggest at least a metaphorical resemblance. Being able to see through the imposed separation, the addressees had received Paul as Christ Jesus. Thus, they are praised for recognizing the positive implications at work in negative and dishonorable circumstances, reversing their temptation even to the point of self-sacrifice ("you would have torn out your eyes"). They had been capable of inverting what appeared evil and dishonorable, turning it into a perception of strength and honor in disguise (an "epiphany of the ἐσταυρωμένος"),[70] and they had done it at great personal risk (see below).

Fifth, we need to determine what the despicable and repulsive "weakness of the flesh" in v. 13 refers to. As Troy Martin has pointed out: "If Paul desired to say he were ill, ἀσθένεια alone communicates this idea better than the addition of τῆς σαρκὸς. The addition would have been confusing, since illness was viewed as a problem of the *body,* not the flesh."[71] The expression "weak flesh" could be ascribed to both healthy and sick bodies, since "weak" functioned simply to distinguish between different kinds of flesh within a body. The weakness of the flesh may be the *material cause* of experienced pain, whereas the *efficient cause* of that pain consists of an improper diet, bad climate, or some other factor that causes an imbalance in the bodily fluids or powers. Utilizing these distinctions for the references to flesh in Gal 4:13–14, the focus turns from what effects something to what is being affected. The "weakness of the flesh" that Paul is experiencing is thus referring to the condition in which he found himself. It is the "vulnerable condition" that was perceived as shameful.[72]

Finally, in 4:15 Paul is confirming—albeit clothed in a disparaging rhetorical question—the Galatian Christ-believers' former enthusiasm (ὁ μακαρισμὸς ὑμῶν) even to the point of self-sacrifice. According to Richard Longenecker, the question

---

[67] B. Longenecker, *Triumph,* 156: "In Paul's day, hatred spells and separation curses were frequently employed as a means of dissociating persons from others by the power of demonic spirits of gods of chaos. Separation curses introduced enmity between previously allied parties, and promoted the interest of the one inducing the curse."

[68] R. Longenecker, *Galatians,* 192; Goddard and Cummins, "Ill-Treated," 105–7; B. Longenecker, *Triumph,* 152.

[69] Cf. Nanos, *Irony,* 186–91, 279–80. Consider also Gal 5:20, where φαρμακεία and ἔχθραι are listed next to each other, and Plutarch, *Inv. od.* 2, 7; *Quaest. conv.* 680C–683B. For further references, see B. Longenecker, *Triumph,* 155–56.

[70] Güttgemanns, *Apostel,* 185.

[71] T. Martin, "Whose Flesh?" 69–70. Aristotle, for instance, differentiates between different kinds of weaknesses of flesh, asserting that internal flesh is the weakest because it is more permeable than external flesh (*Probl.* 31.21) Along the same lines, Hippocrates describes the flesh of the elderly as "thin and weak" (*Morb.* 1.22). In non-Christian contexts up to the sixth century C.E., "weakness" refers to sickness only when used absolutely. Combined with "flesh," it never refers to sickness. The frequently cited 2 Cor 12:7 is no parallel (Mullins, "Paul's Thorn"; contra Hafemann, "Role," 169–70).

[72] These are not Martin's conclusions; he rejects any affiliation of "weakness of the flesh" with persecution. For pro arguments see Goddard and Cummins, "Ill-Treated," 95).

implies that this former state of the addressees had come to an end.[73] This assertion of Paul's, however, has to be recognized for being a recipient instruction, which can only be assessed as a cognition of Paul.[74] The accepted point of departure, where reference is made to a past experience of which both Paul and the addressees have first-hand knowledge, is found in the statement "you would have torn out your eyes and given them to me." Thus, whereas the present enthusiasm of the addressees is a matter of dispute, their former enthusiasm can be taken at face value.

Most commentators agree that Paul is referring to "readiness of the highest sacrifice."[75] As has been identified in a number of ancient sources,[76] the eye represents the most precious thing a man possesses, and the true mark of friendship is a person's willingness to sacrifice what is most precious to him.[77] That the addressees would have supplied Paul with precious gifts of any kind seems far-fetched. Thus, supported by the prominence of *topoi* of friendship in 4:12–20, we may presume that their sacrifice concerned personal involvement, giving true friendship to a stranger, and doing it at great personal risk.

Summing up, the following can be taken as accepted points of departure: a) the addressees had been approached by Paul as he was in a vulnerable and dishonorable condition; b) enthusiastically they had offered their lives in order to care for and assist him; and c) they had accepted Paul's identification of his hardship with Christ. In light of the affirmative motivation in 4:12a, "I also as you" (κἀγὼ ὡς ὑμεῖς), vv. 13–15 are supposed to parallel Paul's vulnerable condition *then* with the addressees' circumstances *now*. The petition, on the other hand ("Become as I"), is a recipient instruction that seeks to obtain the addressees' appreciation of the cruciform life and perception of it as a blessing in disguise. It is a call to equal loyalty, a call to "follow his paradigmatic example of faithfulness in suffering."[78]

Galatians 3:1–5

Paul's determination to maximize the persuasive force of what he is about to argue is underscored by a double recipient coercion: an accusation of foolishness (᾽Ω ἀνόητοι Γαλάται) and the provocative question "Who has bewitched you?" (τίς ὑμᾶς ἐβάσκανεν). The evil-eye imagery implied in βασκαίνειν does not only suggest a possible cause for the addressees' foolishness but also carries with it the idea

---

[73] R. Longenecker, *Galatians*, 192.

[74] Important to note, the supposed loss of enthusiasm is linked to the need for Christ to be formed in them (μορφωθῇ Χριστὸς ἐν ὑμῖν) 4:19; see Güttgemanns, *Apostel*, 189 n. 112. This correlation has to be taken into account as one tries to make sense of 5:4.

[75] Betz, *Galatians*, 227.

[76] For references, see Michaelis, "ὁράω," 5:375–78.

[77] For references to Plato, Aristotle, and Lucian(!) see Betz, *Galatians*, 227–28. R. Longenecker, *Galatians*, 193, suggests that the idiom is telling more than the modern idiom: "giving the shirt off one's back."

[78] Goddard and Cummins, "Ill-Treated," 99; cf. Hansen, *Abraham in Galatians*, 157; Nanos, *Irony*, 88, 187.

that those casting the spell were envious of the addressees.[79] Considering the address-ees' situation, such a suggestion reveals that Paul is being ironic.[80] Rhetorically speak-ing, it is an accomplished move, doing two things in one blow: suggesting that the addressees should reverse their own perception and preparing their receptiveness for the programmatic statement that is to follow. In addition, the reference to evil-eye imagery anticipates 4:14.

In direct continuation, the focus of the whole section is highlighted: "before whose eyes Christ was publicly portrayed [προεγράφη] as crucified." By combining προεγράφη[81] with "before whose eyes," the coercive objective of the whole section is further amplified. The addressees' unequivocal experience of the crucified Christ could simply not be misconstrued by anyone in possession of a healthy perception. Placing ἐσταυρωμένος at the end of the sentence puts an extra emphasis on the word[82] and directs the attention to Christ as being crucified.

Having recognized the connection between Paul's vulnerable condition and the recognition of Christ in 4:12–15, the interpreter should be alerted by the affirmation of 3:1.[83] Instead of the supposition of a technique of impersonation[84] or an exclusive con-cern with theological issues,[85] a comparison of 3:1–5 with 4:12–15 seems to suggest it-self: the passages converge in references to the incipient experience and in the focus on visual experience. The paradoxical experience of the Christ-likeness is highlighted in both places, being at one and the same time an appreciation of spiritual beauty within "fleshly" abhorrence. And there is the contrast between then and now, focusing on right and wrong cognition: *then* they had perceived Christ within the paradox; *now* they are foolish for not appreciating the implications concerning their own lives.

In 3:2 the addressees are confronted with the next rhetorical question, asking them to recount the circumstances surrounding their reception of the Spirit. The question divides into two alternative suggestions, one affirmative (by the hearing of faith [ἐξ ἀκοῆς πίστεως]), the other unreal ("by works of the law" [ἐξ ἔργων νόμου]). Whether or not ἐξ ἀκοῆς πίστεως means "by faith-hearing"[86] or "by the faith-message,"[87] the phrase makes sense only if it refers to how the initial Spirit re-ception was mediated, and correlates to the initial experience, namely, the portrayal

---

[79] See above, n. 69.

[80] Nanos, ("Inter- and Intra-Jewish," 398–99; *Irony*, 32–61, passim) interprets Paul's admoni-tion of the addressees throughout the letter as one of ironic rebuke (typical for the parent-child rela-tion and with a natural tendency toward exaggeration). The term "ironic rebuke" was first suggested for the epistolary formula θαυμάζω ὅτι in 1:6 by Mullins ("Formulas," 385–86).

[81] The word does not simply imply "written beforehand" but connotes a visible presentation, "a painted or chiseled image" (Zahn, *Galater*, 141; see also Dunn, *Theology*, 152).

[82] Rohde, *Galater*, 130.

[83] See also Hafemann, "Role," 174, who has emphasized the importance of the connection be-tween 4:14 and 3:1, albeit with different implications than mine.

[84] Witherington, *Grace*, 205. For a description of the means of mimesis, cf. Lausberg, *Hand-buch*, 554–601.

[85] Betz, *Galatians*, 132: "the original kerygma"; R. Longenecker, *Galatians*, 100; Dunn, *Theol-ogy*, 152.

[86] Williams, *Galatians*, 83–84 ("the state of *being* captivated").

[87] Hays, *Faith*, 149. For a discussion of the options, see 143–49. An update on the debate is available in Johnson and Hay, *Looking Back*, 35–92.

of Christ crucified. There is no indication of a "faith-hearing versus works of law" antithesis. Rather, articulating an accepted point of departure, Paul simply asserts that works of the law were not involved at the initial "encounter" with Christ crucified.[88] To be sure, there is a contrast involved in terms of the superiority of Christ over the works of the law, but there is no antithesis.[89]

It is constructed as a rhetorical question, and a rebuke is implied; but the content of the rebuke is not yet made clear. The explicit assertion so far is simply that the Spirit was received during the portrayal of the crucified Christ. A similarly rebuking rhetorical question about the correlation of Spirit, works of the law, and ἀκαῆ πίστεως is reasserted in v. 5, but there it is directed towards the *present* circumstances.

In 3:3–4 the relationship between accepted points of departure, recipient instruction and recipient coercion, takes another turn. The argument is headed by a repetition of the earlier recipient coercion that intensifies the reprimand for foolishness, perhaps pointing to the fact that now the actual controversy is going to be articulated. In a rhetorical question, the incipient Spirit reception is compared to the present state of the addressees, and the potential implications are affirmed to be detrimental: "Having begun with the Spirit, are you now ending it with the flesh?" And the implications are spelled out in a further question: "Have you suffered so much in vain—if it really is in vain?"

Important to note, 3:1–2 relates an accepted point of departure, namely, the *independence* of Spirit reception from works of law; 3:3–4 adds a recipient instruction, posing an *antithesis* between Spirit-blessedness in the beginning and flesh-vanity now. With the presentation of the antithesis comes a reference to the sufferings of the addressees. Paul affirms that as they were living according to the Spirit, they were suffering (ἐπάθετε). By implication, the absence of suffering belongs to the present danger of flesh-vanity.

The flow of argument in 3:1–5 can be illustrated in this way:
| = independence; ↔ = antithesis

3:1–2	*Beginning*	Christ crucified/Spirit	|	works of law
		faith message	|	works of law
3:3–4	*Now*	Spirit/suffering	↔	flesh
3:5		Spirit/miracles	|	works of law
		faith message	|	works of law

How would the addressees have responded to this line of argument? Leaving recipient instruction and recipient coercion aside for a moment, I think they would have agreed with Paul: "Yes, it was the portrayal of Christ crucified before our eyes

---

[88] Contra Räisänen, *Paul and the Law*, 163, who recognizes, however, that the focus is only on *result*.

[89] R. Longenecker, *Galatians*, 103, points out that the antithesis is between Spirit and flesh, but regrettably, I think, dilutes the observation by interpreting σάρξ as "human effort."

that captivated us in the beginning and resulted in our receiving the Spirit. Yes, works of the law had nothing to do with that. Yes, Spirit and flesh contradict each other. Yes, living in the flesh must contradict living according to the image of Christ crucified."

Considering the rhetoric woven into the argument, they may have wondered, however, what the questions ". . . are you now ending it with the flesh?" "Have you suffered so much in vain?" were supposed to imply. Surely, works of the law were as irrelevant for *their* perception of the conditions for salvation now as they were then. On those grounds, there was no reason for Paul's calling them foolish (cf. 5:6, 6:15). The addressees would simply have been stunned and bewildered. But they would, of course, also have realized that the issue of suffering—Christ's, Paul's, and their own— was introduced into the argument. And as the letter readers reached 4:12–15, 29 and finally 6:12–17, they would have realized that their initial bewilderment was part of the letter-writer's rhetorical strategy. In 3:1–5 they were being initiated emotionally to what was to become ever clearer. participation in Christ's sufferings was not a potential option; it was a requisite.

Against this interpretation one may want to point to the flow of argument that puts flesh and works of law together on the negative side, suggesting that works of law, in effect, "come into the picture on the wrong side of the same antithesis."[90] Yet in none of the other arguments in Galatians where πνεῦμα and σάρξ are juxtaposed are works of law implicated in the antithesis. In 4:29, where the one κατὰ σάρκα is juxtaposed to the one κατὰ πνεῦμα, not works of the law are in view but persecution (see below). In 5:16–26, where the desires of the flesh are juxtaposed to the Spirit, and the works of the flesh to the fruit of the Spirit, Paul affirms that against the fruit of the Spirit there is no νόμος and that those who belong to Christ have crucified their flesh with its passions and desires (5:23–24). The νόμος is explicitly separated from the antithesis of Spirit and flesh. And most important, preparing the antithesis in 5:13–14, the law stands on the side of love, juxtaposing the whole law to "the pretext of the flesh" (ἀφορμὴν τῇ σαρκί).

The most explicit antithesis between Spirit and flesh (τὸ δὲ πνεῦμα κατὰ τῆς σαρκός. ταῦτα γὰρ ἀλλήλοις ἀντίκειται) is followed by the assertion "But if you are led by the Spirit you are not under the law" (5:18). Here again the antithesis between Spirit and flesh is not followed up by an antithesis between Spirit and law. Rather in v. 23 Paul explicitly asserts that the law is not against the fruits of the Spirit (κατὰ τῶν τοιούτων οὐκ ἔστιν νόμος), the point being that Gentile Christ-believers are blessed by the Spirit and have no need of the law. It is therefore not appropriate to translate σάρξ in 3:3 with "human effort."[91] As σάρξ is put into antithesis to the Spirit in Galatians, the antithesis is obviously not right versus wrong effort, but ability versus inability.

To sum up, it is important to note the difference established in 3:1–5 between what is *not related* and what is *antithetical* to the Spirit reception. Works of the law play no part in the construction of the situation of the addressees, except for the as-

---

[90] Cf. Dunn, *Theology*, 155.
[91] See above, n. 89.

sertion that they were not related to it then and are not now. Paul's first order of concern is with the memory and imitation of the crucified Christ and how that imitation is being violated by what he describes sarcastically as "completing in the flesh" (σαρκὶ ἐπιτλεῖσθε). Nothing, of course, can be completed in the flesh, since flesh, as the antithesis to Spirit, articulates incompleteness, passions, desires, licentiousness, selfishness. Instead the motive behind the addressees' desire to get circumcised is unmasked for being a work of the flesh.

Persecution, a Theme of Galatians?

In 4:28–29 Paul argues, "Now we, brethren, like Isaac are children of promise. But as at that time he who was born according to the flesh persecuted [ἐδίωκεν] him who was born according to the Spirit, so it is now." By means of the short addition οὕτως καὶ νῦν, the implications of the preceding allegory are brought to bear on the addressees' present situation. The son of the slave woman is identified with the persecutors, and both Paul and the addressees ("we") with the persecuted. But who are the present persecutors?

If we remember the stereotypical characterizations of the influencers in the letter as a whole, it should come as no surprise if the phrase "those who are κατὰ σάρκα" would refer to the influencers.[92] Yet not even the denigrating characterization of the influencers throughout the letter, and especially not 4:17, supports the idea of them persecuting the addressees. With διώκω being used consistently of actual persecution,[93] it would seem more likely that Paul is referring to the suffering inflicted on the addressees by other than the influencers, supposedly Jews in Galatia.[94]

Moreover, the statement encompasses the history from Abraham up to now, articulating that children of the promise should expect persecution. Ernst Baasland states cautiously, "It is more or less normal that those who are κατὰ πνεῦμα are persecuted by those who are κατὰ σάρκα."[95] The special interest in persecution is further indicated by the strained interpretation of Gen 21:9, justifiable neither from the Hebrew text nor from the LXX. Ishmael's playing with (possibly mocking of) Isaac is interpreted by Paul as "persecution." He may be following an already existing tradition (that is also taken up later on in *Gen. Rab.* 53:11), yet the tour de force of the interpretation still suggests that "the subject of persecution [is] so important to Paul, that he has to strain קחצ/παίζω the way he does."[96]

In 5:11 the reference to persecution does not concern the addressees but Paul's present situation. It has bearing on the situation of the addressees, however, since it

---

[92] So Zahn, *Galater*, 244; Burton, *Galatians*, 266; Mussner, *Galaterbrief*, 331; Martyn, *Galatians*, 445; Witherington, *Grace*, 338; and others.
[93] Baasland, "Persecution," 136: "more or less a technical term for persecution of Christians." See also Cosgrove, "Law," 229.
[94] Schlier, *Galater*, 162; Betz, *Galatians*, 250; Lührmann, *Galatians*, 92; and many others.
[95] Baasland, "Persecution," 135.
[96] Ibid., 136.

comes close to restating the normality of persecution for Christ-believers that has been affirmed already in 4:29. In the form of a rhetorical question, Paul intends to put a rumor to rest that was having an undesirable effect on the addressees: "If I still [ἔτι] preach circumcision, why am I still [ἔτι] persecuted?" And then he adds, "In that case [ἄρα] the scandal of the cross has been abolished." By vouching proof to the contrary, Paul ascertains the falseness of the rumor. But if the proof is real, then the backdrop of the rumor cannot be simply hypothetical.[97] And for the rumor to have any impact on the addressees or the influencers' advice to them (cf. the preceding verse), it would seem to have to be a reference to activities of the Christ-believing Paul.[98]

The real issue of 5:11, however, is the immovable bond between persecution and the cross. The Galatians' concern is this: "Why may we not get circumcised if that would allow us to overcome shame, dishonor, and persecution?" But "Paul's concern is that the 'stumbling block of the cross' not be eliminated from the Christian gospel and Christian experience."[99] If persecution is removed, then (ἄρα) the offense (σκάνδαλον)[100] of the cross is removed. As we read 5:11 in light of the "I as you" of 4:12, we can see why such a statement would fit well into a discourse unit with direct situational pertinence. Paul wants to make sure the addressees understand that, even though absent in body, he is sharing their predicament. Most important, he is accepting persecution as the necessary requisite of the offense of the cross. The Christ-like life must bear witness to the marks of the cross, so uncircumcision of Gentile Christ-believers, being the permanent inducement of the scandal of the cross, must be maintained.

The RSV translates 3:4 (τοσαῦτα ἐπάθετε εἰκῇ) as "Have you experienced so many things in vain?" But the verb πάσχω is used everywhere in the NT and also in the LXX in the unfavorable sense of "experiencing suffering."[101] Walther Michaelis represents many others when he concludes that when πάσχω is used absolutely, it always implies *unpleasant* suffering, except when the context demands a more positive reading. Since "neither the context nor the contents of the epistle [to the Galatians] support the idea of suffering under persecution,"[102] we must accept that it is used

---

[97] Since the second ἔτι has to be temporal, it seems natural to take the first ἔτι the same way (contra Mussner, *Galaterbrief*, 358–59, who reads the first ἔτι as indicating addition).

[98] So also Munck, *Paul*, 91: "Paul's Jewish past, where he stresses his zeal and progress in Judaism (1:14), can hardly have been related by his opponents with any controversial intent." Most interpreters acknowledge the presence of a real condition and agree that the insertion of a pre-Christian affirmation seems enigmatic. Still, the notion that Paul could ever have been advocating circumcision of Gentiles as a Christ-believer (except for Timothy, who is considered a special case) is generally rejected. Galatians 5:11 must refer either to activities of the pre-Christian Paul (e.g., Betz, *Galatians*, 268; R. Longenecker, *Galatians*, 232; Williams, *Galatians*, 140; Witherington, *Grace*, 372–73) or to Paul's continued practice of circumcision among Jews (Dunn, *Theology*, 279). McKnight, *Light*, 152 n. 14, argues that Judaism was "not truly a missionary religion" (117), yet maintains that Gal 5:11 must refer to Paul's pre-Christian zeal for God-fearer circumcision (104, 152). Howard, *Crisis*, 9, 11, assumes a complete misconception on the part of the influencers.

[99] Betz, *Galatians*, 269, but with different implications.

[100] Σκάνδαλον means "trap," "snare," but the word is also used as a metaphor for provocation that causes revulsion, resentment, and resistance (some LXX examples: Josh 23:13; 1 Macc 5:4; Sir 7:6; 27:23; Jdt 5:20).

[101] Cf. R. Longenecker, *Galatians*, 104.

[102] Michaelis, "πάσχω, κτλ," 5:912; contra Lightfoot, *Galatians*, 134.

here *sensu bono.* Baasland rightly observes that persecution in Galatians "is an aspect which the exegetic literature has more or less neglected."[103]

In 6:12 Paul argues that the Galatians are compelled to be circumcised by those who want to make a good showing in the flesh "*only* in order that *they* may not be persecuted for the cross of Christ." Except for 4:17, this is the only explicit affirmation of motive regarding the influencers, and in both cases we find the same stereotype. Many interpreters are so impressed by "only" and "they" that they take 6:12 to exclude the possibility of persecution in Galatia. Thus, they assert that avoidance of persecution cannot have been *the addressees'* motive for circumcision. But such a view can only be sustained if one neglects the rhetorical strategy throughout the letter.[104] Consistently, Paul has been characterizing the actions and motives of the supposed opponents in a completely derogatory manner, so why should one expect anything different this time? The coercive force of the exaggerating "only" (μόνον) in 6:12 gives the accusation away for being, in fact, a less sophisticated case of stereotyping. The eagerness to point out the selfishness of the influencers is conspicuously immoderate especially when the addressees' hardship is taken into consideration. By implication Paul is asserting, "Even though you also are facing persecution, be assured that the influencers could not care less. Their exclusive interest is with their own well-being."[105] Galatians 6:12 fits the stereoptype of the influencers promoted throughout the letter and in 4:17 in particular (ζηλοῦσιν ὑμᾶς οὐ καλῶς).

Much has been inferred from the expression "they compel [ἀναγκάζουσιν] you" for the construction of the influencers' activities. Granted, there is historical evidence that Jewish authorities compelled the inhabitants of conquered lands or refugees to their towns to be circumcised.[106] But those instances can scarcely be paralleled with the exigencies of the influencers. In 2:14, addressing Peter, Paul asserts, "If you, being a Jew, live like a Gentile and not like a Jew, how can you compel [ἀναγκάζουσιν] the Gentiles to judaize?" According to Paul's own representation of the incident at Antioch in 2:11–14, Peter was under considerable pressure and participated in hypocrisy for fear of the circumcised (2:13). Even in Paul's own words, then, "compel" does not have to be about persecution; it can be a rhetorically exaggerated depiction of fearful disengagement. And this would square with circumcised Christ-believers in Galatia who were concerned both for their own and for the uncircumcised Christ-believers' safety, being under the pressure of agents of social control.[107]

---

[103] Baasland, "Persecution," 136. Baasland suggests that πάσχω should be interpreted together with διώκω and πορθέω. See also Nanos, "Inter- and Intra-Jewish," 406; *Irony*, 189–91, 279–80.

[104] For a careful assessment of the caricature of the influencers including 6:12, cf. Barclay, "Mirror-Reading," 368–70, 373–74; *Obeying the Truth*, 45–46. The lack of alertness to stereotyping and rhetorical nuance evident in statements such as "Paul can here only refer to the situation in Jerusalem" (Suhl, "Galaterbrief," 3082) is stunning.

[105] Somewhat overstated, this is Jewett's assessment of the influencers' motive when compelling the addressees into taking the "first visible steps" (cf. Jewett, "Agitators," 342–47).

[106] E.g., Josephus, *Ant.* 13.9.1, 13.11.3, 15.7.9; *Life* 113, 149; and also the historian Ptolemaios, *GLAJJ* 1:146, discussed in Breytenbach, *Paulus,* 128–30.

[107] Nanos, *Irony,* 219–24; Nanos argues, however, that the influencers are non-Christ-believers.

At the end of the letter, Paul summarizes his concern, as it were, in his own hand-writing (6:11). To the reader who is waiting for the final argument against circumcision as a means of securing salvation, these verses must seem puzzling. Why would Paul conclude his letter by asserting the influencers' disinterest with law compliance? Why would he reiterate once more the indifference of both circumcision and uncircumcision? Having taken into account, however, the distinction articulated throughout the letter between concerns of the second and the first order—circumcision as such, and the effect of circumcision—we are prepared to appreciate the forceful and explicit conjunction of the suffering Christ with the suffering servant Paul: "The world has been crucified to me and I to the world" (6:14), followed by "I bear on my body the stigmata of Jesus" (6:17).[108]

We may have considered 3:1 as "simply" a forceful reference to the appropriation of the atonement (albeit prepared for in 2:19–21: "I have been crucified with Christ . . ."). We may still have been unsure as we read 5:11: "Why am I still persecuted. In that case the stumbling block of the cross has been removed." But by the time we reach 6:14–17, the implications are plain. Being crucified with Christ and to the world must be taken as resounding assertions of the life conditions Paul is expecting for himself in this evil world.

Conclusions

This final section will sketch some of the circumstances that may have brought about the writing of the Letter to the Galatians. As Paul came to Galatia, he encountered at least four categories of people: native Jews (φύσει Ἰουδαῖοι, 2:15), proselyte Jews, Gentile liminals (God-fearers), and Gentiles. Paul perceived his mission to be to Gentiles and not to Jews (2:9), but in order to build a platform for himself, he probably began preaching the good news of a crucified Christ among his fellow Jews, insisting that a new creation was being formed within the present evil order (1:4; 6:15). *Now* the blessings of Abraham were being distributed to Gentiles solely on the basis of faith (3:6–9, 26–29). Thus, Gentiles who committed themselves to the crucified Christ should be accepted as equal members of the community of the righteous without further requirements.

The Jewish community, at least those in social and political control, must have been alerted not only by Paul's claim to the equality of uncircumcised Gentiles with Jews (cf. 2:15) but also by the potential political threat inherent in any public proclamation of an executed criminal who was supposed to have risen from the dead, deliv-

---

[108] Helmut Mödritzer has argued that by an act of self-stigmatization Paul was turning a stigma into a charisma. The idea of self-stigmatization entails turning a shameful stigmatization by others into an honorable self-stigmatization. The central thesis is that stigma and charisma belong together. Self-stigmatization had a powerful impact in a culture of shame (Mödritzer, *Stigma*, 213, 222). Mödritzer's interpretations are based on Lipp, *Stigma* and "Social Deviation." The reference to the stigmata of the crucified may also allude to the public shame experienced by the condemned on their path to crucifixion (Nanos, "Inter- and Intra-Jewish," 406, who cites for evidence the *Declamationes* by Pseudo-Quintilian).

ering his followers from this present evil age (1.4). To begin with, they may have tried to put a lid on the situation. But since Paul was not to be silenced, they treated him as they would treat one of their own and punished him.[109] Unable to control his fervor and thus in fear of having their fragile political and social privileges (from which all Jews, including Paul, profited) threatened, they may also have reported their noninvolvement to the city magistrates and thus contributed to making Paul's activities public.

Consequently, Paul the learned man from Tarsus and Jerusalem, was shamed immensely and found himself in a vulnerable and reproachful condition (4:13–14). But this did not keep him from proclaiming his gospel. Instead it served as the occasioning cause for turning to the Gentiles. The first of his converts were probably liminals to Judaism who had been kept from becoming proselytes before, both by the requirement of circumcision and the social disruption that denying one's own cultic affiliations brought with it (cf. 4.9: ἐπιστρέφετε πάλιν).[110] Despite his vulnerable condition, or perhaps because of it, Paul succeeded in making an impression on these people that was stronger than that of other Jews before him. In fact, what surfaces in the text is that the addressees were enthused with love for this messenger, who did not only proclaim but lived his message of the crucified Christ. Their hearts were kindled with a willingness to put their own lives at risk (4:15), and they seem to have been rewarded with pneumatic experiences and miracles (3:2, 5).

Somehow Paul managed to portray his stigmatization as a charisma of Christ[111] and, with his presence, to enthuse the new converts with a similar attitude. In the neighborhood where they were gathering, he may even have been able to exert an influence, so that, for the time being, people were under the impression that is was a legitimate socioreligious group. As Paul moved on, however, the tension increased, and fairly soon the Gentile Christ-believers found themselves squeezed between a rock and a hard place. As liminals to Judaism, their communal identity had been functional. They had been able to fluctuate between obligations to different social and religious contexts, including their native contexts, their obligations to Rome, and their affiliations with Jewish groups (albeit only as "guests"). Having begun to confess Christ as the Lord of their lives, they were now restrained from performing their Gentile community obligations both regarding the cults to which their families

---

[109] E. Sanders, *Paul, the Law*, 192.

[110] Shaye Cohen's investigation into the ways by which a Gentile in antiquity became less a Gentile and more a Jew lead him to propose seven categories (*Beginnings*, 140–74). On the basis of implications from Gal 4:8–11, I conclude that the former association of the Galatian addressees with Judaism would have been closer to category 4 ("practicing some or many ritual of the Jews") than to category 5 ("venerating the god of the Jews and denying or ignoring all other gods").

[111] Baasland, "Persecution," 138–39. Having established my case from within Galatians, I may now be permitted to point to the fact that identification of his sufferings with the suffering Christ is a common theme in Paul's writings (Phil 3:10; Col 2:24; 1 Cor 2:2–3; cf. D. Hill, *Prophecy*; Hodgson, "Paul"; Pobee, *Persecution*; Sumney, "Paul's Weakness"). Persecution is a necessary part of the life in and with Christ (cf. 1 Cor 4:16, 11:1; Phil 3:17; also 1 Thess 2:14; Col 1:24). In asserting these things, Paul is firmly rooted in his Jewishness (see 2 Macc 7:37; Dan 3–6; Bel 4:1; Josephus, *Ant.* 3.2.2, 4.6.6, 7.12.2, 7.13.2, 10.7.3; cf. Hodgson, "Paul," 70–72; Sumney, "Paul's Weakness," 76; Barré, "Qumran"; Pobee, *Persecution*, 38–45 [suffering as part of the messianic woes]).

and relatives were obligated and regarding participation in the emperor cult. Denied at the same time status equality by the larger Jewish community, they found themselves in a social, political, and religious void. They were required to deny idolatry fully yet lacked the societal status that provided a livable environment for such a commitment.[112]

There probably were some proselytes—possibly acquaintances of the former liminals—who had become Christ-believers as proselytes and to whose circumcision Paul would have had no objections. From Paul's point of view, they had become Jews and belonged to a different category than the former liminals. But from the liminals' point of view, their neighbor proselytes were in some ways still like them. And even those proselytes, having become Christ-believers, may have shared some of that sentiment, so that Paul can refer to them as not keeping the law (οὐ νόμον φυλάσσουσιν, 6:15).[113] Through their affiliation with the uncircumcised Christ-believers, the proselyte Christ-believers may have drawn negative attention to themselves, felt threatened, and therefore urged them to consider circumcision both for their own and for the uncircumcised Christ-believers' sake.

In any case, the enthusiasm of the uncircumcised and thus marginalized Christ-believers was put to the test. They were faced with two alternatives: 1) compromising the confession to Jesus as Lord and returning in effect to their communal identity as liminals or 2) being circumcised and receiving equality of status within the community of the righteous, and thus doing nothing else but becoming like their Christ-believing proselyte neighbors, *and, indeed, like Paul.* They had perceived circumcision as a trial, but given the situation they were in as Christ-believers, circumcision had become the lesser of two trials. In considering circumcision, they had reason to assume that they were within the confines of the accepted rule and that their desire to find a workable arrangement of their life circumstances was in agreement with Paul both on a theological and on a personal level: 1) he himself had alerted them to Abraham, the prototype of faith righteousness (3:6–9), who also was the quintessential proselyte,[114] circumcised long before Israel received the law, and 2) he had accepted their comfort and protection in his time of need and should be sympathetic with their hardship. On the other hand, being aware of Paul's zeal for the cruciform life and his previous insistence on their uncircumcision, the addressees did also expect his disfavor.

---

[112] Cf. Nanos, *Irony,* 257–71.

[113] It seems likely that the discussions in the rabbinic sources on whether proselytes retained a certain liminality as compared to Israelites (= native Jews) reflect sentiments of the first century. Even though converts are declared Jews "in all respects" (*b. Yebam.* 47b) and are obligated to observe all the commandments of the Torah (see above, n. 5), according to *m. Bik.* 1:4–5 they could not recite the Deuteronomic declaration upon presenting their firstfruits ("God of our fathers"), since only native Jews have Abraham, Isaac, Jacob, and Jacob's twelve sons as their fathers. Converts did have no share in the land and could not give their daughters in marriage to priests. Important to note, a similar logic was implemented by the Athenian assembly as it awarded full citizenship to 212 Plataeans. Even though the Plataeans were given a share in all things, their foreign birth disqualified them from certain functions that were hereditary. (For details on these and for additional references, see S. Cohen, *Beginnings,* 168–74, 308–40).

[114] Nanos, "Inter- and Intra-Jewish," 397.

Thus, they sought the advice of other counselors within the early Christ-believing movement who could be expected to have a more pragmatic view on discipleship and were able to appreciate the unexpected scenario in which Gentiles were in danger of falling away from Christ on account of their noncircumcision. This constellation made the agreement not to lay burdens on the Gentiles who turn to Christ appear in a different light. Circumcision of Gentiles was, of course, to be preferred to apostasy. And so the Galatian Christ-believers were encouraged by these counselors to proceed.

With astonishment (1:6) Paul heard of these deliberations and recognized that his children in Galatia (4.19) had abandoned their central conviction (4:29). And so the former persecutor of the Judean ἐκκλησίαι in Christ (1:2) sets out to admonish the Galatian ἐκκλησίαι to accept persecution. This being a sensitive matter for a former persecutor, he prepares the task carefully. First he turns their shameful position, with ironic sarcasm, into something that is envied by the influencers (3:1, evil eye). Then he censures their discernment for being fleshly and opposed to the Spirit. Finally, he presents himself as crucified with Christ, presenting his challenge indirectly and hoping to kindle their enthusiasm for that same passion once again.

As the addressees were pondering Paul's challenge, including his reminder of their selfless enthusiasm, an agonizing astonishment, similar to Paul's own (1:6), may have troubled them: "Why," they may have thought, "can Paul not grant us from a distance what we granted him at great personal risk? 'Think right' is what he has to offer us in *our* time of tribulations. But how is it that he accepted our comfort, our protection and help, in *his* time of need and even now commends us for it?"

In conclusion, neither Paul nor the addressees seem to have been concerned with the question that became so prominent among interpreters: "How can I find peace with God?" Instead, the addressees were asking themselves, "How can we find peace in this world?" assured that peace with God was given them by grace. Paul's concern was the *imitatio Christi crucifixi,* the primary conviction of which he considered himself the supreme representation. Indeed, he was rejecting the usefulness of the law for Christ-believing Gentiles, but he was not arguing against compliance with the law in general.

GLOSSARY

adscriptio—statement of the address or addressees for a letter.

agonistic—oriented to competition.

akotropē (ἀκοτροπή)—"dissuasion."

amanuensis—secretary.

amplificatio—"enlargement," "amplification."

antitheton (ἀντίθετον)—a proof or composition constructed from contraries.

apophasis (ἀπόφασις)—a response or answer to an affirmation or charge (κατάφασις).

auctoritas—"influence" or "authority."

auxēsis (αὔξησις)—"amplification," generally of a point already proven.

causa—"cause" or problem at issue.

chiasm or chiasmus (χιασμός)—(based on the Greek letter X) inverted parallels or sequences of ideas, words, phrases, sentences, and even discourse units; e.g., an argument that proceeds A to B to C, then C to B to A.

chreia (χρεία)—a short, intelligent pointed statement (maxim) or action, usually referring to a person or the equivalent of a person, often witty.

conclusio—used by the author of *Rhetorica ad Herrenium* for *enthymeme* (see *enthymeme*).

confirmatio—adducing of proofs to "strengthen" or "confirm" an argument; this is the body of the speech.

conquestio—a loud complaint that seeks to arouse the pity of the audience.

correctio—straightening out; amending a word or phrase just stated, often to state what it is not.

covenantal nomism—The observation of the Torah (law of Moses), which Israelites understand to be incumbent upon them because of a covenant relationship with God (*nomos* is Greek for "law").

deliberative rhetoric (συμβουλευτικός; *deliberativus*)—the genre best suited to exhortation or dissuasion, such as in the political assembly or in giving private advice, with a concern for what direction to take in the future (see Aristotle *Rhet.* 1.3–8). The goal of such rhetoric is to set out the advantage, the course of action recommended as better, or the harmful, the course from which the audience is dissuaded as being worse. Within this persuasive purpose, the elements characteristic of the other two genres may be incorporated, such as concern for justice and injustice (forensic), or honor and disgrace (epideictic). The emphasis is upon the self-interests of the audience; this genre is thus especially suited to a call to the expedient or useful course, such as the declaration of war, even if, for example, the concern for justice (in terms of those who will incur the resultant loss) may be thereby subordinated or subverted. Thus what will be deliberated is not just the end but the means to the end—in other words, what is considered to be good for the audience as well as expedient.

demonstrative—see *epideictic.*

diachronic—with a chronological perspective, referring to phenomena as they change over time.

digressio—departure from the line of argument.

dubitatio—wavering in opinion; doubt; uncertainty.

encomium (ἐγκώμιον)—Laudatory speech (or a composition) praising a person or thing, generally synonymous with epideictic rhetoric (for details, see Hester, "Epideictic Rhetoric and Persona.")

enthymeme (ἐνθύμημα)—"consideration"; a rhetorical counterpart to the syllogism (deductive reasoning with a major and minor premise [often left unstated, assuming the audience will supply this] and a conclusion or proof); also, an argument based upon contraries.

enumeratio—the recapitulation or summary enumerating the main points of an argument.

ephebos (ἔφηβος)—a youth just arriving at manhood.

epicheirēma (ἐπιχείρημα)—"argument," usually from fully stated syllogistic reasoning (which Aristotle, however, referred to as an enthymeme).

epistolography—the study of letters.

epideictic, demonstrative, or panegyric rhetoric (ἐπιδεικτικός; *demonstrativus*)— the genre especially appropriate to the matters of honor, for which one is praised, and disgrace (shamelessness), for which one is blamed (see Aristotle *Rhet.* 1.3, 9; 3.12). These topics occur, e.g., in funeral orations and tend to focus upon the condition one wishes to be held or affirmed presently, perhaps recalling the past or anticipating the future as well as in making a point. It is suited to inculcating or challenging a value without thereby necessarily calling for a course of action. Within this genre, like each of the others, the topics of the other genres may be considered, but they are subordinated to the concern for honor or disgrace. This genre is thus particularly suited to a call to take up an honorable course, such as loyalty to a friend, even if it may be less expedient or perhaps result in disadvantageous or undesirable consequences. The functional aspects of this rhetoric were expanded upon by Perelman and Olbrechts-Tyteca (*New Rhetoric*, 47–54, 193–95, 261–63, 350, 411–15), by emphasizing its application to argument that seeks to enhance adherence to a set of values and the course of action that should follow, which may take many shapes depending upon the elements considered necessary, including the incorporation of elements of forensic or deliberative rhetoric. The intensification of such adherence is the goal of this argumentation, although it may emphasize either association (from shared premise to specific conclusion) or dissociation (separation of language or tradition previously held together) in order to prevail in the face of a rival set of values.

ergasia (ἐργασία)—the "working out" or elaboration of a proposition, usually in detail, step by step.

ethos or *ēthos* (ἦθος)—character of the speaker.

exordium—"beginning," "source"; the introduction of the argument, in which the orator states the purpose and seeks to ingratiate himself or herself with the decision maker(s).

fantasy theme analysis—see *Symbolic Convergence Theory.*

forensic or judicial rhetoric (δικανικός; *iudicialis*)—the genre best suited for accusation or defense in a legal situation such as a court of law, with its natural focus upon judging events that have occurred in the past (see Aristotle *Rhet.* 1.3, 10–15). The goal of such oration may be measured by the concern to establish justice or injustice, although the topics central to the other two genres may be accessory points of appeal as well. Although an act may be admitted, the justice or injustice of the act will still be in view. It is in the context of this concern that "stasis" theory developed to provide a highly technical methodology for clarifying and arguing a case.

genre (or species) of rhetoric—formal category of kind or type.

gnome (γνώμη)—wise or pithy saying, maxim.

halakah (variously transliterated from Hebrew, e.g., halakhah, halachah, halakha; plural, halakhot)—the rules and details of prescribed and proscribed behavior in Jewish tradition; how a person or group should "walk."

inclusio—enclosed section.

indignatio—"indignation," "anger," "disdain"; what the orator seeks to incite against those being opposed.

invention—*Invention* is the first of five elements that characterize an oration or rhetorical discourse. Invention is deciding (literally, "finding") which genre is fitting for the occasion. After doing this, the orator will determine the *arrangement* (composition of the various parts into a coherent whole) and the *style* of the elements (e.g., word choices, sentence structure, figures of speech to employ), commit them to *memory,* and finally execute the oral *delivery.*

judicial—see *forensic.*

kataphasis (κατάφασις)—affirmation or accusation.

lalia (λαλιά)—speech, way of speaking.

logos (λόγος)—persuasive speech by way of inductive and deductive argument.

lysis (λύσις)—statement.

macarism— a "beatitude" or blessing formula, such as "blessed are the . . . , for they shall . . ."

maxim—a short and pithy saying.

mimesis (μίμησις)—"imitation."

narratio—the "narration," or statement of the facts or events of a case; it follows the *exordium* (introduction).

Noahide laws (also Noahic, and other spellings)—the standard expectations of "righteous" behavior for Gentile "children of Noah" that evolved during Diaspora Judaism. These became known in rabbinic Judaism as the Noahide or Noachian commandments, usually consisting of seven elements, such as turning from idolatry. A probable example of one of the variations of such expectations in the first century is contained in the reasoning and list developed in Jerusalem for Christ-believing Gentiles, according to Acts 15:19–32 (the so-called apostolic decree).

nomism/nomistic—see *covenantal nomism.*

oneidistic (ὀνειδιστικός) **letter**—a letter of reproach.

orthodidactic—concerning proper instruction.

orthopractical—concerning proper practice or behavior (orthopraxy).

panegyric—laudatory speech, such as high praise of someone or some event at a public meeting (see *epideictic*).

paradeigma or *paradigma* (παράδειγμα)—persuasion or dissuasion by appeal to "example."

paraenesis (παραίνεσις)—ethical exhortation.

partitio or *divisio*—a logical or rhetorical division; after the *narratio,* the speaker outlines the argument in accordance with the stated issue *(stasis).*

pathos (πάθος)—appeal to emotions.

peroratio—"conclusion," where the argument is summarized and the final appeal made.

persona—"mask," referring to the character or personality a person represents (acts out).

polyptoton (πολύπτωτον)—a form of wordplay in which a word is repeated in, e.g., a different case, number, or gender.

praeiudicium—a previous decision.

praxis (πρᾶχις)—"practice" or "course of action."

probatio—"proof," "demonstration." A supporting argument that strengthens the reasons for accepting the proposition of the speaker.

proem—prologue.

progymnasmata (προγυμνάσματα)—exercises for students of rhetoric.

prooemium (προοίμιον)—prologue.

propositio—"proposition." It states the major premise or problem at issue, summing up the points of agreement and disagreement between the parties and enumerating and briefly explaining the argument to come.

protreptic—speech of exhortation.

protropē (προτροπή)—"exhortation," a call to action.

quotidian—ordinary or daily.

recapitulatio—recapitulation or summarizing of an argument.

refutatio—refutation of the opponent's arguments following the argumentative proofs *(confirmatio).*

salutatio—salutation, greeting.

sententia—a short, pithy saying.

species—see *genre.*

stasis (στάσις; *status, constitutio*)—a way to distinguish the chief issue at dispute in a judicial case; the topic that the parties agree constitutes the matter to be resolved, which may imply that agreement is assumed on certain other topics. The lists of issues were not standardized from one rhetorical practitioner to another but provided topical lines of argument that he or she could apply depending upon the case. In general, four stases were employed according to the specific kind of matter at dispute: a case revolved around either (1) the *fact* of the matter at dispute (did the accused do it?); (2) how the facts should be *defined* (was it murder or self-defense?); (3) how those facts should be *qualified* (was it justified by mitigating circumstances); or (4) whether the court should have *jurisdiction* in this case (was this the appropriate court?). (For additional details, see T. Martin's essay in this volume, "Apostasy to Paganism.")

subscript—closing words.

symbouleutic—see *deliberative rhetoric.*

synchronic—not primarily concerned with change or development but with analysis or description of phenomena at a single point in time.

superscriptio—opening words.

syllogism—the basic structure of deductive reasoning in logic, usually by stating two premises and a conclusion (see *ethymeme; epicheirēma*).

Symbolic Convergence Theory—"a general theory of communication that attempts to offer an explanation for the presence of a common consciousness on the part of members of a group" (see Hester, "Epideictic Rhetoric and Persona," nn. 15 and 60).

topos (τόπος; **plural,** *topoi*)—the *locus* or source of arguments, often lists of subjects, prior arguments, or argumentative patterns, to be inserted in a speech.

BIBLIOGRAPHY

Aalders H. Wzn, G. J. D. "Political Thought and Political Programs in the Platonic Epistles." Pages 145–75 in vol. 1 of *Pseudepigrapha*. Edited by Kurt von Fritz. Entretiens sur l'antiquité classique 18. Vandoeuvres-Geneva: Fondation Hardt, 1972.

Abrahams, I. *Studies in Pharisaism and the Gospels*. First Series. 1917. Repr., New York: Ktav, 1967.

Achtemeier, P. J. "Omne verbum sonat: The New Testament and the Oral Environment of Late Antiquity." *Journal of Biblical Literature* 109 (1990): 3–27.

Adamietz, J. *Ciceros De inventione und die Rhetorik ad Herennium*. Marburg: Philipps-Universität zu Marburg, 1960.

Aletti, J.-N. "La 'dispositio' rhétorique dans les épîtres pauliniennes: Propositions de méthode." *New Testament Studies* 38 (1992): 385–401.

———. Review of H. D. Betz, *Galatians*. *Recherches de science religieuse* 69 (1981): 601–2.

Allison, D. C., Jr. "Peter and Cephas: One and the Same." *Journal of Biblical Literature* 111, no. 3 (1992): 489–95.

Alkier, S., and R. Brucker. *Exegese und Methodendiskussion*. Tübingen: Francke, 1998.

Alon, G. *Jews, Judaism, and the Classical World*. Jerusalem: Magnes, 1977.

Alvarez-Cineira, D. *Die Religionspolitik des Kaisers Claudius und die paulinische Mission*. Herders biblische Studien. Freiburg: Herder, 1999.

Amir, Y. "Die messianische Idee im hellenistischen Judentum." *Freiburger Rundbrief* 25 (1973): 195–203.

Anderson, R. D., Jr. *Ancient Rhetorical Theory and Paul*. Kampen: Kok Pharos, 1996.

Applebaum, S. *Jews and Greeks in Ancient Cyrene*. Leiden: E. J. Brill, 1979.

———. "Judaism: Jews in North Africa." Pages 1072–73 in vol. 3 of *Anchor Bible Dictionary*. Edited by D. N. Freeman. 6 vols. New York: Doubleday, 1992.

Armstrong, B. G., et al., eds. *Ioannis Calvini Opera omnia: Denuo recognita et adnotatione, critica instructa, notisque illustrata*. Series 2. *Opera exegetica Veteris et Novi Testamenti*. Geneva: Librairie Droz, 1992–.

Attridge, H. W., and G. Hata, eds. *Eusebius, Judaism, and Christianity*. Leiden and New York: Brill, 1992.

Aune, D. E. *The New Testament and Its Literary Environment*. Library of Early Christianity. Philadelphia: Westminster, 1987.

———. Review of H. D. Betz, *Galatians: A Commentary on Paul's Letter to the Churches of Galatia*. *Religious Studies Review* 7 (1981) 323–28.

———. Review of B. H. Brinsmead, *Galatians—Dialogical Response to Opponents*. *Catholic Biblical Quarterly* 46 (1984): 147.

Austin, J. L. *How to Do Things with Words*. Cambridge: Harvard University Press, 1975.

Baarda, T. "Openbaring—traditie en Didaché." Pages 152–67 in *Zelfstandig geloven: Studies voor Jaap Firet*. Edited by F. H. Kuiper, J. J. van Nijen, and J. C. Schreuder. Kampen: Kok, 1987.

Baasland, E. "Persecution: A Neglected Feature in the Letter to the Galatians." *Studia theologica* 38 (1984): 135–50.

Bachmann, M. *Sünder oder Übertreter*. Wissenschaftliche Untersuchungen zum Alten und Neuen Testament 59. Tübingen: Mohr Siebeck, 1992.

Backus, I., ed. *Enarratio in evangelion Iohannis*. 2 vols. in *Martini Buceri Opera omnia*. Second Series, *Opera latina*. Leiden: Brill, 1988.

Bacon, B. W. "Paul's Triumph at Antioch." *Journal of Religion* 9 (1929): 204–23.

Bahr, G. J. "The Subscriptions in the Pauline Letters." *Journal of Biblical Literature* 87 (1968): 27–41.

Baldwin, C. S. *Medieval Rhetoric and Poetic (to 1400) Interpreted from Representative Works*. Gloucester, Mass.: Peter Smith, 1959.

Balz, H. "φοβέω." Page 207 in vol. 9 of *Theological Dictionary of the New Testament*. Edited by G. Kittel and G. Friedrich. Translated by G. W. Bromiley. 10 vols. Grand Rapids: Eerdmans, 1964–1976.

Bamberger, B. J. *Proselytism in the Talmudic Period*. New York: Ktav, 1968. Translation of the German original, 1939.

Bammel, E. "Judenverfolgung und Naherwartung: Zur Eschatologie des ersten Thessalonicherbriefs." *Zeitschrift für Theologie und Kirche* 56 (1959): 294–315.

Barclay, J. M. G. *Jews in the Mediterranean Diaspora: From Alexander to Trajan (323 B.C.E.-117 C.E.)*. Edinburgh: T&T Clark, 1996.

———. "Mirror-Reading a Polemical Letter: Galatians as a Test Case." *Journal for the Study of the New Testament* 31 (1987): 73–93. Repr., pages 247–67 in *The Pauline Writings: A Sheffield Reader*. Edited by S. E. Porter & C. A. Evans. Sheffield: Sheffield Academic Press, 1994. Reprinted in *The Galatians Debate*, 367–82.

———. *Obeying the Truth: A Study of Paul's Ethics in Galatians*. Edinburgh: T&T Clark, 1988.

———. "Paul among Diaspora Jews." *Journal for the Study of the New Testament* 60 (1995): 89–120.

Baron, S. *A Social and Religious History of the Jews*. Vol. 1. 2d ed. New York: Columbia University Press, 1954.

Barr, J. *Old and New in Interpretation: Study of Two Testaments*. London: SCM, 1966.

Barré, M. L. "Qumran and the 'Weakness' of Paul." *Catholic Biblical Quarterly* 42 (1980): 216–27.

Barrett, C. K. "The Allegory of Abraham, Sarah, and Hagar in the Argument of Galatians." Pages 1–16 in *Rechtfertigung: Festschrift für Ernst Käsemann zum 70.*

Geburtstag. Edited by W. Pöhlmann, J. Friedrich, and P. Stuhlmacher. Tübingen: Mohr Siebeck, 1976.

———. *Freedom and Obligation: A Study of the Epistle to the Galatians.* London: SPCK, 1985.

———. "Paul and the 'Pillar' Apostles." Pages 1–19 in *Studia paulina in honorem Johannis de Zwaan septuagenarii.* Edited by W. C. van Unnik and J. Nicolaas Sevenster. Haarlem: De Erven F. Bohn, 1953.

———. Review of H. D. Betz, *Galatians. Interpretation* 34 (1980): 414–17.

Bauckham, R. "Barnabas in Galatians." *Journal for the Study of the New Testament* 2 (1979): 61–70.

———. "James and the Jerusalem Church." Pages 415–80 in *The Book of Acts in Its Palestinian Setting.* Edited by R. Bauckham. Grand Rapids: Eerdmans, 1995.

Bauer, W. "Cerinth." Col. 1632 in vol. 1 of *Religion in Geschichte und Gegenwart.* Edited by K. Galling. 7 vols. 3d ed. Tübingen: Mohr Siebeck, 1957–1965.

Bauer, W., W. F. Arndt, F. W. Gingrich, and F. W. Danker. *A Greek-English Lexicon of the New Testament and Other Early Christian Literature.* 2d ed. Chicago: University of Chicago Press, 1979.

Bauer, W., F. W. Danker, W. F. Arndt, and F. W. Gingrich. *A Greek-English Lexicon of the New Testament and Other Early Christian Literature.* 3d ed. Chicago: University of Chicago Press, 2000.

Bauernfeind, O. "Der Schluss der antiochenischen Paulusrede." In *Theologie als Glaubenswagnis: Festschrift für K. Heim.* Hamburg: Furche, 1954. Repr., pages 449–63 in *Kommentar und Studien zur Apostelgeschichte.* Tübingen: J. C. B. Mohr, 1980.

Baum, G., E. Cunitz, and E. Reuss, eds. *Ioannis Calvini Opera quae supersunt omnia.* 59 vols. Braunschweig: C. A. Schwetschke, 1863–1900.

Baumgarten, A. I. "The Name of the Pharisees." *Journal of Biblical Literature* 102 (1983): 411–28.

Baur, F. C. *Church History.* 2 vols. London and Edinburgh: Williams & Norgate, 1878. Translation of the German original, 1853.

———. *Paul the Apostle of Jesus Christ: His Life and Works, His Epistles and Teachings: a Contribution to a Critical History of Primitive Christianity.* Translated from the German original, 1845, by E. Zeller and A. Menzies. 2d ed. 2 vols. London and Edinburgh: Williams & Norgate, 1873–1875.

———. *Paulus, der Apostel Jesu Christi—sein Leben und Wirken, seine Briefe und seine Lehre: Ein Beitrag zu einer kritischen Geschichte des Urchristentums.* Stuttgart, 1845.

Becker, J. *Die Brief an die Galater.* Das Neue Testament Deutsch Neues Göttinger Bibelwerk 8. Göttingen: Vandenhoeck & Ruprecht, 1976.

Bedouelle, G. *Lefèvre d'Etaples et l'intelligence des Écritures.* Geneva: Droz, 1976.

Behm, J. "ἀνατίθημι." Pages 353–54 in vol. 1 of *Theological Dictionary of the New Testament.* Edited by G. Kittel and G. Friedrich. Translated by G. W. Bromiley. 10 vols. Grand Rapids: Eerdmans, 1964–1976.

Beker, J. C. *Paul the Apostle: The Triumph of God in Life and Thought.* Edinburgh: T&T Clark, 1980.

Belleville, L. L. " 'Under Law': Structural Analysis and the Pauline Concept of Law in Galatians 3:21–4:11." *Journal for the Study of the New Testament* 26 (1986): 53–78.

Benoit, P. "La deuxième visite de Saint Paul à Jerusalem." *Biblica* 40 (1959): 778–92.

Bentley, J. H. *Humanists and Holy Writ: New Testament Scholarship in the Renaissance.* Princeton: Princeton University Press, 1983.

Benzing, J., and M. Claus. *Lutherbibliographie: Verzeichnis der gedruckten Schriften Martin Luthers bis zu dessen Tod.* 2 vols. Bibliotheca bibliographica aureliana 143. Baden-Baden: V. Koerner, 1989–1994.

Berchman, R. M. *From Philo to Origen: Middle Platonism in Transition.* Chico, Calif.: Scholars Press, 1984.

———. "Galatians (1:1–5): Paul and Greco-Roman Rhetoric." Pages 1–15 in *Judaic and Christian Interpretation of Texts: Context and Contexts.* Edited by J. Neusner and E. S. Frerichs. New Perspectives on Ancient Judaism 3. Lanham, Md.: University Press of America, 1987. Reprinted in *The Galatians Debate,* 60–72.

———. "Rabbinic Syllogistic: The Case of Mishnah Tosefta Tohorot." Pages 81–98 in vol 5 of *Approaches to Ancient Judaism.* Edited by W. S. Greene. Brown Judaic Studies. Atlanta: Scholars Press, 1985.

Berg, H. G. vom, ed. *Exegetische Schriften aus den Jahren 1525–1527.* Part 3, vol. 1 of *Heinrich Bullinger Werke.* Zurich: Theologischer Verlag, 1983.

———, ed. *Unveröffentlichte Werke der Kappeler Zeit: Theologica.* Part 3, vol. 2 of *Heinrich Bullinger Werke.* Zurich: Theologischer Verlag, 1991.

Berger, K. "Almosen für Israel: zum historischen Kontext der paulinischen Kollekte." *New Testament Studies* 23 (1976–1977): 180–204.

———. "Hellenistische Gattungen im Neuen Testament." *ANRW* 25.2:1031–1432, 1831–85. Part 2, *Principat,* 25.2. Edited by W. Haase. New York: de Gruyter, 1984.

———. "Die impliziten Gegner: Zur Methode des Erschließens von "Gegnern" in neutestamentlichen Texten." Pages 372–400 in *Kirche: Festschrift für Günther Bornkamm zum 75. Geburtstag.* Edited by D. Lührmann and G. Strecker. Tübingen: Mohr Siebeck, 1980.

Berger, P. L., and T. Luckmann. *The Social Construction of Reality: A Treatise in the Sociology of Meaning.* New York: Doubleday, 1966.

Berwald, O. *Philipp Melanchthons Sicht der Rhetorik.* Wiesbaden: Harrassowitz, 1994.

Betz, H. D. *Der Apostel Paulus und die sokratische Tradition.* Tübingen: Mohr Siebeck, 1972.

———. *Der Galaterbrief: Ein Kommentar zum Brief des Apostels Paulus an die Gemeinden in Galatien.* Munich: Chr. Kaiser, 1988.

———. *Galatians: A Commentary on Paul's Letter to the Churches in Galatia.* Hermeneia. Philadelphia: Fortress, 1979. 2d ed., 1984.

———. "Geist, Freiheit, und Gesetz: Die Botschaft des Paulus an die Gemeinden in Galatien." *Zeitschrift für Theologie und Kirche* 71 (1974): 78–93.

———. "In Defense of the Spirit: Paul's Letter to the Galatians as a Document of Early Christian Apologetics." Pages 99–114 in *Aspects of Religious Propaganda in Judaism and Early Christianity.* Edited by Elisabeth Schüssler Fiorenza. Notre Dame: University of Notre Dame Press, 1976.

———. "The Literary Composition and Function of Paul's Letter to the Galatians." *New Testament Studies* 21 (1975): 352–79. Reprinted in *The Galatians Debate*, 3–28.

———. *Paulinische Studien*. Tübingen: Mohr Siebeck, 1994.

———. "Das Problem der Grundlagen der paulinischen Ethik." *Zeitschrift für Theologie und Kirche* 85 (1988): 199–218.

———. "The Problem of Rhetoric and Theology according to the Apostle Paul." Pages 16–48 in *L'apôtre Paul: Personnalité, style, et conception du ministère*. Edited by A. Vanhoye. Bibliotheca ephemeridum theologicarum lovaniensium 73. Leuven: Leuven University Press, 1986.

———. Review of G. A. Kennedy, *New Testament Interpretation. Journal of Theological Studies* 37 (1986): 166–67.

———. *Second Corinthians 8 and 9: A Commentary on Two Administrative Letters of the Apostle Paul*. Hermeneia. Philadelphia: Fortress, 1985.

———. "Spirit, Freedom, and Law: Paul's Message to the Galatian Churches." *Svensk exegetisk årsbok* 39 (1974): 145–60. Translation of "Geist, Freiheit, und Gesetz: Die Botschaft des Paulus an die Gemeinden in Galatien." *Zeitschrift für Theologie und Kirche* 71 (1974): 78–93.

———. *Zweiter Korinther 8 und 9: Ein Kommentar zu zwei Verwaltungsbriefen des Apostels Paulus*. Gütersloh: Mohn, 1993.

Beuttemüller, O. *Vorläufiges Verzeichnis der Melanchthon-Drucke des 16. Jahrhunderts*. Halle, 1960.

Bezzel, I. *Verzeichnis der im deutschen Sprachbereich erschienenen Drucke des 16. Jahrhunderts*. 25 vols. Stuttgart: Hiersemann, 1983–2000.

Birnbaum, P., ed. *Ha-Siddur ha-Shalem*. New York: Hibru Poblishing Kompani, 1949.

Bitzer, Lloyd F. "The Rhetorical Situation." *Philosophy and Rhetoric* 1 (1968): 1–14.

Bizer, E., ed. *Texte aus der Anfangszeit Melanchthons*. Neukirchen-Vluyn: Neukirchener Verlag, 1966.

Bjerkelund, C. *Parakalô: Form, Funktion, und Sinn der parakalô-Satz in den paulinischen Briefen*. Bibliotheca theologica norvegica 1. Oslo: Universitets-forlaget, 1967.

Bjorck, R. G. *Der Fluch des Christen Sabinus*. Papyrus upsaliensis 8. Uppsala: Almqvist & Wiksells, 1938.

Black, E. "The Second Persona." Pages 161–72 in *Landmark Essays in Rhetorical Criticism*. Edited by T. W. Benson. Davis, Calif.: Hermagoras, 1993.

Blass, F., and A. Debrunner. *A Greek Grammar of the New Testament and Other Early Christian Literature*. Translated and revised by Robert W. Funk. Chicago: University of Chicago Press, 1961.

Bligh, J. *Galatians*. London: St. Paul, 1969.

Bockmuehl, M. "Antioch and James the Just." Pages 155–98 in *James the Just and Christian Origins*. Edited by Bruce Chilton and Craig A. Evans. Leiden: Brill, 1999.

———. *Revelation and Mystery in Ancient Judaism and Pauline Christianity*. Grand Rapids: Eerdmans, 1997.

Boissevain, J. *Friends of Friends: Networks, Manipulators, and Coalitions*. Oxford: Basil Blackwell, 1974.

Bonnard, P. *L'épître de Saint Paul aux Galates.* Commentaire du Nouveau Testament 9. Paris: Delachaux & Niestlé, 1972.

Booth, W. *Rhetoric of Fiction.* 2d ed. Chicago: University of Chicago Press, 1983.

Borgen, P. "Judaism in Egypt." Pages 1061–72 in vol. 3 of the *Anchor Bible Dictionary.* Edited by D. N. Freeman. 6 vols. New York: Doubleday, 1992.

———. "Observations on the theme 'Paul and Philo': Paul's Preaching of Circumcision in Galatia (Gal. 5.11)." Pages 85–102 in *Die paulinische Literatur und Theologie.* Edited by S. Pedersen. Arhus: Aros, 1980.

———. "Paul Preaches Circumcision and Pleases Men." Pages 37–46 in *Paul and Paulinism: Essays in Honour of C. K. Barrett.* Edited by M. D. Hooker and S. G. Wilson. London: SPCK, 1982.

———. "Philo of Alexandria." Pages 333–42 in vol. 5 of the *Anchor Bible Dictionary.* Edited by D. N. Freeman. 6 vols. New York: Doubleday, 1992.

Bormann, C. von, L. Schmidt, and W. Schenk. "Hermeneutik." Pages 108–50 in vol. 15 of *Theologische Realenzyclopädie.* Edited by G. Krause and G. Müller. Berlin: de Gruyter, 1977–.

Bormann, E. *Communication Theory.* New York: Holt, Rinehart, 1980.

———. *Force of Fantasy: Restoring the American Dream.* Carbondale: Southern Illinois Press, 1985.

———. *Small Group Communications: Theory and Practice.* 3d ed. New York: Harper Collins, 1990.

Bormann, E., J. Cragan, and D. Shields. "In Defense of Symbolic Convergence Theory: A Look at the Theory and Its Criticisms after Two Decades." *Communications Theory* 4 (1994): 259–94.

Bornkamm, G. *Paul.* London: Hodder & Stoughton, 1971.

———. *Paulus.* Urban-Taschenbücher 119. Stuttgart: Kohlhammer, 1969.

Bornkamm, G., G. Barth, and H. J. Held. *Tradition and Interpretation in Matthew.* London: SCM, 1963. Translation of the German original, 1960.

Botha, P. J. J. "Letter Writing and Oral Communication in Antiquity: Suggested Implications for the Interpretation of Paul's Letter to the Galatians." *Scriptura* 42 (1992): 17–34.

Bourdieu, Pierre. "The Sentiment of Honour in Kabyle Society." Pages 191–241 in *Honour and Shame: The Values of Mediterranean Society.* Edited by J. G. Peristiany. London: Weidenfeld & Nicolson, 1965.

Bousset, W. *Die Schriften des Neuen Testaments.* 2 vols. Göttingen: Vandenhoeck & Ruprecht, 1917.

Bouwman, G. " 'Christus Diener der Sünde': Auslegung von Galater 2:14b–18." *Bijdragen* 40 (1979): 44–54.

Bowker, J. *Jesus and the Pharisees.* London: Cambridge University Press, 1973.

Boyarin, D. *A Radical Jew: Paul and the Politics of Identity.* Berkeley: University of California Press, 1994.

Bradley, D. G. "The TOPOS as a Form in the Pauline Paraenesis." *Journal of Biblical Literature* 72 (1953): 238–46.

Brandenburger, E. *Fleisch und Geist.* Wissenschaftliche Monographien zum Alten und Neuen Testament 29. Neukirchen-Vluyn: Neukirchener Verlag, 1968.

Brandy, H. C. *Die späte Christologie des Johannes Brenz.* Tübingen: Mohr Siebeck, 1991.

Braude, W. G. *Jewish Proselytism in the First Five Centuries.* Providence: Brown University Press, 1940.

Braun, H. *Spätjüdisch-häretischer und frühchristlicher Radikalismus.* 2d ed. 2 vols. Beiträge zur historische Theologie 24. Tübingen: J. C. B. Mohr, 1969.

Braun, W. *Feasting and Social Rhetoric in Luke 14.* Society for New Testament Studies Monograph Series 85. Cambridge: Cambridge University Press, 1995.

Brecht, M. "Brenz, Johannes." Pages 170–81 in vol. 7 of *Theologische Realenzyclopädie.* Edited by G. Krause and G. Müller. Berlin: de Gruyter, 1977–.

———. *Die frühe Theologie des Johannes Brenz.* Beiträge zur historische Theologie 36. Tübingen: Mohr Siebeck, 1966.

Brenz, J. *Opera.* 8 vols. Tübingen, 1576–1590.

Bretschneider, C. G., and H. E. Bindseil, eds. *Philippi Melanchthonis Opera.* 28 vols. Halle, 1834–1860.

Breuer, D. *Einführung in die pragmatische Texttheorie.* Uni-Taschenbücher 106. München: W. Fink, 1974.

Breytenbach, C. *Paulus und Barnabas in der Provinz Galatien: Studien zur Apostelgeschichte 13f; 16.6; 18.23 und den Adressaten des Galaterbriefs.* New York: E. J. Brill, 1996.

Brinckmann, W. "Der Begriff der Freundschaft in Senecas Briefen." Ph.D. diss., Köln, 1963.

Brinsmead, B. H. *Galatians—Dialogical Response to Opponents.* Chico, Calif.: Scholars Press, 1982.

Brisson, J.-P. *Autonomisme et christianisme dans l'Afrique romaine de Septime Severe à l'invasion vandale.* Paris: Editions E. de Boccard, 1958.

Bronson, D. B. "Paul, Galatians, and Jerusalem." *Journal of the American Academy of Religion* 35 (1967): 119–28.

Brown, P. *The Body and Society: Men, Women, and Sexual Renunciation in Early Christianity.* New York: Columbia University Press, 1988.

Brown, R., and J. P. Meier. *Antioch and Rome.* New York: Paulist, 1983.

Bruce, F. F. *The Epistle to the Galatians: A Commentary on the Greek Text.* New International Greek Testament Commentary. Grand Rapids: Eerdmans, 1982.

———. "The Curse of the Law." Pages 27–36 in *Paul and Paulinism: Essays in Honour of C. K. Barrett.* Edited by M. D. Hooker and S. G. Wilson. London: SPCK, 1982.

———. "Further Thoughts on Paul's Autobiography: Galatians 1:11–2:14." Pages 21–29 in *Jesus und Paulus: Festschrift für Werner Georg Kümmel zum 70. Geburtstag.* Edited by E. E. Ellis and E. Grässer. Göttingen: Vandenhoeck & Ruprecht, 1975.

———. "Galatian Problems 1: Autobiographical Data." *Bulletin of the John Rylands University Library of Manchester* 51 (1968–1969) 302–6.

———. "Galatian Problems 2: North or South Galatia." *Bulletin of the John Rylands University Library of Manchester* 52 (1969–1970): 243–66.

————. *Men and Movements in the Primitive Church.* Exeter: Paternoster, 1979.

————. *New Testament History.* New York: Doubleday Anchor Book, 1972.

————. *Paul, Apostle of the Heart Set Free.* Grand Rapids: Eerdmans, 1982.

Brucker, R. "Versuche ich denn jetzt, Menschen zu überreden . . . ?—Rhetorik und Exegese am Beispiel des Galaterbriefes. Pages 211–36 in *Exegese und Methoden-diskussion.* Edited by S. Alkier and R. Brucker. Tübingen: Francke, 1998.

Brunt, J. C. "More on the TOPOS as a New Testament Form." *Journal of Biblical Literature* 104, no. 3 (1985): 495–500.

Bucer, M. *Martini Buceri Opera latina.* Paris: Presses Universitaires de France, 1954–1955.

————. *Martini Buceri Opera omnia.* Gütersloh and Leiden: Brill, 1960.

Büchler, A. "The Levitical Impurity of the Gentiles in Palestine before the Year 70." *Jewish Quarterly Review* 17 (1927): 1–81.

Buffière, F. *Les mythes d'Homère et la pensée grecque.* Paris: Belles Lettres, 1956.

Bullemer, K. "Quellenkritische Untersuchungen zum I. Buche der Rhetorik Melanchthons." Ph.D. diss., Erlangen, 1902.

Bullinger, H. *In omnes apostolicas epistolas, divi videlicet Pauli XI. et VII. canonicas, commentarii.* Zurich: Froschouer, 1539.

————. *Werke.* Zurich: Theologischer Verlag, 1972–.

Bultmann, R. "πείθω." Pages 1–11 in vol. 6 of *Theological Dictionary of the New Testament.* Edited by G. Kittel and G. Friedrich. Translated by G. W. Bromiley. 10 vols. Grand Rapids: Eerdmans, 1964–1976.

————. *Der Stil der paulinischen Predigt und die kynistisch-stoische Diatribe.* Forschungen zur Religion und Literatur des Alten und Neuen Testaments 13. Göttingen: Vandenhoeck & Ruprecht, 1910.

————. "Zur Auslegung von Galater 2:15–18." 1952. Repr., pages 394–99 in *Exegetica.* Tübingen: J.C.B. Mohr, 1967.

Bünker, M. *Briefformular und rhetorische Disposition im 1. Korintherbrief.* Göttingen: Vandenhoeck & Ruprecht, 1984.

Burchard, C. "Joseph and Aseneth." Pages 177–247 in vol. 2 of *Old Testament Pseudepigrapha.* Edited by James H. Charlesworth. 2 vols. New York: Doubleday, 1983, 1985.

Burgess, T. "Epideictic Literature." *University of Chicago Studies in Classical Philology* 3 (1902): 89–261.

Burke, K. "Fact, Inference, and Proof in the Analysis of Literary Symbolism." Pages 283–306 in *Symbols and Values—an Initial Study: Thirteenth Symposium of the Conference on Science, Philosophy, and Religion.* Edited by L. Bryson et al. New York: Harper & Brothers, 1954.

————. *A Grammar of Motives.* New York: Prentice Hall, 1945.

————. *A Rhetoric of Motives.* Berkeley: University of California Press, 1969.

————. *The Rhetoric of Religion: Studies in Logography.* Berkeley and Los Angeles: University of California Press, 1970.

————. "Rhetoric Old and New." *Journal of Education* 5 (1951): 202–9.

Burkert, Walter. *Greek Religion.* Oxford: Blackwell, 1985.

Burkitt, F. C. *Christian Beginnings*. London: University of London Press, 1924.

Burton, E. *A Critical and Exegetical Commentary on the Epistle to the Galatians*. International Critical Commentary. Edinburgh: T&T Clark, 1921. New York: Scribner, 1920.

Büsser, F. "Bullinger, Heinrich." Pages 375–87 in vol. 7 of *Theologische Realenzyclopädie*. Edited by G. Krause and G. Müller. Berlin: de Gruyter, 1977–.

———, ed. *Bibliographie*. Part 1 of *Heinrich Bullinger Werke*. Zurich: Theologischer Verlag, 1960–.

Bussmann, C. *Themen der paulinischen Missionspredigt auf dem Hintergund der spätjüdisch-hellenistischen Missionsliteratur*. Bern: Lang, 1975.

Calvin, J. *Commentarius in epistolam ad Galatas. Ioannis Calvini Opera quae supersunt omnia*. Edited by G. Baum, E. Cunitz, and E. Reuss. 59 vols. Corpus reformatorum 29–87. Braunschweig: Schwetschke, 1863–1900.

———. *The Epistles of Paul the Apostle to the Galatians, Ephesians, Philippians, and Colossians*. Translated by T. H. C. Parker. London: Oliver & Boyd, 1965.

Cameron, P. S. "An Exercise in Translation: Galatians 2.11–14." *The Bible Translator* 40, no. 1 (1989): 135–45.

Campbell, J. K. *Honour, Family, and Patronage: A Study of Institutions and Moral Values in a Greek Mountain Community*. New York: Oxford University Press, 1964.

Campbell, K. K., and K. H. Jamieson. "Form and Genre in Rhetorical Criticism: An Introduction." Pages 9–32 in *Form and Genre: Shaping Rhetorical Action*. Edited by K. K. Campbell and K. H. Jamieson. Falls Church, Va.: Speech Communication Association, 1978.

Cancik, H. *Untersuchungen zu Senecas Epistulae morales*. Hildesheim: Georg Olms, 1967.

Cancik, H., and H. Schneider, eds. *Der neue Pauly: Enzyklopädie der Antike*. Stuttgart: J. B. Metzler, 1996–.

Capelle, W., and H. I. Marrou. "Diatribe." Pages 990–1009 in vol. 3 of *Reallexikon für Antike und Christentum*. Edited by T. Kluser et al. Stuttgart: Hiersemann, 1950–.

Catchpole, D. R. "Paul, James, and the Apostolic Decree." *New Testament Studies* 23 (1976–1977): 428–44.

Chadwick, H. *The Sentences of Sextus*. Cambridge: Cambridge University Press, 1959.

Chapa, J. "Is First Thessalonians a Letter of Consolation?" *New Testament Studies* 40 (1994): 150–60.

Charlesworth, J. A., ed. *Old Testament Pseudepigrapha*. 2 vols. New York: Doubleday, 1983–85.

Chesnutt, R. "Joseph and Aseneth." Pages 969–71 in vol. 3 of the *Anchor Bible Dictionary*. Edited by D. N. Freeman. 6 vols. New York: Doubleday, 1992.

Chilton, B., and C. A. Evans, eds. *James the Just and Christian Origins*. Leiden: Brill, 1999.

Christiansen, I. *Die Technik der allegorischen Auslegungswissenschaft bei Philon von Alexandrien*. Tübingen: Mohr, 1969.

Church, F. F. "Rhetorical Structure and Design in Paul's Letter to Philemon." *Harvard Theological Review* 61 (1978): 17–33.

Ciampa, R. E. *The Presence and Function of Scripture in Galatians 1 and 2*. Wissenschaftliche Untersuchungen zum Alten und Neuen Testament 2.102. Tübingen: Mohr Siebeck, 1998.

Cicero. *De inventione*. Translated by H. M. Hubbel. Loeb Classical Library. Cambridge: Harvard University Press, 1949.

―――. *De oratore*. Translated by J. S. Watson. Carbondale and Edwardsville: Southern Illinois University Press, 1970.

Clarke, M. L. Review of G. A. Kennedy, *Art of Rhetoric*. *Gnomon* 46 (1974): 87–89.

Classen, C. J. *Die Bedeutung der Rhetorik für Melanchthons Interpretation profaner und biblischer Texte*. Nachrichten der Akademie der Wissenschaften in Göttingen 1: Philosophisch-historische Klasse, 1998, no. 5. Göttingen: Vandenhoeck & Ruprecht, 1998.

―――. "Cicero, orator inter Germanos redivivus." *Humanistica lovaniensia* 37 (1988): 79–114; 39 (1990): 157–76.

―――. "Cicero 'Pro Cluentio' 1–11 im Licht der rhetorischen Theorie und Praxis." *Rheinisches Museum für Philologie* 108 (1965): 104–42.

―――. "Cicerostudien in der Romania im 15. und 16. Jahrhundert." Pages 198–245 in *Cicero: Ein Mensch seiner Zeit*. Edited by G. Radke. Berlin: de Gruyter, 1968.

―――. "Paul and Ancient Rhetoric." *Rhetorica* 10 (1992): 319–44.

―――. "Paulus und die antike Rhetorik." *Zeitschrift für die neutestamentliche Wissenschaft und die Kunde der älteren Kirche* 82 (1991): 1–33.

―――. "Philologische Bemerkungen zur Sprache des Apostels Paulus." *Wiener Studien* 107–108 (1994–1995): 321–35.

―――. *Recht, Rhetorik, Politik: Untersuchungen zu Ciceros rhetorischer Strategie*. Darmstadt: Wissenschaftliche Buchgesellschaft, 1985.

―――. Review of R. D. Anderson, Jr., *Ancient Rhetorical Theory*. *Rhetorica* 16 (1998): 324–29.

―――. Review of O. Berwald, *Philipp Melanchthons Sicht*. *Gnomon* 70 (1998): 81.

―――. "Rhetoric and Literary Criticism: Their Nature and Their Functions in Antiquity." *Mnemosyne* 48, no. 5 (1995): 513–35.

―――. *Rhetorical Criticism of the New Testament*. Tübingen: Mohr Siebeck, 2000.

―――. "The Rhetorical Works of George of Trebizond and Their Debt to Cicero." *Journal of the Warburg and Courtauld Institutes* 561 (1993): 75–84.

―――. "Die Rhetorik im öffentlichen Leben unserer Zeit." Pages 247–67 in *Die Macht des Wortes*. Edited by C. J. Classen and H.-J. Müllenbrock. Marburg: Hitzeroth, 1992.

―――. "St. Paul's Epistles and Ancient Greek and Roman Rhetoric." Pages 265–91 in *Rhetoric and the New Testament: Essays from the 1992 Heidelberg Conference*. Edited by S. E. Porter and T. H. Olbricht. Sheffield: Sheffield Academic Press, 1993. Rev. ed., pages 1–28 in *Rhetorical Criticism of the New Testament*. Tübingen: Mohr Siebeck, 2000. Revised version published in *The Galatians Debate*, 95–113.

Classen, C. J., and H.-J. Müllenbrock, eds. *Die Macht des Wortes*. Marburg: Hitzeroth, 1992.

Cohen, A. P. *Self Consciousness: An Alternate Anthropology of Identity*. New York: Routledge, 1994.

Cohen, S. J. D. *The Beginnings of Jewishness: Boundaries, Varieties, Uncertainties*. Berkeley and Los Angeles: University of California Press, 1999.

———. "Conversion to Judaism in Historical Perspective: From Biblical Israel to Post-biblical Judaism." *Conservative Judaism* 36, no. 4 (1983): 31–45.

———. "Crossing the Boundary and Becoming a Jew." *Harvard Theological Review* 82, no. 1 (1989): 13–33.

———. "The Origins of the Matrilineal Principle in Rabbinic Law." *Association for Jewish Studies Review* 10 (1985): 19–53.

———. "Respect for Judaism by Gentiles in the Writings of Josephus." *Harvard Theological Review* 80 (1987): 409–30.

Cohn-Sherbok, D. "Some Reflections on James Dunn's 'The Incident at Antioch.'" *Journal for the Study of the New Testament* 18 (1983): 68–74.

Collins, J. J. "Jesus and the Messiahs of Israel." Pages 287–302 in vol. 3 of *Geschichte-Tradition-Reflexion: Festschrift für Martin Hengel*. Edited by H. Cancik et al. Tübingen: Mohr Siebeck, 1996.

———. "Sybilline Oracles." Pages 317–472 in vol. 1 of *Old Testament Pseudepigrapha*. Edited by James H. Charlesworth. 2 vols. New York: Doubleday, 1983.

———. "A Symbol of Otherness: Circumcision and Salvation in the First Century." Pages 163–86 in *"To See Ourselves as Others See Us": Christians, Jews, "Others" in Antiquity*. Edited by J. Neusner and E. S. Frerichs. Chico, Calif.: Scholars Press, 1985.

Conzelmann, H. *History of Primitive Christianity*. Translated by John E. Steely from the German original, 1969. Nashville: Abingdon, 1973.

Cooper, S. "*Narratio* and *Exhortatio* in Galatians according to Marius Victorinus Rhetor." *Zeitschrift für die neutestamentliche Wissenschaft und die Kunde der älteren Kirche* 91 (2000): 107–35.

Cosby, M. R. "Galatians: Red Hot Rhetoric." In *Rhetorical Argumentation in Biblical Texts: Proceedings from the Lund Conference (July 24–27, 2000)*. Edited by Anders Eriksson et al. Harrisburg: Trinity International, forthcoming.

Cosgrove, C. H. *The Cross and the Spirit*. Macon, Calif.: Mercer University Press, 1988.

———. "The Law Has Given Sarah No Children (Gal 4.21–30)." *Novum Testamentum* 19 (1978): 219–35.

Cotter, W. "The Collegia and Roman Law: State Restrictions on Voluntary Associations, 64 BCE–200 CE." Pages 74–89 in *Voluntary Associations in the Graeco-Roman World*. Edited by John S. Kloppenborg and Stephen G. Wilson. New York: Routledge, 1996.

Cousar, C. *Galatians*. Atlanta: John Knox, 1982.

Cranfield, C. E. B. "Changes of Person and Number in Paul's Epistles." Pages 280–89 in *Paul and Paulinism: Essays in Honour of C. K. Barrett*. Edited by M. D. Hooker and S. G. Wilson. London: SPCK, 1982.

———. "'The Works of the Law' in the Epistle to the Romans." *Journal for the Study of the New Testament* 43 (1991): 89–101.

Cronje, J. van W. "The Stratagem of the Rhetorical Question in Gal 4:9–10 as a Means toward Persuasion." *Neotestamentica* 26 (1992) 417–24.

Crouch, J. E. *The Origin and Intention of the Colossian Haustafel.* Göttingen: Vandenhoeck, 1972.

Crownfield, F. R. "The Singular Problem of the Dual Galatians." *Journal of Biblical Literature* 44 (1945): 491–500.

Cummins, S. A. *Paul and the Crucified Christ in Antioch: Maccabean Martyrdom and Galatians 1 and 2.* Society for New Testament Studies Monograph Series 114. Cambridge: Cambridge University Press, 2001.

Dahl, N. A. "Letter." Pages 538–41 in *The Interpreter's Dictionary of the Bible.* Supplementary volume. Nashville: Abingdon, 1976.

———. "Die Name Israel I: Zur Auslegung von Gal. 6,16." *Judaica* 6 (1959): 161–70.

———. "The Particularity of the Pauline Epistles as a Problem in the Ancient Church." Pages 261–71 in *Neotestamentica et patristica: Eine Freundesgabe, Herrn Professor Dr. Oscar Cullmann zu seinem 60.* Novum Testamentum Supplements 6. Leiden: Brill, 1962.

———. "Paul's Letter to the Galatians: Epistolary Genre, Content, and Structure." Edited by M. D. Nanos. Paper presented at the Seminar on Paul at the Annual Meeting of the SBL, 1973. Pages 12–36 and 76–101 have been edited and published in *The Galatians Debate,* pages 117–42, and referred to as "Galatians"; references to pages in the original and not published in *The Galatians Debate* are referred to as "Paul's Letter."

———. *Studies in Ephesians: Introductory Questions, Text- and Edition-Critical Issues, Interpretation of Texts and Themes.* Edited by D. Hellholm, V. Blomkvist, and T. Fornberg. Wissenschaftliche Untersuchungen zum Alten und Neuen Testament 131. Tübingen: Mohr Siebeck, 2000.

Dalbert, P. *Die Theologie der hellenistisch-jüdischen Missionsliteratur unter Ausschluss von Philo und Josephus.* Hamburg-Volksdorf: H. Reich, 1954.

Danby, H. *The Mishnah.* London: Oxford University Press, 1933.

Dascal, Marcello, and Alan G. Gross. "The Marriage of Pragmatics and Rhetoric." *Philosophy and Rhetoric* 32 (1999): 107–30.

Daube, David. "Jewish Missionary Maxims in Paul." *Studia theologica* 1 (1948): 158–69.

Davies, W. D. *Christian Origins and Judaism.* Philadelphia: Fortress, 1962.

———. "A Note on Josephus, *Antiquities* 15.136." *Harvard Theological Review* 47 (1954): 135–40.

———. "Paul and Jewish Christianity according to Cardinal Daniélou: A Suggestion." Pages 164–71 in *Jewish and Pauline Studies.* Philadelphia: Fortress, 1984.

———. "Paul and the People of Israel." *New Testament Studies* 24 (1977–1978): 4–39. Reprinted in *Jewish and Pauline Studies.* Philadelphia: Fortress, 1984, 123–52.

———. *Paul and Rabbinic Judaism.* London: SPCK, 1955.

———. *Torah in the Messianic Age.* Philadelphia: Fortress, 1952.

Davies, W. D., and D. C. Allison, *A Critical and Exegetical Commentary on the Gospel of Saint Matthew.* International Critical Commentary. Edinburgh: T&T Clark, 1988–1997.

Davies, W. D., P. W. Meyer, and D. E. Aune. Review of H. D. Betz, *Galatians*. *Religious Studies Review* 7 (1981): 310–28.

Demosthenes. *De corona and De falsa legatione*. Translated by C. A. Vince and J. H. Vince. Loeb Classical Library. Cambridge: Harvard University Press, 1963.

Dibelius, M. *An die Thessalonicher I, II, An die Philipper*. 3d ed. Handbuch zum Neuen Testament. Tübingen: Mohr Siebeck, 1937.

———. *Die Formgeschichte des Evangeliums*. 3d ed. Tübingen: Mohr Siebeck, 1959.

———. *Geschichte der urchristlichen Literatur*. Vol. 2. Leipzig and Berlin: Walter de Gruyter, 1926.

———. *James: A Commentary on the Epistle of James*. Revised by Heinrich Green. Translated by M. A. Evans. Hermeneia. Philadelphia: Fortress, 1976.

Dieter, O. A. L. "Stasis." *Speech Monographs* 17, no. 4 (1950): 345–69.

Dix, G. *Jew and Greek: A Study in the Primitive Church*. London: Dacre Press Westminster, 1953.

Dockhorn, K. Review of H. Lausberg, *Handbuch der literarischen Rhetorik*. *Göttinger gelehrte Anziehungen* 214 (1962): 177–96.

Dodd, B. J. "Christ's Slave, People Pleasers, and Galatians 1.10." *New Testament Studies* 42 (1996): 90–104.

———. *Paul's Paradigmatic "I": Personal Example as Literary Strategy*. Journal for the Study of the New Testament: Supplement Series 177. Sheffield: Sheffield Academic Press, 1999.

Donaldson, T. L. "The 'Curse of the Law' and the Inclusion of the Gentiles: Galatians 3.13–14." *New Testament Studies* 32 (1986): 94–112.

———. " 'The Gospel That I Proclaim among the Gentiles' (Gal. 2.2): Universalistic or Israel-Centered?" Pages 166–93 in *Gospel in Paul: Studies on Corinthians, Galatians, and Romans for Richard N. Longenecker*. Edited by L. Ann Jervis and P. Richardson. Sheffield: Sheffield Academic Press, 1994.

———. *Paul and the Gentiles: Remapping the Apostle's Convictional World*. Minneapolis: Fortress, 1997.

Donneyer, D. "Die Kompositionsmetapher 'Evangelium Jesu Christi, des Sohnes Gottes' Mk 1.1: Ihre theologische und literarische Aufgabe in der Jesus-Biographie des Markus." *New Testament Studies* 53 (1987): 452–68.

Doty, W. G. *Letters in Primitive Christianity*. Philadelphia: Fortress, 1973.

Douglas, M. "Deciphering a Meal." Pages 249–75 in *Implicit Meanings: Essays in Anthropology*. Boston: Routledge and Kegan Paul, 1975.

———. "Pollution." Pages 47–59 in *Implicit Meanings: Essays in Anthropology*. Boston: Routledge and Kegan Paul, 1975.

Downey, G. *A History of Antioch in Syria: From Seleucus to the Arab Conquest*. Princeton: Princeton University Press, 1961.

Drane, J. W. *Paul: Libertine or Legalist?* London: SPCK, 1975.

Duncan, G. S. *The Epistle of Paul to the Galatians*. Moffat New Testament Commentary. London: Hodder & Stoughton, 1934.

Dunn, J. D. G. "Echoes of Intra-Jewish Polemic in Paul's Letter to the Galatians." *Journal of Biblical Literature* 112, no. 3 (1993): 459–77.

————. *The Epistle to the Galatians.* Black's New Testament Commentary. Peabody, Mass.: Hendrickson, 1993.

————. "The Incident at Antioch (Gal. 2:11–18)." *Journal for the Study of the New Testament* 18 (1983): 3–57. Repr., pages 129–74 in *Jesus, Paul, and the Law: Studies in Mark and Galatians.* Louisville: Westminster/John Knox, 1990. Reprinted in *The Galatians Debate,* 199–234.

————. *Jesus, Paul, and the Law.* Louisville: Westminster/John Knox, 1990.

————. "The New Perspective on Paul." Pages 183–206 in *Jesus, Paul, and the Law.* Louisville: Westminster/John Knox, 1990.

————. *The Partings of the Ways between Christianity and Judaism and Their Significance for the Character of Christianity.* Philadelphia: Trinity Press International, 1991.

————. "The Relationship between Paul and Jerusalem according to Galatians 1 and 2." *New Testament Studies* 28 (1982): 461–78.

————. *The Theology of Paul's Letter to the Galatians.* New Testament Theology. Cambridge: Cambridge University Press, 1993.

————. *Unity and Diversity in the New Testament.* Philadelphia: Westminster, 1977.

————. "Works of the Law and the Curse of the Law (Galatians 3:10–14)." *New Testament Studies* 31 (1985): 523–42.

————. "Yet Once More—'The Works of the Law.'" *Journal for the Study of the New Testament* 46 (1992): 99–117.

Du Plessis, P. J. ΤΕΛΕΙΟΣ: *The Idea of Perfection in the New Testament.* Kampen: J. H. Kok, 1959.

Dupont, J. *Études sur les Actes des Apôtres.* Paris: Editions du Cerf, 1967.

————. "Pierre et Paul à Antioche et à Jérusalem." *Recherches de science religieuse* 45 (1957): 42–60, 225–39. Repr., pages 185–215 in *Études sur les Actes des Apôtres.* Paris: Editions du Cerf, 1967.

Du Toit, A. B. "Vilification as a Pragmatic Device in Early Christian Epistolography." *Biblica* 75 (1994): 403–12.

Earth, M. "Die Stellung des Paulus zu Gesetz und Ordnung." *Evangelische Theologie* 33 (1973): 508–11.

Ebeling, G. *Evangelische Evangelienauslegung: Eine Untersuchung zu Luthers Hermeneutik.* 2d ed. Darmstadt: Wissenschaftliche Buchgesellschaft, 1962.

————. *Die Wahrheit des Evangeliums: Eine Lesehilfe zum Galaterbrief.* Tübingen: Mohr Siebeck, 1981.

Eckert, J. *Die urchristliche Verkündigung im Streit zwischen Paulus und seinen Gegnern nach dem Galaterbrief.* Regensburg: Pustet, 1971.

Eco, U. *Zeichen: Einführung in einen Begriff und seine Geschichte.* Frankfurt: Suhrkamp, 1977.

Edelstein, L. *Plato's Seventh Letter.* Leiden: E. J. Brill, 1966.

Egli, E., et al., eds. *Huldreich Zwinglis sämtliche Werke.* 14 vols. Berlin and Zurich: C. A. Schwetschke und Sohn, 1905–1963.

Ehrman, B. D. "Cephas and Peter." *Journal of Biblical Literature* 109, no. 3 (1990): 463–74.

Ellicott, C. J. *St. Paul's Epistle to the Galatians*. 3d ed. London: Longmans, Green, 1863.

Elliott, N. *The Rhetoric of Romans: Argumentative Constraint and Strategy and Paul's "Debate" with Judaism*. Journal for the Study of the New Testament: Supplement Series 45. Sheffield: JSOT Press, 1990.

Elliott, S. M. "Paul and His Gentile Audiences: Mystery Cults, Anatolian Popular Religiosity, and Paul's Claim to Divine Authority in Galatians." *Listening* 31, no. 2 (1996): 117–36.

Ellis, E. E. "The Circumcision Party and the Early Christian Mission." *TU* 102 (1968): 390–99.

———. *Prophecy and Hermeneutic in Early Christianity*. Wissenschaftliche Untersuchungen zum Alten und Neuen Testament 18. Grand Rapids: Eerdmans, 1978.

Encyclopaedia Judaica. 16 vols. Jerusalem: Keter, 1972.

Erasmus, Desiderius. *Novum instrumentum omne, diligenter ab Erasmo Roterodamo recognitum et emendatum*. Basel, 1516.

Erdt, W. "Marius Victorinus Afer, der erste lateinische Pauluskommentator." Ph.D. diss., Hamburg, 1979.

Erichson, A. *Bibliographia calviniana: Catalogus chronologicus operum Calvini*. Berlin: C. A. Schwetschke, 1900.

Ernesti, J. C. G. *Lexicon technologiae Graecorum rhetoricae*. Leipzig: Sumtibus Caspari Fritsch, 1795.

———. *Lexicon technologiae Latinorum rhetoricae*. Leipzig: Sumtibus Caspari Fritsch, 1797.

Esler, P. F. *Community and Gospel in Luke–Acts: The Social and Political Motivations of Lucan Theology*. Cambridge: Cambridge University Press, 1987.

———. *The First Christians in Their Social Worlds: Social-Scientific Approaches to New Testament Interpretation*. London: Routledge, 1994.

———. *Galatians*. New Testament Readings. New York: Routledge, 1998.

———. "Making and Breaking an Agreement Mediterranean Style: A New Reading of Galatians 2:1–14." *Biblical Interpretation* 3, no. 3 (1995): 285–314. Reprinted in *The Galatians Debate*, 261–81.

———. Review of C. C. Hill, *Hellenists and Hebrews*. *Biblical Interpretation* 3 (1995): 119–23.

———. "Sectarianism and the Conflict at Antioch." Pages 52–69 in *The First Christians in Their Social Worlds: Social-Scientific Approaches to New Testament Interpretation*. London: Routledge, 1994.

Etaples, J. Lefèvre, d', ed. *S. Pauli epistolae XIV ex Vulgata, adiecta intelligentia ex Graeco, cum commentariis*. Paris, 1512.

Fairweather, J. "The Epistle to the Galatians and Classical Rhetoric: Parts 1 & 2. *Tyndale Bulletin* 45, no. 1 (1994): 1–38.

———. "The Epistle to the Galatians and Classical Rhetoric: Part 3. *Tyndale Bulletin* 45, no. 2 (1994): 213–43.

Faraone, C. A., and D. Obbink. *Magika hiera: Ancient Greek Magic and Religion*. New York: Oxford University Press, 1991.

Farmer, W. R. "Jesus and the Gospels." *Perkins (School of Theology) Journal* 28, no. 2 (1975): 31–36.

———. *Maccabees, Zealots, and Josephus: An Inquiry into Jewish Nationalism in the Greco-Roman Period.* New York: Columbia University Press, 1957.

Feld, H. " 'Christus Diener der Sünde.' " *Theologische Quartalschrift* 153 (1973): 119–31.

Feldman, L. H. *Jew and Gentile in the Ancient World: Attitudes and Interactions from Alexander to Justinian.* Princeton: Princeton University Press, 1993.

———. "Jewish Proselytism." Pages 372–408 in *Eusebius, Judaism, and Christianity.* Edited by H. W. Attridge and G. Hata. New York: Brill, 1992.

———. "Josephus." Pages 981–98 in vol. 3 of the *Anchor Bible Dictionary.* Edited by D. N. Freeman. 6 vols. New York: Doubleday, 1992.

Filson, F. V. *A New Testament History.* London: SCM, 1965.

Finkel, A. *The Pharisees and the Teacher of Nazareth.* Leiden: E. J. Brill, 1974.

Finn, T. M. *From Death to Rebirth: Ritual and Conversion in Antiquity.* New York and Mahwah, N. J.: Paulist, 1997.

Finsler, G. *Zwingli-Bibliographie: Verzeichnis der gedruckten Schriften von und über Ulrich Zwingli.* Zurich, 1897. Repr., Nieuwkoop: B. de Graaf, 1962.

Fischel, H. A. *Rabbinic Literature and Greco-Roman Philosophy.* Leiden: Brill, 1973.

Fishbane, M. *Biblical Interpretation in Ancient Israel.* Oxford: Clarendon, 1985.

Fitzmyer, J. "Crucifixion in Ancient Palestine, Qumran Lierature, and the New Testament." *Catholic Biblical Quarterly* 40 (1978): 493–513. Repr., 125–46 in *To Advance the Gospel.* New York: Crossroad, 1981.

———. *To Advance the Gospel.* New York: Crossroad, 1981.

Foerster, R., and E. Richtsteig, eds. *Libanii Opera.* Vol 9. Leipzig, 1927.

Foerster, W. "Abfassungszeit und Ziel des Galaterbriefes." Pages 135–41 in *Apophoreta: Festschrift für Ernst Haenchen zu seinem 70.* Edited by U. Eickelberg. Beihefte zur Zeitschrift für die neutestamentliche Wissenschaft 30. Berlin: Töpelmann, 1964.

———. "Die δοκοῦντες in Gal 2." *Zeitschrift für die neutestamentliche Wissenschaft und die Kunde der älteren Kirche* 36 (1937): 286–92.

Forbes, C. "Comparison, Self-Praise, and Irony: Paul's Boasting and the Conventions of Hellenistic Rhetoric." *New Testament Studies* 32 (1986): 1–30.

Fortna, R. T., and B. R. Gaventa, eds. *Studies in Paul and John.* Nashville: Abingdon, 1990.

Foss, S. K., compiler. *Rhetorical Criticism: Exploration and Practice.* Prospect Heights, Ill.: Waveland, 1989.

Fowler, R. M. Review of G. A. Kennedy, *New Testament Interpretation. Journal of Biblical Literature* 105 (1986): 328–30.

Frank, G. "Melanchthons Dialektik und die Geschichte der Logik." Pages 125–45 in *Melanchthon und das Lehrbuch des 16. Jahrhunderts.* Edited by J. Leonhardt. Rostocker Studien zur Kulturwissenschaft 1. Rostock: Universität Rostock, Philosophische Fakultät, 1997.

Fredriksen, P. "Apocalypse and Redemption in Early Christianity: From John of Patmos to Augustine of Hippo." *Vigiliae christianae* 45 (1991): 2–30.

———. *From Jesus to Christ: The Origins of the New Testament Images of Jesus.* New Haven: Yale University Press, 1988.

———. "Judaism, the Circumcision of Gentiles, and Apocalyptic Hope: Another Look at Galatians 1 and 2." *Journal of Theological Studies* 42, no. 2 (1991): 532–64. Reprinted in *The Galatians Debate,* 235–60.

———. "Paul and Augustine: Conversion Narratives, Orthodox Traditions, and the Retrospective Self." *Journal of Theological Studies* New Series 37 (1986): 3–34.

Freedman, D. N., ed. *The Anchor Bible Dictionary.* 6 vols. New York: Doubleday, 1992.

Freyne, S. *Galilee from Alexander the Great to Hadrian, 323 B.C.E. to 135 C.E..* Wilmington: Michael Glazier; Notre Dame: University of Notre Dame Press, 1980.

Fridrichsen, A. "Die Apologie des Paulus Gal. 1." Pages 53–76 in *Paulus und die Urgemeinde: Zwei Abhandlungen.* Edited by Lyder Brun and Anton Fridrichsen. Giessen: Töpelmann, 1921.

———. *The Apostle and His Message.* Uppsala Universitetsårsskrift 3. Uppsala: Lundequistska Bokhandeln; Leipzig: Harrassowitz, 1947.

Friedrich, R., and K. A. Vogel, eds. *500 Jahre Philipp Melanchthon (1497–1560).* Pirckheimer Jahrbuch 1998. Wiesbaden: Harrassowitz Verlag, 1998.

Fritz, K. von, and K. Horna. "Gnome, Gnomendichtung, Gnomologien." *RE Sup* 6:74–90.

Fuhrmann, M. *Das systematische Lehrbuch: Ein Beitrag zur Geschichte der Wissenschaften in der Antike.* Göttingen: Vandenhoeck & Ruprecht, 1960.

Fuhrmann, M., ed. *Anaximenis ars rhetorica.* Leipzig: B. G. Teubner, 1966.

Fung, R. Y. K. *The Epistle to the Galatians.* New International Commentary on the New Testament. Grand Rapids: Eerdmans, 1953.

Funk, R. "The Apostolic Parousia: Form and Significance." Pages 249–68 in *Christian History and Interpretation: Studies Presented to John Knox.* Edited by W. R. Farmer, C. F. D. Moule, and R. R. Niebuhr. Cambridge: Cambridge University Press, 1967.

———. *Language, Hermeneutic, and Word of God: The Problem of Language in the New Testament and Contemporary Theology.* New York: Harper & Row, 1966.

Furnish, V. P. *The Love Command in the New Testament.* Nashville: Abingdon, 1972.

———. *Theology and Ethics in Paul.* Nashville: Abingdon, 1968.

Gäbler, U. *Huldrych Zwingli im 20. Jahrhundert: Forschungsbericht und annotierte Bibliographie, 1897–1972.* Zurich: Theologischer Verlag, 1975.

Gaechter, P. *Matthäus.* Innsbruck, Vienna, and Munich: Tyrolia, 1963.

———. *Petrus und seine Zeit.* Innsbruck, Vienna, and Munich: Tyrolia, 1958.

Gager, J. *Kingdom and Community: The Social World of Early Christianity.* Englewood Cliffs: Prentice-Hall, 1975.

———. *The Origins of Anti-Semitism: Attitudes toward Judaism in Pagan and Christian Antiquity.* Oxford: Oxford University Press, 1983.

———. "Some Notes on Paul's Conversion." *New Testament Studies* 27 (1981): 697–704.

————, ed. *Curse Tablets and Binding Spells in Ancient Mediterranean Culture*. Oxford: Oxford University Press, 1991.

Gaiser, K. *Protreptik und Paränese bei Platon: Untersuchungen zur Form des platonischen Dialogs*. Tübinger Beitrage zur Altertumwissenschaft 40. Stuttgart: W. Kohlhammer, 1959.

Ganoczy, A., and S. Scheld. *Die Hermeneutik Calvins*. Wiesbaden: F. Steiner, 1983.

Gardiner, A. H., and K. Sethe, eds. *Egyptian Letters to the Dead, Mainly from the Old and Middle Kingdoms*. London: Egypt Exploration Society, 1928.

Garnsey, P. *Food and Society in Classical Antiquity*. Key Themes in Ancient History. Cambridge: Cambridge University Press, 1999.

Gartner, B. *The Theology of the Gospel according to Thomas*. New York: Harper & Brothers, 1961.

Gaston, L. "Paul and the Law in Galatians 2–3." Pages 37–58 in *Paul and the Gospels*, vol. 1 of *Anti-Judaism in Early Christianity*. Edited by Peter Richardson with David Granskou. Waterloo, Ont.: Wilfrid Laurier University Press, 1986.

————. *Paul and the Torah*. Vancouver, B.C.: Wilfrid Laurier University Press, 1988.

Gasque, W. W. *A History of the Criticism of the Acts of the Apostles*. Grand Rapids: Eerdmans, 1975.

Gaventa, B. R. *From Darkness to Light: Aspects of Conversion in the New Testament*. Philadelphia: Fortress, 1986.

————. "Galatians 1 and 2: Autobiography as Paradigm." *Novum Testamentum* 28 (1986): 309–26.

————. "The Singularity of the Gospel: A Reading of Galatians." Pages 147–59 in *Thessalonians, Philippians, Galatians, Philemon*, vol. 1 of *Pauline Theology*. Edited by J. M. Bassler. Minneapolis: Fortress, 1991.

Geiger, A. *Urschrift und Ubersetzungen der Bibel in ihrer Abhangigkeit von der innern Entwicklung des Judentums*. Frankfurt: Madda, 1928.

Georgi, D. *Die Geschichte der Kollekte des Paulus für Jerusalem*. Theologische Forschung 38. Hamburg-Bergstedt: Reich, 1965.

————. *The Opponents of Paul in Second Corinthians*. Philadelphia: Scholars Press, 1986.

————. "Weisheit Salomos." Pages 389–478 in *Jüdische Schriften aus hellenistisch-römischer Zeit*. Edited by W. G. Kümmel. Gütersloh: Mohn, 1973.

Geyser, A. S. "Paul, the Apostolic Decree, and the Liberals in Corinth." Pages 124–38 in *Studia paulina in honorem J. de Zwaan*. Haarlem: De Erven F. Bohn N.V., 1953.

Giomini, R., and M. S. Celentano, eds. *C. Iulii Victoris Ars rhetorica*. Leipzig: Teubner, 1980.

Girardin, B. *Rhétorique et théologique: Calvin—le Commentaire de l'Épître aux Romains*. Paris: Beauchesne, 1979.

Gnilka, J. *Der Philipperbrief*. Herders theologischer Kommentar zum Neuen Testament 10.3. Freiburg, Basel, and Vienna: Herder, 1968.

Goddard, A. J., and S. A. Cummins. "Ill or Ill-Treated? Conflict and Persecution as the Context of Paul's Original Ministry in Galatia." *Journal for the Study of the New Testament* 52 (1993): 93–126.

Goetchius, E. V. N. *The Language of the New Testament*. New York: Scribner, 1965.

Goguel, M. *The Primitive Church.* London: George Allen & Unwin, 1964. Translation of the French original, 1947.

Goldin, J. *The Fathers according to Rabbi Nathan.* New Haven: Yale University Press, 1955.

Goldstein, J. A. *The Letters of Demosthenes.* New York: Columbia University Press, 1968.

Goodman, M. "Jewish Proselytizing in the First Century." Pages 53–78 in *The Jews Among Pagans and Christians in the Roman Empire.* Edited by J. Lieu, J. North, and T. Rajak. London: Routledge, 1992.

————. "Nerva, the Fiscus Judaicus, and Jewish Identity." *Journal of Roman Studies* 79 (1989) 40–44.

————. "Proselytising in Rabbinic Judaism." *Journal of Jewish Studies* 40 (1989): 178–85.

————. *State and Society in Roman Galilee, A.D. 132–212.* Towtowa, N.J.: Rowman & Allanheld, 1983.

————. *Who Was a Jew?* Yarton Trust. Oxford: Oxford University Press, 1989.

Goppelt, L. *Apostolic and Post-apostolic Times.* London: A. & C. Black, 1970. Translation of the German original, 1962.

Gordon, T. D. "The Problem at Galatia." *Interpretation* 41 (1987): 37–40.

Görgemanns, H. "Epistolographie." Pages 1166–69 in vol. 3 of *Der neue Pauly: Enzyclopädie der Antike.* Edited by H. Cancik and H. Schneider. Stuttgart: J. B. Metzler, 1996–.

Görgemanns, H., and M. Zelzer. "Epistel." Pages 1161–66 in vol. 3 of *Der neue Pauly: Enzyclopädie der Antike.* Edited by H. Cancik and H. Schneider. Stuttgart: J. B. Metzler, 1996–.

Gori, F., ed. *Opera exegetica.* Part 2 of *Marii Victorini Opera.* Corpus scriptorum ecclesiasticorum latinorum 82, vol. 2. Vienna: 1986.

Gowers, E. *The Loaded Table: Representations of Food in Roman Literature.* Oxford: Clarendon, 1993.

Griffiths, J. G. "Allegory in Greece and Egypt." *Journal of Egyptian Archaeology* 53 (1967): 79–102.

————. *Plutarch's De Iside et Osiride.* Edited and translated by J. G. Griffiths. Cardiff: University of Wales, 1970.

Grondin, J. "Hermeneutik." Pages 1350–74 in vol. 3 of *Historisches Wörterbuch der Rhetorik.* Edited by G. Ueding, G. Kalivoda, and F-H. Robling. Tübingen: Max Niemeyer, 1992.

Grundmann, W. *Matthäus.* Theologischer Handkommentar zum Neuen Testament. Berlin: Evangelische Verlagsanstalt, 1968.

————. "χρίω, κτλ." Page 551 in vol. 9 of *Theological Dictionary of the New Testament.* Edited by G. Kittel and G. Friedrich. Translated by G. W. Bromiley. 10 vols. Grand Rapids: Eerdmans, 1964–1976.

Guelich, R. A. *The Sermon on the Mount: A Foundation for Understanding.* Waco: Word Commentary, 1982.

Gulley, N. "The Authenticity of the Platonic Epistles." Pages 103–30 in vol. 1 of *Pseudepigrapha.* Edited by Kurt von Fritz. Entretiens sur l'antiquité classique 18. Vandoeuvres-Genève: Fondation Hardt, 1972.

Gummere, R. M. *Seneca the Philosopher and his Modern Message.* Boston: Marshall Jones, 1922.

Guthrie, D. *Galatians.* New Century Bible. London: Oliphants, 1969.

Güttgemanns, E. *Der leidende Apostel und sein Herr: Studien zur paulinischen Christologie.* Edited by Ernst Käsemann and Ernst Würthwein. Forschungen zur Religion und Literatur des Alten und Neuen Testaments. Göttingen: Vandenhoeck & Ruprecht, 1966.

Haacker, K. "Paulus und das Judentum im Galaterbrief." Pages 95–111 in *Gottes Augapfel: Beiträge zur Erneuerung des Verhältnisses von Christen und Juden.* Edited by E. Brocke and J. Seim. Neukirchen-Vluyn: Neukirchener Verlag, 1986.

Hadot, I. *Seneca und die griechisch-römische Tradition der Seelenleitung.* Quellen und Studien zur Geschichte der Philosophie 13. Berlin: de Gruyter, 1969.

Haenchen, E. *Acts.* Oxford: Blackwell, 1971.

———. "Matthäus 23." Pages 30–40 in *Gott und Mensch.* Tübingen: J. C. B. Mohr, 1965.

Hafemann, S. J. "The Role of Suffering in the Mission of Paul." Pages 165–84 in *The Mission of the Early Church to Jews and Gentiles.* Edited by J. Ådna and H. Kvalbein. Tübingen: Mohr Siebeck, 2000.

———. *Suffering and the Spirit: An Exegetical Study of II Cor. 2:14 -3:3 within the Context of the Corinthian Correspondence.* Wissenschaftliche Untersuchungen zum Alten und Neuen Testament 19. Tübingen: Mohr Siebeck, 1986.

Hahn, F. "Das Gesetzesverständnis im Römer- und Galaterbrief." *Zeitschrift für die neutestamentliche Wissenschaft und die Kunde der älteren Kirche* 67 (1976): 26–63.

———. *Mission in the New Testament.* London: SCM, 1965. Translation of the German original, 1963.

Hall, R. G. "Historical Inference and Rhetorical Effect: Another Look at Galatians 1 and 2." Pages 308–20 in *Persuasive Artistry: Studies in New Testament Rhetoric in Honor of George A. Kennedy.* Edited by Duane F. Watson. Journal for the Study of the New Testament: Supplement Series 50. Sheffield: Sheffield Academic Press, 1991.

———. "The Rhetorical Outline for Galatians: A Reconsideration." *Journal of Biblical Literature* 106, no. 2 (1987): 277–88. Reprinted in *The Galatians Debate,* 29–38.

Hansen, G. W. *Abraham in Galatians: Epistolary and Rhetorical Contexts.* Journal for the Study of the New Testament: Supplement Series 29. Sheffield: JSOT Press, 1989.

———. *Galatians.* Downers Grove, Ill.: InterVarsity, 1994.

———. "A Paradigm of the Apocalypse: The Gospel in the Light of Epistolary Analysis." Pages 194–221 in *Gospel in Paul: Studies on Corinthians, Galatians, and Romans for Richard N. Longenecker.* Edited by L. A. Jervis and P. Richardson. Sheffield: Sheffield Academic Press, 1994. Reprinted in *The Galatians Debate,* 143–54.

Hare, D. R. A. *The Theme of Jewish Persecution of Christians in the Gospel of Matthew.* Cambridge: Cambridge University Press, 1967.

Harnack, A. von. *Mission and Expansion of Christianity in the First Three Centuries.* Vol. 1. 4th ed. New York: Harper, 1924.

Hartfelder, K. *Philipp Melanchthon als Praeceptor Germaniae.* Berlin: A. Hofmann, 1889.

Harvey, A. E. "The Opposition to Paul." Pages 319–32 in vol. 4 of *Studia Evangelica.* Edited by F. L. Cross. Berlin: Akademie, 1968. Reprinted in *The Galatians Debate,* 321–33.

Harvey, G. *The True Israel: Uses of the Names Jew, Hebrew, and Israel in Ancient Jewish and Early Christian Literature.* Arbeiten zur Geschichte des antiken Judentums und des Urchristentums 35. Leiden: Brill, 1996.

Haseloff, O. W. "Über Wirkungsbedingungen politischer und werblicher Kommunikation." In *Kommunikation.* Edited by O. W Haseloff. Berlin: Colloquium, 1969.

Hauck, F. "κοινός." Pages 789–809 in vol. 3 of *Theological Dictionary of the New Testament.* Edited by G. Kittel and G. Friedrich. Translated by G. W. Bromiley. 10 vols. Grand Rapids: Eerdmans, 1964–1976.

Hausammann, S. Römerbriefauslegung zwischen Humanismus und Reformation: Eine Studie zu Heinrich Bullingers Römerbriefauslegung von 1525. Zurich: Zwingli, 1970.

Hawkins, J. G. "The Opponents of Paul in Galatia." Ph.D. diss., Yale University, 1971.

Hay, D. M. "Paul's Indifference to Authority." *Journal of Biblical Literature* 88 (1969): 36–44.

Hayd, S. *Introductio hermeneutica in sacros Novi Testamenti libros.* Vienna, 1777.

Hays, R. *Echoes of Scripture in the Letters of Paul.* New Haven: Yale University Press, 1989.

———. *The Faith of Jesus Christ: An Investigation of the Narrative Substructure of Galatians 3:1–4:11.* Society of Biblical Literature Dissertation Series 56. Chico, Calif.: Scholars Press, 1983.

Henderson, J. R. "Erasmus on the Art of Letter-Writing." Pages 331–55 in *Renaissance Eloquence: Studies in the Theory and Practice of Renaissance Rhetoric.* Edited by J. J. Murphy. Berkeley: University of California Press, 1983.

Hengel, M. *Acts and the History of Earliest Christianity.* London: SCM, 1979. Translation of the German original, 1979.

———. *Between Jesus and Paul.* Philadelphia: Fortress, 1983.

———. "Ἰουδαία in the Geographical List of Acts 2:9–11 and Syria as 'Greater Judea.'" *Bulletin for Biblical Research* 10, no. 2 (2000): 161–80.

———. "Die Ursprünge der christlichen Mission." *New Testament Studies* 18 (1971–1972): 15–38.

———. *Die Zeloten: Untersuchung zur jüdischen Freiheitsbewegung in der Zeit von Herodes I bis 70 n. Chr.* Leiden and Cologne: E. J. Brill, 1961.

Hercher, R., ed. *Epistolographi graeci.* Paris, 1873.

Herkenrath, E. *Beschreibendes Verzeichnis der Literatur über Heinrich Bullinger.* Vol. 2 of *Bibliographie.* Edited by F. Büsser. Part 1 of *Heinrich Bullinger Werke.* Zurich: Theologischer Verlag, 1977.

Hermann, C. "Eine Fragment gebliebene Rhetorik von Johannes Brenz." *Blätter für Württembergische Kirchengeschichte* 64 (1964): 79–103.

Hertz, R., ed. *Chumash.* London: Soncino, 1988.

Herzog, J. J., A. Hauck, and H. Caselmann. *Realencyklopädie für protestantische Theologie und Kirche.* Leipzig: J. C. Hinrichs, 1896.

Hester, J. D. "The Invention of 1 Thessalonians: A Proposal." Pages 251–79 in *Rhetoric and the Bible: Papers at the Pretoria Conference.* Edited by S. Porter and T. Olbricht. Sheffield: Sheffield Academic Press, 1995.

———. "Placing the Blame: The Presence of Epideictic in Galatians 1 and 2." Pages 281–307 in *Persuasive Artistry: Studies in New Testament Rhetoric in Honor of George A. Kennedy.* Edited by Duane F. Watson. Sheffield: JSOT Press, 1991.

———. "The Rhetorical Structure of Galatians 1:11–14." *Journal of Biblical Literature* 103, no. 2 (1984): 223–33.

———. "Sanders and the New Perspective." July 27, 2001, post on "Corpus-Paul" list (http://franklin.oit.unc.edu/cgi-bin/lyris.pl?enter=corpus-paul).

———. "Speaker, Audience, and Situations: A Modified Interactional Model." *Neotestamentica* 32, no. 1 (1998): 251–71.

———. "The Use and Influence of Rhetoric in Galatians 2:1–14." *Theologische Zeitschrift* 42, no. 5 (1986): 386–408.

Hill, C. C. *Hellenists and Hebrews: Reappraising Division within the Earliest Church.* Minneapolis: Fortress, 1992.

Hill, D. *Matthew.* New Century Bible. London: Oliphants, 1972.

———. *New Testament Prophecy.* Atlanta: John Knox, 1979.

Hirsch, E. "Zwei Fragen zu Gal 6." *Zeitschrift für die alttestamentliche Wissenschaft* 29 (1930): 192–97.

Hock, R., and E. O'Neill. *The Progymnasmata.* Vol. 1 of *The Chreia in Ancient Rhetoric.* Atlanta: Scholars Press, 1986.

Hodgson, R. "Paul the Apostle and First Century Tribulation Lists." *Zeitschrift für die neutestamentliche Wissenschaft und die Kunde der älteren Kirche* 74 (1983): 59–80.

Hoffman, L. A. *Covenant of Blood: Circumcision and Gender in Rabbinic Judaism.* London: University of Chicago Press, 1996.

Hoffmann, M. *Rhetoric and Theology: The Hermeneutics of Erasmus.* Toronto: University of Toronto Press, 1994.

Hogg, M. A., and D. Abrams. *Social Identifications: A Social Psychology of Intergroup Relations and Group Processes.* New York: Routledge, 1988.

Holladay, C. R. "Aristobulus (OT Pseudepigrapha)." Pages 383–84 in vol. 1 of the *Anchor Bible Dictionary.* Edited by D. N. Freeman. 6 vols. New York: Doubleday, 1992.

Holloway, P. A. "The Enthymeme as an Element of Style in Paul." *Journal of Biblical Literature* 120, no. 2 (2001): 329–43.

Holmberg, B. "Jewish *versus* Christian Identity in the Early Church?" *Revue biblique* 105, no. 3 (1998): 397–425.

———. *Paul and Power: The Structure of Authority in the Primitive Church as Reflected in the Pauline Epistles.* Coniectanea neotestamentica or Coniectanea biblica: New Testament Series 11. Philadelphia: Fortress, 1978.

Holmes, D. H. *Index lysiacus.* Bonn: F. Coheni, 1895.

Holmstrand, J. *Markers and Meaning in Paul: An Analysis of 1 Thessalonians, Philippians, and Galatians.* Coniectanea neotestamentica or Coniectanea biblica: New Testament Series 28. Stockholm: Almqvist & Wiksell International, 1997.

Holtz, T. "Die Bedeutung des Apostelkonzils für Paulus." *Novum Testamentum* 16 (1974): 243–66.

Holtzmann, H. J. *Lehrbuch der historisch-kritischen Einleitung in das Neue Testament.* Freiburg: Mohr, 1886.

Holtzmann, O. "Zu Emanuel Hirsch: Zwei Fragen zu Galater 6." *Zeitschrift für die neutestamentliche Wissenschaft und die Kunde der älteren Kirche* 30 (1931): 76–83.

Holub, R. C. *Reception Theory: A Critical Introduction.* London: Methuen, 1984.

Hong, I-G. "The Law in Galatians." Th.D. diss., University of Stellenbosch, 1991. Rev. version, *The Law in Galatians.* Sheffield: Sheffield Academic Press, 1993.

Hooker, M. D. "Were There False Teachers in Colossae?" Pages 315–31 in *Christ and Spirit in the New Testament: Essays in Honour of C. F. D. Moule.* Edited by B. Lindars and S. S. Smalley. Cambridge: Cambridge University Press, 1973.

Horsley, R. A., and J. S. Hanson. *Bandits, Prophets, and Messiahs: Popular Movements in the Time of Jesus.* San Francisco: Harper & Row, 1987.

Howard, G. *Paul—Crisis in Galatia: A Study in Early Christian Theology.* 2d ed. Society for New Testament Studies Monograph Series 35. Cambridge: Cambridge University Press, 1990.

Hubbard, B. J. *The Matthean Redaction of a Primitive Apostolic Commissioning: An Exegesis of Matthew 28:16–20.* Society of Biblical Literature Dissertation Series 19. Missoula, Mont.: Scholars Press, 1974.

Hübner, H. "Galaterbrief." *Theologische Realencyclopädie* 12 (1984): 5–14.

———. *Das Gesetz bei Paulus.* Göttingen: Vandenhoeck & Ruprecht, 1978. 2d ed., 1980.

———. *Law in Paul's Thought.* Studies of the New Testament and Its World. Edinburgh: T&T Clark, 1984.

———. Review of H. D. Betz, *Galatians. Theologische Literaturzeitung* 109 (1984): 241–50.

Hübner, H., and D. Flusser. "Paulus." Pages 133–60 in vol. 26 of *Theologische Realenzyclopädie.* Edited by G. Krause and G. Müller. Berlin: de Gruyter, 1977–.

Hughes, F. W. *Early Christian Rhetoric and 2 Thessalonians.* Sheffield: Sheffield Academic Press, 1989.

Hultgren, A. "Paul's Pre-Christian Persecutions of the Church." *Journal of Biblical Literature* 95 (1976): 97–111.

Hutcheon, L. *Irony's Edge: The Theory and Politics of Irony.* New York: Routledge, 1994.

In omnes M. Tullii Ciceronis orationes, quot quidem extant, doctissimorum virorum enarrationes. Basel: Ioannes Oporinus, 1553.

Jegher-Bucher, V. "Formgeschichtliche Betrachtung zu Galater 2, 11–16." *Theologische Zeitung* 47 (1991): 305–21.

————. *Galaterbrief auf dem Hintergrund antiker Epistolographie und Rhetorik: Ein anderes Paulusbild.* Abhandlungen zur Theologie des Alten und Neuen Testaments 78. Zurich: Theologischer Verlag, 1991.

Jenkins, R. *Social Identity.* New York: Routledge, 1996.

Jeremias, J. *Abba.* Göttingen: Vandenhoeck & Ruprecht, 1966.

————. *Infant Baptism in the First Four Centuries.* London: SCM, 1960. Translated from the German original, 1958.

————. *Jerusalem in the Time of Jesus.* London: SCM, 1969. Translated from the German 3d ed., 1962.

————. *Jesus' Promise to the Nations.* Studies in Biblical theology. Translated by S. H. Hooke from the German original, 1956. Naperville, Ill.: A. R. Allenson, 1958.

————. *The Proclamation of Jesus.* Vol. 1 of *New Testament Theology.* London: SCM, 1971. Translated from the German original, 1971.

————. "Zum Quellenproblem der Apostelgeschichte." 1937. Repr., pages 238–55 in *Abba.* Göttingen: Vandenhoeck & Ruprecht, 1966.

Jewett, R. "The Agitators and the Galatian Congregation." *New Testament Studies* 17 (1970–1971): 198–212. Reprinted in *The Galatians Debate,* 334–47.

————. *A Chronology of Paul's Life.* Philadelphia: Fortress, 1979.

————. *Dating Paul's Life.* Philadelphia: Fortress, 1979.

————. *Paul's Anthropological Terms: A Study of Their Use in Conflict Settings.* Leiden: Brill, 1971.

————. "Romans as an Ambassadorial Letter." *Interpretation* 36 (1982): 5–20.

————. *The Thessalonian Correspondence: Pauline Rhetoric and Millenarian Piety.* Philadelphia: Fortress, 1986.

Johanson, B. C. *To All the Brethren: A Text-Linguistic and Rhetorical Approach to I Thessalonians.* Stockholm: Almquist & Wiksell, 1987.

Johnson, E. E., and D. M. Hay, eds. *Looking Back, Pressing On.* Vol. 4 of *Pauline Theology.* Society of Biblical Literature Symposium Series. Atlanta: Scholars Press, 1997.

Johnson, L. T. *The Letter of James.* Anchor Bible 37A. New York: Doubleday, 1995.

————. "The New Testament's Anti-Jewish Slander and the Conventions of Ancient Polemic." *Journal of Biblical Literature* 108, no. 3 (1989): 419–41.

Jones, F. S. *An Ancient Jewish Christian Source on the History of Christianity: Pseudo Clementine Recognitions 1.27–71.* Atlanta: Scholars Press, 1995.

Jones, S., and S. Pearce, eds. *Jewish Local Patriotism and Self-Identification in the Graeco-Roman Period.* Journal for the Study of the Pseudepigrapha: Supplement Series 31. Sheffield: Sheffield Academic Press, 1998.

Josephus. Translated by H. St. J. Thackeray et al. 10 vols. Loeb Classical Library. Cambridge: Harvard University Press, 1926–1965.

Junghans, H. *Der junge Luther und die Humanisten.* Göttingen: Vandenhoeck & Ruprecht, 1985.

Juster, J. *Les juifs dans l'empire romain.* 2 vols. Paris: Geuthner, 1914.

Karlsson, G. *Idéologie et ceremonial dans l'épistolographie Byzantine.* 2d ed. Uppsala: Almqvist & Wiksell, 1962.

Käsemann, E. *Commentary on Romans*. Translated by G. W. Bromiley. Grand Rapids: Eerdmans, 1980.

Kasher, A. *Jews, Idumeans, and Ancient Arabs*. Tübingen: Mohr Siebeck, 1988.

Kassel, R., ed. *Aristotle ars rhetorica*. Berlin: de Gruyter, 1976.

Kennedy, G. A. *The Art of Persuasion in Greece*. Princeton: Princeton University Press, 1963.

———. *The Art of Rhetoric in the Roman World, 300 B.C–A.D. 300*. Princeton: Princeton University Press, 1972.

———. *Classical Rhetoric and Its Christian and Secular Tradition from Ancient to Modern Times*. Chapel Hill: University of North Carolina Press, 1980.

———. *Greek Rhetoric under Christian Emperors*. Princeton: Princeton University Press, 1983.

———. *New Testament Interpretation through Rhetorical Criticism*. Chapel Hill: University of North Carolina Press, 1984.

Kern, P. H. *Rhetoric and Galatians: Assessing an approach to Paul's Epistle*. Society for New Testament Studies Monograph Series 101. Cambridge: Cambridge University Press, 1998.

Kertelge, K. "Zur Deutung des Rechtfertigungsbegriffs im Galaterbrief." *Biblische Zeitschrift* Neue Folge 12 (1968): 211–22.

Kieffer, R. *Foi et justification à Antioche: Interprétation d'un conflit (Ga 2,14–21)*. Lectio divina 111. Paris: Cerf, 1982.

Kilpatrick, G. D. "Galatians 1:18: ΙΣΤΟΡΗΣΑΙ ΚΗΦΑΝ." Pages 144–49 in *New Testament Essays: Studies in Memory of T.W. Manson*. Edited by A. J. B. Higgins. Manchester: Manchester University Press, 1959.

King, D. H. "Paul and the Tannaim: A Study in Galatians." *Westminster Theological Journal* 45 (1983): 368–69.

Kinneavey, J. L. *Greek Rhetorical Origins of Christian Faith: An Inquiry*. New York: Oxford University Press, 1987.

Kittel, G., and G. Friedrich. *Theological Dictionary of the New Testament*. 10 vols. Translated and edited by G. W. Bromiley. Grand Rapids: Eerdmans, 1964.

———, eds. *Theologisches Wörterbuch zum Neuen Testament*. 10 vols. Stuttgart: W. Kohlhammer, 1932–1979.

Klawans, J. *Impurity and Sin in Ancient Judaism*. Oxford: Oxford University Press, 2000.

———. "Notions of Gentile Impurity in Ancient Judaism." *Association for Jewish Studies Review* 20, no. 2 (1995): 285–312.

Klijn, A. F. J., and G. J. Reinink. *Patristic Evidence for Jewish-Christian Sects*. Leiden: Brill, 1973.

Kluser, T., et al., eds. *Reallexicon für Antike und Christentum*. Stuttgart, 1950–.

Knape, J. *Philipp Melanchthons Rhetorik*. Tübingen: Niemeyer, 1993.

Knox, J. *Chapters in a Life of Paul*. New York: Abingdon-Cokesbury, 1954.

Koehn, H. "Philipp Melanchthons Reden: Verzeichnis der im 16. Jahrhundert erschienenen Drucke." *Archiv für die Geschichte des Buchwesens* 25 (1984): 1277–1486.

Koenig, E. *Stilistik, Rhetorik, Poetik in Bezug auf die biblische Literatur*. Leipzig: Dieterich, 1900.

Koepp, W. "Die Abraham-Midraschimkette des Galaterbriefes als das vorpaulinische heidenchristliche Urtheologumenon." Pages 181–87 in *Wissenschaftliche Zeitschrift der Universität Rostock;* Reihe Gesellschafts- und Sprachwissenschaften 2, no. 3. Rostock: The University, 1952–1953.

Koester, H. *Einführung in das Neuen Testament.* New York: Walter de Gruyter, 1980.

———. "ΓΝΩΜΑΙ ΔΙΑΦΟΡΟΙ: The Origin and Nature of Diversification in the History of Early Christianity." *Harvard Theological Review* 58 (1965): 279–318.

———. "Häretiker im Urchristentum." Cols. 17–21. in vol. 3 of *Religion in Geschichte und Gegenwart.* Edited by K. Galling. 7 vols. 3d ed. Tübingen: Mohr Siebeck, 1957–1965.

Köhler, W. *Bibliographia brentiana.* Berlin, 1904.

Koniaris, G. L., ed. *Maximus Tyrius: Philosophumena—ΔΙΑΛΕΞΕΙΣ.* Berlin: Walter de Gruyter, 1995.

Koptak, P. E. "Rhetorical Identification in Paul's Autobiographical Narrative: Galatians 1.13–2.14," *Journal for the Study of the New Testament* 40 (1990): 97–115. Reprinted in *The Galatians Debate,* 157–68.

Koskenniemi, H. *Studien zur Idee und Phraseologie des griechischen Briefes.* Annales Academiae scientiarum fennicae 102, no. 2. Helsinki: Suomalainen Tiedeakatemie, 1956.

Kraabel, A. T. "The Disappearance of the 'God-Fearers.'" *Numen* 28 (1981): 113–26.

———. "Social Systems of Six Diaspora Synagogues." Pages 79–91 in *Ancient Synagogues: The State of Research.* Edited by Joseph Gutmann. Chico, Calif.: Scholars Press, 1981.

———. "Synagoga Caeca: Systematic Distortion in Gentile Interpretations of Evidence for Judaism in the Early Christian Period." Pages 219–46 in *"To See Ourselves as Others See Us": Christians, Jews, "Others" in Late Antiquity.* Edited by Jacob Neusner and Ernest S. Frerichs. Chico, Calif.: Scholars Press, 1985.

Kraeling, C. H. "The Jewish Community at Antioch." *Journal of Biblical Literature* 51 (1932): 130–60.

Kraftchick, S. J.. "Why Do the Rhetoricians Rage?" Pages 55–79 in *Text and Logos: The Humanistic Interpretation of the New Testament.* Edited by T. W. Jennings, Jr. Atlanta: Scholars Press, 1990.

Krieger, C. *Martin Bucer and Sixteenth Century Europe.* 2 vols. Leiden: Brill, 1993.

Krüger, F. *Humanistische Evangelienauslegung: Desiderius Erasmus von Rotterdam als Ausleger der Evangelien in seinen Paraphrasen.* Tübingen: Mohr, 1986.

Kuhn, K. G. "προσήλυτος." Pages 727–44 in vol. 6 of *Theological Dictionary of the New Testament.* Edited by G. Kittel and G. Friedrich. Translated by G. W. Bromiley. 10 vols. Grand Rapids: Eerdmans, 1964–1976.

Kumaniecki, K., ed. *M. Tulli Ciceronis de oratore.* Leipzig: B. G. Teubner, 1969.

Kümmel, W. G. "Die älteste Form des Aposteldekrets." Pages 83–98 in *Spiritus et Veritas.* San Francisco, 1953. Repr., pages 278–88 in *Heilsgeschehen und Geschichte: Gesammelte Aufsätze, 1933–64.* Marburg: N. G. Elwert, 1965.

———. " 'Individualgeschichte' und 'Weltgeschichte' in Gal 2:15–21." Pages 157–73 in *Christ and Spirit in the New Testament: Studies in Honour of C. F. D. Moule.*

Edited by B. Lindars and S. S. Smalley. London: Cambridge University Press, 1973.

———. *Introduction to the New Testament.* Rev. translation. Nashville: Abingdon, 1975. Translated from the German original, 1973.

LaGrand, J. "Proliferation of the 'Gentile' in the New Revised Standard Version." *Biblical Research* 41 (1996): 77–87.

Lagrange, M. J. *Galates.* 2d ed. Études bibliques. Paris: Gabalda, 1925.

Lake, K. *The Acts of the Apostles.* 5 vols. The Beginnings of Christianity, Part 1. London: Macmillan, 1933.

———. *Earlier Epistles of St. Paul.* London: Rivingtons, 1911.

Lambrecht, J. "The Line of Thought in Gal 2:14b–21." *New Testament Studies* 24 (1977–1978): 484–95.

———, ed. *The Truth of the Gospel (Galatians 1:1–4:11).* Monographic Series of "Benedictina." Biblical-Ecumenical Section 12. Rome: St. Paul's Abbey, 1993.

Lampe, G. W. H., ed. *A Patristic Greek Lexicon.* Oxford: Oxford University Press, 1961–1968.

Landes, R. "Lest the Millennium Be Fulfilled: Apocalyptic Expectations and the Pattern of Western Chronography, 100–800 C.E." Pages 137–211 in *The Use and Abuse of Eschatology in the Middle Ages.* Edited by W. Verbeke, D. Verhelst, and A. Welkenhuysen. Mediaevalia lovaniensia 1.15. Leuven: Leuven University Press, 1988.

Lategan, B. C. "The Argumentative Situation of Galatians." *Neotestamentica* 26, no. 2 (1992): 257–70. Reprinted in *The Galatians Debate,* 383–95.

———. "Is Paul Defending His Apostleship in Galatians? The Function of Galatians 1:11–12 and 2:19–20 in the Development of Paul's Argument." *New Testament Studies* 34 (1988): 411–30.

Lategan, B. C., and W. S. Vorster. *Text and Reality: Aspects of Reference in Biblical Texts.* Philadelphia: Fortress, 1985.

Lausberg, H. *Handbuch der literarischen Rhetorik: Eine Grundlegung der Literaturwissenschaft.* Munich: Hueber, 1960.

Leeman, A. D. *Orationis ratio:* The Stylistic Theories and Practice of the Roman Orators, Historians, and Philosophers. 2 vols. Amsterdam: A. M. Hakkert, 1963.

Lemmer, H. R. "Why Should the Possibility of Rabbinic Rhetorical Elements in Pauline Writings (e.g., Galatians) Be Reconsidered?" Pages 161–79 in *Rhetoric, Scripture, and Theology: Essays from the 1994 Pretoria Conference.* Edited by S. E. Porter and T. H. Olbricht. Sheffield: Sheffield Academic Press, 1996.

Leonhardt, J. "Melanchthon als Verfasser von Lehrbüchern." Pages 26–47 in *500 Jahre Philipp Melanchthon (1497–1560).* Edited by R. Friedrich and K. A. Vogel. Pirckheimer Jahrbuch 1998. Wiesbaden: Harrassowitz, 1998.

———, ed. *Melanchthon und das Lehrbuch des 16. Jahrhunderts.* Rostock: Universität Rostock, Philosophische Fakultat, 1997.

Lerle, E. *Proselytenwerbung und Urchristentum.* Berlin: Evangelische Verlagsanstalt, 1960.

Levine, A.-J. " 'Traversing Sea and Land': The Search for the Origin of Matthew 23:15." Unpublished paper.

Levy, B. J. "Torah in the Messianic Age." *Gesher* 7 (1979): 167–81.

Liddell, H. G., R. Scott, and H. S. Jones. *A Greek-English Lexicon.* 9th ed. With revised supplement. Oxford: Oxford University Press, 1996.

Lietzmann, H. *Galater.* 3d ed. Handbuch zum Neuen Testament. Tübingen: J. C. B. Mohr, 1932.

Lieu, J. M. "Circumcision, Women, and Salvation." *New Testament Studies* 40 (1994): 358–70.

Lightfoot, J. B. *The Epistle of St. Paul to the Galatians.* Zondervan Commentary. Grand Rapids: Zondervan, 1957.

Lindars, B., and S. S. Smalley, eds. *Christ and Spirit in the New Testament: Studies in Honour of C. F. D. Moule.* London: Cambridge University Press, 1973.

Linton, O. "The Third Aspect: A Neglected Point of View." *Studia theologica* 3 (1950): 73–95.

Lipp, W. "Social Deviation, Leadership, and Cultural Change: A Sociology of Deviance Approach." *Annual Review of the Social Sciences of Religion* 1 (1977): 59–77.

———. *Stigma und Charisma: Über soziales Grenzverhalten.* Schriften zur Kultursoziologie 1. Berlin: Duncker & Humblot, 1985.

Locher, A., ed. *Marii Victorini Afri Commentarii in epistulas Pauli ad Galatas, ad Philippenses, ad Ephesios.* Bibliotheca scriptorum graecorum et romanorum teubneriana. Leipzig: Teubner, 1972.

Lofthouse, W. F. "Singular and Plural in Paul's Letters." *ExpTim* 58 (1946–1947): 179–82.

Loheit, F. "Untersuchungen zur antiken Selbstapologie." Ph.D. diss., Rostock, 1928.

Longenecker, B. W. *The Triumph of Abraham's God: The Transformation of Identity in Galatians.* Edinburgh: T&T Clark, 1998.

Longenecker, R. N. *Galatians.* Word Biblical Commentary 41. Dallas: Word, 1990.

———. "The Pedagogical Nature of the Law in Galatians 3:19–4:7." *Journal of the Evangelical Theological Society* 25 (1982): 57–59.

Loubser, J. A. "Orality and Pauline 'Christology': Some Hermeneutical Implications." *Scriptura* 47 (1993): 29–36.

Lubac, H. de. *H. de. Exégèse médiévale.* 2 vols. Paris: Aubier, 1959–1964.

Lüdemann, G. *Antipaulinismus im frühen Christentum.* Vol. 2 of *Paulus der Heidenapostel.* Forschungen zur Religion und Literatur des Alten und Neuen Testaments 130. Göttingen: Vandenhoeck & Ruprecht, 1983.

———. *Paul, Apostle to the Gentiles: Studies in Chronology.* Translated by F. S. Jones. London: SCM, 1984.

———. *Studien zur Chronologie.* Vol. 1 of *Paulus der Heidenapostel.* Forschungen zur Religion und Literatur des Alten und Neuen Testaments 123. Göttingen: Vandenhoeck & Ruprecht, 1980.

Lührmann, D. *Galatians.* Continental Commentaries. Minneapolis: Fortress, 1992.

Lull, D. J. *The Spirit in Galatia.* Society of Biblical Literature Dissertation Series 49. Chico, Calif.: Scholars Press, 1980.

Lund, N. *Chiasmus in the New Testament.* Chapel Hill: University of North Carolina Press, 1942.

Lütgert, W. "Gesetz und Geist: Eine Untersuchung zur Vorgeschichte des Galaterbriefes." *Beiträge zur Förderung christlicher Theologie* 22 (1917): 473–576.

———. *Gesetz und Geist: Eine Untersuchung zur Vorgeschichte des Galaterbriefes.* Gütersloh: Bertelsmann, 1919.

Luther, M. *A Commentary on St. Paul's Epistle to the Galatians.* Westwood, N.J.: Fleming Revell, 1953.

———. *D. Martin Luthers Werke.* 68 vols. Weimar: H. Bohlau, 1883–1999.

Luz, U. "Der alte und der neue Bund bei Paulus und im Hebräerbrief." *Evangelische Theologie* 27 (1967): 318–36.

———. *Matthew 1–7: A Commentary.* Edinburgh: T&T Clark, 1989.

———. *The Theology of the Gospel of Matthew.* Cambridge: Cambridge University Press, 1995.

Lyons, G. *Pauline Autobiography: Toward a New Understanding.* Society of Biblical Literature Dissertation Series 73. Atlanta: Scholars Press, 1985.

Maccoby, H. "The Washing of Cups." *Journal for the Study of the New Testament* 14 (1982): 3–15.

Machen, J. G. *Machen's Notes on Galatians.* Edited by J. H. Skilton. Nutley, N.J.: Presbyterian and Reformed, 1977.

Mack, B. L., and V. Robbins, *Patterns of Persuasion.* Sonoma, Calif.: Polebridge, 1989.

Majercik, R., T. B. Dozeman, and B. Fiore. "Rhetoric and Rhetorical Criticism." Pages 710–19 in vol. 5 of the *Anchor Bible Dictionary.* Edited by D. N. Freeman. 6 vols. New York: Doubleday, 1992.

Malherbe, A. J. "I Thessalonians as a Paraenetic Letter." Paper presented to the Paul Seminar at the annual meeting of the SBL, 1972.

———. *Ancient Epistolary Theorists.* Edited by Bernard B. Scott. Society of Biblical Literature Sources for Biblical Study 19. Atlanta: Scholars Press, 1988.

———. " 'Gentle as a Nurse': The Cynic Background to I Thess ii." *Novum Testamentum* 12 (1970): 203–17.

———. *Moral Exhortation, a Greco-Roman Sourcebook.* Philadelphia: Westminster, 1986.

———. "Paul: Hellenistic Philosopher or Christian Pastor?" *Harvard Theological Review* 68 (1986): 3–13.

Malina, B. J. *The New Testament World: Insights from Cultural Anthropology.* London: SCM, 1983. Rev. ed., Louisville: Westminster/John Knox, 1993.

Malina, B. J., and J. H. Neyrey. "First-Century Personality: Dyadic, Not Individual." Pages 67–96 in *The Social World of Luke–Acts: Models for Interpretation.* Edited by J. H. Neyrey. Peabody, Mass.: Hendrickson, 1991.

Manson, T. W. "The Problem of the Epistle to the Galatians." Pages 168–89 in *Studies in the Gospels and Epistles* by T. W. Manson. Edited by Matthew Black. Manchester: Manchester University Press, 1962.

Margolin, J.-C., ed. *Opera omnia Desiderii Erasmi Roterodami.* New York: North-Holland, 1971.

Martin, J. *Antike Rhetorik: Technik und Methode.* Handbuch der Altertumswissenschaft 2/3. Munich: C. H. Beck, 1974.

Martin, T. "Apostasy to Paganism: The Rhetorical Stasis of the Galatian Controversy." *Journal of Biblical Literature* 114, no. 3 (1995): 437–61. Reprinted in *The Galatians Debate,* 73–94.

———. "Pagan and Judeo-Christian Time-Keeping Schemes in Gal 4:10 and Col 2:16." *New Testament Studies* 42 (1996) 120–32.

———. "Whose Flesh? What Temptation? (Galatians 4.13–14)." *Journal for the Study of the New Testament* 74 (1999): 65–91.

Martyn, J. L. "Apocalyptic Antinomies in Paul's Letters to the Galatians." *New Testament Studies* 31 (1985): 410–24.

———. "*Clementine Recognitions* 1,33–71, Jewish Christianity, and the Fourth Gospel." Pages 265–95 in *God's Christ and His People: Studies in Honor of Nils Alstrup Dahl.* Edited by J. Jervell and W. A. Meeks. Oslo: Universitetsforlaget, 1977.

———. *Galatians: A New Translation with Introduction and Commentary.* Anchor Bible 33A. New York: Doubleday, 1997.

———. "A Law-Observant Mission to Gentiles: The Background of Galatians," *Scottish Journal of Theology* 38 (1985): 307–23. Rev. ed., "A Law-Observant Mission to Gentiles." Pages 7–24 in *Theological Issues in the Letters of Paul.* Nashville: Abingdon, 1997. Rev. ed. reprinted in *The Galatians Debate,* 348–61.

———. *Theological Issues in the Letters of Paul.* Nashville: Abingdon, 1997.

Marx, F., ed. *Incerti auctoris de ratione dicendi ad C. Herennium libri IV.* Leipzig: B. G. Teubner, 1923.

Marxsen, W. *Einleitung in das Neue Testament.* 4th ed. Gütersloh: Gerd Mohn, 1978.

———. *Introduction to the New Testament.* Oxford: Basil Blackwell, 1968.

Matera, F. J. *Galatians.* Sacra pagina 9. Collegeville, Minn.: Liturgical Press, 1992.

Maurach, G. *Der Bau von Senecas Epistulae morales.* Heidelberg: C. Winter, 1970.

———. Review of H. Cancik, *Untersuchungen zu Senecas Epistulae morales. Gnomon* 41 (1969): 472–76.

Maurer, W. *Der junge Melanchthon zwischen Humanismus und Reformation.* 2 vols. Göttingen: Vandenhoeck & Ruprecht, 1967–1969.

McEleney, N. J. "Conversion, Circumcision, and the Law." *New Testament Studies* 20 (1973–74): 319–41.

McGiffert, A. C. *A History of Christianity in the Apostolic Age.* Edinburgh: T&T Clark, 1897.

McGuire, M. R. P. "Letters and Letter Carriers in Christian Antiquity." *Classical World* 53 (1960): 148–53.

McKnight, S. *A Light among the Gentiles: Jewish Missionary Activity in the Second Temple Period.* Minneapolis: Fortress, 1991.

McNeile, A. H. *Matthew.* London: Macmillan, 1915.

Meecham, H. G. *Light from Ancient Letters: Private Correspondence in the Non-literary Papyri of Oxyrhynchus of the First Four Centuries, and Its Bearing on New Testament Language and Thought.* New York: Macmillan, 1923.

Meeks, W. A. *The First Urban Christians: The Social World of the Apostle Paul*. New Haven: Yale University Press, 1983.

———. "Jews and Christians in Antioch in the First Four Centuries." Pages 33–65 in *SBL Seminar Papers, 1976*. Edited by George MacRae. Society of Biblical Literature Seminar Papers. Missoula, Mont.: Scholars Press, 1976.

———. *The Origins of Christian Morality: The First Two Centuries*. New Haven: Yale University Press, 1993.

———. Review of H. D. Betz, *Galatians*. *Journal of Biblical Literature* 100 (1981): 304–7.

Meeks, W. A., and R. H. Wilken. *Jews and Christians in Antioch in the First Four Centuries of the Common Era*. Society of Biblical Literature Sources for Biblical Study. Missoula, Mont.: Scholars Press, 1978.

Melanchthon, P. *Compendiaria dialectices*. Leipzig, 1520.

———. *De rhetorica libri tres*. Wittenberg, 1519.

———. *Dialectices libri quatuor*. Hagenau, 1528.

———. *Elementorum rhetorices libri duo*. Wittenberg, 1531. Rev. ed., 1536.

———. "Ἐξήγησις methodica in epistolam Pauli πρὸς τοὺς Γαλάτας." *Texte aus der Anfangszeit Melanchthons*. Edited by Ernst Bizer. Texte zur Geschichte der evangelischen Theologie 2. Neukirchen-Vluyn: Neukirchener Verlag, 1966.

———. *Erotemata dialectices*. Wittenberg, 1547.

———. *Institutiones rhetoricae*. Hagenau, 1521.

———. *Operum Philippi Melanthonis tomi quinque*. Basel, 1541.

Mendelson, A. *Secular Education in Philo of Alexandria*. Monographs of the Hebrew Union College 7. Cincinnati: Hebrew Union College, 1982.

Merk, O. "Der Beginn der Paränese im Galaterbrief." *Zeitschrift für die neutestamentliche Wissenschaft und die Kunde der älteren Kirche* 60 (1969): 83–104.

Merkelbach, R. *Roman und Mysterium in der Antike*. Munich: Beck, 1962.

Meyer, H. A. W. *Kritisch exegetisches Handbuch über den Brief an die Galater*. 4th ed. Kritisch-exegetischer Kommentar über das Neue Testament (Meyer-Kommentar). Göttingen: Vandenhoeck & Ruprecht, 1870.

Meyer, R. "πάροικος." Page 850 in vol. 5 of *Theological Dictionary of the New Testament*. Edited by G. Kittel and G. Friedrich. Translated by G. W. Bromiley. 10 vols. Grand Rapids: Eerdmans, 1964–1976

———. "περιτέμνω." Pages 72–84 in vol. 6 of *Theological Dictionary of the New Testament*. Edited by G. Kittel and G. Friedrich. Translated by G. W. Bromiley. 10 vols. Grand Rapids: Eerdmans, 1964–1976.

———. "φαρισαῖος." Pages 15–18 in vol. 9 of *Theological Dictionary of the New Testament*. Edited by G. Kittel and G. Friedrich. Translated by G. W. Bromiley. 10 vols. Grand Rapids: Eerdmans, 1964–1976.

Meynet, R. "Histoire de 'l'analyse rhétorique' en exégèse biblique." *Rhetorica* 8 (1990): 291–320.

Michaelis, W. "ὁράω." Pages 315–82 in vol. 5 of *Theological Dictionary of the New Testament*. Edited by G. Kittel and G. Friedrich. Translated by G. W. Bromiley. 10 vols. Grand Rapids: Eerdmans, 1964–1976.

————. "πάσχω." Pages 896–939 in vol. 5 of *Theological Dictionary of the New Testament*. Edited by G. Kittel and G. Friedrich. Translated by G. W. Bromiley. 10 vols. Grand Rapids: Eerdmans, 1964–1976.

Millar, A., and J. K. Riches. "Interpretation: A Theoretical Perspective and Some Applications." *Numen* 28 (1981): 29–53.

Miller, C. R. "Genre as Social Action." *Quarterly Journal of Speech* 70 (1984): 151–67.

Minear, P. "The Crucified World: The Enigma of Gal. 6.14." Pages 395–407 in *Theologia crucis-signum crucis: Festschrift fur Erich Dinkier*. Edited by C. Andersen and G. Klein. Tübingen: Mohr Siebeck, 1979.

Misch, G. *A History of Autobiography in Antiquity*. London: Routledge & Kegan Paul, 1950.

Mitchell, M. M. *Paul and the Rhetoric of Reconciliation: An Exegetical Investigation of the Language and Composition of 1 Corinthians*. Louisville: Westminster, 1992.

Mitternacht, D. *Forum für Sprachlose: Eine kommunikationspsychologische und epistolär-rhetorische Untersuchung des Galaterbriefs*. Coniectanea biblica: New Testament Series 30. Stockholm: Almqvist & Wiksell International, 1999.

Mödritzer, H. *Stigma und Charisma im Neuen Testament und seiner Umwelt: Zur Soziologie des Urchristentums*. Novum Testamentum et orbis antiquus 28. Freiburg, Switzerland: Universitätsverlag; Göttingen: Vandenhoeck & Ruprecht, 1994.

Momigliano, A. *The Development of Greek Biography: Four Lectures*. Cambridge: Harvard University Press, 1971.

————. *Second Thoughts on Greek Biography*. Amsterdam: North-Holland, 1971.

Mondolfo, Rodolfo, and Leonardo Tarán, *Eraclito. Testimonianze e imitazioni*. Firenze: La nuova Italia, 1972.

Moore, G. F. "Christian Writers on Judaism." *Harvard Theological Review* 14 (1921): 197–254.

————. *Judaism*. 3 vols. Cambridge: Harvard University Press, 1927.

Morland, K. A. *The Rhetoric of Curse in Galatians: Paul Confronts Another Gospel*. Atlanta: Scholars Press, 1995.

Most, G. W. "The Stranger's Stratagem: Self-Disclosure and Self-Sufficiency in Greek Culture." *Journal of Hellenistic Studies* 109 (1989): 114–33.

Moule, C. F. D. *An Idiom Book of New Testament Greek*. Cambridge: Cambridge University Press, 1959.

————. "Sanctuary and Sacrifice in the Church of the New Testament." *Journal of Theological Studies* New Series 1 (1950): 29–41.

Muilenberg, James. "Form Criticism and Beyond." *Journal of Biblical Literature* 88 (1969): 1–18.

Müller, G. Review of L. Edelstein, *Plato's Seventh Letter*. *Göttinger gelehrte Anziehungen* 221 (1969): 187–211.

Müller, J. *Martin Bucers Hermeneutik*. Gütersloh: Gerd Mohn, 1965.

Müller, W. G. "Brief." Pages 60–76 in vol. 2 of *Historisches Wörterbuch der Rhetorik*. Edited by G. Ueding, G. Kalivoda, and F-H. Robling. Tübingen: M. Niemeyer, 1994.

Mullins, T. Y. "Disclosure: A Literary Form in the New Testament." *Novum Testamentum* 7, no. 1 (1964): 44–50.

———. "Formulas in New Testament Epistles." *Journal of Biblical Literature* 91 (1972): 380–90.

———. "Paul's Thorn in the Flesh." *Journal of Biblical Literature* 76 (1957): 299–303.

———. "*Topos* as a New Testament Form." *Journal of Biblical Literature* 99 (1980): 541–47.

Munck, J. *Christ and Israel: An Interpretation of Romans 9–11.* Translated by I. Nixon. Philadelphia: Fortress, 1967.

———. *Paul and the Salvation of Mankind.* Translated by Frank Clarke. Richmond: John Knox, 1959.

Murphy, J. J., ed. *Renaissance Eloquence: Studies in the Theory and Practice of Renaissance Rhetoric.* Berkeley: University of California Press, 1983.

Mussner, F. *Der Galaterbrief.* 3d ed. Herders theologischer Kommentar zum Neuen Testament 9. Freiburg, Basel, and Vienna: Herder, 1977.

Nadeau, R. "Classical Systems of Stases in Greek: Hermagoras to Hermogenes." *Greek, Roman, and Byzantine Studies* 2 (1959): 53–71.

———. "Hermogenes' On Stases: A Translation with an Introduction and Notes." *Speech Monographs* 31(1964): 361–424.

———. "The Progymnasmata of Aphthonius." *Speech Monographs* 19 (1952): 264–85.

Nanos, M. D. "The Inter- and Intra-Jewish Context of Paul's Letter to the Galatians." Pages 146–59 in *Paul and Politics: Ekklesia, Israel, Imperium, Interpretation.* Edited by R. A. Horsley. Harrisburg: Trinity, 2000. Reprinted in *The Galatians Debate,* 396–407.

———. "Intruding 'Spies' and 'Pseudo' Brethren: The Intra-Jewish Context of 'Those of Repute' in Jerusalem (Gal. 2:1–10)." Paper presented at the 1997 International Research Consultation: Ideology, Power, and Interpretation. Birmingham, England, 1997. (Forthcoming in *Paul and His Opponents.* Edited by S. E. Porter and B. W. R. Pearson. Brill.)

———. *The Irony of Galatians: Paul's Letter in First-Century Context.* Minneapolis: Fortress, 2002.

———. *The Mystery of Romans: The Jewish Context of Paul's Letter.* Minneapolis: Fortress, 1996.

———. " 'O Foolish Galatians, Who Has Cast the Evil Eye [of Envy] upon You?' (Gal 3:1a–b): The Belief System and Interpretive Implications of Paul's Accusation." Paper presented at the annual meeting of the SBL. Boston, Mass., Nov. 22, 1999.

Neumeister, C. *Grundsätze der forensischen Rhetorik gezeigt an Gerichtsreden Ciceros.* Munich: M. Hueber, 1965.

Neusner, J. "The Fellowship (חבורה) in the Second Jewish Commonwealth." *Harvard Theological Review* 53 (1960): 125–42.

———. "First Cleanse the Inside." *New Testament Studies* 22 (1975–1976): 486–95.

———. *From Politics to Piety: The Emergence of Pharisaic Judaism.* Englewood Cliffs: Prentice-Hall, 1973.

———. *A History of the Mishnaic Law of Purities.* 22 vols. Leiden: E. J. Brill, 1974–1977.

————. *The Idea of Purity in Ancient Judaism.* Leiden: E. J. Brill, 1973.

————. *The Rabbinic Traditions about the Pharisees before 70.* 3 vols. Leiden: E. J. Brill, 1971.

Neusner, J., and E. S. Frerichs, eds. *"To See Ourselves as Others See Us": Christians, Jews, "Others" in Antiquity.* Chico, Calif.: Scholars Press, 1985.

Newton, D. *Deity and Diet: The Dilemma of Sacrificial Food at Corinth.* Journal for the Study of the New Testament: Supplement Series 169. Sheffield: Sheffield Academic Press, 1998.

Neyrey, J. *Honor and Shame in the Gospel of Matthew.* Louisville: Westminster John Knox, 1998.

Nickelsburg, G. W. E. "Revealed Wisdom as a Criterion for Inclusion and Exclusion: From Jewish Sectarianism to Early Christianity." Pages 73–82 in *"To See Ourselves as Others See Us": Christians, Jews, "Others" in Late Antiquity.* Edited by J. Neusner and E. Frerichs. Chico, Calif.: Scholars Press, 1985.

Nicholas, B. *An Introduction to Roman Law.* Oxford: Clarendon, 1963.

Nickle, K. F. *The Collection: A Study in Paul's Strategy.* London: SCM, 1966.

Nock, A. D. *Conversion.* Oxford: Oxford University Press, 1933.

Nolland, J. "Proselytism or Politics in Horace, *Satires* i, 4, 138–43?" *Vigiliae christianae* 33 (1979): 347–55.

————. "Uncircumcised Proselytes?" *Journal for the Study of Judaism in the Persian, Hellenistic, and Roman Periods* 12 (1981): 173–94.

Norden, E. *Die antike Kunstprosa.* 5th ed. Stuttgart: B. G. Teubner, 1958.

Novak, D. *The Image of the Non-Jew in Judaism: An Historical and Constructive Study of the Noahide Laws.* New York: Edwin Mellon Press, 1983.

O'Brien, P. T. *The Epistle to the Philippians: A Commentary on the Greek Text.* Grand Rapids: Eerdmans, 1991.

O'Neill, J. C. *The Recovery of Paul's Letter to the Galatians.* London: SPCK, 1972.

Oepke, A. *Der Brief des Paulus an die Galater.* Edited by J. Rohde. Theologischer Handkommentar zum Neuen Testament 9. Berlin: Evangelische Verlagsanstalt. 1984.

Ollrog, W. H. *Paulus und seine Mitarbeiter.* Wissenschaftliche Monographien zum Alten und Neuen Testament 50. Neukirchen: Neukirchener Verlag, 1979.

Oltramare, A. *Les origines de la diatribe romaine.* Lausanne, Geneva, and Neuchâtel: Payot, 1926.

Opitz, P. *Calvins theologische Hermeneutik.* Neukirchen-Vluyn: Neukirchener Verlag, 1994.

Oppenheimer, A. *The Am Ha-aretz: A Study in the Social History of the Jewish People in the Hellenistic-Roman Period.* Leiden: E. J. Brill, 1977.

Otto, E. *Die biographischen Inschriften dcr ägyptischen Spätzeit, ihre geistesgeschichtliche und literärische Bedeutung.* Leiden: Brill, 1954.

Otto, G., et al. "Christliche Rhetorik." Pages 197–222 in vol. 2 of *Historisches Wörterbuch der Rhetorik.* Edited by G. Ueding, G. Kalivoda, and F-H. Robling. Tübingen: Max Niemeyer, 1992.

Overbeck, F. "Über die Anfange der patristischen Literatur." *Historische Zeitschrift* 48 (1882): 417–72.

————. *Über die Auffassung des Streits des Paulus mit Petrus in Antiochien (Gal. 2:11ff)* *bei den Kirchenvätern.* Basil: Schultze, 1877. Repr., Darmstadt: Wissenschaftliche Buchgesellschaft, 1968.

Paget, J. C. "Jewish Christianity." Pages 731–75 in *The Early Roman Period,* vol. 3 of *The Cambridge History of Judaism.* Edited by William Horbury, W. D. Davies, and John Sturdy. New York: Cambridge University Press, 1999.

Parker, T. H. L., ed. *Iohannis Calvini Commentarius in epistolam Pauli ad Romanos.* Vol. 22. Leiden: Brill, 1981.

Parkes, J. *The Foundations of Judaism and Christianity.* London: Vallentine, Mitchell, 1960.

Parks, E. P. *The Roman Rhetorical Schools as a Preparation for the Courts under the Early Empire.* Baltimore: Johns Hopkins Press, 1945.

Patte, D. *Paul's Faith and the Power of the Gospel: A Structural Introduction to the Pauline Letters.* Philadelphia: Fortress, 1983.

Patton, J. H. Review of G. A. Kennedy, *New Testament Interpretation. Quarterly Journal of Speech* 71 (1985): 247–49.

Pedersen, S., ed. *Die paulinische Literatur und Theologie.* Aarhus: Forlaget Aros; Göttingen: Vandenhoeck & Ruprecht, 1980.

Pépin, J. *Mythe et allégorie: les origines grecques et les contestations judeo-chretiennes.* Paris: Aubier, 1958.

Perelman, C. *The Realm of Rhetoric.* Notre Dame: Notre Dame University Press, 1982.

Perelman, C., and L. Olbrechts-Tyteca. *The New Rhetoric: A Treatise on Argumentation.* Notre Dame: University of Notre Dame Press, 1969.

Peristiany, J. G., ed. *Honour and Shame: The Values of Mediterranean Society.* London: Weidenfeld & Nicolson, 1965.

Peristiany, J. G., and J. Pitt-Rivers, eds. *Honor and Grace in Anthropology.* Cambridge: Cambridge University Press, 1992.

Perosa, A., ed. *Collatio Novi Testamenti.* Florence: Sansoni, 1970.

Peter, H. *Der Brief in der römischen Literatur.* Leipzig: Teubner, 1901. Repr., Hildesheim: Olms, 1965.

Petersen, N. R. *Rediscovering Paul: Philemon and the Sociology of Paul's Narrative World.* Philadelphia: Fortress, 1985.

Pitta, A. *Disposizione e messagio della lettera ai Galati: Analisi retorico-letteraria.* Analecta biblica 131. Rome: Editrice Pontificio Istituto Biblico, 1992.

Pitt-Rivers, J. "Honor." Pages 503–11 in vol. 6 of *International Encyclopedia of the Social Sciences.* Edited by D. Sills. New York: Macmillan, 1968–.

————. "Honour and Social Status." Pages 19–77 in *Honour and Shame: The Values of Mediterranean Society.* Edited by J. Peristiany. London: Weidenfeld & Nicolson, 1965.

Pobee, J. S. *Persecution and Martyrdom in the Theology of Paul.* Journal for the Study of the New Testament: Supplement Series 6. Sheffield: JSOT Press, 1985.

Porter, S. E. "Ancient Rhetorical Analysis and Discourse Analysis of the Pauline Corpus." Pages 249–74 in *The Rhetorical Analysis of Scripture: Essays from the 1995 London Conference.* Edited by S. E. Porter and T. H. Olbrecht. Sheffield: Sheffield Academic Press, 1997.

―――. *The Paul of Acts: Essays in Literary Criticism, Rhetoric, and Theology.* Tübingen: Mohr Siebeck, 1999.

―――. "Paul of Tarsus and His Letters." Pages 533–85 in *Handbook of Classical Rhetoric in the Hellenistic Period, 330 B. C.–A. D. 400.* Edited by S. E. Porter. Leiden: Brill, 1997.

―――. "The Theoretical Justification for Application of Rhetorical Categories to Pauline Epistolary Literature." Pages 100–22 in *Rhetoric and the New Testament: Essays from the 1992 Heidelberg Conference.* Edited by S. E. Porter and T. H. Olbricht. Sheffield: Sheffield Academic Press, 1993.

―――, ed. *Handbook of Classical Rhetoric in the Hellenistic Period, 330 B. C.–A. D. 400.* Leiden: Brill, 1997.

Porter, S. E., and T. H. Olbricht, eds. *Rhetoric and the New Testament: Essays from the 1992 Heidelberg Conference.* Sheffield: Sheffield Academic Press, 1993.

―――, eds. *Rhetoric, Scripture, and Theology: Essays from the 1994 Pretoria Conference.* Sheffield: Sheffield Academic Press, 1996.

―――, eds. *The Rhetorical Analysis of Scripture: Essays from the 1995 London Conference.* Sheffield: Sheffield Academic Press, 1997.

Porton, G. G. *The Stranger within Your Gates: Converts and Conversion in Rabbinic Literature.* Chicago: University of Chicago Press, 1994.

Poster, C. "A Conversation Halved: Epistolary Theory in Graeco-Roman Antiquity." In *Letter Writing Instruction from Antiquity to the Present.* Edited by C. Poster and L. Mitchell. University of South Carolina Press, forthcoming.

―――. "The Economy of Letter Writing." In *Rhetorical Argumentation and the New Testament.* Edited by T. Olbricht et al. Harrisburg, Pa.: Trinity Press International, forthcoming.

Preisigke, F., and E. Kießling. *Wörterbuch der griechischen Papyrusurkunden.* 3 vols. Berlin: Selbstverlag der Erben, 1925–1931.

Preuss, S. *Index demosthenicus.* Leipzig: In aedibus B. G. Teubneri, 1892.

Price, S. R. F. *Rituals and Power: The Roman Imperial Cult in Asia Minor.* Cambridge: Cambridge University Press, 1984.

Prior, M. *Paul the Letter-Writer and the Second Letter to Timothy.* Journal for the Study of the New Testament: Supplement Series 23. Sheffield: JSOT Press, 1989.

Pucci Ben Zeev, M. *Jewish Rights in the Roman World: The Greek and Roman Documents Quoted by Josephus Flavius.* Texte und Studien zum antiken Judentum 74. Tübingen: Mohr Siebeck, 1998.

Pucket, D. L. *John Calvin's Exegesis of the Old Testament.* Louisville: Westminster/John Knox, 1992.

Quintilian. *Institutio oratoria.* Translated by H. E. Butler. Loeb Classical Library. Cambridge: Harvard University Press, 1920.

―――. *Institutio oratoria.* Edited by M. Winterbottom. 2 vols. Oxford: Clarendon, 1970.

Rabbow, P. *Seelenführung: Methodik der Exerzitien in der Antike.* Munich: Kosel, 1954.

Rabe, Hugo, ed. "On Invention." Pages 93–121 in *Hermogenis opera.* Leipzig: B. G. Teubner, 1913.

Radermacher, L., ed. *Demetrii Phalerei qui dicitur De elocutione liber.* Leipzig: B. G. Teubner, 1901.

Räisänen, H. "Galatians 2.16 and Paul's Break with Judaism." *New Testament Studies* 31 (1985): 543–53.

———. "Legalism and Salvation by the Law." Pages 63–83 in *Die Paulinische Literatur und Theologie.* Edited by S. Pedersen. Aarhus: Forlaget Aros; Göttingen: Vandenhoeck & Ruprecht, 1980.

———. *Paul and the Law.* Philadelphia: Fortress, 1983.

Rajak, T. "Jewish Rights in the Greek Cities under Roman Rule: A New Approach." Pages 19–35 in *Approaches to Ancient Judaism.* Edited by W. S. Green. Studies in Judaism and Its Graeco-Roman Context 5. Atlanta: Scholars Press, 1985.

———. "Jews and Christians as Groups in a Pagan World." Pages 247–62 in *"To See Ourselves as Others See Us": Christians, Jews, "Others" in Late Antiquity.* Edited by Jacob Neusner and Ernest S. Frerichs. Chico, Calif.: Scholars Press, 1985.

———. "Was There a Roman Charter for the Jews?" *Journal of Roman Studies* 74 (1984): 107–23.

Ramsay, W. M. *St. Paul the Traveller and the Roman Citizen.* London: Hodder & Stoughton, 1895. 14th ed., 1920.

Reed, J. T. "The Epistle." Pages 171–93 in *Handbook of Classical Rhetoric in the Hellenistic Period, 330 B. C.–A. D. 400.* Edited by S. E. Porter. Leiden: Brill, 1997.

———. "Using Ancient Rhetorical Categories to Interpret Paul's Letters: A Question of Genre." Pages 292–324 in *Rhetoric and the New Testament: Essays from the 1992 Heidelberg Conference.* Edited by S. E. Porter and T. H. Olbricht. Sheffield: Sheffield Academic Press, 1993.

Reeve, A., and M. A. Screech, eds. *Erasmus' "Annotationes" on the New Testament: Acts, Romans, I and II Corinthians.* Leiden: Brill, 1990.

Regt, L. J. de, et al., eds. *Literary Structure and Rhetorical Strategies in the Hebrew Bible.* Assen: Van Gorcum, 1996.

Reicke, B. "Der geschichtliche Hintergrund des Apostelkonzils und der Antiochia-Episode, Gal. 2, 1–14." Pages 172–87 in *Studia paulina: In honorem Johannis de Zwaan septuagenarii.* Edited by J. N. Sevenster and W. C. van Unnik. Haarlem: De Erven F. Bohn, 1953.

———. "The Law and This World according to Paul." *Journal of Biblical Literature* 70 (1951): 259–76.

———. *The New Testament Era.* Translated by David E. Green. Philadelphia: Fortress, 1968.

Reitzenstein, R. *Die hellenistischen Mysterienreligionen: Ihre Grundgedanken und Wirkungen.* Leipzig and Berlin: B. G. Teubner, 1920.

Rengstorf, K. H. "ἁμαρτωλός." Pages 317–33 in vol. 1 of *Theological Dictionary of the New Testament.* Edited by G. Kittel and G. Friedrich. Translated by G. W. Bromiley. 10 vols. Grand Rapids: Eerdmans, 1964–1976

———. "ζυγός." Pages 896–901 in vol. 2 of *Theological Dictionary of the New Testament.* Edited by G. Kittel and G. Friedrich. Translated by G. W. Bromiley. 10 vols. Grand Rapids: Eerdmans, 1964–1976.

Reusch, F. "Hayd, Stephan." Page 123 in vol. 11 of *Allgemeine Deutsche Bibliographie.* Edited by R. V. Liliencron, et al. 56 vols. Leipzig: Duncker & Humblot, 1875–1912.

Reuters, F. H. *Die Briefe des Anacharsis: Griechisch und Deutsch.* Schriften und Quellen der Alten Welt 14. Berlin: Akademie Verlag, 1963.

Reventlow, H. Graf. *Epochen der Bibelauslegung.* 3 vols. Munich: C. H. Beck, 1990–1997.

Reynolds, J., and R. Tannenbaum. *Jews and Godfearers at Aphrodisias.* Cambridge: Cambridge University Press, 1987.

Rhetorica ad Herennium. Translated by H. Caplan. 5th ed. Loeb Classical Library. Cambridge: Harvard University Press, 1981.

Ribbeck, O. *Kolax: Eine ethologische Studie.* Abhandlungen der [K.] Sächsischen Gesellschaft der Wissenschaften. Phil.-hist. Klasse 9. Leipzig: Hirzel, 1883.

Richardson, P. *Israel in the Apostolic Church.* Cambridge: Cambridge University Press, 1969.

———. "Pauline Inconsistency: I Corinthians 9.19–23 and Galatians 2.11–14." *New Testament Studies* 26 (1979): 347–62.

Riches, J. *Jesus and the Transformation of Judaism.* London: DLT, 1980.

Ricoeur, P. *Interpretation Theory: Discourse and the Surplus of Meaning.* Fort Worth: Texas Christian University Press, 1976.

———. *The Rule of Metaphor: Multi-disciplinary Studies of the Creation of Meaning in Language.* London: Routledge & Kegan Paul, 1978.

Ridderbos, H. N. *The Epistle of Paul to the Churches of Galatia.* New International Commentary on the New Testament. Grand Rapids: Eerdmans, 1956.

Rigaux, B. *Saint Paul et ses lettres.* Paris: Desclée, 1962.

Ritschl, A. *Entstehung der altkatholischen Kirche.* Bonn: A. Marcus, 1850.

Robbins, V. K. *Jesus the Teacher: A Socio-rhetorical Interpretation of Mark.* Philadelphia: Fortress, 1984.

———. Review of G. A. Kennedy, *New Testament Interpretation. Rhetorica* 3 (1985): 145–49.

Roberts, W. R. *Greek Rhetoric and Literary Criticism.* New York: Longmans, Green, 1928.

———, trans. *Aristotle, The Poetics; Longinus, On the Sublime; Demetrius, On Style.* Rev. ed. Loeb Classical Library. Cambridge: Harvard University Press, 1945.

Robertson, A. T. *A Grammar of the Greek New Testament in the Light of Historical Research.* London: Hodder & Stoughton, 1914.

Robinson, D. W. B. "The Circumcision of Titus and Paul's 'Liberty.'" *Australian Biblical Review* 12 (1964): 24–42.

———. "The Distinction between Jewish and Gentile Believers in Galatians." *Australian Biblical Review* 13 (1965): 29–48.

Rohde, J. *Der Brief des Paulus an die Galater.* Theologischer Handkommentar zum Neuen Testament 9. Berlin: Evangelische Verlagsanstalt, 1989.

Ropes, J. H. *The Singular Problem of the Epistle to the Galatians.* Cambridge: Harvard University Press, 1929.

Roussel, B. "Bucer Exegete." Pages 39–54 in vol. 1 of *Martin Bucer and Sixteenth Century Europe.* 2 vols. Edited by C. Krieger and M. Lienhard. Leiden: Brill, 1993.

———. "Martin Bucer lecteur de l'épître aux Romains I–II." Diss. theol., typescript. Strasbourg, 1970.

Rowland, C. "The Parting of the Ways: The Evidence of Jewish and Christian Apocalyptic and Mystical Material." Pages 213–37 in *Jews and Christians: The Parting of the Ways, A.D. 70 to 135*. Edited by J. D. G. Dunn. Tübingen: Mohr Siebeck, 1992.

Rowley, H. H. "Jewish Proselyte Baptism and the Baptism of John." *Hebrew Union College Annual* 15 (1940): 313–34.

Ruckert, L. I. *Commentar über den Brief Pauli an die Galater*. Leipzig: Köhler, 1833.

Rummel, E. *Erasmus' Annotations on the New Testament: From Philologist to Theologian*. Toronto: University of Toronto Press, 1986.

Russell, W. B. "Rhetorical Analysis of the Book of Galatians." *Bibliotheca sacra* 150 (1993): 341–58, 416–39.

Sæbø, M., ed. *Antiquity*. Part 1 of *From the Beginnings to the Middle Ages (until 1300)*, vol. 1 of *Hebrew Bible/Old Testament: The History of Its Interpretation*. Göttingen: Vandenhoeck & Ruprecht, 1996.

Safrai, S., and M. Stern, eds. *The Jewish People in the First Century*. 2 vols. Assen and Amsterdam: Van Gorcum, 1974–1976.

Sampley, J. P. "Before God I Do Not Lie (Gal 1:20): Paul's Self Defense in the Light of Roman Legal Praxis." *New Testament Studies* 23 (1977): 477–82.

———. *Pauline Partnership in Christ: Christian Community and Commitment in the Light of Roman Law*. Philadelphia: Fortress, 1980.

Sand, A. "Uberlieferung und Sammlung der Paulusbriefe." Pages 11–24 in *Paulus in den neutestamentlichen Spätschriften*. Edited by K. Kertelge et al. Freiburg: Herder, 1981.

Sanders, E. P. *Jesus and Judaism*. London: SCM, 1985.

———. "Jewish Association with Gentiles and Galatians 2:11–14." Pages 170–88 in *The Conversation Continues: Studies in Paul and John in Honor of J. Louis Martyn*. Edited by R. T. Fortna and B. R. Gaventa. Nashville: Abingdon, 1990.

———. *Jewish Law from Jesus to the Mishnah*. Philadelphia: Trinity Press International, 1990.

———. *Paul and Palestinian Judaism*. Philadelphia: Fortress, 1977.

———. *Paul, the Law, and the Jewish People*. Philadelphia: Fortress, 1983.

Sanders, J. T. "Paul's 'Autobiographical' Statements in Galatians 1–2. " *Journal of Biblical Literature* 75 (1966): 335–43.

———. "The Transition from Opening Epistolary Thanksgiving to Body in the Letters of the Pauline Corpus." *Journal of Biblical Literature* 81 (1962): 348–62.

Sandnes, K. O. *Paul, One of the Prophets? A Contribution to the Apostle's Self-Understanding*. Wissenschaftliche Untersuchungen zum Alten und Neuen Testament 2.43. Tübingen: Mohr Siebeck, 1991.

Saw, I. *Paul's Rhetoric in First Corinthians 15: An Analysis Utilizing the Theories of Classical Rhetoric*. Lewiston: Edwin Mellen, 1995.

Schafer, A. "De rhetorum praeceptis quae ad narrationem pertinent." Ph.D. diss., Freiburg, 1921.

Schäfer, P. *Judeophobia: Attitudes toward the Jews in the Ancient World.* Cambridge: Harvard University Press, 1997.

Schäfer, R. "Melanchthon's Intepretation of Romans 5.15: His Departure from the Augustinian Concept of Grace Compared to Luther's." Pages 79–104 in *Philip Melanchthon (1497–1560) and the Commentary.* Edited by T. J. Wengert and M. P. Graham. Sheffield: Sheffield Academic Press, 1997.

Schechter, S. *Aspects of Rabbinic Theology.* New York: Schocken, 1961. Translated from the German original, 1909.

Scheible, H. "Melanchthon." Pages 371–410 in vol. 22 of *Theologische Realenzyclopädie.* Edited by G. Krause and G. Müller. Berlin: de Gruyter, 1977–.

———. Review of E. Bizer, ed., *Texts aus der Anfangzeit Melanchthons. Zeitschrift für Kirchengeschichte* 79 (1968): 417–419.

Scheible, H., and W. Thüringer, eds. *Melanchthons Briefwechsel: Regesten.* 10 vols. Stuttgart: Frommann-Holzboog, 1977–1998.

Schenke, H. M. "Das Weiterwirken des Paulus und die Pflege seines Erbe durch die Paulus-Schule." *New Testament Studies* 21 (1974–75): 505–18.

Schiffman, L. H. "At the Crossroads: Tannaitic Perspectives on the Jewish-Christian Schism." Pages 115–56 in *Aspects of Judaism in the Graeco-Roman Period,* vol. 2 of *Jewish and Christian Self-Definition.* Edited by E. P. Sanders. London: SCM, 1981.

———. *The Halakhah at Qumran.* Leiden: E. J. Brill, 1975.

———. *Who Was a Jew?* Hoboken: KTAV, 1985.

Schlier, H. *Der Brief an die Galater.* Kritisch-exegetischer Kommentar über das Neue Testament (Meyer-Kommentar) 7. Göttingen: Vandenhoeck & Ruprecht, 1971.

Schlueter, C. J. "1 Thessalonians 2:14–16: Polemical Hyperbole." Ph.D. diss., McMaster University, 1992.

Schmid, W. Review of H. Lausberg, *Handbuch der literarischen Rhetorik. Archiv für neueren Sprachen und Literatur* 115 (1964): 451–62.

Schmidt, P. L. "Brief." Pages 771–75 in vol 2 of *Der neue Pauly: Enzyclopädie der Antike.* Edited by H. Cancik and H. Schneider. Stuttgart: J. B. Metzler, 1996–.

Schmithals, W. "Die Häretiker in Galatien." *Zeitschrift für die neutestamentliche Wissenschaft und die Kunde der älteren Kirche* 47 (1956): 25–67. Repr., pages 9–46 in *Paulus und die Gnostiker: Untersuchung zu den kleinen Paulusbriefen.* Hamburg-Bergstedt: Reich, 1965.

———. "The Heretics in Galatia." Pages 13–64 in *Paul and the Gnostics.* New York: Abingdon, 1972.

———. "Judaisten in Galatien?" *Zeitschrift für die neutestamentliche Wissenschaft und die Kunde der älteren Kirche* 74 (1983): 27–58.

———. *Paul and James.* Translated by D. M. Barton. Studies in Biblical Theology 46. Naperville, Ill.: Allenson, 1965.

———. *Paul and the Gnostics.* Translated by J. E. Steely. Nashville and New York: Abingdon, 1972.

Schneider, J. "Brief." Cols. 564–85 in vol. 2 of *Reallexikon für Antike und Christentum.* Edited by Th. Klauser et al. Hiersemann Verlag: Stuttgart, 1950–.

————. "ὄρκος." Pages 457–62 in vol. 5 of *Theological Dictionary of the New Testament.* Edited by G. Kittel and G. Friedrich. Translated by G. W. Bromiley. 10 vols. Grand Rapids: Eerdmans, 1964–1976.

Schneider, N. *Die rhetorische Eigenart der paulinischen Antithese.* Hermeneutische Untersuchungen zur Theologie 11. Tübingen: Mohr Siebeck, 1970.

Schnider, F., and W. Stenger. *Studien zum neutestamentlichen Briefformular.* New Testament Tools and Studies 11. New York: Brill, 1987.

Schoeps, H. J. *Paul: The Theology of the Apostle in the Light of Jewish Religious History.* Translated by H. Knight. Philadelphia: Westminster, 1961.

Schoon-Janssen, J. *Umstrittene "Apologien" in den Paulusbriefen.* Göttinger theologischer Arbeiten 45. Göttingen: Vandenhoeck & Ruprecht, 1991.

Schrage, W. *Ethik des Neuen Testaments.* Göttingen: Vandenhoeck & Ruprecht, 1982.

Schubert, P. *Form and Function of the Pauline Thanksgiving.* Zeitschrift fur die neutestamentliche Theologie 20. Berlin: Topelmann, 1939.

Schuler, M., and J. Schulthess, eds. *Huldreich Zwinglis Werke.* 8 vols. Zurich, 1828–1842.

Schürer, E. *Geschichte des jüdischen Volkes im Zeitalter Jesu Christi.* Leipzig: J. C. Hinrichs, 1901.

————. *History of the Jewish People.* Rev. ed. by G. Vermes et al. 4 vols. Edinburgh: T&T Clark, 1978–1987.

Schutter, W. L. *Hermeneutic and Composition in I Peter.* Wissenschaftliche Untersuchungen zum Alten und Neuen Testament 2.30. Tübingen: Mohr, 1989.

Schütz, J. H. *Paul and the Anatomy of Apostolic Authority.* Society for New Testament Studies Monograph Series 26. Cambridge: Cambridge University Press, 1975.

Schweitzer, A. *The Quest of the Historical Jesus: A Critical Study of Its Progress from Reimarus to Wrede.* Translated by W. Montgomery from the original German, 1906. New York: Macmillan, 1910.

Schweizer, E. "Bibelrhetorik." Pages 1548–72 in vol. 1 of *Historisches Wörterbuch der Rhetorik.* Edited by G. Ueding, G. Kalivoda, and F-H. Robling. Tübingen: Max Niemeyer, 1992.

————. *Matthäus.* Das Neue Testament Deutsch. Göttingen: Vandenhoeck & Ruprecht, 1973.

Scott, J. M. *Paul and the Nations: The Old Testament and Jewish Background of Paul's Mission to the Nations with Special Reference to the Destination of Galatians.* Tübingen: Mohr Siebeck, 1995.

Segal, A. F. *Paul the Convert: The Apostolate and Apostasy of Saul the Pharisee.* New Haven: Yale University Press, 1990.

————. *Rebecca's Children: Judaism and Christianity in the Roman World.* Cambridge: Harvard University Press, 1986.

Seneca the Elder. *Declamations.* Translated by M. Winterbottom. 2 vols. Loeb Classical Library. Cambridge: Harvard University Press, 1974.

Sieben, H. J. *Exegesis patrum: Saggio bibliografico sull'exegesi biblica dei Padri della Chiesa.* Rome: Istituto Patristico Augustinianum, 1983.

Sieffert, F. *Der Brief an die Galater*. Kritisch-exegetischer Kommentar über das Neue Testament (Meyer-Kommentar) 7. Göttingen: Vandenhoeck & Ruprecht, 1899.

Siegert, F. *Argumentation bei Paulus gezeigt an Röm 9–11*. Tübingen: Mohr, 1985.

———. "Gottesfürchtige und Sympathisanten." *Journal for the Study of Judaism in the Persian, Hellenistic, and Roman Periods* 4 (1973): 109–64.

Sigal, P. *The Foundations of Judaism: Part 1, From the Origins to the Separation of Christianity*. Vol. 1 of *The Emergence of Contemporary Judaism*. Pittsburg Theological Monograph Series 29. Pittsburgh: Pickwick, 1980.

Simon, M. *St. Stephen and the Hellenists in the Primitive Church*. London: Longmans Green, 1958.

Smalley, B. *The Study of the Bible in the Middle Ages*. Oxford: Oxford University Press, 1941. 3d ed., 1985.

Smallwood, E. M. *The Jews under Roman Rule*. Leiden: E. J. Brill, 1976.

Smiga, G. M. *Language, Experience, and Theology: The Argumentation of Galatians 3:6–4:7 in Light of the Literary Form of Letter*. Rome: Pontifica Universitas Gregoriana, Facultas Theologiae, 1985.

Smit, J. *Brief aan de Galaten*. Belichting van het bijbelboek. Boxtel: Katholieke Bijbelstichting, 1989.

———. "Hoe kun je de heidenen verplichten als joden te leven? Paulus en de torah in Galaten 2,11–21." *Bijdragen* 46 (1985): 118–40.

———. "The Letter of Paul to the Galatians: A Deliberative Speech." *New Testament Studies* 35 (1989): 1–26. Reprinted in *The Galatians Debate*, 39–59.

———. "Naar een nieuwe benadering van Paulus' brieven: De historische bewijsvoering in Gal. 3,1—4,11." *Tijdschrift voor theologie* 24 (1984): 207–34.

———. *Opbouw en gedachtengang van de brief aan de Galaten*. Nijmegen: n.p., 1986.

———. "Paulus, de Galaten, en het judaisme: Een narratieve analyze van Galaten 1–2." *Tijdschrift voor theologie* 25 (1985): 337–62.

———. "Redactie in de brief aan de Galaten: Retorische analyze van Gal. 4,12–6,18." *Tijdschrift voor theologie* 26 (1986): 113–14.

Smith, C. "Ἐκκλεῖσαι ΕΌΕ in Galatians 4:17: The Motif of the Excluded Lover as a Metaphor of Manipulation," *Catholic Biblical Quarterly* 58 (1996): 480–99.

Smith, D. E. "Table Fellowship as a Literary Motif in the Gospel of Luke." *Journal of Biblical Literature* 106, no. 4 (1987): 613–38.

Smith, J. Z. "Fences and Neighbors: Some Contours of Early Judaism." Pages 1–25 in vol. 2 of *Approaches to Ancient Judaism*. Edited by William Scott Green. Brown Judaic Studies 9. Chico, Calif.: Scholars Press, 1980.

Smith, M. "The Gentiles in Judaism, 125 BCE–CE 66." Pages 192–249 in *The Early Roman Period*. Vol. 3 of *The Cambridge History of Judaism*. Edited by W. Horbury, W. D. Davies, and J. Sturdy. New York: Cambridge University Press, 1999.

Solmsen, F. Review of L. Edelstein, *Plato's Seventh Letter*. *Gnomon* 41 (1969): 29–34.

Sottas, H. *La préservation de la propriété funéraire dans l'ancienne Égypte avec le récueil des formules d'imprécation*. Paris: H. Champion, 1913.

Souter, A. *The Earliest Latin Commentaries on the Epistles of St. Paul*. Oxford: Clarendon, 1927.

Staedtke, J. *Beschreibendes Verzeichnis der gedruckten Werke von Heinrich Bullinger.* Vol. 1 of *Bibliographie.* Edited by F. Büsser. Part 1 of *Heinrich Bullinger Werke.* Zurich: Theologischer Verlag, 1972.

Staehlin, G. "Galaterbrief." Cols. 1187–89 in vol. 2 of *Religion in Geschichte und Gegenwart.* Edited by K. Galling. 7 vols. 3d ed. Tübingen: Mohr Siebeck, 1957–1965.

———. "φίλος, κτλ." Pages 113–71 in vol. 9 of *Theologisches Wörterbuch zum Neuen Testament.* Edited by G. Kittel and G. Friedrich. 10 vols. Stuttgart: W. Kohlhammer, 1932–1979.

Stamps, D. "Rhetorical Criticism of the New Testament: Ancient and Modern Evaluations of Argumentation." Pages 129–69 in *Approaches to New Testament Studies.* Edited by S. E. Porter and D. Tombs. Journal for the Study of the New Testament: Supplement Series 120. Sheffield: Sheffield Academic Press, 1995.

Standaert, B. "La rhétorique ancienne dans saint Paul." Pages 78–92 in *L'apôtre Paul: Personnalité, style, et conception du ministère.* Edited by A. Vanhoye. Bibliotheca ephemeridum theologicarum lovaniensium 73. Leuven: Leuven University Press, 1986.

Stange, E. "Diktierpausen in den Paulusbriefen." *Zeitschrift für die neutestamentliche Wissenschaft und die Kunde der älteren Kirche* 18 (1917): 109–17.

Stanton, G. Review of G. W. Hansen, *Abraham in Galatians. Journal of Theological Studies* 43 (1992): 615.

Starcke, C. "Die Rhetorik des Apostels Paulus im Galaterbrief und die 'πηλίκα γράμματα' Gal. 6:11." *Programm Stargard* i. P. 1911.

Steinmetz, F. A. *Die Freundschaftslehre des Panaitios: Nach einer Analyse von Ciceros "Laelius de amicitia."* Wiesbaden: F. Steiner, 1967.

Stendahl, K. "The Apostle Paul and the Introspective Conscience of the West." *Harvard Theological Review* 56 (1963): 199–215.

———. *Paul among Jews and Gentiles and Other Essays.* Philadelphia: Fortress, 1976.

Stern, M. *Greek and Latin Authors on Jews and Judaism.* 2 vols. Jerusalem: Israel Academy of Sciences and Humanities, 1980.

Sternberg, M. *The Poetics of Biblical Narrative: Ideological Literature and the Drama of Reading.* Bloomington: Indiana University Press, 1985.

Sternberger, G., et al. "Schriftauslegung." Pages 422–99 in vol. 15 of *Theologische Realenzyclopädie.* Edited by G. Krause and G. Müller. Berlin: de Gruyter, 1977 .

Stirewalt, M. L., Jr. "Official Letter-Writing and the Letter of Paul to the Churches of Galatia." Paper presented to the Paul Seminar at the annual meeting of the SBL, 1973.

———. *Studies in Ancient Greek Epistolography.* Resources for Biblical Study 27. Atlanta: Scholars Press, 1993.

Stogiannou, B. P. "Ἡ ὑπὸ τοῦ Παύλου ἰδιόχειρος ἀνακεφαλαίωσις τῆς πρὸς Γαλάτας." Δελτίον βιβλικῶν μελετῶν 1 (1971): 59–79.

Stowers, S. K. *The Diatribe and Paul's Letter to the Romans.* Chico, Calif.: Scholars Press, 1981.

———. *Letter Writing in Greco-Roman Antiquity.* Library of Early Christianity. Philadelphia: Fortress, 1986.

———. "Social Typification and the Classification of Ancient Letters." Pages 78–90 in *The Social World of Formative Christianity and Judaism: Essays in Tribute to Howard Clark Kee.* Edited by J. Neusner, P. Borgen, E. S. Frerichs, and R. Horsley. Philadelphia: Fortress, 1988.

Strack, H. L., and P. Billerbeck. *Kommentar zum Neuen Testament aus Talmud und Midrasch.* 6 vols. Munich: C. H. Beck, 1922–1961.

Strecker, G. "Autonome Sittlichkeit und das Proprium der christlichen Ethik bei Paulus." *Theologische Literaturzeitschrift* 104 (1979): 865–72.

———. "The Kerygmata Petrou." Pages 102–27 in vol. 2 of *New Testament Apocrypha.* Edited by E. Hennecke, W. Schneemelcher, and McL. Wilson. Philadelphia: Westminster, 1963.

Stroebel, E., ed. *M. Tulli Ciceronis rehetorici libri duo.* Leipzig: B. G. Teubner, 1915.

Strohm, S., et al. *Griechische Bibeldrucke: Die Bibelsammlung der Württembergischen Landesbibliothek Stuttgart.* Stuttgart–Bad Cannstatt: Frommann-Holzboog, 1984.

Strugnell, J., and H. Attridge. "The Epistles of Heraclitus and the Jewish Pseudepigrapha: A Warning." *Harvard Theological Review* 64 (1971): 411–13.

Stuart, D. R. *Epochs of Greek and Roman Biography.* Berkeley: University of California Press, 1928.

Stuckelberger, A. *Senecas 88e Brief: Über Wert und Unwert der freien Kunste.* Heidelberg: C. Winter, 1965.

Stuhlmacher, P. "Erwägungen zum ontologischen Charakter der kaine ktisis bei Paulus." *Evangelische Theologie* 27 (1967): 1–35.

———. *Vorgeschichte.* Vol. 1 of *Das paulinische Evangelium.* Göttingen: Vandenhoeck & Ruprecht, 1968.

Stupperich, R. "Bibliographia bucerana." *Schriften des Vereins für Reformationsgeschichte* 169 (1952): 45–67.

———. "Bucer, Martin." Pages 258–70 in vol. 7 of *Theologische Realenzyclopädie.* Edited by G. Krause and G. Müller. Berlin: de Gruyter, 1977–.

Stupperich, R., et al., eds. *Melanchthons Werke in Auswahl.* 7 vols. Gütersloh: Mohn, 1951–83.

Suhl, A. "Der Galaterbrief—Situation und Argumentation." *ANRW* 25.4:3066–3134. Part 2, *Principat,* 25.4. Edited by H. Temporini and W. Haase. New York: de Gruyter, 1987.

———. *Paulus und seine Briefe: Ein Beitrag zur paulinische Chronologie.* Studien zum Neuen Testament 11. Gütersloh: Mohn, 1975.

Sullivan, D. L. "The Epideictic Discourse of Science." *Journal of Business and Technical Communication* 5 (1991): 229–45.

———. "The Ethos of Epideictic Encounter." *Philosophy and Rhetoric* 26 (1993): 113–33.

Sullivan, D. L., and C. Anible. "The Epideictic Dimension of Galatians as Formative Rhetoric: The Inscription of Early Christian Community." *Rhetorica* 18:2 (2000): 117–45.

Sumney, J. L. *Identifying Paul's Opponents: The Question of Method in 2 Corinthians.* Journal for the Study of the New Testament: Supplement Series 40. Sheffield: Sheffield Academic Press.

―――. "Paul's Weakness: An Integral Part of His Conception of Apostleship." *Journal for the Study of the New Testament* 52 (1993): 71–91.

Swetnam, J. Review of H. D. Betz, *Galatians. Biblica* 62 (1981): 594–97.

Sykutris, J. "Epistolographie." *RE Sup* 5:185–220.

Talbert, C. H. "Again: Paul's Visits to Jerusalem." *Novum Testamentum* 9 (1967): 26–40.

Tarazi, P. N. *Galatians: A Commentary.* Orthodox Biblical Studies. Crestwood, N.Y.: St. Vladimir's Seminary Press, 1994.

Taylor, N. *Paul, Antioch, and Jerusalem: A Study in Relationships and Authority in Earliest Christianity.* Journal for the Study of the New Testament: Supplement Series 66. Sheffield: JSOT Press, 1992.

Tcherikover, V. "Jewish Apologetic Literature Reconsidered." *Eos* 48 (1956): 119–93.

Theissen, G. *The Social Setting of Pauline Christianity.* Edited and Translated by J. H. Schütz. Philadelphia: Fortress, 1982.

Theon, A. *Progymnasmata.* Pages 59–130 in vol. 2 of *Rhetores graeci.* Edited by L. Spengel. 1854. Repr., Frankfurt: Minerva, 1966.

Thompson, L. "Social Location of Early Christian Apocalyptic." ANRW 26.3:2617–56. Part 2, Principat, 26.3. Edited by H. Temporini and W. Haase. New York: de Gruyter, 1996.

Thornton, T. C. G. "The Crucifixion of Haman and the Scandal of the Cross." *Journal of Theological Studies* New Series 37 (1986): 419–26.

―――. "Trees, Gibbets, and Crosses." *Journal of Theological Studies* New Series 23 (1972): 130–31.

Thraede, K. *Grundzüge griechisch-römischer Brieftopik.* Munich: Beck, 1970.

Thurén, L. *Argument and Theology in 1 Peter: The Origins of Christian Paraenesis.* Journal for the Study of the New Testament: Supplement Series 114. Sheffield: Sheffield Academic Press, 1995.

―――. *Derhetorizing Paul: A Dynamic Perspective on Pauline Theology and the Law.* Edited by M. Hengel and O. Hofius. Wissenschaftliche Untersuchungen zum Alten und Neuen Testament 124. Tübingen: Mohr Siebeck, 2000.

―――. *The Rhetorical Strategy of 1 Peter with Special Regards to Ambiguous Expressions.* Åbo: Åbo Academy, 1990.

―――. "Was Paul Angry? Derhetorizing Galatians." Pages 302–20 in *The Rhetorical Interpretation of Scripture: Essays from the 1996 Malibu Conference.* Edited by D. Stamps and S. Porter. Sheffield: Sheffield Academic Press, 1999.

Tomson, P. J. *Paul and the Jewish Law: Halakha in the Letters of the Apostle to the Gentiles.* Compendia rerum iudaicarum ad Novum Testamentum. Section 3: Jewish Traditions in Early Christian Literature 1. Minneapolis: Fortress, 1990.

Trapp, M. B., ed. *Maximus of Tyre. Dissertationes.* Stuttgart: B. G. Teubner, 1994.

Trebilco, P. R. *Jewish Communities in Asia Minor.* Cambridge: Cambridge University Press, 1991.

Treu, K. "Freundschaft." Pages 418–34 in vol. 8 of *Reallexikon für Antike und Christentum.* Edited by T. Kluser et al. Stuttgart: Hiersemann, 1950–.

Trigg, J. W. "Augustine/Jerome, *Correspondence.*" Pages 250–95 in *Biblical Interpretation.* Message of the Fathers of the Church 9. Wilmington: Michael Glazier, 1988.

Trillitzsch, W. *Senecas Beweisführung.* Berlin: Akademie, 1962.

Trobisch, D. *Die Entstehung der Paulusbriefsammlung: Studien zu den Anfängen christlicher Publizistik.* Edited by M. Küchler and G. Theissen. Novum Testamentum et orbis antiquus 10. Freiburg, Switzerland: Universitätsverlag; Göttingen: Vandenhoeck & Ruprecht, 1989.

———. *Die Paulusbriefe und die Anfänge der christlichen Publizistik.* Kaiser Taschenbuch 135. Gütersloh: Chr. Kaiser, 1994.

Tyson, J. B. "Paul's Opponents in Galatia." *Novum Testamentum* 10 (1968): 241–54.

———. " 'Works of the Law' in Galatians." *Journal of Biblical Literature* 92 (1973): 423–31.

Übelacker, W. G. *Untersuchungen zu exordium, narratio, und postscriptum (Hebr 1–2 und 13:22–25).* Vol. 1 of *Der Hebräerbrief als Appell.* Stockholm: Almqvist & Wiksell, 1989.

Ueding, G. *Klassische Rhetorik.* Munich: C. H. Beck, 1996.

Ulonska, H. "Die Funktion der alttestamentlichen Zitate und Anspielungen in den paulinischen Briefen." Ph.D. diss., Munster, 1963.

Urbach, E. E. *The Sages: Their Concepts and Beliefs.* Jerusalem: Magness Press, Hebrew University, 1975.

Valla, L. *In latinam Novi Testamenti interpretationem ex collatione Graecorum exemplarium adnotationes apprime utiles.* Paris, 1505.

Van Iersel, B. *Marcus.* Bruges: Tabor, 1986.

Van Stempvoort, P. A. *De Allegorie in Gal 4: 21–31 als hermeneutisch Probleem.* Nijkerk: G. F. Callenbach, 1953.

Van Voorst, R. E. *The Ascents of James.* Atlanta: Scholars Press, 1989.

Vanhoye, A., ed. *L'apôtre Paul: Personnalité, style, et conception du ministère.* Bibliotheca ephemeridum theologicarum lovaniensium 73. Leuven: Leuven University Press, 1986.

Verbeke, W., D. Verhelst, and A. Welkenhuysen, eds. *The Use and Abuse of Eschatology in the Middle Ages.* Leuven: Leuven University Press, 1988.

Verseput, D. J. "Paul's Gentile Mission and the Jewish Christian Community: A Study of the Narrative in Galatians 1 and 2." *New Testament Studies* 39 (1993): 36–58.

Vielhauer, P. *Geschichte der urchristlichen Literatur: Einleitung in das Neue Testament, die Apokryphen, und die Apostolischen Väter.* Berlin: de Gruyter, 1975.

———. *Oikodome.* New ed. Munich: Neudruck, 1979.

Voegtle, A. *Die Tugend- und Lasterkataloge im Neuen Testament.* Munster, 1936.

Vogels, H. J., ed. *Ambrosiastri qui dicitur Commentarius in epistulas paulinas. Pars tertia: In epistulas ad Galatas, ad Efsios, ad Filippenses, ad Colosenses, ad Thesalonicenses, ad Timotheum, ad Titum, ad Filemonem.* 3 vols. Vienna: Hoelder-Pichler-Tempsky, 1966.

Volkmann, R. von. *Die Rhetorik der Griechen und Romer in systematischer Übersicht.* Leipzig: B. G. Teubner, 1885.

Vos, J. S. "Paul's Argumentation in Galatians 1–2." *Harvard Theological Review* 87, no. 1 (1994): 1–16. Reprinted in *The Galatians Debate,* 169–80.

Vos, C. S. de. *Church and Community Conflicts: The Relationships of the Thessalonian, Corinthian, and Philippian Churches with Their Wider Civic Communities.* Society of Biblical Literature Dissertation Series 168. Atlanta: Scholars Press, 1999.

Vouga, F. *An die Galater.* Edited by A. Lindemann. Handbuch zum Neuen Testament 10. Tübingen: Mohr Siebeck, 1998.

———. "Der Galaterbrief: Kein Brief an die Galater? Essay über den literarischen Charakter des letzten großen Paulusbriefes." Pages 243–58 in *Schrift und Tradition: Festschrift Josef Ernst.* Edited by K. Backhaus and G. Untergassmair. Paderborn: Schöningh, 1996.

———. "Zur rhetorischen Gattung des Galaterbriefes." *Zeitschrift für die neutestamentliche Wissenschaft und die Kunde der älteren Kirche* 79 (1988): 291–92.

Wainwright, A. "Where Did Silas Go? (And What Was His Connection with Galatians)." *Journal for the Study of the New Testament* 8 (1980): 66–70.

Walker-Ramisch, S. "Graeco-Roman Voluntary Associations and the Damascus Document: A Sociological Analysis." Pages 128–45 in *Voluntary Associations in the Graeco-Roman World.* Edited by J. S. Kloppenborg and S. G. Wilson. New York: Routledge, 1996.

Wallace, D. *Greek Grammar beyond the Basics.* Grand Rapids: Zondervan, 1996.

Walter, N. "Die 'als Säulen Geltenden' in Jerusalem—Leiter der Urgemeinde oder exemplarisch Fromme?" Pages 78–92 in *Kirche und Volk Gottes: Festschrift für Jürgen Roloff zum 70. Geburtstag.* Edited by M. Karrer, W. Kraus, and O. Merk. Neukirchen-Vluyn: Neukirchener Verlag, 2000.

———. "Hellenistische Diaspora-Juden an der Wiege des Urchristentums." Pages 37–58 in *The New Testament and Hellenistic Judaism.* Edited by P. Borgen and S. Giversen. Aarhus: Aarhus University Press, 1995.

———. "Paulus und die Gegner des Christusevangeliums in Galatien." Pages 351–56 in *L'apôtre Paul: Personnalité, style, et conception du ministère.* Edited by A. Vanhoye. Bibliotheca ephemeridum theologicarum lovaniensium 73. Leuven: Leuven University Press, 1986. Revised and translated in *The Galatians Debate,* 362–66.

———. "Paulus und die Gegner des Christusevangeliums in Galatien." Pages 273–80 in *Praeparatio evangelica: Studien zur Umwelt, Exegese, und Hermeneutik des Neuen Testaments.* Edited by W. Kraus and F. Wilk. Wissenschaftliche Untersuchungen zum Alten und Neuen Testament 98. Tübingen: Mohr Siebeck, 1997.

———. *Der Thoraausleger Aristobulos.* Berlin: Akademie, 1964.

Watson, D. F. *Invention, Arrangement, and Style: Rhetorical Criticism of Jude and 2 Peter.* Atlanta: Scholars Press, 1988.

———. "Rhetorical Criticism of the Pauline Epistles since 1975." *Currents in Research: Biblical Studies* 3 (1995): 219–48.

———, ed. *Persuasive Artistry: Studies in New Testament Rhetoric in Honor of George A. Kennedy.* Sheffield: Sheffield Academic Press, 1991.

Watson, D. F., and A. J. Hauser. *Rhetorical Criticism of the Bible: A Comprehensive Bibliography with Notes on History and Method.* Leiden: Brill, 1994.

Watson, F. *Paul, Judaism, and the Gentiles: A Sociological Approach.* Cambridge: Cambridge University Press, 1986.

Wechsler, A. *Geschichtsbild und Apostelstreit. Eine forschungsgeschichtliche und exegetische Studie über den antiochenischen Zwischenfall (Gal. 2,11–14).* Beihefte zur Zeitschrift für die neutestamentliche Wissenschaft 62. New York: Walter de Gruyter, 1991.

Wedderburn, A. J. M. "Some Recent Pauline Chronologies." *Expository Times* 92 (1980–1981): 103–8.

Wegenast, K. *Das Verständnis der Tradition bei Paulus und in den Deuteropaulinen.* Neukirchen: Neukirchener Verlag, 1962.

Weichert, V., ed. *Demetrii et Libanii qui feruntur* ΤΥΠΟΙ ΕΠΙΣΤΟΛΙΚΟΙ *et* ΕΠΙΣΤΟΛΙΜΑΙΟΙ. Leipzig: In aedibus B. G. Teubneri, 1910.

Weima, J. A. D. "The Function of I Thessalonians 2:1–12 and the Use of Rhetorical Criticism: A Response to Otto Merk." Pages 114–31 in *The Thessalonians Debate: Methodological Discord or Methodological Synthesis.* Edited by K. P. Donfried and J. Beutler. Grand Rapids: Eerdmans, 2000.

———. "What Does Aristotle Have to Do with Paul? An Evaluation of Rhetorical Criticism." *Calvin Theological Journal* 32 (1997): 458–68.

Weinrich, H. *Sprache in Texten.* Stuttgart: Klett, 1976.

Weintraub, K. J. *The Value of the Individual: Self and Circumstance in Autobiography.* Chicago: University of Chicago Press, 1978.

Weiss, B. *Die paulinischen Briefe im berichtigten Text.* Leipzig: Hinrichs'sche Buchhandlung, 1896.

Weiss, J. "Beiträge zur paulinischen Rhetorik." *Theologische Studien: Festschrift für Bernhard Weiss.* Edited by C. R. Gregory. Göttingen, 1897.

———. *Earliest Christianity.* First English translation 1937. 2 vols. New edition with a new introduction and bibliography by F. C. Grant. New York: Harper Torchbook, 1959. Translated from the German, 1914.

———. *Das Urchristentum.* Göttingen: Vandenhoeck & Ruprecht, 1917.

Wendland, P. *Die hellenistisch-römische Kultur in ihren Beziehungen zu Judentum und Christentum: Die urchristlichen Literaturformen.* 2d/3d ed. Tübingen: Mohr, 1912.

Wengert, T. J. *Philip Melanchthon's* Annotationes in Johannem *in Relation to Its Predecessors and Contemporaries.* Geneva: Dros, 1987.

Wengert, T. J., and M. P. Graham, eds. *Philip Melanchthon (1497–1560) and the Commentary.* Sheffield: Sheffield Academic Press, 1997.

Westerholm, S. Review of S. McKnight, *A Light among the Gentiles. Journal of Biblical Literature* 113 (1994): 330–32.

Westman, R., ed. *M. Tulli Ciceronis* orator. Leipzig: B. G. Teubner, 1980.

Wettstein, J. J. (Joannis Jacobi Wetstenii). *Novum Testamentum graecum editionis receptae cum lectionibus variantibus codicum mss., editionum aliarum versionum et patrum.* Amsterdam, 1752.

Wetzel, R., and H. Scheible, eds. *Melanchthons Briefwechsel: Kritische und kommentierte Gesamtausgabe.* 3 vols. Stuttgart-Bad Cannstatt: Frommann-Holzboog, 1991–2000.

White, J. L. "Apostolic Mission and Apostolic Message: Congruence in Paul's Epistolary Rhetoric, Structure, and Imagery." Pages 145–61 in *Origins and Method: Towards a New Understanding of Judaism and Christianity—Essays in Honour of John C. Hurd.* Edited by B. H. McLean. Sheffield: JSOT Press, 1993.

———. *The Body of the Greek Letter.* Society of Biblical Literature Dissertation Series 2. Missoula, Mont.: Scholars Press, 1972.

———. *The Form and Function of the Body of the Greek Letter.* Society of Biblical Literature Dissertation Series 2. Missoula, Mont.: Scholars Press, 1972.

———. "Introductory Formulae in the Body of the Pauline Letter." *Journal of Biblical Literature* 90 (1971): 91–97.

———. *Light from Ancient Letters.* Minneapolis: Fortress, 1986.

———. "New Testament Epistolary Literature in the Framework of Ancient Epistolography." *ANRW* 25.2:1730–56. Part 2, *Principat,* 25.2. Edited by W. Haase. New York: de Gruyter, 1984.

———. "The Structural Analysis of Philemon." Paper presented to the Paul Seminar at the annual meeting of the SBL, 1970.

Whittaker, M. *Jews and Christians: Graeco-Roman Views.* Cambridge Commentaries on Writings of the Jewish and Christian World 200 BC to AD 200 6. Cambridge: Cambridge University Press, 1984.

Wilamowitz-Moellendorff, U. von. "Die Griechische Literatur des Altertums." In Teil 1, Abteilung 8 of *Die Kultur der Gegenwart.* 2d ed. Berlin and Leipzig: B. G. Teubner, 1907.

Wilcken, U., ed. *Urkunden der Ptolemäerzeit (ältere Funde).* Berlin and Leipzig: Walter de Gruyter, 1927.

Wilckens, U. "Was heisst bei Paulus: 'Aus Werken des Gesetzes wird kein Mensch gerecht'?" 1969. Repr. in *Rechtfertigung als Freiheit: Paulusstudien.* Neukirchen: Neukirchener Verlag, 1974.

———. "στῦλος." Pages 732–36 in volume 7 of *Theological Dictionary of the New Testament.* Edited by G. Kittel and G. Friedrich. Translated by G. W. Bromiley. 10 vols. Grand Rapids: Eerdmans, 1964–1976.

Wilcox, M. "The 'God-Fearers' in Acts: A Reconsideration." *Journal for the Study of the New Testament* 13 (1981): 102–22.

———. " 'Upon the Tree'—Deut. 21:22–3 in the New Testament." *Journal of Biblical Literature* 96 (1977): 85–99.

Wilder, A. N. *The Language of the Gospel: Early Christian Rhetoric.* New York: Harper & Row, 1964.

Wilken, R. "The Jews of Antioch." Pages 67–75 in *SBL Seminar Papers, 1976.* Edited by George MacRae. Society of Biblical Literature Seminar Papers. Missoula, Mont.: Scholars Press, 1976.

Williams, S. K. *Galatians.* Abingdon New Testament Commentaries. Nashville: Abingdon, 1997.

Wilson, R. McL. "Gnostics—in Galatia?" Pages 358–67 in vol. 4 of *Studia Evangelica*. Edited by F. L. Cross. Berlin: Akademie, 1968.

Wilson, S. *Luke and the Law*. Cambridge: Cambridge University Press, 1983.

Winninge, M. *Sinners and the Righteous: A Comparative Study of the Psalms of Solomon and Paul's Letters*. Coniectanea neotestamentica or Coniectanea biblica: New Testament Series 26. Stockholm: Almqvist & Wiksell International, 1995.

Winston, D. "Solomon, Wisdom of." Pages 120–27 in vol. 6 of the *Anchor Bible Dictionary*. Edited by D. N. Freeman. 6 vols. New York: Doubleday, 1992.

Winter, B. W. *Seek the Welfare of the City: Christians as Benefactors and Citizens*. Grand Rapids: Eerdmans, 1994.

Witherington, B., III. *Grace in Galatia: A Commentary on Paul's Letter to the Galatians*. Grand Rapids: Eerdmans, 1998.

Wolfson, H. A. *Philo: Foundations of Religious Philosophy in Judaism, Christianity, and Islam*. Rev. ed. 2 vols. Cambridge: Harvard University Press, 1962.

Wrede, W. "Paulus." Pages 1–97 in *Zur neueren Paulusforschung*. Edited by Karl H. Rengstorf. Wege der Forschung 24. Darmstadt: Wissenschaftliche Buchgesellschaft, 1964.

Wright, N. T. *The Climax of the Covenant: Christ and the Law in Pauline Theology*. Edinburgh: T&T Clark, 1991.

———. *The New Testament and the People of God*. Minneapolis: Fortress, 1992.

Wuellner, W. "Paul's Rhetoric of Argumentation in Romans." *Catholic Biblical Quarterly* 38 (1976): 330–51.

———. "Where Is Rhetorical Criticism Taking Us ?" *Catholic Biblical Quarterly* 49 (1987): 448–63.

Zahn, T. *Der Brief des Paulus an die Galater*. 3d ed. Kommentar zum Neuen Testament 9. Leipzig and Erlangen: Deichert, 1922.

Zeitlin, S. "Proselytes and Proselytism during the Second Commonwealth and the Early Tannaitic Period." Pages 407–17 in vol. 2 of *Solomon Zeitlin's Studies in the Early History of Judaism*. New York: Ktav, 1974.

Zetterholm, M. *The Formation of Christianity in Antioch: A Social-Scientific Approach to the Separation Between Judaism and Christianity*. London: Routledge, forthcoming.

Ziegler, K., and W. Sontheimer. *Der Kleine Pauly: Lexicon der Antike*. Stuttgart: Alfred Druckenmuller, 1964.

Ziesler, J. *The Meaning of Righteousness in Paul: A Linguistic and Theological Inquiry*. Society for New Testament Studies Monograph Series 20. Cambridge: Cambridge University Press, 1972.

INDEX OF MODERN AUTHORS

INDEX OF ANCIENT SOURCES